Reasoning Together

THE NATIVE CRITICS COLLECTIVE

by
Janice Acoose, Lisa Brooks, Tol Foster, LeAnne Howe,
Daniel Heath Justice, Phillip Carroll Morgan,
Kimberly Roppolo, Cheryl Suzack, Christopher B. Teuton,
Sean Teuton, Robert Warrior, and Craig S. Womack

Edited by
Craig S. Womack, Daniel Heath Justice, and
Christopher B. Teuton

Library of Congress Cataloging-in-Publication Data

Reasoning together : the native critics collective / by Janice Acoose ... [et al.] ; edited by Craig S. Womack ... [et al.].
p. cm.
Includes bibliographical references and index.
ISBN 978-0-8061-3887-9
1. American literature—Indian authors—History and criticism—Theory, etc. 2. Indians of North America—Intellectual life. 3. Indigenous peoples—North America—Intellectual life. 4. Indians of North America—Ethnic identity. 5. Indians in literature. I. Acoose, Janice. II. Womack, Craig S.
PS153.I52R33 2008
810.9'897—dc22 2007024442

The paper in this book meets the guidelines for permanence and durability of the Committee on Production Guidelines for Book Longevity of the Council on Library Resources. ∞

1 2 3 4 5 6 7 8 9 10

Contents

Reasoning Together

A Single Decade

Book-Length Native Literary Criticism between 1986 and 1997

CRAIG S. WOMACK

From the late 1960s to the end of the 1980s, more federal legislation affecting Indian country was passed than during any comparable period in U.S. history. Within that same period literary studies were in an upheaval over the question as to what constitutes literature, which books should be considered the proper objects of study, how they should be read, and the very ability of language itself to effectively name the world. The crosscurrents emanating from these juxtaposed events culminated in a brief span of years that saw the publication of seven seminal studies in Native literary criticism. Now, a decade later, a group of scholars has come together to reflect on the history of their discipline and to pool their thoughts in a dialogue in print—this coauthored book you hold in your hands, *Reasoning Together: The Native Critics Collective*. At the end of this essay I describe the creative process behind the book, but first I want to lay out the path that brought us here.

Interpenetrating Histories: The Literary and the Political

Mikhail Bakhtin's book, *The Dialogic Imagination*, is not published in Russia until 1975, the year of his death. In the United States that same year, Congress passes the Indian Self-Determination Act, legislation intended to remedy the failed polices of relocation and termination that sought to end the sovereign status of tribes during the late 1940s and 1950s. The act gives tribes more power to regulate their own housing, law enforcement, health, social service, and community development programs rather than having these services managed by the Secretary of the Interior.

Bakhtin writes that formalist attempts to view texts as autonomous objects,

---

Craig S. Womack (Oklahoma Creek-Cherokee) is the author of Red on Red, Drowning in Fire, *and* American Indian Literary Nationalism, *the last coauthored with Robert Warrior and Jace Weaver. He teaches American Indian literature in the English department at Emory University.*

which should be analyzed according to their internal unity rather than external contexts, cuts narratives off from the living world of language evident in their sociological backdrops. Rather than a systematic display of language, Bakhtin says, the novel can be celebrated for its "heteroglossia," its diversity of speech that is as often measured by contradiction, tension, competition, and doubt as by its ultimate cohesiveness. This multivoiced discourse involves interplay among different kinds of language, an essential characteristic of novels. And it is perhaps this communal orientation of Bakhtin's that will attract so many scholars of Native American literature to his work in the early 1990s.

The same year Jacques Derrida's translated work *Of Grammatology* is published in English—1976—the U.S. Congress passes a bill to terminate the Indian Claims Commission. Derrida's writings mount a forceful critique against structuralism. The implications of his work change the way many people view reality by problematizing the referentiality of language and rejecting truth as a stable ahistorical foundation rather than as socially constituted, shaped by culture, and subject to change in different time periods and places. According to French theory, a literary thesis is persuasive rather than definitive, and readings of literature are just as valuable for their ultimate undecidablity as their conclusions, given that they proceed by way of language, which always involves multiple and changing meanings. While some scholars have emphasized the fixed nature of the written word and the flexibility of its oral counterpart, Derrida decenters all language by rooting it in ever-changing, infinitely variable meanings.

The demise of the Indian Claims Commission marks the end of an era. Established in 1946 as the economic arm of the federal termination and relocation policies, it was a plan whereby the United States would once and for all get out of the Indian business and end its historic trust relation with the tribes. All outstanding treaty claims were to be taken care of, largely through monetary compensation for unremunerated land cessions and other outstanding government debts; the plan was that the claims would be settled by 1952, when the United States would conclude its treaty obligations to the tribes by terminating their governments and jurisdictions, permanently relocating their members to U.S. cities. The program focused more on compensation than on land redress, since it was an attempt to end tribal jurisdictions. Reservation status would be dissolved in the homelands, which would be converted to counties under state authority. By 1952, however, only 370 of some 850 claims have been settled by the ICC. And, by 1976, even though the commission has awarded some $800 million, many treaty claims are still outstanding. The bill that terminates the Indian Claims Commission sends the rest of the claims over to the U.S. Court of Appeals. The claims continue under a new era of self-determination after tribes win back a degree of sovereignty in the 1970s. Many of the terminated tribes, the most well-known case being that of the Wisconsin Menominees, regain reservation status.

In 1978, the same year French philosopher Michel Foucault's landmark study, *The History of Sexuality*, is published in the United States in its English translation, American Indians are granted religious freedom—almost exactly two hundred years after the Christian majority gained such freedom—when Congress passes the American Indian Religious Freedom Act (AIRFA), which promises to "protect and preserve for American Indians their inherent right of freedom to believe, express and exercise traditional religions."[1]

Foucault's study suggests that sexuality is not an ahistorical universal phenomenon but an idea with a history, as his title indicates. Sexuality, including concepts such as heterosexuality and homosexuality, are not innate conditions but socially regulated constructions of identity that are related to systems of power that affect both conformity and resistance.

In Indian country AIRFA acknowledges that First Amendment rights extend to America's indigenes, though one might note that the Native American church, the peyote religion, will remain in a precarious legal position. As is often the case in regard to congressional legislation affecting Indian country, few federal agencies change their regulations and even fewer state courts uphold religious decisions in a tribe's favor. In the same year as Foucault's study is published and AIRFA becomes law, Congress passes the Indian Child Welfare Act, which gives tribal courts jurisdiction over Native children living on reservations. Now the tribes will make the decisions as to whether children should be removed from their families—and where they should be placed in the event of their removal—rather than leaving these decisions to state workers, or in earlier times, to the whims of priests and Indian agents.

Why mention the American Indian Religious Freedom Act in the same breath as *The History of Sexuality* or relate the end of the Indian Claims Commission to Jacques Derrida's deconstructive theories? Bakhtin and self-determination? What, if anything, do these disparate events have to do with one another? If one believes in the weblike metaphysics of a novel like Laguna writer Leslie Marmon Silko's *Ceremony* (1978), one hesitates to say they have no relationship whatsoever. We know that Marx and Engels, for example, quoted extensively from Lewis Henry Morgan's 1877 book, *Ancient Society*, about Iroquoian culture. Given the huge influences of Marxism on literary theory, it is not impossible to imagine Native people having some bearing on the theoretical outpouring of the last four decades.

The decade when American Indian critics began to publish book-length works of literary criticism coincides with seismic shifts in literature departments as well as in federal Indian policy. The Indian Self Determination Act, the Indian Child Welfare Act , the American Indian Religious Freedom Act, and the end of the Indian Claims Commission were not the only pieces of legislation that would change the future in Indian country. In the years leading up to and encompassing the decade that I am considering—a decade that begins with Laguna Pueblo author Paula Gunn Allen's 1986 publication of *The Sacred Hoop: Recovering the Feminine in American Indian Traditions* and ends with Cherokee scholar Jace Weaver's 1997 book, *That the People Might Live: Native American Literature and Native American Community*—everyday tribal realities would shift dramatically because of the laws coming out of the U.S. Congress.

Other major legislation would include the Indian Tribal Government Tax Status Act (1982), which gave to tribes many of the tax advantages exercised by states, such as the right to issue tax-exempt bonds to finance governmental projects; the Indian Mineral Development Act (1982), which established the power of tribes to enter into joint-venture agreements with mineral companies to develop their own mineral resources; the Indian Gaming Regulatory Act (1988), which required compacts between states and tribes to govern the scope of casino operations; the Tribally Controlled Schools Act (1988), which provided grants to tribes to operate their own schools; and the Native American Graves Protection and Repatriation Act (NAGPRA) (1990).

NAGPRA is a law with wide-ranging implications. It not only provides for the return of the skeletal remains of ancestors housed in museums to their tribes of origins but for the repatriation of remains and artifacts found on tribal lands after November 16, 1990, to their lineal descendants or to the tribe if the descendants cannot be identified. NAGPRA also contains a criminal provision against trafficking in such items. Federal agencies and museums have to provide an inventory of remains and cultural artifacts in their possession for tribes who want to repatriate them. It is worth mentioning that the repatriation provisions of NAGPRA do not apply to private collections, and as a result the law is limited in terms of stemming the trafficking of burial goods.

Given these landmark events in literature and public policy, it should cause little wonder that unpacking whatever has happened to Native literature for even one single decade, the years between 1986 and 1997, is a monumental chore. This gargantuan task has contributed to this unruly beast of an essay and a methodology here that some may find cumbersome, so let me offer a word or two about this curious dance between policy and literature that may have some readers scratching their heads by now.

Toward an Ethics of Criticism

This introduction is organized along a timeline for theoretical reasons that relate to the efforts of my coauthors to present a credible theoretical integrity. The most consistent and damaging critique against Native intellectuals involves labeling them as "essentialists." Essentialism has to do with making universal claims in ahistorical modes. In short, one could describe this as writing without dates, without historical references. This chapter, however, makes dates, and particular events, a cornerstone of its approach because I want it to be an embodiment of the kind of antiessentialism we hope to uphold in this volume (while asserting that not all essentialisms are "bad" or should be automatically dismissed). Instead of making universal, overarching assumptions about Indians, we want to delve into particulars. We are trying to avoid the kind of literary work that has been so very popular in our field in which people avoid historical research and base their criticism exclusively on tropes and symbols. We want to show some kind of commitment to archival sources and other kinds of knowledge rather than atemporal, nonhistorical, clichéd analyses such as, "Well, . . . I think the frybread probably symbolizes. . . ."

Indeed, many of the essays that follow can be located within particular geographies and historical moments, whether it is Lisa Brooks's eighteenth-century New England Native intellectuals, Cheryl Suzack's discussion of the 1986 White Earth Land Settlement Act, Tol Foster's analysis of Will Rogers in relation to 1930s regionalism, Robert Warrior's claiming that closest of geographies, the human body, in his study of literary erotica, or any other number of the historical and place-specific references made by my coauthors. If we were to scrutinize our own theory, the following questions might define it: What date did it occur? Can you locate it on a map? How is jurisdiction exercised in this particular space?

Another reason for all the dates, and the anecdotes that go with them, in this opening chapter is because this is a period piece. I want to evoke some kind of feeling for the events occurring in the eighties and nineties rather than keep my discussion in the abstract. I want to create a theoretical milieu that has the sense of a story unfolding, a history of ideas, rather than philosophy in a timeless vacuum. I am interested in the culture of theory, the places it lives in, the people it hangs out with, though I know this will be less than a perfect process.

Some purists may say that our efforts together here do not even qualify as theory, since they apply to work that might be called analysis or criticism or historical investigation or advocacy or protest instead. As this mongrel of an introduction demonstrates, however, we are anything but pure. We are not attempting a *Teacher's Guide to the Norton Anthology of Theory* that provides all the correct answers as to what theory is and is not. In fact, recent theory itself has become skeptical of such formulas. We are of the mindset, as are many theorists, that theory is not cancelled out by application or praxis; nor does it cease to be theory in the event one actually discovers something meaningful about it, something that can be applied to the real world or to a particular work of literature. We believe theory, in fact, can emerge from novels, poems, plays, and many other forms, including life itself. We even claim these as prominent emergence points, important creation stories for theory. This introduction tells stories because stories are the birthplace of theory (and, in this case, I think the converse is true as well).

We want to create some kind of methodology for the emergence of Native literary criticism, which is too often interpreted along thematic lines rather than according to historical particulars. We also hope to provide a context for this anthology in terms of how it came about in a particular moment of time—thus this attempt to say something about our authorial ancestors, even if we can only examine them through one decade. We want to turn the anthology into a story, well, into a whole bunch of stories that are a part of a larger whole. History is his and her story. This is our story, the story of Native literary theory during a particularly striking ten-year period, at least as much as we know how to tell right now.

Let me say a bit more about the call-and-response structure of this chapter that attempts to link political and literary history. Some strong positions form a part of this book's introduction. There is an underlying protest against the Iraq war that runs throughout, for example, a war being waged at the time of this writing. This particular view does not necessarily represent the opinions of my fellow authors, but it moves toward what I would like to think of as an interventionist approach to theory consistent with the other essays. In his recent book, *After Theory* (2003), which is an attempt to predict what comes next after the decades of French, and other, theories in the 1970s and 1980s, Terry Eagleton criticizes a detached hypothetical analysis of the effects of colonialism and recommends instead an advocacy that names specific ways the United States must change its imperial thinking and practices. I hope this anthology, as well, represents a commitment to theory rooted in activism, where political outcomes are as important as underlying philosophies. That is to say, we hope for both smart theory and smart praxis. In this regard, the way in which Cheryl Suzack moves back and forth between an analysis of Winona LaDuke's vice presidential campaigns in 1996 and 2000, her efforts as a novelist, and her involvement in the White Earth land claim serves as a strong example.

For most American Indian artists, including the ones in this anthology, it is impossible to simply walk away from the social ills that threaten our communities to engage in an art that prioritizes aesthetics at the cost of ignoring the things that are killing us. We all know the statistics: shorter lives, higher unemployment, younger suicides, and a host of other depressing realities. We know the foundation of these problems is loss of land, and these statistics can only be changed through its return, a grim prospect in light of the unlikelihood of land reform in America. A major dilemma for the Indian artist, then, is commenting in one's art on social policy and articulating community strategies for increased health, while keeping the work artful. Such a conundrum shapes the kind of theory that will be generated by those interested in an ethical criticism. It is our belief that an increased commitment to social realism can actually generate new artistic experimentation rather than shut it down.

Think of it this way: some people might claim that if you write metered or rhymed poetry formal constraints limit your word choices. Those who have tried it, however, know that it also causes you to choose words you would not have considered without the demands of the metrical or rhyming structures. Sociology is not, by default, the death of art any more than meter is the death of poetry. Bad sociology is the death of art (also of sociology), and bad art is the death of art. The question "What might a land-reform novel look like?"—one that has been intimated by Elizabeth Cook-Lynn over the years—is certainly intriguing, and rather than making art impossible, it asks us to find new ways to be artful. It is an endeavor that requires vision, dreaming of things that do not yet exist. An ethical theory, I believe, has to be built on dreams as much as realities, another conundrum in our effort to achieve a theory that both depicts the world as it is and looks beyond to what it might be. This theory then will move in and out of historical dates—in them to assess the state of Native America and out of them to dream of something better. We claim a commitment to a realism that can also embrace artistic vision. Reality does not straddle us and hold us earthbound; it is the necessary beginning point for artistic flights of fancy.

In relation to vision, this is a materialist criticism with a difference: it makes religious matters a central concern. I see two reasons for this. The deplorable situation in Indian country is a spiritual crisis that has to do with the breach of relationship between humanity and creation. Land theft was engineered by the Christian church from the very beginning, a fact that can be established by simply reading Pope Alexander VI's papal bull *Inter Caetera*, issued after first contact, calling for conquest of the so-called New World: "Among the works well pleasing to the Divine Majesty and cherished in our heart, this assuredly ranks highest, that in our times especially the Catholic faith and the Christian religion be exalted and everywhere increased and spread, that the health of souls be cared for and that the barbarous nations be overthrown and brought to the faith itself."[2]

Whether or not it is true, majority culture views the United States as a Christian nation, proclaiming this now more loudly (if less sincerely) than ever. The church has not only offended Indians; it has cut itself off from a relationship with the God it says it serves and who claims, among other things, to be a God of justice, to have created peoples for a reason, and to have put them in particular environments according to Her will. This means the church not only needs to reconcile itself with Native peoples but with God.[3] Until the church rectifies this situation, it is fraudulent. The church has breached a fundamental relationship with creation and its Creator through its massive disruption of the environment of the New World and its inhabitants. Early Christian Indian writers, especially William Apess, seemed to realize that U.S. society had to understand—if in fact it was capable of any self-analysis whatsoever—that its offenses against Indians were a part of its broken relationship with God. Apess knew that otherwise he could not reach his audience.

The second reason for making religious studies a cornerstone of a materialist theory is that spiritual matters are paramount for Indian people themselves and no discussion of art or politics can proceed without referencing them.

As with any call and response, where to leave off one song and take up another always involves infinite choices, something I have learned on those occasions I am called on to sing myself. Perhaps we can answer our foray into the policy world of the 1980s with some Native literary history that leads up to the outpouring of recent creative and nonfiction work among Native people.

A fundamental question might be: How did the invention of Native American literary criticism come about, allowing Native critics to write book-length works about the topic and facilitating the publication of collections of Native writings? Certainly other earlier Native authors preceded contemporary Native critics; we can trace the beginnings of a Native literature in English all the way back to Mohegan author Samson Occom's "A Short Narrative of My Life," published in 1768. We also recognize a significant body of literature, much, but not all, of it nonfiction, that appeared in print in the nineteenth century and included tribal histories, autobiographies, travel narratives, political analysis, theological works, and a wide range of materials appearing in periodicals.

Yet in earlier periods we do not find Native writers referring to a unified body of discourse they call Native literature (or calling it by any other term), though we might note at least two instances where Native authors critique non-Indian representations of Native people in popular literature. One is found in Mohawk writer E. Pauline Johnson's (1861–1913) much-overlooked essay, "A Strong Race Opinion" (1892), perhaps Johnson's strongest piece of writing. The essay laments the lack of individuality in fictional representations of Native women, who are cast all too frequently in the nineteenth century as stereotypes—women who act like they've just stepped out of an essay about Indians rather than like human beings with the capacity to surprise and delight. They are often named Wynona or, as Johnson says, "Once or twice she has borne another appellation, but it always has a 'Winona' sound about it,"[4] and Johnson sets out to prove this by identifying the various Ramonas, Wandas, Wacoustas, and Ienas that populate the pages of non-Indian portrayals of Native women in the nineteenth century. It is a wonderful piece of criticism and satire. The fact that Johnson identifies writings *about* Indians but not *by* Indians is informative, especially given the fact that work of the latter type existed. Johnson, as did other Native writers, even if they knew of such writings, did not speak of them as a coherent body of literature that could be identified as Native.

Another Native critique of popular representations of Indians is found in a scene in Okanogan author Mourning Dove's novel *Cogewea; the Half-blood* (1927). The protagonist, Cogewea, is reading a novel authored by a non-Native "Indian expert" whose short time on the Flathead Reservation of Montana has resulted in assimilating a bunch of nonsense about Indians from the mixed-blood cowboys. The author turns this "information" into a full-blown fictional account. Cogewea's criticism of the passage is as forceful as E. Pauline Johnson's critique, if not as convincing:

> "Bosh!" she mused half aloud. "Show me the Red 'buck' who would *slave* for the most exclusive white 'princess' that lives. Such hash may go with the whites, but the Indian, both full bloods and the despised *breeds*

> know differently. And, that a 'hero' should be depicted as hating his own mother for the flesh and heart that she gave his miserable frame. What a figure to be held up for laudation by either novelist or historian! No *man*, whether First American, Caucasian, or of any other race, could be so beastly inhuman in real life; so low and ungratefully base as to want to hide his own mother. The lower animals respond to this instinct, and can people suppose that the Indian, who is of the heroic, has not the manhood accredited to even the most commercialized of nations? The truth is, he has more love of the undying type than his 'superior' brother ever possessed."[5]

The campy list of predisposed impossibilities for "red bucks" and others (slaving for white women, hating their own mothers, expressing shame over their Indianness) gives us pause, since we know that Indians, like any other humans, can, and sometimes do, experience self-hatred, assimilation, internalized oppression, and other negative behaviors. We might wonder about their natural tendency, on the positive end of the spectrum, to be "of the heroic," because, among other things, the Indian man has "more love of the undying type than his 'superior' brother ever possessed." No doubt Cogewea is reading a really lousy book, but we might suspect there are better ways to point out its faults. And this is not even to mention all the assumptions about men, women, the role of novels, and history as "laudation."

How then did we move from a critique of non-Indian writings to the emergence of a Native literary criticism? The answer, of course, is *not* that no Native literature existed during Johnson's and Mourning Dove's time, a facile assumption that many have made. When did Native authors begin to think of themselves as a community of artists and how did this come about?

This is a difficult question with many paths for us to investigate and more than one of them thorny. Obviously, there is no way my answer can be comprehensive. I want to begin with an observation about publications. The year 1973, somehow, becomes a pivotal point. Any Indian worth her salt knows what happened in Indian country in 1973, but before I say something about activism, there is a fascinating shift in art that occurred around this time in relation to Native people. Any book published before 1973 that might have called itself something like *Native American Literature* would have contained creation stories, songs, and chants translated into English from the original Native languages (often the original text would not be provided, only the English version). After 1973, a book calling itself *Native American Literatur* would contain short stories, poems, plays, excerpts from novels. Literature that called itself something like *Native American Art* before 1973 would have pictures of things like Anazasi pottery shards and would discuss archaeological matters. After 1973, the book would have pictures of paintings, drawings, and sculptures created by contemporary Native artists.

By 1973 a critical mass had been reached so that Native people were no longer considered an exclusively historical phenomenon but a modern one.

The fact that American Indians had taken over Alcatraz in 1969, occupied the BIA building in Washington, D.C., in 1972, and laid siege at Wounded Knee in 1973, no doubt gave rise to the notion that they still existed and that they had demands. Among Native people themselves, a shift of consciousness had occurred from an integrationist tendency that had been inculcated in the boarding-school generation to a view of the inherent worth of Indian identity that became part of the Red Power movement that rejected assimilationist notions. These shifts are brilliantly chronicled in Paul Chaat Smith's (Comanche) and Robert Warrior's (Osage) *Like a Hurricane: The Indian Movement from Alcatraz to Wounded Knee* (1996).

Without this change of consciousness, the conception of the Indian artist is nearly impossible. Before this time there were a number of Indians who did art but few Indians who spoke of themselves as Indian artists. Given the vocational tendencies of boarding schools, graduates often did not imagine their futures as intellectuals, authors, painters, novelists, poets, cultural critics. The shift of consciousness evidenced in the activism of the 1970s was instrumental in the rise not only of militants but of Native artists, and it had a lot of wide-ranging effects, such as the beginning of Native studies courses and programs in universities that came out of the demands of the young Indian protesters.

It was also the wild-and-woolly sixties. Mainstream society was being questioned on a large scale outside of Indian country; for many people, it was a time of self-expression more than of blending in. This worked itself out in a number of ways in the Indian world as well as in the literary one, where various manifestations of antiauthoritarianism would eventually contribute to an attack on institutions as sacred as the literary canon.

In Indian country in 1962, a unique art school was founded that is known today as the Institute of American Indian Art (IAIA). At first, the place was called the Santa Fe Indian School, and kids with problems were sent there from so-called broken homes. The school was a social experiment with a unique emphasis—nowadays we might call it art therapy.

Not everything was as happily progressive as it might sound, however. Let's see, now, we've got all these problem Indian kids, many of them from the Southwest. What are we going to do with them? What are they good at? I know; let's have them make jewelry! So turquoise it was at first, but increasingly IAIA became an Indian arts school instead of an Indian problem-kids school, a key factor being the hiring of more and more Native faculty who wanted to teach students things that would engage their minds as much as their hands. A new critical discourse arose that was much different from the low-level vocational training of federal boarding schools, and it had to do with the creation, expression, analysis, and interpretation of art.

Faculty and students began searching for a new kind of art, one rooted in their home cultures and the cultures of their fellow students, who were to be the teachers along with the faculty. Dorms and buildings were set up to maximize contact, Indians sharing ideas about art with other Indians. important precept was not only to root art in home traditions, and to exp one's own art to the home traditions of Indians of other tribes, but to open up to as many realms as possible beyond traditional definitions. Students were taught art and art history from cultures around the world and from different time periods. Personal expression was encouraged as far as carrying these influences in whatever direction was true to one's artistic vision rather than a strict dictate such as "This is not really what they make at San Ildefonso." Students learned new designs, techniques, materials, styles that went way beyond Indian silversmithing. They were thinking of themselves as artists, not as workers in handicrafts.

Native artists with national reputations came out of IAIA in the late 1960s and throughout the 1970s, and, indeed, a reading of their names sounds like a who's who of Native artists: Gorman, Hauser, Cannon, and many others. During this time period over three thousand Native students attended classes at IAIA, and, given the size of the Native art world at the time, this was to have a tremendous impact.

Drama and poetry were also taught at the school. Every Native drama troupe that emerged in the 1970s was composed of students and directors who had gone to IAIA or had taught there; most Native playwrights themselves have a history with the school. No literary critic, strangely enough, has ever even mentioned, much less examined, the effect of IAIA on Native letters, in spite of the powerful concepts erupting in the school—for instance, Indian cultures as a source for artistic achievement and intellectual development rather than as an impediment to integration; the role of a pan-tribal artistic aesthetic fostered by exchange among Indians of various tribes and even an international perspective fostered by the study of European art and techniques; Indian control of things Indian in terms of teaching, interpreting, and creating art; the notion that Indian tradition could be a beginning point for improvisation in the arts rather than an end point; the belief that Indian artistic integrity could hold up when merged with European artistic practices; an exploration of the emergence of tribal viewpoints in English—which would all prove matters of vital importance to literature and tribal aesthetics in the years to come.

In the world of publishing a number of non-Indian-edited collections had existed before the 1970s that tended toward ethnographic material. Important Indian-authored anthologies were published in the late 1970s and 1980s that not only reinforced the idea of Indians speaking on their own behalf and defining artistic standards for themselves but made a community of Native writers visible to each other in a way they had never been before.

Quapaw-Cherokee writer Geary Hobson's *The Remembered Earth: An Anthology of Contemporary Native American Literature* (1979) not only contained poetry and fiction—instead of creation stories and chants—but within its pages were extremely important Indian-authored critical statements such as N. Scott

Momaday's "The Man Made of Words," Joy Harjo's "Oklahoma: The Prairie of Words," and Hobson's own "The Rise of the White Shaman as a New Form of Cultural Imperialism." The Momaday essay is a groundbreaking exploration of an Indian view of imagination in relation to Native and non-Native traditions. The Harjo piece discusses tribal aesthetics in relation to particularities of place. The Hobson political critique examines issues of appropriation and who can say what about Native literature. In many ways, virtually all the theories we explore here will lead back to these three critical issues.

Acoma author Simon Ortiz's *Earth Power Coming: Short Fiction in Native American Literature* was published in 1983 by the Navajo Community College Press. It was different from Hobson's work in that it included only fiction. The fact that it was published by a tribal college also represented a new zeitgeist in terms of Indians controlling their own artistic output, and it is still exemplary today in terms of a tribally published work getting broad distribution. A number of Native poems and stories have included scenes of the Indian artist having to negotiate her wares with the non-Indian trading post owner, and this has functioned as a metaphor for much more than the best price a character might obtain for her jewelry, reaching, as it does, for broader issues of representation, control, and hegemony. The Ortiz anthology was a landmark for tribal control of tribal literature.

A strong, groundbreaking work followed the next year when Mohawk writer Beth Brant published *A Gathering of Spirit* (1984), a collection composed of poetry, fiction, and personal statements from Native women writers, including a strong representation of lesbian writers and women prisoners. More than anything that had been published to that point, it broke with established notions of literary merit, the makeup of the canon, and modernist aesthetics. And this was before cultural studies was really beginning to take hold. By virtue of its very existence it demonstrated the hegemonic nature of literary inclusion in mainstream society.

It is interesting to consider the names in the Ortiz anthology and how many of them had also been published in Hobson's earlier collection. Part of the power of these books was the way in which they created community, drawing together a group of Native writers who at least knew each other's work. If any given author had not met all his peers, he could read their work in the same book where his own work was published. E. Pauline Johnson, of course, had no such reference materials to draw on in terms of Native collections of poetry and prose. Our own anthology builds on these Native traditions initiated by Hobson, Ortiz, and Brant by gathering together not only a number of Native writers who know each other but who will address each other's work within its pages, a second necessary step once a community of thinkers becomes evident to each other.

The early anthologies had a ripple effect, I believe: the recognition *within* Indian country led to an increased awareness *outside* it in the critical world. Early non-Indian authored book-length studies of Indian writing included

Alan Velie's *Four American Indian Literary Masters* (1982), Kenneth Lincoln's *Native American Renaissance* (1983), and Andrew Wiget's *Native American Literature* (1985). I am not certain one could ascribe to these three works any uniformity of approach, although certainly all of them consider what is tribal about tribal literature and remark its negotiations between oral and written modes. What is more interesting, it seems to me, is their contradictions of each other and sometimes even the disparities within single texts. Velie, for example, defends Native literature on aesthetic grounds lest anyone call it "protest fiction," citing James Baldwin's supposed commitment to aesthetics over politics and his oft-quoted statements about Richard Wright. Velie titles one of his chapters, "*House Made of Dawn:* Nobody's Protest Novel." Some who are more cynical than I might argue that defending Momaday against charges of polemics is a little like worrying if anyone will accuse the pope of being Protestant. While *House Made of Dawn* certainly has political implications, its politics, some critics have argued, seem to be more covert than overt. Velie's idea of literary "masters," as will be pointed out in another part of this essay, came to be questioned in later years under the auspices of cultural studies, but one can certainly appreciate his intent here to demonstrate the excellence of Native literature in relation to other great writings.

In Velie's volume we see many other aspects of a modernist orientation in terms of the books he chooses for analysis and the way he approaches them: he discusses the surrealism in James Welch's poetry, the comedy in his novel *Winter in the Blood,* an epic search theme indicative of a grail motif in Leslie Marmon Silko's *Ceremony,* and Gerald Vizenor's postmodernism, arguably a diversion from the modernism just alluded to. Though Indians might be militant, as Velie seems to admit, and though he might like their radical politics and the time period that produced them, their novels hold back their political opinions in favor of artistic accomplishment, as if the two are contrary endeavors. One might suspect it depends on *which* novel one looks at and *how* (there is all that atomic bomb stuff in *Ceremony,* after all)— and, especially, if one meanders a little off the beaten path and considers the vast body of work outside that of Velie's four "masters."

Velie is one of our academic elders, a pioneer of Native literature instruction at the university level, having taught one of the first, if not *the* first, Native literature courses in the country in 1971. His critical study has several strengths. One is it shows just what a stellar group of Indian novelists had arisen who could outmodern the modernists, employing some of their techniques—achronicity, multiple viewpoints, stream of consciousness, and other internal perspectives—with extreme skill. Secondly, Velie points to an aspect that is essential to any literature, minority or not: it has to have some element of universalism, a point of recognition that can speak across cultures to the human condition. One of the implications of Velie's work, I believe—it is, after all, the product of a Shakespeare scholar—is that one can read Shakespeare more richly having read Indian literature and one can read Indian literature with greater pleasure by considering Shakespeare. Pointing to these intersections between European literatures and Indian ones is a worthwhile endeavor, even when I have a hard time with particulars, such as seeing the grail cup in *Ceremony* or, more importantly, seeing apoliticism as a virtue.

Kenneth Lincoln seems to disagree with Velie, although it is not entirely clear why: "Alan R. Velie looks at Momaday, Welch, Silko, and Vizenor in *Four American Indian Literary Masters* (1982), but he slides away from the texts with questions of biography, theme, and non-Indian artistic influence. Whether the literatures carry 'the power to move us,' raised by Dell Hymes, still begs critical response." Lincoln is not exactly clear what rocks his world, what has the power to move him, although one suspects it is deeply tribal: "Grounded Indian literature is tribal; its fulcrum is a sense of relatedness."[6]

Emerging out of the Lincoln book is a term whose definition is as ambiguous as Lincoln's arguments. The term will be a source of controversy for years to come: "The Native American renaissance here targeted," Lincoln says, "less than two decades of published Indian literature, is a written renewal of oral traditions translated into Western literary forms."[7] The term "Native American renaissance"has been something of a floating signifier in the years since its proclamation. Just what has been revived? What was it like before its resuscitation? Why was it only two decades old in 1983, especially given the overwhelming evidence otherwise (two hundred years of books in English, for example)? Is the claim that it originates in an oral tradition a given fact? Could it have any textual precedents? What kinds of translations are occurring —are they the same as translating one language into another? In the synthesis that is the result of oral and written convergence, how are Indian viewpoints affected? Western viewpoints? If Indian literature is actually oral in its origins, might Western literature be also?

Lincoln was right, of course, in a certain sense. Something *had* happened, most noticeably in the area of fiction writing and poetry: there was more of it than there had ever been, and the content differed from earlier works and even in the way the stories were being told. There were also some strong continuities with earlier writers that could have been established with a little attention to literary history. The "homecoming" impulse, for example, a phrase used by critic William Bevis to describe novels about Indians returning home to the reservation, had long been established in fiction from the 1920s and 1930s, a point Louis Owens would later clarify in *Other Destinies.*

If Lincoln seems uncertain about what constitutes the field itself, he appears equally unclear about what to do with it: "There is no codified discipline to approach these materials in their cultural diversities. A scholar should attend to cultural-specific differences among tribes but also recognize the pan-Indian acculturations that reunify tribal Americans among themselves and across tribes."[8] Lincoln himself might somewhat contradict his critique of Velie's attention to Western influences, since Lincoln recommends, with great frequency, a scholarship that is multidisciplinary, though it seems more rooted in ethnography, oral traditions, Indian worldviews than, for example, in any sense of Native nationalism, tribal governments, jurisdictions, and sovereignties. It is multidisciplinary only to the degree one excludes political science from the disciplines.

Louis Owens would later go on to examine the themes of the novels of the 1920s and 1930s in relation to a kind of cloud of uncertainty about the Indian future that hangs over these works. In the earlier book-length critical works of the 1980s one might detect an uncertainty in regard to the future of Indian criticism. Andrew Wiget's somewhat generically titled *Native American Literature* at least tries to account for a written literature in the eighteenth and nineteenth centuries as well as the prevalence of novelists in the 1920s and 1930s, histories that are necessary before conclusions can be arrived at in terms of just what has been revived in the renaissance and the general state of affairs before Native literature's supposed transformation. Wiget lays out much of this history without speculating as to how it shaped later fiction, poems, and plays; but he seems to be aware that important connections exist. If our own anthology also demonstrates a certain tenuousness as to the question "What to do with Native-authored work?" one clear step has been made that differentiates us from the Velie, Lincoln, and Wiget milestones: we have ventured beyond the work of N. Scott Momaday, Leslie Silko, Louise Erdrich, James Welch, and Gerald Vizenor. In fact, most of the essays collected here focus on "noncanonical" texts, or whatever one might call the work of the great majority of writers who are not identified as one of the "masters." Some of our authors have even written on works that might not have been considered literature in these early studies or by a few of the more stodgy contemporary critics.

These early critical works, and other predominantly non-Indian scholarship, promoted the canonization of five Native novels in particular: *House Made of Dawn* (1968), *Winter in the Blood* (1974), *Ceremony* (1978), *Darkness in Saint Louis Bearheart* (1978), and *Love Medicine* (1984). By 1990, though more than two thousand books had been authored by Native people in twenty years, a huge proportion of the critical attention had been focused on these five novels. Even today literary journals run special issues on the same five Native authors over and over again, with an occasional bow to Louis Owens, Sherman Alexie, maybe one or two others at best. Most Native authors of fiction have a greater chance of batting in next year's World Series than receiving critical recognition, even in an Indian literary journal.[9] Much of this, I think, has to do with pedagogy. Those who write the articles teach these particular canonical works in their classes. They would have to rethink the Indian world if they began teaching fiction outside of recovery, ethnography, homecoming, retribalization, and oral tradition modes that have been prevalent in the popular fiction and its attendant criticism.

By the 1980s, because of the high-modernist techniques of the canonical writers themselves and their validation by the non-Indian critics, a bias toward modernism had emerged. A very large body of Indian writings was ignored, such as the theological discussions of the early Christian authors; women's autobiographies as well as men's; the sentimental poetry and prose of E. Pauline Johnson; formula fiction like Mourning Dove's *Cogewea; the Half-blood;* a host of tribal histories that also serve as potential aesthetic discussions; and political writings like William Apess's remarkable communal composition, *Indian Nullification of the Unconstitutional Laws of the State of Massachusetts Relative to the Marshpee Tribe; or, The Pretended Riot Explained* (1835), which today might be regarded as an early sovereignty primer. Many other works were avoided that did not fit easily into old-fashioned notions of what constitutes the literary and, moreover, what is authentically Indian.

While the 1980s critical approaches may have been marked by many of the formulas of modernism in terms of what is recognized as a legitimate literary text and how those works should be read, Native critical aesthetics seemed to insist on modernism with a tribal difference, a revised modernism. Though these assumptions were mostly left unstated, the criticism still reinforced its own premises—particularly the widely held assertions about the prominence of mixed-blood authors and their role of mediation between non-Indian and Native worlds. This notion seems to have become particularly pronounced in the 1980s as a slight revision of the much-earlier "torn between two worlds" views of mixed-bloods. While in *The Sacred Hoop* Paula Gunn Allen would attribute the predominant theme of the alienated tribal protagonist to the mixed-blood identities of contemporary Native authors and their own alienation from both white and Indian cultures,[10] one might wonder if alienation isn't at least equally attributable to modernism itself, with its tragic orientation toward an oppressive world and its dehumanizing technologies.

A pure formalism that elevated texts over contexts and emphasized the New Critical tenets of the 1930s—featuring dense poetic language, ambiguity, and the internal unity of literary works in spite of their difficulty to read—did not emerge; that is, the New Critical repudiation of sociological readings of literature did not gain a foothold in Native literary studies. One might note, however, certain limitations of culturally based Native literary criticism during this time period. Unlike the advent of cultural studies that would spring up all over the country and take command of U.S. literature classes in the early 1990s, here culture was almost always defined as ethnography rather than politics. This is to say that tribes were always viewed as cultures rather than governments. Culturally based arguments in relation to literature involved claims that virtually all Indian writing is based on oral tradition and ceremony. Yet there was little actual tribally specific analysis or consideration of how oral tradition itself had a literary history and had changed over time.

Avoidance of these issues diverted attention to superficial generalizations about "the Indian mind," whatever that might be ("it" was always described as "nonlinear"). Indian writing became circular, non-Aristotelian, lacking a beginning, middle, and end since oral stories, supposedly, do not have linear plots—and what else could Native writing be based on if not oral stories? Textual contributions from earlier generations of Native writers were seldom considered in relation to today's literature.

Every Indian story was actually about tricksters if one looked deeply enough. There were tricksters in every teapot. The job of the critic was to locate the trickster in the story. The simple fact that there is no such thing as a trickster in indigenous cultures, that tricksters were invented by anthropologists, that no Indian language has the word "trickster" in it, that many people from home would not know what literary critics were talking about when using terms such as "trickster" were simply ignored. Of course, Native cultures, and many cultures around the world, including European ones, have story characters who behave in ways that are very much like the ways of what are often called "tricksters," but early critical formulations often existed apart from historical specificity. No doubt a lingua franca with terms like "trickster" was necessary, but many had not considered the possibilities, and limitations, of the emerging terminology, having assumed its universal applicability.

The problems of considering the field a unified body of discourse called "Native literature" went unexamined, as well as the history of arriving at such a viewpoint. While disclaimers about tribal differences were often uttered, few explored what those differences might actually be or how tribally specific approaches rather than Native literature approaches might change the way Native works were read. In our own collection this debate is ongoing and ranges from, on one side of the spectrum, Janice Acoose's highly specific Cree readings of Canadian literature, what one might call a Cree performance of Cree texts, to Tol Foster's insistence that failing to account for broader regions that surround Native writings will inevitably result in missing significant aspects of their meaning.

In the 1980s criticism, Native writings that failed to measure up to their supposed roots in oral tradition or trickster games were simply ignored or made to fit. The radically assimilationist writings of the Society of American Indian leader Carlos Montezuma, for example, were treated as if they did not exist. Christian Indian writers were either ignored or analyzed as if they could not possibly be actually talking about Christianity—a good trickster reading would reveal that Christianity was just a subversive guise for something more Indian. Given the diversity of Native perspectives, there was surprisingly little engagement in the field with some of the more uncomfortable texts—unless the critic became an apologist, revealing the true Indian meaning hidden behind the assimilationist subterfuge. Critics outlined many literary approaches without any attention to history, politics, language, or other factors that could move theoretical claims beyond clichés. Even today, obviously, many of these problems still need to be worked through.

At the beginning of our story, that is, the opening of this introduction, I mentioned some European texts that rocked the theoretical world. All men, all old-world European. Not an auspicious beginning for a Native critic. So I hasten to add that against the backdrop of the all-male, all old-world texts, feminism came along in the 1980s to cause a radical shift in theoretical and literary modes. Feminism would alter poststructuralism, psychoanalytic theory, postcolonial studies, gay and lesbian studies, cultural studies, and semiotics. Then, confronted with ideas from gender studies, feminist literary theory greatly expanded its focus:

> Like feminism, which critically analyzes and attempts to transfrom contemporary social systems, feminist literary theory entails a twofold movement encompassing both the critique of already existing sociolinguistic structures and the invention of alternative models of reading and writing.
>
> In its earliest phases, this double movement focused almost exclusively on female-gendered issues; however, the increased participation of feminists of color, coupled with the rise of gender studies during the early 1980s, has expanded feminism's field of study considerably. Generally, feminist literary theory is divided into four stages or trends focusing in various ways on gender-based textual issues:
>
> 1. an analysis of representations of women in male-authored texts;
> 2. "gynocriticism," a term coined by Elaine Showalter that refers to the development of a uniquely female aesthetic and an alternative, women's literary tradition;
> 3. "gender studies," or an analysis of the ways all texts, including those written by men, are marked by gender; and
> 4. explorations of how racial, sexual, and class differences among women expand previous models of gendered reading and writing.[11]

Some critics during the late 1970s and 1980s insisted that feminists recognize, rather than simply ignore, a dynamic relationship between feminism and lesbianism. In her 1980 essay, "Compulsory Heterosexuality and Lesbian Existence,"[12] Adrienne Rich develops the idea that all bonds between women, not merely sexual ones, are part of a lesbian continuum, thus making lesbianism central to any understanding of feminism or even of women's relations generally. Rich exposes the arbitrary nature by which Western culture naturalizes male-female bonds. By questioning this singular trajectory of man and woman, she opens up other possibilities, which she presents as part of her continuum. Most radically, given the time it is written, Rich's essay goes beyond simply arguing that homosexuality is as natural as heterosexuality; she argues that heterosexuality itself is an invention reinforced by "compulsory" dictates guided by economic forces, class structures, governments, and punishment for those who do not conform. Heterosexuality is not a universal, inherent, inevitable, or even natural state, even though its proponents often pretend it is.

We note Showalter's invention of the term "gynocriticsm" here in acknowledging that it might have had some effect on Paula Gunn Allen's description of what she calls "gynecentric" cultures throughout *The Sacred Hoop*, as well as on earlier work, and it might have contributed to her bravery in publishing a chapter on lesbianism in a Native studies book.

Paula Gunn Allen's Indigenous Feminism

The evolution of feminism is central to understanding how *The Sacred Hoop* ended up in print as the first book-length work of literary criticism published by an American Indian author, though the question of whether feminism is relevant to Native cultures has had much to do with its cautious application to American Indian literatures. This very question is addressed in this anthology, where Cheryl Suzack takes on Navajo writer Laura Tohe's claims in Tohe's essay, "There Is No Word for Feminism in My Language."

An important contribution of women of color to feminism in the 1980s was the anthology *This Bridge Called My Back: Writings by Radical Women of Color* (1981). Both editors of the volume, Gloria Anzaldua and Cherrie Moraga, identify as Chicana and lesbian, and the book contains lesbian writers in all sections rather than a token, often unacknowledged, representation in a broader feminist offering. Many of its writers critique the racism and classism of canonized feminist writings of the 1970s and earlier time periods. In the preface, Moraga "declares that Women of Color are revolutionary forces, bridges who straddle the divisions within society."[13]

It is interesting to note that Gloria Anzaldua's book *Borderlands/La Frontera: The New Mestiza* was published in 1986, the same year as *The Sacred Hoop*. In it, Anzaldua "refuses to prioritize any one component of her identity . . . [instead choosing] multiple and enigmatic self-positioning and social relegation in and outside canons . . . and institutions. . . . Anzaldua contests liberal pluralist delineations of lesbian and gay subjectivity merely in terms of identity or lifestyle, instead positing a politicized queerness that reclaims the revolutionary roots of gay liberation in its radical interconnectedness with all struggles against oppression."[14] In Anzaldua's writing we see many of the traits of the later gender and queer studies that would challenge feminism, particularly in relation to the way queer theory resists defining its own parameters, instead searching out all things betwixt and between, emphasizing border crossings of various sorts, complicating identities, and transgressing boundaries. Anything that confuses the distinctions between male and female, hetero and homo, that points to their interrelatedness rather than their oppositional nature is of interest; even better is whatever can demonstrate that the categories themselves are fictitious.

To make another connection of interest to us, these same open-ended, infinitely variable traits provide Gerald Vizenor's justification for associating postmodern theories with the traits of the so-called trickster of Native North America. More on this later. This also marks, if not the beginning, at least the continuance, of the opening of a can of worms in relation to identities and relativism. Just exactly what can be claimed as an Indian identity in the context of all this border crossing is an ongoing debate that will also be taken up in this book you hold. Daniel Justice's essay argues that Elizabeth Cook-Lynn's criticism of mixed-blood ideologies sometimes fails to pay attention to a complicated matrix of kinship, and Cheryl Suzack claims that both those who celebrate and those who denigrate "mixed-bloodedness" organize arguments around a category (the mixed-blood) that tells us little about an individual's cultural and political affiliations.

This bit of feminist history helps to locate Paula Gunn Allen's book, which appears early, just before a critical shift in feminism as the new gender studies sought to destabilize gender categories themselves—where terms like "female" and "feminine," the latter term appearing in Allen's subtlitle, would be problematized. In the radical subversion of gender that came after these earlier stages, the categories male and female become socially constructed ideas that are historically unstable, differing in various historical periods and cultures. Famously, in Judith Butler's 1990 *Gender Trouble: Feminism and the Subversion of Identity,* a work published three years after Allen's *The Sacred Hoop,* gender became something we do rather than who we are.

By referring to Butler's later publication of *Gender Trouble,* I am not trying to put Allen and Butler in some kind of ranking order, with the Butler work representing an advancement in thought, nor do I wish to speculate as to whether or not Allen would have rallied to the cry of gender as performance had she read Butler before writing her own book. I am not the kind of critic who believes that literary criticism, or the world at large, gets better every year.

I do wish to point out the transitional timeframe in which *The Sacred Hoop* hangs suspended—contemporary with the early theorists who sought a woman's literature, often drawing attention to silenced or forgotten women's voices and attempting an articulation of a female literary aesthetic that could be formulated from a reading of neglected texts. *The Sacred Hoop* predates the later theorists who problematized the very term "female" itself, while safeguarding their own set of favorite books that demonstrate their principles, books that undermine distinctions between genders, where the categories themselves seem to break down.

It is important to note that women of color made significant contributions to gender theory because of their insistence that not all women are the same, since factors such as race and class affect how women experience both oppression and resistance. By contesting a universalized, "one-size-fits-all" feminism that seemed to have a white, middle-class audience as its constituency, women of color, with their commitment to difference, contributed significantly to a burgeoning antiessentialist critique.

Today we might see this with some irony, at least in Paula Gunn Allen's case, given the many charges of essentialism that are frequently levied against her. The critique of Allen often centers around her treatment of Indian identity, as well as reductive statements about what seems to be a universalized Indian worldview, consciousness, and epistemology. To make matters overly simple for the point of illustration, some might come away from the Allen book having reached the facile conclusion that Indians are radically different from white folks and radically similar to each other.

Indian identity may very well may have been a key factor in Allen's essentialism because gender identity and Indian identity are not necessarily the same thing. It is one thing to say gender is not who we are but what we do, as the later gender theorists said; it is quite another to say Indians are not who we are but what we do (although there are some who make such claims). This is to say, there are a good number of people in Indian country who still believe Indian identity has something to do with who we are, no matter how difficult it is to define exactly what this means. "Indian as performance" is not an idea that has caught on, unless one is referring to notorious fakers—the likes of Grey Owl and Jamake Highwater. If Allen has problems working out her own relationship to issues of authenticity and identity, so do the rest of us who call ourselves Native critics. The notion of just what makes tribal literature tribal is a vexing problem that ends up a focus, in one way or another, of each essay in our own collection. It is much easier to describe the tribalness of tribal literature as a process than to pin down a definition; the frustrating paradox has to do with the fact that one is, nonetheless, often put in the position of having to come up with a definition.

Allen's essentialism deserves further consideration than what it has been given. At the time she wrote *The Sacred Hoop*, many Native American studies departments were just establishing themselves as academic disciplines, some of them brand-new. It was probably not very profitable during this time period to approach university administrators, many of whom are conservative by nature—certainly few have read Foucault or Butler— and say, "We would like to have a Native American studies department or a major. And, oh, by the way we don't think Indians really exist" (or "Indians are just a matter of performance"). Early histories of academic units usually involve strong claims to an identity and the initial establishment of a protectionist mode, preserving cherished ideals rather than deconstructing them. Allen's critics need to do a better job of analyzing the historical moment that surrounds *The Sacred Hoop* and contributes to her views of women's and Native identities.

By insisting on essential differences from Euroamerican cultures and even Eurofeminism, Allen was attempting to deal with the thorny problem of theorizing difference, one that has stumped many critics besides Allen who do not get called essentialists. While contrasting Indians with Europeans, however, Allen often reduced diversity among Native people to a gynocratic utopia and made other totalizing statements about a singular Indian consciousness. She pointed to Indian differences from Europeans but did not extend the notion to Indian diversity across and within tribes, at least in any way that might have challenged her problematic gynocracy. The critics of her essentialism, however, often overlook the vast knowledge of historical and cultural particulars that she drew on (particularly in regard to Keres culture) and that somewhat mediated her sweeping statements. Instead they focus on her lapses into generalizations, which are, in fact, frequent. This first book-length work is truly a wonderful and thorny beginning, as fascinating for the problems it created as the questions it answered, a state of affairs that some people, myself being one of them, would call a great literary success.

The Sacred Hoop, which probably outsold all other Native American literary critical works before and after its publication, has had an impact on other disciplines besides Native literature—women's studies, gender studies, and queer studies, for instance. It has also found a popular reading audience outside the academy. Perhaps at the time of its publication the book spoke to those interested in a spirit-based view of the universe often ignored in other theoretical discussions, which tended to back away from religious issues that critics associated with foundationalism. This was a time when even religious studies departments would debate the social construction of religious ideology. Some academic departments went as far as asserting that the only ones qualified to teach religion objectively were those who did not believe in it—those who would emphasize that religious experience, like all human experience, is constructed by culture rather than revealed by God. In minority studies, especially, a fear existed among academics in regard to speaking out about spirituality and being perceived as a throwback, someone representing himself as an academic while still listening to his ancestors on the sly. Allen's book recognized that religious issues could not be left out of theoretical discussions, since they are central to the ways we construct reality.

Thornier issues such as how cultural specificity, politics, and history limit access to the spirituality of other cultures go unexamined in the book though both Geary Hobson and Leslie Marmon Silko had addressed these problems in their white shaman essays that predated the publication of *The Sacred Hoop.*

Allen's failure to historicize and theorize the problematics of insider and outsider status sometimes lends itself to universalist readings of her book. The fact that the book contains no references to the legal basis for American Indian tribes does not help clarify these matters. *The Sacred Hoop* implies a cultural basis for tribes, one originating in various forms of tradition, especially ritual, rather than a governmental one that has evolved through treaties, court cases, and federal Indian law. A more dynamic middle ground, where traditions and politics inform each other, does not seem to be Allen's aim. Systems of tribal governance before and after contact are notably absent from her discussion. There is something of an antimaterialist bias in Allen, a real irony since the focus of her book is a pan-tribal analysis, which includes a central argument that there is a concrete physical and verifiable manifestation of ritual. And her chapter, "Something Sacred Going on Out there: Myth and Vision in American Indian Literature" is a brilliant tour de force analysis of Black Elk's vision, arguing for its materiality. Nonetheless, at other times, Allen seems to reject the very notion of materiality that she argues for elsewhere: "Ritual based cultures are founded on the primary assumption that the universe is alive and that it is supernaturally ordered. That is, they do not perceive economic, social, or political elements as central; rather, they organize their lives around a sacred, metaphysical principle. If they see a cause-and-effect relationship between events, they would ascribe the cause to the operation of nonmaterial energies or forces."[15] Tell that to the tribal treasurer writing the annual budget report!

Writing about the poetry of Wendy Rose, Allen states, "In poems that speak to her dispossession, as in most of her work, Rose maintains a clear, steady, spiritual basis. She often futhers her point with spirit-based imagery, so that the thrust of her work moves steadily toward a nonmaterial, nonsocial, and nonpolitical significance. The social, political, interpersonal, and personal images and statements she forms become metaphors for spirit-infused consciousness—a thrust toward uniting fragmented elements of her life that she shares with the other Indian women writers."[16]

In spite of the obvious problems in keeping one's metaphysics and politics separate, those who would eventually accuse Allen of essentialism center their critique around the monolithic quality of her work, which they say reduces wide cultural diversity in Native North America to a single Indian consciousness. I have yet to hear a critic say, in relation to Allen, How can one separate spirituality from governance? This reveals something about the nature of the resistance Native scholars face in relation to critics who are themselves extremely limited by the narrow range of what they consider to be "literary" or even "Native." And this despite an enthusiasm for a widely pervasive cultural studies movement that has opened up the rest of literature to a much broader field.

Reminiscent of Velie's earlier study that defended Native novelists against polemical charges, Allen writes,

> Western novels of protest are aesthetic responses to oppression and cultural dissolution and generally focus on the oppressor rather than on the oppressed, a focus different from that taken by American Indians in this century. American Indians in general have more often than not refused to engage in protest in their politics as in their fiction and poetry. They have chosen rather to focus on their own customs and traditions and to ignore the white man as much as possible. As a result they have been able to resist effectively both colonization and genocide.[17]

Velie had at least recognized a radical time period that surrounded a conservative fiction. At times, Allen makes her antimaterialism a foundational cornerstone of her study: "The oral tradition, based on a mystical understanding of unity that is not as material as it is psychic, provides an axis for the work of contemporary American Indian writers, and this axis is as present in the work of 'marginal' Indians like Rose, Hogan, Harjo, and TallMountain as it is in the work of the more traditional women writing today."[18] Yet one might argue that *The Sacred Hoop* owes much more to protest than Allen seems to realize—

if one considers the role of sixties and seventies activism in the evolution of Native studies courses at the university level and the corresponding literature of the period.

It is interesting to note that in Allen's subtitle are the words "recovering," "feminine," and "traditions," in that order. Such themes are possible in the retribalization period of the sixties and seventies in ways they had not been earlier. Partially as a result of the Indian movement, Native people sought renewed connections to traditions that had, in some cases, been outlawed, and, in others, discouraged in boarding schools and various assimilation programs in previous generations. As mentioned earlier, Paul Chaat Smith and Robert Warrior, in *Like a Hurricane,* trace out the multifaceted changes that occurred in Indian country in the decades that precede the sixties and seventies, arguing that internal shifts in Indian thinking, very different from that of the boarding-school generation, had to occur before events such as Alcatraz, the takeover of the BIA, and Wounded Knee could even be imagined.

Native imaginative literature owes much to the activism that surrounded it, even though we might be frustrated in seeking evidence of such a relationship in novels, poems, and plays. While Canada saw the publication of a "movement novel" one year before *The Sacred Hoop*, Okanogan author Jeannette Armstrong's *Slash* (1985), the United States had yet to produce one.

Red Power movements, however, whatever lack of overt references to them seemed to permeate the pages of U.S. Native fiction, created a shift in consciousness by implanting Indian pride, without which it was impossible to imagine oneself an Indian writer. If a potential Native intellectual operates from a set of assumptions based on the boarding-school mentality of the previous generation—that all traces of residual Indianness need be eliminated before a successful integration into mainstream society can occur—that individual is not going to imagine himself or herself as a Native writer, painter, or intellectual. Such terms seem oxymoronic in an environment of such radical assimilation. Native activism of the 1960s and '70s was an important part of what made the *idea* of the Native artist possible.

Further, if one considers the themes prominent in the imaginative literature of the same time period, as well as the realities in American Indian life as tribes sought to relearn languages and renew ceremonies that, in some cases, had not been practiced or had gone underground for many years, one sees that activism was central, not peripheral to these endeavors: One does not try to relearn her language or a dance or a ceremonial role if one does not believe there is any inherent worth in Indian identity, that it should be traded for integration in the mainstream, that modern life and traditional life are two incongruities. In Indian country there is sometimes a tension between those who do cultural recovery work, such as language classes and ceremonial leadership, and political activists—yet both kinds of work are deeply interdependent. It is a mistake to attribute one to the metaphysical untouched by material realities.

It fascinates me that in Métis writer D'Arcy McNickle's 1936 novel, *The Surrounded,* its protagonist Archilde Leon doodles, draws pictures on hats, plays the fiddle, and even wanders around the Pacific Northwest for a spell, getting paid as a musician. Yet at no point does Archilde imagine himself a *Native* artist, even when he considers going to Paris to take up the violin more seriously than he can on the Flathead Reservation. The novel even mentions an Indian string quartet whose members, like Archilde (and McNickle himself, coincidentally), were trained in music at boarding school; yet, afterwards the musicians fall into dissipated lives. McNickle writes, "Only a few of the several dozen he [Mr. Duffield, boarding-school teacher] had taught continued in the direction he had given them. Among those few were some older boys who had played as a quartette at the Sunday teas. They organized an Indian String Quartette which won something of a reputation in Pacific Coast cities. Archilde knew them later, and though there was no doubt of their success, something had gone wrong with them and even they had lost the track."[19]

The Surrounded, as remarkable a novel as it is, is not a portrait of the Indian artist by any stretch of the imagination, and the reason is that few during McNickle's time could quite imagine themselves as Indian artists, even though there were Indians who did art. McNickle himself seemed to feel that leaving the Flathead Reservation and never returning was an essential part of any progress he might make as an intellectual.

In choosing the terms dealing with recovery and traditions for her subtitle, Allen mediates in the retribalization period by also bringing to bear the idea of the feminine, drawing on those concerns contemporary to the feminism of her time that had to do with recovering a body of women's writing and theorizing a feminist aesthetic for it. Allen sets about doing this by drawing heavily on her own Laguna tradition, emphasizing creation stories in which the thought processes of powerful female figures account for the beginnings of Laguna institutions. Like the early feminism that sought to unearth forgotten works written by women and give voice to women silenced in the past, Allen emphasizes the way that historical and ethnographic records have left out women's contributions to Native cultures.

Where Allen has drawn fire in more recent years has had to do with a monolithic treatment of Native and European cultures in which Indian culture is measured in relation to its difference from a white totalized Other. Indian culture is characterized by harmony, European culture by hierarchy; Indians by balance because of an emphasis on relationships and responsibility, Europeans by dualistic splits that originate from a sin-based view of the universe; Indians by a merging of physical and spiritual realities, Europeans by various bifurcations of body and soul. One of Allen's chapters is subtitled, "From Gynecentric to Patriarchal"; the chapter itself opens with the sentence, "During the five hundred years of Anglo-European colonization, the tribes have seen a progressive shift from gynecentric, egalitarian, ritual-based social systems to secularized structures closely imitative of the European patriarchal system."[20] Such a claim seems to be based on the assumption that no tribe could ever be patriarchal and no aspect of European culture gynecentric (whatever such a term might mean).

Many with a historical bent that leans toward a dynamic, interactive view of history, see the matter as much more complicated than "Feminist utopia goes downhill after invasion," and feminists themselves might insist on a greater agency for women than this view might entail. Some might remark a similarity with other falls from various graces that turn history into a simplistic before and after. Sometimes my students, both Indian and non, tell me that Indian women are treated better in Native cultures than white women are in European ones, which seems to me problematic, given not only the reductive nature of the generalization but the number of Native women who are fighting the good fight in relation to terrible systems of sexism and abuse every day of their lives. To some degree overly idealistic depictions of these matters in books and articles have contributed to such viewpoints.

Yet we need to understand the moment from which Allen writes in order that we might give her work the great deal of credit it deserves. Not only had early feminism opposed a feminine aesthetic against a masculine one (if women ran the world there would be no war, for example), one of the most influential books in the history of Native studies had embraced a similar methodology. Standing Rock Sioux writer Vine Deloria, Jr.'s landmark 1973 work, *God Is Red,* a comparative religious study, had treated Native religion and Christianity as two reducible phenomena so that Deloria could make certain points about ways of viewing temporal and spatial realities. In spite of Deloria's claims about the incommensurability of the two religions, in the historical record we could find evidence of Christian sects such as the Gnostics, for example, who might closely resemble the practically minded Indian religious practitioners Deloria describes. Or we might find evidence of Indian religious thought deeply concerned with temporality in ways that might remind us of the Christians Deloria sets out to critique. Yet in spite of the oppositional framework, Deloria produces an eminently useful text that seems tailor-made for many of the surveys we find ourselves teaching in Native American studies—in spite of some of its philosophical problems and inconsistencies. In a Native philosophy course, in particular, it seems almost criminal to leave Deloria's book off the syllabus. It asks students to think about time and space in a way that many of them haven't before. As different as *The Sacred Hoop* is from Deloria's book in terms of its orientation toward feminism and literature, still in the way arguments are organized around Indian and European universals, it is quite similar.

In addition to the monolithic outlook that structures many of its chapters, another notable characteristic of *The Sacred Hoop* is its lack of attention to nineteenth- and early-twentieth-century Native writers; in fact, a kind of uneasiness about what to do with them seems to surround their mention:

> There are various kinds of American Indian novels. Some of them, though written by American Indians, have little or nothing to say about Indian life. The first novel published by a Native American, the Cherokee breed John Rollin Ridge's *The Life and Adventures of Joaquin Murieta, the Celebrated California Bandit* (1854), and the three novels written in the 1920s by another Cherokee breed John Milton Oskison are largely of this category, though each in its way takes up themes that pervade later Native American fiction proper. Ridge's novel, while not about Indians, is about native response to invasion and conquest. Joaquin Murieta is a California Mexican who avenges the murders of his people that occur as a result of the gold rush, the Mexican-American War, and the takeover of California by the United States. The novel contributed to Chicano/Latino protest lore more than a hundred years after its writing. Oskison's three novels do not treat identifiably Indian themes, but they are each set in Indian Territory and include Indians as minor characters. In his last novel, *Brothers Three,* Indians (breeds like himself) appear as major characters, and the futile struggle to function in the white world is that book's major theme. In *Brothers Three,* Oskison is the first Native American writer to take as a theme the prejudice experienced by breeds. In various guises, that theme would pervade Native American novels throughout the twentieth century.[21]

One might note that the first section of the chapter that follows this statement is a discussion of the work of Mourning Dove and D'Arcy McNickle, and one wonders if this implies that these are authors who *do* have something to say about Indian life. The phrase "Native American fiction proper" is certainly telling, especially for those of us who would go on to study or write the *im*proper ones. Allen's own novel, *The Woman Who Owned the Shadows* (1983), with its lesbian protagonist, probably had its own difficulties with "proper" behavior.

The vacillation between the first sentence quoted here—the one that opens the chapter about Oskison's lack of attention to Indian matters—and the last three sentences about Oskison, where Allen concludes that he has things to say about Indians, is interesting. Rather than claiming Oskison explores Cherokee realities, Allen says he writes about breeds. *Brothers Three,* however, does not simply take place in some undefined geography; its events occur on Cherokee land within the Cherokee Nation, and its protagonists are three Cherokee citizens. Why is the novel about breeds rather than about the faction of Cherokee citizenry that made their living as cattlemen? Is "breed" really their most salient characteristic? *Brothers Three* relentlessly interrogates the meaning of land, and since the land is within Cherokee jurisdiction and is discussed in relation to its Cherokee inhabitants, it does not take much of a leap to call this a Cherokee discussion. Perhaps the "gynecentricity" of these characters is not marked enough for Allen, or maybe she has a hard time locating their Indian minds. Yet some might argue that the novel, especially because of its naturalism, is a more convincing Cherokee portrayal than some Cherokee works written today that trot out all the beads and feathers and try too hard to prove their Cherokeeness.

One of the ways, then, we might account for the absence of the nineteenth-century writers in Allen's study is that they do not present the kind of Indians she is looking for. In fairness, her book focuses on novels and poetry, and the great majority of nineteenth-century Native writing is nonfiction. Yet one might wonder if this larger body of Native thought, especially in a book like *The Sacred Hoop*, which talks about thought incessantly, might provide a useful framework for understanding the burgeoning fiction being published in the decade in which Allen is writing.

Robert Warrior raises a similar point in a work that appeared nine years later, *Tribal Secrets: Recovering American Indian Intellectual Traditions* (1995), which argues that opening up Native literary analysis to earlier nonfiction writers helps us reject the illusion that Native literature began in the late twentieth century and the idea that our critical forbears are all non-Indian. *The Sacred Hoop* does not even mention the names of writers like Samson Occom, William Apess, George Copway, Sarah Winnemucca, and a host of others. Perhaps the Christian orientation of these early male writers, and Winnemucca's defense of her morality and her pleas to allow her people to return to the Malheur Reservation in Oregon do not meet the kind of literary expectations Allen associated with "recovery," "tradition," and the "feminine."

A less theoretical consideration is the fact that many nineteenth-century works we have today in reprints were only available in special library collections at the time Allen was writing, another shift we have to factor in terms of sheer physical availability. It might be said, however, that history, literary or otherwise, is not the main focus of *The Sacred Hoop*, which tends to dehistoricize its broader cultural concerns by making them universal worldviews.

Our own book moves away from the notion of "masters" and "literature proper" because it is really the only strategic move that allows a theory to emerge that (1) extends beyond a narrow range of Native texts that keeps us stuck in the fab five and their attendant criticism and (2) challenges the assumption that there is no such thing as Native theory so one simply has to adapt whatever legacy is handed down in literature departments.

When we step away from demands for the "proper" Indian writer whose authenticity is apparent enough to us, whatever the minimal standard might be, all of a sudden we open up a vast territory of work that might be considered a potential source of criticism. Paradoxes, as has already been mentioned, are inescapable, and one will also be faced with the task of evaluating the worth or lack of worth of the various materials according to some kind of criteria that must be worked out. We hope this collection has something to do with puzzling over these standards in ways that go beyond the materials' most superficial Indian features or claiming a radical incommensurability with European culture.

It is interesting how many times the word "breed" appears in the quoted paragraph, where Allen describes John Rollin Ridge's work, and in Allen's references to herself throughout *The Sacred Hoop*. Ridge is identified as a breed, but nothing is said about the Ridges as one of the most important families in nineteenth-century Cherokee history in terms of the drastic impact their decisions had on the rest of the tribe. What makes them breeds instead of prominent Cherokee citizens who would affect Cherokee destiny (including that of full-blood citizens) forever? Allen's work is part of an impulse that would be continued throughout the 1980s—that of viewing American Indian writers as mixed-bloods who mediate between the white and Indian worlds. In the next decade Elizabeth Cook-Lynn, a Crow Creek Sioux writer and critic, would question the wisdom of promulgating such a role and focusing Native literary studies around mixed-blood issues rather than political ones such as sovereignty, jurisdiction, and land redress. Cook-Lynn's writings question the validity, in light of tribal communal realities, of obsessing over personal identity.[22]

Paula Gunn Allen, rather ironically, endorses a linear view of literary history that prioritizes modern works over older ones. Modern novels are ritualistic, earlier ones colonialistic and exploitative: "Most of these contemporary novels are ritualistic in approach, structure, theme, symbol, and significance, the novels *most properly termed American Indian novels* because they rely on native rather than non-Indian forms, themes, and symbols and so are not colonial or exploitative. Rather, they carry on the oral tradition at many levels, furthering and nourishing it and being furthered and nourished by it [my emphasis]."[23] Once more we have Native literature proper and its improper predecessors. Some might wonder why the earlier writers do not constitute ancestral voices as much as the storytellers Allen constantly celebrates.

Allen provides a thoughtful reading of Laguna writer Leslie Marmon Silko's novel *Ceremony*, one that initiated a long-lasting discussion that would continue into the next decade, regarding the way in which encounters with powerful Laguna women are an essential part of Tayo's—the novel's protagonist—recovery. While *Ceremony* would have succeeded as a novel purely because of its excellence—indeed, it had already done so by the time of *The Sacred Hoop*—the feminist reading that Allen gives it is surely a contributing factor that makes it one of the works most frequently taught and written about in Native literary history, partially because of Allen's exploration of an ecofeminist strain in the book which resonated with movements that transcended narrow academic specialization or even a strictly Laguna reading of the text.

Paula Gunn Allen, among others, not only pioneered a space for Native studies in universities, she pioneered a space for Native literature within Native studies. The broad appeal of *The Sacred Hoop* made it useful as a primer for NAS surveys, which, by necessity, had to rely on some way of reducing 537 federally recognized U.S. tribes, and other tribal societies, to a manageable discussion—and Allen's book certainly seeks commonalities across tribal boundaries. In addition to all of this, anyone who throws in a chapter on Native lesbianism in a work that is sure to be used as a Native studies textbook has my vote as one of our foremothers. (And Allen named gay and lesbian contributions to Native cultures in other chapters as well.)

In the years following the 1986 publication of *The Sacred Hoop*, sovereignty continues to face serious threats in Indian country. A group calling itself "Protect American Rights and Resources" has its first national conference on March 28–29, 1987, in Wausau, Wisconsin, to protest "tribal claims to wildlife and fisheries, land, timber, water, minerals, shoreline claims, resources, and clouded titles [as well as] [t]ribal taxation over non-Indians and non-tribal people, constitutional losses, and additional tax burdens being placed on existing taxpayers because of these claims." A major partner of PARR is the National Rifle Association, which calls for the "Non-discriminatory application of conservation laws against Indian and non-Indian alike, and a transfer of the responsibilities from the Federal government and Indian tribes to the states." PARR is part of a rock-throwing mob of some four hundred treaty protesters who attack four boats of Lac du Flambeau Chippewa spearfishers and fifteen other tribal people on the landing.[24]

The Lac du Flambeau spearers—as well as the Lac Courte Oreilles, Bad River, Red Cliff, Mole Lake, and St. Croix bands of Chippewa Indians—are guaranteed rights to take walleye, pike, and other fish under the treaties of 1837 and 1842 between the United States and the Lake Superior Chippewas, and the rights are affirmed by the federal district court for the Western District of Wisconsin in March 1987.[25]

In 1987 Wilma Mankiller is the first woman elected chief of the Cherokee Nation, a position she held after Ross Swimmer resigned in 1985. The North American Indian Women's Association is seventeen years old in 1987. That year the group passes the following resolutions at their annual conference:

> The North American Indian Women's Association, Inc. (NAIWA), hereby opposes in the strongest terms any transfer of the BIA schools or educational programs serving Indian students to the states' public school systems or any third party in all fifty states. NAIWA strongly recommends that the Indian Preference Law be legally enforced for all the Indian people with emphasis on hiring, promotion and training Indian women.
>
> NAIWA recommends and strongly urges Congress to provide job opportunities such as meaningful public work projects on all Indian reservations, boundaries and reserves.
>
> NAIWA shall provide a substance free environment (no alcohol, drugs, or other substances) during NAIWA sponsored functions (i.e., business meetings, group, community, and family activities). That NAIWA members individually and collectively serve as role models at such events.[26]

Some individuals begin to wake up and realize that HIV and AIDs are not the white man's disease but the reason their cousin is sick. Many more continue not to wake up. On July 31, 1990, William Bettelyoun files a suit stating "that employed members of the Indian Health Service in Rosebud, South Dakota and Aberdeen, S.D., Administrative Office released medical information [about his HIV status] to his employer and the public. As a result, Bettelyoun alleges he was forced to leave his job as a Senior Planner for the Rosebud Tribe and was fired from another part-time job."[27]

In the literary world several books appear claiming a traditional basis for acceptance of various sexual orientations, including Walter Williams's 1986 publication, *The Spirit and the Flesh: Sexual Diversity in American Indian Culture,* and Will Roscoe's 1988 *Living the Spirit: A Gay American Indian Anthology* and his 1991 *The Zuni Man-Woman.*

By January of 1991, twelve thousand American Indians are in the Middle East putting their lives on the line for George Herbert Walker Bush's Operation Desert Storm. Indian communities hope for the return of their sons and daughters, name and remember them at ceremonies and powwows across the country. Sixty-two-year old White Earth Chippewa tribal member Bea Swanson and four supporters spend five days beating the Ojibway-made Minnesota Peace Drum across the street from the White House in protest of the war. Stephen Bentzlin, twenty-three, a Dakota Sioux citizen of the Sisseton-Wahpeton band becomes the first combat casualty from the state of Minnesota, succumbing to multiple shrapnel wounds and dying alongside ten of his fellow U.S. Marines in the battle for the Kuwaiti town of Khafji on January 29, 1991.

On July 28, 1991, Gen. Colin Powell breaks ground at a memorial to the "buffalo soldiers" of the 9th and 10th Cavalry Regiments at Fort Leavenworth, Kansas. The buffalo soldiers waged war on the Apache, Comanche, Ute, Kiowa, Cheyenne, Shoshone, Bannock, Kickapoo, Lipan, Mescalero, Blackfoot, and Sioux tribes. The general, the first African American chief of staff, keeps a picture of a buffalo soldier across from his desk and says that it reminds him of "the thousands of African-Americans who went before me and who shed their blood and made their sacrifices so that I could sit where I sit today."[28]

In a nationwide televised broadcast on February 18, 1991, Marine Brig. Gen. Richard Neal, speaking of the rescue of an American F-16 pilot, refers to Iraqi-held territory in Kuwait as "Indian Country." Protests are lodged by a number of tribal leaders across the nation. Some wonder why their sons and daughters are fighting a war in which the enemy is referred to as Indians. Lt. Col. John Tull, a spokesman for the U.S. Central Command in Saudi Arabia, says, "I am not exactly sure where it [the term Indian Country] originated. If you think in common sense terms, where might it have come from? From the days of the Wild West and something like that."[29]

When actor Kevin Costner comes to South Dakota in 1990 to star in the movie *Dances with Wolves,* he is determined to recruit Doris Leader Charge to play the role of Pretty Shield, the wife of Chief Ten Bears, a role Leader Charge turned down several times. In disbelief, Costner himself takes her out for a long walk on the prairie and asks "if [she] had been offered the role of Pretty Shield, and if [she] had turned it down." Leader Charge affirms that this is the case, and Costner asks her why. "Your film will only show for a few months," she says, "but I'll need this job [teaching at a Sioux tribal college] long after that." Costner then asks if it would be okay if he called the college president to ask him to extend Leader Charge's leave. Leader Charge agrees, and as a result she ends up in the film. Her annual teaching salary is seventeen thousand dollars; she earns twenty-three thousand for six months of work on *Dances with Wolves*. She uses the money to fix her fifty-five-hundred dollar, two-bedroom frame house in the reservation town of Parmelee, South Dakota, where vandals have broken windows and punched holes in the walls. She also buys a new refrigerator, stove, washer, and dryer with her windfall."[30]

1991 is the year Wisconsin Ojibways have to get a court injunction from federal judge Barbara Crabb in order to exercise their treaty fishing rights when protesters try to stop them from fishing and holler at them, "Timber niggers, go home where you came from" (which in itself says something about groups like Equal Rights for Everyone and Protect American Rights and Resources). The court injunction specifies no "rock throwing, boat swamping, physical harassment and intimidation, and assault and battery against spearers and their families."[31] The Indian fishers have suffered all of these indignities at the hands of the "equal rights" protesters.

One hour before President George H. W. Bush declares on February 27, 1991, that "Aggression is defeated, the war is over," Manuel Michael Davila, of the U.S. Army's 2nd Armored Division, an Oglala Sioux husband and father of a three-year-old daughter, is killed when his armored tank is hit by hostile fire and he is trapped inside, succumbing to third-degree burns.[32]

In 1991 a special program to encourage Native American students to study print and broadcast journalism is established at the University of Missoula in Montana. The same year, the Carlson School of Management at the University of Minnesota establishes a business leadership program for American Indians, a two-year course that leads to a master's degree in business administration, and admits its first participants into the program—Aurolyn Stwyer of the Confederated Tribes of Warms Springs, Oregon, and Terry Mason Moore, an Oklahoma Osage. *National Native News*, which began as a program with the Alaska public radio network in 1987, is, by 1991, a daily radio news program airing on 150 public radio stations across the United States.

On Friday, March 22, 1991, Darrell Doxtdator of the Six Nations Reserve in Canada stands by his convictions and refuses to take the oath of allegiance to the queen as he and 403 other law graduates are being admitted to the bar. Doxtdator says, "The Iroquiois Confederacy are not subjects of the Queen; we are allies of the Queen."[33]

In 1991 Arlene and Irving Crandall give back to the Narragansetts the three hundred and fifty acres their ancestors got from the tribe in 1659. The land is valued at $41 million, but the Crandalls cannot afford to pay the eleven thousand dollars they owe in back taxes and are afraid the town of Westerly will auction off the property and tear up the woodlands for development.

In the early 1990s cultural studies is taking hold in English departments across America. But it is also meeting strong resistance because of the perceived threat it poses to the canon and to traditional views of literature. While some regard cultural studies as the "Cole Porter approach" to English, where anything goes, cultural studies has a specific history that began in England with books like Richard Hoggart's *The Uses of Literacy* (1957) and Raymond Williams's *Culture and Society, 1780–1950,* published in 1958. Especially important to early British formations of cultural studies is the University of Birmingham's Centre for Contemporary Cultural Studies, founded in 1963. Cultural studies draws on specific Marxist theories in its origins and its concerns for materialist readings. The movement has picked up momentum in the United States with the introduction of several works, such as Patrick Brantlinger's *Crusoe's Footprints: Cultural Studies in Britain and America* (1990), Anthony Easthope's *Literary into Cultural Studies* (1991), and Fred Inglis's *Cultural Studies* (1993).

Proponents of cultural studies make the point that their approach is nothing new—until the early nineteenth century the term "literature" itself indicated all writing, and its study, by definition, was an interdisciplinary affair, often encompassing science and philosophy as well as poetry and fiction.

Cultural studies involves a shift from the exclusive study of literary texts to an inclusion of the study of societal institutions, from texts to contexts. Cultural studies questions the close-reading principles of the earlier New Critics, who claimed that everything one needed for interpreting a literary work resided in the work itself rather than in its sociological backdrop. A prominent, and controversial, aspect of cultural studies is the legitimization of what has formerly been considered "low culture." The shift is propelled by a view of culture as multifaceted and a conviction that literature both influences and is influenced by a wide array of signifying practices.

The "anything goes" rap has to do with the meanderings of cultural studies outside high-brow culture, its interest in everything from soap operas to newscasts to Victorian leisure habits to advertising images to Beavis and Butt-Head. Science fiction, Gothic novels, Harlequin romances, and other books previous generations of critics turned their noses up at are now studied, sometimes alongside works formerly upheld as masterpieces. One critic says cultural studies involves the "reconceptualization of culture as everyday social practice rather than the elite product of society."[34]

The theory that drives this egalitarian impulse is based on a conviction that the literary canon is not a sacred tradition inspired by God or a muse or even the inherent, transcendent talent of its authors. The bequeathing of the label

"Great Works" reflects, instead, the biases of those who bequeath the label. The canon is a construct of the social attitudes of the times. Claiming literary worth is not an objective endeavor. What makes a work superior in any given time period or culture can be different in another. The earlier New Critics claimed that the interpretational principles one needs reside in the text itself, rather than its sociological contexts. Whether or not they intended to, the formalists chose works for study that most clearly illustrated their principles and avoided those that did not, relegating the latter to low culture and placing them outside the realm of literary analysis.

According to cultural studies, the earlier formalist aesthetics reflected power relations in society rather than some God-given or universally applicable principle about "good" ways to read literature. In *Culture and Imperialism* (1993), for example, "Edward Said shows that modernist features like self-consciousness, discontinuity, and irony may be seen as responses to the legitimacy crisis in Western culture, whose hegemony overseas can no longer be taken for granted."[35] This places claims about how to read texts in a historical framework rather than assuming them to be timeless and universal.

Some would claim that the New Critics themselves were politically conservative and opposed to the ideology of the working classes and the left, even if that opposition often went unexamined in their own writings. One might remember Malcolm Cowley's gem of a rejection letter in response to a 1936 request from D'Arcy McNickle, who had asked to write an article on Salish water rights: "We have so little space in the *New Republic* at present," Cowley wrote, "what with the election and the counter revolution in Spain—that we couldn't possibly print an article about the Flathead Indians and the Rocky Mountain Power Company dam."[36]

Cultural studies opens up the canon to forgotten and erased authors, many of them women and minorities. Cultural studies also considers nonauthors and nontextual areas of inquiry. One critic says, "Cultural studies brings into view social groups who may not have created much literature but who have clearly participated in cultures—the poor and illiterate, the working classes, slaves, peasants, women, people of color, people with disabilities, the deaf, and so on."[37]

Increases in mass-communication technologies make cultures increasingly global and interdependent; thus, cultural studies emphasizes issues of cosmopolitanism and hybridity, the fact that cultures do not exist in a vacuum apart from the influences of other societies. Global electronic communications and mass migrant movements that intersect with and influence other cultures are contemporary realities. Attempts to locate pure or authentic cultures are frequently problematized in cultural studies, which instead focus on various aspects of cross-cultural dialogue. When the ideology of the nation-state is examined, it is often either problematized or placed in a global context that questions its autonomy. Because of the transnational and comparative interests of cultural studies, national literatures are also questioned. The denaturalization of the nation, so to speak, has been part of the process of opening up the canon to those who have been marginalized within the construct of the nation, questioning, especially, the totalizing structures within the nation-state that create a monolithic story that overlooks diverse relations within, without, and across its real and imagined borders.

While cultural studies contributes to the environment within English departments that allows for institutional validation of Native American literature as a field of study, as well as other minority literatures, it also creates some interesting challenges. Cultural studies emphasizes resistance to the literary specialization of the 1930s-style New Criticism that foregrounded the autonomy of the individual text; instead, cultural studies opts for a much broader, comparative field of interest. While Native literary studies has found some institutional support to whatever degree it mimics broadly construed multicultural and ethnic literature models, its footing becomes less secure in terms of Native literature's role as an academic specialization and an insistence on building Native literature programs in departments outside of the comparative framework. It is often easier, for example, to build a Native literature program under the auspices of American literature than to argue for Native literature to be included as one of a department's areas of specialization, with the same autonomy as British lit, rhetoric, and American lit, for instance.

This problem is intensified when Native literature becomes even more focused, seeking out tribally specific approaches. There is the tendency in cultural studies to view nationalism as a pathology and a contrary tendency in Native studies to view it in terms of the survival of tribes. Some critics are stymied by the transnational turn in cultural studies and the seemingly contrary sovereigntist emphasis in Native studies. These critics are puzzled as to how the two viewpoints can be reconciled.

These problems would be addressed some years later. With the publication of Robert Warriors' s *Tribal Secrets: Recovering American Indian Intellectual Traditions* (1996), sovereigntist readings are increasingly applied to Native American literary texts rather than relegating political discussions solely to Native studies departments. A healthy impulse is the recognition that federal Indian law is not the exclusive domain of Native studies any more than metaphors are the exclusive domain of Native literature. Within Native literature, however, accusations of isolationism have arisen in regard to Native critics, attributing to the sovereigntists a naive belief in cultural purity and to the cosmopolitans a more theoretically advanced commitment to hybridity. A resistance literature is building that argues that sovereignty is not an isolationist position, since tribal governments exist in complex relationships with municipal, state, and federal powers that demand constant movement between and across borders. Sovereignty (by definition, government-to-government relations) has a profound cosmopolitanism at its core—a genuine cosmopolitanism that can be claimed for its Indian integrity rather than as a hybrid mess that is constantly measured in relation to ethnographic rather than legal criteria.

One of the thorny theoretical areas in cultural studies is the theorization of difference. On the one hand, difference, particularities, specifics, the local, historical details, and so on, allow one to avoid reductive universalized statements about the world that might be labeled as essentialist. On the other hand, naming differences, such as claims about coherent racial or cultural identities, seems to contradict the way in which theory has emphasized the fluidity between insider and outsider positionalities, the breakdown of oppositional categories, cross-cultural exchanges, hybridities, the interdependency of ideas and the people who express them, the global aspects of contemporary life.

Native literature has its own examples of these paradoxes. Those claiming an essentialized Native paradigm, or worldview based on principles of "harmony," organize such a claim around both sameness and difference: uniformity among Indians who all share the harmony principle but embody a marked difference from those pesky linear-minded Europeans. European diversity is ignored; instead, it's said that a lack of holistic knowledge somehow overshadows the multiplicity of "old world" governments, languages, and histories that encompass a very large continent and thousands of years of diverse cultures. Both a radical commensurability among Indians and incommensurability between Indians and Europeans are claimed at the same time. What to do with all of this is often puzzling.

In her critical study, *Contemporary American Indian Literatures and the Oral Tradition* (1999), Susan Brill de Ramirez includes an appendicized list of the characteristics of Native novels, which she calls "oral novels," traits that include multiple viewpoints, achronological plot lines, and so on. The problem is that many of the traits on Brill de Ramirez's list could easily be applied to the writings of James Joyce, Virginia Woolf, William Faulkner, and any other number of modernist works. One comes away from the Brill de Ramirez study wondering what, if anything, can be concluded. Do such traits really originate in the oral tradtion? Maybe modernism orignates in the oral tradition, a possibility that Brill de Ramirez acknowledges, if briefly. If one deems the criteria for what makes an Indian novel Indian to be based on a universalized set of cultural traits rooted in the oral tradition that differentiates it from "white" writing, one, ironically, runs the risk of reducing difference, making these traits much the same as the European literary movement that dominated a good deal of the twentieth century—given modernism's similar characteristics of disrupted chronology and so forth that Brill claims for the oral tradition and for oral novels. This seems a case in point where history, politics, and legal issues might shed some light on highly aestheticized thematics.

In naming these conundrums, I do not wish to discourage young critics who might throw their hands up in the air and proclaim in dismay "What's the point?" Given the complexity of these philosophical traps, it might seem whatever one writes is bound to be faulty. The answer is not a descent into inarticulateness. I do not want to scare off the very group we so desperately need. Rather, I hope to make clear the importance of those who are willing to think for themselves instead of accepting prevailing assumptions, critics who realize that their statements have both philosophical ramifications and the potential to affect the real world in both positive and negative ways. Simply put, we are still at a point in the discipline where we need to lay a lot more historical groundwork in order to map our way through these philosophical dilemmas. Historical specificity, in my view, is a correct direction—not the only direction, but a useful one.

A second problem in relation to cultural studies, a more general one, has affected other disciplines besides Native literature. By the 1990s cultural studies had been significantly influenced by poststructuralist ideas gathered from French theory that was authored in the seventies and translated into English in the eighties. One characteristic of this influence relates to queer theory which, more fully than almost any other discipline, embraces poststructuralism. This characteristic is the refusal of queer theory to define its own parameters, that is, to state explicitly what its field of studies is—what is queer and what is not. In fact, queer theory is most interested in the gray areas, those identities and practices that are the hardest to characterize as gay or straight, whereas gay and lesbian studies tends to search out silenced or erased gay authors, artists, and their contributions to history, a task that requires looking for "gay evidence," so to speak, from the past.

Queer theory problematizes the notion of gay identity or gay cultural production during earlier time periods when such terms or gender concepts did not even exist. By doing so, queer theory also undermines the dominant culture's sense that hetero is something that can be distinguished from homo and thus rewarded or punished on the basis of a sense of a coherent identity category. Queer theory accepts the fluidity of such categories in the past, when people did not think about the distinctions between straight and gay in the same way.

Queer theory, like cultural studies, is sometimes seen as an "anything goes" discipline since it is difficult to disqualify anything as a potential subject for its scrutiny. Queer theory constantly raises questions about whether or not a gay identity is even possible; instead it prioritizes any idea or behavior that might be scrutinized relevant to its deviance, its abilities to disrupt, its resistance to normative values. (Here is an example: A student of Louise Erdrich's novel *Love Medicine* could analyze Lipsha's effeminacy and transgression of traditional gender roles without speculating as to whether or not Lipsha is a gay character. Whether or not he is gay, he can be understood as queer in terms of his deviance. A gay and lesbian studies reading, in contrast, might look for gay evidence in the novel and thus try to answer the question, Is Lipsha gay or straight?)

Some gay and lesbian activists have wondered how queer theory can contribute to gay and lesbian civil rights in America if it begins with the proposition that gay people do not exist or, at least, cannot be defined. Further, in terms of integration issues, if queer theory values all things weird that challenge the status quo, gay and lesbian activists might well ask, "Just how weird do you want to be if you want to gain acceptance in mainstream society?" Queer theorists might respond, "Just how normal do you want to become in order to gain acceptance?" The latter point involves a recognition that one of the disadvantages of integration is the degree to which a marginalized group has to become like those who oppress it in order to achieve "equality." Queer theory might be seen as an antiassimilationist strategy taken to its most logical extreme. Gay and lesbian activists might argue that the guarantee of some kind of basic civil rights is paramount if an oppressed group is to get any kind of foothold in society before it can start deconstructing everything.

While a critical movement, like queer theory, that proposes more questions than answers has a good deal of validity—especially in totalitarian periods such as the present, when the country desperately needs those with questions more than it needs fundamentalists with clear-cut (and very frightening) answers—court decisions often depend on definitions rather than open-ended questions. One queer theorist has written recently in a prominent Canadian English journal:

> . . . queer theory does not indulge in that messianic project of creating a better future—the one Michel Foucault distinctly disallows in *The History of Sexuality*—out of a wretched past, or of schooling its children into liberation and clear-thinking. The value—and the threat—of queer theory, then, is precisely that we haven't allowed it to ossify into formulas and programs. There is no singular agenda to queer studies, and that's what makes them queer. For queer theory to continue it must theorize; it must continue to discover itself anew, rather than trading in the truths that, to any thinking person, are irrefutable (racism is bad, discrimination is bad, slavery is bad).

The same critic writes, "[I]t is the refusal of queer theory to ground 'homosexual oppression' in some stable material field from which to denounce it that troubles those academics who prefer the comforting pieties of race and ethnicity criticism and the stabilizing empirical assumptions from which these proceed."[38]

Another group of critics, Marxist in orientation, after critiquing what some might call the bourgeois left for having more interest in literary tropes than in a reallocation of wealth, made the following statement in their volume about a socially responsible, socially engaged postmodernism: "The goal of *Transformation* is to produce effective knowledge for understanding the world in order to change it."[39] In terms of cultural studies, which is not the same as queer theory yet affected by some of the same poststructuralist tendencies that have been embraced by queer studies, some would argue that the irony of the theoretical fascination with all things unanswerable is that cultural studies has moved away from its early Marxist and materialist orientation. Early cultural studies had an interventionist aim rather than an exclusively analytical one. These critics might argue that deconstruction should lead to reconstruction, that critique must relate to vision, that theorists should consider the political outcomes of their theories.

In terms of Native literary theory, then, some express fears of an overly theoretical scholarship that might separate itself from activism, and, indeed, evidence of this kind of work has recently come to light with the publication of Elvira Pulitano's *Toward a Native American Critical Theory* (2003), which claims that Native identities, perspectives, histories, and sovereignties are impossible apart from a fundamental hybridity that involves a profound European foundation stemming from five hundred years of contact. What remains for tribes, after a radical deconstruction of their identities, is a political question the Pulitano book fails to address.

The role of history is especially important to this discussion. Native literature has often, either directly or indirectly, claimed the role of telling the truth about history, the Indian side of the story we might say. Naming particular historical events and reevaluating them in the light of Indian viewpoints is a central endeavor in Native novels, poems, plays, and the attendant criticism of these works. Postmodern theory, with its problematization of master narratives, and its study of the power structures that undergird them, has both supported Native American counternarratives for their resistance to the official story and expressed a leeriness for them inasmuch as they are rooted in any kind of notion of normative truth claims. Some Native critics are frustrated to find out that just when they might finally have an audience for their side of the story, the non-Indian world has discovered that all stories are subjective. This might strike some as a little too convenient, another abdication of responsibility—in short, a further manifestation of colonialism.

In terms of positive outcomes, however, opening up literary studies to nonliterary texts, an important early cultural studies commitment, is of great value to Native literary analysis, simply because of the lack of an obvious body of Native criticism—as a unified body of knowledge—in earlier time periods (*not* its lack of existence, that is, but its lack of recognition. There is certainly a substantial body of early work with theoretical implications, even though its authors and readers might not have called it Native criticism at the time). In Charles Eastman's writings, for example, one does not find references to "Native literature" or "Native criticism," even though other Native authors were writing in Eastman's own time and in the century before. A cultural studies approach allows us to look at Eastman, for instance, in relation to the fiction of Momaday rather than assuming that no Indian texts precede Momaday that might shed light on his work. This is a point Robert Warrior makes in defense of his own selection of nonfiction work as part of the literary study in *Tribal Secrets*.

I have taken quite a bit of time here to survey cultural studies—and for good reason. Cultural studies theories that question the inherent superiority of the canon, explore the infinite variability of textual meanings, give attention to cultures that surround literary production, analyze power relations that inform judgments of literary merit, and politicize interpretive acts, all these efforts, raise central issues that American Indian critics have had to address, if for no other reason than because the places where such debates take place also happen to be their places of employment where they draw their monthly paychecks. More to the point, these issues also speak to Indian realities. In one way or another they show up in all the critical studies written in the 1990s.

Louis Owens and the Identity Theorists

In 1992, while the rest of the country was celebrating the Columbus quincentennial, Louis Owens's *Other Destinies: Understanding the American Indian Novel* appeared. Owens's study was the most comprehensive analysis of Native fiction up to that time. Reading the book is equivalent to an undergraduate semester-length course introducing students to the works and major themes of a select group of contemporary Indian writers[40] and some works from the 1920s and 1930s, as well as one foray into the nineteenth century to look at John Rollin Ridge's novel, *The Life and Adventures of Joaquin Murieta*.

In keeping with the book's orientation toward an audience of Indian and non-Indian readers alike, one of its continuous themes is popular culture's representation of Indians. Because of the support Native literature garnered in the academy during the cultural studies and multicultural decade of the nineties, as well as the prevalence of non-Indian scholars in the field, as much of the energy in the discipline has been directed to the way non-Indians view Indians as to the way Indians view themselves or as to how Native communities might become involved in the evaluation of Native literature (or Native literature in the evaluation of Native communities).

In terms of identity questions, which are pronounced in *Other Destinies*, Owens contrasts those Indian characters in fiction whose identities are intact, that is, those who have a strong sense of connection to traditions, with characters whose identities are fragmented and who are experiencing difficulties adjusting to the modern world. Owens is especially interested in the recovery of identity. Other critics before him had remarked on the "homecoming impulse" of contemporary Native novels, which had to do not only with physical returns to reservations but also with spiritual accommodation of Indian values, languages, stories, songs, and ceremonies.

Owens observes in the works of the contemporary writers he studies a more assured restoration of tribal tradition than the uncertainty evident in the 1920s and 1930s novels authored by Mourning Dove, John Joseph Mathews, and D'Arcy McNickle, whose fictional outcomes he finds ambiguous in relation to the prospect of a positive Indian future. He also contrasts an interest in restoration in contemporary Native fiction with the alienation and tragic orientation of modernist literature, as well as with the indeterminacy of postmodernism, its contestation of identities and sense of an incoherent self. The prevalence of the alienated protagonist of Native fiction, a person marked by an acute inarticulateness early in the novel who progresses toward speech that contributes to appropriate relations in his environment as the story unfolds, centers much of Owens's character analysis. Overall, he uncovers a general movement toward healing in Native fiction.

The "Indianness" of the Indian text is a major interest of Owens's, and, in spite of recent criticism in Pulitano's *Toward a Native American Critical Theory* that has placed Owens on one end of a spectrum that represents an antiessentialist view and Paula Gunn Allen on the end associated with essentialized reductive claims for an Indian consciousness, the two critics have much in common. Owens, for example, contrasts an Indian harmonized worldview with European fragmentation over and over again. A striking example of the continuities between the two critics might be seen in the statement from Allen's *The Sacred Hoop* that would eventually draw a lot of attention to her supposed essentialism:

> Only a participant in mythic magic can relate to the myth, can enter into its meaning on its own terms. This is not to say that only a devout Oglala can comprehend the Myth of White Buffalo Woman or that only a practicing Cheyenne can comprehend the presence of Sweet Medicine. It does mean that only those who experientially accept the nonmaterial or nonordinary reality of existence can hope to comprehend either figure in their own terms; all others are, of necessity excluded.[41]

In his analysis of James Welch's historical novel *Fools Crow* (1986), Owens writes,

> In the Blackfoot world rendered so completely in this novel, there is no disjunction between the real and the magical, no sense that the magical is metaphorical. In the world Welch recovers, Raven talks to men and women, the sacred and the profane interpenetrate irresistibly, and this is reality. If the reader can pass through that conceptual horizon, if the reader acknowledges and accepts this reality, he or she experiences an Indian world, that world forever distanced from the airplane man of *Winter* [*in the Blood*] and, more tragically, from the doomed Loney. In *Fools Crow*, Welch has accomplished the most profound act of recovery in American literature.[42]

Like Allen, Owens also maintains the divide between fiction and nonfiction, even though his work appeared in the beginning of the cultural studies movement that would break down such distinctions. While there are occasional references to nonfiction works—important ones would include John Joseph Mathew's *Talking to the Moon* (1945) and D'Arcy McNickle's 1973 sociohistorical work, *Native American Tribalism: Indian Survivals and Renewals*—these are brief interludes that provide comparisons with the fiction itself, which is the main interest. Nonfiction is not Owens's subject of study here. We still have a sense of "Native American literature proper," to cite Paula Gunn Allen's phrase once again. Although Owens's work is not as devoid of historical references as is Allen's book, an analysis of federal Indian policy is not his major focus, and Owens stays comfortably within cultural rather than legal definitions of Indiannness.

In keeping with the theme of uncovering the Indianness of Indian literature, a frequent discussion in Owens is the representation of oral performance in written novels. Here, we should note an early 1980s discussion of these matters that has become central to ethnopoetics. Dennis Tedlock, Dell Hymes, and Jerome Rothenberg are cited endlessly in relation to the challenges of representing verbal performances in print. In Dennis Tedlock's *The Spoken Word and the Work of Interpretation* (1983), the author devises a scheme in which the aural and physical interactions of his Zuni storytellers and their listening audience can be represented in writing. Tedlock's representations of storytelling sessions might be likened to an orchestral score, with indications for changes in volume, pauses, interjections of listeners, and a host of other performative aspects of storytelling.

Dell Hymes's *In Vain I Tried to Tell You: Essays in Native American Poetics* (1981) takes a slightly different turn. Hymes, working mostly in the Northwest, studied stories told in English rather than those that needed translation. He examined various versions of the same story, assuming that enough of them could be scrutinized for their commonalities in order to piece together an accurate, authoritative version. Hymes represents the stories he collects as poetry rather than prose, the poetic line breaks meant to emphasize units of breath where the storyteller paused before moving on to the next line. Hymes, then, in using recordings, still relied on live performances in order to determine where to break off his poetic lines.

Jerome Rothenberg's *Shaking the Pumpkin: Traditional Poetry of the Indian North Americas* (1972) strayed the furthest from actual story performances. Rothenberg's "transliterated" songs, incantations, and stories had already been translated into English and published in anthologies. His aim was to take the stories that had suffered from textual representations that stymied their performative qualities and re-create the energy of the oral performance. The result is often ecstatic poems (lots of exclamation points!) that seem reminiscent of some of the beat poetry of the 1950s. Rothenberg was much less interested than Hymes or Tedlock in rendering the literary work in a way that might be consistent with its reception in the culture where it originated than he was in making it exciting.

After the early 1980s, virtually every discussion of Native orality at some point invoked these three authors, often to the exclusion of other topics of oral performance such as the literary history of oral traditions, the dynamic nature of a particular verbal tradition in terms of the way it changes over time, the political ramifications of oral narratives, or a consideration of the narrow way in which most representations had prioritized certain kinds of Indian stories (such as talking animal stories, for example) over others (such as histories of treaty signings). Leslie Marmon Silko had successfully integrated oral stories represented in poetic lines into the prose format of her novel *Ceremony*, surely another big influence on both oral expression in novels and its analysis in criticism.

The "oral into written" analysis that dominates Owens's book is part of an overall trend during the time, pointed out in relation to *The Sacred Hoop*, where those Indian authors whose oral influences are less evident—such as the nineteenth-century Christian and nonfiction writers—are simply left out of the discussion, the exception being Owens's interesting reading of Cherokee author John Rollin Ridge's 1854 potboiler, *The Life and Adventures of Joaquin Murieta*. Owens interprets that novel as one that seems to be about Mexicans but is really about Indians. His reading in some ways seems determined to locate the Indian essence of the novel along the lines of the apologist work mentioned earlier. The possibility that an Indian author might have a lot to say about Mexicans, California, the Gold Rush, and other matters, for some reason, seems rather incidental in Owens's discussion, which seeks out the hidden Cherokee message behind these seemingly Mexican themes that are actually secret codes for Indians. (I myself have read some of Lynn Riggs's work for coded gay subject matter, and I am not claiming that such strategies are entirely without merit).

Another consistency with the earlier critical work of Paula Gunn Allen is both the great frequency with which Owens mentions mixed-bloods and the relevance he attributes to the topic. Owens traces a general improvement in the fictional lot of mixed-bloods compared with their earlier counterparts, who were depicted in the novels of the 1920s and '30s as tragic victims torn between two worlds. Owens emphasizes reconnections to tribal tradition that seem to outweigh matters of blood in the contemporary fiction; for instance, in the work of Gerald Vizenor, mixed-blood identity is associated with transformative trickster powers that can shake things up in important ways that challenge static definitions of Indians.

At times, Owens's mixed-blood readings seem a little reductive, however. In his analysis of Mourning Dove's 1927 novel, *Cogewea; the Half-blood*, Owens concludes in the last sentences of his chapter, "Very literally allowed a place in neither the Indian nor white races, Cogewea will marry Jim LaGrinder and produce children who will, like the parents, be halfbloods. The novel ends on a note of stasis, with nothing resolved, none of the many questions answered."[43] Such a reading manages to erase the important ways in which both Cogewea and Jim identify as Salish people throughout the novel, as well as their increasing connection to Salish tradition as the novel progresses, through listening to the stories of the Stemteema, involvement in ceremonies in the sweat lodge, and Cogewea's growing attention to Salish spirit guides that culminates in the voice that speaks to her out of the buffalo skull. Throughout the novel buffalos are associated with vanishing species and linked with terminal cultures; yet in the end the very same buffalo skull that seemed to earlier represent vanishing Indians shows a surprising vitality and relevance to Cogewea's everyday life—advising her on affairs as basic as the man she is to marry.

At one point in the novel, when the half-blood James LaGrinder is called to the Stemteema's tipi, she simply turns to him and says, "You are an Indian."[44] You gotta love old ladies like that. In a better world she might have been a Native literary critic. She does not say, "You are torn between two worlds, or a fraction determined by the size of your numerator in relationship to your denominator, or a mediator between the white and Native world, or a mixed-blood trickster breaking down terminal creeds." She says, "You are an Indian," when she knows fully well that Jim has a white parent.

Owens overlooks these passages as well as the many times Cogewea, in arguments with the evil dandy from the East Coast, Alfred Densmore, insists that she identifies with her Salish culture rather than her non-Indian one. At the end of the novel, Cogewea's "most Indian" sibling marries a European guy named Frenchie and moves to Paris. How are we to read this?

One observation might be that Cogewea is ahead of her time. No doubt today there is someone living on the Flathead Reservation who is the result of just such a union, and the question "What might the Salish identities of such progeny be like?" goes unanswered in Owens's analysis. The reductive term "mixed-blood," divorced as it is from history and culture, really does not tell us much about these people, a point Cheryl Suzack makes in her contribution to this collection when analyzing the celebration and denigration of mixed-bloods in contemporary criticism.

Similarly, while Owens makes much of the mixed-blood identity of Chal Windzer, the protagonist of John Joseph Mathews's novel *Sundown* (1934), a close reading of the text reveals that Chal's mother is an Osage full-blood, and his father is three-quarters Osage. Chal's mixed-blood identity is more of an ideological matter that relates to his father's political alliances with the progressive faction of the tribe than a racial one, a fact Robert Warrior handles much more adroitly in *Tribal Secrets.* A significant issue is whether or not the models that have developed in relation to mixed-blood identity, in Owens's work and elsewhere, are all that relevant. One critic in this volume, Sean Teuton, recommends dispensing with the term altogether, a reasonable proposition in my view.

Mikhail Bakhtin is the most obvious theoretical influence on Owens in two important ways. First of all, Owens draws on Bakhtin's notion of the heteroglot nature of novels that become a showcase for competing ideologies, diverse linguistic styles, multiple viewpoints, and other ways in which the literary work involves contradictions and tensions. Secondly, Owens uses Bakhtin's notion of authoritative and internally persuasive discourse as a means of understanding colonizer and colonized.

Authoritative discourse is the means of external coercion and pressure that causes people to accept definitions of their lives that may not be consistent with their own values. Internally persuasive discourse involves self-definition, what I like to think of as personal sovereignty, one's imagining of himself or herself in ways that are consistent with internal values that feel right, whether or not they match up with societal expectations. Owens's analysis of the recovery of the protagonists he studies has to do with their growing acceptance of an internally persuasive discourse. There is some difference from Bakhtin here: Since Owens is discussing marginalized communities, the recovery is not simply rooted in individuality but in acceptance of the values of a home territory, which itself suffers a silenced relationship to the dominating discourse.

Another theoretical influence on Owens is James Clifford. *Writing Culture: The Poetics and Politics of Ethnography* (1986), edited by Clifford and George Marcus, takes ethnography beyond the issues of textual representations of performances alluded to earlier that were part of the work of Tedlock, Hymes, and Rothenberg and into ethical areas regarding the relationship between the ethnographer and those he or she studies. This problematizes the emphasis of earlier Boasian anthropology on the objective representation of culture based on scientific principles of accurately recording and analyzing the subject of the ethnographic encounter.

In drawing connections between cultural studies and anthropology, Owens follows up on the earlier work of Clifford Geertz in *The Interpretation of Cultures: Selected Essays* (1973). Owens draws on Clifford's work—and, by implication, Geertz's—to examine ways that colonizing agents create Indians in their own image, that is, how their perceptions strongly influence what they see. Much more fully than Owens, Greg Sarris, in *Keeping Slug Woman Alive: A Holistic Approach to American Indian Texts*, which appeared in print in 1993, the year after Owens's study, made the ethics of ethnography one of his central focuses, drawing out fascinating connections between readers' relationships to texts and their relationships to "Other" cultures.

One question that may occur to readers of *Other Destinies* is whether or not its Bakhtinian framework is capable of transforming readings of Native literature. In other words, would Owens's book remain much the same without the Bakhtinian mantra that occurs throughout its pages? In the bigger picture, do Euroamerican literary theories have what it takes to create a lively, empowering, challenging Native American literary criticism?

A good deal of the answer, of course, depends on how these theories are applied. In *Keeping Slug Woman Alive*, the work of Geertz and Clifford, along with that of reader-response theorists, makes a deeper penetration into the very structures and styles of Sarris's book rather than being applied as a topical ointment as it is in Owens's text. Sarris not only uses these theories to illuminate Pomo culture and texts, he uses Pomo culture and texts to illuminate these theories. In other words, Sarris creates a two-way dialogue, where the Euro theorists are held accountable to Pomo ideas, demonstrating, powerfully, that in any given literary encounter, Pomo literature is not merely the passive partner but potentially the active one—just as capable of exerting its own influences on European theory as being influenced *by* it. Euro theory does not become the lens through which Sarris views Native literature; it becomes one participant in a multifaceted dialogue about the meaning of ideas.

Sarris is just as likely to examine—and often does examine—these theories through the lens of Pomo culture, and the result is fascinating, given that European literary theory is seldom held up to this kind of scrutiny. The question "How might Bakhtin be revised in light of Native culture and literature?" is not considered in *Other Destinies.* One section of Sarris's book is about ways in which Pomo basketmaking might serve as a model for ways to read texts.

This is not to prioritize one of these books over the other. Owens's book is quite powerful as a survey, and it also has many of the limitations of one. I want to understand something about the historical factors that surround these texts rather than create a hierarchy out of them.

Owens's chapter on Gerald Vizenor, a compelling reading of Native America's most theoretically engaged fiction writer, discusses the ways Vizenor likens postmodernism's awareness of infinite signification to possibilities for liberating static definitions. Throughout the book, Owens maintains that Native worldviews are consistent with postmodern understandings of relational rather than absolute truth without taking on some of the aspects of postmodernism's indeterminacy and incoherent sense of identity formations; thus Owens tries to steer a safe course between Indian and postmodern seas, even in the case of Vizenor, who seems to approach postmodernism in a celebratory rather than a cautious mode. This is a delicate balancing act, of course, and Owens comes up with passages such as this one:

> The key to reconciling, or at least containing, this apparent dialectic lies once again in Vizenor's trickster pose. Embodying contradictions, all possibilities, trickster ceaselessly dismantles those imaginative constructions that limit human possibility and freedom, allowing a signifier and signified to participate in a process of "continually breaking apart and re-attaching in new combinations." In "Trickster Discourse" Vizenor quotes Jacques Lacan, who warns us not to "cling to the illusion that the signifier answers to the function of representing the signified, or better, that the signifier has to answer for its existence in the name of any signification whatever." At the same time, however, trickster shows by negative example the necessity for humanity to control and order our world. Within the straitjacket of a fixed, authoritative discourse the self is made lifeless, like Belladonna, by stasis; within the unordered infinitude of pure possibility, the self deconstructs schizophrenically, the way trickster's body is continually coming apart in the traditional stories. Through language, stories that assert orders rather than order upon the chaos of experience, a coherent, adaptive, and syncretic hu-

> man identity is possible without the "terminal" state of stasis. Every such utterance than becomes not "the telling of a story" but the "story of a telling," with responsibility falling upon the teller.[45]

After almost three decades of French theory and manifold debates about its relevancy, including recent reactions to poststructuralist extremes in which theorists have tried to reclaim the validity of identities and normative truth claims, present-day readers may wonder if these speculations of Owens about Native authors and theory, which are brief and infrequent in *Other Destinies,* are enough to really unpack these complicated theoretical matters or even reasonably defend Vizenor's grab-bag relationship to postmodernism. Simply saying "trickster" over and over again, as years of this kind of criticism have shown, does not guarantee one is actually communicating anything. To his credit, rather early on, Owens seems to sense that something else is in order rather than an embrace of all things postmodern, even if he does not seem quite able to say what it might be—that is, what such a literature or criticism might look like. This may have something do with the book's curious missing conclusion—it is as if the author was not sure what he wanted to conclude.

In July of 1992 the Returning the Gift festival takes place on the University of Oklahoma campus. It is an unprecedented gathering of over three hundred Native authors, many of them poets, from all over the United States, Canada, Mexico, and Central America. I remember two things about the historic meeting. Gathered at Mr. Bill's, a Norman bar, in the evenings, we visit and karaoke. Two non-Indian frat guys get up to sing the Johnny Horton unfortunate classic, "Running Bear Loves Little White Dove." Mr. Bill's is full of Indians, another historic first, and the crowd rises up and boos the frat guys down. It's all in good fun, but I think the guys are honestly frightened.

Perhaps, in the end, this kind of camaraderie is the strongest thing to come out of the meeting, given that the contact will lead to Indian institutions such as the Wordcraft Circle, which begins as an organization to match up young Native writers with mentors, and the Native Writers Circle of the Americas, which will go on to present lifetime achievement awards chosen by Native writers themselves.

The second thing I remember from Returning the Gift is Leslie Silko's impassioned speech. She wants us to look toward the south, to Mexico, where things are going to happen, she says. This speech seems to prefigure the Zapatista uprising, which will occur two years after this meeting, three after the appearance of Silko's monumental opus, *Almanac of the Dead.*

On December 2, 1993, at the opening address of the National Congress of American Indians in Reno, Nevada, the Indian pledge of allegiance is presented by its Lummi author, Jewel Praying Wolf James, for the first time. This is how it goes: "I pledge allegiance to my Tribe, to the democratic principles of the Republic and to the individual freedoms borrowed from the Iroquois and

Choctaw Confederacies, as incorporated in the United States Constitution, so that my forefathers shall not have died in vain."[46]

During the winter solstice, on December 21, 1993, Siletz Indians from Oregon and California publicly celebrate their Feather Dance. It's held for the first time in over a century, since their people were massacred around their plank dancehouse near Crescent City, California, in 1855. The dancehouse itself was burned, and the U.S. government officially outlawed the Feather Dance, confiscating the tribe's ceremonial regalia. The Feather Dance goes underground —until winter, 1993.

1993 is also the year the California Indian author Greg Sarris publishes a remarkable book entitled, *Keeping Slug Woman Alive: A Holistic Approach to American Indian Texts,* which draws on his Pomo and Miwok cultures and asks compassionate questions about the many cultural vantage points that shape the ways we read and experience.

In the cultural studies environments of the 1990s, cross-cultural dialogue becomes increasingly important, and many different aspects of isolationism and specialization are questioned. The social relations that surround literature, often discussed as systems of power involved in both authoring texts and reading them, become as important as the content of any given literary work. One critic writes that "the literary is the ground for a self-reflexive disclosure of the ways in which cultural construction works, revealing how Western subjectivities and writing practices constitute themselves in the continually changing contexts of Western (cultural) hegemony and non-Western resistance."[47]

Cultural studies not only overlaps the literary with anthropology, history, sociology, and other disciplines, it causes the "nonliterary" disciplines to reevaluate their mission and work; if literature has taken a sociological turn, these other fields have taken a literary one and now question the assumptions behind keeping fiction and nonfiction apart, social science away from literary theory. During this period, which is marked by critical skepticism, many methodologies across disciplines are no longer as safe as they used to be, when it was often assumed that as long as given scientific principles were adhered to, or a particular documentation style followed, or a close reading made in relation to convincing literary arguments a project was assured of some degree of objectivity or accuracy. Increasingly, with the theories that reject truth as a universal foundation, objectivity is viewed as a mediated rather than a transparent endeavor. Indians, of course, do not need cultural studies to understand that the scientific methods of ethnographers and anthropologists do not always guarantee unbiased viewpoints.

Greg Sarris and the Ethics of Education

A central idea in *Keeping Slug Woman Alive* is the role of participants' subjectivities in various kinds of cultural encounters, especially how their perspectives shape their views of culture, and, ultimately, how such views affect writings and the interpretations of experiences. Reading is of key interest in Sarris's study. By the time of its publication in 1993, cultural studies had long rejected the notion that reading involves a lone encounter between a reader and text; cultural studies had also rejected New Criticism's assumption that the responses of readers, supposedly outside the formal structures of the text itself, are irrelevant. Cultural studies had been deeply affected by theories that emphasized the interdependence of the formal structures of a work and the perceptions of those analyzing them. One critic wrote,

> Cultural studies has accented the context or the social relations of reading. Because the technologies of textuality and representation have long since outstripped any solely literary determination, reading can no longer be imagined as a singular encounter between subject and text but must instead be reconceived as a historically variable bundle of norms, codes, capacities, and techniques, whose precise configuration at any time (including the forms of agency and effectivity that reading supports) remain a topic for detailed examination. In cultural studies there can be no general, uncontroversial answer to the question of what it means to read or how reading is accomplished, no matter how final the pedagogical solutions of close reading may sometimes deceptively appear to be.[48]

Reader-response theories are of central importance in *Keeping Slug Woman Alive,* and by the time of its publication reception aesthetics had uncovered a host of different kinds of readers: ideal readers, superreaders, implied readers, virtual readers, real readers, historical readers, resisting readers, critical readers, and so on. Greg Sarris's approach to reader-response theory might be paraphrased thusly, "Everybody's talking about it; nobody's doing it." While a survey of the different kinds of reader response is not possible here, Sarris argues that even those theorists most centrally involved in reception aesthetics who emphasize the dynamic impact that a reader's own life story has on the story she is encountering in the text she is reading, that those theorists seldom tell their own stories in their critical writings. One of the best footnotes in the book reads,

> In his essay "Intersubjective Reading," David Bleich, for example, notes: "In very few instances does the critic actually study his or her own readings, much less the readings of others, while the great majority of discussions give all the attention to the texts" (402). Bleich goes on to discuss the work or ideas of others (i.e., Gadamer, Barthes). The language, tone, and narrative format of the essay is typical of contemporary academic prose, specifically that of literary criticism and theory. Bleich is analytical and detached. Nowhere does he discuss his reading or historicize his position as the writer of this essay. He concludes the essay by commending that work which "lead[s] toward a rationality of multiple voices and common interests, toward readings 'responsible for the meaning of each other's inner lives'" (420). Can he commend his own work?[49]

Sarris, in illuminating reader-response theory and particular texts, tells stories about his own life, frequently about his interactions with the Pomo medicine woman Mabel McKay, rather than giving abstract summarizations of some hypothetical reader and what might happen when this anonymous being encounters a literary text. Sarris contends that he cannot convey Mabel's life apart from revealing his own. Sarris, more profoundly than any other reader-response theorist before him, locates readings in time and space. He is a fiction writer and a biographer, and he brings to reader response the skills of such writers: the use of dialogue, setting, narrative action, sensory details, images, symbols. Abstractions about what might happen to readers during their encounters with texts are replaced with a reader and happenings, the reader bearing a name and the happenings identifiable on a map in relation to where they take place. Sarris's chapters often conclude with astonishingly evocative storytelling, sometimes reminiscent of the kind of cumulative power with which Louise Erdrich wraps up chapters in her novels.

One of the most significant aspects of Sarris's text, in relation to the Allen and Owens books that precede it, is Sarris's ability to work within an integrative rather than oppositional framework. Instead of pitting a totalized Western culture against a similarly monolithic Native one, where traits such as hierarchies in Western culture are compared with harmonies in Native culture, Sarris emphasizes the multifaceted production of cultural meanings. Sarris's phrase for those describing Indian or non-Indian cultures in reductive terms is "[o]ne says what the other is," a position that fails to reveal the complexities of culture in terms of its interrelationships.[50]

A telling story, explicated in beautiful detail in the book's second chapter, is "The Woman Who Loved the Snake." When Mabel McKay tells the story to Greg, one of his friends from Stanford, a non-Indian Shakespeare scholar by the name of Jenny is with him. Jenny keeps asking, "What does the snake symbolize?" in relation to the story's central character. She is apparently unable to understand the concept of a real man who turned into a snake, a problem that one might easily attribute to her European background and inability to see the fluidities between natural and supernatural phenomena. Sarris, instead of going for a superficial conclusion about the story in relation to Jenny's inadequacies as a non-Indian outsider, in a surprising revelation confesses that he, a Pomo, had also misunderstood the meaning of a related story, which he assumed had to do with first contact between whites and Pomo people. In regard to his inquiries about the story, Mabel had asked him, "How can that be? You ever know white people with four legs and two heads?" Sarris says, "I had assumed a literal, linear relation between prophecy, or Old Man's dream, and so-called empirical reality, a relation which posits a kind of fundamental difference between the two states that Mabel may not share."[51]

Sarris challenges a non-Indian/Indian oppositional framework in many different ways throughout the book. His aim is not to deny Indian ownership of Native texts, perspectives, or worldviews or the importance of reading

Native authors and listening to Native voices after a five-hundred-year non-Indian monopoly on Native discourse. Sarris need not be viewed in an antagonistic relationship with Native literary nationalism. He is interested in working beyond some of the facile clichés that have turned us away from strong critical thinking. He goes beyond the Native studies search for the most traditional interpretation—the analysis elders are most likely to endorse—asking the question, instead, of what happens to the elders and those who listen to them, when they engage in conversation. The conversations of one such elder, Mabel McKay, Sarris insists, expose a "vast territory" that is oral, a production of meaning that depends on many participants, not just elders, not even only Indians. Mabel's talk often exposes various critical frameworks, different kinds of assumptions people are operating from, and all of this is part of the story, not just the man and the snake, which is the version that is most likely to be chosen as the Indian story to the exclusion of the conversations that precede and follow it that reveal the critical assumptions of participants in the story-making process. Sarris writes, "This book should not be taken simply as an insider's record of things 'Indian.' I am not privileging an Indian's point of view regarding the texts and topics considered. I am not interested in pitting Indians against non-Indians, insiders against outsiders, or in showing that any one group of people is necessarily privileged or better or worse than another. Instead, these essays try to show that all of us can and should talk to one another, that each group can inform and be informed by the other."[52]

Sarris argues that what has often been considered the oral tradition has been a narrow representation of a much broader, dynamic complex of interrelationships. Many reductive studies of orality are "no more the whole story than a cup of water is the river."[53] The stories Sarris includes as Indian ones are narratives that would most likely be overlooked in ethnographic, anthropological, and literary works that opt for the "stories proper" rather than the conversations that surround them.

We might say that the first line of the trickster, creation, monster slayer, or otherwise categorized and canonized story in an Indian anthology is not the first line at all, according to Sarris, nor is the ending line of the text truly the end. Telling about Jennie's, and Greg's own, "mistaken" assumptions about the woman who loved the snake, as well as their personal histories with Mabel and each other, should also be considered important parts of the story. Transcriptions of oral stories have often failed to reveal these interrelationships, assuming instead some kind of transparent, unmediated narrative.

This has not been merely a matter of the white anthropologist distorting the story, as has often been claimed in Native studies, but a reflection of the complex nature of the stories themselves and the interrelationships that create their meanings. What has often been missing in scholarship, Sarris says, is an effective way of upsetting things, exposing the critical assumptions behind the claims critics make: "How do scholars see beyond the norms they use to frame the experiences of others unless those norms are interrupted and exposed so that scholars are vulnerable, seeing what they think as possibly wrong, or at least limited?"[54]

One of the most powerful aspects of Sarris's analysis is that while avoiding an oppositional framework, he does not fall prey to the radical skepticism that would become apparent in the deficit approaches applied some years later by hybridity theorists who seem unable to progress beyond claiming the foundational nature of the European underpinnings of Indian stories, insisting that the narratives, as well as their contexts, cannot be claimed as Indian without confessing their profound hybridity, given five hundred years of contact and the inevitablility of cultural exchange. Sarris, in contrast, identities a Pomo storytelling tradition and works within a tribally specific framework that assumes the existence of Indian viewpoints (though not prioritizing them in relation to other critical modes in terms of their relevance and not claiming them as pristine).

Sarris's book is different from *The Sacred Hoop* and *Other Destinies* in that Sarris works in a tribally specific mode at least to the degree that he chooses Pomo stories and texts as his focus—with the exception of a chapter on Chippewa writer Louise Erdrich's novel *Love Medicine* (1984), although it might be pointed out that Erdrich's novel receives scrutiny from various Pomo perspectives as well. Paula Gunn Allen had drawn extensively on Keres cultures in *The Sacred Hoop,* but it is not focused primarily on Laguna literature. The Owens book is also written in the undefined "Native literature" mode, as were most of the critical works then and now.

While Sarris is quite interested in Euroamerican literary theory, he also saturates his book with a wide range of Pomo viewpoints. He assumes a Pomo body of tradition to work from, whereas later hybridity theorists would question whether or not such an autonomous body of work could even be identified or claimed as the subject of one's study because of the way tribally specific texts and oral stories, as well as tribal identities, are already deeply reflective of non-Indian influences. While not claiming that a Native interpretation of an Indian text or experience is guaranteed to be insightful, neither does Sarris ever say that Indian experience, and interpretation of things Indian by Indians, is fated to some fundamental indeterminacy because of its inherent hybridity. Sarris's work does not necessarily imply that Native perspectives are impossible outside of hybridist frameworks, a theoretical position that is religious rather than critical in terms of its claim for "One True Theory," the theory of hybridity, an inherent contradiction to the hybridists' own insistence on interdependencies as well as their rationalist tendencies.

Sarris's participatory view of textual communities is especially interesting in light of his analysis of Elizabeth Colson's work, *Autobiographies of Three Pomo Women* (1974). Sarris argues that an accurate rendering of the life stories of the Pomo women who are the subject of the book is not the only issue, nor is the corrrect analysis of Pomo cultural concerns that might inform the text.

The autobiography of Elizabeth Colson is a key determinant in her depictions of Pomo women, the autobiography of the autobiographer. Of particular importance are Colson's encounters with the women, the account of her account. She does not reveal her presence in the text; she leaves no tracks in the story that might explain her own relationship to her subjects and subject matter.

The older Boasian anthropology would have discouraged Colson from writing about these relationships as part of the Pomo story she is unfolding; an experiential, first-person methodology would be seen as unscientific, subjective, even unprincipled. In addition to Colson's effect on the women's life stories, Sarris points out the issue is more complex than white distortion of Indian texts, because Native storytellers make decisions, whether conscious ones or not, as to how to edit stories as they tell them. Sarris's analysis of these issues carries forward some of the important earlier work of Clifford and Geertz; however, Sarris adds another layer to these complexities by insisting that the autobiography of the reader who encounters Colson's text is a key factor in the outcome of the story too.

Sometimes students in my courses despair at these complexities, concluding that the thrust of Sarris's analysis is the hopeless inaccuracy of texts because of the almost limitless layers of translation they go through. This is not the point at all, however. The idea is a self-awareness of our own role as readers in shaping what we encounter and a resistance to reading where we talk back to texts, where we ask questions, rather than view the texts as the authoritative final word that has come down to us in some pure form. When teaching these issues to students, I emphasize that this can be as simple a matter as writing questions in the margins of a textbook rather than simply highlighting the lines with a yellow Magic Marker as if the text, indeed, is magic and can and should be assimilated without question. I tell students that they will be amazed at how much better they will remember material for tests if they talk back to the materials—write questions in the margins of their book regarding passages they disagree with, do not understand; notice contradictions with other pages in the book, and so on, rather than just underscoring the typescript, which exercises their wrists, a very little, their brains even less.

In criticizing representations of Indians in popular culture, Sarris moves beyond simply relegating this to a "white problem." He believes that Allen, Native herself, when referring to Pomo religious traditions in *The Sacred Hoop*, seems unable to escape a methodology that summarizes and speaks on behalf of Mabel McKay and Kashaya religious traditions rather than finding ways to give voice to Pomo women like Mabel and Essie Parish—even by doing as little as including direct quotations from the sources Allen names. Of equal importance, Allen, according to Sarris, does not acknowledge her own methodology or interrogate it: "Allen does not ask questions about how she reads each of the Pomo women's words and performances she translates and discusses in her scholarship." She misses aspects of Pomo culture, such as the role of men dreamers, but more to the point, Sarris says, is the problem that Allen replicates in practice what she sets out to criticize: she silences Indian women. He writes, "How does what Essie Parrish demonstrates in her healing show [Allen's claim of] the basic understanding the tribal peoples generally have about how sickness comes about?" Which tribal peoples? Where? When? Neither Mabel McKay nor Essie Parrish is allowed to talk to or inform Allen's conclusions about them. Neither woman has an individual voice represented in the text. Allen provides no direct quotations. . . . Allen has shaped what she heard and saw to inform the Indian presence in the text she reads.[55]

This discussion is reminiscent of a fascinating chapter in Sarris entitled, "Culture under Glass: The Pomo Basket," which emphasizes the way in which museum displays cut off contact between those viewing Native material objects and those making them, allowing neither group to ask questions of each other, thus diluting the spiritual possibilities of the items themselves. Ultimately, Sarris compares baskets under glass to academic specializations that fail to communicate across disciplinary, and other kinds of, boundaries.

The book concludes with two powerful final chapters about teaching that again break down an Indian/Euro oppositional framework. Sarris discusses the failure of teachers'attempts to instruct Pomo school children in traditional Pomo stories, culture, and language, analyzing the way the children resisted their own culture when it felt like something imposed from the outside (and this was not simply a matter of non-Indian teachers or texts) rather than self-generated. Students had to be allowed some creative means of generating their own stories, rather than being told what constituted Pomo culture; in order for them to engage the materials they had to be its cocreators.

Sarris applies these ideas to university instruction, where often times we teach cultural norms rather than critical thinking. Even in more dialogic classroom environments, students can still channel back the "right answers," and the discussions we lead can encourage this. Sarris advocates what he calls "strong-sense critical thinking," which involves the inclusion of experience in a twofold dialogue: How does one's experiences cause her to read the text differently and how does the text cause one to read her experiences differently?

I do not wish to create a hierarchy of Native criticism by privileging one book over the other, so here I want to make a personal observation rather than claim some kind of universal critical truth: While I learned a lot of information from Owens's *Other Destinies,* Sarris's *Keeping Slug Woman Alive* changed the way I think. It made me reconsider the way I evaluate the kind of information about Native novels that Louis Owens doles out. I felt I had experienced a paradigm shift after I read Sarris. After I read Owens I felt I had completed a really useful survey. Sarris's ideas about exposing one's methodologies and uncovering personal stories that relate to the research one undertakes have influenced my writing, including the approach of this introductory chapter you are reading.

—

On January 1, 1994, Maya Indians in Chiapas, calling themselves Zapatistas after Emiliano Zapata, an Indian leader who organized landless peasants in the Mexican revolution, execute a brilliant takeover of eight Mexican cities on a date carefully chosen to mark the exact time the North American Free Trade Agreement is to take effect. The takeover is so effective the Mexican news media speculate that it could have only been masterminded by Cuban Communists, not Indian campesinos. The Mexican army counterstrikes with some fifteen thousand troops, tanks, and bombers. As many as four hundred people die, roughly half of them from the Mexican army. The Zapatistas organize a worldwide protest over the Internet and through the international press, voicing their claims that NAFTA will make Mexico's elite richer and push more and more Indians off their traditional home lands.

In a 1994 visit to Arkansas, the chief of the United Keetoowah band, John Ross, discovers that President Bill Clinton's late mother claimed to be of Cherokee descent. The Keetoowahs, who supported Clinton in the presidential race, bring the information before the tribal council and vote in Bill Clinton as an honorary affiliate, thinking that making him a member of a federally recognized Indian tribe might help all Native people. The White House, evidently unimpressed, does not respond to the news. Some years later Spokane/Coeur d'Alene author Sherman Alexie will meet Clinton at the White House. Clinton will tell him that he's "part Cherokee." Alexie will reply, "That's what all white people say." Clinton will laugh.

On April 29, 1994, Clinton himself greets more than three hundred leaders of federally recognized Indian nations, the first time tribal leaders have been invited to the White House to discuss issues with a sitting president since President James Monroe hosted a group of Native leaders in 1822.

In 1994 I am a Ph.D. student at the University of Oklahoma. During the spring semester police try to break in on the freshman composition class I am teaching. They intend to arrest a young American Indian woman, who at that moment is in the middle of a presentation. I plead with them to wait until class is over. They refuse. They demand that I identify the student they are looking for. The class is on the third floor of the football stadium, no way in hell the student can escape, I say, if they'll just wait. The police insist they are going to arrest me for aiding and abetting a criminal. I respond, too bad, wait until class is over. The police then threaten to interrogate every student in the classroom until someone identifies the person they're after. In order to avoid humiliating the student in front of the entire class, I relent and quietly tell her about the officers outside the door who want to "visit" with her. They handcuff her and drag her off in front of all of us. Many of my students call home to their parents that night, quite frightened, and we have to spend the rest of the semester doing damage control. More angry than I've ever been before or since, I start my own investigation and find out that city cops have no jurisdiction on the OU campus, and they had no right to enter my class. I consider this a major violation of the sanctity of the classroom, the rights of my students, and my personal sovereignty. I am still angry all these years later. I publish an article in the school newspaper entitled, "No Where Is Safe in Occupied Territory." The student, who had been with friends when a car was stolen, is not held for custody. The lieutenant from the Norman Police Department who tries to smooth things over with me in a later interview begins the conversation with "My next door neighbor is an Indian, and he's a nice guy."

Days after that arrest, twelve drunk and naked members of Phi Kappa Psi fraternity knock over a tipi in front of Bizell Library and piss on it. Native students are inside praying, getting ready for the opening of Native American Heritage Week on campus. Someone calls OU police who don't bother to take a statement or investigate. Protests ensue, many of us are involved, and OU claims for months that the university must protect the confidentiality of the fraternity members, which seems to mean granting them immunity from all their actions. Some of the blame for the deaths of drunk fraternity members involved in accidents over the years, I'm now convinced, can be attributed to OU's good ol' boy hands-off relationship with fraternities, whose members will probably end up future Bubbas on governing boards that run the place.

This is a definitive year for me as a writer, a critic, and a human being in terms of understanding about safety and risk, what it means in life and in criticism.

Robert Allen Warrior: Debunking the Alienated Protagonist

The year 1995 saw the publication of Osage writer Robert Warrior's *Tribal Secrets: Recovering American Indian Intellectual Traditions.* The book more closely resembles the cultural studies modes of the 1990s, given the scope of its attention to those works not immediately recognizable as "literary" or "theoretical" in the conventional sense of these terms as was the case with the "literature proper" in *The Sacred Hoop* and *Other Destinies.* Recent accusations regarding Warrior's rejection of theory, and a separatist approach that dismisses non-Indian contributions to the field, are somewhat ironic, for the book has a striking similarity to other cultural studies works that sought to open up "the vast territory," to borrow a phrase from Greg Sarris, of that which is literary. Some of the critique has centered around whether or not Warrior, and other Native critics, expose the critical assumptions that inform their work by examining their own methodologies, especially in terms of whatever Euroamerican theoretical underpinnings inform what they do.

Warrior's approach seems to me a highly pragmatic one, with much to commend it. He seems to ask the question, "Why not use what we already have?" Since American Indian intellectuals had authored a large number of books in the nineteenth and early twentieth centuries, how could a responsible criticism proceed as if none of these works existed? Warrior has never claimed that Euroamerican theory should be rejected by Native critics. Instead, he makes a case for considering Native-authored works of previous generations so that critics might make better-informed decisions about the relevance of Euroamerican theory. Warrior seeks to discard the earlier widely held assumptions that Native fiction began in 1968 and critical thought originated outside Indian country. He works as a historian who is interested in Native literature that has grounded "itself in its own history the way that African-American, feminist, and other oppositional discourses have."[56]

An important observation has to do with the historical mode that Warrior works in. Passages in the book are identified as "1890–1916: Assimilationism and Apocalypticism," "1925–1960: John Joseph Mathews and a Generation of Free Agents," "1960–1973: The Battle to Define Red Power," "1973 to the Present: Diversity, Party Lines, and the Need for a Generational Perspective." This is much different than the ahistorical analysis of cultural traits in Allen and Owens, where a circularly minded Native world is set off against a linear-obsessed Western Other. It is also different from Sarris, who does not scrutinize historical periods in terms of how a particular era might affect literary production, instead theorizing the meaning of cross-cultural encounters and readings.

Warrior works across historical spans to discuss the nature of changes in Indian country, rather than emphasizing a universalized "Native paradigm." He points out differences, for example, in some of the community-born writers of the twenties and thirties in relation to those Society of American Indian (SAI) authors who preceded them and who were dislocated from their original homes. He observes the lack of a national Native organization in the twenties and thirties and compares that lack to the integrationist lobbying of the SAI a generation before. He contrasts the nostalgic viewpoints of the SAI writers in relation to depictions of an Indian past , noting that the authors of the twenties and thirties at least located their stories in contemporary Indian settings, no matter how uncertain they may have been about a narrative's outcome.

I offer two quotes, the first from Allen, the second from Owens, for comparison with Warrior: "The major difference between most activist movements and tribal societies is that for millennia American Indians have based their social systems, however diverse, on ritual, spirit-centered, woman-focused worldviews."[57] Some might wonder which activist movements are being contrasted with which Indians, or find perplexing the notion of cultural constants that hold up for millennia, or even wonder if all tribal groups are as "woman-focused" as Allen says. The seeming schism between Indians and activism is perplexing. Warrior, in contrast, suggests changes had occurred in the mere twenty years between the SAI writers and the writers of the twenties and thirties. He does not try to create a stable, ahistorical category for two decades, much less millennia.

Owens writes, "in spite of the fact that Indian authors write from very diverse tribal and cultural backgrounds, there is to a remarkable degree a shared consciousness and identifiable worldview reflected in novels by American Indian authors, a consciousness and worldview defined primarily by a quest for identity: What does it mean to be "Indian"—or mixedblood—in contemporary America?"[58] In addition to their concerns about personal identity issues, both critics much less frequently cite particular historical dates than does Warrior, instead embracing shared worldviews that transcend time.

Warrior describes his approach to history and literature, thusly: "The intellectual historical mode of chapter 1 served to create a context for understanding the place of Mathews and Deloria among American Indian writers in terms of the impact of history on their works. In this chapter the focus shifts to the ways in which literature promotes a deeper insight into history."[59] Like many cultural studies advocates in the nineties, Warrior sets out to demonstrate that an interest in sociology need not mean an abandonment of close reading, that history informs literature and vice versa.

One of the real strengths of Warrior's work has always been his aversion to romanticism and his commitment to social realism instead of a naive nativism that celebrates all things Indian. Warrior, for example, points out the racism of some in the SAI leadership in regard to African Americans that kept them from building broader alliances; the sexism of John Joseph Mathews's novel *Sundown*, in which Chal's mother is never even named, and the erasure of women's roles in *Talking to the Moon;* and the varied Osage opinions about Mathews in his own times and now. In the Native paradigm approaches, such inequities can only be attributed to non-Indians or to Indians who are no longer "traditional." Warrior works as a historian rather than an apologist for a harmonious utopia contrasted with a "white" world of imbalance and oppositions.

One of the most important aspects of *Tribal Secrets* is that Warrior is the first Native critic to examine public policy as a central concern in relation to fiction. The book's working vocabulary not only includes the Dawes Act of 1887, the Indian Reorganization Act of 1934, the Collier reforms of the 1930s, and termination and relocation of the 1950s, but it also includes frequent refernces to organizations such as SAI, Carlisle Indian Boarding School, the National Indian Youth Council, the National Congress of American Indians, and the American Indian Movement.

I am a reader of *Tribal Secrets* who believes that the way I approach criticism was forever altered by my encounter with this particular text. Warrior analyzes Challenge Windzer, the protagonist of John Joseph Mathews's novel *Sundown,* outside the identity frameworks that dominated Native literary critique at the time Warrior wrote the book. Warrior argues that Chal's struggles are linked with the abrogation of Osage national government, the dislocating effect of having grown up in a sovereign nation that is dismantled under the Dawes and Curtis acts. Chal's problems are as much ideological as personal. The status of Osage sovereignty can be read in relation to Chal's identity, a relationship, we might note, between the state and one's state of being. Warrior moves beyond an analysis that is "strictly biological-cultural rather than political-ideological. Quite obviously . . . Mathews did not intend *Sundown* to be merely a story of how an individual deals with personal identity. Rather, Mathews evokes a historical period of intense importance for Osage people and communities and attempts to sort out how the political strategies of various groups of Osages played out and what possible future might exist."[60]

These sentences changed the way I view Native literature; they redirected my energies toward a broader style of Native literary analysis than simply turning to the life of the protagonist with every reading. Two characters named Tayo and Abel had dominated Native criticism and were viewed as the central focus of the novels that depicted them. It was a little bit like the theatrical world before modernism when theater was a vehicle for a leading man who produced, directed, promoted, starred, tacked up handbills, fed, hired, fired, and took the loudest applause or the scariest boos at the end of the show. The sentences just quoted from *Tribal Secrets* are, for me, among the most important in the book. Yet they are seldom, if ever, cited.

Recent critics like Elvira Pulitano, author of the mistitled *Toward a Native American Critical Theory* (2003), turn, instead, to passages they can use to point out what they see as Warrior's overly separatist act in examining Native-authored texts—or to insist that his use of terms like "intellectual sovereignty" are ill-defined. Warrior's prioritization of communal rather than personal identity, however, seems neither overly separatist nor lacking in clarity to me. Warrior reads *Sundown* as a novel about a community in a crisis involving land, jurisdiction, and sovereignty, rather than the story of an alienated protagonist, the one-size-fits-all model that had dominated contemporary Native literary criticism. Warrior, like earlier critics, also has "recovery" in his subtitle, but it seems to be recovery of a different sort, recovery of a tradition rooted in politics as much as culture in the narrow ethnographic sense of the term.

Another highlight of *Tribal Secrets* is Warrior's lucid explication of Mathews's rather difficult concept of ornamentation, a philosophy Mathews articulated in relation to a ten-year observation of Osage land. Mathews eventually turned his musings on Osage land into an Osage political philosophy with ramifications beyond Osage country. In spite of an intense sense of Osage land and culture—maybe I should say *because of* his knowledge of such things—Mathews developed his ideas regarding ornamentation into a theory with global implications for international political relations, an arena few people consider within the purview of Native studies. Mathews's nonfiction demonstrates that Indians can comment on other things besides Indians, a simple insight that holds rich possibilities for literary studies. If non-Indian scholars, as we all agree, can study and write about Native literature and theory, perhaps we should turn ourselves loose on some of their literatures and histories too. Most impressive is the fact that Mathews locates his international musings within an Osage theory with origins in Osage landscape. (Of course, the hybridists would point out the obvious here—its "Osageness" cannot be claimed in absolute or purist terms. Those of us mounting a resistant critique to the deficit theorists, however, would point out it can still be claimed as Osage.)

Warrior's impressive handling of Mathews's foray into political science on a global level—he warned against the U.S. vision of itself as in a state of eternal virility between World Wars I and II—should have made Warrior the leading proponent of anti-isolationism in Indian studies instead of the one most likely to be identified as parochial for his lack of consideration of non-Indian sources, Euroamerican theory, and the non-Indian world at large. These reactions are a little hard to scrutinize, since cultural studies approaches have long since opened up literature to sociology, and those who find shortcomings in Warrior's work claim to be theoretically advanced in comparison to his "theoretical naivete." Go figure.

In the critique of Warrior as an isolationist, a central issue seems to be his focus on Indian-authored books and sources; that is probably the real issue creating all the sparks, rather than his analysis of social policy in relation to fiction. The idea that Indians might be the subject of Indian criticism seems obvious to some of us, but the theoretical modes in cultural studies have leaned toward cross-cultural analyses with an emphasis on interdependency rather than an exclusive focus on one group.

Perhaps it is not so much Warrior's focus on Indians that has created the controversy as his focus on Indian source material, which some regard as an exclusion of non-Indian-authored works about Native people or, more generally, a denial of outside cultural influences. Cross-cultural work is, no doubt, important, but how is it altered in a historical moment in which Indian-authored books still constitute a miniscule fraction of the total number of books about Indians? In such an environment, reading Indian statements about Indians can reasonably be seen as simply sound research.

Warrior also provides a reading of Vine Deloria, Jr.'s Native studies classic, *God Is Red* (1973) in relation to Deloria's discussion of temporal and spatial ideas in theology. Deloria criticizes Christianity for what he views as a lack of concern for material conditions. Warrior, rather ingeniously, finds a link between Deloria's contrast of temporal and spatial religions—temporal religion's focus on dogma and spatial religion's orientation toward land—and the interest of identity critics in personal growth in comparison with the interest of materialist critics in social realities. Warrior looks beyond narratives of personal, or cultural, recovery to an engagement with material culture, history, and politics.

In the mid-1990s Congress considers several bills that will gut some Indian programs and end others. Assistant Secretary of Indian Affairs Ada Deer (a member of the Menominee tribe) accuses Congress of "returning to a termination mentality," calling the bills being debated "unethical and immoral." "This country's first Americans deserve better treatment," she says. "They deserve honesty, candor, and respect. The United States, at the very least, should keep its promises." The bills are defeated.[61]

In 1996 the Utah Senate Judicial Committee unanimously passes SB128 guaranteeing Indian inmates the right to "practice traditional ceremonies, meet with spiritual leaders, and have a place to worship on prison grounds."[62] Although federal law has earlier acknowledged the rights of prisoners, the new law specifies which ceremonial items can be brought in or maintained in prisons.

On April 6, 1996, in Winnebago, Nebraska, the Great Lakes Running Strong, a men's basketball team composed primarily of players from the Lac du Flambeau Ojibway Reservation, win the National Indian Athletic Association Men's 40 and Over basketball championship. Down by eight points at half-time, Great Lakes comes from behind to defeat the Lakota Spirit in the title game by a score of 76 to 67.[63]

In July of the same year the Confederated Umatilla tribes get back their first sacred possession when the Wallula Stone is returned under NAGPRA. Taken by a railroad engineer to Portland in 1910, this basalt boulder, covered with fifteen-thousand-year-old petroglyphs, is returned in a public ceremony, and Portland mayor Vera Katz apologizes for its theft. The stone becomes the centerpiece of the Umatilla veterans' memorial, dedicated on July 4.[64]

Gerald Vizenor: A Little Upsetting Is Necessary

In 1996 Kimberly Blaeser's book, *Gerald Vizenor: Writing in the Oral Tradition*, was published. Since Vizenor himself had featured literary criticism in works such as *Manifest Manners: Postindian Warriors of Survivance* (1994) and had contributed an essay and an introduction to *Narrative Chance: Postmodern Discourse on Native American Indian Literatures* (1993), some might wonder, Why not go directly to the source instead of to a study of the author in question? *Manifest Manners,* however, is not exclusively a work of literary criticism; one chapter, for example, is about Indian casinos. And his introduction to *Narrative Chance* is a brief one.

Moreover, distinguishing between genres traditionally described as literary criticism, fiction, cultural critique, autobiography, and journalism is difficult in Vizenor's oeuvre, where any given writing could contain all these elements and more. Looking at a book such as Blaeser's, an overview of Vizenor's prolific output, and one written by a Native critic of his own tribe, helps to locate Vizenor's attention to literary criticism in the wide range of the genres he writes in, since an examination of the more than twenty-five books he had written by the time of Blaeser's study is impossible. Blaeser's book, further, contains many continuities with the first two works of this study, *The Sacred Hoop* and *Other Destinies*.

I want to make a personal observation about Gerald Vizenor at the outset: this is a writer I greatly admire. To engage a fellow author at the level of ideas, and to critique those ideas, is not to dismiss the man or his work; rather, it is to take him seriously. The heterodoxy of Vizenor's work is one of the best things to have ever happened to Native studies. But, like all heterodoxies, as well as all orthodoxies, it is fraught with its own set of problems. This statement is necessary in order to point out that here I neither dismiss Vizenor nor do I analyze other critics (with whom I might have certain affinities) in purely celebratory terms. I want readers to be clear about my intent. I often reveal my biases in terms of critical stances I agree and disagree with—this introduction is not a purely descriptive effort—but I try to point to the philosophical underpinnings that influence my stance, and I hope to reveal a little bit of literary history that surrounds my choices. This is not a party for friends nor a snubbing of enemies. For reasons I am not quite sure I understand, saying anything about Vizenor, whether positive or negative, has a tendency to get people all riled up. One camp says one is only allowed to praise him, another that it is one's moral duty to bring the man down. I ascribe to neither of these positions.

Given that Vizenor, more than any other Native critic, is often associated with poststructuralism, I want to say more about its impact on cultural studies. Poststructuralism has influenced a diverse range of disciplines—feminist criticism, postcolonial theory, film studies, and queer theory, to name a few. An important concept in poststructuralism is the infinite capacity for language to take on different meanings. According to Vincent Leitch:

> Because the signifier (word) is disconnected from the signified (concept) and the referent (thing), language floats or slides in relation to reality, a condition made more severe with the additional sliding introduced into language by figurative language, such as metaphors and metonymies. Such rhetoricity (as it is called) adds layers of substitutions and supplements (more differences) to floating signifiers. Textuality and rhetoricity are conditioned by yet a third sliding or differential element, intertextuality—a text's dependence on prior words, concepts, connotations, codes, conventions, unconscious practices, and texts. Every text is an intertext that borrows, knowingly or not, from the immense archive of previous culture. The term *(inter)textuality,* with parentheses, captures the sense of textuality as being conditioned by this inescapable historical intertest.[65]

One might see, especially in the last part of this definition, some compatibilities with orality, particularly the notion of a passed-on tradition, the way storytellers are informed by those tellers who came before them, those contemporary to them, and those to come. In terms of the first part of Leitch's definition, Vizenor borrows from the poststructural idea of liberating signifier from signified to open up static definitions of Indianness (in simple language, to challenge stereotypes). Labeling ossified or overly generalized definitions as "terminal creeds," Vizenor has expended great energy on attempting to open up the signifier "Indian" to a wider range of signification. Vizenor's sophisticated take on stereotypes is not only related to popular non-Indian representations of Native peoples but to the stereotypes Natives cling to about themselves.

One might also worry, however, about some of poststructuralism's incompatibilities with oral traditions, instead of assuming a perfect fit, a subject Blaeser largely avoids in her study, as does Vizenor in his own work. This might be of particular concern in relation to the way words seem to be moving away from the things they represent in poststructuralist thought. Some might wonder how to reconcile notions of nonrepresentation with certain ceremonial settings, where spoken words are sometimes seen as having a physical component or a physical effect on the world: *words* cause *things* to happen, a very special relationship between signifier and signified. Often the very things words represent come to be, and the happenings are not exclusively the domain of human efforts, influences, mediations. These are complicated matters. Ceremonial language is also mediated by the humans who speak it and the ritual circumstances that surround it where humans are involved, but in some tribal worldviews the powers of language are not created exclusively by humans. In puzzling through these realities, we might wonder what N. Scott Momaday means, for example, when he says, "A word has power in and of itself. It comes from nothing into sound and meaning; it gives origin to all things."[66] If all language is socially mediated, as some would claim, some Native thinkers might respond, "Yes, but it is also mediated by others besides humans."

A further word of caution might be appropriate. How much free rein do we want to give definitions? Do we want to remove "Indian" so far from its social referents that definitions are no longer possible? How would tribes manage in the world of federal Indian law if "Indian" is a matter of infinite signification and ultimately undecidable? Can historical claims be made from a philosophical vantage point that emphasizes that events can never be separated from perceptions, thereby denying any kind of certitude? What happens if a historically silenced minority group wants to amend the historical record to include their side of the story? Can they do this if normative truth claims are no longer considered viable? Is simply presenting a competing narrative very satisfying if one's community is telling its story for the first time while the dominating group has controlled the discourse for centuries? Does Native studies want to become like queer studies in its refusal to define the parameters of its own discipline so that anything and everything becomes its potential subject matter? Does this ambiguity of audience and mission help or hurt in light of a history of erasure and underrepresentation? What of the goal of Native critics who might want to focus on their own communities for a change instead of making everybody else central to their efforts? Blaeser's focus, for better or worse, does not include a discussion of the broader ramifications of the theoretical field Vizenor plays in, at least in terms of the more problematic aspects of poststructuralism.

On the other hand, in terms of poststructuralism's power to disrupt, Native studies needs a good, strong kick in the butt to move it beyond some of the static clichés that have kept it from addressing difficult issues. The temptation has been to fall back on the opposition of a balanced, communal utopia offset against a menacing Western hierarchical society. Native people might want more agency than this; they might want the freedom to imagine themselves anew, to act in ways that intervene in their destinies, to view themselves as more than the victims of Western dystopias or the happy inhabitants of a communal lark. Native studies practitioners might want to expand into other subject areas that heretofore have been ignored. Tol Foster's essay in our own collection here analyzes the way Native studies has largely ignored Will Rogers because he does not signify "Indian" in a fashion familiar to the public at large, or even to people in contemporary Native studies. Vizenor's work provides some of the tools for this rearticulation of an expanded field.

Blaeser demonstrates how Vizenor's poetics, which allow for opening up texts, can contribute to such liberation by allowing Native people to go beyond fixed, terminal definitions and empowering them to articulate identities whose only limits are their imaginations. One of the jobs of poststructuralism, then, is to break down conventional oppositions by questioning binary pairs such as writing/orality, male/female, nature/culture, purity/contamination, civilization/savagery, straight/gay, and white/black. Poststructuralism questions the reasons for privileging one half of the binary pair over the other and demonstrates how each half is dependent on the other for its existence. For example, taking the nature/culture opposition, we might ask how metropolitan centers such as New York City, often seen as the mecca of literate culture and art in the so-called New World, can exist apart from a relationship to nature? Is there not earth under New York streets? The city's inhabitants, being human and a part of the natural world, breathe air, shovel snow, give birth, return to the earth, and experience other natural phenomena, as do people everywhere. Poststructuralists might question a viewpoint that presents a big city as a threatening menace because of its distance from the natural world.

Meaning is a key issue in poststructural theory, as it is in every theory. In the New Criticism of the 1930s meaning was difficult, a puzzle composed of ambiguity, paradox, irony, contradictions, and tensions. With enough patience, however, a puzzle can be put together by the person who is smart enough to figure out how all the pieces fit.

In poststructural thought meaning is undecidable in the sense of yielding one definition that remains the same in all times and places. Meaning is there, somewhere, and we can even describe it, but we cannot say definitively what it is in singular terms—it always has multiple possibilities. Some skeptics might say poststructuralism makes meaning impossible; in reality, it makes meaning infinitely possible: words that depend on other words that depend on . . . well, you get the point. Here our puzzle does not have five hundred pieces; it has more pieces than anyone could ever count, given all the words that have been spoken and written and thought throughout history and all the different ways people meant them and did not mean them and the meanings their listeners or readers attributed or did not attribute to them. Meanings, then, are not stable but infinitely contextual. If we ask thirty people to define the word "table," few, if any, will have the exact same words in their definition. When my students start throwing around terms like "European mindset" in order to point out Native people do not think like Them, I ask the class what would happen if we went around the room and had each person decide who there has a European mindset and who does not and explain the reasons why. We never do that, of course, since I like to avoid bloodshed whenever possible, but the statement makes a certain point about monolithic clichés.

Extending these issues to literature, readings, from a poststructuralist point of view (given that they are readings of language), are undecidable. One can make a literary claim; one cannot make a *definitive* literary claim. Poststructuralism, however, is not necessarily a descent into meaninglessness (whether or not it is a descent into relativism is a thornier issue): "The redoubled reading typical of much deconstruction rests on claims of interest and insight, not of validity and truth. A reading or interpretation of a text does not prove but persuades; it is more or less compelling, productive, original, or useful. This pragmatic set of criteria links deconstruction with contemporary U.S. neopragmatism, an influential philosophy that insists on the contingency of all human arrangements and concepts."[67]

My reading might be more convincing than yours; however, it cannot be inherently more valuable. Yours might be more convincing than mine in the right set of circumstances. In Native literary studies these ideas will come back to haunt us later when it becomes theoretically difficult (although I would argue not impossible) to mount an argument for prioritizing Indian readings of Indian literature, as it will also create a serious disruption in other areas of minority studies in terms of trying to base academic disciplines on distinctions between insiders and outsiders by privileging one group over the other.

In describing Vizenor's oral influences, Blaeser draws on the theories of Walter Ong's *Orality and Literacy: The Technologizing of the Word* (1982). Ong studied the dynamics of oral performance, especially emphasizing the role of audience, which is immediate, for an oral storyteller as opposed to imagined for a writer. Ong describes how stories in societies that are primarily oral evolve systems that allow narratives to be remembered through various forms of rhythms, repetitions, and multiple reinforcement. Ong argues that oral storytelling depends on strong narrative styles that emphasize action over abstraction. Primary orality changes the very way people think, according to Ong.

Unfortunately, when one reads Ong, the characteristics that he attributes to the thought processes of communal cultures, which he claims are resistant to conceptualization and abstraction, sound a bit like the way his Jesuit forefathers described the people they encountered in the New World. A further problem is the opposition Ong creates between writing and orality, which seems to contradict the poststructuralist theories Vizenor relies on. One might well argue, for example, that a writer finds ways to try to compensate for an oral performance, as do readers, even if those processes are often subconscious ones. We might also find ways in which orality is created by writing. In Native American studies, for example, we might point out trends in which written texts, that is, oral tradition collections, are passing into verbal tellings in Native communities these days.

The same kind of oppositions that make Ong's work troubling are sometimes part of the Blaeser analysis. In the introduction, for example, Blaeser says that Vizenor "strives to compensate for the inadequacies of written language." She goes on to show how Vizenor's story "Almost Browne" "comments on the origin and existence of the words outside the static written tradition, on the authenticity of the oral and the actual, on the presence and power of sound and language, on the 'almost' quality of mere words."[68]

Blaeser seems to privilege orality over writing, as evidenced by the phrase "static written tradition." One question might be to what degree does Vizenor himself do the same thing? Blaeser's comments about his work seem to point to an innate inauthenticity in writing. One of Derrida's famous theoretical postulates was that he "deconstructed the speech/writing opposition by showing how writing precedes speech; characteristically, he reinscribes the concept of writing *(ecriture* in French) to mean any and all forms of inscription and at the same time undercuts the privileging of speech as face-to-face spontaneous utterance."[69]

One might compare Blaeser's statements about Vizenor, for example, with Warrior's *Tribal Secrets,* published in the previous year, that made a case for a written tradition that had been understudied, a claim Warrior makes without privileging the written over the oral or vice versa. While Blaeser seems to inadvertently demonstrate Vizenor's problematic relationship with poststructuralism, not much is said up front about his philosophical inconsistencies and sometimes haphazard relationship with theory.

Vizenor's life story includes an early involvement with Indian activism in the Twin Cities in the mid-1960s, which in later years evolved into a writerly relationship with activism as a cultural critic rather than a physical participant. Some might say that Vizenor's interest in the nonrepresentational modes of postmodernism, in this case liberating fiction from social realism, freeing it up for the world of imagination (Vizenor would argue that the oral tradition is not based exclusively on a mimetic realism), marks a similar movement in his fiction away from the real world—that he has traded tropes for reality.

In understanding these controversies, however, a challenge for any critic of Vizenor is the enormous breadth of his creative output—fiction is only one element. A gritty, antiromantic, journalistic commitment composes another significant aspect of Vizenor's writing, which has dealt with Sand Creek, AIM members, incarcerated Indians, and many other topics profoundly engaged with the world of daily Indian life. Vizenor also often writes of popular culture stereotypes and the ways that Native people themselves fall prey to them, a point he makes in regard to what he calls the tribal "kitschymen," in *Manifest Manners*. He uses the term to describe "bone-choker Indians" and the way prominent activists have posed as simulations of Indianness in order to capture the public's attention, feeding into preconceived notions. Vizenor's personal critiques are almost always surrounded by ambiguities—while he might be making fun of these individuals, he also seems strangely appreciative of the opportunities they provide for laughter. If someone becomes the target of Vizenor's irony, he or she at least might be comforted by the fact that readers may not quite be able to tell if the person is being made fun of or not, given the ambiguities with which Vizenor loves to surround these depictions.

Vizenor is particularly interested in the manifestations, so to speak, of Manifest Destiny in the modern world, where the notion of divinely ordained American exceptionalism seems to be even more pervasive today than it was in the nineteenth century. He coined the term "manifest manners" as a neologism for triumphalism, and there is a whole vocabulary of Vizenor words that do not exist in any dictionary. Some find this playfulness liberatory, others simply annoying.

The strength of Blaeser's analysis lies in her description of the ways in which Vizenor parts company with realistic representation—and the reasons he does it. Vizenor disrupts journalistic and autobiographical claims to objectivity, bringing to bear the skills of a fiction writer on his nonfiction efforts. He works in narrative forms and brings a sense of mythic traditions to an interpretation of factual events. While journalism and autobiography often explore causality, Vizenor allows for competing versions of stories that complicate explanations as to why things happened. He is interested in the "shadows" of stories, the truths behind the facts, that which does not get reported, the meanings of what goes unsaid, those things that can be imagined, the larger, ongoing tribal story beyond its textual representation. Vizenor believes that a metaphorical approach to nonfiction can often reveal more than a "factual" one that claims realistic representations. Readers can be empowered if they can be encouraged to create their own shadows, their own interpretations, rather than simply reading the story as transparent, unmediated discourse.

In these regards Vizenor's nonfiction might be related to the gonzo journalism of the 1960s made famous by Tom Wolfe and Hunter S. Thompson, as well as to poststructural notions of infinite signification, undecidability, multiple interpretations. Journalism and autobiography, like fiction and poetry, rely on language that "floats or slides in relation to reality."[70] Important to all of Vizenor's writing, no matter the genre, is the idea of the reader's responsibility to participate in the creation of the text and the writer's responsibility to facilitate that participation, to leave part of the story open for the reader's completion. The text becomes an invitation for the reader to go beyond the words on the printed page, an encouragement for her to seek out her own experiences. Blaeser does an especially good job of discussing how the poetics of haiku, an early form Vizenor wrote in, become the basis for all his writing. Tribal songs, dreams, and haiku, because of its extreme beauty, leave a space open for the reader to imagine his own meaning, a space that "propel[s] the reader beyond mere words toward the imaginative dream vision."[71]

Blaeser characterizes Vizenor's fiction in relation to what Vizenor has called a "trickster consciousness." The ideology Vizenor has developed around an analysis of tricksters is his strongest link to poststructuralist theory. I want to begin here by questioning a common assumption. Tricksters do *not* originate in Native American cultures. The word "trickster" is not a term indigenous to an Indian language; it is an ethnographic one. While many Native American cultures, as well as many European, American, African American and Asian cultures, have story characters that resemble what we often call tricksters, it is a mistake to assume that tricksters originate in Indian stories. One might approach the current universal application of trickster theories to Native cultures with some caution. Certainly, the use of the word "trickster" in Native literature has sometimes meant simply resorting to laziness—the substitution of a cliché for substantive analysis with attention to historical and cultural particulars.

Trickster then is a trope rather than a reality within Native cultures. Yet it is the very nature of this nonrepresentational aspect of trickster that most interests Vizenor. He wants fiction to accomplish more than simply repeat social science definitions of Indians, pop culture representations, litanies of Indian tragedies at the hands of whites, accounts of reservation poverty, reports on Indian activism, and so on. Vizenor allows his characters to take flight beyond the literal, to have access to imaginary worlds as much as real ones. Mythic vision itself embodies worlds of possibilities rather than reports on reality.

Vizenor borrows the shape-shifting abilities of tricksters to explain his own understandings of language, poststructural theory, and issues of representation. Postmodern interpretations of literature have questioned the role of mimesis—of the idea of literature holding up a mirror to society—instead emphasizing the mediated nature of the representation that is the product of a whole host of culturally shaped institutions as well as processes that occur while reading. Language, with its tricksterlike capacity to take on many guises, shapes, and manifestations, has the potential to liberate Indians from static definitions, and Vizenor is especially critical of the tendencies within the social sciences to categorize Native people rather than open up the signifier "Indian" to multiple possibilities. One of the qualities of the trickster that seems to most attract Vizenor is his inscrutability, and this is beautifully illustrated in the symbolism of the story "Ice Tricksters," from *Landfill Meditations:* before you can figure trickster out, he melts on you. Vizenor's life and body of work might be described as a resistance to easy definitions.

Another important aspect of Vizenor's tricksters is the way in which they are linked to mixed-blood identity. Mixed-bloods, in Vizenor's writing, become "cross-bloods." The name change is significant. Critics writing in the 1980s and 1990s often claimed that early Native writers had depicted the mixed-blood as a tragic victim torn between two worlds, unable to fit in either. These critics had emphasized that the more contemporary mixed-blood writer was able to mediate between the white and Indian worlds and was inclined toward much less negative depictions, as we observed in our discussion of Louis Owens's *Other Destinies.*

In Vizenor's work this is carried a step further than much of the 1980s criticism and certainly further than in the novels from the early part of the twentieth century. The cross-blood is inextricably linked to comic, rather than tragic, modes of representation. Tragedy often works toward an inexorable conclusion, comedy toward multiple possibilities where endings only kick off new beginnings with lots left for the reader's imagination. Because of its open-endedness, the comic mode was extremely important in postmodern fiction after World War II. Mixed-bloods, in Vizenor's fiction, like tricksters, are not easy to define. They are betwixt and between. Poststructural theories have been interested in those identities that break down oppositions, that challenge distinctions between insider and outsider status, that remain ambiguous. Fluid boundaries, cross-cultural exchange, skepticism about pure culture, and challenges to cultural authenticity have all been a part of the movements we have been tracing. Mixed-bloods obfuscate clear-cut distinctions between Indian and non-Indian.

At times such theories have gotten Vizenor in trouble. Native people have not always responded enthusiastically to statements, for example, that Indians are anyone who imagines himself or herself to be Indian, one of Vizenor's attempts to "liberate" Indians from static definitions. The Blaeser book would have been better, to my way of thinking, if it had more thoroughly acknowledged some of the counterarguments. Particularly damning book reviews, for example, by Robert Berner and other occasional critics, might have been acknowledged, at least to the point of defending Vizenor against the charges levied against him.

A real value of Blaeser's book is her ability to provide an explanation of Vizenor's famously difficult style; its impenetrability, abstraction, theoretical jargon, puzzling contradictions. Parsing Vizenor's prose and coming up with a reasonable explanation is a formidable task, and Blaeser takes on her mission with great aplomb. Yet even after reading Blaeser's plausible defense, some readers might be left wondering why Vizenor does not simply say what he means. Others more prone to provide a justification for what Vizenor does might see a reflection of contemporary theory in Vizenor's writing, especially in relation to French deconstruction and its U.S. version in the 1980s, where communicating with an audience does not exactly seem to be the goal of the writer; a proliferation of prose styles during this time period seemed to mirror the notion of indeterminacy. Still, some might wonder if a theoretical approach that values obfuscation as much as clarification is consistent with Native worldviews. Skeptics might question the relevance of an inaccessible prose style toward intervening in the real world, where every year Native people face issues of land loss, threats to jurisdiction, new calls from redneck politicians for the federal government to end the trust relationship with tribes, and so on.

Vizenor's oeuvre is so varied that a generalized critique is almost always reductive. For all the post-Indian gobbledygook in *Manifest Manners* and some more recent works, other writings are entirely straightforward in their use of terminology. *Manifest Manners,* in fact, has a perfectly lucid chapter on the problems caused by Indian casinos. Many readers would defend the wisdom of the neologisms in more obtuse passages, seeing much more than gobbledygook, noting, in fact, the power of Vizenor's playfulness to open up a dialogue between theory and Indian studies.

A larger problem is the grab-bag relationship with theory, latching on to ideas without much consideration of their broader implications. In her chapter on the difficulties of Vizenor's style, Blaeser does explain that he often purposefully exposes the artifice of written language so that the usual process of suspending disbelief is interrupted. When this happens, the reader sees not so much the story but how the story is made—the nature of its construction—and is encouraged to consider the world outside the text. Blaeser points out that Vizenor's is a style that requires a response, not just a consumption of the literary work. His writing is composed of a multilevel discourse, a network of literary, social, and critical subtexts that break down distinctions between genres. Ambiguity and indeterminacy are reinforced by contestatory views within the same story. Characters speak in puzzling and contradictory ways, plot lines are seldom smooth, and sometimes little is resolved.

Like much of postmodern fiction, basic story development of character, plot, and setting is sometimes missing. Old-fashioned critics might see postmodern works as simply bad writing in which authors fail to do the work of a writer in terms of fleshing out the story for readers. Postmodern writing, however, is often based on the assumption that readers can and should flesh out the story for themselves. Vizenor's writing, likewise, "gesture[s] broadly beyond itself";[72] it is strongly allusive.

Given the history of cultural studies and poststructuralism we have traced out, it is somewhat problematic when Blaeser says in her introduction that "Vizenor's work runs counter to the dominant literary aesthetic."[73] Vizenor's writing is deeply reflective of "the dominant literary aesthetic," not counter to it. If his work runs counter to anything, it would be the formalism of the 1930s New Critics, not the "dominant literary aesthetic." It is not very convincing to claim Vizenor as a remarkable exception in relation to contemporary aesthetics, astonishingly gifted as he may be in his ability to draw from theory and incorporate it into a tribal perspective.

Along somewhat different lines, it is not fruitful to consider Vizenor's work as the embodiment of another kind of exceptionalism. Elvira Pulitano, in *Toward A Native American Critical Theory,* argues that Vizenor completely escapes any essentialist traps in his writing while other Indian writers are immersed in them: "More forcefully and more provocatively than the other theorists I have discussed, Vizenor combines revolutionary content and revolutionary style, presenting a significant alternative to Western hermeneutics. Rejecting any form of separatism and essentialism as far as Indian identity is concerned, he celebrates a discourse that is communal and comic."[74] Vizenor's exceptionalism is not the case. No one can write, or say, anything about the world without ever using generalizations. Essentialism can be mediated; it cannot be escaped or "rejected" in "any form."

Monolithic treatments can be tempered by citing historical and cultural particulars, emphasizing differences as often as similarities. To escape essentialism entirely one would have to quit writing and speaking. This is one of the reasons why naming essentialists sometimes feels more like a witch hunt than a scholarly endeavor—to point out an essentialist will always require having four fingers pointed back at oneself. This is not a call to end the critique of monolithic treatments. Obviously, we have to question some such claims when they become overly reductive if we are to engage in serious scholarship.

———

In September 1996, the Chinook, a tribe seeking federal recognition, announce their claim to Long Island, a two- by eighty-mile stretch of land off the coast of Washington—a wildlife refuge with one of the highest black bear concentrations in the country and a five-thousand-year-old cedar grove. The Chinooks made thirteen treaties in the 1850s, but Congress did not ratify them. Consequently, the Chinooks have never made any land cessions of their original territory.[75]

In 1996 the Ralph Nader/Winona LaDuke Green Party ticket wins six hundred thousand write-in votes in nineteen states, ranking fourth among more than a dozen political parties across the country.[75]

Elizabeth Cook-Lynn: Literature and Land Redress

In 1996 Elizabeth Cook-Lynn published *Why I Can't Read Wallace Stegner and Other Essays: A Tribal Voice.* If critics have viewed Gerald Vizenor as the most postmodern of Native writers, they have tended to regard Cook-Lynn as his opposite, a throwback to an antiquarian literature based on polemics instead of theory. This is a most unfortunate perception, given the urgency of Cook-Lynn's pleas for an ethical relationship between literature and Native communities. If critics were to take her seriously instead of dismissing her,

Cook-Lynn's insistence that land redress should be regarded as a central tenet of Native literary criticism could push us to examine literature in really fresh, exciting ways.

To what degree has American Indian literature, and its attendant criticism, addressed the always endangered status of tribal sovereignty? Is there a gap between Native social realities and Native literature? Should Native literature demonstrate a commitment to social realism? Is literary imagination bound to a different kind of reality? Is political commentary the job of novelists, poets, and playwrights, as well as those who write about their work? Are demands for a politicized literature restrictive—or liberatory with the potential to open up tribal writings to rich possibilities? Can any set of rules address all tribal literatures? To what degree are contemporary Native novels already inherently political, and is this enough? All of these questions are either addressed directly or implied in Cook-Lynn's work, and they are important ones.

The critics have mostly chosen to ignore the questions she raises by creating various smokescreens that dismiss her, charging parochial and reductive views of identity. Criticism, for example, of her statements about the problems of mixed-blood ideology seem to obscure these other issues. It is probably true that her critique of certain writers could have been more convincing if it had remained focused on their ideology rather than naming the problem a "mixed-blood" one. Some critics have raised important concerns about the ways she has addressed Adrian Louis, Michael Dorris, and Louis Owens by placing them in categories that diminish their complexity.

Confusions abound, and I suspect this is why Cook-Lynn has tried to articulate clear-cut definitions that some have seen as overly reductive. Tribal critics who formerly endorsed the concept of sovereignty (and perhaps still do in spite of their recent skepticism about terminology) have jumped into the fray by claiming that it is a European, not an Indian, concept, that the modern nation-state is inconsistent with Native cultures. Sometimes they suggest an alternate terminology, or, in other cases, simply protest without articulating what might replace sovereignty or the language used to describe it.

The positive aspect of these objections is that alternative definitions suggest that sovereignty is an ongoing, dynamic process, that Native people can hope for more than the way sovereignty is often limited by courts, that sovereignty can be opened up to other arenas—the personal, artistic, and communal lives of American Indians, for instance—than the legal one.

The problems ensue when critics demand a European barometer for all things Indian, measuring indigenous integrity by the degree to which it diverges from some incommensurable white Other or conforms to a precontact past. This is the etymological approach to Native studies that evaluates concepts in relation to their point of origin rather than their relevance in the modern world.

Sovereignty, for all its problems and contradictions, is a reality in Indian country, embedded in the U.S. Constitution and two centuries of federal Indian law. In short, it is what Native people have to work with, the hand that has been dealt us. This, of course, does not mean Native people should not dream of more, or even advocate for more, but present realities must also be acknowledged. Some make strong cases that sovereignty does not work for their particular community, but this hardly provides an argument that it should be dismissed for all of Indian country.

Cook-Lynn subtitles her book *a tribal voice*. A recent criticism by Elvira Pulitano in *Toward a Native American Critical Theory* challenges the possibility of any such voice, given the way American Indian critics are situated after five hundred years of cross-cultural contact. Cook-Lynn, like many before her, argues that something tribal can still transcend and transform the work of Native authors, critics, and their cultures. To claim a tribal voice, contrary to Pulitano, is not an isolationist act of claiming *the* tribal voice, an inherent zealousness that would overlook tribal diversity, choose to ignore the relationship of tribes and their people with the outside world, and represent a naive commitment to cultural purity.

There is no theoretical justification for claiming that a tribal perspective, a sovereigntist perspective, or a Native perspective is an inherently isolated one, particularly if these terms are pluralized and stated as tribal perspectives, sovereigntist perspectives, Native perspectives. (Although any given Native perspective could be isolationist, depending on whatever its proponents claim, the point is that there is nothing purist or isolationist about Native perspectives simply by default.) Sovereignty— by definition, government-to-government relations—has everything to do with inside and outside, with relations across and between borders. It is far from the fly in the ointment of everything postmodern, and literary critics who embrace sovereignty, given its realities in Indian country, deserve more than the knee-jerk reaction they have received.

Cook-Lynn recognizes that the appeal of such a tribal voice is not its cultural purity—its protection from contamination from outside European influences—but the importance of a people speaking on their own behalf. In relation to Mesquakie writer Ray Young Bear's remarkable novel, *Black Eagle Child: The Face Paint Narratives* (1992), Cook-Lynn contrasts Young Bear's book with ethnographic depictions and literary collaborations between Indians and non-Indians: "For the first time, we encounter an articulate, bilingual, tribal Phaedrus wrestling with his imperfect life vis-à-vis his own value system without the intervention of a Christian monitor or omniscient literary interpreter, and it is an inspiring event."[77] This statement could apply to much of modern Native literature that is energized by the inspiration of speaking on one's own behalf, which is not the same thing as claiming some kind of purity—the phrase "his imperfect life" is an important one here.

In another section of the book Cook-Lynn writes,

> The emergence of this [tribal] voice has little to do with the fear that the very concept of academic standards must be altered, though perhaps it must. It has less to do with the inaccuracies or simplistic views of

> cultural difference which are deplored as racist or politically correct or incorrect depending upon matters of taste, and even less to do with the fact that Western values have been inherently oppressive to native peoples. Its emergence has to do with the need of human beings to narrate, to tell the story of their own lives and the lives they have known, the intellectual need to inquire and draw conclusions which is simply a part of being human. . . .
>
> Perhaps those of us who have been making the argument in recent years that individual works are comprehensible only within the context of the economic, behavioral, and political forces of the culture from which they emerge are simply pleading for cultural autonomy. It is a powerful argument and a poignant plea. Thoughtful American Indian critics do not see this argument as dangerous, hostile, or as a denial of history and art. In fact, they find it is the most liberating reflection of all.[78]

Some critics, however, *have* seen these claims as dangerous, especially problematizing ideas such as autonomy, arguing instead for the inevitable hybridity of all cultural perspectives that they claim are, by definition, interdependent. A defense of Cook-Lynn's work, of course, rests on the argument that autonomy and purity are not the same thing, and no sovereigntist that I know of sees them as such. A reading of Cook-Lynn's work reveals that her understanding of political autonomy does not equate to cultural purity. In the quote just cited, Cook-Lynn does not claim a purity for the tribal voice she sees as a real, contemporary, ongoing necessity—only the human right to tell one's story.

A more problematic statement in relation to the more recent debates is the word "only" that appears in her statement, "individual works are comprehensible only within the context of the economic, behavioral, and political forces of the culture from which they emerge." Of course, those same forces in those cultures outside tribal society influence tribal works as well, a point Cook-Lynn makes frequently in other parts of the book, especially in terms of vested interests that threaten sovereignty, even if she does not make that point here. The hybridity critics would problematize the very notion of emergence, that is, the "forces of the culture from which they emerge." They would say that any given culture is already the profound result of these outside influences from the time that it emerges; the notion of some pure emergence, they would say, is fictitious.

Cook-Lynn makes important claims for a tribally specific, partisan criticism that serves her home community, the Sioux Nation and its national bands. One is reminded of a somewhat different critic in these regards, Edward Said, who was clear about his commitment to the Palestinian people. The Sioux Nation is not Cook-Lynn's only constituency; she is engaged in a literary criticism with a distinctive Native studies, rather than an English department, emphasis. She demonstrates that having an audience in mind, rather than writing for "everyone," is an act that focuses her in important ways, a reasonable claim in light of composition theory and much else. One of the questions that has yet to be answered in criticism is the role of those of us who write Native literary criticism from a Native studies perspective in comparison with those who write Native literary criticism from an English department perspective. Who is the audience for these two endeavors? In what ways do the two approaches reinforce each other? Contradict one another? What are some of the distinctions in content? What is the value of each?

In relation to her vocation as a Sioux critic, Cook-Lynn writes, "Works which directly affect the political well-being of the Sioux Nation are, naturally, given priority for examination."[79] The title essay examines such work, that of the Pulitzer Prize–winning author Wallace Stegner, whose writings are focused on the northern plains. Cook-Lynn criticizes Stegner's depictions of vanishing Indians:

> Following a compelling description of the Sioux Chieftain Sitting Bull's return to the United States from his Canadian exile at the close of the nineteenth century, Stegner said, as so many American writers and historians had said before him, "The Plains Indians were done."
>
> He does not say how this could be so in the face of evidence that representatives of Plains Indians nations signed peace treaties with the United States federal government, reserved land bases and rights for themselves and their future generations, and set up governments which continued to adapt to the inevitable changes of the modern world.
>
> He does not say how this could be so when native populations exist all over the American landscape, identified by cartographers as occupying space on maps, by linguists as speaking hundreds of languages; people who have been reenacting their own mythologies at significant moments, cherishing the desire to sundance in the summer sun at Devil's Tower, Wyoming, and to pray with the pipe at Green Grass, South Dakota. These people who continue to reproduce themselves biologically and tell their children to whom they are related cannot be wished away either through the deception of the imagination or by any other distractions which are probably more political than artistic.[80]

What strikes me about the quotation is not so much its description of inaccurate popular representations of Indians. No doubt there is much truth in Cook-Lynn's assertions that just such fictional depictions make dispossessions possible, that "continued actions emerge from these imaginings,"[81] and that legislation and social action evolve from them. What is further disturbing to me as a literary critic is the striking resemblance of this description to those aspects of contemporary Native literature and criticism that are devoid of references to treaties, tribal governments, and historical particulars that are replaced by oral tradition and culture in the narrowest sense of these two terms.

Federal Indian policies, court decisions, land claims, tribal governments, and politics are not the only factors important to an analysis of Native literature, since artistic imagination is more than a legal case study. On the other hand, complete disavowal of them leads to a largely romantic vision of the field. Unfortunately, it is just such a romanticism that dominates our criticism today; it hinges on culturally based studies, in the ethnographic sense of culture, rather than a consideration of tribes as legal entities. It does not consider the broader ramifications of cultural studies practices as they have evolved in literature departments, with their attention to a much broader field of play than ethnography.

Cook-Lynn makes a compelling case that legal acts are creative processes, too:

> The quiet voice of American Indians, and the intellectual voice of the Sioux Nation in particular, began to be heard at the turn of the century when the Sioux sought to file suit against the federal government for the theft of the Black Hills. This was not just politics. It was a creative process which, like any artful activity, would follow the stress lines of history and validate the mythology which was and is at the heart of the people. The Sioux were among the first of the indigenes to do this creative thing when American Indians who did not already have access to American court systems were heavily stereotyped by American scholars and writers as "vanishing," "degraded," or "caught between two cultures."[82]

There is some hope that future work may begin to reflect this interdependence between legal matters and literature. Robert Warrior, for example, in *The People and the Word: Reading Native Nonfiction*, makes the case that the Osage constitution can be read as literature. Cook-Lynn argues that if political happenings "are examined as essentially literary events, actions, and ideas, it may be that the incorporation of such concrete praxis can affect canon theory and literary theory (as it always has in oral societies) by challenging intellectual orthodoxies which do not appreciate—indeed, negate and omit—a nationalistic approach to the development and interpretation of any works, including contemporary fiction." The irony of this statement is that cultural studies has, in fact, endorsed just such work—at least to the point of linking literature to a wide array of social institutions if not its nationalistic impulses—but Indian literary studies have been slow to catch up. Cook-Lynn breaks down oppositions between fiction and politics by claiming that "the imagination plays a functional role in political and social life."[83]

The literary arguments in the book become impassioned pleas for critics to make just such connections. One of the foundations for Cook-Lynn's case for a politicized literary criticism has to do with the canon itself. She warns that opening up the canon is not the same thing as transforming the canon or invigorating Native literature. Literary integration does not necessarily mean

Native literature will take on some of the political and aesthetic issues Cook-Lynn sees as essential to tribal life:

> The significance of the study of aesthetics and politics cannot be overemphasized, since American Indian fiction writers, clearly, have been instrumental, intentionally or not, in legitimizing the struggle to open up the American literary canon to include minority literatures, as though that were the major function of third world writers. This effort may be appealing to some, especially in the face of the Bennett/Bloom hysteria that such an effort simply attempts to abolish the idea of canon altogether in American schools and is, therefore, almost treasonous. Even if the open-canon movement were to succeed, however, there remain for American Indian (First Nation) scholars two issues over which they will have little influence: first, opening up the canon is a little like opening world trade markets: exploitation abounds—a few legends here, a myth there. Seattle's famous oration, some poetry, and Momaday's "Man Made of Words" essay are inserted between the Age of Romanticism and T. S. Eliot just to illustrate some cross-cultural interest and fairness.
>
> The second worry for the nativist is the question of whether or not opening up the American literary canon to include native literary traditions and contemporary works will have much relevance, given its own set of unique aims—the interest in establishing the myths and metaphors of sovereign nationalism; the places, the mythological beings, the genre structures and plots of the oral traditions; the wars and war leaders, the treaties and accords with other nations as the so-called gold standard against which everything can be judged. These are the elements of nationalism which have always fueled the literary canon of tribal peoples and their literary lives. In my own tribal literary traditions there is a fairly long list of Dakota/Lakota writers and storytellers as well as a huge body of ritual and ceremony against which everything may be compared. Reference to the body of nationalistic myths, legends, metaphors, symbols, historical persons and events, writers and their writings must form the basis of the critical discourse that functions in the name of the people; the presence of the Indian nation as cultural force a matter of principle.[84]

While opening up the canon to Indian writers may have some advantages (such as confronting U.S. readers with the fact that their readings take place in the Americas and that no study of American literature is complete without a consideration of Native literatures), will it contribute to a Sioux criticism that takes into consideration a long tradition of Sioux writers in some kind of substantial way or will it remain oriented toward the literary survey? Can the canon do that, or is this the job of Sioux literary specialists and the role of other tribal specialists to work out in relation to their own nations?

Sioux studies, and other such tribally oriented work, has become difficult recently in relation to theory. Some theoretical modes problematize the idea of a coherent body of tribal tradition that can be drawn on to analyze the literature of a particular tribe. Both the tribe, and its literature, it is argued, exist only to the degree that they can be claimed as hybridities, profoundly influenced by five hundred years of contact. Sioux studies, in this view, cannot adequately account for Sioux literature unless it is combined with other cross-cultural approaches. I am biased in these matters, but there is some doubt in my mind as to whether these scholars believe in the validity, perhaps even the existence, of the Sioux Nation, and other tribal governments, since every time they say the word "sovereignty" the next word out of their mouths is deficit-oriented, some problematization of the tribal nation's coherence, a reaction to something they see as isolationist and naively committed to cultural purity.

Cook-Lynn is not making a case for tribal literature's lack of contamination, its purity; she is asking, among other political questions, who is going to talk about treaties? One cannot help but notice the theorists' evasion of the questions she has raised with smokescreens about hybridity. One is struck by the politicized nonfiction that dominated Native literature in the nineteenth century and its authors' involvements in tribal politics. (Sean Teuton and Lisa Brooks both take up, in this collection, the political content of these works and the activism of their authors.) The politicization of early-twentieth-century fiction and its creators has to also be considered. *Cogewea; the Half-blood, The Surrounded,* and *Sundown,* for example, all contain discussions of the effect of the Dawes Act on reservation life. Mourning Dove was the first woman on the Colville tribal council, D'Arcy McNickle was a long-term employee of the BIA; and John Joseph Mathews served on the Osage council for several terms as well as founding the Osage museum at Pawhuska. Much of the abstraction about hybridity has avoided the historical work necessary for a discussion of the meaning of the modernistic turn of some of the prominent Native novels of the late 1960s and 1970s—a radical period, given the events of those years in Indian country as well as in America at large—and a relatively conservative fiction that prioritizes issues of personal and cultural recovery over political analysis.

Of the recovery mode that dominates contemporary Native literature, Cook-Lynn even cites what she sees as the shortcomings of her own novel, *From the River's Edge,* claiming that while her protagonist "may be attempting to say how it is that he may return to a moral world, the reality of our lives as tribal people is that without effective politics, such a return can be at best temporary."[85]

Cook-Lynn problematizes the cosmopolitanism that was a central feature of cultural studies in the 1990s, claiming that its application to tribal literary studies might create confusion about the nature of criticism and the role of critics, an argument that seems quite prescient given recent developments in the field. She writes,

> The tacit worry that Native American writers are thought by critics and readers to be in some important way representative of modern tribal nationalistic perspective and the failure to be clear about authorial intent suggest several things about tribal sovereignty or First Nation status: that the tribes are not nations, that they are not part of the Third World perspective vis-à-vis colonialism, and that, finally, they are simply "colonized" enclaves in the United States, some kind of nebulous sociological phenomena. It is crucial to understand that such an assessment is in direct opposition not only to the historical reality of Indian nations in America, but also to the contemporary work being done by tribal governmental officials and activists, politicians, and grassroots intellectuals to defend sovereign definitions in the new world.
>
> Thus, the violation of nationalistic or Third World models in fiction and criticism should be of legitimate concern to scholars and should become part of the discourse in literary theory as it is applied to the works of Native American writers. While the writers themselves may disclaim any responsibility, and even while the critical, scholarly discussion is nonexistent or misdirected, the existence of such postcolonial incoherence on the part of writers who claim to be indigenous people can only contribute to the confusion about the role of minority intellectuals within the United States and, more important, their influence. Scholarship and art must say something about the real world, mustn't they? As Vine Deloria, Jr., asked the anthropologists in 1970, "Where were you when we needed you?" Indians may well ask of their writers, two decades later, "Where were you when we defended ourselves and sought clarification as sovereigns in the modern world?"[86]

Cook-Lynn's fiction contains many of the same mimetic impulses that she recommends in theory; the flooding of the Missouri River in the 1940s is a pervasive theme that is traced out in a complicated matrix of cultural and social movements that are referenced by dates and the places throughout her entire body of work, across fiction, poetry, and essays. Other important historical events she takes up in fiction are the 1980 Supreme Court case that recognized the theft of the Black Hills, the Wounded Knee occupation in 1973, the murder of an Indian woman in Walworth County, South Dakota, in 1980, and the trial of the murderers in 1995, some of the actual court transcription being incorporated into *Aurelia: A Crow Creek Trilogy.*

Especially refreshing is Cook-Lynn's partisanship in today's intellectual environment of philosophical relativism, where, we are told, all things are equally fictitious, a most distressing revelation to minorities whose truths are finally being acknowledged. According to Cook-Lynn, historical truth can, and should, be sought out. A major theme in all her work is the fiction writer's and the critic's responsibility to history. She seems to recognize what she is up against in relation to resistance to such efforts. In *Anti-Indianism in Modern*

America: A Voice from Tatekeya's Earth (2001), Cook-Lynn writes, "it becomes a crime to revise a well-loved, scrupulously cleansed, and largely mindless history while the attempt to do better, to correct, to investigate is seen as inappropriate scholarship."[87] Rather than a historical relativism that problematizes all forms of objectivity, Cook-Lynn seeks an interventionist role for Native critics interested in truth telling and amending the historical record.

In reading Cook-Lynn over the years, I am reminded of Ralph Ellison's claim in his nonfiction essays that morality is an essential aspect of novel writing. Ellison felt that many of the modernists writers of the 1920s had turned away from issues of race, which Ellison believed were essential to any discussion of America. While Ellison, obviously, did not always agree with American novelists Mark Twain or William Faulkner in respect to race issues, he claimed that they at least were responsible enough to contemplate America's racism, a tendency he believed was being abandoned in modernist aesthetics. Ellison saw this as a moral challenge.

Personally, I am inspired by old-fashioned critics like Cook-Lynn, who still claim morality as not only theoretically tenable but socially imperative, even when this seems like an uphill battle. Her work, I believe, is part of what makes this anthology on an ethical Native literary criticism possible. Cook-Lynn says, "For now I have to be content in my own realization that the partisan struggle in which I've been engaged will eventually matter. Indian studies scholars who have been studying Indian histories and lifeways in the past two or three decades have been doing so for the purpose of petitioning for redresses of grievances in this democracy."[88]

Cook-Lynn's claims warrant further discussion and qualification. One can argue that *some* Native novels should make sovereignty a central concern; one might argue, rather convincingly, that in the present historical moment a great many *more* of them should have a much stronger nationalist orientation; one could say that in comparison with other periods and genres they seem strangely devoid of politics. But can we say that *all* Native novels have to be cast in a particular political mold? Might futuristic tribal pilgrims—in a kind of Mad Max postapocalyptic road journey a la *Darkness in Saint Louis Bearheart*—have something to teach us about the human, and the tribal, condition, the real Indian world? As an admirer of that particular work, one challenged by its resistance to easy formulations, I would say it can. In literature one hopes that flights of fancy can be instructive, that metaphors service truth telling, and that tropes can be historically and socially engaged. Can we make the very definition of a Native novel a sovereigntist text if we wish novel writing to remain an artistic endeavor? These important questions depend on how we define Native novels, art, and sovereignty, and working out these implications would become an important focus in future works of Native literary criticism.

Jace Weaver: The Religious Underpinnings of Indian Literatures

Jace Weaver's *That the People Might Live: Native American Literatures and Native American Community* (1997) seems to mark a moment in Native literary criticism in which a threshold had been crossed. Weaver comments, "Until recently, most analysis of Native literary production has been left to non-Native scholars. Now, however, a small number of critical voices is being raised among Natives, but much more work needs to be done from Native perspectives."[89] Indeed, by 1997, enough book-length works of Native literary criticism existed to teach an undergraduate- or graduate-level course whose reading list could consist of all Native writers, a possibility that had occurred long before in Native fiction and nonfiction courses.

One of the advantages for the literary specialist in Native studies is that we can teach courses that draw on a wide variety of readily available books authored by Indians, whereas historians, anthropologists, and other specialists face a greater challenge in prioritizing Native texts. The challenge is not impossible, however, for scholars who teach in the social sciences if they are creative about text selections. When I was a member of an NAS department at Lethbridge, Alberta, I taught U.S. Indian history with only Native-authored books. I figured if I could not at least prioritize Native authors I might as well offer the course in the history department. I drew on a wide array of Indian autobiographies, tribal histories, novels, religious conversion accounts, Indian-edited oral tradition collections, and other Indian-authored sources. To me this was a serious matter that had to do with being a Native studies practitioner interested in thinking through what makes Native studies courses unique in relation to courses about Indians in other academic departments as well as giving Native people opportunities to speak for themselves. Such a process is never perfect, but the least we can do is teach books written by Indians in Native American studies. If we do not, who will?

Like Robert Warrior's *Tribal Secrets*, Weaver's book makes a case for the inclusion of Native nonfiction as part of Native literary studies. He writes, "I define literature broadly as the total written output of a people." This links Weaver to movements in cultural studies that resuscitated older, broader definitions of literature. Weaver also values a religious studies orientation in his particular approach to Native literature, which he claims as a necessary perspective for an understanding of reality: "Like philosophical metaphysics, the subject of theology is ultimate reality. It deals with the noumenal in a Kantian sense, asserting 'that there is a dimension other than the material one generally recognized as real.'"[90]

Such statements are important, given the possibility that a doctrinaire materialist criticism might limit reality to the tangible or literal. Weaver also argues that if language, and thus storytelling, has the power to transform, as many claim, then such transformations might fall just as much in the realm of religious analysis as linguistic analysis: "This power of language to transform has religious implications as well."[91] Such a statement underscores an issue that needs further exploration in Native literary studies: how a materialist approach to culture can include Native religious perspectives regarding the effects of spirits on physical existence. Much of materialist criticism—in this regard true to its Marxist roots—has shown a strong rationalist bias. Critics have yet to demonstrate how epistemic categories such as race, gender, and class are mediated by spiritual forces. Materialist critics have been resistant to definitions of religion in any other terms besides human mediation and the social construction of religious beliefs. Native critics may very well want to consider revisionist strategies in relation to materialist criticism.

The most concrete realization of the religious studies mode of Weaver's book is the inclusion of the Christian writers William Apess (Pequot), Samson Occom (Mohegan), and Peter Jones (Ojibway), all Christian converts and ministers, very different writers than those who had been analyzed in the 1980s-style criticism. What remains to be seen is whether or not a Native or non-Native critic will emerge who is sympathetic to these writers' Christianity rather than treating it in a defensive mode, arguing that the writers represent an authentic nativism *in spite of* their faith rather than *because of* it. Many contemporary Creek Christians, to use an example close to home in my case, believe that their Christian faith is the most profound expression of their Indianness. We have yet to see a literary critic who operates from this particular set of Indian assumptions.

Weaver examines these Christian writers in relation to their tribal community commitments—as he does in the case of all the writers in his study—claiming that Native literature both shapes, and is shaped by, community. Weaver coins a term, "communitism," for the way Native literature embodies both community and activism, claiming, in fact, this characteristic as the literature's most predominant trait:

> *Comunitism* is related to Vizenor's "survivance," Warrior's "intellectual sovereignty," and Georges Sioui's "autohistory." Its coining, however, is necessary because none of these terms from Native intellectuals nor any word from the Latin root *communitas* carries the exact sense implied by this neologism. It is formed by a combination of the words "community" and "activism." Literature is communitist to the extent that it has a proactive commitment to Native community, including what I term the "wider community" of creation itself.[92]

Weaver's study, I hope, will inspire others to consider what specific forms some of this literary activism might take.

Weaver's introduction begins with the questions that undergird Native literature, questions that many avoid because of their undecidability: Who is an Indian and what constitutes Native literature? These issues are difficult because the answers are always contained inside other questions. Who is asking?

Why do they want to know? Who creates the definitions? Which community is being referred to? Which individual or author or literary work are we talking about? Rather than weighing in on these challenges, Weaver provides a survey of the way in which others have tried to address them and how the formulations have been contested, placing a number of voices in conversation in a dialogic style in his introduction.

In addition to a good survey of the problems located in these identity and authenticity issues, Weaver provides an impressive overview of postcolonial theory, one of the major influences on his study, distinguishing between settler and colonial societies, the role of the dominant and indigenous languages, indigenous nationalism in relation to colonialistic nationalism, various views of hybridity, representations of Others, internalization of dominant-culture attitudes by indigenous populations, the colonists' sense of a foreign relation to Native soil and their attempts to indigenize themselves, and the other major themes that have characterized postcolonial studies since the African writers' books of the 1960s and 1970s and Edward Said's *Orientalism* (1978). Weaver is impressively well-read in these matters.

One of the more interesting aspects of this discussion in terms of debates to come is Weaver's observation about mediation critics like James Ruppert, who wrote a book on the subject entitled *Mediation in Contemporary Native American Fiction* (1995). Weaver quotes Ruppert's definition of mediation as "an artistic and conceptual standpoint, constantly flexible, which uses the epistemological frameworks of Native American and Western cultural traditions to illuminate and enrich each other." Ruppert continues, "Whether by blood or experience, Native Americans today, especially writers, express a mixed heritage. As old and isolating world views give rise to new ones, the writer acts out his role as mediator-creator."[93]

While, ostensibly, mediation criticism seems to be about Indians, its ideas may interest non-Indians more. As Weaver says, "The concern with getting rid of 'old and isolating world views' and 'unbridgeable chasm[s]' has always been more of a concern for Amer-Europeans than for Natives, who do not view their own cultural responses as 'old and isolating' and who often express scant interest in bridging their worldviews with that of dominant culture." A mediated literature, logic would suggest, requires non-Indian participation in its analysis. Weaver himself makes this observation when he says, "Ruppert writes as an Amer-European about Native literature, so mediation becomes important to him as an entry point."[94]

Weaver argues that it is not a given that a particular Native reader, or Native readers generally, will see themselves as mediators or view literature as mediated discourse. Weaver also takes issue with critics who claim orature as the primary Native American literature (another "Native literature proper") because of its links with a performative authenticity. By prioritizing orality, Native novels, poems, and plays then become a secondary form of artistic expression, distanced even further from cultures of origin than are traditional stories.

In terms of issues of canonicity, Weaver expresses concerns similar to those of Cook-Lynn:

> . . . to insist, as Krupat and others do, on a "genuinely heterodox national canon" inclusive of American Indian literature (orature or otherwise) has equally undesirable implications. It becomes equally an instrument of control as Eurocentric standards of judgement are employed to claim into the national canon only those works of which the *métropole* approves, those which best legitimate the existing social order. "Indigenous writing has suffered many of the general historical problems of post-colonial writing, [including] being incorporated into the national literatures of the settler colonies as an 'extension' rather than as a separate discourse." Such incorporation denies Native literature recognition of its distinct existence, specific differences, and independent status as literary production and, as Owens contends, retards consideration of Native works in their own cultural contexts. As I noted earlier, Natives have never been great respecters of national borders. The very fact that Thomas King (Cherokee}, E. Pauline Johnson (Mohawk), Peter Jones (Anishinaabe), and George Copway (Anishinaabe) —among others—can be, and have been, claimed at various times and for various purposes as part of the national literatures of both the United States and Canada says that something more important and complex is occurring in Native literature, something that merits special recognition as a separate discourse.
>
> Finally, by bringing Native literature into the canon of the United States, Krupat helps establish the indigeneity of Amer-European settler literature as part of a national literature rooted in the new soil of this continent. This quest for indigeneity has been a constant in settler colonies from their inception . . . it validates attempts by Amer-Europeans, such as those of Jerome Rothenberg and the ethnopoetics movement, to incorporate or utilize indigenous forms and aesthetics as part of "an enriching cultural appropriation." Begged, of course, is the question of precisely who is "enriched" and who is diminished in the process.[95]

In relation to canonical inclusion, one might wonder whether those writers who have a sense of the local, of grassroots movements, of sovereigntist perspectives, and a commitment to nationalism have as much chance of canonical inclusion as Native writers engaged in cross-cultural projects or having a more global outlook. What are the chances, for instance, of the quirky, difficult, inaccessible, brilliant, extremely localized writings of Ray Young Bear, one of the most talented Native writers in the Americas, being canonized?

A strong feature of Weaver's approach is that it opens up his study to some very unusual inclusions, such as Natachee Momaday, the Cherokee mother of the famous Pulitzer Prize–winning author, N. Scott Momaday. The former is almost never included on anyone's list of Native writers, yet she was Cherokee and wrote a Native novel, *The Owl in the Cedar Tree* (1965), and edited one of the very earliest anthologies of Native American literature, *American Indian Authors* (1972), which contains, I might note, the most overlooked, and possibly one of the finest, short stories in American Indian literature, Creek writer Durango Mendoza's "Summer Water and Shirley."

Weaver's inclusion of another Cherokee, playwright Lynn Riggs, has contributed to renewed interest in Riggs's plays, which had almost faded into obscurity, a real loss to Native studies, given Riggs's prolific output of some thirty plays and his prominence in the literary world in the 1930s and 1940s. Weaver not only analyzes Riggs's play *The Cherokee Night* (1936) according to Cherokee social history, he shows us how Riggs's less obvious Indian plays, such as *Green Grow the Lilacs* (1930), can be reimagined as Indian ones. These readings were important to me personally because—even though Weaver does not take on this subject directly—I have always felt that if the plays could be reimagined as Cherokee, many of them could also be reimagined as gay. (Some of them, like *The Cream in the Well* (1940) and *The Year of Pilar* (1940), need no reimagining; gay content is overt in these two works, although it is cast in a weird tragic light that has to do with, of all things, incest between siblings.) Weaver's book considers Native writings that many would overlook as Native, and this is a great contribution.

Weaver admits that his book is not exhaustive: "All of this is to say that this work makes no claim to being definitive."[96] This is certainly true of the religious studies analysis, where the scrutiny of the Christian writers' theology is not as nuanced as it could be. Weaver, for example takes issue with Arnold Krupat, who dismisses the Christian writers as "not Indian enough" and therefore does not include them in his study of Indian autobiographies. Weaver writes, "Though Krupat is inclined to dismiss Occom's writings, including his autobiography, as nothing more than Christian 'salvationism,' the subtle critical nature of them reveals an underlying communitist theme."[97] Weaver's response to this is to search the letters and autobiography of Occom and demonstrate that, contrary to Krupat, they contain significant Indian content. Weaver also examines Occom's best-seller, "Sermon Preached at the Execution of Moses Paul an Indian" (1772), locating its antialcohol message and arguing that this is addressed to an Indian audience as well as a vehicle for a strong anticolonial critique.

Weaver also criticizes Krupat's dismissal of William Apess:

> In Apess's writing [Krupat] detects no unique individual voice. Rather, he hears only "a voice to be heard commonly in the early nineteenth century"—salvationism. According to Krupat, although Apess is proud to acknowledge "his Indian ancestry," "even his understanding of what it means to be a 'Native' is filtered through Christian perspective." Apess's identity as a Native derives not from any indigenous, Pequot

> understanding but from a purely Western, Christian one. He defines himself "exclusively in relation to salvationist discourse," without any Pequot dimension whatsoever. This reflects the writer's "wish to be the licensed speaker of a dominant voice that desires no supplementation by other voices"—the "mouthpiece of the Lord." The only voice that he wants to be heard is "the only voice that came to count for him," that of the Christian God.[98]

Weaver's response to Krupat's seemingly deficit view of Apess's Indianness is to set out to prove that Apess does, in fact, take on Indian themes and engages in a resistant, anticolonial discourse.

I think Weaver is quite right in asserting that Occom's and Apess's Christianity contains significant Native viewpoints and dominant cultural critique. In Occom's autobiography, his protest of the racism that dominates the missionary field is apparent for anyone who reads it, a point Weaver himself makes. Apess's criticism of Christianity in his essay, "An Indian's Looking-Glass for the White Man" (1833), is one of the strongest indictments in print, one strangely redolent of Malcolm X in his most querulous "white devils" days.

Here is my point: Why does a religious studies scholar need to prove that a Christian Indian is still an Indian? Why would he not be? Let me play devil's advocate for just a minute to demonstrate what I mean. Let us say these two men actually were "mouthpieces for salvationism." Should we show no interest in what two Indians have to say about Christianity and salvation? Could we not, for example, as part of our Native studies analysis, scrutinize the two men's Christian theology for its own sake without converting it to Indianness? Are we missionaries? Do all Christian Indians have to be converted to Indian Indians before we can include them as worthy studies? Must Christian theology be decoded as a subterfuge for an underlying Indianness? Can tribal sovereignty include an individual's, or a community's, right to choose one's own religion, including Christianity? Are Indians always victims of Christianity? Have they ever made choices about it? What about contemporary Muscogee Christians, for example, who believe that their Christianity is the most profound expression of their Indianness—might such patterns have been possible in the late eighteenth and early nineteenth centuries as well? Maybe we could simply recognize the personal and communal religious sovereignty of Occom and Apess.

In other words, I appreciate Weaver's demonstration of Occom's and Apess's communitism. I question, however, the need to supplement the Christianity with a conclusive Indian sign that demonstrates that the theology transcends its "Christianness," especially in response to a critic who might claim an opposition between Christian and Indian identities. I reject the notion that Christian theology is not a potential subject of Native studies unless it is amended with just the right amount of beads and feathers. My sense of Occom and Apess—and I get this from comparing them with George

Copway, who had a much slippier, deceptive relationship to Christian faith, as well as from primary textual evidence in Occom and Apess's own work—is that both men, as best as I can tell, viewed their Christian identities as a central core of their humanity and their Indianness. I think they were also Indian activists, but should a religious studies emphasis avoid matters of religion? If John Rollin Ridge chose to write about Mexicans in California, Samson Occom might have chosen to talk about Christian salvation.

I think where Weaver is on to something and deserves credit is that we cannot simply let the church off the hook for its criminal actions in the New World by declaring some fundamental compatibility between Christianity and Native life and letters, another form of a monolithic treatment. I'm simply asking questions about possibilities for contextualization and interpretation and digging into historical particulars.

Weaver realizes, I believe, that a religious critical orientation must recognize that the "critical" part of the phrase is as important as the "religious," and this is what he is trying to do when he outlines the way both Occom and Apess are far more than the mouthpieces of salvation in their strong critiques of the colonialist impulses of Christian praxis. One can be both a Christian and a Christian critic. My point has to do with erring toward either a commensurability or an incommensurability that either equates Christianity and Native religion or reduces them to total difference.

The last concern I want to express has to do with a larger problem in Native literature more than a specific criticism of the Weaver book. Weaver, as had Warrior before him and, to a lesser extent, Sarris before that, made an argument for a wide range of literary sources rather than an adherence to a strict line between fiction and nonfiction. In explaining this approach, Weaver writes,

> Penny Petrone subsumes a wide variety of forms including speeches, letters, reports, petitions, diary entries, essays, history, protest literature, journals, and journalism, under the definition of literature in *Native Literature in Canada.* In so doing, she deliberately forgoes "the purist attitude of Western literary critics toward literature that does not conform totally to their aesthetic criteria." Not to do so, she argues, leads to neglect of Native literary output. I have, however, in deference to literary purists, adopted the formulation of "literatures," in the plural, to avoid any confusion. Such an expansive definition has the advantage of covering the full spectrum of whatever Natives have produced.[99]

Neither Native literary scholars, Penny Petrone or Jace Weaver, of course, invented these approaches to the study of a wide range of literary sources outside of fiction, poetry, and drama. Even more importantly, such an approach is not opposed to Western literary criticism. Purist attitudes have been significantly revised for several decades now: consider the beginnings of North American cultural studies by 1990, the year of the publication of the

Petrone book; its earlier history in Britain in the 1950s; and its widespread effect on literature departments in the United States by 1997, the year of the publication of the Weaver book—and, coincidentally, the same year as the Professional Modern Language Association (PMLA) forum "Thirty-Two Letters on the Relation between Cultural Studies and the Literary," many of which make the same arguments for opening up literary studies as Petrone and Weaver do.

This is not a major fault. Those of us who have read T. S. Eliot's "Tradition and the Individual Talent" (1919) know that it is human nature for all critics to view the originality of their own work to the exclusion of the tradition that creates it, and Eliot urges a conscious consideration of the ways in which we are the outcome of those who came before.

I only want to use this passage as a stepping-stone to the discussion of a larger problem, one endemic in the field of Native literary studies, rather than use it to find fault with Penny Petrone and Jace Weaver who, I believe, are simply trying to make points about the validity of a wide variety of sources. The problem has to do with critics who claim an incommensurable relationship to the very theories that support their own work. This is illustrated by this particular example that attributes to Western literary scholarship a "purity" that critics themselves had widely questioned for decades.

Too often in Native literary studies we assume that Western critical theory is the enemy, largely because we have not read widely enough in it. (This is definitely not the case with Weaver, who is one of the most widely read intellectuals I know, and his survey of postcolonial theory aptly demonstrates this.) It is easier to claim an oppositional relationship than to actually study something. We become the movie critic who has not seen the movie, the book critic who has not read the book, the theory critic whose only familiarity with theory is his criticism of it. Recently, I heard a Native filmmaker criticize Michael Moore's *Fahrenheit 9/11* because of the way it embodied "the cult of personality." Later, during the same talk, she openly admitted to not having seen Moore's film, an act that struck me as indicative of a little personality cult of her own.

This is not to say that I think everything about cultural studies is wonderful, and I understand the challenges it has created for a Native literary criticism that has nationalistic impulses. We have to at least admit, however, that cultural studies exists. It has been very difficult to get Native critics to examine their own theoretical assumptions, a problem I have to admit that has generated criticism of my own work. Some of that criticism I have deserved.

If we continue to avoid disclosure of our own methodologies, the field is going to become an even bigger mess than it is now, a hotbed for ad hoc opinions and unexamined accusations. At recent conferences I have been dismayed at the way in which people were all over the map in relation to important matters such as sovereignty. Some were ready to throw away the term in exchange for one "more traditional," as if they were returning something they no longer wanted to Wal-Mart for a refund. I am not advocating a party line in relation to sovereignty. I am convinced by Robert Warrior's call in *Tribal Secrets* for an open-ended, process-oriented consideration of it so that we can apply the notion more broadly than the legal arena and more creatively in all our endeavors. I would, however, hope for a studied philosophical consideration as to why a concept like sovereignty has carried so much historical weight and thus remains relevant. I hope more literary books follow that make history and analysis a central feature.

In the case of *That the People Might Live,* especially useful is Weaver's avoidance of ranking literary merit; rather, Weaver follows the impulses of cultural studies to debunk notions of intrinsic worth and thereby opens up his study to overlooked authors such as Lynn Riggs, who tends to get dismissed as a minor-league player in relation to the dramatic majors: O'Neil, Miller, Williams, and, to a lesser extent, Odetts.

Some questions future works in religious studies might address could include how religious viewpoints might affect debates about foundationalism; the ways religious history could contribute to a discussion in Native literature that revises a dominant ahistorical inquiry focused on inherent oral and communal traits; the ways religious viewpoints could be applied to an ethical criticism; discussions of strategies in which indigenous Christianity manages forms of resistance in colonial societies (rather than always being viewed as capitulation); a consideration of what makes Christianity appealing to Indians, assuming Native people have agency; and, especially, formulations of a materialist criticism that could take into account spirits (or we might say, how a religious studies view could reinvigorate a Marxist-influenced materialist analysis).

Among the five thousand people standing in front of West Hollywood's Metropolitan Community Church on a November evening in 1998, there for a candlelight vigil protesting the brutal killing of Matthew Shepard, an openly gay Wyoming college student, is a contingent of fifty people representing Indian communities throughout the greater Los Angeles area. "We've come all the way from the High Desert," says Priscilla Collins of Mojave. "I'm Dineh/Navajo and my partner is Chevehuevi; we're here with my Mom in support of [mourning] this young man's death. We, as Indian people, know what hate is. It's good to see all the people from different tribes here representing . . . tribes throughout Southern California."[100] The intertribal group represented in the crowd includes members from the Southern California Indian Center, the UCLA Indian Studies Program, the American Indian Church, and other Native individuals interested in uniting against hate crimes.

In 1999 the Institute of American Indian Arts faces drastic budget cuts. President Della C. Warrior says,

> It's kind of ironic that President Clinton proclaimed November as the Native American Heritage month and then the only college that is devoted solely to preserving the heritage of Native people gets their

> budget cut by fifty percent, and with the language in it that this is the last year of funding. Over the last five years this is an overall decrease of nearly eighty percent of the Institute's funding. What they [federal government] expect the Institute to do is to become self-supporting. I don't know how they came to that conclusion; we are an educational Institution. Educational institutions are supported by their state and federal governments. We were part of the boarding school under the BIA and came out of that system in 1986, but we really don't start until 1989 as a federally chartered college with a museum. So they've expected us to become self-sufficient in ten years.[101]

(IAIA still exists, though each year it faces major obstacles in its vision of expansion into the larger field of applied arts.)

In 2000 writer and activist Winona LaDuke, a White Earth Chippewa, runs for vice-president of the United States on the Green Party ticket with consumer advocate Ralph Nader. LaDuke is "instrumental in crafting specific provisions of [the party's] platform, which includes transforming the federal budget to meet real human needs; responsible alternative energy development and a phaseout of nuclear power (and an end to nuclear waste dumping on reservations); return of public land holdings to Native communities; fixing the badly-broken BIA trust fund system; protection of Yellowstone bison and restoration of the Buffalo Commons; support for a living wage; breaching of dams; and clemency for Leonard Peltier."[102] LaDuke is also a novelist, author of *Last Woman Standing* (1997), which takes place on the White Earth Reservation in Minnesota and deals with ongoing issues of land redress and legislation like the White Earth Land Settlement Act.

On September 11, 2001, Deborah Laezza, who works in the health department of the American Indian Chapter House, is in a subway with her sixteen-year-old-son as it crosses the bridge from Brooklyn to Manhattan. Getting off at Canal Street, about fifteen blocks from the World Trade Center, Laezza watches "Seas and seas of people running north, away from the area and to the train station. . . . There was too much smoke everywhere that we couldn't see, first, that the first tower had just fallen. Then the ground shook like an earthquake and Tower Two collapsed."[103] The Mashantucket Pequots provide ferry boats to get folks in and out of the area as well as substantial donations. Other tribes give money as well. The Mohegans donate a million dollars toward relief efforts, and similar sizeable gifts come from the Tulalip tribes in Washington state, the Morongo band of Mission Indians in California, the Prairie band of the Potawatomi Nation in Kansas, and many others. Blood drives and the roundup of supplies take place all over Indian country.

In 2002 the United Nations tries to pass a draft declaration on the Rights of Indigenous Peoples. The United States is the most vocal opponent of the resolution and brings the process to a standstill by demanding that terms like "self-determination" be changed to "internal self-determination" and "collective rights" be replaced with "individual rights." The United States has been raising such roadblocks for eight years. The session ends without any of the forty-three remaining articles of the draft declaration being passed. Only two have been passed in the eight previous years. In comparison, the United States passed its own Bill of Rights in two years, discussion beginning in 1787, amendments proposed by James Madison in 1789, three months of debate beginning in June, and passage in Congress on September 25, 1789.

In 2003 Anishinaabe author Kateri Akiwenzie-Damm, from the Cape Croker reserve in Canada, publishes an edited collection entitled *Without Reservation: Indigenous Erotica.* "I kept asking why we don't write about it because sexuality is part of being alive,"[104] Akiwenzie-Damm says on a book tour.

On September 21, 2004, twenty thousand Native people show up in Washington, D.C., for the opening of the National Museum of the American Indian on the National Mall. The medicine maker of Tallahassee and Hillabbee Creek ceremonial grounds, everybody's favorite elder, Sam Proctor, returns home complaining of the price of a cup of coffee in D.C.—and of a fish dinner for which he paid fourteen dollars.

On a much more somber note, as this anthology goes to press, we are engaged in the obscenity of another Gulf War, this one even more senseless than the previous one, and more Indians are dying on foreign soil far from the resting places of their ancestors.

By now some have noticed that the dates of my study, comprising an eleven-year span, are something of a baker's decade. I hope at this point that the title is understood ironically in that rather than a single decade it seems like a rather *singular* one, and the possibilities for the paths that lead into and away from it are endless. What route have we taken to get from these years to a decade later and the appearance of this anthology in 2008?

The decades leading up to this collection, as I have tried to demonstrate in this introduction, were monumental ones in terms of literary developments based on the French theory of the 1970s and 1980s, the rise of cultural studies in the 1990s, and a tribal literature that did not originate in these decades but burgeoned during them. The Euroamerican theoretical outpouring has left critics puzzled in its wake, wondering what will come next—indeed, what *can* come next after such radical shifts in notions about language, representation, and power. This kind of exponential growth has also characterized federal Indian law during the same time period. What this leaves us with as tribal critics is a lot to wade through and make sense of. Little wonder many of us are confused. To my way of thinking we can keep poking around in the dark, hoping at best we do not hurt ourselves, or we can try to shed some light on this history, if only by simply trying to tell some of the story. This introduction is itself a baby step; what follows in my coauthors' chapters are descriptions of the kind of tribal criticism that might emerge out of all these movements.

The Idea behind This Anthology

First, a word about how this book came about. In 2002 a non-Indian scholar approached me in regard to contributing an essay for an anthology of Native literary criticism. In addition to my own participation he wanted me to recommend some other people. My definition of Native literary criticism is the same as my definition of Native literature: criticism or literature authored by Native people. As I have often said, this includes valuing non-Native participation in the field. I mentioned the name of a young Native scholar who I thought would be good. I was told that person was not "famous enough." I began suggesting other names, only to be met with the same response until I had named about ten different people, none of them famous enough. Many had books out; some were published in multiple genres of poetry, fiction, and criticism. I wondered how I had made the list myself. The critic would love to have an essay from these folks, he told me, but he knew in his "heart of hearts" the big-name outfit that wanted to do this anthology wanted big names *in* it.

I am sure the critic was telling the truth—that the people I mentioned would not be considered for a Native literature handbook. I therefore declined to participate myself—which I think is something Indian authors ought to do with greater frequency. I have some problems when scholarship becomes a version of the MTV music awards, and I asked the critic if he had thought about what it means to publish a segregated anthology solely on the basis of fame. I like the person who contacted me, and my question gave him pause. His book is now in print, both of its editors non-Indian, though Native scholars have provided the endorsements and a bit of the content.

Suffice it to say our efforts here represent something different. Like William Apess and the Mashpees, after a lot of conversation and writing together, we have managed our own woodland revolt, choosing to elect our own selectmen—and women—rather than submitting to the usual overseers. I dream of the day when those putting together panels on Native literature, and books about the subject, will refuse to go forward with their projects unless significant Native participation is at the very core of their efforts. In the meantime more of us need to say no when inclusion amounts to tokenism.

I am about the most antianthology guy you could ever meet, but after that conversation I wondered if a collection of essays on Native literature that contained the work of Native literary critics might not be in order. I also wondered if it might not be time for an "unfamous" anthology. This was something of an epiphany to me because I thought all of us were "unfamous" anyway. I can't imagine that even someone like N. Scott Momaday has ever been plagued by paparazzi, but I could be wrong.

Thus began a conversation about an anthology that would address Native literary theory. Some early participants included Sean Teuton, Daniel Justice, Malea Powell, Jim Ottery, Janice Gould, Jace Weaver, Robert Warrior, and myself. We began with the assumption that Native cultures and literatures are theory-laden and that the act of theorizing—the right kind of theorizing—is an appropriate Indian response to them. We did not want the anthology to serve as a place to vent the usual clichés: "Nobody understands us," "The academy does not respect Native knowledge," "Literary theory is irrelevant," and so on, true as those objections may be in particular cases. We hoped to *create* Native knowledge rather than complain about its reception in the non-Indian world.

The idea that Native literary criticism is criticism authored by Native people was to serve as a baseline for the essays. By no means did we want to dismiss our non-Indian colleagues who were writing high-quality literary criticism about Native literature. There could be—and we assumed would continue to be—a valuable critical response written by non-Indians that would contribute to the discussion of Native literature. I have yet to meet a Native literary critic, including those of us singled out as the most separatist in our approaches, who claims that non-Natives should not write about Indian literature. These colleagues, however, are not the focus of this particular anthology. For works that give prominence, if not priority, to them, readers could examine virtually every critical anthology that has been published to date, including the most recent ones.

We wanted the anthology to mark a certain historical threshold, to celebrate a turning point. Just as it had been possible for some time by the year 2002 to teach a Native literature course using all Native authors (there had, in fact, probably been enough book-length works to do this since at least the early 1900s, although accessibility was always a problem and courses calling themselves "Native literature" did not come along until the early 1970s), it was also possible by the year 2002 to teach a course on Native literary criticism using all Native authors.

If the resulting anthology is less than perfect, it has something to do with our commitment to a book that would challenge us, push us, hard, to our limits. Instead of allowing contributors to dig an already-written essay out of a slush pile, we assigned everyone the same question to write about: "Describe an ethical Native literary criticism." Our exact instructions in the original letter were these:

> *Describe an ethical Native literary criticism.*
> Some considerations might be—but need not be limited to—the following:
>
> 1. What areas are lacking in Native theoretical discussions? What are the missing pieces of the puzzle yet to be examined? What could be done to fill in these gaps? What areas of historical inquiry still need to be undertaken?
> 2. Is the debate on essentialism relevant to Native theorizing? Why or why not? Should Native theorists take a different approach to the

topic of essentialism than the way it is being debated by mainstream theorists?
3. Is social construction, especially in relation to language, relevant to Native theorizing? Why or why not?
4. Can we include spirituality in our theorizing in ways that are both ethically and epistemologically sound?
5. What is the role of pan-tribalism in Native theorizing? Of tribal specificity?
6. Can sovereignty be theorized in meaningful ways? If, so, how?
7. What are some specific examples of praxis, of literary theory that has benefited, or could benefit, Indian communities?
8. Do current models such as hybridity, cosmopolitanism, mediation, oral tradition analysis, the Native perspective, intellectual sovereignty, tribally specific approaches (to name a few among many possibilities) work? Why or why not?

These questions might seem impossible in terms of addressing all of them, but we submitted them as a list to choose from according to the authors' interests as a means of getting people started. In other words, they were intended as "free choice" questions, and no one was asked to take on all of them. It is also important to note that they were generated by the group itself, not assigned by me. The criteria for the completion of this book is born of endless ongoing conversations up to the minute the type was set on the printing press.

The first question (the missing pieces of the puzzle) seemed especially important to me because it called people to do the historical groundwork that has been missing. Rather than venturing off into abstract never-never land, we asked contributors to answer the questions by means of exemplification, to apply them to a reading of a particular Indian text. We created an internal review board composed of those who would read and comment on all the essays because we knew that manuscript reviewers for university presses do not always provide the in-depth critique we wanted for our book. The three people who ended up volunteering to be readers were myself, Chris Teuton, and Daniel Justice, and I am infinitely grateful to these two guys, who took up this task when they were both first-year professors, an incredible gift to all of us. Thank you.

I have not yet named the most unique feature of the anthology. Contributors not only received their rough drafts back with extensive comments on their own essays. They received the comments on *every* essay in the entire manuscript. Their rewrites, then, contained their responses to the essays of their fellow contributors. The subject matter of their final essays was the book itself as they cited and discussed the ideas in other contributions. We wanted to get beyond essentialized abstractions about community and try our hand at *performing* community. We were not looking for the kind of pastoral lark, however, that is usually falsely assumed about communal societies. We wanted to challenge one another, even to disagree, because we believed there had been a lack of healthy debate in the field. We asked that contentions be undertaken in a spirit of collegiality, even generosity.

This anthology then is not a collection of disparate essays where "anything goes" or, as Will Rogers might put it, "We never met a topic we didn't like." The aim was to create a conversation among the essayists. Given the importance of trees in the world, we did not want an anthology for an anthology's sake: we hoped to produce the best one ever written in Native literary studies. We decided to give an authorship credit to every participant who contributed an essay to the final product. This is why all twelve participants are coauthors.

We brainstormed a list of every single Native person we could think of who teaches and writes about Native literature. We tried to err toward inclusivity rather than exclusivity. We especially hoped to get people to join the project whose viewpoints we disagreed with. We weren't always successful. We invited the senior scholars in the field, including the ones who are, evidently, famous. Interestingly, almost every single senior critic turned us down, even though we expressed an interest in hearing whatever advice our academic elders might have for the younger Native critics coming up in the discipline. None of them expressed any hostility toward the collective, but they named writing projects that would keep them from participating. In fact, these senior critics have continued to show support and enthusiasm for the book—though one told me the project sounded a little like "herding ducks."

He was right.

The results of the duck herding, however, proved rather interesting. Some of the ways the ducks refused to herd in the early part of the process included the submission of initial drafts sporting an extreme level of abstraction about ethics without any application to particular texts. These drafts lacked engagement with other essayists; at best, the name of a fellow contributor was dropped in with a sentence or two about his or her ideas, as if the author had just skimmed the piece for the requisite quote. These essays proceeded as if theory simply did not exist; they exhibited a refusal to name even the writer's own theoretical commitments; there was a lack of historical references, minimal attention to the question on ethics, and a host of other shortcomings.

These issues were addressed in ongoing drafts and conversations. Given the way this project was set up, I believe these problems were inevitable, and I am even more convinced that the challenges indicate the importance of the work we did together. My intention here is to simply describe some of the difficulties that have occurred along the path toward realizing this project, not to express disappointment in it.

A turning point occurred when a roadblock loomed that had us thinking the book might not ever get published. Instead of giving up, the group rose to the challenge and took to heart some of the criticism we had been subjected to. Never has a group of people remained more diligent in terms of sticking to it for the long haul, since it took us six years to get this book in print. One contributor who kept all her notes from the process says she wants to submit them to a library as evidence of what Indians have to go through to get published in the new millennium. We came up with a plan to regroup into smaller units, where we each looked at the essays of three participants rather than responding to everyone's. This seemed to create a more manageable working environment, and people really started digging into one another's work.

This collective is an important statement in our own voices. The problems inherent in the book are as instructive as its clarities in that they represent challenges in the field at large. This collective publication, I believe, manifests a level of engagement between Native critics and texts, Native critics and each other, that has not quite happened anywhere else in the same way.

I think one of the revelations of this experience is that it is easy to talk about all the ways in which Native cultures, texts, and criticism are communal. It is a lot harder to *perform* community. I am reminded a little of the novel *Waterlily*, which demonstrates, among many other things, that communal life inside a camp circle is no easy row to hoe if one considers, for example, the restrictions on Waterlily when she is living among her in-laws. Reciprocity is highly valuable; it is seldom very easy.

Our aim was not so much to come up with a unified body of theory, a new "school" as it were, because we were not ready to ask people to shape their ideas around a given body of precepts (the reason for assigning questions rather than criteria). I have observed recent reactions to postmodernism, for example, that are already declaring themselves as "fields" and shutting themselves off too early from questions that still need to be asked, and their position is the weaker for it. I wanted to avoid that finality, the emergence of a school of thought that had prematurely set its rules in stone.

Sean Teuton's contribution recalls his experiences teaching Native literature at Auburn Prison in New York and the prisoners' politically charged responses to that literature in his piece, "The Callout: Writing American Indian Politics." Teuton then discusses the early American Indian writers of the late eighteenth and nineteenth centuries and the activist issues they examined in their works, calling into question the dearth of direct political analysis in some contemporary Native writing and criticism that centers around fiction. The relevance of Teuton's essay is its proactive approach. Many of us complain that the university does not understand us. Teuton's essay suggests that rather than succumb to the restrictions of academe we can take our knowledge to other places. To prisons? Why not?

Phil Morgan's essay, "'Who Shall Giansay our Decision?' Choctaw Literary Criticism in 1830," is a living example of recovering Native intellectual knowledge in his "discovery" of the writing of J. L. McDonald, a Choctaw who authored a critical piece in the 1830s that discusses the differences between Choctaw oral performance and their representations in print some 150 years before the debate that surrounds the work of Dennis Tedlock, Dell Hymes, and Jerome Rothenberg, who are often assumed to be the originators of the discussions of oral performance in relation to American Indians.

In " 'Go Away, Water!': Kinship Criticism and the Decolonization Imperative," Daniel Heath Justice analyzes a controversial exchange between the Native critics Louis Owens and Elizabeth Cook-Lynn in which they argue over the role of mixed-blood authors and the identity-based ideology that has tended to characterize mixed-blood emphases. Justice argues that both critics avoid crucial questions about kinship.

Cheryl Suzack, author of "Land Claims, Identity Claims: Mapping Indigenous Feminism in Literary Criticism and in Winona LaDuke's *Last Standing Woman,*" makes a strong argument for the relevance of feminist theory in Native critical work, challenging those Native thinkers who have claimed a cultural incompatibility with feminism. Suzack analyzes Winona LaDuke's novel *Last Standing Woman* and draws parallels between LaDuke's activism and literary themes, insisting that neither is possible without a strong feminist commitment.

Chris Teuton' s three different approaches to Native literary criticism are organized into "modes" that move from issues of personal identity to accountability to communities in his essay, "Theorizing American Indian Literature: Applying Oral Concepts to Written Traditions." He applies his theoretical framework to N. Scott Momaday's well-known introduction to *The Way to Rainy Mountain*, which Teuton analyzes as a progressive movement away from an individualistic viewpoint and toward a more communally centered vision.

Janice Acoose's essay, "Honoring *Ni'Wahkomakak,*" is the most tribally specific of the contributions, and it focuses on the way Cree literatures reach both inside and outside Cree culture. Its strength is in its Cree performance of a Cree reading of Cree texts, especially in light of the theoretical debates that might tend to claim that no such Cree performance is possible in any "pure" sense. It adds a further important dimension to our book, given the predominance of U.S. literature. It is important to note that events like repatriation, the Royal Commission reports, Mohawk resistance at Oka, the three phases of James Bay flooding and the resistance of the Grand Council of Crees, the evolution of the Assembly of First Nations, and many other events could, and should, be part of this study—if only I had another hundred pages to devote to an introduction.

For now, I do want to say that our anthology is not exactly the first of its kind. In 1993 Jeannette Armstrong's *Looking at the Words of Our People,* an all-Native collection of literary criticism, was published in Canada by the En'owkin Centre at Penticton, B.C. Although the interactive nature of our own collection and its particular theoretical orientation make it different from this Canadian work, Armstrong's volume represents a historical moment in terms of gathering together Native critics, one that contributes to our own efforts a decade later.

In "Digging at the Roots: Locating an Ethical, Native Criticism," Lisa Brooks applies a concept of participative, deliberatory thinking to Native literary criticism by demonstrating the extent of networking among eighteenth-century New England Native intellectuals, writers whom most critics have treated as isolated spokesmen who had little contact with each other. The essay draws on archival work that has not been examined before and explores the meaning of regionalism in terms of the flow of Indian ideas across a particular geography. Brooks traces the cooperation of these critics all the way back to northeastern oral traditions that caution against the dangers of thinking without checking ideas with others who form the backdrop of one's intellectual community.

Tol Foster's essay, "Of One Blood: An Argument for Relations and Regionality in Native American Literary Studies," intervenes between recent tribally specific approaches and pan-tribal ones, arguing that much clarification for literary and historical issues comes from examining the surrounding tribes and geographies that strongly affect any particular community. Foster is interested in the power Native literature has to reach outside itself and make connections rather than only sustain its adherents, arguing for a nuanced cosmopolitanism.

Kim Roppolo scrutinizes rhetorical theory in her essay, "Samson Occom as Writing Instructor: The Search for an Intertribal Rhetoric," outlining a set of criteria for making critical language consistent with the texts to which it is applied. One valuable pedagogical asset of her piece is that it names the composition and rhetoric essays that have been authored by Native people in relation to Indian writing issues.

LeAnne Howe's essay, "Blind Bread and the Business of Theory Making," tells the story of Embarrassed Grief, a fictional character who represents problematic identity categories. After laying out the young woman's story, Howe turns toward nonfiction to discuss the way Embarrassed Grief complicates simple formulations about insiders and outsiders. Howe also analyzes her own novel *Shell Shaker,* recent winner of the American Book Award, in terms of her own process of historical inquiry.

By reminding us that theorizing is an embodied experience in his essay, "Your Skin Is the Map: The Theoretical Challenge of Joy Harjo's Erotic Poetics," Robert Warrior's writing might suggest an important baseline criteria for a materialist criticism: it must acknowledge and address physical human and nonhuman suffering as well as physical pleasure. This strikes me as an important point, given the way in which "desire" has become such a dominant trope in postmodern criticism. The fact that a very significant proportion of the world is experiencing malnutrition, dying of AIDS, being abused in their own habitats in the case of animals (and humans), and being bombed by the U.S. military in Iraq and Afghanistan should be somewhere on our radar screen as we formulate theory. We should remember this because of the way theory originates in the physical body, the site of much pleasure and pain.

A celebratory essay, Warrior's piece is also a sobering one in light of recent antibody, antispirit legislation against gay marriage being passed by some tribes. Native thinkers need to challenge such laws rather than simply accept the formulation that any tribal legislation is normative. I heard a high-profile critic recently say that while he hated a particular tribe's position on gay marriage he respected their sovereign right to make these decisions for themselves. This misses the point. It is a given that tribes can pass legislation, a right that was broadened in the late twentieth century under the Indian Self-Determination Act. But this hardly dismisses Indian people from the responsibility of evaluating whether or not tribes are passing *good* legislation.

My own contribution, "Theorizing American Indian Experience," turns toward the challenge of validating Indian claims regarding experience in a theoretical environment where many critics have told us that no experience in these postcontact, postcolonial, and postmodern times can be claimed as "Indian." These critics insist that only hybridity is possible. I make an argument for the possibility of insider status by searching for meaningful aspects of essentialist viewpoints, and other strategies, that allow personal experience to be claimed for its insights.

The way I see it, a continuity that sometimes exists between these essays is a commitment to grounding literary theory in social practice—whether it is a fellow southeastern author who makes his volunteer work among prisoners a basis for literary readings, a feminist who links a novel to a particular land-claim case at the White Earth Reservation, an Abenaki intellectual uncovering the interactions between eighteenth-century New England Indian intellectuals, or an Osage scholar who, ultimately, claims the human body as an important literary reference. We ask that those who cannot root their literary practice in social activism, for whatever reasons, at least do us the kindness of refraining from using their own divergent viewpoints as an occasion for simply dismissing ours. We ask for debate rather than dismissal.

While I am hestitant to generate a concluding theoretical summary about our own efforts in this collective—though tempted to do so by making points about a materialist criticism that allows for the presence of both spirits and history—I want to avoid a premature final word. I will say we need to do much more historical work instead of relying so heavily on thematic studies. In some sense, this is preaching to the choir, since some of this work is emerging here and elsewhere. The real value of this book may be the potential of the essays to raise tension, contradiction, even disagreement in the dialogue I hope will follow. This collection allows Native critics to speak for themselves, and I hope we can all celebrate it for that opportunity, even when it comes time to subject it, as all criticism must be, to a rigorous scrutiny.

Notes

1. O'Brien, *American Indian Tribal Government*, 90.
2. Quoted in Weaver, "From I-Hermeneutics," 8.

3. This idea that the dominant culture has to reconcile itself with God in order to reconcile with Indians is born out of a conversation I had with Ron Blackburn on a flight back to Oklahoma from the Claremont Theological Forum in the summer of 2005.

4. This essay is reprinted in Johnson, *Tekahionwake*, 178–79.

5. Mourning Dove, *Cogewea*, 91.

6. Lincoln, *Native American Renaissance*, 10, 8.

7. Ibid., 8.

8. Ibid., 9.

9. This may not be so much the fault of the journals as the fact that the articles submitted to them still focus on the big names. This has become such a problem that *American Indian Quarterly* has a published submission statement that lists the canonical authors they will *not* accept articles on.

10. See the chapter, "A Stranger in My Own Life," in Allen, *Sacred Hoop*.

11. Keating, "Feminist Literary Theory," 267.

12. Rich, "Compulsory Heterosexuality," 631–60.

13. Gilley, "Cherrie Moraga," 496.

14. Barnard, "Gloria Anzaldua," 57.

15. Allen, *Sacred Hoop*, 80.

16. Ibid., 177.

17. Ibid., 82.

18. Ibid., 175.

19. McNickle, *Surrounded*, 95–96.

20. Allen, *Sacred Hoop*, 195.

21. Ibid., 76–77.

22. See, for example, Cook-Lynn, "American Indian Intellectualism" and "Who Gets to Tell the Stories?"

23. Allen, *Sacred Hoop*, 79.

24. *News from Indian Country*, February 28, 1987.

25. Ibid., June 30, 1987, 1.

26. Ibid., December 31, 1987, 17.

27. Ibid., January 15, 1991, 2.

28. Ibid., January 15, 1991, 3.

29. Ibid., March 15, 1991, 1.

30. Ibid., February 15, 1991, 14.

31. Ibid., March 31, 1991, 7, and April 15, 1991, 7.

32. Ibid., March 31, 1991, 3.

33. Ibid., August 15, 1991, 4.

34. Phillips, "Thirty-two Letters," 273.

35. Goebel, "Thirty-two Letters," 260.

36. Quoted in Owens, *Other Destinies*, 80.

37. Davis, "Thirty-two Letters," 259.

38. Bruhm, "Queer Today," 31, 29.

39. Zavarazadeh, Elbert, and Morton, *Post-Ality*, i.

40. This is an idea I got from a conversation with Steven Sexton, a graduate student at OU.

41. Allen, *Sacred Hoop*, 107–106.

42. Owens, *Other Destinies*, 165–66.

43. Ibid., 48.

44. Mourning Dove, *Cogewea*, 216.

45. Owens, *Other Destinies*, 235.

46. *News from Indian Country*, February 28, 1994, 11.

47. Goebel, "Thirty-two Letters," 260.

48. Glover, "Thirty-two Letters," 260.

49. Sarris, *Keeping Slug Woman Alive*, 111n16.

50. Ibid., 113.

51. Ibid., 44.

52. Ibid., 7.

53. Ibid., 40.

54. Ibid., 29.

55. Ibid., 126.

56. Warrior, *Tribal Secrets*, 2.

57. Allen, *Sacred Hoop*, 2.

58. Owens, *Other Destinies*, 20.

59. Warrior, *Tribal Secrets*, 45.

60. Ibid., 54.

61. Pevar, *Rights of Indians and Tribes*, 13–14.

62. *News from Indian Country*, March 15, 1996, 8A.

63. Ibid., April 30, 1996, 10B.

64. Ibid., September 15, 1996, 10A.

65. Leitch, ed., *Norton Anthology*, 21.

66. Momaday, *Way to Rainy Mountain*, 33.

67. Leitch, ed., *Norton Anthology*, 22.

68. Blaeser, *Gerald Vizenor*, 13, 160.

69. Leitch, ed., *Norton Anthology*, 22.

70. Ibid.

71. Blaeser, *Gerald Vizenor*, 12.

72. Ibid., 13.

73. Ibid.

74. Pulitano, *Toward a Native American Critical Theory*, 185.

75. *News from Indian Country*, October 15, 1996, 3A.

76. Ibid., November 30, 1996, 1A

77. Cook-Lynn, *Why I Can't Read Wallace Stegner*, 17.

78. Ibid., 77.

79. Ibid., 21.

80. Ibid., 32.

81. Ibid., 33.

82. Ibid., 64–65.

83. Ibid., 86, 89.
84. Ibid., 84–85.
85. Ibid., 85.
86. Ibid., 82–83.
87. Cook-Lynn, *Anti-Indianism*, 175.
88. Cook-Lynn, *Why I Can't Read Wallace Stegner*, 39.
89. Weaver, *That the People Might Live*, ix.
90. Ibid., ix, 32.
91. Ibid., 4.
92. Ibid., xiii.
93. Ibid., 35.
94. Ibid. 35, 36.
95. Ibid., 23–24.
96. Ibid., xi.
97. Ibid., 51.
98. Ibid., 54.
99. Ibid., ix–x.
100. *News from Indian Country*, November 15, 1998, 1A.
101. Ibid., December 31, 1999, 9A.
102. Ibid., November 15, 2000, 9A.
103. Ibid., October 15, 2001, 14A.
104. Ibid., December 15, 2003, 13B.

The Callout

Writing American Indian Politics

SEAN TEUTON

For Ashley

There are so many strifes within our people. Between nations, tribes, and clans that they have weakened our sacred hoop! Inside this iron house, we've put those differences, those strifes aside. To become *one* as our Great Spirit Grandfather wants us to be! If we on the inside can do this, why, we ask, cannot our brothers and sisters do this out there? Recently a brother and sister have come into our circle; at first not all of us could be sure of their hearts. But now we know and feel they are *one* with us. For them, some of my brothers are writing, drawing, painting to share with you out there! You see, I for myself wish to make your faith stronger, your hoop larger. By bringing you into our circle in this iron house, we make all our peoples' sacred hoop that much stronger and beautiful.

Matthew, Lakota prisoner
Auburn Prison, January 1, 1998

The guards glare down from their towers as I approach the prison. On the roof stands a life-size statue of the Department of Corrections logo, "Copper John," a Revolutionary War soldier with bayonet at his side. After teaching Indian men at Auburn Correctional Facility, in the heart of Iroquoia, almost every Friday night for five years,[1] I still feel a yawning dread when I pass through these walls. The Christians wait in line with their Bibles, but they no longer speak to me and have stopped handing me their *Watchtowers* with the crying Indian on the cover. In the lobby hang prints of products the prisoners

---

Sean Teuton, a citizen of the Cherokee Nation, is assistant professor of English and American Indian studies at the University of Wisconsin–Madison. He is the author of Red Land, Red Power: Grounding Knowledge in the American Indian Novel.

are paid to produce at fewer than two dollars an hour, among which are cotton straight jackets. The stern guards in gray search, then escort, me through a series of barred doors. Finally I enter the cool night air of the central yard. Not a tree stands on this huge square of asphalt, though some of the older men recall when the last lone tree was cut down in the early seventies. When birds fly over the yard, Native prisoners collect their fallen feathers. On each side of the yard ascend cell blocks seven stories high and sealed with one massive pane-glass wall. The bodies behind the glass and bars surrounding the yard hoot, holler, and curse us, and the sound and smell of iron and sweat emanate into the yard. I soon enter the hot classroom and wait, hoping the men got the "callout"—when the guards slide back the iron bars and call a waiting man to step from his cell. I am happy to suddenly hear the men's own callouts as they shout hello to me from down the hall. On entering the classroom, one of the men usually approaches me with his writing. In his statement above, Matthew, for example, beseeches his fellow prisoners to recognize their achievement of intertribal unity and to widen their circle to include me and my colleague from beyond the prison walls. In resisting his confinement by engaging those outside his world, Matthew expands his Native consciousness to grow intellectually as well as politically. Written in prison, Matthew's work is inherently political, but it's the writing beyond the walls that makes him a threat to the prison.[2]

I begin with this narrative of work with Native prisoners to invoke the centrality of political writing to the liberation of Native America but, more importantly, to consider the influence of political intervention on scholarship. As an Indian scholar in graduate school, I laid bare our colonial relations through these visits to Auburn Prison and relentlessly grounded my ideas about American Indian culture, literature, and our collective struggle for decolonization. In my work with American Indian prisoners, I was finally able to see the operation of USA[3] imperial power, made more transparent in prison. There I discovered the hidden risks one takes to write about domination. Most of all, I found in Native prisoners a model for true intellectual and political development. Like Matthew, I had to encounter another world if I was ever going to challenge my own. To go beyond the walls that divide by class and education is perhaps the most empowering activity an indigenous intellectual can pursue. This essay traces a similar political transformation in our literary tradition, as Native intellectuals through the generations harnessed their experiences of colonial subjugation to inform their ideas, uniting theory and practice. I thus argue, perhaps too simply, that an ethical American Indian theory must enter the world to change and be changed by the world. To do so, I turn to our intellectual tradition of historically engaged political writing to introduce a theory of Native praxis. Then, in closing, I return to the classroom—to the writing of indigenous prisoners—to demonstrate this theory. What drives Indian intellectuals to political action? In moments such as described above, when we are overwhelmed by the experience of Native criminalization—and, more broadly, other observations of anti-Indianism[4]—American Indian scholars awaken politically and begin putting their ideas to work. I term that demand for justice "the callout."

The Callout in Native Critical Traditions

On a stormy day in 1772 in New Haven, before a crowd of Europeans, Africans, and Indians, Samson Occom, an ordained Christian minister, delivered "A Sermon, Preached at the Execution of Moses Paul, an Indian":

> *My poor kindred,*
> You see the woful consequences of sin, by freeing this our poor miserable country-man now before us, who is to die this day for his sins and great wickedness. And it was the sin of drunkenness that has brought this destruction and untimely death upon him. There is a dreadful ire denounced from the Almighty against drunkards; and it is this sin, this abominable, this beastly and accursed sin of drunkenness, that has stript us of every desirable comfort in this life; by this we are poor, miserable and wretched; by this sin we have no name of credit in the world among polite nations; for this sin we are despised in the world, and it is all right and just, for we despise ourselves more; and if we don't regard ourselves, who will regard us?[5]

Both Occom and Paul were Mohegan. In spite of colonial attacks on his people, Paul made a life in an altered world: he served in the colonial militia, worked as a sailor, and converted to Christianity.[6] But Paul began to drink heavily and, while drunk, killed a wealthy white man. For this offense he was sentenced to be hanged, and he asked Occom to preach at his execution. Years later, his plans betrayed by Eleazor Wheelock to found Dartmouth College for American Indians, Occom, like Paul, began drinking and later died.[7] How strange and sad that day in New Haven must have been: two men of the same tribal homeland standing in the rain, divided by a gallows, divided by European education and occupation, divided before a crowd who saw perhaps only the law-abiding and the lawless. One could attribute the opposed yet parallel lives of Paul and Occom to mere coincidence if not for the same colonial fate both men ultimately met. Moses Paul is an American Indian criminalized for killing a white man; he would not have been missed were the crime reversed.[8] For a time, Occom escapes Paul's criminality by luck of a Western education, only to die from the very alcoholism he preached against.

Working closely with American Indian prisoners often encourages the above meditations on indigenous "immediacy," a term I propose to describe this shared colonial experience among Indians in otherwise different social and economic locations that serves to unite our intellectual work in American Indian studies. Shared experiences of colonial oppression often join Indian people across distinctions of privilege in Indian country, even today. On this socially leveling fact of modern Native existence, American Indian intellectuals base their deepest commitments to making ideas defend the real lives of those around us.[9]

As a plea to indigenous people to refuse the weapons of their destruction—the colonizer's liquor—so that American Indians can recover their lives and revitalize their communities, Occom's call finds its place in a tradition of Indian intellectual discourse concerned with empowering tribal members. Indeed, the minister dares even to rebuke those who attempt to corrupt young Native people: "And here I cannot but observe, we find in sacred writ, a wo against men who put their bottles to their neighbours mouths to make them drunk, that they may see their nakedness: and no doubt there are such devilish men now in our days, as there were in the days of old." Occom doesn't censure only Indians: he calls on all for a humanistic, antimperialist resistance to the insidious intrusion of whiskey traders and their unfamiliar drug into American Indian communities. Then, turning to Native people, he objects to using alcohol because it feeds the cycle of racial self-hatred begun by colonial invasion: "[F]or this sin we are despised in the world, and it is all right and just, for we despise ourselves more." Occom's message speaks to American Indian communities even today. In the end, he asserts that our recovery must begin within ourselves: "[I]f we don't regard ourselves, who will regard us?" Native wellness of both body and mind must begin with a love of self, a "regard" to resist and overthrow those who endeavor to harm us.[10]

Occom's sermon is thought to be the first publication in English by an American Indian. It's most significant, though, that this first work is a piece of political criticism. Occom's public rebuke of those who degrade the community for their own personal gain represents a moment in a long history of politically engaged Native intellectualism.

Native criticism as politics has been central to discussions of culture and art probably as long as American Indians have possessed a self-conscious language.[11] A concern for the practice of power—and politics, above all, is the negotiation of power—is, in fact, built into tribal governance, where debate is a public and social obligation.[12] Early accounts of Cherokee social life, for example, value public deliberation over community and individual moral behavior as a basic requirement of social existence. Cherokee and Osage legal scholar Rennard Strickland lists "social postulates" in his study of Cherokee law, two of which deal directly with moral public life:

1. Popular consensus is essential to effective tribal action. Leadership depends upon popular support, which may be withheld to prevent action. Withdrawal of factions may provide the solution when agreement by consensus is impossible. Social harmony is an element of great value.
2. Society is divided into separate classes and ranks which were created by the Spirits. There is no significant stigma and only limited privilege

> attached to class membership. All classes, both men and women, are of great value socially and have important and useful roles in Cherokee society.[13]

Many other Native cultures share this pluralistic organization of public government. In fact, it is often argued that the founders of the United States modeled their democracy on the government of the Iroquois Confederacy.[14]

Steeped in this discourse of public politics, it's not surprising that American Indians in the nineteenth century began to adapt European political writing to defend the sovereign status of their nations. While I will not provide here an extensive Native intellectual history,[15] I would like to identify a few writers whose work is intensely political as well as intellectual, conveying the sense of immediacy I have been describing. Though less known than William Apess, Cherokee statesman Elias Boudinot appeared with the Pequot minister to lecture publicly against the impending 1830 Removal Act to force Indians west of the Mississippi. Boudinot is credited with founding in 1828 the first Native newspaper, the *Cherokee Phoenix*. His commitment to the public discussion of politics is best represented in his famous "Address to the Whites," a speech he delivered in the First Presbyterian Church in Philadelphia in 1826 to raise money for a school in the Cherokee Republic. In this public discussion, Boudinot masterfully negotiates between opposing political forces: the USA government coveting indigenous lands, the Christian Board of Missions demanding the destruction of traditional Cherokee culture, the plantation-owning Cherokees seeking a capitalist economy, and the traditional Overhill Cherokees resisting the intrusion of Western ways. Given in a public forum before a Christian congregation, Boudinot's "Address" recalls the political grace of Occom's "Sermon": "I now stand before you delegated by my native country to seek her interest, to labour for her respectability, and by my public efforts to assist in raising her to an equal standing with other nations of the earth."[16]

This immediacy of American Indian political criticism is probably most painfully felt in the writings of Charles Eastman, who fled with his people from the USA military to Canada, and returned as a young man to become a physician and a major voice in the Society of American Indians (SAI). Like Occom, Apess, and Boudinot, Eastman delivered public lectures, which could be politically charged. Though Eastman had become a part of European society, having been accepted in eastern social circles and having married into a well-to-do white family, his distance from the severe colonial issues facing a branch of his own people, the Dakota Sioux, was suddenly truncated when he became the doctor at the Pine Ridge agency. On December 28, 1890, Eastman witnessed the aftermath of the Wounded Knee Massacre, when five hundred soldiers opened fire on the men, women, and children of Big Foot's encampment. Like Occom, Eastman found himself in an uncanny moment of immediacy:

> A majority of the thirty or more Indian wounded were women and children, including babies in arms. As there were not tents enough for

> all, Mr. Cook offered us the mission chapel, in which the Christmas tree still stood, for a temporary hospital. We tore out the pews and covered the floor with hay and quilts. There we laid the poor creatures side by side in rows, and the night was devoted to caring for them as best we could. Many were frightfully torn by pieces of shells, and the suffering was terrible. General Brooke placed me in charge and I had to do nearly all the work, for although army surgeons were more than ready to help as soon as their own men had been cared for, the tortured Indians would scarcely allow a man in uniform to touch them.[17]

As a Native intellectual viewing the brutal force of USA empire building, Eastman was challenged to either face or turn away from this cataclysmic event. Perhaps to escape the closeness of this colonial reality, Eastman participated in the SAI's near-collective denial of Indian hating in the United States. Today, Indian scholars wonder about this response to material reality. In a sentence, Osage scholar Robert Warrior explains the bleak social context in which turn-of-the-century Native scholars struggled for an attainable politics: "This generation was the integrationist legacy of post-Wounded Knee existence."[18] In the face of such deplorable USA treatment of Indian nations, Eastman nonetheless incorporates his testimony of Wounded Knee into *From the Deep Woods to Civilization*, which at the time attracted a large USA audience for whom this murderous event would be difficult to ignore. As the simple story of an Indian becoming an American, his autobiography will contradict and confuse, for against that narrative, Eastman ultimately indicts the USA for "the savagery of civilization."[19]

On another front of the nineteenth-century Indian wars, the United States had forced Native nations to allot their collective lands to individual tribal members and to surrender to the USA the "surplus" land to sell to European homesteaders. White settlers, railroaders, oilmen, and miners flooded into formerly Native national lands. The General Allotment Act, later called the Dawes Act of 1887, devastated Native economies, ecologies, and societies: individual property eroded communal moral consciousness. Unable to pay their newly imposed property taxes, American Indians by the thousands were again dispossessed of their lands. The craven Dawes Act precipitated the loss of 26 million acres of Indian land.[20] The dream of a Native state to be called Sequoyah dissipated when Indian Territory was forced into Oklahoma statehood in 1907, and white settlers participated in yet another land rush on Indian lands in the former Cherokee Outlet. In these desperate times, early- and middle-twentieth-century Native literature is thus marked by a reduction in overt political writing for a mass market.[21] Its major writers began to disengage politically and remained cautious about raising their anticolonial voices. Perhaps with the exception of Luther Standing Bear's *Land of the Spotted Eagle*, political writing went underground or became more indirect, regrouping from colonial defiance to community preservation, from public address to novel. Writing during this time of daunting social upheaval for American Indians, Native intellectuals such as Gertrude Bonnin , D'Arcy McNickle, and John Joseph Mathews were nonetheless concerned with protecting tribal lands and cultural practices by supporting the 1934 Indian Reorganization Act to restore tribal governments.[22] So, even though McNickle and Mathews pursued social and political projects to benefit their tribal communities and American Indian–European American relations in general, they concurrently wrote novels such as *The Surrounded* (1936) and *Sundown* (1934), respectively, which were surprisingly tentative about the survival of tribal cultures. They often represented the colonial conflicts between Native nations and the United States as nihilistic, culturally incommensurable collisions between radically different peoples, as in McNickle's *Wind from an Enemy Sky* (posthumously, 1978). Like Eastman, their colonial experiences and political demands appear somewhat restrained in their fiction.

McNickle was Cree Métis but was enrolled in the Confederated Salish Kootenai tribes on the Flathead Reservation in Montana, where he was born. Though he never stayed long in his community after leaving for Oxford in 1925, McNickle worked closely with John Collier on his "Indian New Deal" and helped found the National Congress of American Indians (NCAI). In contrast to the despairing tone of his fiction, McNickle's books on tribal histories and political theory present more affirmative views of American Indians in the twentieth century. In *Indians and Other Americans: Two Ways of Life Meet*, coauthored with Harold Fey, McNickle writes a statement of Native diplomacy and attempts to explain the troubled history of Indian policy in terms of differing philosophical and political views to a broad USA audience, including members of the U.S. Congress.

Unlike McNickle, Mathews pursued his politics more locally, by helping to organize and build his Osage community. In his commitment to explaining to USA citizens the history and lifeways of his social world at home, Mathews carried on the political commitments of Sioux anthropologist Ella Deloria and Alexander Posey, a Creek journalist, both of whom wrote about their tribal histories and the contemporary political challenges facing their home places in such works as *Speaking of Indians* and the Fus Fixico letters, respectively. Mathews grounds his writing in the needs of the people of his home place in an era fraught with doubt. Cherokee scholar Jace Weaver terms this tribal persistence to defend American Indian communities "communitism": "In their efforts, one can see the continuing communitist struggle for Natives as Natives that was the predominant theme during the period, in literature as in politics."[23] To this political purpose, Mathews worked in Osage government and even established the Osage Tribal Museum in 1938. These real world practices no doubt informed his critical writing, but not as forcefully as one would expect. He wrote a history of the Osage people, *Wah'Kon-Tah*, which became a selection in the Book-of-the-Month Club. In *Talking to the Moon*, an ecological memoir of his home deep in the Osage Blackjacks region, where he walked daily through the lands, Mathews meditates on the relationship of Osages to the earth and its rhythms, imagining the human place in the living world, and the actual consequences of the destructive oil business on life's delicate balance.

The years following World War II, in which we see a relative scarcity of American Indian intellectual writing, can be understood as a time of cultural germination and of political planning for the social and literary outpouring of the 1960s and 1970s. When in 1969 Alfonso Ortiz published the controversial *The Tewa World*, he drew on both his experience as a tribal member of the San Juan Pueblo and his Western scientific knowledge of cultural systems of meaning. Ortiz also authored numerous articles on Native lifeways that presented the real, very personal emotional and intellectual lives of American Indians.[24] Significantly, the literature of the Indian movement departs from earlier forms influenced by modernism in its use of the dialogic narrative. Although Red Power authors are said to implement modernist forms characterized by the fractured narrative and the privileging of a character's psychological internality, their works remain rooted in and concerned with the meaning of tribal experience. In *House Made of Dawn*, for instance, N. Scott Momaday infused his narrative with historical and anthropological fact as well as with oral tradition.[25] Other Native writers such as Leslie Marmon Silko and Simon Ortiz composed works grounded in Native communities, novels and poems in which actual tribally significant places were named and described. To forgo this textual attachment to actual territories, indeed, would be to commit a symbolic surrender of nationhood, to cede "not only vast territories of land, but also the territories of imagination and of voice," writes Nahkawè scholar Janice Acoose, an essayist in this collection. American Indian intellectuals of the Indian movement realized their commitment to tribal communities by creating art and writing criticism attendant to the social facts of everyday Native existence in the real world.

Since the Red Power era in Native intellectual history is already well documented,[26] let me merely emphasize here the fundamental role of "history" in sgrounding American Indian political struggles.[27] Like earlier moments, the Indian movement drew its strength from scholars, activists, and writers taking seriously the linkage between self-conception and tribal experience, with the public display of this connection registered in the popular media when Red Power organizers described their own lives and the poverty in national territories. What became a popular form of testimony at demonstrations relentlessly linked American Indian experience to identity. For this reason, Native scholars and activists of this period such as Vine Deloria, Jr., and Clyde Warrior held social location as a primary means of calling attention to the deplorable colonial relations between the United States and Native nations. Native intellectuals of the Indian movement didn't seek to escape the demands of history, for they viewed them as hardly a trap; instead, they harnessed the force of experience to fortify a radical politics.

Even this historical sketch of American Indian political criticism displays a tradition of indigenous cultures developing theoretical paradigms to serve practical actions in the midst of an ongoing USA colonial invasion of Native homelands.[28] Responding to the immediacy of direct and startling experiences of colonialism within their communities, Native intellectuals have been driven to defend their people not with war but with ideas, as American Indian scholar-activists meet and debate, often publicly, the crucial issues frequently masked by racist assumptions of superiority and a manifest destiny to control Native nations. When Native scholars recall experiences of colonial domination and cultural privation within their own communities or families, they discover the necessity of theories relevant to the real lives of their people, those whom their scholarship can serve. This exhortation to us by our tribal constituents is often characterized as "heeding the voices of our ancestors," in the words of Mohawk scholar Taiaiake Alfred.[29] It's the call of a history that lays claim to our tribal selves. As our tradition shows, a practical criticism in American Indian studies should thus recognize that what we call "theory" must refer closely to our real worlds: the social, economic, and ecological conditions in which we live. As an empirically tested process, theoretical inquiry works better to explain and challenge the political subjugation of Indian country.

Those American Indian scholars who remain close to the daily life of their tribal communities have often been best prepared to pursue this kind of political scholarship. Readers might bear with this controversial claim, for it can be supported theoretically. As we know, the inherited and lived colonial circumstances of political subjugation and cultural destruction, the incontrovertible facts of social location, shape but do not entirely determine the experiences American Indians are likely to have. Such experiences inform cultural identity, and identity, in turn, serves to interpret these experiences. On this often-undisclosed understanding of tribal social location, experience, and identity, Indian people reserve an advanced knowledge of a Native world that others are not likely to have.[30] When we lay claim to those experiences to fortify our tribal selves, we forge a political identity. Worthy political identities are thus made from the very same experiences that the dominated undergo, but they are consciously created through self-reflection on, and disclosure of, that domination. From this view, it also stands that indigenous political identities can be borne out of interpretations of a formerly unknown, dominated world we seek to experience. In coming closer to our own and others' colonial experiences, we can *choose*, that is, self-consciously construct, our political identities. When we experience a political awakening to anticolonial resistance, we often do so through this increased access to the actual material conditions facing our tribal constituents. So doing, such scholars deepen their knowledge—and their political investment—in the liberation struggle for Indian people.[31]

If American Indian intellectuals have long held the discussion of politics as a cultural value inseparable from the body of Native understanding, we might ask why some Native intellectuals and writers of the recent decade have not been more politically engaged. Surely the caution cannot be attributed to an aggressive colonial circumstance similar to that of the early twentieth century. The 1990s nonetheless at times marked the obscuring of political issues facing the real lives of American Indians in their communities, a change in intellectual and artistic focus begun just after the slowing of the civil rights movement. Some American Indian scholars began to seek a more sophisticated theoretical framework from which to challenge the myth of the Vanishing American and other tragic views of Native cultures and literatures. Employing postmodern theory, Native intellectuals such as Betty Louise Bell, Kimberly Blaeser, Laura Donaldson, Louis Owens, Kathryn Shanley, and Gerald Vizenor sought to deconstruct harmful representations of American Indian identity and lifeways.

Cherokee scholar Betty Louise Bell advocated replacing the colonized identity "half-breed" with the postmodernist subject position of "cross-blood," from which hybrid Native writers would negotiate power in the space between colonizer and colonized: "The Native American 'I' has, from colonization, been a hybrid identity, composed and mediated by the settler's language, experience, and imagination. . . . For the crossblood, . . . the stories of tribal lives before and after conquest survive in coexistent individualized narratives, neither succumbing to the other, neither being colonized by the language or history of the other, but creating a space where memory and imagination actively interact with the world."[32] The cross-blood position attempted to account for a colonial history that, in this view, has often taken the ability to write one's own history. Cross-blood intellectuals tended to consider external social and material forces, such as the imposition of colonial languages and the displacement of tribal peoples from their lands, to erode one's ability to write with indigenous agency. Some postcolonial theorists influenced by this version of poststructuralism, such as Gayatri Spivak, doubted whether the subaltern can speak at all, because the colonized are always already at least partially invented by the colonizer. Accepting that colonized Indians are, on some level, always constructed, even to themselves, by their colonizers, cross-blood scholars thus sought the small freedom promised in ideological and cultural indeterminacy. Drawing on poststructuralist theorists of the postcolonial like Homi Bhabha, such trickster criticism often claimed that Native people today live hybrid lives that liberate by remaining permanently dislocated: "Tricksters exist on the borders of splintered lives and divided opposing cultures, speaking and healing in a divided crossblood space," writes Bell.[33] Like other cross-blood theorists of Native culture and literature, Bell was drawn to Anishinaabe writer Gerald Vizenor's ahistorical trickster fiction, perhaps because it evades and thus must not defend a history that American Indians are forced to forget.

In Vizenor's novel *Bearheart*, for instance, Belladonna Darwin-Winter

Catcher is confused about her Indianness. Her name suggests multiple interactive cultural determinants: the Christian worshiper of a "Beautiful Lady" or the Virgin Mary, the rational evolutionary, and the tribal historian. She encounters "the hunter," a trickster who is of little help in discerning how she should behave or define herself. He says: "Indians are an invention. . . . You tell me that the invention is different than the rest of the world when it was the rest of the world that invented the Indian. . . . An Indian is an Indian because he speaks and thinks and believes he is an Indian, but an Indian is nothing more than an invention."[34] The hunter insists that Indian identity is a pervasive colonial construction beyond which Native people cannot conceive a genuine tribal identity. While we should not assume that the hunter represents Vizenor's views on identity, *Bearheart* nonetheless provides little guidance on how to construct one's own Native selfhood. American Indian scholars advocating this position thus inadvertently subverted the goal of Native oral tradition to morally ground individuals within the tribe. Indian postmodernists made of that trickster an indiscriminate subverter of all claims to self-knowledge. In *Bearheart*, Vizenor suggests that the cultural specificity of tribal values constitute a "terminal creed." The white hunter corners Belladonna: "My father said the same things about the hunt that you said is tribal. . . . Are you telling me that [what you identify as a tribal value] is exclusive to your mixedblood race?" "Yes!" snapped Belladonna. "I am different than a whiteman because of my values and my blood is different."[35] Because Belladonna asserts cultural difference but cannot name essential tribal values that no white man shares, the hunters execute her with a poison cookie, announcing that she "is a terminal believer and a victim of her own narcissism."[36] Holding that claims to knowledge can only be terminal, the trickster position on indigenous culture and identity was thus oddly reliant on essentialism.

Whether as Coyote, Rabbit, Raven, or Naanabozho, the trickster in the traditional tribal narrative, however, most often serves as a negative example to remind tribal people to regulate tribal values. In *American Indian Thought*, the first collection of Native philosophical essays ever produced, Indian philosophers find trickster behavior, for example, to diverge from, and thus underscore, normative moral behavior: "The idea is simply that the universe is moral. Facts, truth, meaning, even our existence are normative. In this way, there is no difference between what is true and what is right. On this account, then, all investigation is moral investigation. The guiding question for the entire philosophical enterprise is, then: what is the right road for humans to walk?" writes Cherokee philosopher Brian Yazzie Burkhart.[37] This Ojibway story, for example, teaches by showing how Naanabozho often acts impulsively on his unexamined appetite, and so thwarts his own interests. He finally attains his goal only after he learns to deliberate before he acts: "While walking along the river he saw some berries in the water. He dived down for them, but was stunned when he unexpectedly struck the bottom. There he lay for quite a while, and when he recovered consciousness and looked up, he saw the berries hanging on a tree just above him."[38] That oral traditional trickster reminds us through his hasty and unself-aware behavior that we should reflect before diving in for our desires, for what we truly need might be right in front of us. Within traditional stories, the trickster restores Vizenor's supposed terminal creeds of "balance" and "harmony" as normative principles self-critically valued within the community. To restore balance to the world, for example, the trickster must invoke a moral theory through which to evaluate which tribal values might be helpful or harmful in achieving balance. It's this process of evaluation that postmodern tricksters precluded, for while Native critics agree that tricksters work to challenge colonial definitions, they can't evaluate among definitions on this position. To do so, from this view, would be to support a terminal creed. In the service of postmodernism, moreover, such ahistorical narratives might not be the most politically enabling genre at this time.[39] Liberation is not won by escaping the colonial context, but instead by creating the social conditions to enable political knowledge so that tribal cultures may flourish.[40]

Returning to American Indian political realities, Native scholars such as Elizabeth Cook-Lynn, Robert Warrior, Jace Weaver, Michael Wilson, and Craig Womack began to question the usefulness of postmodern theories and fiction, most all with book-length studies that appeared between 1995 and 2001 and directed the critical focus to the material needs of Native people in their communities. I dare to suggest that these scholars hearken to the Indian movement just described in order to recover its relational view of social location, identity, experience, and political transformation as they build the Indian theories of our times. Crow Creek Sioux scholar Cook-Lynn shows concern for the postmodernist direction of Native literary criticism: "When writers and researchers and professors claim a mixed-blood focus on individualism and liberation, they often do not develop ideas as part of an inner-unfolding theory of Native culture; thus, they do not contribute ideas as a political practice connected to First Nation ideology. No one will argue that Native studies has had as its central agenda the critical questions of race and politics. For Indians in America today, real empowerment lies in First Nation ideology not in individual liberation or Americanization."[41]

Cook-Lynn locates the problem of Native writers and scholars producing less politically engaged fiction and criticism, their inattention to "race and politics," in what she calls a misdirected "mixed-blood focus." Such a focus, she claims, is more accepted and promoted in the university, a primary site for the investigation, representation, and transmission of American Indian intellectualism. Furthermore, in privileging this mixed-blood focus on colonial interaction as the most productive site of Indian culture, Native scholars, in the midst of intellectual struggle, often place themselves in a hostile world with "a lack of communal interests or goals . . . a lack of trust," as Cherokee/Choctaw/Creek contributor Kim Roppolo describes this hybrid space.

My understanding of Cook-Lynn's critique might differ from that of Cherokee contributor Daniel Justice. According to Justice, Cook-Lynn attacks self-identified mixed-blood writers such as Louis Owens for their conversion to dominant culture by intermarriage with Europeans. While such a statement is potentially damning for Cook-Lynn, she more often disagrees with the individualist, nontribal values she sees often promoted by such mixed-bloods. In other words, Cook-Lynn, in my view, objects not to the multiheritage but rather the social values of mixed-bloods, who, she contends, undermine nationhood by providing only self-absorbed narratives of displacement, and who are promoted in the academy for doing so. This said, I find it impossible to separate race from ideology in the concept of the mixed-blood, and so I ask that we reject the term altogether. I should be clear that I do not deny *the political reality of racialization*. Indeed, we must be accountable for the privileges of light skin, maleness, and straightness in a world that invests these social registers with great power. In these I recognize my own privilege. But, as Choctaw scholar Michael Wilson argues,[42] the mixed-blood as a category cannot escape the discourse of purity and corruption, a binary that, ironically, Justice also recognizes in Cook-Lynn's claims. Of course, Cook-Lynn can surely attack the values of particular writers as detrimental to nationhood and sovereignty without ever turning to identity politics, and other Native scholars can recast our discussions to evaluate the tribal values we come to hold and promote in our research. I thus submit that Native scholars exchange the mixed-blood for the tribal citizen and begin to discuss the merit of particular social values to serve our ethical goals, as Justice rightly does in writing on the concept of kinship in this collection. On this principle of kinship, we can justify the granting of tribal national citizenship to nonenrolled Indians, for example. Like other countries, Native nations can stand by their sovereignty and thus develop ethically just standards of membership.

The task facing today's American Indian intellectuals, then, is to recover a trusted real world space through which to inform and test our research, as the above scholars have begun to show. That is to say, in focusing their work on more socially relevant topics that consider the lives of American Indians in the world and their political transformations, scholars reground and empower their studies. That world is often a painful, dominated space, but one that nonetheless reclaims ground from the colonial matrix. Recalling Antonio Gramsci's philosophy of praxis, Cook-Lynn calls the study of this process an "inner-unfolding theory of Native culture."[43] At this time, our readings of culture and books should provide cogent explanations that refer accurately to the real and literary lives of American Indians. At the same time, the practical demands of oppressive economic and social conditions on reservations may be a call to action for Native scholars and activists. For American Indian studies to have a real impact in the lives of the people, it should become *located* in the real world.

Praxis in the American Indian Classroom

Placing our intellectual selves in the Native community, classroom, or prison, we can derive an indigenous moral and political criticism with profound anticolonial implications. Paulo Freire draws a similar conclusion regarding the liberating potential of public political discussions: "The insistence that the oppressed engage in reflection on their concrete situation is not a call to armchair revolution. On the contrary, reflection—true reflection—leads to action,"[44] for in examining literary texts and attaching them to our shared world, we collectively struggle for social knowledge and social justice, in the way that bell hooks approaches the classroom, as a site of social struggle in which oppressed people imagine a freed self.[45] The American Indian prison classroom is eminently political. While race and class certainly work to criminalize indigenous men in the United States, colonialism still remains the most relevant means of understanding how the structures of power persist in constructing the "savage." The federal incarceration of Native people today extends a long history of USA imperialism by displacing American Indian leaders from their homelands and depriving them of their tribal communities and clan members. In resistance to this ongoing imperialist project to destroy culture by removing Native men from their ancestral social location, American Indian prisoners gather in solidarity and devise strategies for overturning the prison's aggressive attempts to erode their indigenous cultural selves.

On a given Friday night at Auburn Prison, the men and I gather in the classroom, pull out the drum, and sing a few songs. In the midst of an often chaotic evening, we eventually settle down to discuss a prearranged topic such as the social role of Indian women, varying tribal warrior traditions, or a particular tribal history. The discussion often begins with the men giving statements, which at times emerge in a form similar to the testimony of Occom or Apess. In their writing assignments, the men often transcribe their oral testimonies into impassioned written statements full of rhetoric and imagination that transcend the prison walls.

Chico is a heavy Navajo man who wears his hair undone and down to his belt. He uses a cane to serve an old injury, and he likes to sit and do beadwork while he warns the younger men about reckless, colonized thinking. Chico types his "Surviving behind the Wall" with great care and in capital letters, ending the statement with "I have spoken," and signing his name. Chico opens his statement this way: "There is a battle going on behind the wall with the Native community. It's a battle against alcohol and drug abuse, against physical and mental abuse, against poverty and ignorance, against racism and anger. It is a battle for dignity, independence, freedom, justice, health, and happiness. This battle is being fought in the hearts and minds of our people in the New York State prison communities and in all the Native communities across the United States."

Perhaps drawing on the warrior tradition, Chico portrays the struggle facing imprisoned Native men as a "battle," a war, ironically, against all the dysfunctional activities for which the men are charged, such as alcohol and drug abuse. But the other abuses—physical and mental abuse—are imposed on the men by the prison. Interestingly, in announcing a war against poverty and ignorance, Chico could be referring to Indian prisoners or to the guards who often abuse them, who, ironically are also impoverished and undereducated. Shifting his declaration from those values the battle opposes to those it wishes to promote, Chico proclaims those human rights that anyone—white, Native, or otherwise—would support. Chico declares this battle to be fought both with our emotions as well as our intellects, not only by American Indians in prison, but also by Indian people throughout the United States. Chico calms down some in the second half of his statement to recognize his Creator, who helps him survive imprisonment: "In these walls, we can't ever feel that we are alone. A lot of times there is no one who can be physically there when you need support. That is why we always give thanks to the Creator for all the blessings and that he is always with us."

The men's writings often reflect the oscillations of hope and despair, calm and rage that prison life promotes. Even though daily life is strictly controlled, the known world can be completely and immediately destroyed when, for example, a man is transferred to another prison without a moment's notice—often as unofficial punishment for resisting confinement. While the prisoner agonizes over losing his prison family and having to defend and establish himself in a new and unknown prison, back at the former prison, his friends and allies hear of his abrupt departure in the morning mess hall. Chico's piece, "The People's Feeling," displays outrage at these deliberate abuses. It opens with an autoethnographic description, almost presenting an aesthetic figure study of Indian people: "The Native Americans, as I have before said, are copper-coloured, with long black hair, black eyes, short, tall, straight, and elastic forms. We are less than two/three millions in number. We were originally the undisputed owners of this soil. We got our title to our lands from the Great Spirit who created them for us. We were once a happy and flourishing people, enjoying all the comforts and luxuries of life which we knew of and consequently cared for. We gave thanks daily and prayers to the Creator, thanks for his goodness and protection."

Chico begins with this idealized description of pre-Columbian life in North America to prepare his Western readers for the alternative indigenous history of the European conquest and colonization of Native people he leads us through: "First, you must follow me a vast way from the civilized world. Now you should forget the many theories you have read in the books of or about Indian barbarities, butchers, and murders." He begins by correcting the tragic portrait of the Vanishing American: "What poor miserable victims to suffer such death and destruction. That is the portrait that they have painted of us. What beautiful lies they tell for their amusement, for their information, so that we can again trust them and help them finish what their forefathers started back in the 1400s. They are unthinkable and unmerciful, their starvation is to finish us and wipe us out forever!!!!" Chico challenges his fellow Indian prisoners to reconsider the dominant culture's representation of Native people as passive victims and reminds prisoners not to internalize this portrait. He insightfully suggests that the image of the helpless fallen Indian actually serves the colonial imagination set on the eventual disappearance of Native people and the discovery of territories and resources.

Chico then asks us to question who is the true savage, defined not by a superior culture but by humanity, reminiscent of the best of Eastman: "You should consider why they have call[ed] us savages of our North American [*sic*] without looking at what they did to our people and what they are doing to us. Our Indian pride has never been cut down." Chico ends this statement with pathos to balance his earlier outrage: "So great and unfortunate are the disparities between the savage and the civil. Now you must ask yourself one question: Who is the savage here? My eyes are full of tears and my heart is full of pain. What I feel is such pain and I still want to know the true answer to this question of pain and cruelty against us." I imagine Chico chooses to leave the term "civilization" abbreviated to evoke the related notion, "civility," a universal value of courtesy or polite action to understate the brutality of the American invasion of Indian country. At the threshold of his emotion and intellect, Chico awaits a logical response to the spectacle of empire and genocide. He was shipped out one night.

Of all group members, Whitehorse, a Lakota man, is the most volatile. Without fail, he arrives with his sheaf of papers, written in an angry slash of ink and scratched-out corrections. On a piece of lined paper he writes: "It makes me sad because when the white man came to our people they came with this little black book and told us wonderful things about their God! But we did not see these things. All we got to see was destruction of our identity and death." Whitehorse writes with similar perplexity of earlier America Indian leaders who could not understand the separate roles of priest and soldier; then again, these servants often worked together. Whitehorse then lashes out with an alternative history of missions in Indian America: "My brother and sister, we all know the real history. The one that they don't tell us about! Mystic River, you smelled the Pequot flesh burning. Or how about the pubic hairs of our women scalped at Sand Creek." With visceral accuracy, Whitehorse assaults his readers with the dark side of Christian conversions, the hypocrisy of the New Canaanites who, by divine instruction, intended to destroy the old in the so-called Pequot War of 1637. The second image recalls "the Fighting Parson," Colonel John Chivington, who in 1864, with his drunken 3rd Colorado Volunteers, rode all night to Sand Creek and massacred women and children of the Southern Cheyenne in the name of Jesus.

I end this selection of writings with a poem from Alex, a twenty-four-year-old Seneca guy who got into college and paid for it with a football scholarship. When he was injured, he lost his scholarship and, out of money, had to quit school and return to his reservation. Deeply depressed, Alex began drinking recklessly and eventually landed in prison. The poem is titled "Ongwehonwe," which roughly translates, "The Real People":

> I once knew a man.
> who carried strong drink in his hand.
> He worked from dark to dark,
> then the partying would start.
> As the years did pass,
> he kept a strong grasp on the glass.
> Bad thinking came with his fierce drinking.
> The taste of Bud or Beam
> made a good man mean.
> Friends and family could only stand by
> as they watched him die inside.
> He would not be stopped
> not by a long shot.
> The day came at bay,
> when he would pay for his ways.
> 25 to life,
> cut his spirits like a knife.
> Sitting behind a giant wall
> has he missed his call?
> Now with a clear mind,
> all he has is time.
> What does the Creator have planned for him?
> After all, he did spare his life again.
> He is so sorry for what had transpired.
> His heart will never be free,
> from that tragedy.
> His new brothers in prison,
> are the only ones who will listen.
> He wants to do good,
> and make it understood.
> He sings earth songs in early day,
> and tries to live true Ongwehonwe.

Ending by beginning, Alex "sings earth songs in early day" as he works to get his mind on the inside, as the men say, to stop the yearning for home and begin to discover new ways, often through language, to gather the men and transcend the confinement of the walls. In the lines above, Alex wonders, "sitting behind a giant wall," if he has "missed his call," invoking both the call of life to pursue one's expressive course as well as the call from the guards to leave his cell for a visit from family or teacher. These two cruelly opposed callings resonate with the call of history and the call to action I have been developing in this essay. Trace that call and response through our intellectual history, from the public exhortations of Samson Occom to the impassioned pleas of Taiaiake Alfred, and find only a few shadowy moments when Native intellectuals hesitated. Instead, American Indian scholars have honored the call from our relations, who,from the prison or the street, request our advocacy. This callout can often be heard from quite near, bringing to light our privilege as Western-educated scholars who nonetheless find, in a startling moment of immediacy, the collapse of class and social boundaries.

Perhaps more than any other boundary, the walls of imprisonment divide and discard our people. For this reason, I open and close this essay with the callout of indigenous prisoners. Though we might not always live close to real-world Indian struggles, we can certainly seek them out. Entering prisons, we gather more hands-on experience of colonial privation, which not only discloses the workings of domination in Indian country but also, most importantly, informs our understanding of our political selves. When I began working in prisons, I defended a simplified view of the dealers and victims of domination. Over the years, however, I came to understand the deadening frustrations of underpaid white prison guards in a rust-belt town and to discover the stunning acts of self-possession in Indian men I thought conquered. Such corrections in my vision of Indian territory galvanized my political identity. As we empower our political identities with such experiences, so we challenge and inform our understanding of true freedom for Native America, "freedom as connection to others, rather than freedom from others," as Michael Hames-García puts it.[46]

Thus my theoretical view of political activity as fundamental to knowledge production. Yet I suppose any ethical Native theory ultimately grows from encounters such as those described above. My own interest in prison work began when, as a young adult, I learned that, unlike my own family, most American families don't have regular visits from the police or to jail. Since undertaking this contribution to the anthology, my eighteen-year-old niece has been imprisoned. I dedicate this essay to her.

Notes

1. I taught at Auburn with my Tuscarora friend and colleague, Vera Palmer. The prisoners gave me permission to share some of their writings in an exhibit called *Art across* Walls. In this volume I have changed the prisoners' names to protect their privacy, but where I quote their writings I have chosen to stay true to the original phrasings rather than editing any of the passages.

2. Indigenous people incarcerated in their own lands by an occupying colonial power such as the United States are unavoidably political prisoners who engage in unavoidably political writing. See Ross, *Inventing the Savage,* 2. Such extradition violates federal Indian treaties. See, for instance, the 1868 Fort Laramie Treaty, in Prucha, *Documents*, 110. Chomsky,'s *On Power and Ideology* (12–13) refers to the Sullivan campaign through western New York in 1779 as one of the founding

events of United States imperialism. Said's *Orientalism* (40) shares a similar thesis on the West's imperialist containment of the East. The imprisonment or accumulation of the Native might correspond to the accumulation of their capital; see Lenin, *Imperialism*, 62–63. To understand the men's world, I draw on the experiences of criminality in my own family. See Howe, *Punish and Critique*, and the introduction to Rosaldo, *Culture and Truth*. Scarry *The Body in Pain* (3–5), shares this challenge in the resistance of pain to language. Of all minority groups, American Indians are the most disproportionately incarcerated: "On any given day, one in 25 Indian adults is under the control of the criminal justice system—63,000 individuals. The number of Indians in state and federal prisons is 38 percent above the national average. In South Dakota, according to a report in 1991, Indians comprise 7 percent of the general population, but 25 percent of the prison population" (O'Brien, "The Struggle to Protect," 32).

3. In this essay, I use the abbreviation USA to emphasize a relationship to the Americas, in which the United States is *of*, that is, beholden to, the hemisphere and its original peoples.

4. Cook-Lynn defines anti-Indianism as "a form of discrimination and ideological bias in scholarship as well as in practical politics and mainstream thinking." See Cook-Lynn, *Anti-Indianism*, 3.

5. Occum, "A Sermon," 478.

6. Citing Occom's evangelical rhetoric, Krupat suggests Occum has lost his culture (*Voice in the Margin*, 146). Murray disagrees with Krupat: "[Occom] actually exploits the ambiguities of his position as a civilized Indian in his writing" (*Forked Tongues*, 57).

7. For historical background on the execution of Paul, Occom's sermon, and Occom's eventual despair, see Love, *Samson Occom*, especially chapters 9 and 10, and Blodgett, *Samson Occom*, 105–168.

8. As late as 1755, a royal proclamation "Given at the Council Chamber in Boston . . . require[d] his Majesty's subjects of the Province to embrace all opportunities of pursuing, captivating, killing and destroy[ing]all and every of the [Penobscot] Indians. [T]he premiums of bounty following viz: For every scalp of a male Indian brought in as evidence of their being killed as aforesaid, forty pounds. For every scalp of such female Indian or male Indian under the age of twelve years that shall be killed . . . , twenty pounds. Quoted in Vine Deloria, Jr., *Custer*, 6.

9. The term "intellectual" might aspire to Muscogee historian Donald Fixico's definition of Indian "genius," as "keepers of traditional knowledge who have insightful life experiences and who possess gifts of special insights to life, and whose actions benefit their people" ("Call for Native Genius," 44).

10. Occum, "A Sermon," 480, 478.

11. Criticism is unavoidably political as long as power plays a role in cultural production. Creek critic Jana Sequoya-Magdaleno explains: "At issue in that struggle . . . are the emergent institutional interests of Indian-identified cultural producers to define and control the signifier 'Indian'" ("Telling the *différance*,"

93). In *Marxism and Form*, Fredric Jameson explores the problem of politics and criticism: "The artist himself is merely an instrument. . . . This is why our judgments on the individual work of art are ultimately social and historical in character" (329).

12. For a similar European model, see Habemas, *Structural Transformation*.

13. Strickland, *Fire and the Spirits*, 22.

14. See Seneca historian John Mohawk, "Indians and Democracy," 70–71, and Taino intellectual José Barreiro, *Indian Roots*.

15. Robert Warrior, in "Native American Scholar," and Jace Weaver, in *That the People Might Live*, organize political moments in American Indian intellectual history. See also LaVonne Ruoff, *American Indian Literatures*.

16. Boudinot, "An Address to the Whites," 69. Theda Perdue comments in *Cherokee Editor*, "Boudinot portrayed the Cherokees as a 'civilized' people in part because he believed their society was in the process of of complete transformation but also because he knew that a charge of 'savagery' by whites might lead to their extermination" (21).

17. Eastman, *From the Deep Woods*, 110.

18. Robert Warrior, *Tribal Secrets*, 7.

19. See Eastman, *From the Deep Woods*.

20. Wilkinson, *American Indians*, 20.

21. On SAI writing, see Lucy Maddox, *Citizen Indians*. For a discussion of Maddox, see Sean Teuton, "A Questions of Relationship."

22. See Gertrude Bonnin, *American Indian Stories*; D'Arcy McNickle, *The Surrounded* and *Wind from an Enemy Sky*; and John Joseph Mathews, *Sundown, Talking to the Moon*, and *Wah'Kon-Tah*.

23. Weaver, *That the People Might Live*, 88.

24. Alfonso Ortiz also received criticism from his community for revealing Tewa religious knowledge.

25. See Selinger, "*House Made of Dawn*."

26. See Smith and Warrior, *Like a Hurricane*; and Sean Teuton, *Red Land, Red Power*.

27. Marxist theories of criminality, for example, specify the role of historical forces in our definitions of criminal acts, "the socially structured inequalities of wealth and power that shape human action" (Greenberg, *Crime and Capitalism*, 6). For poststructuralist critiques of historicization, see Williams, *Marxism and Literature*, 108–114, and Laclau and Mouffe, *Hegemony and Socialist Strategy*.

28. See also the archival work of Konkle, *Writing Indian Nations*, and Littlefield and Parins, eds., *Native American Writing*.

29. Alfred, *Heeding the Voices*, 73.

30. On the realist theory of identity, see Mohanty, *Literary Theory*, chapter 5. For a realist view of Indian country, see Sean Teuton, "Placing the Ancestors."

31. According to Hau, political development, then, is achieved through the interaction of differing Native social locations ("On Representing Others," 138). Mao explains this engagement between intellectuals and "the people" and the

resulting creative transformation with his concept of "contradiction." See Mao, *On Contradiction*, 6. Recall Marx's famous eleventh thesis on Feuerbach: "The philosophers have only *interpreted* the world, in various ways; the point, however, is to *change* it" ("Theses on Feuerbach," 145). On this process in Native internationalism, see Sean Teuton, "Internationalism and the American Indian Scholar."

32. Bell, "Almost the Whole Truth," 184, 185.

33. Ibid., 185.

34. Vizenor, *Bearheart*, 195.

35. Ibid., 194.

36. Ibid., 145.

37. Burkhart, "What Coyote and Tales Can Teach Us," 17.

38. Quoted in Thompson, *Tales of North American Indians*, 54.

39. In "Here's an Odd Artifact," her review of Louise Erdrich's *The Beet Queen*, Silko suggests that Erdrich is canonized because her fiction avoids colonial realities in self-conscious, postmodern language. See also Castillo, "Postmodernism." On the need for a criticism based in the lived world of American Indians, see Robert Warrior, "The Native American Scholar," 50.

40. If social and historical forces construct what we call "subjectivity," then it follows that we can change these conditions so new forms of selfhood may emerge. Institutions must be reformed. Writing in 1969, Noam Chomsky makes this very demand of the American university (*For Reasons of State*, 315). In American Indian studies, Elizabeth Cook-Lynn presents this view of political transformation by answering "the questions which must be asked of Native American novelists for appropriate nation centered theory to emerge from praxis" ("Literary and Political Questions," 50). See also Stripes, "Beyond the Cameo School."

41. Cook-Lynn, "American Indian Intellectualism," 70–71.

42. See Wilson, "Speaking of Home."

43. Cook-Lynn, "American Indian Intellectualism," 71.

44. Freire, *Pedagogy of the Oppressed*, 52.

45. hooks, *Teaching to Transgress*, 89.

46. Hames-Garcia, *Fugitive Thought*, xii.

"Who Shall Gainsay Our Decision?"

Choctaw Literary Criticism in 1830

PHILLIP CARROLL MORGAN

Utilizing tribally specific criticism to help us read and find usefulness in American Indian literatures is a sound approach. To suggest otherwise is analogous to saying that Samuel Taylor Coleridge had nothing particularly more insightful to write about early-nineteenth-century British literature than, say, Pushmataha, the Choctaw chief, would have had. Though it seems self-obvious to many Native critics, the clear defense of the premise remains a thorny problem in a contemporary academic atmosphere in which history and tradition are too frequently dismissed as shaky, subjective ground. In this essay I am proud to introduce to the debate another Native voice from the nineteenth century, that of James L. McDonald. His analyses and his comparisons of Choctaw language arts and storytelling styles to their counterparts in the English language suggest that a tribally specific approach is not a new one. McDonald, a gifted Choctaw intellectual, working between 1824 and 1831 in the preremoval Mississippi Choctaw Nation, wrote what I am calling the "Spectre Essay" in December of 1830. I will argue that his essay represents the earliest example yet found of Choctaw literary criticism and that his "performance" of oral traditional forms in the new literacy presuppose what have become some of the defining features of late-twentieth and early-twenty-first-century Native American literary criticism.

I think that if McDonald were with us today, he might be amused, perhaps perplexed, by the modern preoccupation with traditionalism. In McDonald's writing we are privileged to have commentary that has not yet encountered the need to react to what Cherokee scholar Daniel Heath Justice has termed "colonialist constructions of absence."[1] McDonald was still a citizen of a sovereign nation, still present in his ancestral Mississippi homeland at the time he

---

Phillip Carroll Morgan (Choctaw) is completing his doctorate in English at the University of Oklahoma; his dissertation focuses on nineteenth-century Choctaw literature. He is the author of The Fork-in-the-Road Indian Poetry Store.

wrote the "Spectre Essay," albeit only a matter of months before Choctaws embarked upon the Trails of Tears to their new sovereign nation in Indian Territory west of the Mississippi River. I uncovered his essay amid a lively body of preremoval correspondence between him and his young Choctaw intellectual peers—Peter Pitchlynn, Henry Vose, David Folsom, and others—preserved in the Western History Collection at the University of Oklahoma.

I was struck with a sentiment early in my reading of these handwritten treasures very much like what Abenaki critic Lisa Brooks (this volume) declares about her readings of Mohawk and Mohican leaders Joseph Brant and Hendrick Aupaumut: that "we may have as much to learn from the relations between early Native writers as we do from the writings themselves." Contrary to portrayals of Choctaws and other Native nations facing removal as powerless victims, readings of their correspondence reveal an optimism, a confidence, even an exalted enthusiasm for reestablishing Choctaw education, agriculture, culture, and commerce in their new sovereign nation. I sense in reading McDonald that he regards oral tradition not as a dead artifact but more an art, importing a phrase from Brooks, in an "active state of transformation." The concept in Abenaki philosophy of one's natality (the transformation of birth connected to homeland) contrasted with a consciousness of one's mortality, Brooks (this volume) writes, "provides a striking contrast to the stereotypical European constructions of Native 'tradition' as static and potentially destructible (mortal), while confirming the idea of tradition, so present in much of contemporary Native literature, as an ongoing process, both cyclical and transformative." McDonald, in the immediate throes of leading the incorporation of literacy into Choctaw discourses, seems very excited by the transformation going on; he is certainly not perplexed by the end of one tradition and the beginning of another. Though his evaluations tend to romanticize and perhaps overestimate the superiority of Choctaw to English, his essay is not nostalgic, wounded, nor defensive.

Transregional Similarities in Early Indigenous Writing

Working on independent projects examining original manuscripts from diverse, geographically and culturally separated Native nations, Abenaki scholar Lisa Brooks comes to surprisingly similar observations to my own. In "Digging at the Roots: Locating an Ethical, Native Criticism," an essay within this collaborative volume, she reports that besides the more-often-studied published works of northeastern Native authors William Apess and Samson Occom, Mohawk leader Joseph Brant and Mohican leader Hendrick Aupaumut "each produced enough writing to fill volumes, and both men's influence on early American Indian policy was considerable." Choctaw leaders/writers like J. L. McDonald and Peter Pitchlynn also produced volumes, especially if we consider the multiple postremoval revisions of the constitution of the Choctaw Nation, as well as petitions to the U.S. government, correspondence, treaties, and intervening negotiations with the Chickasaw and other Native nations.

The most interesting writing, however, as Brooks suggests, may be the written communications between the Native writers themselves. Brooks's admonition relative to sometimes united, sometimes conflicting, written debates between Brant and Aupaumut, that "[a]ny reading of their journals demonstrates the need for those of us who analyze their writings to be highly educated in and aware of the nuances of those [respective] traditions" applies with equal force to Pitchlynn, McDonald, and their contemporaries. I will state the obvious. Some scholars from each band, tribe, and nation need to realize both the responsibility and the opportunity to discover the roots of their own intellectual traditions. An excellent place to begin this voyage of discovery is with primary research in the library, museum, tribal government, and private archives that have in the past been the academic terrain of historians and folklorists but largely ignored by literary critics. The search and discovery experiences for me rank among the most personally and professionally enriching of my life, because to actually *read* (rather than to imagine the dispositions of) McDonald, Pitchlynn, Brant, or Aupaumut connects and validates me as a writing Indian across a gulf of time with relatives grappling with virtually identical issues 175 or more years ago.

Brooks emphasizes how the writing Indian William Apess employed the creative, regenerative, and reconstructive power of language, both written and spoken, to establish "a refuge from tyranny and persecution."[2] Apess's postmodern-like use of a multiple-voiced narrative in *Indian Nullification* not only included various newspaper authors in support of the Mashpees, but also included published voices in opposition to the Mashpee argument for restoration of their rights to self-determination. The final showdown of opposing orators in the Massachusetts statehouse resulted in a spontaneous ovation after the Mashpees finished their speeches. Their arguments accomplished the passage of the Mashpee Act, restoring Mashpee rights, without a single dissenting vote. I, as she, regard this remarkable historical event and its written traces as illustration of the foundational importance in any Native critical methodology of the early writers.

I agree further with Brooks that analyzing how ancestral indigenous writers viewed certain pan-tribal issues, like common-cause dealing with the then young United States, affords tight relevance to our current conversation. The ways Joseph Brant, for example, developed his ideas to build a multinational Indian alliance called the United Indian Nations may inform our current grappling with an ethical Native literary criticism. We indigenous writers of the twenty-first century are not defining ourselves so much as separatists as we are writing from an already separated context as circumscribed and imposed by U.S. treaty, law, and doctrine. The Aupaumut, Brant, and McDonald documents exhibit this separateness. Echoing Osage intellectual historian Robert Warrior's call in *Tribal Secrets* "to root our work in analysis that is spatially and historically specific," Brooks asserts that the early Native writers of the Northeast were "thinkers who inhabited many spaces of interaction, just as we do today." Though their metaphors and theoretical dispositions are in important ways uniquely Mohawk, Mohican, Abenaki, or Choctaw, the early writers from these traditions lead both Brooks and myself to remarkably similar conclusions. Aupaumut's and Brant's narratives, Brooks writes, "attest to this interrelationship between oral and written literature within northeastern Native communities, where writing is informed and infused by oral tradition, and the continuance of oral tradition is aided by the tool of literacy."

J. L. McDonald in his "Spectre Essay" argues with expressive passion that the force and precision of Choctaw oral storytelling modes and styles exceed those same features in their analogue in the English language. Whether we regard orality and literacy in our intellectual traditions as old, as new and dichotomous techniques, or as reciprocal and indivisible, it is imperative that we inform ourselves fully of the thematics, usages, and critical dispositions of our literary ancestors.

Warrior writes in his latest book, *The People and the Word: Reading Native Non-fiction*, that "Native non-fiction writing grows alongside modernity in its own development, and from that can emerge a much stronger sense . . . of how Native writers have engaged modernity."[3] He prefaces this accurate observation with the critical directive that "examining Native writing with nonfictional writing at its center" illuminates Native writing as "a literature with a long history rather than seeming faddish" and as a body of writing which "relies more on its own terms rather than the tastes and mandates of the contemporary conventions of modern literary studies."[4] J. L. McDonald's letters examined in this essay are exemplary of just such an engagement with modernity.

Intertextuality in the "Spectre Essay"

An interesting feature of McDonald's essay is its presentation of a fictional story from the Choctaw oral archives translated into written-down English, alongside a nonfiction commentary and contextualization of the story. Where my analysis diverges from Brooks's examinations is in the immediate intertextuality of this side-by-side presentation. She shows how the human origins story of Sky Woman both generates and reflects Abenaki philosophy. She then demonstrates effectively how that philosophy informs the largely political texts of Aupaumut, Brant, and Occom, the early-day writers of the Northeast. In McDonald's essay we have text drawn from a deep vein of Choctaw mythos and metatext that seeks to situate that primary text for "modern" readers. His critical performance is very similar to what the essayists in this volume are doing.

The logical question here becomes: If McDonald is doing literary criticism, what kind of lit crit is it? First, McDonald's criticism is different from the romantic expressivist criticism that Coleridge, among others, was doing at the turn of the nineteenth century, which hinges on the view that poetry and other literatures grow out of, and are organic expressions of, nature. This expressivism is what one might expect of someone like McDonald, who was educated in English-language schools of the period. Rather, in my view at least, McDonald's commentary reads as a formalist type criticism, since he more strongly focuses on form than on content, more on the techniques of telling the story than on the material of the story.

His particular focus may reveal a significant relationship between text and criticism in indigenous writing. When inscribed texts perform in such close proximity to dominant oral traditions, as McDonald's does, and as many current productions by indigenous authors consciously do, the forms and structures of the oral stories duplicate themselves to varying degrees in the written texts. Even though many Native critics acknowledge poststructuralist and postmodern dispositions in Native literature—carefully situating that literature in the complex social spaces in which it originates—few would deny the militancy of centuries-old forms, tropes, and structures in determining the products of Native poets, novelists, playwrights, and even critical writing, like that of the essayists in conversation in this volume. Conversely, few would deny the dramatic and dynamic impact of Native writing upon Native oral performance and upon what we regard as oral tradition. Considering the paradigms of the culture studies era we find ourselves operating within in twenty-first-century English departments, a critical revolution or two removed from the formalisms of the early- and mid-twentieth century, one might describe some of the propensities of current Native scholars as a neo-formalism, or more specifically, Native formalism.

Formalism is an inherently ambiguous term that the twentieth-century formalists (who often eschewed the label for its connotations of aridity) could never unanimously agree on a definition for. The sense of formalism that I'm referring to here is the idea that *what* a work of literature says cannot be separated from *how* the literary work says it. A formalist, as I understand formalism, would say that the form and structure of a work are, in fact, part of the content of the work, rather than just the package for its content. The rigorous attention to recognized and ancient forms, structural elements, and artistic techniques is prominent in Native literary criticism.

Brooks, for example, extensively uses the forms, tropes, and structures of Sky Woman as a model to explicate not only Brant's and Aupaumut's political philosophies reflected in their prolific writings, but also to ground her own claims that participatory and relational schemes are to be preferred over oppositional schemes in criticizing the world, its people, or the literature we create. She asks, "How might we follow the example of the water animals, of Sky Woman, of Skyholder in our own writing? The academy asks us to think about our careers, our professional progress as individuals, and our production of knowledge, with little regard for our position as members of Native communities. Does this necessitate following Flint's rocky path? How can we ensure that our scholarship does not destroy our mother? What would it mean to participate in criticism, to make our writing participate in and create community?" It is an intriguing reality in Native writing that poets, novelists, and critics hold so tenaciously to the mythos of our respective tribes. Although essentialism has been thoroughly indicted as a negative trend in twentieth-century Native literary criticism, one might regard the tendency to zealously match contemporary literate work with ancient oral forms as an almost universal essence in Native writing. Perhaps this is one area where essentialism, as Craig Womack argues, may not always be a dirty word.

An early example, on the other hand, of how literacy impacts oral tradition is McDonald's "Spectre Essay," which he titled,"The Spectre and the Hunter, a Legend of the Choctaws." My first impression as a reader of the legend in its marvelous handwritten form was that it has a markedly literate quality. Just the fact that a writer of letters has to accomplish so much in the writing that would be accomplished in a face-to-face conversation by gesture, inflection, and other languages of the human body results in the transformation of a story that may have existed viably for centuries only in the memory of tellers.

"The Spectre and the Hunter" is a tale of horror. It is also a cautionary tale that tragically portrays what happens to a tribal member, the great hunter/warrior/athlete, Ko-way-hoom-mah, the Red Tiger, who "questioned the existence of It-tay-bo-lahs [invisible things] and Nan-ish-ta-hool-ahs [witches], and as to Shil-loops [ghosts] he said he had never seen them—then why should he fear them? –Dangerous it is to trifle with beings that walk unseen among us."[5] Even though McDonald interrogates beliefs about witchcraft, labeling them absurd, waning superstitions, he explains that the unnamed young Choctaw narrator of the story has been run out of his hometown after being accused of witchcraft by a conjurer. The narrator remained in his employment, McDonald relates, until he could earn enough money to buy a good rifle and ammunition and emigrate to the new nation in the western Indian Territory. The inescapable implication here is that Choctaw mythic values, and the language forms they reside in, embodied in people like the young storyteller, are moving west, intact with the nation.

"Young men now are not what their fathers have been," the "Legend" claims in its first paragraph, suggesting strongly that the central motif of the story represents cultural values that deserve revival and preservation. Ko-way-hoom-mah's derision of the power of the spirits and his fierce individualism prove to be his downfall. After setting out on a hunting trip accompanied only by his loyal dog, "Ko-way-hoom-mah kindled a fire, and having shared a portion of his provisions with his dog, he spread his deer skin and blanket by the crackling fire, and mused on the adventures of the day already past, and on the probable success of the ensuing one."[6] As he settles into a dreamy state of slumber, soothed by his expectations of the next day's successful hunt, he is startled by a cry in the distance. "He listened with breathless attention," the legend continues, "and in a few minutes he again heard the cry—keen—long—

and piercing, as that which the Tik-ba-hay-kah [leader or conductor] gives in the dance preceding the Ball play."[7] The cry was distinctly human, not animal, even though he could summon no reasonable explanation for its source.

Fearful, he rekindled his fire, folded his blanket around him, and waited, for the voice was evidently approaching his camp. Soon, a ghastly figure emerged from the woods surrounding his campfire. "It seemed to be the figure of a hunter like himself. Its form was tall and gaunt—its features livid and unearthly. A tattered blanket was girded round his waist, and covered his shoulders; and he had what seemed to have been a rifle, the barrel corroded with rust, the stock decayed and rotted, and covered here and there with mushrooms."[8] Ko-way-hoom-mah felt his flesh and hair creep as the spectre advanced and stretched forth his bony hands to the fire, shivering with cold. He fixed his hollow gaze upon the hunter, but spoke not a word. With instinctive courtesy, Ko-way-hoom-mah offered his grim visitor his deerskin as a seat. The spectre shook his head and instead plucked up some briars from the nearby thicket, spread them like a bed by the fire, and reclined as if to fall asleep.

After a tense interval during which Ko-way-hoom-mah was "petrified with mingled fear and astonishment," his dog miraculously begins to speak. "Arise and flee for your life. The spectre now slumbers; should you also slumber you are lost," said the dog. "Arise and flee, while I stay and watch."[9]

Ko-way-hoom-mah takes flight, runs for miles, finally stopping to rest on the banks of a roaring river. He feels safe for a moment, but then he hears the spectre crashing through the woods toward him, with the dog baying in the chase. Ko-way-hoom-mah dives into the stream and swims across the cold current. By the time he reaches the center of the river, the spectre reaches the riverbank and plunges in after him. Ko-way-hoom-mah imagines the macabre ghost glaring at him with glassy eyeballs and reaching for him from the air right above the river with skeleton-like hands. "With a cry of horror, he was about giving up the struggle for life and sinking beneath the waves, when his faithful dog, with a fierce yell, seized upon his master's enemy. After a short and desperate struggle, they both sank, the waters settled over them, and our exhausted hunter reached the shore in safety." Ko-way-hoom-mah returned home an altered man, "shunned the dance and the Ball play, and his former hilarity gave place to a settled melancholy. In about a year after his strange adventure, he joined a war party against a distant enemy and never returned."[10]

It is difficult to determine what McDonald's agenda may be in transcribing a story from the oral tradition and making it the centerpiece of a critical commentary. It is probably what it purports to be—a story that will entertain and instruct an audience and a comparative analysis of how the forms and techniques of Choctaw storytelling stack up against English modes. One thing seems certain. McDonald is fascinated with the interplay of oral and written texts.

Indigenous Criticism: Assimilating English Writing

The only commissioner representing the Choctaw Nation in its treaty with the United States in the winter of 1824–25 who signed his name in English was J. L. McDonald. Other Choctaw commissioners—Moshulatubbee, Robert Cole, Daniel McCurtain, Talking Warrior, Nittackachee, and David Folsom—signed with an 'x' mark, and their names were recorded by a clerk of the treaty conference.[11] This excursion to Washington City has been mentioned most often in history books as the one where two Choctaw chiefs died. Chief Apuckshunubbee died en route to the conference in Marysville, Kentucky, as the result of an accident, and the more famous Chief Pushmataha died of the croup on Christmas Eve, 1824, after indulging in a six-thousand-dollar cornucopia of oysters, liquor, lodging, and other festivities provided by the U.S. government.[12]

The few white people that McDonald had encountered growing up in the old Choctaw Nation in Mississippi had adopted Indian customs and dress. After receiving an education in the English language and experiencing increasing levels of contact with white people, he began to analyze the differences between the two cultures. He was certainly not the first Choctaw to engage in this sort of analysis, but he appears to have been the first to attempt to formally set down such evaluations in writing. Of specific interest to the field of Native American literary criticism are comparisons he makes between English and Choctaw language characteristics and between Choctaw and English storytelling methods and styles. These comparisons are carefully articulated in a ten-page letter to another prominent Choctaw political figure, Peter Perkins Pitchlynn, composed in two dated writing sessions during a cold week in December 1830. McDonald's presentation of a traditional story situated in a critical context is important because, among other reasons, the essay was written *before* the dissolution of the original nation—that is, before the invasion of their land by Europeans.

Virginia Woolf, in a famous essay written in 1942, referred to letter writing as "the humane art," the art "which owes its origin to the love of friends" and its texture to the primacy of the conversational paradigm.[13] McDonald's letters deserve our attention in several degrees of valuation. First, and perhaps foremost, he occupied a vantage point that twenty-first-century literary critics cannot personally experience and that, at best, we can only roughly estimate. McDonald was an important Choctaw intellectual living and writing in a colonial contact zone together with a burgeoning population of white American citizens on the expanding U.S. southwestern frontier in the early nineteenth century.

Mary Louise Pratt, linguist and ethnographer, defines "contact zones" as "social spaces where cultures meet, clash, and grapple with each other, often in contexts of highly asymmetrical relations of power, such as colonialism, slavery, or their aftermaths."[14] In Pratt's view, the concept of the contact zone helps us understand "why subordinate cultures feel invisible, why they may feel self-hatred, why they feel such powerful pressures to be like (or assimilate to) the dominant culture, and why they need to be so resilient and inventive as they find ways to negotiate, resist, or undermine the dominant culture."[15] I find this contact-zone abstraction useful in understanding McDonald's work, except for (at least) one essentially flawed presupposition—that McDonald and his peers assimilated "to" the dominant culture that was treating and litigating Choctaws out of their ancestral homeland in Mississippi. Choctaws were preparing, both materially and culturally, to emigrate to a new sovereign country. On the basis of a reading of his correspondence, it would seem that McDonald's project was more evidently one of active assimilation "of" the English language and the technology of literacy, a lively negotiation with the problems and potentialities inherent to literacy.

Important questions come to mind when examining Choctaw writing from this period. Was McDonald aware that scholars would someday read his letter as an example of comparative literary analysis? Were he and Pitchlynn and others, perhaps, involved in ongoing discourse about the impact of dramatic shifts underway among Choctaws from the oral intellectual traditions to written productions? How do Choctaw and other indigenous letter writings rank in importance with published articles? How do we read these commentaries in the context of political upheavals during the 1820s and 1830s? What can we know about McDonald just from his writing? I believe that at least partial answers to these questions are available from an examination of written correspondence between these members of the first generation of Choctaws to incorporate literacy into their lives as a tool of discourse.

McDonald's letter to Pitchlynn fulfilled a promise he had made "to reduce to writing a tale which I have repeated to you, as illustration of the imaginative powers of our countrymen." McDonald thanked his "esteemed friend" for the "hint that has recalled it to mind: For I am confined to the house by the gloomy weather which prevails without, and a little exercise of the pen will be an agreeable relief." McDonald explains that "The Spectre of the Hunter," was typical of stories he had heard as a child of five or six ("some twenty years since"), when it was the custom of Choctaw boys to assemble together on pleasant summer evenings and tell stories in rotation. "These stories they facetiously styled 'shookha noompas,' or hog stories," he relates, "but the reason why they were so styled, I have now forgotten if I ever knew." He declares that he remembers distinctly a number of these stories, and "compares them with others which I have heard in after years among the white people, and I can truly say that the Indian loses nothing in comparison" (1). He goes on to write that, regarding the stories designed to captivate the attention and enlist the feelings of children, "the Indian has decidedly the advantage."[16]

One could read McDonald's essay as romanticized self-adulation, not criticism at all. His claims about the advantages of Indian stories over the whites' stories are not supported with any textual evidence from white writers or orators, and the only non-Indian title he even mentions is Irving's "Rip Van Winkle," which he alludes to in an ironic postscript at the end of the essay. Nevertheless, the more I read this communication the more I come to believe that McDonald meant it to be, perhaps naively, an enduring essay of comparative language and literature. His argument is discreetly constructed, consciously aimed at contending with the counterargument that his is simply a nostalgic view of a "vanished" culture. The tone of the letter suggests that Choctaw writers are carefully and selectively assimilating the English language and literary styles into older, more established language art forms. The distinction between "assimilating" a contact-zone culture, as opposed to "being assimilated by" a colonial culture, is an important one. This is one of the pivot points in the elaboration of Native literary criticism articulated by Creek novelist and scholar Craig Womack in *Red on Red*. "We need, for example, to recover the nineteenth century," Womack writes, "especially in terms of understanding what Native writers were up to during that time and how their struggles have evolved toward what Indian writers can say in print today, as well as the foundational principles they provide for an indigenous criticism."[17] McDonald seems to be reaching for some of these foundational principles.

"He [the Choctaw storyteller] is in general more familiar with the objects of nature than the white man," McDonald argues, "and hence can enliven his stories with more apposite and striking illustrations."[18] Alluding to previous conversations with Pitchlynn on these issues of technique and epistemology, McDonald writes, "You have remarked how exactly he [the Indian] can name the different trees of the forest, and the almost numberless plants of the field. You know that not a beast ranges the hills, not a reptile crawls on the plains which he cannot name. The fowls that sail the air, and the birds that warble in the grove are equally familiar. In his lonely wanderings, they have become as dear and cherished companions. He has learned all their names and can describe to you their habits and distinctive histories."[19] In a few sentences McDonald sketches a picture of nineteenth-century Indian versions of silvaculture, botany, zoology, and ornithology. I find that this part of McDonald's argument resonates interestingly with Cheryl Suzack's twenty-first-century argument contained in this volume. She calls for a criticism that "eschews the self-evident in critical engagements with Native literary texts to construct instead a form of critical discourse that reads across the genres of literary, legal, and social positioning." McDonald, I think, is saying essentially the same thing. The Choctaw storyteller can enhance his/her stories with "more apposite and striking illustrations" precisely because the telling of stories ranges across a broad geography of arts and sciences, each informing the other. Using Suzack's term, McDonald is "positioning" the typical Choctaw producer of a language art form as one unwilling to divorce the arts from the sciences. He concludes this paragraph with a quantitative estimation of the difference between white and Indian experience and education: "Almost every Indian can do this, and nine tenths of white people cannot."[20]

Trying to be even-handed in his comparative analysis, but without devoting even an entire sentence to the concession, McDonald declares, "I believe that in tales of high imagination the Indians are deficient; but it is, as I conceive, simply for the want of improvement." Perhaps suggesting a direction in national education policy, an arena toward which correspondent Pitchlynn devoted a lot of his professional career energy, McDonald writes, "They have the stamina, if in early life it could be drawn out, cultivated and polished." Turning to a direct comparison of indigenous and colonial languages, the author observes, "There is also, it seems to me, much more force and precision in the Choctaw language, than in English;—or do I only think so because it is my mother tongue? It may not be so varied, so rich as the English language; its vocabulary is far from being so copious; but as far as it goes, is it not stronger, more nervous?"[21]

He supports this admittedly overromanticized claim of linguistic force by explicating in rich detail how a warrior or hunter describes his adventures "with a clearness and distinctness which make you feel as if you had been with him. . . . You become completely identified with the narrator;—in short, you enjoy the pleasures of the chase, without the fatigue."[22] McDonald's central point in this passage is that the selection of animated details by a Choctaw storyteller gives a high degree of presence to his story and creates a clear connection with his audience. Again, he is arguing that technique and form tend to trump content or context as a critical consideration.

These metalinguistic and metadiscursive comments by McDonald, a Choctaw intellectual immersed in the early stages of incorporating literacy into Choctaw intellectual traditions, are crucially important. When any writer, worker, or professional is in the dialectical crunch of blending older conventions with newer conventions, both conventions are laid bare. This is especially true of language conventions, which govern our discourses routinely on a subconscious plane. McDonald is metaphorically standing in a doorway through which are passing into his possession exciting new language art forms. His conviviality in welcoming what he perceives to be the promising potentials of literacy is surprising. There is no evidence in his scrutiny that suggests that he expects literacy to replace orality, or orality to subdue literacy. It is more accurately inferred that he expects each to perform a transforming and edifying work on the other. We may choose to regard this as what Womack refers to as a foundational principle of indigenous criticism.

McDonald's Critical Project

I will interject the important question here: What was J. L. McDonald's purpose in writing what is essentially a ten-page essay on Choctaw storytelling? Why, for example, is there not a single reference to politics as such in this correspondence between two young and prominent Choctaw political leaders, a letter crafted within a tense national setting just two-and-a-half months after the signing of the Treaty of Dancing Rabbit Creek (September 27–28, 1830), which sealed the fate of Choctaw removal from their ancestral homeland? The answer may be that literary criticism is itself very much a political act. Education is an intensely political process of indoctrination. Literary criticism informs these doctrines, not only in the vital terms of what texts are employed in the literacy-based classroom, but also in terms of *how* and *why* these texts are taught. I will speculate that McDonald's and Pitchlynn's stewardly concerns for the integrity of Choctaw institutions and traditions were, in fact, heightened by the impending emigrations, that paramount among a plethora of cultural concerns were the directions they would lead in the reconstitution of the Choctaw Nation west of the Mississippi. Pitchlynn did, in fact, become the primary leader in the establishment of the Choctaw school system in the new Choctaw Nation in what is now Oklahoma.[23]

It seems safe to me to speculate that Pitchlynn's request, *after* the treaty and *before* emigration, for McDonald to begin writing down Choctaw stories and his critical commentary on rhetorical practice, hinged on two important recognitions. The first recognition was that if Choctaws failed to develop their own school curricula, much would be lost in terms of Native epistemology, belief, and practice. The second recognition was that J. L. McDonald was the most gifted and skilled literary person in the nation and was, therefore, the man for the job.

Other than an occasional trapper or trader who had married into the Choctaw Nation, McDonald knew few Europeans as a child, experiencing little but Choctaw tradition, speaking and hearing almost exclusively the Choctaw language. In the spring of 1819, at the urging of chiefs Pushmataha and Moshulatubbee, and with a commitment of tribal monies from them, missionary teachers from the American Board of Commissioners for Foreign Missions opened the first literacy-based school, the Eliot School, on the Yalobusha River in the Choctaw Nation.[24] Like the Cherokees in Georgia, Choctaws felt that assimilating literacy and associated technologies would give them the best odds for maintaining control of their homeland. "Choctaw leaders were eager for education, not Christian salvation," Clara Sue Kidwell writes. "They were willing to follow the civilization policy of the federal government and learn to live with their white neighbors."[25] The advent of Eliot School was likely the first opportunity that McDonald, fifteen years old in 1819, had for learning to read and write in English.

Choctaw scholar D. L. Birchfield reports that while still a teenager McDonald was sent east to study law and lived as a ward in the home of Thomas L. McKenney, who later became commissioner of Indian affairs. After being admitted to the bar, McDonald returned to the Choctaw Nation to see his mother and was appointed to the Choctaw delegation, which departed in late 1824 for treaty negotiations in Washington, D.C. As mentioned earlier, chiefs Apuckshunubbe and Pushmataha both died before the treaty talks started.

Having lost their great elder leaders, the delegation turned to twenty-year-old McDonald, and, according to Birchfield, a lawyer himself, it was McDonald's skill in the complex arguments that prevented the Choctaws from losing in the 1825 treaty what they had gained in the treaty of 1820. Unfortunately, McDonald's untimely death in 1831, nine months after he penned the "Spectre Essay," tragically cut short what surely would have been a stellar career as a lawyer and as a writer.[26]

Another question we may ask of the "Spectre Essay" is "What can we know about J. L. McDonald just from his writing? Letter writing has been termed by various scholars as a dying art.[27] "Lacking a basic instrument for surveying, let alone criticizing, the letter," Leslie Mittleman writes, "scholars have tended to treat collections as discrete entities rather than according to general principles that might elucidate the letter as an art form."[28] In the absence of prescribed methodology, I have found myself studying this and other letters more like a detective: one who examines hard evidence for what it is, while at the same time searching—endeavoring to remain open to "clues" to larger unsolved mysteries.

An examination of the four letters from McDonald to Pitchlynn in the Western History Collection at the University of Oklahoma reveals an interesting feature of the "Spectre Essay." McDonald, in all four letters, exhibits a skilled penmanship as well as a sophisticated command of the English language. The "essay" letter, however, was written in a more beautiful and controlled handwriting and with more careful organization than the other three letters, suggesting perhaps one or more rough drafts before the final letter of December 13–17, 1830, was produced.

Even though "the letter has remained a kind of stepchild of literary affections,"[29] it seems safe to say that McDonald intended his "essay" letter to endure as a work of literature. We can speculate that his intent was to see it published, perhaps in a journal or newspaper. Even more likely, based on McDonald's claim in the December 17 installment that the young man who told him the story entitled "The Spectre of the Hunter" had drawn it from "his store of *shookha noompas*,"[30] he intended to publish a collection of these stories and commentaries. McDonald wrote in one of the more conversational, less literary letters to Pitchlynn, dated March 28, 1831: "I finished the story of the Hunter and the Spectre some time ago, and will send it to you some time or other. But I am not pleased with it on paper."[31] The critical comment on his writing disciplines confirms the "Spectre Essay" as a work in progress that had demanded the careful editing that a physical examination of the documents suggests.

In the section of the essay, which is a preamble to the legend, McDonald describes in great detail the methods employed by a typical Choctaw hunter, and then by a typical Choctaw warrior, in telling the stories of their adventures. Of the first, he writes, "You may have heard a young hunter giving the stirring details of a bear hunt, and what sportsman would not warm with the tale?" McDonald is pointing out here what he regards as a level of universal appeal in this form of storytelling. "The first cry of the dogs—the rushing of the animal through the tangled underwood—the snapping of cane—the confusion of the fight—the inspiring calls of the hunter—and the death scene when gun after gun is discharged into the head of the bear." The exposition of essential elements of style, rhetorical delivery, and the estimation of audience impact enumerated by McDonald, I would argue, are features of an analytical criticism. Our critic concludes the hunter storytelling paragraph with an emphatic statement of comparative analysis: "According to Indian custom:—all is told with a clear connection, and depicted with a vividness, which I should despair of hearing in the English language."[32] If McDonald had not died young, it would have been fascinating and valuable to see how this claim would have been fleshed out in subsequent analyses.

McDonald then turns to the story-narrating techniques of a warrior to further support his claim that Indian storytelling is, in important aspects, superior to its counterpart in English. "He shall be a warrior in the prime of life—not young, nor yet aged. . . . Imagine him returned from his war expedition."[33] McDonald flexes his critical muscles by asking the reader to "imagine" he/she is hearing the oral presentation. I believe McDonald is conscious of the metadiscursive quality of his evaluations at this point in the essay. In other words, he is engaged with perhaps the most enthralling feature of criticism—that it is discourse about discourse—in this case, writing to readers (the practice of literacy) about a story being told to another audience (oral discourse). "He is seated; his friends are around him, silent but attentive; not one obtruding a question; but all waiting for his pleasure to begin."[34] McDonald infuses his essay with the sense of theater that is such an integral part of the storytelling/hearing experience. Actors have told me that a stage play is relatively meaningless in rehearsal, that a play takes its fully intelligible form as art only in the presence of an audience. Further, they say that different audiences substantially alter the overall experience, resulting in the pleasant organic feel of live acting.

McDonald seeks to convey the organic-dynamic of Choctaw storytelling/hearing to a reader of inscribed language. This is a bold critical move in my opinion. With the finesse of a playwright, McDonald combines what might be regarded as set directions and script in his example:

> He has just smoked his pipe, and adjusts himself for the narration. He tells of the days and nights he travelled before he approached the hunting ground of his enemy. He describes the different objects he saw in his route, the streams he crossed, and his camping places. Here he killed a bear, there a buffalo.He marks on the ground a rude map of the country, to give a better idea of his travels. He describes where he first discovered the trail of his enemy. In such a quarter lay their town; here he concealed himself until he should discover some straggling foe. He

> describes the rivulet that quenched his thirst and the tree that sheltered him. Not an incident is forgotten; and every incident heightens the interest of his perilous situation.

McDonald's story of the warrior's story continues in marvelous and compelling detail. The protagonist determines to elude his enemies if possible but is prepared to die like a warrior if conflict is unavoidable. "He puts in requisition every wile and stratagem of which he is master," McDonald continues. "At length he discovers an Indian, recognizable as foe by his painted face and peculiar head dress."[35]

At this point in the story of a story, I, a twenty-first-century reader, am hanging on every word of this page-turner. "Our warrior crouches low, takes a deadly aim, and brings. . . ." Tragically, in my view, the next page of McDonald's manuscript is missing. I prayed that the archivist had simply failed to copy one of the pages, but upon returning to the collection and reviewing the original manuscript, I found that, alas, that page was, in fact, not there. We may never know what his conclusions were on that final page in this first half of the essay. He had already made his case convincingly, however, for the potency of Choctaw orality.

Fortunately, the last half of the essay, containing the text of "The Spectre of the Hunter," is complete, intact. In his introduction to that second part of the essay, the section dated December 17, 1830, containing the legend, McDonald reiterates that his project is "an attempt to prove that our vernacular tongue is more expressive than the English." Implying communality with Pitchlynn in the rhetorical undertaking, he asks a powerful question concerning rhetorical sovereignty:[36] "Should you coincide with me in opinion who shall gainsay our decision?" He then addresses the problem of competing criticism. "It may indeed be said that parties interested will generally decide in their own favour. But let the question for the present rest."[37]

Letters as Literature

The question no longer rests. A great deal of brain power has been expended in this era of culture studies to create what Robert Warrior terms a praxis, or guiding principles, for delineating Native intellectual histories. "After more than two centuries of impressive literary and critical production," he writes, "critical interpretation of those writings can proceed primarily from Indian sources."[38] Warrior's scholarship has been influential in laying the groundwork for reading across time and genre barriers in Native literature. This approach to texts "provides a new historical and critical site that invites us to see contemporary work as belonging to a process centuries long, rather than decades long, of engaging contours of Indian America,"[39] Warrior argues. Debates occur and recur in English, social science and humanities departments across the country in which scholars brood over how to classify and criticize Native literature. Broad definitions of intrinsically problematic terms like American studies and Native American studies cast stumbling blocks into our pathways. In a narrower sense, however, all literature scholars grapple with the questions governing our judgments of "What is literary?" Can readers regard J. L. McDonald's letter essay as literary, for example, and if judged literary, how do such writings rank or compare with published articles and books?

By way of comparing things literary, McDonald's framing of "stories within stories" immediately brings to my mind a couple of N. Scott Momaday's well-known works and also *Heart of Darkness* by Joseph Conrad. In *House Made of Dawn* and *The Names,* Momaday frames his stories in more or less present time within the bookends of ancient myth. In *Heart of Darkness*, five men sit on board the *Nellie*, a boat docked on the Thames. An unnamed narrator introduces the four other characters besides himself to the reader: the owner of the boat, a lawyer, an accountant, and Charlie Marlow. The author lets Marlow's story of his journey into the African jungle spin out of their casual conversation.

Similarly, in his introduction to the "Spectre Essay," McDonald claims that the legend was told to him by a young orphaned Choctaw while employed in his household. McDonald writes:

> He worked with us faithfully during the busy part of the season, and with the avails of his labour, purchased a good rifle and ammunition, and started west of the Mississippi. During his stay with us, I found he was remarkably intelligent for his opportunities. He did not speak a word of English. His father and mother, as he informed me, were both dead; and he had but few near relatives living. He had been charged with witchcraft by a conjurer of his neighborhood—(I am glad this absurd superstition is wearing away among the Choctaws)—and had been obliged to fly from the nation to save his life. This young man frequently entertained us with tales during the intervals of labour. He possessed an easy flowing elocution and from his store of "shookha noompas" one evening told us the following story.[40]

Again, McDonald cleverly employs several rhetorical devices to historicize and legitimate the legend. Overall, in this passage, he accomplishes three, essentially literary, tasks.

First, and perhaps most importantly, our author connects the story being told in the present with the past and with the future of Choctaw artistic/intellectual and mythic tradition. The young, monolingual storyteller's harrowing escape from "his neighborhood" after being accused of witchcraft (a capital offense) by a conjurer rhetorically certifies his placement squarely within the heart of Choctaw mythic tradition. Furthermore, it places him definitively *outside* the English language and other European discourses. "Purchasing a good rifle and ammunition" for his journey to the new nation west of the Mississippi serves to rhetorically and materially "transport" that mythic tradition and its store of story forms, structures, and tropes into the future. McDonald leaves no gaps that would require an imaginative stretch to make this interpretation of rhetorical purpose.

Second, McDonald places *himself*, the critic, within this tightly connected stream of Choctaw intellectual history. He not only cites how mainstream ("this young man frequently entertained us") these stories are within the leisure schedule of his family, but also harks back to the December 13 half of the essay in which he declared the importance of the *shookha noompas* tradition in his own boyhood.

Third, he establishes his essay, essentially a critical analysis of a story within a story, as a work of literature. *Webster's Unabridged Dictionary* defines "literary" as "appropriate to literature rather than everyday speech or writing." That lexicon defines "literature," in one of its important senses, as "the class of writings distinguished for beauty of style or expression, as poetry, essays, or history, in distinction from scientific treatises which contain positive knowledge." Certainly, in my view at least, McDonald's essay fits both definitions. In this passage just set forth, he contextualizes the legend within an ancient oral tradition, within a complex contemporaneous cultural and political landscape, within the materializing future landscape of the Choctaw Nation West, and within a tradition inherently implicit in what he is practicing—the written tradition. These are brilliantly self-conscious and self-critical moves.

I will finish the discussion here by examining the epilogic remarks McDonald makes at the end of the legend, which serve as the conclusion of the "Spectre Essay." "Such, my dear sir, is the substance of the tale as related to me; and as I review what I have written, it seems to me faint and feeble compared with the animated and vivid touches of my Choctaw narrator,"[41] McDonald writes. Again self-conscious, McDonald alludes to the reflective and recursive problems of literacy compared to the enlivened discourse of the storyteller. This is, he continues, "another evidence which I might assign of the superior force of our own vernacular, were I not aware that it might be said (perhaps very justly) that I am ignorant of the force and power of the English language, and therefore, not a competent judge."[42] With this thinly modest caveat, wholly confounded by the force and power most readers would have perceived in what they had just read in English, he signs off the essay with a typical epistolary closing sentiment to Pitchlynn. In a postscript, however, he references "a singular story" he once read "of one Rip Van Winkle, who went out hunting and, feeling somewhat fatigued, lay down to take a nap. His nap it seems proved to be a long one; for when he awoke, he found his gun covered with mushrooms. I remember having been particularly struck with the 'mushroom gun' in my Indian's story—and I think I can safely affirm he had never heard of Rip Van Winkle."[43] In the end, perhaps more so in 1830 when Washington Irving's tale was fresher and more popular than today, the reader is presented with a captivatingly literary twist.

Striking parallels, in fact, exist between "The Spectre of the Hunter" and

Irving's short story. In spite of dramatically different settings and characterizations, both are tales of men who wander off alone, except for the companionship of their loyal dogs, experience encounters with supernatural beings, and return home to tell their stories. Both stories, as McDonald points out in his postscript, contain the symbolically rusty, timeworn rifle. Irving frames his tale of "Rip Van Winkle," published in 1819–1820 in *The Sketch Book of Sir Geoffrey Crayon, Gent,* as a "discovery" within the (obviously fictional) posthumous writings of Diedrich Knickerbocker. McDonald's oral tradition story is similarly situated within the voice of a shadowy narrator, the unnamed young Choctaw sojourner.

Ultimately, McDonald's highly ironic postscript leaves his essay wide open to a variety of interpretations. Perhaps McDonald's recording of the legend, as told by the young Choctaw outcast, is entirely a fiction—not simply a fiction, but a Choctaw revision or parody of Irving's "Rip Van Winkle." McDonald immediately subverts this tempting explanation, however, by disavowing the possibility of a direct connection between the two short stories. If not a parody, or an example of Choctaw assimilation of an English language story, then perhaps McDonald is highlighting the humanistic similarities between stories crafted primarily for children springing from seemingly diverse cultures. McDonald's allusions to "Rip Van Winkle" remind me of what Acqumeh poet laureate Simon Ortiz observes in his famous essay about the Native nationalistic impulse—how his people had absorbed and transformed Catholic rituals received from the Spanish into their own celebrations and art forms. This "speaks of the creative ability of Indian people," Ortiz writes, "to gather in many forms of the socio-political colonizing force which beset them and to make these forms meaningful in their own terms."[44] Whatever his intent in his references to "Rip Van Winkle," McDonald leaves the nineteenth-century, or the twenty-first-century, reader or critic much to imagine in terms of language, tradition, and literature.

The Ethic

It must have taken most, if not all, of us a while to get into the conversation that this book set out to be. Writing within the individualistic confines of my university office, like a monk in an abbey, I felt the *individual* honor of being asked to join the group of notable scholars writing for this volume. But what I felt was the typical self-conscious, competitive, and hierarchical honor that so pervades the academic experience. Embarrassingly, my motive to write more or less evaded the concern for Indian people as communities, and as *a community*, that propelled me—after another professional career and after raising a family—to enter the academy in the first place. The conversation imperative never fully crystallized in my thinking until I read Daniel Justice's confession in the second formal revision of his essay, "Go Away, Water!: Kinship Criticism and the Decolonization Imperative" (this volume). He writes, "This essay is written in Fire; it's about relationships and the attentive care we give to the ongoing processes of balanced rights and responsibilities that keep kinship going in a good way. Kinship, like Fire, is about life and living; it's not about something that *is* in itself so much as something we *do*—actively, thoughtfully, respectfully."

I expect that every essayist in the volume was moved by this passage, and for good reason. Only after we have considered the epistemologies of our ancestors, our kin, especially epistemologies reflected in writing, do we fully realize what Lisa Brooks regards as the regenerative power of the written word. And only after this realization do we realize the primacy in language of the conversational paradigm. It is by, and only by, engaging in fruitful conversation that we guarantee the survival and flourishing of our communities.

I recently heard a sage and respected scholar from another component of the University of Oklahoma English department say that the next new wave of theory after postmodernism will be ethics. I do not wish to fully explicate the idea, but I think she meant, translated into Indian, something like what follows. Postmodern theorists feel more or less comfortable in trashing old reliable metanarratives like the Bible or Sky Woman, by asserting the hybrid unreliability of individual subject identities, like Native American or feminist. The postmodern paradigm further succeeds in reducing the historically central concept in the United States of the individual from a civic-minded voting capitalist to a lone wolf in chaos. If ethics is the codes, laws, or just rules of thumb that govern our discourses, forming an invisible cement that holds social groups like Native lit crit specialists together, then groups composed of lone wolves in chaos are in big trouble. This is the case because the first goal of any group must be to agree on its ethics, if it desires to be, and to continue to be, viable. I'm going the long way around to arrive at the point I want to repeat and emphasize. We can't have coherent ethics without coherent conversation. We couldn't be having a coherent conversation in an overly competitive, anticonversational, and purely individualistic collection of essays. Like postmodernism will find that its most constraining dismissal is that of ethical talk, Native literary critics must not speak and listen just to a screen but must, like the nineteenth-century Choctaw writers examined here, speak and listen to each other.

It is an ignoble tribute to the success of the United States' westward expansion that it has taken James L. McDonald's essay 175 years to come to its first published use as a critical text. On the other hand, the fact that McDonald and his peers heartily engaged literacy and allowed the new technology to amplify an already rich language arts tradition should stand as a credit to their generation and as an inspiration to ours. Craig Womack declares in his treatise on Creek national literature that "without Native American literature, *there is no American canon*."[45] Osage critic Robert Warrior asserts that sovereignty is a way of life and a decision, "a decision we make in our minds, in our hearts, and in our bodies—to be sovereign and to find out what that means in the process."[46] Similarly, in his epistolary conversation with Peter Pitchlynn, J. L.

McDonald asks his colleague concerning their critical project: "Should you coincide with me in opinion, who shall gainsay our decision?"[47]

Indeed, I certainly coincide in opinion and decision with McDonald, though I claim no "radical incommensurability" in how a reader or critic outside the Choctaw Nation might read Choctaw literature. I do, nonetheless, claim knowledge and an aesthetic and intellectual trajectory that are mine and that I share with my kin. Choctaw novelist LeAnne Howe (this volume) describes this trajectory as a "tribalography" that "comes from the native propensity for bringing things together, for making consensus, and for symbiotically connecting one thing to another. It's a cultural bias, if you will."[48] I say that it is our right as free intellects, our privilege as Choctaws, and our duty to our local and professional communities to criticize, interpret, and integrate our present, past, and future tribal literatures as we walk a centuries-old road.

J. L. McDonald probably didn't learn all he knew about critical analysis in Mississippi missionary schools or in Ohio law offices. The confident tone with which he delivers his critiques strongly suggests that his ideas and ours are part of an ongoing, perhaps ancient, discourse—a discourse that in his day was admirably coming to terms with literacy. Especially in what sometimes seems like an overly legalistic debate, precedent is important. An appeal to precedent is rooted in the human desire not to reargue issues that were settled in the past. McDonald's treatment of Choctaw literature is a commendable attempt to establish a clearly outlined ethic—that Choctaw intellectuals are uniquely and peculiarly qualified to evaluate Choctaw literature. What is called for, further, is perhaps a blend of Native formalist discourse that acknowledges and articulates the irresistibly powerful story forms and mythic structures that determine, as they should, a lot of what Native authors write with the poststructuralist notions of a freeplay of signifiers that help us interrogate and destabilize obstinate residues of colonialism, which constrain our work not only as human beings trying to contribute to healthy communities but as critics carrying out the missions of scholarship.

Notes

1. Justice, "Indigenizing the Post-Apocalyptic Frontier," 1.
2. Apess, *Indian Nullification*, 179–80.
3. Robert Warrior, *People and the Word*, v.
4. Ibid.
5. McDonald to Pitchlynn, December 13–17, 1830 (hereafter D13–17), 5.
6. Ibid., 6.
7. Ibid., 7.
8. Ibid., 7–8.
9. Ibid., 9.
10. Ibid.
11. Debo, *Rise and Fall*, 51.

12. Ibid., 50.
13. Woolf, *Death of the Moth*, 58.
14. Pratt, "Arts of the Contact Zone," 530.
15. Ibid., 531.
16. D13–17, 1, 2.
17. Womack, *Red on Red*, 3.
18. D13–17, 2.
19. Ibid.
20. Ibid.
21. Ibid.
22. Ibid., 3.
23. Pitchlynn's role in establishing the new Choctaw Nation's school system, as well as the interesting politics of reconstituting an entire nation, is richly detailed in Baird, *Peter Pitchlynn*.
24. Kidwell, *Choctaws and Missionaries*, 30–38.
25. Ibid., 28.
26. Birchfield, *Oklahoma Basic Intelligence Test*, 165–67.
27. See, for example, Guillen, "On the Edge of Literariness," 1–24.
28. Mittleman, "Is Letter-Writing a Dying Art?" 221–26.
29. Ibid.
30. D13–17, 6.
31. McDonald to Pitchlynn, March 28, 1831, 3.
32. D13–17, 3.
33. Ibid.
34. Ibid., 4.
35. Ibid.
36. Lyons, "Rhetorical Sovereignty," 449–50. Lyons defines rhetorical sovereignty as "the inherent right and ability of peoples to determine their own communicative needs and desires in this pursuit [of self-determination], to decide for themselves the goals, modes, styles, and languages of public discourse."
37. D13–17, 6.
38. Robert Warrior, *Tribal Secrets*, xvi.
39. Ibid., 2.
40. D13–17, 7.
41. Ibid., 12.
42. Ibid.
43. Ibid.
44. Simon Ortiz, "Towards a National Indian Literature," 8–19.
45. Womack, *Red on Red*, 7.
46. Robert Warrior, *Tribal Secrets*, 123.
47. D13–17, 6.
48. Howe, "Story of America," 42.

"Go Away, Water!"

Kinship Criticism and the Decolonization Imperative

DANIEL HEATH JUSTICE

It was the unlikely alliance of the Thunders and Water Spider that brought Fire to the world. The world was wet, cold, and cheerless in those days. Taking pity on the Animals who shivered in the darkness (this was before the time of Humanity), the Thunders sent lightning to the Middle World, where it burned in a hollow log on an island. The Animals tried to get Fire, but each was unprepared for the dangers of the strange red glow: it singed Raven's feathers a glossy black, scarred Screech Owl's face, and ringed the eyes of other Owls with clinging black soot. Other Animals made the attempt, but those who did always returned to their companions in soggy defeat, their bodies charred and blackened from the strange smoke and heat.

At last, when all the larger Animals had failed, the little Water Spider made the attempt. She didn't have Raven's swiftness or Blacksnake's agility, but she had a gift that was unlike anything her friends had: she knew how to weave. For a long time she drew the silk from her body, weaving it into a stout translucent bowl, broad in the center and tapered slightly at the top. When she was satisfied that the bowl would serve her purpose, she skittered across the waters, grabbed a hot coal of the lightning-struck wood, dropped it into her silken bowl, and carried it on her back to the others.

Water Spider could have hidden this rare and wondrous warmth from the others; she could have dropped it into the water to punish the other Animals for doubting her, for scorning this small, shy creature who was so easy to overlook and dismiss. But she honored her kinship obligations and brought Fire to share with all the Animals in the Middle World. Fire gave warmth and light; the cold shadows now had a limit to their reach. Darkness didn't disappear when Fire

---

*Daniel Heath Justice, a member of the Cherokee Nation, was raised in the mining town of Victor, Colorado. He now lives in Toronto, Ontario, where he teaches aboriginal literatures and aboriginal studies at the University of Toronto. He is the author of a book-length study of Cherokee literature—*Our Fire Survives the Storm: A Cherokee Literary History*—as well as the indigenous fantasy trilogy,* The Way of Thorn and Thunder.

came to the Animals; it still stalks at the edge of the flickering light, greedier now that it has resistance.

But our eyes ever seek the firelight through the shadows. This is the gift of the Thunders and Water Spider: we want to join others around the dancing flames, not wander alone in the dark waters of the night.

This essay is written in Fire; it's about relationships and the attentive care we give to the ongoing processes of balanced rights and responsibilities that keep kinship going in a good way. Kinship, like Fire, is about life and living; it's not about something that *is* in itself so much as something we *do*—actively, thoughtfully, respectfully.

This essay is one part of a larger project that puts kinship principles in practice. In this essay, my aims are threefold: to propose the interpretive significance of the relationship between kinship, peoplehood, and decolonization; to employ the concerns of this mutually affecting relationship as a critical lens through which to regard recent controversies in Native literary criticism; and to offer reflections on the complicated possibilities promised by work that attends to similar concerns.

This essay speaks to others in the volume; the texts (and their authors) are also engaged in a relationship and a community. Together we respond to the ideas and questions of other Native literary critics; we travel through the imaginative mindscapes of indigenous writers; we respond to the driving call for decolonization that echoes through those mindscapes; we attend to many of the values and concerns of our families and tribal nations.

Yet we write in Fire. This book isn't the allotted boundary of the conversation. The pages are brittle and crumble to dust or ash too easily; they don't share anything on their own. We have to be the ones to feed them, to take them beyond white space and root them—and ourselves—in rich red earth and memory.

We have to give voice to Fire, even if it means our tongues will burn.

"Go Away, Water!"

In her analysis of Seminole continuity in what is now Florida, *The Tree That Bends: Discourse, Power, and the Survival of the Maskókî People*, Patricia Riles Wickman relates the following episode: "In 1736 . . . ostensibly Christianized Natives left Spanish hegemony, both ideologically and geographically, when a viable alternative presented itself. They transferred their allegiance to the British, because the British offered them arms and more trade goods and did not require them to commit cultural suicide in order to get those things. Baptized Natives simply struck themselves on the forehead saying, "Go away water! I am no Christian!"[1]

This event intrigues me for a couple of reasons. First, it's a (literally) striking example of indigenous agency and self-determination, wherein outside impositions are named, defined, and challenged in a ritual repudiation of Christian baptism. Second, and no less important, is the way in which this concise ritual of verbal exorcism and physical action—and with it, the implied return of indigenous specificity—speaks to one of the larger goals of this collection, namely, the turn of the critical discussions in indigenous literatures to the centrality of indigenous contexts, both through a direct response to those creeds and definitions that have been imposed upon Native peoples and through the affirmation of a renewed way of understanding the ethical relationship between the critic and indigenous literatures.

In thinking of an ethical Native literary criticism, it seems to me to be quite fruitful to reflect on community and kinship—both in their broadly theoretical forms and in their context-specific manifestations—as interpretive concepts in our analyses. In this way, we can be fully attentive to the endurance of indigenous peoples against the forces of erasure and determine, in various ways, how the survival of indigenous peoples is strengthened by the literature we produce and the critical lenses through which we read them.

Toward that end, I want to return again to Wickman's account. Its inclusion is not provided simply as a critique of Christianity, even though I generally tend to take a rather jaded view of all monotheistic traditions, and this particular creed's militant impacts on the world. Neither is it the symbolism of water itself that is being rejected; indeed, the ritual of "going to water" was and remains one of the most significant components of the Muscogeean ceremonial calendar shared among traditional Creeks, Seminoles, Cherokees, and other southeastern nations.[2] Rather, I read the episode above as an empowered response to the forced *imposition* of any outside definition—here, the coercive transformative ritual of Christian baptism—and the accompanying assertion of self-definition.[3]

Similarly, in applying the example to the realm of the literary, this isn't a slam against a wide range of interpretive lenses, either, for, like the example of Christianity, it's much less about which lens we choose to read through than it is about which options are available to us, and how clear or distorted our understanding may be depending on the choice we make. I'm a literary nationalist, but I've never believed that literary nationalism is the only intellectually defensible way to approach a thoughtful understanding of indigenous literatures. On the other hand, principles of nationhood and the tribal-specific study of our own texts certainly have an important role to play in the analysis, interpretation, and dissemination of indigenous literatures—particularly if there is any hope of making such study relevant to Native communities and the larger issues of concern to the indigenous Americas. Such relevance can only take place in an intellectual environment wherein respect and equality are guiding principles.

Thus, to my mind, "Go away, water!" isn't a statement or ritual that's fundamentally about rejection, because rejection for its own sake is ultimately impotent and self-defeating. Rather, it's about shifting away from the terms of "cultural suicide" that Wickman notes above, and opening room for the return of those models of self-determination that speak to the survival and presence of indigenous *peoples*, not simply the durability of individuals of indigenous ancestry. Certainly, to open that space, we have to uproot those rank ideologies of fragmentation that have defined us and our scholarship against our will, which lay claim to our words but offer little but angst and alienation in exchange. We have to challenge the idea that the hyperindividualist creeds of industrialization and atomization are the wellsprings of intellectual sophistication. Indigenous intellectual traditions have survived not because they've conceded to fragmenting Eurowestern priorities, but because they've *challenged* those priorities.We exist today as indigenous nations, as peoples, and the foundation of any continuity as such is our relationships to one another—in other words, our kinship with other humans and the rest of creation. Such kinship isn't a static thing; it's dynamic, ever in motion. It requires attentiveness; kinship is best thought of as a verb rather than a noun, because kinship, in most indigenous contexts, is something that's *done* more than something that simply *is*. As such, the relationship of our literatures to our communities—and the role of that relationship in ensuring the continuity of indigenous nations into the future—is the primary interest of this exploratory essay, and, indeed, the larger collection as a whole.

Peoplehood and the Decolonization Imperative

Literary expression—in its broadest and most inclusive definition—is a profoundly powerful exercise of the ways in which that relationship is made manifest. This is the heart of the decolonization imperative of indigenous literatures: the storied expression of continuity that encompasses resistance while moving beyond it to an active expression of the living relationship between the People and the world. Spokane writer Gloria Bird reminds us that "writing remains more than a catharsis; at its liberating best, it is a political act. Through writing we can undo the damaging stereotypes that are continually perpetuated about Native peoples. We can rewrite our history, and we can mobilize our future."[4]

The decolonization imperative in our literature both *reflects* indigenous continuity of the past and present and *projects* that continuity into the future. Stories—like kinship, like fire—are what we do, what we create, as much as what we are.[5] Stories expand or narrow our imaginative possibilities—physical freedom won't matter if we can't imagine ourselves free as well. To assert our self-determination, to assert our presence in the face of erasure, is to free ourselves from the ghost-making rhetorics of colonization. Stories define relationships, between nations as well as individuals, and those relationships imply presence—you can't have a mutual relationship between something and nothingness.

Indigenous nationhood is predicated on this understanding of relationship. The idea of "the nation" has fallen into disfavor over the last decade; it's no longer viewed by most scholars as an inevitable or even desirable way of constituting group identity. Yet for indigenous peoples in North America and elsewhere, community is the constitutive measurement of selfhood. Indigenous nationhood should not, however, be conflated with the nationalism that has given birth to industrialized nation-states. Nation-state nationalism is often dependent upon the erasure of kinship bonds in favor of a code of assimilative patriotism that places, and emphasizes, the militant history of the nation above the specific geographic, genealogical, and spiritual histories of peoples.

Indigenous nationhood is more than simple political independence or the exercise of a distinctive cultural identity; it's also an understanding of a common social interdependence within the community, the tribal web of kinship rights and responsibilities that link the People, the land, and the cosmos together in an ongoing and dynamic system of mutually affecting relationships. It isn't predicated on essentialist notions of unchangeability; indeed, such notions are rooted in primitivist Eurowestern discourses that locate indigenous peoples outside the flow and influences of time. In his contribution to this book, Creek scholar Tol Foster addresses this dynamic state of being (and the presumptions of agents of nation-state nationalism) with enviable clarity. He writes:

> Others who act on tribal people will certainly be considered Other, but they will not be considered "modern" against some sort of tribal premoderns. This is a construct, we should notice, of the antitribal nation-state, which wishes to posit historical breaks as a way of building up an incommensability between then and now, just as tribal stories often construct a vague rupture between now and the time when crucial myths were in play. That was then, but this is now, we hear the government judge proclaim, but for tribal people, such explanations are inadequate, and indeed dangerous. Following from Native epistemology we must add to such narratives of difference the notion of the relational. History and events are part of the story, but they are not the determinate parts. Relations are the primary axis through which we can understand ourselves and each other.

Agents of change exist in relationship to one another and demonstrate by those interactions their ability to both influence others and to be self-determining; as Foster points out, the representations of Indians as absolute Others relegates us to the role of museum artifacts of ever-diminishing authenticity. The recognition of some sort of relationship between and among peoples—the ever-contextual contours of kinship—returns us to the physical realm of the participatory. At their best, these relationships extend beyond the human to encompass degrees of kinship with other peoples, from the plants and animals to the sun, moon, thunder, and other elemental forces. The central focus of indigenous nationhood, then, is on *peoplehood* (or, to use Chickasaw scholar Amanda Cobb's term, *peopleness*), the relational system that keeps the people in balance with one another, with other peoples and realities, and with the world. Nationhood is the political extension of the social rights and responsibilities of peoplehood.

Peoplehood, too, is the abiding concern of indigenous literatures. Jace Weaver (Cherokee) defines this emphasis as "communitism"—a synthesis of "community" and "activism" that implies an active, participatory engagement in the creation and maintenance of a people as a culturally distinctive body. Under this definition, community isn't a stable or static group of people; rather, it's an ever-adaptive state of being that requires its members to maintain it through their willingness to perform the necessary rituals—spiritual, physical, emotional, intellectual, and familial—to keep the kinship network in balance with itself and the rest of creation. The ground is always shifting, the People are always responding to change within and without, new challenges require new or revised responses. A community—with all its constituent members and social concerns, past and present—is alive, and the People are responsible for its survival through attention to their kinship rights and responsibilities and through their response to the continuity fueled by the decolonization imperative.

Though related, the decolonization imperative is not the root of indigenous peoplehood and self-determining sovereignty, as Amanda Cobb, points out: "[A]lthough the journey of sovereignty moves from survival to continuance, taking into account the colonization experience and providing for decolonization, it is important to note that sovereignty and decolonization are not synonymous terms. Tribal sovereignty existed before colonization and does (or will depending on your point of view) exist after colonization. Sovereignty is *the going on* of life—the living. The path to survival and the path to continuance each consist of more than 'step' or what I choose to call, 'action,' a term I use to underscore Native agency in a given moment or context."[6] The decolonization imperative gives fuel to sovereignty and continuity, but without "the going on" that Cobb addresses, it runs the risk of being merely reactionary, not creative or transformative. At its best, peoplehood is shaped by relationships and lived purpose, fueled by a desire to create something that will last beyond the pains of oppression. Indigenous writing, in this context, is both an act of love for the People and the product of that love, whether it speaks of joy and possibility or pain and alienation. "Going on" is more than endurance; it is, as Cobb demonstrates in her analysis of the work of Acoma Pueblo poet Simon Ortiz, the expression of a sovereignty of hope and possibility.

The intersections between community, continuity, and purpose, then, seem a useful relational constellation to analyze in an essay on ethical Native literary criticism. If peoplehood is a fundamental concern of our literature, then it follows that it should also be a fundamental concern of our criticism of that literature. Native critics have responsibilities to our tribal nations, but we also have responsibilities to the broader community of Native literary studies, and it's the latter that is sometimes the most vexing and difficult to navigate, as the individualist ethos of Eurowestern academe doesn't fit very smoothly with the communitistic principles of indigenous nationhood. Yet we must find a way to travel these difficult waters if we have any hope of bringing the study of literature and the social concerns of indigenous peoples together in a meaningful way.

Of course, broad notions like "community," "people," and "nation" are tricky to work with. We can't very well use them without immediately qualifying them: Each community is different; no community is monolithic and without dissent or even conflicting ideas about what exactly constitutes the group; the principles underlying tribal nationhood aren't necessarily those that give rise to the nationalism of industrialized nation-states; and so on. Yet we can still talk about ideals as functional principles without erasing the specific contexts in which those principles operate; though members of a group might differ in their understandings of that community's composition, they nonetheless work to articulate the shifty, unstable, but ultimately embodied notion of purposeful collectivity.

It's this struggle between different definitions of community that interests me, and the spaces between, within, and among those definitions. For example, this volume is an engagement with multiple communities: those of our respective tribal nations as well as the larger field of Native literary criticism and the smaller group of Native scholars participating in the project. All the contributors have read the essays of others and have revised their work with the words and ideas of the others firmly in mind. These community influences have, to varying degrees, shaped both the questions we've asked and our responses. Some of the early contributors weren't able to participate in the final version, but their ideas, too, were invaluable in our collective considerations. We don't speak with a unified voice, even on a topic as ostensibly straightforward as proposing an ethical literary criticism, and the differences give as much shape to the broader concern as the similarities.

Similarly, early in my studies of the Cherokee literary tradition, I realized that my initial supposition that there was a single, unitary idea of "Cherokeeness" was both naive and, ultimately, impossible, especially given the long and tangled realities of Cherokee social history. Yet I also came to realize that though there are many different ways of understanding what it is to be Cherokee—some more suited to the preservation of Cherokee nationhood, communitism, and decolonization than others—each way is still an attempt to give shape to an idea of what it is to be, think, and live Cherokee. Thus, easy assertions of a unitary definition break down, and the complicated living realities of the Cherokee people are revealed. The definitions might differ, but all the definitions still speak to the idea of Cherokeeness. The fires of Cherokee nationhood still burn: around the kitchen table, in the council house, in the churches, in the ceremonial grounds, and in the classroom.

As a literary critic studying literature in which metaphor and symbolism are so powerfully evocative, I too easily fall back upon uncritical language, assume an easy, uncomplicated certainty that so rarely exists in the messy realities of life. We can talk about words giving shape to meaning, literature as a social force that can enhance our sovereignty, poetry as rebellion, without ever really grappling with all the difficulties of those assertions. I did it with the earlier drafts of this essay, and I'm probably doing it now, too, in spite of my cautious hopes otherwise. It's the bigger concepts—the ones we so often assume to have a uniform meaning among all readers—that really get us into difficulties. What happens, for example, when a concept like sovereignty shifts from indigenous empowerment and responsibility and is instead used as a hammer to stifle dissent within the community, especially when it comes from client chiefs and sell-out council members who feel a larger obligation to the colonialist nation-state than to the dignified survival of their own people? What happens when appeals to "tradition" are used to justify bigotry, abuse, neglect, or corruption, or when the traditions of one indigenous community are used to dismiss the very existence of other indigenous peoples? What do we do when Eurowestern values of individualism, antagonistic dualism, and market-driven commodification and commercialism replace older traditions of sacred kinship, communal concern, and complementarity, thus becoming the de facto constitutive traditions of the community? We can advocate the contextualized principles of political sovereignty and tradition without assuming that political independence or appeals to a context-specific tradition alone will be the cure-all for Native empowerment, or that empowerment without ethical consideration or reflection is inevitably a good thing. Those kinds of certainty are comforting in the short term—and for those who desire power over others—but they are ultimately ineffective in revealing truth, giving respectful voice to experience, or pushing us to face the big challenges facing indigenous peoples today.

Indigenous communities are shaped by principles of kinship, and kinship itself is a delicate web of rights and responsibilities. In order to explore ethical criticism, we have to be prepared for complexity and eschew simplistic explanations that do little to illuminate the world and much to obscure it; the texts I examine here—both within the larger collection and beyond it—are intended to be more suggestive of complexity than to be sweeping or comprehensive in scope. Similarly, I engage here with texts about Indian identity more to question their significance to issues of kinship than to privilege notions of "race," which are fundamentally incompatible with indigenous epistemologies.

Rather than simply presenting a linear list of ethical considerations for Native literary scholars, I'm interested in a more philosophical reflection on current indigenous realities and the possibilities for a responsible relationship between the sociopolitical realities of Native America and the literary criticism that emerges from our diverse and complicated communities. In other words, I want to explore how the principles of kinship can help us be more responsible and, ultimately, more useful participants in both the imaginative and physical decolonization and empowerment of ndigenous peoples through the study of our literatures.

"To Cut Off the Remembrance of Them from the Earth"

We should never forget that the very existence of indigenous literatures, not to mention the decolonization imperative of indigenous peoplehood, is a rebellion against the assimilationist directive of Eurowestern imperialism. Empire is driven as much by expedience and simplification as by hunger for power or resources. Simplification is essential to the survival of imperialism, as complications breed uncertainty in the infallibility of authoritative truth claims. Empire contains within it the insistence on the erasure of the indigenous population, through overt destruction or co-optation; indeed, the very *memory* of an unbroken Native presence is often furiously repressed by the colonizers.

Two telling examples illustrate this point. The first is the destruction of the Maya codices by the Spanish invaders. As Craig Womack (Muscogee Creek-Cherokee) notes, this act can quite clearly be seen as an "act of cultural genocide [with] one culture finding itself threatened by the profundity of the Other's literacy. These were illiteracy campaigns, sponsored by the group claiming to be the most literate."[7] The destruction of the means of knowledge dissemination was crucial to the policy of colonization, as the dominating creeds of Europe could only flourish in the perceived absence of the indigenous epistemologies. And the written codices themselves were not the only target; the Spanish also destroyed the sites of indigenous learning.[8]

Take, too, the case of the Pequots. In his masterful introduction to the writings of William Apess (Pequot), Barry O'Connell writes: "In 1637 [the Pequots] were the objects of the first deliberately genocidal war conducted by the English in North America. . . . Some Pequots survived but were compelled to sign a treaty that declared them extinct as a people and forbade the use of their name forever."[9] Historian Michael Freeman adds: "[T]he colonial authorities forbade the use of the Pequot name in order, in Captain [John] Mason's words, 'to cut off the remembrance of them from the earth.'"[10] In reflecting on the work of Apess within a larger Native intellectual genealogy, Robert Warrior (Osage) observes that "while the Pequots managed to survive the genocidal designs of the New England Puritans, their existence for the next three hundred years would be marked by social deprivation and constant threats to the status of their lands. And their reservation-based population continued to decrease."[11]

Empires can't survive by acknowledging complexity, so whatever complications they can't destroy or ignore are, if possible, commodified, co-opted, and turned back against themselves. The struggle to uproot imperialism then too often becomes myopic, as the colonized in many cases too often seek to find expedient, simplistic solutions to their many difficulties. The result is turning against one another in frustration, thereby destroying themselves and one another in service of the very empire they seek to dismantle. Although between one-third to three-quarters of the Pequots survived the English campaign, the symbolic erasure of the Pequot presence in the Northeast didn't stop with the English colonists. It's continued into the present age, contributing today to an enduring prejudice that presumes the inauthenticity of the Pequots and other eastern Native communities—and given unfortunate voice by high-profile Native people.

An illuminating example: in December 2002, a letter appeared in the *Hartford Courant* that caused quite a stir on various Native academic e-mail lists. (The letter has since been republished in the *American Indian Quarterly*, and all citations here are from this publication.) In her letter, Oglala Sioux writer and scholar Delphine Red Shirt, an adjunct professor at Yale University, castigates those "newly born" Indians of Connecticut—and, by extension, the entire East—whom she does not recognize as "real" Indians. She writes, "What offends me? That on the outside (where it counts in America's racially conscious society), Indians in Connecticut do not appear Indian. In fact, the Indians in Connecticut look more like they come from European or African stock. When I see them, whether they are Pequot, Mohegan, Paugussett, Paucatuck or Schaghticoke, I want to say, 'These are not Indians.' But I've kept quiet. I can't stay quiet any longer. These are not Indians."[12]

Red Shirt goes on to assert that "[t]here are no remnants left of the indigenous peoples that had proudly lived in Connecticut. . . . The blood is gone." She follows the line of logic used by many anti-Native forces, namely, that blood quantum and phenotypically "Indian" features are the fullest measure of cultural authenticity and that those who are lacking in these qualities are, by definition, no longer Indian—if they ever were. The success of Indian casinos in Connecticut draws Red Shirt's particular scorn, as she connects the U.S. recognition process to "a new arena for profit making," whereby "[p]eople who had been indigent elsewhere can come here and claim lineage and book a cruise to the Caribbean islands or move into a spanking new retirement home on casino income as a tribal member."[13]

There's no intellectual engagement in this letter with the histories or contemporary realities of these communities; it's all hyperbolic Sturm und Drang. In spite of brutal cultural oppression, forced migrations of much of the population, and material suffering, the Pequots have maintained an active presence in their homelands, which Robert Warrior addresses in his recent discussion of William Apess:

> Clearly, just the continuing existence of the Pequots in the face of all they experienced is testimony to the resilience of generations of political leadership that refused to give up on the idea of the Pequots as a people. That idea, of course, required a land base, and some Pequot people held on to that land base with ferocious tenacity. In the process, those Pequots managed to carve out a place for themselves in which they man-

> aged to endure. Their descendants would be the ones who, much later, set the stage for the contemporary rebirth of the Pequots as a people.[14]

Red Shirt's rhetoric both ignores and perpetuates the racist inconsistencies and genocidal practices of U.S. Indian policy and those of its invader predecessors on eastern tribes.[15] When she asserts that "on the outside (where it counts in America's racially conscious society), Indians in Connecticut do not appear Indian," she overtly subjugates Indian identity to the slippery perceptions of bigoted, self-interested observers who generally refuse to see even the Indians who, like her, "appear Indian." Visual recognition is a dangerous thing to put one's faith in; it's all too easy to close your eyes.

Disconnected from history or the current kinship practices of the peoples she dismisses, Red Shirt's argument draws instead on longstanding Eurowestern stereotypes about Indians, which Robert F. Berkhofer, Jr., addressed over twenty years earlier:

> In spite of centuries of contact and the changed conditions of Native American lives, Whites picture the "real" Indian as the one before contact or during the early period of that contact. . . . Since Whites primarily understood the Indian as an antithesis to themselves, then civilization and Indianness as they defined them would forever be opposites. Only civilization had history and dynamics in this view, so therefore Indianness must be conceived of as ahistorical and static. If the Indian changed through the adoption of civilization as defined by Whites, then he was no longer truly Indian according to the image, because the Indian was judged by what Whites were not. Change toward what Whites were made him ipso facto less Indian.[16]

Red Shirt's recognition of Indianness requires both a tacit acceptance of the Eurowestern stereotype of the unchanging Indian and, at the same time, a tribally specific assertion that places her own cultural identity—that of an Oglala Sioux—as the absolute standard against which all other Indians are measured: "I am Indian and have had to live with all that means. I do not claim to descend from a full-blooded Indian. I am it. What I am witnessing in this casino-mad state is a corruption of my heritage. I am outraged by it. These are not Indians."[17] While the Pequots, Mohegans, Paugussetts, Paucatucks, and Schaghticokes make no claim to being Oglala Sioux, their assertion of a broader identity as "Indian" is seen by Red Shirt not merely as inaccurate but as insulting, deeming it a "corruption" of her own Oglala heritage.

It might seem a bit gratuitous or self-serving for a light-skinned mixed-blood Cherokee to devote so much attention to a single letter, yet my interest here isn't so much to justify the Indianness of the Pequots and others who don't appear phenotypically Native. Rather, I've chosen this document to illustrate what I see as a widespread avoidance of kinship and context, both on the part of Red Shirt herself and others of like righteousness as a preemptive response to some of the more predictable (but no less vexed) responses to her arguments. Her letter exemplifies both the complexity of the sociopolitical status of American Indians today and a significant lack of sensitivity to the larger significance of kinship to indigenous continuity. Her fierce response to the claims of eastern tribes can be seen as mere geographic and blood-quantum bigotry, but to dismiss it simply as such would be to ignore some of the very historical realities that she herself erases. Those communities from the eastern edge of the continent have a much longer history of dealing with the immediate effects of European invasion than do many of the communities in the northern U.S. and southern Canadian prairie: for at least two hundred years, the tribal peoples Red Shirt dismisses acted as a buffer that protected many western communities from the full brunt of white expansion. The bodies that Red Shirt doesn't recognize are the living testaments to that legacy —a legacy that her people now benefit from in a country that prizes blood purity above kinship obligations.

Similarly, among most eastern indigenous nations—indeed, among most tribal nations in this hemisphere—intermarriage was an honored method of developing kinship bonds with other peoples, either indigenous or invader, an act both intimately familial and overtly political—and many of us reflect that tradition in our skin and features.But as colonization spread its crimson claws across the continent, and as traditional kinship structures became increasingly weakened by Eurowestern values (patriarchy, capitalism, rampant individualism, etc.), this tradition also became a site of conflict, even among communities with previously liberal traditions of intermarriage.[18]

While examining these conceptual weaknesses in Red Shirt's argument, it's also vital to keep firmly in mind the culturally specific contexts from which they themselves emerge. The current home of the Oglala Sioux tribe—the Pine Ridge Reservation in South Dakota—has one of the most devastated ecologies and economies in the United States, as Winona LaDuke (Anishinaabeg) points out: "Alcoholism, unemployment, suicide, accidental death, and homicide rates [among the Oglala Lakota of Pine Ridge] are still well above the national average. Indian Health Service statistics indicate that alcoholism death rates in the Aberdeen, South Dakota, area are seven times the national average and almost three times that of all Indian people. The suicide rate on one of the Lakota reservations is almost seven times the national average and generally is at least three times the suicide rate of all non-Indians in the state of South Dakota."[19] Add to these grim statistics an unemployment rate of at least 80 percent, the brutal racism of their white neighbors (and a number of unsolved murders of Lakota men whose bodies have been found on the edge of the reservation), decades of conflict between the BIA-endorsed government and the grassroots Oglala leadership, loss of lands to allotment and flooding, destruction of the buffalo herds, Wounded Knee I and II, and the incursions of white ranchers into the area. For the Oglalas, and for many western Native peoples, this is the immediate reality of being Indian: "Pine Ridge is a testimony to survival. It is also a testimony to genocide. . . . The

Oglalas are survivors. They are like the Yellowstone [buffalo] herd: besieged, shot down, but still alive."[20]

The sad reality is that the Oglalas are among the most brutalized Native communities in the continental United States, and still they endure. Given the immediacy of the Oglala struggle, it's not difficult to imagine that the phenomenal economic success of the Connecticut tribal casinos and their relatively recent federal recognition is a difficult pill for Red Shirt to swallow, especially when the Native people who benefit economically and politically do not share the physical or cultural characteristics that she recognizes as "Indian" and yet benefit from that designation.

If kinship and context are important to the indigenous scholarly enterprise, we have no choice but to challenge Red Shirt's claims, especially those that view indigenousness in solely racial terms—a product of nineteenth-century Eurowestern science—rather than the relevant indigenous epistemologies and familial relationships. The color coding of "race" in America may be a material reality, but it's not a natural state of affairs—it was constructed by human minds and biases, and it can be unmade in ways that are more responsive to the complicated realities of indigenous value systems. While addressing the problematic nature of Red Shirt's claims and examining the historical contexts of Pequot assertions of nationhood, however, we also have to embed those claims in a context that recognizes the continuing racism and oppression suffered by the Oglala Lakotas.

To erase the endurance of either the Pequots or the Lakotas requires a dangerous movement away from the expansive qualitative standard of kinship toward that of race, which depends on an ever-diminishing quantitative standard. Kinship is adaptive; race, as a threatened constitutive commodity, always runs the risk of becoming washed out to the point of insignificance. Extending this discussion to both this text and to Native literature in general, we find that kinship criticism is far more responsive to the historicized contexts of Indian communities in all their complexity, whereas race-reading—rooted as it is in Eurowestern stereotypes and deficiency definitions—can only view Indians through a lens of eventual Indian erasure. If, as is the consensus of communitistic analyses, our literatures assert a consciousness of land and ancestry, of community and kinship ties, of traditions and ceremonies, of survival and presence outside of colonialist death narratives shouldn't our criticism attempt to do the same? As Native literature is arguably centered in the continuation of the People, the aesthetic moral imperative from which indigenous meaning, purpose, and identity are derived would be well served by a similar concern in our criticism.

Continuation doesn't matter if we continue in the image of individualized Eurowesterners—it is as *peoples* that we endure, through our obligations to kinship and balanced relationships. A solitary flame without fuel dies quickly. This is as much the case for Native writers and scholars as it is for tribal nations themselves; as Chris Teuton (Cherokee Nation) demonstrates so masterfully in his detailed genealogy of Native literary criticism, we who are contributing to this volume do so because our literary peers and ancestors gave shape and substance to these discussions (and were themselves engaged with those of non-Native scholars in the field) and because we want to contribute to the endurance of this flame beyond the short flicker of our own warmth. Our ideas and voices are now being woven into those conversations, and we add to the continuity of this small community. By participating in these acts of kinship, we keep the community and its history alive.

This isn't to say, however, that all the conversations are harmonious; if anything, the intimate relationship between our nations and our scholarship pretty well guarantees that the stakes are high. Our investment in these issues is more than an anemic intellectual exercise. We ask questions of the literature and its writers that generally aren't asked in other fields, and we place a lot of weight on the answers that emerge. At times, our kinship duties are pushed aside in our insistence on the answer we want to hear.

For example, what relationship does Native literature and criticism have to the protection of lands and treaty rights? Given that so much of this material is, at least superficially, concerned with affirming the author's Indianness, can such literature be considered ethical? Can it even be considered indigenous? Ostensibly simple questions, but—as with most things—far more complicated than they seem. Examining these complications through a relational lens might provide us with an option beyond false either/or binaries, where the conversation and the opinions it elicits become part of the process of kinship. In this way, divisive debates are stripped of some of their corrosive qualities, and they become oriented more clearly toward continuity.

Embodied Sovereignties

Over half of American Indians and large numbers of Mexican and Canadian Natives do not live on traditional lands. In the United States and Canada, government policies of removal, land seizure and allotment, erosion of successful indigenous trade networks and sufficiency economies, excessive taxation, termination of government-to-government relationships with tribal nations, boarding and residential schools, disruption of families and kinship communities, forced assimilation and relocation were the primary forces of Native land dislocation in the nineteenth and twentieth centuries. These issues, connected with government definitions of Indianness that disenfranchised tens of thousands of Native peoples while simultaneously undermining indigenous conceptions of peoplehood, have resulted in large populations of Native peoples who, while not grounded to an ancestral land base, nonetheless maintain their Native identities and struggle to reestablish their survival. Community recognition at a local level is, as a result, often difficult to establish or maintain, particularly for multiracial Native writers. When one is uprooted from ancestral lands, the next landscape under siege becomes the body and its identities.

The indigenous body is more than flesh, blood, and bone; as both Womack and Warrior point out in their discussions of Native erotica, Native bodies are sites of both colonized conflict and passionate decolonization. Some of the earliest European iconography of the "New World" imagined the Americas as an exotic/erotic brown-skinned woman, open and yielding to the penetrating thrust of European imperialism. Invasion depended on the subjugation of indigenous women and their frequent positions of authority as much as it depended on the erosion of affirming sexual pleasure and diversity of gender roles and identities. It's no surprise, then, that as part of a larger movement of indigenous empowerment and decolonization, queer Native women like Joy Harjo (Muscogee), Chrystos (Menominee), and Beth Brant (Mohawk) have worked tirelessly to reclaim sexuality from centuries of myopic misogyny and homophobia.

Yet in speaking of sex and bodies, we must also attend to other dimensions of that relationship. These are the particular landscapes/bodyscapes that provoke some of the most incendiary discussions between Native intellectuals, between those who would see it fully mapped and clearly navigable, and those who desire a more amorphous and ambiguous terrain. The vexed relationships between individuals, tribal communities, and colonialist governments make easy answers or unyielding positions difficult to maintain, as unflinching attention on any one of these elements blinds the viewer to the powerful influences of the others. This is nowhere more evident than in the debates regarding the nature of sovereignty and Native cultural identities between Crow Creek Sioux scholar Elizabeth Cook-Lynn and the late mixed-blood (Choctaw-Cherokee) theorist Louis Owens. The nature of their often heated discussions regarding the place of the mixed-blood narrative in Native literature in many ways mirrors the role that blood quantum plays among Cherokees (and other early white-contact tribes) and those tribes who experienced the full impact of white colonization toward the latter half of the nineteenth century.

Cook-Lynn has long been warning Indian country of the dangers inherent in a strong focus on mixed-bloodedness rather than on sovereignty and asserting tribal land rights; she founded *Wicazo Sa Review* in part to ensure that there was one venue for Native scholars and writers to focus their attention toward those latter aims. For Cook-Lynn, the stories we tell are, above all, moral stories, and the strongest ethical position that Native scholars and writers can take is one of dedication to the exercise of political, social, spiritual, and territorial sovereignty. As she noted in 1993, "If history is to tell us anything, it tells us that land seekers are, and always have been, the dangerous ones. And, if the study of literature tells us anything, it is that the stories hold the secrets to our lives as much as does the land. That is the dilemma in American literature and particularly in the Great Plains, and that is why the question, 'Who gets to tell the stories?' is not only never far from our thoughts, it is the political question of our time.[21] Cook-Lynn has also written about mixed-blood tribal groups and what she sees as their dangers to Indian communities—the unspoken implication being that they are no longer Indians or indigenous themselves:

> [Wallace Stegner's] description of the metis, or half-breeds, as a buffer race, which means that they are "a small, neutral race or state lying between potentially hostile ones," is, in terms of their relationship to Indians, the beginning of a deception which allows the turning away from what was really happening in Indian communities. The metis would hardly have been called neutral by any of the plains peoples and societies for whom the arranged marriage patterns of ancient times were a tool of cultural survival. Instead, the metis were and probably still are seen by native peoples as those who were *already converts* to the hostile and intruding culture simply through their marriage into it.[22]

Similar to the rhetorical avoidances in Red Shirt's letter, Cook-Lynn's focus on mixed-bloodedness as *the problem* draws attention away from the colonial powers that turned intermarriage into a colonizing state. Bonita Lawrence (Mi'kmaq) points out in reference to urban mixed-bloods that because "it appears as if 'the problem' resides solely with mixed-bloodedness or urbanity, not with dehumanizing identity legislation[, t]he role that identity legislation has played in *creating* mixed-bloodedness (and urbanity) as problems for one's Indianness falls out of the picture."[23] Cook-Lynn's focus on a purity/assimilation binary and conflation of multiraciality with lack of national spirit seems counterproductive to an argument on sovereignty that respects tribal specificity; it also betrays a particularly U.S. bias that doesn't reflect the general recognition of the Métis in Canada on both social and political levels. The autobiographical writings of Maria Campbell, the poetry of Gregory Scofield, the political historiography of Howard Adams, and the work of other Métis writers and scholars have demonstrated time and again the degree to which their distinct communities have suffered under colonialism, yet without the same treaty and land-base protections of other First Nations peoples in Canada, writings that Cook-Lynn does not discuss or acknowledge.

Indeed, this larger argument overlooks what is one of the most fundamental concerns in the struggle for land and sovereignty: the *relationship* of the People to the earth. Womack's question—"Is human knowledge the only kind of knowledge there is?"—can guide us well here, as it speaks to the vital significance of the rest of creation to the lives and intellectual concerns of indigenous peoples. While the land herself is of central concern to most indigenous epistemologies, we don't know her outside of our relationship(s) to her (or to the other peoples who depend on her for survival). We often call her Mother; we—like the Animal-people and Tree-people—are her kindred, and ours is a relationship of reciprocity. She gives life and sustenance to us; we (ideally) give her respect, honor, and care. Beyond the earth itself are our relationships with other spirit-beings and peoples, all of which depend on attentive engagement; as Kimberly Blaeser (Anishinaabe) indicates, kinship on the microcosmic level gives evidence of the health and significance of the macrocosm: "Perhaps we rejoice at the smallest encounter of relatedness because it signals the greater."[24] While the language of treaties all too often erases relational understandings and replaces them with the Eurowestern language of land-as-object, the guiding purpose behind the defense of treaty rights is as much (or more) about ensuring the ongoing maintenance of the ceremonies and rituals that ensure good relationships with the rest of creation as it is the defense of limited natural resources.

When Cook-Lynn focuses on land and treaty rights to the exclusion of kinship, she leaves important questions unaddressed. Louis Owens takes up some of these questions when he responds to Cook-Lynn's assertions; in doing so, he illuminates some of the different ways in which various tribal nations have experienced the ravages of colonialism, yet he falls into something of the same avoidance of kinship concerns. Owens comes from communities deeply impacted by diaspora—the Choctaw and Cherokee removals and their subsequent social upheavals—and he approaches Native literature and issues with a significantly different perspective than does Cook-Lynn, whose people have remained generally in the same geographic location for many generations (and who themselves have long been regarded by many of their Indian neighbors such as the Omahas and Poncas as imperialists). For Owens, Native self-determination isn't simply about the physical land itself; it's also about the interior sociopsychic landscape:

> Tribal people have deep bonds with the earth, with sacred places that bear the bones and stories that tell them who they are, where they came from, and how to live in the world they see around them. But of course almost all tribal people also have migration stories that say we came from someplace else before finding home. The very fact that tribal nations from the Southeast were so extraordinarily successful in making so-called Indian Territory a much beloved home after the horrors of Removal and before the horrors of the Civil War underscores the ability of indigenous Americans to move and in doing so to carry with them whole cultures within memory and story.[25]

Owens responds to Cook-Lynn's assumption that the most valid Indian narratives are those embedded in the ancestral homelands of the writer's community; such an assumption would erase any land ethic or spiritual relationship of those Indians removed from their homelands by the U.S. government and would certainly erase the voices of nearly every Indian in what is now Oklahoma:

> . . . there are indeed countless thousands of people in the positions of a Momaday, Silko, [Thomas] King, Vizenor, and so forth: people who do not live in reservation communities and who, if they are artists, may create art about urban or rural mixedblood experience at a distance

> from their tribal communities. Should the stories of such people, the products of colonial America's five hundred years of cultural wars against indigenous peoples, not be told because they do not fit the definition of what one Lakota critic thinks is tribally "real"? Are their stories not ones that "matter" or have "meaning"? Contrary to what Cook-Lynn asserts, this is a powerful literature of resistance, a counter-voice to the dominant discourse that would reduce Indians to artifactual commodities useful to tourist industries.[26]

While Owens perhaps oversimplifies Cook-Lynn's point—after all, rootedness in the land is a central ethic of most indigenous worldviews—he quite accurately represents the reality of a large number of indigenous people in this hemisphere.

Yet Owens's argument, too, suffers from a lack of engagement with kinship principles, namely, because he places individual and family stories of displacement at the center of analytical concern, asserting the Indianness of "movement," "distance," and the "products of colonial America's five hundred years of cultural wars" without placing this "powerful literature of resistance" firmly within a conversation about the relationship of the People to one another, to their histories, their futures, and to the rest of creation. In challenging Cook-Lynn's erasure of these narratives of motion and displacement, Owens goes to the other side, representing motion as a push away from the land that features so significantly in the orature and written literatures of the People, not a back-and-forth movement of departure *and* return, separation *and* (re)integration.

Owens's voice is most resonant, his understanding most incisive, when he engages specific places, specific voices, and his relationships to them. He embeds his response to Cook-Lynn in a larger discussion of his family's complicated "blood trails" across Oklahoma, Mississippi, and California, including photographs, family stories, and reflections on the relationships between those travelers of the past and his own experiences as an inheritor of those experiences. Even then, however, the "blood trails" Owens follows here exist at a distance from this specificity of landed relationship, except as a reflection of past connection or as a more generic commentary about large-scale indigenous values related to land and history. He writes, "If loss of parents or grandparents or tribal community is the residue of difficult history, then you recreate community beginning with the nucleus of family and extending through memory and imagination and nation."[27] Yet when a family, a community, or a nation is fully removed from the land of its origins, that land doesn't cease to shape the People's cosmos, even when they're building new relationships with a new land; their links to it change, but they rarely vanish, just as separation from a loved one inevitably changes but doesn't necessarily erase our relationship to that person. "Memory and imagination" are important, but so too are the relational rituals that bind the People to both their rights and responsibilities within the larger familial web. Besides, even migration accounts take place in a world of identifiable features—each landscape has a distinctive personality, and as the People come to understand that personality and their own relationship to it, they weave it into their understanding of themselves and the rest of creation.

The Cook-Lynn/Owens debate, then, is less about which vision of the purpose of Native literature is "right" or "wrong," but how both arguments are limited by their partial attention to the principles within which both indigenous lands and identities are rooted. Just as Red Shirt's argument about Pequot survival attends only to her own kinship contexts and not those of the Pequots, Mohegans, Paugussetts, Paucatucks, and Schaghticokes in whose land she now lives, both Cook-Lynn and Owens place their own contextualized experiences as the sole defining lens of North American indigenousness, to the diminishment of all.

A Sacred Trust

What, then, might be a useful approach to thinking about ethical Native literary criticism, one that (hopefully) avoids the blistering burn of fire left neglected? For me, at this time, the best approach is about relationships, about attending to the cultural, historical, political, and intellectual contexts from which indigenous texts emerge. This engagement provides a rich range of interpretive possibility, and it sensitizes us to the multiple relationships and contexts that make such study morally meaningful. It reflects many of the complicated realities influencing our lives, not just theoretical considerations. Cherokee literary critic Sean Teuton's essay (this volume) speaks directly to this concern when he reminds us, through the consideration of the writing of Native prisoners in Auburn Prison, that indigenous writing is, at its heart, a political assertion of the "going on" addressed earlier by Amanda Cobb. It is, in all the best ways, a *worldly* exercise of peoplehood and continuity:

> I thus argue . . . that an ethical American Indian theory must enter the world to change and be changed by the world. To do so, I turn to our intellectual tradition of historically engaged political writing to introduce a theory of Native praxis. Then, in closing, I return to the classroom—to the writing of indigenous prisoners—to demonstrate this theory. What drives Indian intellectuals to political action? In moments such as described above, when we are overwhelmed by the experience of Native criminalization—and, more broadly, other observations of anti-Indianism—American Indian scholars awaken politically and begin putting their ideas to work. I term that demand for justice "the callout."

In this book, we are, I hope, expressing our own versions of "the callout," and doing so in a way that does honor to those whose own voices have been (and remain) silenced, marginalized, and unheard.

Teuton and others call out; it's an invitation for response. This project expresses, in its own small way, peoplehood in practice. Janice Acoose's insistence on the necessary relationship between the "cultural integrity" of nation-specific literatures and the health of their status as "sovereign nations and self-determining peoples" is a powerful reminder that the (self)representation of a community is inextricably linked to the dignified ability of its members to participate in the web of rights and responsibilities that make them a People. Other contributors explore this relationship as well, including the meaningful "epistemological roots" and geographic contexts in Lisa Brooks's analysis of northeastern U.S. Native literatures, LeAnne Howe's narrative reflections on the aesthetic and intellectual dimensions of being a "practicing Choctaw," and Cheryl Suzack's incisive reading of the complicated Anishinaabeg kinship contexts of Winona LaDuke's *Last Standing Woman.*

The living kinship traditions and literatures of each People—from ancient ceremonialism to Christian syncretism and pan-Native perspectives, from birch-bark scrolls and wampum belts to poems, novels, and web pages—rather than being perceived as a frozen set of principles or texts of merely ethnographic interest, are instead seen in their own enduring beauty as a strong but flexible structure that gives guidance for continuity even in the winds of change. The green cedar bends with the wind and endures; when the sapwood dies and the tree grows rigid, sometimes even the slightest wind can bring it crashing down. Dead wood burns too quickly; green wood warms longer. Trusting in the principles of kinship and their relevance to our lives today and tomorrow keeps our work flexible, because the roots are strong. We won't always agree with one another, and that, too, is a vital aspect of this work: it's important to remember that dissent is an important aspect of self-determination. Debate and discussion are time-honored intellectual and social practices shared in the older political traditions of most indigenous peoples in the Americas, with status conferred on eloquence, not coercion. To return to earlier reflections, by contextualizing Red Shirt's invective against the Connecticut tribes and the Cook-Lynn/Owens debate, we shift from a discursive model of conflict and silencing to one of respectful relationship. The flames might burn white-hot, but they leave rich ash behind. The seeds that survive will be strong . . . and there's room in this fertile soil for many seeds.

This essay ends in Fire.

Kinship—in all its messy complexity and diversity—gives us the best measure of interpretive possibility, as it speaks to the fact that our literatures, like our various peoples, are *alive.* The decolonization imperative gives us hopeful purpose for our "going on." Our council fires burn still. Tobacco, cedar, sweetgrass, and sage still rise up in cleansing smoke and prayer. The heat of passion connects us with others in body and spirit, driving away cold shame and isolation, just as our embodied words burn these connections onto the page, onto the heart, onto the mind. There can be no higher ethical purpose than to answer "the callout" and tend to those kin-fires; it's a sacred trust.

It's what we do for family.

Notes

1. Wickman, *Tree That Bends*, 204.

2. See, for example, Kilpatrick, *Night Has a Naked Soul*, especially 99–100; Conley, *Cherokee Medicine Man*, especially 68–70; and Lewis and Jordan, *Creek Indian Medicine Ways*, especially 48–50.

3. The fact is, most Cherokees—and a good percentage of other Indians in North America—are at least nominally Christian, and for most of these folks, there's no necessary conflict between their Christian beliefs and their identities at Native peoples. Besides, the last five hundred-plus years have seen the gradual indigenization of Christianity among many peoples in the Americas, so, like European languages, one can no longer accurately claim the absolute alienness of these invader ways. To willingly *choose* one particular path among many, or to bring together elements of different traditions in a way that still affirms the nationhood and self-determination of the community, is a very different thing from being forced by outsiders to walk a narrow, painful path to the exclusion of others.

4. Bird, "Breaking the Silence," 30.

5. I've quoted Thomas King's comment on these concerns ad nauseum, but it's still relevant here: "The truth about stories is that that's all we are." See King, *Truth about Stories*, 3.

6. Cobb, unpublished manuscript, in possession of the collective.

7. Womack, *Red on Red*, 13.

8. Leon-Portilla, "Introduction," xlvi. This anthology of extant responses of Aztecs and their descendants to the Spanish invasion is a powerful testament to the endurance of Native voices against nearly overwhelming oppression. A more recent collection, *Mesoamerican Voices* (Restall, Sousa, Terraciano, eds.), gives further context for the literary responses to this bloody era.

9. See O'Connell, ed., *On Our Own Ground*, xxv.

10. Freeman, "Puritans and Pequots," 289.

11. Robert Warrior, *People and the Word*, 11.

12. Red Shirt, "These Are Not Indians," 643.

13. Ibid.

14. Robert Warrior, *People and the Word*, 11.

15. Pequot survivors resisted erasure, however, and maintained their traditions and name, even two centuries later, although their invisibility to outsiders often continued under various institutional means. O'Connell writes of many reasons why New England Natives were marginalized in later years. Many of these reasons focus heavily on the Pequots' loss of lands and economic independence, forcing migration to those places with the best available jobs: "Censuses notoriously miss such people. Those people who might be found and who might have identified

themselves as 'Indian,' or by the name of a cultural group such as 'Mohegan' or 'Pequot,' could not have been registered in most federal censuses in the nineteenth century because there was no category for them. One could only be 'white,' 'colored,' or 'mulatto'" (*On Our Own Ground*, lxiii).

16. Berkhofer, *White Man's Indian*, 28–29.

17. Red Shirt, "These Are Not Indians," 644.

18. Intermarriage has been embraced by many Cherokees, as well as by the majority of non-Native "Generikees" who claim Indian identity through a Cherokee great-great-grandmother (who is often a "princess"), thus leading to the proliferation of jokes in Indian country that have as their premise the diluted blood quantum of Cherokees. Intermarriage is not, however, universally embraced among Cherokees, especially among some traditionalists, who have long asserted that such practices endanger both Cherokee identity and the nation's sovereignty. See, for example, Sturm's *Blood Politics*, a fascinating study of the complications of Cherokee identity.

19. LaDuke, *All Our Relations*, 148.

20. Ibid.

21. Cook-Lynn, "Who Gets to Tell the Stories?" 64.

22. Cook-Lynn, *Why I Can't Read Wallace Stegner*, 35.

23. Lawrence, *"Real" Indians and Others*, 46.

24. Blaeser, unpublished manuscript, in possession of the collective.

25. Owens, *Mixedblood Messages*, 164.

26. Ibid., 158–59.

27. Ibid., 165.

Land Claims, Identity Claims

Mapping Indigenous Feminism in Literary Criticism and in Winona LaDuke's *Last Standing Woman*

CHERYL SUZACK

> [T]he land claims of White Earth will not so simply disappear, but will rise to challenge new generations. . . . Ignored by the public or dismissed by the courts, they will simply become more complex with the passage of time. At White Earth—as in much of Indian Country—one may not inherit the land, but one does inherit the struggle.
>
> "Without Due Process"
> Holly Youngbear-Tibbetts, 1991

On March 13, 1991, Winona LaDuke and thirty-four enrolled members of the White Earth band of Chippewa Indians appeared as appellants before the Minnesota Division of the United States District Court in an action to recover disputed land on the White Earth Indian Reservation in northern Minnesota. Plaintiffs in the case, led by Marvin Manypenny and George Fineday, Sr., asserted approximately "40 claims involving title and possessory interests in 4087 acres of land." They sought "declaratory, injunctive, and monetary relief" against the federal government, including the Department of the Interior and several of its employees, the State of Minnesota and its agents, three Minnesota counties, and "numerous named and unnamed individual holders of, or claimants to, disputed property." They argued that by enacting the White Earth Land Settlement Act (WELSA) in 1986, "Congress affirmatively and expressly waived the federal government's sovereign immunity" and "es-

---

Cheryl Suzack (Batchewana First Nations) is an assistant professor of English at the University of Victoria. Her research focuses on law and literature. Her recent publications include a forthcoming article in Race and Racism in 21st Century Canada *and a review article in* Postcolonial Text.

tablished a[n] independent cause of action for allottees and their heirs seeking return of the land and monetary damages." Plaintiffs stated furthermore that they "opposed the enactment of WELSA" and "continue to oppose the Act's provisions which divest them and other members of the White Earth Band of any interest in the disputed property."[1]

As a contemporary land claim settlement act passed by Congress to "settle unresolved claims to certain allotted lands on the White Earth Indian Reservation," WELSA consolidated imposed colonial definitions of indigenous identity by distinguishing among community members on the basis of "full-blood" and "mixed-blood" inheritance and by grounding dispossessed allottees' claims to their allotment lands in the language of blood-quantum identity. "Full-blood" status, for the purposes of legal verification within the act, designated "a Chippewa Indian of the White Earth Reservation, Minnesota, who was designated as a full blood Indian on the roll approved by the United States District Court for the District of Minnesota on October 1, 1920, . . . or who [was] the biological child of two full blood parents so designated on the roll or of one full blood parent so designated on the roll and one parent who was an Indian enrolled in any other federally recognized Indian tribe, band, or community." "Mixed-blood" status was determined as "a Chippewa Indian of the White Earth Reservation, Minnesota, who was designated as a mixed blood Indian on the roll approved by the United States District Court of Minnesota on October 1, 1920, . . . [and] also refer[ed] to any descendants of an individual who was listed on said roll providing that descendant was not a full blood under the definition in subsection (c) of this section."[2]

Without reference to the imposed identity provisions of WELSA legislation, Judge John R. Gibson affirmed the decision of the district court and dismissed the case against the federal government, the State of Minnesota, and the remaining counties and private landowners. Judge Gibson stated that since Congress proposed WELSA to settle "with finality" "unresolved legal uncertainties" arising out of clouded titles to allotted lands, it could not also "establish a substantive basis for a cause of action" against the federal government as appellants claimed. For this reason, he stated, WELSA could not be read to imply a "waiver of sovereign immunity" of the federal government, and thus the district court's decision to dismiss the plaintiff's claim on the grounds that they "failed to join" the United States "as an indispensable party to the case" was held intact. With the failure of their appeal, appellants in the case had exhausted all avenues of legal recourse for recovering tribal lands outside of the terms established in WELSA, and they forfeited all rights to receive compensation under the act for lost allotments.[3]

The background legal and legislative history of the White Earth Indian Reservation illustrates how the rulings by the Minnesota Supreme Court and Congress depend on identity categories that emerge out of federal policies of colonial management.[4] It also demonstrates that the problem of formulating community affiliations that do not conform to blood-quantum categories remains an important theoretical and practical issue in contemporary literary theory. This essay contends that an ethical Native literary criticism must remain vigilant to the conditions of cultural production from which emerge the identity categories we inhabit and employ in our cultural criticism. It argues for the importance of gender identity to a reading of community relations and tribal histories, and it proposes that contemporary creative writers and community activists, such as Winona LaDuke, offer a progressive vision for reimagining community values and inherited community relationships through indigenous feminist practice.

Because the *Manypenny* case and WELSA legislation reveal the ways in which identity categories for Native peoples have real, material implications, theorizing identity in Native American literature cannot remain an intellectual exercise divorced from social reality. In Native America, identity categories mean all the difference between land and dispossession, between restorative justice and continued oppression. Thus, the study of Native American literature must be constituted through the terrain of political representation in order to transform the relationship between theory and practice and provide articulations for new and emerging political positions. As Laura Kipnis argues, "If the theoretical object prescribes a set of theoretical strategies, it simultaneously describes a field of political possibility."[5] At a historical juncture when land claims settlements coincide with the unrelenting persecution of Native peoples, theorizing identity cannot be divorced from the legal and social implications of colonial identity formation and subjectification. It is out of an understanding of the crucial interlocking effects of the political, social, and theoretical for Native peoples that this essay attends to reasserting the necessity of gender analysis to Native identity.

In what follows, I examine how American Indian feminist critics have theorized a relationship between community identity, tribal history, and women's collective agency in connection with gender identity in order to create an oppositional space from which to restore gender identity as an analytical category in discussions of tribal politics and community values. In contrast to congressional legislation that privileges as normative male tribal identity, American Indian feminist critics negotiate the arena of history and politics by examining the multiple imbrications of race and gender identity that shape the social subjectivities of Native women. Their analyses of communal social arrangements include theorizing the valency of feminism and race identity for reconstructing history, and articulating forms of community identity that do not conform to blood-quantum codes.

Thinking about Native identity theoretically requires an engagement with the literary, the legal, and the social. To situate my analyses of the gender implications of literary texts, I focus on the political and literary activism of Winona LaDuke. LaDuke's cultural politics demonstrate the imbrications of the literary with activist feminist aesthetics and social intervention. Her first novel, *Last Standing Woman*, privileges the interconnections between gender relations and community relations not only as sites of collective identity formation and objectification such that women recognize their common identity and are moved to political action, but also as social positions that explain how relations of power within American Indian communities change in response to transformations in the organization of social relationships. The connections that LaDuke articulates between tribal politics and gender relations suggest that, as a writer, she is beset by a dual and potentially conflicted set of critical and political demands: on the one hand, how to take issue with the call by contemporary American Indian critics for an unproblematized historical representation and reconstruction in American Indian writing, and, on the other, how to participate in a process of cultural reinvention and renewal that illuminates how the revival and preservation of tribal identity must of necessity engage with the inheritances of a colonial past. In LaDuke's novel, issues of community identity and tribal relations are framed by the historical disruption of community ties and the social disintegration of community relations. The literary text not only stages debates about community identity, but also offers a problematization of these issues as they are represented through legal and legislative means.

For LaDuke, feminist literary politics cannot be divorced from cultural and political alliances. Her work as a Green Party candidate, feminist organizer, and indigenous and environmental activist demonstrate these commitments. One of the most widely recognized spokespeople on behalf of environmental, political, and economic issues, LaDuke served as Ralph Nader's vice-presidential candidate for the Green Party in the 1996 and 2000 elections; was chosen by *Time Magazine* in 1994 as one of America's fifty most promising leaders age forty and under; was selected by *Ms. Magazine* in 1997 as one of its women of the year; and, in 1988, received a twenty thousand dollar award from Reebok in recognition of her human rights activism. (She used the money to buy back nearly one thousand acres of reservation land at White Earth.)[6] She has also been instrumental in forming community-based organizations, such as the White Earth Land Recovery Project, to explore other mechanisms for recovering tribal lands after participating as a claimant in the two court cases that exhausted all legal recourse available to the community, and the Indigenous Women's Network, a non—governmental organization that advocates a collective identity for all women as representatives of "Mothers of our Nations."[7]

The potentially conflicted "new ageism" of LaDuke's account of women's collective agency as representative of "Mother Earth in human form" is further complicated by her public activism, which displays a conscientiousness for the collective "marginalization of all women" from environmental collapse and for the erosion of women's self-determination through "colonialism" and "rapid industrialization" in fledgling nations.[8] Although LaDuke defends her views on "the living wage, health care, [and] welfare reform" as "women's issues," she has failed to secure the support of mainstream feminist groups, particularly during the 2000 election in the United States when she was accused by prominent women activists not only of discussing "motherhood" issues at the expense of a concern for "feminis[t]" ones, but also of dividing support for the left by running on behalf of the Green Party and "taking votes away from the Democratic Party."[9] While it is probably more accurate to describe LaDuke's commitments to mainstream feminist concerns as a form of "green feminism" in keeping with her support for the Green Party's core values on women's issues,[10] her engagements with tribal history and gender representation in *Last Standing Woman* demonstrate a form of *feminist* "indigenism" that connects the erosion of intertribal historical ties with transformations to the status of women as a result of the disruption of power relations within the tribal community.

My claims for LaDuke's novel are informed here by Marie Anna Jaimes Guerrero's definition of "indigenism," which she describes as a "struggle against American colonization from the premise of collective human rights." However, I am restoring the term "feminist" to Guerrero's analysis of the relationship between "native women and feminism," even though Guerrero herself claims that the "priorities and sociopolitical agendas" expressed by the "white, middle-class women's movement" are "individualist rather than communal in orientation" and lead to a polarization of interests that she expresses as "feminism versus indigenism." Instead of adopting "Eurocentric paradigm[s]," Guerrero argues for a "universal indigenist worldview" that facilitates the recognition of "struggle[s] between Indian nations and the American state over questions of sovereignty and incorporation into the U.S. polity [as] most visible when one examines the contradictions that emerge over the tribal status of native women."[11]

While I agree with her claims that "patriarchal structures" operate "both inside and outside the tribe," I am concerned with Guerrero's definition of both colonialism and tribalism as undifferentiated forms of "patriarchy." If colonialism is patriarchal and tribalism is patriarchal, then what difference does "race" identity make to the subjectivity of indigenous women—and by extension, of colonial subjects?[12] LaDuke's novel renders a much more complicated formulation of the relationship between race and gender identity through its exploration of the effects of colonialism as a disruption that occurs in the structural relations within the tribe, thus shifting relations of power, and through its examination of the subordination of Anishinaabeg women as a function of the loss of power associated with Anishinaabeg men, thus transforming relations of gender. Her literary activism can thus be understood as strategically reconfiguring aspects of the cultural imaginary that were not accessible through legal and legislative symbolic systems, the material implications of which I have laid out at the beginning of this essay.[13]

An ethical turn in Native cultural criticism must also ask what implications an imposed colonial past has for Native identity that is increasingly determined according to demands for its expression of "authenticity." Debates about the status of "mixed-blood" literature that, on the one hand, deploy an organizing binary of "insider/outsider" status to privilege forms of literary expression in order to construct American Indian literatures as sites for the "identification" of tribally specific cultural practices—or as "authentic" expressions of tribal culture—exist alongside claims that foreground the literature's reflection of tribal identity to privilege its mimetic function. At one end of this spectrum of demands for authenticity, Elizabeth Cook-Lynn's criticisms of the "mixed-blood literary movement" for its repudiation of "tribally specific literary traditions" that are formulated within "the hopeful, life-affirming aesthetic of traditional stories, songs, and rituals," take issue with the "major self-described mixed-blood voices of the decade" who, Cook-Lynn claims, offer "few useful expressions of resistance to the colonial history at the core of Indian/White relations."[14]

Cook-Lynn argues that "there is [in this fiction, nonfiction, and poetry] explicit and implicit accommodation to the colonialism of the 'West,'" with the result that the popularization of its "intellectual characteristics" circulates in cultural discourse "an aesthetic that is pathetic or cynical, a tacit notion of the failure of tribal governments as Native institutions and of sovereignty as a concept, and an Indian identity which focuses on individualism rather than First Nation ideology." The assemblage of writers from distinct tribal and national inheritances who represent the claim that "mixed-blood" writing has become a movement include "Gerald Vizenor, Louis Owens, Wendy Rose, Maurice Kenny, Michael Dorris, Diane Glancy, Betty Bell, Thomas King, Joe Bruchac, and Paula Gunn Allen." Yet, aside from arranging this list according to "mixed-blood" status, it is unclear how these writers are constitutive as a group, especially when they share no common ground according to gender, tribal origin, or national identity. In thus foregrounding these writers as "mixed-blood" rather than through another organizing category, Cook-Lynn appears to be complicitous with her own critique insofar as her discussion of "mixed-blood identity" foregrounds identity categories instituted through federally imposed blood-quantum distinctions, thus lending critical weight to the terms, rather than through other categories of social enablement that might include tribal identity or political affiliation.[15]

In contrast to Cook-Lynn's position, Louis Owens argues for a reading of "mixed-blood" literature that posits its resistant politics as representative of its "exterior" location beyond the literature itself, presumably in the "reality" of social relations as a "place of contact between cultural identities, a bidirectional, dynamic zone of resistance" from which to confront the dominant discourse. The site of political engagement that Owens claims for a "hybridized, polyglot, transcultural frontier" that is "quite clearly internalized" by "mixed-blood" authors, yet provides the common ground from which "Native Americans . . . continue to resist [an] ideology of containment and to insist upon the freedom to imagine themselves within a fluid, always shifting frontier space," relies on the "fixity" of the concept of "mixed-blood" identity as a transhistorical signifier that asserts its timelessness without reference to the literature's internal variation or to its implication in different sociohistorical contexts. In a critical style similar to Cook-Lynn's, Owens analyzes a range of "mixed-blood" literature for its consistency with his advocacy of a social/constructivist approach to American Indian writing.[16]

The literary-critical positions represented by Cook-Lynn and Owens articulate two ends of a spectrum in a debate that is concerned with legitimating the literary politics and oppositional practices of American Indian writing by illustrating how it participates in, or fails to reflect, tribal practices. I have drawn attention to these critical positions in order to illuminate the ways in which identity politics organizes these discussions. Both critics claim an interventionary space for "mixed-blood" literature in cultural discourse, yet in so doing, they homogenize distinctions between tribally distinct American Indian writers: Cook-Lynn through an assertion that the "mixed-blood" story has "taken center stage" and gained momentum in "every genre and most disciplines during this era of the rise of cultural studies, diversity, and multiculturalism," and Owens in his assertion that "the mixedblood is not a cultural broker but a cultural breaker, break-dancing trickster-fashion through all the signs, fracturing the self-reflexive mirror of the dominant centre, deconstructing rigid borders, slipping between the seams, embodying contradictions, and contradancing across every boundary."[17]

What remains unspoken in these considerations of the category of "mixed-blood" writing is the term's implication in a colonial history of land-allotment practice through which the federal government imposed forms of colonial identity on American Indian communities. This recognition and its historical specificity to the dispersal of tribal lands during the allotment period are crucial to understanding how the literary-critical practices we deploy as cultural critics circumvent and thus perpetuate analytical terms that avail colonial politics. The kind of criticism that I have been demonstrating, and one that I would call for, eschews the self-evident in critical engagements with Native literary texts to construct instead a form of critical discourse that reads across the genres of literary, legal, and social positioning. As the social justice implications of the *Manypenny* case disclose for us, not to do so is to absent ourselves from a field of engagement that is critical to the social and cultural histories of indigenous communities. A materialist Native literary practice that identifies the social effects of cultural work and its political imbrications in colonial history would get beyond the self-evident form of discursive practice that relies *solely* on "telling our story" criticism.[18] Such a practice would articulate the relationship between congressional legislation as it has been inherited and imposed within tribal communities and a standpoint feminist perspective[19] that privileges subordinate group claims to politicize identity categories with the material histories of colonial struggle.

Sean Teuton's "The Callout: Writing American Indian Politics" (this volume) represents an important undertaking in this regard. Problematizing the criminalization of Indian men in Auburn Prison, Teuton wields the category of "political writing" across a number of institutional locations to argue that what joins Indian people across positions of privilege and underprivilege in Indian county, even today, are their "shared experiences of colonial oppression." For Teuton, this common cause resonates across culture, history, and politics to "relentlessly" ground our "collective struggle for decolonization." Asking with urgency, "What drives Indian intellectuals to political action?" Teuton defines the demand for decolonization and social justice as a transformative "callout" that reverberates through an intellectual tradition of historically engaged writing to politicize our colonial present. The weight of our implication as cultural critics in this history thus engenders a leveling effect: as American Indian intellectuals, our deepest commitments, Teuton writes, must be "to making ideas defend the real lives of those around us."

The question of where to find a critical purchase for establishing the validity of indigenous knowledge in the service of transforming the social sphere is also skillfully explored in Lisa Brooks's "Digging at the Roots: Locating an Ethical, Native Criticism" (this volume). Arguing for a broader engagement in the intellectual traditions that have formed the "roots" of our cultural present, Brooks suggests a shift in how we conceptualize our responsibility to those early activists who have gone before us to generate a legacy that we might embrace as part of "a long-standing Native intellectual tradition." Challenging us to understand that "What we have at stake is not only the recognition of the validity of our knowledge, but the sustenance of indigenous epistemologies," Brooks examines the "northeastern landscape" of Samson Occom and William Apess to problematize oppositional frameworks that rely on complicity or critique to constitute their subjects of knowledge. Arguing that the degree of corruption "by writing, by Christian religion, and by their presence in European circles" misses the complexity of both Occom's and Apess's attachments to indigenous sovereignty struggles, Brooks extends her historical focus to the contemporary critical moment in which "Indianness" remains situated within a "contrived scale of corruption and purity." Observing the multiplicity of influences that constitute Native subjectivity, Brooks advocates that we let go of inhibiting determinations of "Indianness" to embrace instead the capacity for social intervention modeled by these early activists. Not to do so, as Brooks shows, is to burden our inheritors with the conformist demands of our historical present rather than to imagine a space of social transformation that we hope also to inhabit.

As both Sean Teuton's and Lisa Brooks's essays demonstrate, defining Native ethics or an ethical turn in Native literary criticism represents an enormously difficult task. In what follows, I explore how American Indian feminist critics have participated in similar calls for feminist materialist and ethical analysis, before turning to an examination of Winona LaDuke's first novel to illustrate how it participates in cultural critique in order to facilitate new categories of social enablement and political identity. The call for a recognition of the reciprocal relationship that exists between Native American women's traditions and a standpoint indigenist feminist perspective that can illuminate how feminism's commitment to analyzing the reproduction of gender relations facilitates the reconstruction of American Indian women's historically fractured lives has been raised by critics such as Paula Gunn Allen, Laura Tohe, and Kathryn Shanley. Allen's analysis represents one of the earliest attempts by a cultural critic to restore gender analysis to a consideration of the organizing politics of community practices. In "Kochinnenako in Academe: Three Approaches to Interpreting a Keres Indian Tale," Allen argues that

> Analysing tribal cultural systems from a mainstream feminist point of view allows an otherwise overlooked insight into the complex interplay of factors that have led to the systematic loosening of tribal ties, the disruption of tribal cohesion and complexity, and the growing disequilibrium of cultures that were anciently based on a belief in balance, relationship, and the centrality of women, particularly elder women. A feminist approach reveals not only the exploitation and oppression within the tribes by whites and by white government but also areas of oppression within the tribes and the sources and nature of that oppression. To a large extent, such an analysis can provide strategies for the tribes to reclaim their ancient gynarchical, egalitarian, and sacred traditions.[20]

Allen proposes a "gynocratic" reading of Native American tribal traditions that emphasizes the concepts of balance and interconnectedness and that foregrounds the values of personal autonomy, communal harmony, and egalitarianism found within oral narrative forms. Her reading, however, of the feminist content within the traditional Keres ritual, "How Kochinnenako Balanced the World," seems to enact a form of "tribal feminism" that privileges a self-actualizing feminist consciousness as enabling social transformation at the expense of illustrating how tribal communal cultural values connect with feminist agency. If it is the case that tribal consciousness differs from, yet illuminates, aspects of a feminist-standpoint analysis, then on what grounds is this difference staged? And how is a "tribal-feminist" perspective different from an "information-retrieval" approach to feminist consciousness that provided the basis for second-wave feminist work?[21] These questions remain unanswered in Allen's model, yet they are crucial to articulating the differences in social and cultural location that Allen argues for.

Allen's focus on a tribal "matrilineal" consciousness as self-actualizing and privileged within American Indian communities and through which American Indian women organize and determine for themselves a place within tribal culture resonates with Laura Tohe's assertion of the prominence of "Diné women" and "Diné matrilineal culture" to the survival and continuity of women's cultural practices, despite the "[disruptions of] five hundred years of Western patriarchal intrusion." Tohe notes the important relationship established between Diné cultural traditions such as the Kinaaldá (Walking into

Beauty, or coming-of-age ceremony), matrilineal deities such as Changing Woman or White Shell Woman, the principal mythological deity through which the matriarchal system of the Diné was established, and the reconstruction of positive self-images that have enabled Diné women to resist their portrayal as " 'those poor' Indian women who were assimilated, colonized, Christianized, or victimized." Tohe demonstrates how Diné women have sustained each other during disruptive socioeconomic changes that have altered their social positions in terms of gender relationships. She argues that these women have continued to rely on "kinship" patterns and "clan relationships" that have continued to secure positive relational connections. She refuses, however, to represent or identify these practices as "feminist" in ideology.[22]

Indeed, Tohe seems determined to eschew a relationship between the cultural practices of Diné women, as they sustained them through "five hundred years of colonialism," and feminism as a movement that she characterizes as ethnocentric and performative, a movement that prompted white feminists of the 1970s to "burn their bras" and ignore the "issues that were relevant to [Diné women's] tribal communities." While it is possible to dismiss as reductive the representation of the women's movement of the 1970s in order to recognize the problems of ethnocentrism and strategic performativity that Tohe is pointing to, it is much more difficult to disregard the issue of essentialism through which she argues for the exceptionality of Diné women's cultural systems—much more difficult, because the exceptionality of Diné women legitimates a relational identity that connects Diné women through *identity as sameness* with women "from other tribes."[23]

It is possible to appreciate Tohe's argument as privileging a form of cultural resistance that recognizes tribal identity as enabling for American Indian women, even though tribal identity and matrilineal culture are not discussed in terms of their historical and political specificity. Yet it is hard to forget the "exceptionality" of Chippewa women from the White Earth Indian Reservation who were so different from other Anishinaabeg women that when they married non-Indian men they were excluded from federal recognition.[24] An explanation of the self-actualizing consciousness of Diné matrilineal culture, together with an understanding of why colonial policies targeted this cultural consciousness in other locations, provides a broader recognition of the systematic and uneven colonial processes that affect American Indian women in discrete yet relational cultural locations. Tohe concludes that "[t]here was no need for feminism because of our matrilineal culture. And it continues. For Diné women, there is no word for feminism."[25] This claim rings as a somewhat rhetorical argument for the exceptionality of Diné women's matrilineal culture, since it disavows a larger commitment to building a future for American Indian women's feminist community, a commitment that can work against asymmetrical power relations in several cultural and/or tribal locations.

In contrast to Allen's focus on feminist consciousness and Tohe's emphasis on tribal women's exceptionalism, Kathryn Shanley calls for a shifting, local analysis that can attend to "the gulf" that exists between "feminism as we theorize and practice it in the academy . . . and the way women live their lives in postcolonial times and places." Shanley argues for a cross-cultural feminist perspective that considers the common denominators and communal ties in the experiences and continuing traditions of contemporary American Indian women. She writes, "[w]hether living off-reservation in rural America, on-reservation in America's internal colonies that could be sovereign, or in America's cities, Indian women and their histories cannot be adequately represented or understood if we do not also understand their centuries-old oppressions." The standpoint for Shanley's practice exists in the provisionally known but intimately familiar space of emplacement within her family. She writes,

> [My] "Indianness" is more than blood heritage—it is a particular culture, Nakota, and a history of the place where I grew up, and more. I am also a mixed—blood, though I prefer [the] term "crossblood." . . . Woman, however, is the first skin around me, and I do not entirely know what it is or even how to talk about it. I do know it is not my story alone; my story belongs also to my mother, grandmother, sisters, friends, relatives, and so many others, including non-Indians, and all their perspectives must be respected in whatever I say. So my approach to the subject of American Indian women and history requires a shifting discourse, one that circles its subject and even circles my own subjectivity.[26]

The genealogy that Shanley constructs of a gendered identity dispersed across multiple inheritances of history and family provides a model of American Indian identity that is circular and provisional, yet conceives of the space of feminist critical work as a site for reconstructing and reimagining connections among women through the cross-cultural work of the critic. It is a space that contrasts, on the one hand, with imposed forms of tribal identity that privilege blood-quantum quotas, and thus collude with federally enforced identification policies, and on the other, with a self-constituting feminist subject that privileges individual agency. The question that remains, however, is how to conceive of women's gendered identity over time. Or to phrase the question somewhat differently in accordance with Shanley's recognition of the role of the cultural critic, what critical frameworks within contemporary feminist criticism can read the multiple intersections of race and gender identity in the context of an inherited colonial history?

To provide a provisional answer to this question, I turn to the work of feminist historian Joan Scott, whose analysis of gender as an organizing category in women's scholarship proposes a two-part theorization of gender identity that depends upon conceiving of gender relations both as "constitutive element[s] of social relations based on perceived differences between the sexes" and as "a primary way of signifying relationships of power." Scott argues for a materialist analysis of gender identity as "substantively constructed and [related] to a range of activities, social organizations, and historically specific cultural representations" in order to extend considerations of gender as an analytic category beyond what she characterizes as the "descriptive stage" of gender identifications to a conceptual level of analysis that explains how gender relations occur systematically. For Scott, feminist critics need to pursue not "universal general causality" but "meaningful explanation" through which to understand how gender relations interact with social organizations so as to articulate not only "a concept of human agency as the attempt . . . to construct an identity, a life, a set of relationships, a society within certain limits and with language," but also "[a] conceptual language that at once sets boundaries and contains the possibility for negation, resistance, reinterpretation, the play of metaphoric invention and imagination." Scott's conceptualization of gender both as a site of subject constitution and as a language through which relations of power are articulated thus provides an understanding of "the individual subject" in relation to "social organization[s]" and an explanation for "the nature of [these] interrelationships" toward a recognition of "how gender works, how change occurs."[27]

In drawing on Scott's theorization of gender relations as a conceptual apparatus for reading LaDuke's *Last Standing Woman*, my purpose is not to engage in a form of feminist privileging that deploys one set of critical thinkers against another. That is, I am not arguing for a reading of Joan Scott's work as more interventionary/resistant/enabling than the theorizations of gender and race identity offered by American Indian feminist critics and writers. This is not a form of "identity politics" as it is practiced in Susan Gubar's analysis of feminist criticism.[28] Rather, my aim here is to illustrate how these critical thinkers struggle with a similar set of organizing questions. In Scott's view, "gender as an analytic category" has been enabling for feminist historicism insofar as it "explain[s] the origins of patriarchy" on the basis of "analogies to the opposition of male and female," acknowledges the centrality of a "woman question" to recovery work in women's history by accommodating "feminism within a Marxian tradition," and recognizes "the formation of subjective sexual identity" in different schools of psychoanalysis so as to explain the production and reproduction of the subject's gendered identity."[29]

Nevertheless, Scott argues, "gender as a way of talking about systems of social or sexual relations d[oes] not appear." She claims, rather, that feminist historians, in pursuing "single origins" in terms of gender analysis, have given little attention to the imbrications of the "individual subject [with] social organization" and to "articulat[ing] the nature of their interrelationships." Yet her explanation for this neglect—that feminist critics have had "[difficulty] incorporating the term 'gender' into existing bodies of theory and convincing adherents of one or another theoretical school that gender belongs in their vocabulary"—continues to resonate as an important materialist insight for feminist criticism, especially in light of ongoing reformulations of history that are being written with what Gayatri Chakravorty Spivak calls the "tools for developing alternative histories," that is, with analytic frameworks that read history through the multiple determinations of "gender, race, ethnicity, [and] class."[30] To recognize the conceptual similarities between the issues raised by American Indian feminist critics in conjunction with the formulation of these questions in feminist historical work is to undertake a form of cross-cultural engagement that prioritizes the common ground and conceptual terrain through which to envision a form of feminist community. Such an endeavor, as well as the hopeful insights of this kind of commitment, are aptly represented in fiction by American Indian women writers, especially in fiction by Winona LaDuke.

Last Standing Woman

In *Last Standing Woman*, Winona LaDuke negotiates a space for the recognition of gender identity to community relations and tribal history by configuring the story of the disruption of the Anishinaabeg social order through invasive policies of colonial management as a series of interruptions that lead to the erosion of Anishinaabeg cultural values and to the sexual exploitation of women. Set, initially, during the nineteenth century in the waning moments of Indian resistance to the U.S. government's treaty—making process and to settler incursions on Indian land, the novel begins with the story of Ishkwegaabawiikwe, an Anishinaabeg woman "drawn to the border" between Anishinaabeg and Dakota territories and "drawn to battle" by the discord that surfaces in her marriage when she realizes her mistake in marrying a man "at war" with himself, the spirits, the Creator, and his wife, whom he beats and cuts "until she c[an]not see and c[an]not feel" (27). Isolated from her family, who "would have avenged such an act," by her husband's hunting and trading practices, Ishkwegaabawiikwe seeks to escape the physical abuse of her spouse by traveling with her brother to the border zone that divides Anishinaabeg land from Dakota Territory. There she witnesses the devastating effects of "Little Crow's War" with the United States. Confronted by the "charred remains" of the Dakota village, Ishkwegaabawiikwe searches for the Dakota woman whom she had observed and admired during a previous visit. Weary of the "battles between the Dakota and the Anishinaabeg, the battles between the Indians and the white men, [and] the war in her own lodge," she rescues the Dakota woman Situpiwin ("Tailfeathers Woman") and claims her as her "sister."[31]

By asserting a connection with the Dakota woman as her kin through a courageous act of self—determination, Ishkwegaabawiikwe disavows her community's injunction against offering help to the Dakota people and restores a sense of self—respect to the woman who is bereft of her family and tribe, for in spite of Dakota expectations to the contrary, Ishkwegaabakiikwe acts to bring aid to the Dakota people out of respect for their prior affiliations as the Anishinaabeg people's "most honored enemies," even though the Anishinaabeg leaders rejected the Dakotas' call for support in their war against the United States government for fear of violating Anishinaabeg treaty arrangements. The decision by the war chief, Shingobay, in refusing assistance to the Dakota people and in insisting on the Anishinaabeg people's autonomy results not in their future protection but in a form of administrative extermination that leads to the "terminat[ion] [of] the *Anishinaabe* reservations of Gull Lake, Sandy Lake, Pokegama, Oak Point, and others" within a year. The novel thus privileges women's acts of resistance as engendering an alternative vision of community identity that focuses on intertribal communal relations rather than autonomous ones and foregrounds the necessity for a dual approach to reconfiguring the history of the Anishinaabeg community, one that not only illustrates the multiple identifications through which community affiliations occur, but also represents as constitutive the relationship between the cultural and sexual exploitation of tribal women and the political and territorial dispossession of the Anishinaabeg people.[32]

In a novel that relentlessly explores the issue of community fragmentation for several generations of Anishinaabeg people who struggle to resist the physical erosion of the community's land base by "the white man's law" and his "treaty" and the spiritual destruction of their ceremonies through religious conversion by the "Episcopal and Catholic priests," LaDuke deploys the kinship union between Ishkwegaabawiikwe and Situpiwin as a symbolic act of resistance to the erosion of community values. Their kinship signifies women's cultural connection and interdependence and conveys an ethical consciousness that transcends tribal dissolution and community antagonisms to assume both material and spiritual dimensions within the novel. Thus, when Ishkwegaabawiikwe and Situpiwin learn of the proposal by the "pine cartel" and the Indian agent Simon Michelet to deforest several allotments at Many Point and to eliminate the seasonal round of trapping and wild rice harvesting at Round Lake, they are able to unite with traditional community members to protect the land and destroy the logging equipment in an act of defiance that reestablishes a resistant consciousness within the tribe and that consolidates the spiritual renewal of the community that began with Ishkwegaabawiikwe's re-creation of the drumming ceremonies.[33]

Although the community does not go unpunished for its behavior—several families starve to death when government rations are withheld by the Indian agent and members of the drumming circle are arrested and incarcerated for practicing the ceremonies—Ishkwegaabawiikwe's opposition to the Indian agent and the timber barons, together with the spiritual regeneration initiated within the community by the resurgence of "Ojibway ceremonies," provides a touchstone for subsequent generations at White Earth. The younger people learn of Ishkwegaabawiikwe's courage and her kinship with Situpiwin through intergenerational storytelling and recover the ceremonies as an alternative symbolic framework for countering the material and spiritual devastation that occurs on the reserve through economic disparity and rampant poverty.[34]

Indeed, one of the most compelling features of LaDuke's novel is her representation of the social problems of alcoholism and drug addiction as a trans-historical phenomenon perpetuated by the fragmentation of community ties and the social isolation of community members. Through the story of Janine Littlewolf, set in the contemporary moment, LaDuke links the concept of intergenerational disinheritance and social isolation represented by Situpiwin's deprivation of her family and the loss of Anishinaabeg members through death, disease, and residential schools to the contemporary predicament of Anishinaabeg women who endure systemic poverty and emotional despair as a result of their "accumulation of intergenerational grief." LaDuke illustrates how the expression of Janine Littlewolf's desperation in "drown-[ing]" in alcohol her "pain of loss" for her children, who have been taken by social workers, continues the legacy of disinheritance and isolation that women endure historically through the loss of their children to social-welfare institutions. In keeping with her personal history of absent parents and an institutional upbringing, where her only "memories of intimacy" were represented by "the nuns of nine years of boarding school," Littlewolf suffers from a similar legacy of abjection for "having signed over her parental rights" such that "she never could locate [her children], and they could never know of her, their blood family, or even of each other."[35]

The resonances between Littlewolf's physical act of repudiation in signing away her children reverberates symbolically with the political act of dispossession resulting from the treaty and allotment arrangements through which the Anishinaabeg people were perceived to have sealed away their allotment land with "the stroke of a pen on a sheet of paper." Yet LaDuke's novel struggles to reconfigure the abjection of this reading of Anishinaabeg history by articulating a form of social solidarity between community members that is organized through "the crises and contingencies of historical survival." The figure of George Ahnib, Janine Littlewolf's only remaining son who "huffs" gasoline to escape impoverishment and to enter the world of the drum, exemplifies LaDuke's commitment to expressing a form of community that is not bound by federally imposed identity provisions or paternalistic categories of biological inheritance but emerges out of the community's accumulated identifications with each other and their collective struggles in history. In LaDuke's view, George belongs to the reservation through bonds of personal and group history and political priority, not only because "[it] was his home," but also because "he [was] related by blood to many families, . . . related by the tragedy and joy of the village's collective history."[36]

The central conflict in the novel illustrates LaDuke's concern to articulate a form of collective community identity that enables the social reconstruction of members' historically fractured lives without reassembling them at the expense of individual interest groups and without reconfiguring social justice issues as race relations. The decisive moment occurs during a standoff between a community-based group known as "Protect Our Land"—an organization reminiscent of "Anishinaabe Akeeng"—and FBI officials who are supported by the tribal council and several non-Indian community members because of resentment for the demands made by Protect Our Land and a growing sense of vulnerability after learning that their titles to property on reservation land are clouded.[37] When Alanis Nordstrom, an "Indian reporter" for the *Rocky Mountain News* who grew up off—reserve and whose identification with her inheritance from the Anishinaabeg community is "conveniently Indian," returns to White Earth to cover the story of the occupation of the tribal offices by members of Protect Our Land, she learns of the opposition of the group to the tribal council's decision to construct a mill for logging purposes on sacred reservation land. Following the repeated dismissal of their objections by the tribal council, the members of Protect Our Land resolve to voice their protest through confrontational means, for clear-cutting the land represents both a spiritual and material assault. It not only jeopardizes the tribe's social resources through the possible elimination of their "hunting and trapping lands" and "medicin[al] plants," but also risks their cultural past and future inheritances through the desecration of the grave sites that house the artifacts of beadwork, medicine pouches, and bones of the Anishinaabeg dead. The participation in the resistance by Elaine Mandamin, the great-great-great granddaughter of Mindemoyen, a woman who lost her land in 1915 when the government's representative from the Smithsonian Institution claimed that her "cranial measurements" and "scarable skin" determined that she was "of mixed blood descent," together with the garrison strategies undertaken by Moose Hanford, the great-grandson of Ishkwegaabawiikwe, whose grave site had been desecrated by archaeology students from the university, illustrates how LaDuke represents the conflict over clear-cutting as a social justice issue. This issue, for LaDuke, foregrounds the oppositional consciousness associated with women's collective cultural disinheritance but builds solidarity within the feminist community through inclusive gender politics.[38]

Indeed, one of the most excruciating scenes in the novel occurs in response to the abdication of responsibility to an indigenous feminist community by Alanis Nordstrom. Frightened by the threat of guns arrayed on both sides of her as she enters the tribal offices to report on the activities of Protect Our Land, yet confident that her "adopted survival strategy" of passing as Indian during the cultural events of powwows and rallies participated in "from the stands" will distinguish her from the group, Alanis is stunned by the realization that someone has mistaken her for a "militant" member of the community organization and fired on her. The moment of recognition that Alanis experiences demonstrates LaDuke's uncompromising stance toward race identity as a social position that cannot be appropriated as a site of privilege dissociated from its imbrication in hierarchical social relations. As Alanis struggles to deny her complicity with the material advantages that accrue to race identity through passing as a "weekend Indian," the narrative voice of the storyteller intervenes to assert the epistemic violence of race identity configured through racist doctrine:

> The bullets had not hit her, had not torn into her physical body and shattered bones and spilled blood, but the bullets had hit her just the same, hit her somewhere else deep inside. She was in shock as she stood still, silently fighting to regain her composure. *I am not you*, she had almost said, yet obviously to whomever had leveled the rifle to his shoulder, closed one eye to sight it, placed his finger on the cool steel of the trigger and pulled, obviously to that person she was *one of them*. And that person—whether he had tried to kill her and missed or merely had tried to scare her with a close shot—had taken away a part of her. And now her image of herself as the objective, professional newspaper reporter became confused with her image as the gunman saw her, as an Indian, as an enemy, as someone to shoot. The bullets had destroyed the boundaries in her mind, and the ricochet reverberated through her very soul.[39]

LaDuke resolves the conflict associated with Alanis's experience of disidentification and "miscognition" by illustrating how her experience of physical violation prompts her to abandon her position of objectivity such that she begins to identify with the vision of community and economic sustainability adopted by Protect Our Land, to broadcast the conflict publicly so as to expose the social and ethical commitments of the group, and to return to the reservation as a prodigal member. She acts to reestablish connections in the aftermath of the resolution to the conflict, which includes the cancellation of the "logging permit and mill construction lease," and to help in the funeral arrangements for Hawk Her Many Horses, a member of Protect Our Land who was killed during the standoff. LaDuke settles Alanis's confusion over race identity and race privilege by demonstrating a transformation in her character's consciousness such that she recognizes the material costs of perceiving subordinate-group identity and racist ideology as *optional* issues for political commitment.[40]

Many of the political sentiments expressed in the novel are also reflected in LaDuke's public statements about the relationship between activist engagements and ethical responsibility. In an interview with the *Seattle Times*, when asked how she felt about "white people who want to participate in native-land, environmental or social-justice causes," LaDuke replied, " 'Do it because it's the right thing. . . . Don't do it because of guilt. Do it because it encourages your own humanity.' "[41] That LaDuke articulates a vision of feminist community that is inclusive in terms of gender identity yet organized through a politics of affiliation signals her responsibility to work exhaustively toward her goals of rebuilding community identifications and transforming relations of power in order to establish a desirable and enabling collective future.

One of the most compelling features of LaDuke's novel is her configuration of a site for the establishment of a community formulated on the basis of its "common humanity" and ethical responsibility in her claim for the White

Earth Indian Reservation as an "Anishinaabe homeland." Narrated through the transhistorical feminist consciousness of "Ishkwegaabawiikwe, the Storyteller," the narrative restores to the Anishinaabeg people a vision of their common origins and historical agency that begins with the arrival of the people at Gaawaawaabiganikaag, "White Earth," a place "named after the white clay you find [there]," as the consummate end to a spiritual journey that began with their thousand-year migration from the "big waters in the *Waaban aki*, the land of the east" and concluded with their arrival "*Ningaabii'anong*, [in] the west." LaDuke's vision of the formation of White Earth as a place constructed through divine intervention that transports the Anishinaabeg people from a liminal state of existence, where they "undulated between material and spiritual shadows," to a new beginning in the observance of the "Creator's law" and in recognition of a "season[al] round," not only connects the Anishinaabeg to the land through a spiritual purpose that disavows its formation as a remnant of the treaty process in which the Anishinaabeg people become the victims of colonial management, but also articulates their relationship to the land as a material fact in recognition of their historical agency.[42] Thus, in LaDuke's view, the Anishinaabeg people's right to the land cannot be superseded by secular issues that privilege the relations of law and government over the relations of the metaphysical. For LaDuke, the Anishinaabeg people's material and spiritual connections to the land are fused such that they cannot be distinguished through quantifiable blood connections or illegally imposed colonial patterns of ownership.

The concluding events of the novel emphasize this view as they illustrate the return to the White Earth community of the bones of their ancestors and the cultural belongings that had resided for decades in the Smithsonian Institution in Washington. Organized through the efforts of Elaine Mandamin and Danielle Wabun, two members of Protect Our Land who discover an "inventory of the people and belongings missing from the reservation through the years," and with the aid of Alanis Nordstrom, who researches the "anthropologists and Indian agents' records for White Earth" to match "people [with] documents and sacred items," the community prepares for the return of "funerary objects, human remains, and objects of cultural patrimony" to be reburied on the land. The scene in which Moose Hanford's van breaks down while he's traveling from Washington to White Earth with the remains of ancestors from the Anishinaabeg community, his feelings of vulnerability when several people stop to assist him, including a police officer whom he worries might arrest him, and his buoyant response when he realizes that the people surrounding him have offered their help because they support the rights of American Indian peoples to repatriate their cultural artifacts demonstrates the future moment of cooperation and understanding that LaDuke envisions between Indian and non—Indian peoples.[43] The novel thus offers the issue of repatriation,[44] and its attendant recognition of the rights of First Peoples to reclaim their lands and their cultural effects, as a contemporary problem whose resolution all people can work toward.

Such a recognition on LaDuke's part reconfigures the boundaries of identity politics away from an oppositional stance that privileges race identity and asymetrically organized race relations toward a communal position that envisions a common humanity. What resides at the forefront of this vision of community relations is a feminist indigenous network organized through the values of mutual respect and cultural obligation. LaDuke thus writes from a site of feminist politics and indigenous identification similar in kind to that articulated by authors such as Louise Erdrich, who, in much of her fiction and especially in *The Antelope Wife*, expresses profound concern for the plight of indigenous women and for their exploitation at the hands of indigenous men. Erdrich, like LaDuke, Linda Hogan, Maria Campbell, and Beatrice Culleton Mosionoier, undertakes complex interweavings of character development with plot structure in order to illuminate how women's lack of access to tribal and community cultural resources perpetuates their socioeconomic disempowerment and often violent sexual exploitation. In this respect, these writers articulate an alternative political grounding for their work, one that might best be understood as *indigenous feminist* in conceptual orientation and as a crucial resource for thinking through Native identity across several registers of the social formation.

Notes

1. *Manypenny v. United States*, 948 F. 2d 1057 U.S. Ct. App. 1991 (hereafter *Manypenny* 1991), 1058–1062; White Earth Land Settlement Act, 100 Stat. (1986).

2. White Earth Indian Land Claims Settlement, S. 1396 v, vii, viii. In an attempt to smooth over the uneven historical contradictions inherent in the term and to forestall recognition of community social practices determining membership, Congress included an additional qualifier that defined "mixed-blood" status as follows: "the term 'mixed blood' shall not include an Indian enrolled in any federally recognized Indian tribe, band, or community other than the White Earth Band" (viii). For an excellent account of how the U.S. government uses "theories of race" to "articulate political goals," see Garroutte, "The Racial Formation of American Indians, 224–39.

3. *Manypenny* 1991, 1060, 1063, 1065; *Manypenny v. United States* 125 F.R.D. 497 U.S. Dist. Ct. D. Minn. 1989 (hereafter *Manypenny* 1989), 502.

4. For a brief history of the land transactions, public policies, and government enactments that illustrate the mismanagement of White Earth Reservation lands by federal and state governments, see *Manypenny* 1991, 1060–1062. Melissa Meyer, in *The White Earth Tragedy*, provides an excellent account of the ways in which differences in cultural, social, and religious practices were consolidated at White Earth in terms of "mixed-blood" and "full-blood" distinctions through government legislation and internal political dissension. An invaluable analysis of the "equity suits" by White Earth heirs, together with an examination of legal and legislative dispossession of allottees and a synopsis of WELSA, appears in Holly Youngbear-Tibbetts's "Without Due Process." For a general legal history of the White Earth Indian Reservation and the complicated categories of legal claims

that emerged following the Zay Zah decision, see Peterson, "That So-Called Warranty Deed." The Zay Zah case represents the foundational quiet action title by George Aubid, Jr., that challenged the tax-delinquent status of a White Earth allottee and made clear in its decision that "the language of the Clapp Amendment cannot be taken on its face" (581).

5. Kipnis, "Feminism," 152.

6. Cronin, "Activist/Author," n.p.

7. LaDuke, "Indigenous Women's Network," 1.

8. Ibid.

9. Rampell, "Towards an Inaugural Pow-Wow," n.p. Support was withheld from the Green Party by Gloria Steinem, a board member of the Feminist Majority Foundation, and Dolores Huerta, cofounder of the United Farm Workers, both of whom, according to Ed Rampell, "vigorously backed Gore and called upon women not to vote for Nader." "Many leading feminist organizations and individuals," Rampell noted, were concerned that "a Bush victory would result in the appointment of anti-abortion Supreme Court justices, and the enactment of legislation curtailing or ending women's reproductive rights." He claimed that "many female voters apparently agreed [with mainstream feminist demands] since in the majority of states more men than women voted for Nader, according to gender voting results released by the Feminist Majority" (Rampell, "Feminist Dream or Nightmare," n.p.)

10. LaDuke's commitments include "the replacement of the cultural ethics of domination and control with more cooperative ways of interacting that respect differences of opinion and gender" and "[h]uman values such as equity between the sexes, interpersonal responsibility, and honesty . . . with moral conscience" (Rampell, "Towards an Inaugural Pow—Wow," n.p.).

11. Guerrero, "Civil Rights versus Sovereignty," 101–103.

12. Ibid., 103. Guerrero states that "These two patriarchal structures can, in concert, literally determine whether native women's claims to membership within tribes are honored or ignored" (103). Guerrero's focus on tribal membership is crucial to recognizing how indigenous women fail to gain access to community resources and thus continue in a subordinate position in dominant society, as indicated by the sociological data that takes up the majority of Guerrero's engagement. The problem that I think is overlooked in Guerrero's formulation is that a focus on membership provisions alone does not explain why indigenous women —who are members of the tribe—become objects of abuse by indigenous men. Such an explanation requires a distinction between ongoing colonialism through control of community identity by the state, as it produces normative racial categories, and violence against indigenous women by indigenous men, as it is expressed in terms of gender identity. Writing by Native women is exemplary in this regard. A subcategory within Native literature could usefully be categorized as Native feminist writing; it would include a wide range of authors such as Winona LaDuke, Louise Erdrich, Joy Harjo, Paula Gunn Allen, Maria Campbell, Beatrice Mosionier, and Janet Campbell Hale.

13. In this regard, LaDuke's writing does not distinguish her from a tradition of indigenous authors who have taken up the politics of redress both through writing and political activism. Rather, it firmly locates her within a network of indigenous intellectual exchange. See Robert Warrior's *Tribal Secrets* for an assessment of the work of Vine Deloria, Jr., and John Joseph Mathews as early examples of this strategy of engagement. Warrior argues convincingly for the politicization of literary aesthetics in his contention that American Indian literary practices need to be considered from a materialist perspective that engages both the historical circumstances from which they emerge and the political commitments of their producers (xx).

Note that the tribal name is spelled variously as "Anishinaabe" and "Anishinaabeg." In this essay I have standardized on the latter form.

14. Cook-Lynn, "American Indian Intellectualism," 76, 67.

15. Ibid., 67.

16. Owens, *Mixedblood Messages*, 47, 27.

17. Cook-Lynn, "American Indian Intellectualism, 67; Owens, *Mixedblood Messages*, 41.

18. In this sense, I would suggest that it is equally important to consider Native writing for its self-consciousness with regard to staging the limitations of singular identities privileged at the expense of other aspects of relational selfhood. My reading of LaDuke's writing for its intersectional consciousness of race and gender identity represents an attempt to think through the social implications and political alternatives proposed by a critical stance that illuminates the imbrications of race and gender identifications and disidentifications under different historical conditions.

19. By "standpoint feminist perspective," I mean to invoke Nancy Hartsock's elaboration of the term as not "simply an interested position," which she qualifies as a "bias," but rather a critical stance that is invested in "the sense of being engaged" (Hartsock, "Feminist Standpoint," 107). For Hartsock, a standpoint structures knowledge formations in an invested way that "posits a duality of levels of reality, of which the deeper level or essence both includes and explains the 'surface' or appearance, and indicates the logic by means of which the appearance inverts or distorts the deeper reality" (108). Additionally, the concept of a standpoint, according to Hartsock, "depends on the assumption that epistemology grows in a complex and contradictory way from material life" (108). Hartsock's definition of "standpoint thinking" has not only been important to my analysis of the relationship between gender and history in American Indian women's critical practices, but also to my foregrounding of colonial politics through legal and legislative representations, that is, the presence of American Indian identity in colonial legal texts. For the American Indian critics I cite here, the loss of Indian land represents a deeply historical and material power relationship that is theorized according to several organizing sets of criteria, one of the most urgent of which is gender relations.

20. Allen, *Sacred Hoop*, 223.

21. My use of the term "information-retrieval approach" is indebted to Gayatri Spivak's groundbreaking formulation of the problem in "Three Women's Texts and A Critique of Imperialism." Spivak argues that the recovering the "self-authorizing" female heroine of feminist criticism from the archive of British women's history depends upon the disavowal of the feminist agent's complicity with the discourses of Western imperialism (798–99).

22. Tohe, "There Is No Word," 103, 106.

23. Ibid., 109, 110.

24. During the allotment of land among White Earth residents, the United States Chippewa Commission, set up to enforce the allotment legislation enacted by the 1889 Nelson Act, relied on a ruling by the assistant attorney general dated May 24, 1895, that "a 'Chippewa Indian' must be of 'Chippewa Indian blood'; must have a recognized connection with one of the bands in Minnesota; must have been a Minnesota resident when the act was passed; and must move to one of the reservations with the intention of residing there permanently." The ruling, according to Melissa Meyer, "discriminated against the children of Anishinaabe women who married U.S. citizens after 9 August 1888 denying them rights under the Nelson Act" (Meyer, "White Earth Tragedy," 60).

25. Tohe, "There Is No Word," 110.

26. Shanley, "Blood Ties and Blasphemy," 209, 210, 205.

27. Scott, "Gender," 41, 33.

28. Gubar, "What Ails Feminist Criticism?" 878–902. Gubar argues that "a number of prominent advocates of racialized identity politics and of poststructuralist theories have framed their arguments in such a way as to divide feminists, casting suspicion upon a common undertaking that remains in dispute at the turn of the twentieth century" (880). She notes the work of "feminists of racial identity politics," such as "bell hooks, Hazel Carby, and Chandra Mohanty," as particularly egregious examples of the tendency to "promote consternation among white women" (890).

29. Scott, "Gender," 41, 33.

30. Ibid., 44, 41; Spivak, "Who Claims Alterity?" 271.

31. La Duke, *Last Standing Woman*, 27, 33, 34.

32. Ibid., 32.

33. Ibid., 24, 46, 70, 40. The "pine cartel" is a term I owe to Holly Youngbear-Tibbetts. See "Without Due Process," 97.

34. LaDuke, *Last Standing Woman*, 57, 59.

35. Ibid., 72–80, 117.

36. Ibid., 24, 115, 119. The conceptualization of community through "the crises and contingencies of historical survival" and the compelling project of "enacting historical agency through the slenderness of narrative" both belong to Homi Bhabha's formulation of resistance through narrative in his provocative reading of Toni Morrison's novel *Beloved* in "By Bread Alone," 198–99.

37. LaDuke, *Last Standing Woman*, 133. The novel makes explicit reference to a court case argued in 1977 on behalf of "George Agawaateshkan," a figure reminis-

cent of George Aubid from the Zay Zah decision, who refuses to "sign papers issued to him by a county agent which would relinquish his rights to a parcel of land" at White Earth. Like Aubid, Agawaateshkan pursues the matter in court and legitimates his claim to the land when the Supreme Court of Minnesota rules in his favor and acknowledges that the "county and state had illegally taken the *Anishinaabeg* land almost sixty years before." Rather than authenticate Agawaateshkan's land claim *solely* through mixed-blood status and lines of descent in keeping with the Supreme Court decision in the Zay Zah case, LaDuke illustrates how Agawaateshkan's title emerges out of his affiliations with a transhistorical resistant consciousness that ties him as a descendant to "Bugonaygeeshig, the war chief of the southwestern *Anishinaabeg*," who was the only Anishinaabeg leader during the last of the "Indian wars" with the courage to commit the Anishinaabeg people to Dakota aid (133, 31).

38. Ibid., 183, 148, 143, 65, 138. LaDuke's description of the methods of "scientific racism" painfully captures the humiliating experience of embodiment that White Earth members were forced to endure through their objectification by government officials and scientists. When Mindemoya appears before Dr. Ales Hrdlicka to decide whether or not she is of "mixed blood" or "full blood" descent so as to determine if her land is "saleable," she is forced to endure several uncomfortable minutes while the doctor measures her cranial size and records her physical features. The most distressing moment occurs when she is ordered to disrobe while the doctor "pull[s] his thumb and forefinger across her chest in a deep scratch" in order to discover whether or not her skin is tough enough to resist penetration by sharp objects, which was believed, at the time, to be an indication of "full—blood" status. The debasing psychological and emotional violations are second only to the act of physical dispossession from her land that accompanies Hrdlicka's pronouncement that Mindemoya is of "mixed blood descent" (65).

39. Ibid., 183, 185, 187. Cheryl Harris provides a brief yet fascinating discussion of the relationship between "white privilege" and "racial passing" in relation to her grandmother's experience with race privilege in "Whiteness as Property." See 1710–12.

40. LaDuke, *Last Standing Woman*, 179, 213, 219, 316.

41. Cronin, "Activist/Author," n.p.

42. LaDuke, *Last Standing Woman*, 23, 17, 24. The connections between LaDuke's representation of the formation of the White Earth Indian Reservation as an "Anishinaabe homeland" and the search for a Jewish homeland through the epic journey of the Israelites are most likely not accidental. LaDuke is half-Jewish on her mother's side, although she identifies solely as Anishinaabe and has lived on the White Earth Reserve since 1981 when she moved to the community to become principal of the local school. Her post-secondary educational interests demonstrate an early investment in both political science and economics, both of which have been central to the social reconstruction work that she has undertaken on the White Earth Reservation. She attended Barnard College in New York City before attaining an economics degree from Harvard University; she holds a mas-

ter's degree in rural development from Antioch College. She has also been a fellow at the Massachusetts Institute of Technology. A good, if brief biography is found in Jennifer Baumgardner's interview, "Kitchen Table Candidate" in the April/May 2001 issue of *Ms.* Magazine.

43. LaDuke, *Last Standing Woman*, 270, 269, 271, 274, 276, 278.

44. Of the several articles and special journal issues devoted to the issue of repatriation of Native American remains, the most succinct in terms of its treatment of government policy, legal objectives, and community concerns is by Rebecca Tsosie, who examines the issue in relation to the discovery of "Kennewick Man"; the development of the Native American Graves Protection and Repatriation Act; and the consideration of repatriation as a political policy in its historical, cultural, and legal contexts. See "Privileging Claims," 583–677.

Theorizing American Indian Literature

Applying Oral Concepts to Written Traditions

CHRISTOPHER B. TEUTON

> The earth is a great island floating in a sea of water, and suspended at each of the four cardinal points by a cord hanging down from the sky vault, which is of solid rock. When the world grows old and worn out, the people will die and the cords will break and let the earth sink down again into the ocean, and all will be water again. The Indians are afraid of this.
>
> *Myths of the Cherokee*
> James Mooney, 1900

The old ones tell us this is how the world began. Above the arch of the Sky-Vault lay Galunlati, the sky world. A long time ago the ancient animals found themselves crowded in there; they needed more space to live. These animals were similar to those we have today. There were Rabbit, Bear, Possum, Bat, and all the others. But the animals were larger than they are now, and they could talk; this was before they were completely formed as the creatures we now know, before their forms were finally shaped by their actions.

The animals were curious about the world of water far below the Sky-Vault, which stretched as far as anyone could see. They decided to have a council in which all would have a voice in deciding what should be done about their collective problem. In the end, little Dayunisi, Beaver's Grandchild, also known

---

Christopher B. Teuton, a citizen of the Cherokee Nation, is assistant professor of English at the University of Denver, where he teaches courses in American Indian literature, multicultural literature, and American literature. He is currently researching Cherokee Nation reading practices and is at work on a book, Deep Waters: Orality, Literacy, and American Indian Critical Theory.

as the water beetle, volunteered to search the waters, looking for land for the animals to live upon. Dayunisi searched all over, but there was no land to be found. Finally, he thought to dive underneath the surface. He dove a long way down, and at last came to the bottom. With his last bit of strength, he grabbed a handful of something and brought it back up. It was a clump of mud. When Dayunisi placed it on the surface of the water, it began to spread out in all directions.

I begin this essay concerning an ethical Native literary criticism with the Cherokee creation story because it reminds me what stories and criticism should do: enable us to create our worlds. I have read this story, read about it, and found it referenced in dozens of works, including those by James Mooney, Charles Hudson, Theda Perdue, Robert J. Conley, and Thomas King. I have heard it told. I have seen it in the form of an animated cartoon by Joseph Erb, and I have seen it depicted by a Hollywood actor. I have a painting of it in my home. I have talked about it with family and friends. I have thought about it many, many times, from as many angles as I have discovered. And I have felt it, when once I lay in the middle of a creek deep in the Smoky Mountains and watched out of the corners of my eyes water beetles skitter across the surface of the water all around me. If there is a story that lives in me, it surely is this one. I never tire of its beauty and its meanings; it is both a story and a constant source of reflection on the responsibilities of being. These two aspects of its reality are inextricable.

The creation of Elohi is not simply a material matter; it occurs within and through a complex social context that is structured by clear ethical codes. As the story goes, Elohi was created by the animals of the Ancient Time because they needed more space in which to grow. The animals' goal was survival, and they first approached this goal through harmonious discussion. In council, the animals communicated with each other as equals. In the end, the council of animals relied upon an apparently weak creature, little Dayunisi, who alone could search the great expanse of water and dive deep enough to find earth. Elohi is created as a world of self-sustaining harmonious relationships in which every creature is necessary to the survival of all. Engaging the story as I am doing here, thinking about what it may mean, making claims about its symbolism, and defining some contours of its ethics, is something that has been done for as long as the story has existed. Among the reasons the story is powerful is that it is richly theoretical. Just as Plato's allegory of the cave is about more than climbing out of a hole to catch some sun, the Cherokee creation story is about more than diving into water to bring mud to the surface.

To claim that American Indian oral traditional stories like the Cherokee creation story may be read as theories or may be used as theoretical templates invites critique. The critique begins as a methodological one founded upon an argument that to interpret oral narratives as though they are equivalent to texts that are products of literacy is to confuse and obfuscate the methods and purposes of two very different forms of communication. The obvious differences between the transmission of Native knowledge in oral and written contexts are well known: The oral communicative context is communal, while writing "isolates" the reader; the oral communicative event is, at the very least, dialectic, but the reader's text never responds; the oral event exists in the present, writing exists as a record of past thought.[1] And there are other, well-noted differences between these forms of communication. For American Indian literary theory, what is most crucial about the ways in which orality and literacy have been theorized concerns the prevailing conclusions regarding the ways in which knowledge and critical methods exist in oral and literate thought.

Walter J. Ong makes strict distinctions between primary oral cultures and literate cultures, and those lines have been drawn on the level of conceptualizing critical thought: "Human beings in primary oral cultures, those untouched by writing in any form, learn a great deal and possess and practice great wisdom, but they do not 'study.' They learn by apprenticeship—hunting with experienced hunters, for example—by discipleship, which is a kind of apprenticeship, by listening, by repeating what they hear, by mastering proverbs and ways of combining and recombining them, by assimilating other formulary materials, by participation in a kind of corporate retrospection—not by study in the strict sense."[2] According to Ong, human beings in oral cultures lacked what literates would identify as a critical method. The capacity for innovative, iconoclastic, purposeful thought only came later with the technology of writing. From this perspective, to analyze the Cherokee creation story as I have done above is to reveal my own indebtedness to the technology of writing for enabling me to gain a necessary critical distance from the story in order to analyze it, as "Writing . . . serves to separate and distance the knower and the known and thus to establish objectivity."[3] Taking his lead from Ong, literary scholar Arnold Krupat similarly argues, "Traditional cultures abound in philosophical thought, powerful verbal and visual expression, and deeply felt relations to the divine or supernatural. But traditional cultures neither conceptualize nor linguistically articulate the generalized abstract categories of philosophy, literature, and religion."[4] While Ong's theories are thought-provoking, one danger in overextending the implications of the contrasts he describes has already been realized in Native American literary studies.

Claiming oral cultures do not analyze their worlds portrays our oral contemporaries and ancestors as incapable of objective analysis and critical thought. But apart from implicitly constructing a hierarchy of knowledge, one in which orality is a vehicle of static knowledge and literacy allows for empirical progress, the refusal to acknowledge that philosophical thought, "literary" expression, and religious traditions may have been, and may continue to be, expressed in oral cultures effectively denies scholars of indigenous philosophy, literature, and religion the ability to define and assert what Robert Warrior calls, in another context, a Native American "intellectual patrimony."[5] The critical methodologies that could come from claiming such a patrimony are denied any reality from the outset, as not only the narrative products of Native peoples but the practice of doing "Native American literature" is tied up in non-Native forms of representation and criticism: "In varying degrees, all verbal performances studied as 'Native American literature,' whether oral, textualized, or written, are mixed, hybrid; none are 'pure' or, strictly speaking, 'autonomous.' Native American written literature in particular is an intercultural practice; moreover, so far as it is written for publication, it is offered to a general audience, all of whose members in their own ways 'receive' it, even though none of them can in any reasonable way be said to 'own' it."[6] To extend the logic of this rhetorical position, it can be said that contemporary American Indian critical thought that builds off of any Native utterance is a hybrid product, not simply because the audiences for these utterances may be "intercultural," the texts may be written in English, or even that their authors may claim mixed racial or cultural heritages but because the practice of analyzing the world through linguistic expression is understood as *Western in origin*. As long as this rhetorical position toward Native critical thought prevails, the connections contemporary scholars make with linguistic expressions of the Native past will be labeled critically anachronistic. In a final bitter irony, should we scholars of Native literature assume the rhetorical position that is claimed for oral people—that oral stories exist outside of criticism and are self-evidently truthful—we are labeled "essentialist" thinkers.

The divisions between oral and literate cultures that so often constrain the ways in which Native American thought can be theorized may be specific to the field of literary studies, for it appears that scholars in history and anthropology claim Indians have always theorized their worlds. In his magisterial *The Southeastern Indians*, Charles Hudson states, "It is useful to think of this Southeastern Indian belief system as a kind of theory. Just as a theory in our natural sciences explains a certain range of phenomena, a belief system explains unusual events in everyday life, though it is expressed in terms we generally call religious or magical. But to regard the belief system of the Southeastern Indians as being merely religious or magical is to fail to appreciate it."[7] These "theories," of course, are expressed in ceremonies, rituals, and stories. In *A Forest of Time: American Indian Ways of History*, Peter Nabokov argues that Native oral traditions do not simply replicate belief, but are a form of discourse that extends Native knowledge and history through their diversity of representations: "By identifying the multiple, often quarreling interest groups within any society, and by making each of their claims the measure of any given history's intended relevance or 'scale' (rather than abstract concepts of time or genres of narrative), we arrive at oral tradition's defining benefit and unending pleasure: multiple versions."[8] Nabokov's analysis of oral expression contradicts the portrayal of oral cultures as necessarily conservative in striving to preserve their knowledge: "Rather than being closed systems of fixed symbols, if myths are to remain relevant and recited they must be susceptible to internal tinkerings and updatings."[9] While Hudson and Nabokov approach their studies of Native orality with different methodologies, both scholars assume that oral peoples have concepts, theories, and systems of knowledge, including belief systems and forms of historicizing the past.

The literary scholar who feels compelled to defend within his/her own field a critical interpretation that in other fields is a nonissue is bound to intuit the debate as more concerned about the politics of Native literary interpretation than it is about accurately representing the genealogies of Native American cultural heritage. Maori scholar Graham Smith identifies the attempt to deflect discussion away from pressing indigenous issues as the "politics of distraction," a political dynamic in which indigenous scholars are "drawn into engaging with and justifying ourselves to the dominant society."As an example, in this essay I have been writing about a methodological issue concerning interpretation that, in my experience, has little relevance to the ways in which stories are actually told and valued in contemporary Native communities. The interpretive issue is an academic one, concerning as it does the ways in which texts are understood in an academic context, and, in light of the obvious power dynamics involved, it "puts the colonizer at the centre, and thereby we [indigenous academics] become co-opted into reproducing (albeit unintentionally) our own oppression."[10]

Having justified as much as I feel necessary the reason I may engage the Cherokee origin story as a critical source, I now want to discuss the critical methods and ethics that may be drawn from such an engagement with oral tradition.

In the full origin story, layer upon layer of meaning is added as Cherokees articulate their worldview and model complex strategies for interpreting that world. One way of reading the story is as an allegory concerning the creation and application of knowledge. A tribally centered interpretation of the Cherokee origin story might conceptualize the reader as an analogue of Dayunisi. Like Dayunisi, the reader leaves the ordered world of stable, static knowledge, the Upper World, in order to dive deep into the unexplored depths of chaotic and mysterious potential meaning in the Under World. Like Dayunisi, each reader brings his/her own viewpoint, experience, and unique skills to the task of interpretation. The act of returning with new knowledge and fresh interpretations creates new terrain upon which the community may continue to grow. Knowledge is sought and valued in relation to the collective harmony and survival of the community as a whole.

Read as an allegory about the creation of new knowledge, the Cherokee origin story models criticism as a social practice. The story is built upon relationships: among the animals themselves, between the animals and Galunlati, and between the animals and the Under World. Crucially, the existence of all those relationships depends upon discussion and one individual risking his life for the good of the whole. Dayunisi dives into the water not because it is his duty but because he can; he has the specific tools needed to help others, and his sacrifice is an act of altruism. And it is that act of altruism upon which the world depends. It is the first Cherokee conceptualization of social responsibility, and, coming out of oral tradition, it is a clear articulation of an ethical purpose and motivation for creating new knowledge, which is also at the heart of critical thought.

In spite of the resistance to acknowledge the conceptual continuity between oral and literate modes of critical thought, recent critical works by scholars such as Jace Weaver, Taiaiake Alfred, Maureen Konkle, Lucy Maddox, and Robert Warrior reveal in diverse ways that since the first writings were printed by Indians in North America, criticism as a social practice has been embedded within these works. An apt term for these works is "communitist," to use Jace Weaver's term, as they are committed to community with an activist intent. But, rather than arguing that these works were communitist exclusively because of the social and political contexts in which they were produced, I want to suggest that the sources of the communitism in Native writing have their origins as a sociocritical practice in Native oral traditions.

Robert Warrior's *The People and the Word: Reading Native Nonfiction* illustrates on multiple levels the ways in which Native writers have used their literary skills to serve the interests of Native people. Warrior focuses exclusively on the contributions of Native literacy, as he claims "the history of Native writing constitutes an intellectual tradition, a tradition that can and should inform the contemporary work of Native intellectuals." While tracing out a genealogy of the contributions and effects of literacy in the work and lives of William Apess, the framers of the Osage constitution, N. Scott Momaday, and accounts of Native students in boarding schools, Warrior's text illustrates the ethical dimension common to such temporally and culturally distanced subjects. Warrior is correct in asserting, "Nonfiction writers have brought us impassioned pleas on behalf of Native peoples, accounts of crucial moments in Native history, profiles of people in contemporary Native communities, and explorations of dysfunctions, like substance abuse, in the Native world. But what motivated writers such as Apess to dedicate their lives to support Native people through writing? The question is perhaps impossible to answer with any exactness, but it is worth asking, as Warrior claims: "This tradition of writing is the oldest and most robust type of modern writing that Native people in North America have produced as they have sought literate means through which to engage themselves and others in a discourse on the possibilities of a Native future." What is key here is that Native American nonfiction writers, including scholars, continue to write in support of their communities and Native America as a whole, and they do so, as much as—and perhaps more than—any other group of scholars with an ethical dimension in mind. Witness Warrior's own purpose for writing this text: "My overarching concern is working out how doing the work of the critic and intellectual can contribute to improving the intellectual health of Native America, its people, and its communities." And Warrior approaches his subject matter with a decidedly textual methodology, one soundly grounded in archival work, cultural and literary history, and close readings of texts and contexts.[11]

While reaching for similar goals, Taiaiake Alfred's *Peace, Power, Righteousness: An Indigenous Manifesto* utilizes the Rotinohshonni Condolence ceremony for its structure and methodology. It is fascinating to juxtapose these two texts. Warrior's is dedicated to exploring the tradition of intellectual thought in literacy, while Alfred's is dedicated to reinvigorating Native intellectual traditions through a renewed focus on oral traditional paradigms: "I am advocating a self-conscious traditionalism, an intellectual, social, and political movement that will reinvigorate those values, principles, and other cultural elements that are best suited to the larger contemporary political and economic reality." Warrior focuses on critically neglected writings, and Alfred on critically neglected oral traditions: "The meanings of our traditional teachings are embedded in the structure of the narrative as much as in any words one might write in order to explain them."[12] While on the surface very different, the two works share a commitment to Native community and a focus on the social responsibilities that are crucial aspects of both oral and literate traditions. Speaking of the purposes of intellectual thought, Warrior writes of his work, "These readings, then, are self-consciously committed ones that take seriously the social and existential implications of intellectual work and proceed from the idea that what intellectuals do ought to matter and ought to make a difference in the real lives of real people living in real time."[13] Similarly, Alfred places knowledge in a community context, but links it to a definition of identity: "However knowledgeable and rooted one may be, one cannot be truly indigenous without the support, inspiration, reprobation, and stress of a community as facts of life. Ideas transform when they make the journey from the mind of one person into the collective consciousness; and our peoples' reality is communal."[14] Based on two very different methodological approaches, what ties together the work of Alfred and Warrior is their commitments to Native community within the context of knowledge production, and that ethos of social responsibility runs strong in both the written and oral traditions they discuss and model in their own works.

If writing isolates, creates individualism, then how is it that Native literary studies is so dominated by the concerns of Native community? The ethical dimension of Native literature owes much to the values expressed in oral traditions, values that are now shared and explored in Native nonfiction and fiction. So strong is the ethical dimension of Native American writing that the different ways in which criticism is performed as a social practice may serve as a rubric for defining several approaches to the study of Native American literature and the purposes of Native American literary criticism.

Three Sociocritical Modes of Interpretation

It is often claimed that American Indian literary criticism began as a field of study in the late 1960s and early 1970s during the blossoming of what Kenneth Lincoln named the "Native American literary renaissance," but that system of dating Native American critical writing needs to be pushed back. While much debate surrounds what is considered "writing," it is accepted that at least since the first century B.C. the Maya people of Izapan had systems of writing and iconography. There are assuredly other, more ancient forms of critical writing, but the Quiché Maya *Popol Vuh* stands out as one of the earliest and continuously influential works of critical writing produced in the Americas. Apart from being one of the most complex texts in human history, one that offers a fully integrated and layered astronomical, cosmological, epistemological, agricultural, and religious epic, the *Popol Vuh* is also a postcolonial text that calls attention to itself as both a record of a colonized people and a source of their resistance. Around 1558 it was translated from Quiché Mayan into Spanish by writers who refused to identity themselves, but whose work bears their defiance of the Spanish colonizers. One way of reading the *Popol Vuh* is as a book about a book, the Maya "Council Book," or "The Light That Came from beside the Sea," a text that was "the potential and source for everything done in the citadel of Quiché, the nation of the Quiché people." One imagines that writing in secrecy, transcribing from "the original book and ancient writing," the Quiché authors could see where the colonizers would lead their people. With the destruction of their books and their nation, and with their culture and belief system under attack "now amid the preaching of God, in Christendom now," they used the weapon of language to serve the future needs of their people in order to remain a people. Nearly five hundred years after it was written in Quiché, the *Popol Vuh* continues to live within Maya culture as, among other functions, a Maya critical text that embodies a Maya critical methodology.[15]

The field of American Indian literary studies has only recently begun to reconceptualize what may constitute critical methodologies and the sources, such as the *Popol Vuh*, from which these methodologies may originate. But currently, the academic study of American Indian creative works may be divided into three critical modes of interpretation. These modes are not strictly chronological; all three styles of criticism continue to be published. The three modes may be differentiated not just by the central questions they ask, but by the ethical positions they define in relation to the social contexts they engage. The progression of the modes marks a gradual shift from non-Native-centered to Native-centered epistemologies employed in the analysis of Native literature. Mode one criticism has its roots in ethnographic and anthropological discourse and is inevitably concerned to some degree with issues surrounding the implications of Native American cultural authenticity and cultural identity. A tacit question that haunts mode-one criticism is

"Who and what is an Indian?" Mode-two criticism attempts to correct the misrepresentation of Native peoples and cultures. Functioning similarly to those Native American criticisms that Robert Warrior argues appeal to "idealism" and/or "essentialism" and that hope to provide a "strong counternarrative to received academic and popular understandings of American Indian people and cultures," mode-two criticism often allows its discourse to be determined by that which it would argue against, asking, "Who can say who and what is Indian but an Indian?"[16] Mode-three criticism bypasses questions of representation to theorize how academic work can be made accountable and put in dialogue with Native people, communities, and nations. Mode-three criticism is speculative and process-oriented, asking, "How are we Native people and nations to become who we want to become?" Although each mode asks different types of questions and addresses different audiences' concerns, they often exist side by side; the borders between each mode are potentially fluid. A single article may contain examples of mode-one, -two, and –three criticism, sometimes necessarily so. Nevertheless, particular critical modes have dominated Native literary discourse at different points during the past thirty years or so, and this literary history needs to be explored in order for Native literary discourse to understand its present and future paths.

Mode-one Native American literary criticism began in the mid-1970s and is defined by criticism that applies mainstream critical theories and methodologies, with their epistemological roots in Western thought, to interpret American Indian literature. Works such as Kenneth Lincoln's *Native American Renaissance* use an interdisciplinary methodology based on anthropological, ethnographical, and historical sources and attempt to translate Native cultural thought through analyzing literature: criticism as an act of cultural translation. The use of non-Native evaluative models that do not draw on Native worldviews or knowledge systems for their philosophical bases to critique Native American art is understandable when one considers the historical context. In the early 1970s, when Native literature was first recognized as a field of study, scholars struggled foremost to get Native literature recognized as a legitimate focus of scholarship, worthy of being taught in universities. To this end, Native literary scholarship was mostly interested in developing a canon of Native literature, focusing specifically on questions of definition: "What is Indian literature?" and "Who is an Indian author?"[17] As the field moved into the 1980s, mode-one scholarship continued the process of cultural translation and provided important cultural background research, useful readings of specific texts, and important bibliographic and literary historical research.

Recent works of mode-one discourse have begun to reimagine the relationships between Native American art, culture, and politics in relation to Western culture. Arnold Krupat's *The Turn to the Native: Studies in Criticism and Culture* is indicative of this development, advocating a form of "cross-cultural translation or ethnocriticism" as a "critical language that might mediate" between texts as different as "Proust and Native American fiction."[18] In *Red Matters: Native American Studies*, Krupat argues once again for a cosmopolitan literary pose, one that "cobbles . . . [a] criticism out of a variety of perspectival possibilities" and whose purpose of "cross-cultural translation" claims that the nationalist, indigenist, and cosmopolitan perspectives need each other to "achieve [their] full discursive effectivity."[19] Recently, however, critics such as Maureen Konkle have begun to challenge what they see as an inherent privileging of cultural contexts over political contexts in the study of Native American literature. In her analysis of the politics of Indian intellectual discourse, *Writing Indian Nations*, Konkle writes of the nineteenth-century Cherokee writer Elias Boudinot's use of his education in the struggle to preserve the sovereignty of the Cherokee Nation prior to removal: "The two main points that Boudinot as a Cherokee spokesman tried to get across to whites were, first, that the Cherokees formed a political entity that was separate from and not subordinate to U.S. authority and, second, that the Cherokees and other Native peoples had been misrepresented by whites as static primitives locked in time, when they in fact had changed over time like whites themselves." A Western education equipped nineteenth-century Indian intellectuals like Boudinot to "reject racial difference, claim history and therefore political equality for themselves, and, often through the use of sustained textual analysis, refute whites' knowledge about them as politically self-interested misrepresentations."[20] Konkle shows that not just literacy, but the use of "textual analysis" specifically has an historical precedent in the Cherokee Nation as a crucial tool of decolonization. While mode-one criticism continues to make important contributions to Native literary studies on the academic level, its Western methodological orientation and focus on an academic audience was one of the factors that gave rise to a second mode of criticism that sought to make American Indian literary studies more accountable to Native concerns and to address American Indian audiences directly.

Mode-one and mode-two scholarship developed side by side. Critics such as Vine Deloria, Jr., Paula Gunn Allen, Ward Churchill, and Gerald Vizenor wrote mode-two political, cultural, and literary theoretical criticism throughout the '70s, '80s, and '90s. Despite what may at first appear focused on an academic audience, a great deal of mode-two criticism is addressed to mainstream readers. While often differing widely in terms of methodological approach, mode-two scholarship is defined by two differing critical paths that attempt to reach similar goals. Concerning issues of representation, writers such as Vizenor attempt to show the ramifications of Euroamerican stereotypes on the self-perceptions of Native people. Vizenor's philosophical idealist position attempts to persuade readers of his trickster discourse to reimagine who they are, in all their historical, cultural, and racial complexity, with the aim of freeing them metaphysically. More concerned with the struggles over Native American material reality, mode-two works by scholars such as Elizabeth Cook-Lynn attempt to keep the central focus and goal of Indian studies as a field and scholarship about Indians actively committed to supporting the sovereignty of Native nations and cultures. Cultural critics such as Deloria, whose 1969 groundbreaking work, *Custer Died For Your Sins: An Indian Manifesto*, laid bare the systems of power and repression that have served to subjugate Indians, turned the critical gaze back on mainstream American culture. An important function of this struggle has been the creation of Native critical neologisms, concepts, and strategies, such as Vizenor's "terminal creeds," introduced in his first novel, *Darkness in Saint Louis Bearheart* (1978); Allen's terms "gynocentric" and "gynocratic," discussed in *The Sacred Hoop* (1986); and Cook-Lynn's term "anti-Indianism," articulated in *Anti-Indianism in Modern America* (2001). When mode-two discourse is focused on psychic liberation, it has largely been supported by mainstream literary criticism, but when discussions of real-world political struggles over land and Native nationhood infuse mode-two scholarly works, those texts often draw critiques from scholars who claim they reduce the world-changing effects of cross-cultural exchanges on Native America.

Offering a postcolonial critique of Paula Gunn Allen's *The Sacred Hoop*, Elvira Pulitano writes, "Instead of participating in the critical dialogue from within, showing how it is possible to create new ways of theorizing while adopting the discursive tools offered by the metropolitan center, Allen steps outside, into the margin, and opts for a separatist solution. Such a separatist solution, however, ironically ends up legitimating the binary categories of Western/Eurocentric thinking."[21] Pulitano attempts to recenter the study of American Indian literature within mainstream critical discourse by claiming that a Native critical perspective is untenable. One could imagine a similar critique of Janice Acoose's essay in this volume. In attempting to articulate a culturally specific critical position, such as Allen's Laguna feminist mode of cultural critique, critics who do not foreground and privilege the supposed hybrid nature of Native cultural productions have been labeled essentialists. This tension between what have been called the "essentialist" and the more fluid ideas of Native tradition is a touchstone for the way mode-two criticism has been perceived.

Similarly, some mode-two works such as Ward Churchill's *Fantasies of the Master Race: Literature, Cinema and the Colonization of American Indians* seem reactive and might give the impression that mode two-criticism is more concerned with critiquing misrepresentations of Native cultures than with actually developing Native conceptual models. Seen in historical context, however, it has been crucial that mode-two scholarship create a space in which Native critical thought could develop in its own terms, and, in spite of the charges of "essentialism" leveled at writers of mode-two texts, mode-two scholarship has done this through articulating the differences between Native and non-Native worldviews. Mode-two scholarship has focused on the continued colonial subjugation of American Indian nations by the United States, exposing unlawful land claims, abuses of federal power, and the misuse of

Native lands. By following this course, however, mode-two scholarship at times risks overstating the divisions between the Native and non-Native, and has thus been perceived as overly ideological. Mode-two scholarship has accomplished a great deal in creating Native-centered academic spaces for the articulation and exploration of tribal knowledge systems, worldviews, and political theories. It has not, however, freed itself from an adversarial relationship to the Western institutional world, a fact that limits its interpretive reach.

In the 1990s, a third mode of American Indian literary scholarship began to reshape the field. Building on the work initiated within mode-one criticism, but sharing with mode-two criticism a dedication to bridging the gap between Native American critical writing and the concerns of Native American communities, mode-three criticism focuses on developing American Indian conceptual, theoretical, and methodological discourses to be used in the study of Native American art, culture, and politics. To varying degrees, and sometimes in direct conflict, critical texts by Native intellectuals—Gerald Vizenor, Robert Warrior, Greg Sarris, Craig Womack, Louis Owens, Jace Weaver and, among others, the contributors to this volume—build upon the work of mode-two scholarship by acknowledging the differences between Western and Native worldviews, but they endeavor to shift the focus of Native American literary discourse from a reactive critical position to one that may be both theoretically sophisticated and culturally grounded. Mode-three criticism engages a process of culture-building by imagining the place of critical scholarship within Native communities and by providing terms that may be used to create a space for the articulation of Native epistemologies within academia but are accessible and informative to mainstream audiences. Craig Womack, for example, articulates several important mode-three concerns in his article in this volume: "What is the relationship between our theories and the people we are theorizing about? Do the subjects of our theorizing see themselves in the same way as we describe them in books, journal articles, classroom lectures, and so on? How do we bring their self-representations into our theorizing? I see this as one of the most salient, as well as the most difficult, ethical questions in my life as a scholar."

Firmly committed to the idea of tribal sovereignty, mode-three criticism debates the best means to be used in decolonizing Native American critical studies. As Womack makes clear, one method is to enter into dialogue with one's tribal community. Still, while some mode-three critics argue with Elizabeth Cook-Lynn that Native national sovereignty and community survival should be the goal of Native literary criticism, others, such as Louis Owens, support a more exploratory and transformational critical ethos in keeping with Gerald Vizenor's trickster discourse. In a similar vein, Tol Foster's essay on Will Rogers in this volume argues that a strength of Native American literature has been its ability to have a cosmopolitan constituency and intellectual reach. At the same time, Owens himself acknowledges the skepticism some Native writers have concerning the application of mainstream theory, such as postmodern theory, in Native textual studies.[22] While mode-three criticism continues to work out how, and to what extent, American Indian literary discourse may benefit from judicious use of Western academic theory, it has consistently remained focused on the articulation of Native conceptual models in the struggle for Native national rights and cultural self-actualization. As a part of this process, many works of mode-three criticism return to ideas and concepts first expressed within Native oral traditions, but developed and adapted by Native writers, for models of how to read and understand contemporary Native American literatures.

While all three modes of American Indian literary criticism address, and are informed by, mainstream critical theory, the postcolonial theoretical concept of hybridity has been particularly influential in the development of Native American literary criticism. As articulated in such canonical works as *The Empire Writes Back: Theory and Practice in Post-colonial Literatures* (1989), hybridity and syncretism have deeply influenced the development of postcolonial literatures.[23] If only because Native American writers usually publish in English, a language of American colonization, those who advocate the concept of hybridity argue that these writers occupy a hybrid, mixed, cross-cultural space that forever separates them from the precolonial past and undercuts any "separatist" political positions they may or may not advocate.[24] The political implications of how hybridity is understood have profound ramifications in the study of Native American literatures. Those who advocate hybridity as a concept argue that Native writers and critics delude themselves when they claim to write in support of decolonizing Native nations, for they are already deeply shaped and influenced by colonial power. Once again, this is an argument that is founded upon the idea that the practice of critical thought is Western in origin and is inextricably linked to literacy. Instead of resisting the label "hybrid," those who advocate hybridity might argue, Native Americans should celebrate it, for "cultural syncreticity is a valuable as well as inescapable and characteristic feature of all post-colonial societies and indeed is the source of their peculiar strength (Williams 1969)."[25] However, from the perspectives of mode-two and a growing contingent of mode-three critics, this issue of culture-sharing has little to do with cultural purity/impurity and more to do with the production and aims of knowledge within a colonial context.

Mode-three criticism makes use of, without allowing its purposes to be defined by, academic theory. Robert Warrior illustrates a mode-three critical stance when, in his introduction to *Tribal Secrets*, he justifies privileging Native voices and discourses, stating that while his position may "seem overly separatist to some, [it] accepts the influences and complexities of contemporary and historical American Indian life and prepares the ground for more fruitfully engaging non-Native critical discourses."[26] Despite Warrior's careful defense of his "Blackjacks discourse," an "intellectual space" that "regulate[ed] the process by which visitors entered that space" and allowed him to "sort through the cacophony of voices competing for critical attention," critics such as Pulitano interpreted Warrior's "intellectual sovereignty" as separatist.[27] But to pigeonhole mode-three criticism as separatist is misguided. The real defining characteristic of the mode has less to do with any separatist intellectual agenda than it does with making Native American critical thought respond to the needs of Native communities in a nonreactive, intellectually sophisticated manner. In *The People and the Word*, Warrior proposes the concept of "intellectual trade routes" as something different from but complementing "intellectual sovereignty." Linking the ancient Native tradition of trade across cultural and geographic borders, Warrior argues that the concept of intellectual trade routes enables scholars to find commonalities, differences, and "new knowledge from new places." This new knowledge comes out of the juxtapositions of wildly diverse histories, stories, and even discourses. As Warrior acknowledges, "intellectual trade routes" is a term for a "different agenda" than the "withdrawing into an intellectual space" that the Blackjacks discourse and "intellectual sovereignty" initially depended upon. While this intellectual dynamic of closing in with the Blackjacks discourse and opening up with "intellectual trade routes" may seem like a contradiction, that is only the case if one does not understand that the impetus for exploring these works remains the same: a "genuine love and passion I have for the modern development of intellectualism among indigenous people and the figures who have been instrumental to that development."[28]

Mode-three scholarship strives to create theories that respond to the issues and concerns of Native communities, and in doing so it has expanded the horizon of American Indian critical study by daring to articulate, and then privilege, Native perspectives. Works such as Sarris's *Keeping Slug Woman Alive* develop critical terms and methodologies to interpret Native literature and culture. These new terminologies are opening up ways of reading Native texts from within sociocritical frameworks that support the idea that criticism is a social act. This act of critical self-determination is a philosophical statement that asserts the value of culturally specific ontologies, epistemologies, and critical paradigms.

Mode-three criticism is just beginning to explore the field of Native American critical thought, but as the field develops it is important to recognize one crucial commonality within this form of intellectual engagement: its understanding of criticism as a social practice with the potential to impact material reality. While as of yet mode-three criticism has been largely focused on printed texts, its commitments to studying Native written literature, literary history, and critical theory are informed by the concepts and traditional values articulated within tribal oral traditions.

Building on Paulo Freire's concept of "praxis," Warrior utilizes Deloria's concept of tribal sovereignty as "process-oriented," "constructive group action" that "recognizes that American Indians have to go through a process of building community and that that process will define the future." Instead of defining "sovereignty" as the political act of preserving Native national autonomy, Warrior uses "intellectual sovereignty" to refer to a *tribal discourse* that is founded on constructing "communities and social structures through which those communities exercise political, economic, and spiritual power along with responsibility."[29] The understanding of community and discourse that is "process-oriented" and focused on building group solidarity is not a description of a social commitment immediately associated with a written discourse. As Ong is so often quoted, "Writing and print isolate. There is no collective noun or concept for readers corresponding to 'audience.'"[30] But the ways in which Warrior theorizes intellectual sovereignty assumes that there is a collective group, a readership, an audience that can be united by their commitments and their participation within a written discourse. What is in many ways amazing is that writing as if there were a collective has made that collective come together as it is doing in this volume, speaking to and with each other—and to the other audiences who may engage our discussion. Using this concept of sovereignty as a process of communal self-determination, Warrior applies his ideas to American Indian intellectual and critical discourse: "I contend that it is now critical for American Indian intellectuals committed to sovereignty to realize that we too must struggle for sovereignty, *intellectual sovereignty*, and allow the definition and articulation of what that means to emerge as we critically reflect on that struggle." In keeping with this community-centered critical approach, Warrior emphasizes the relevance of Native critical studies to "issues of economic and social class, gender, and sexual orientation," which have often been ignored.[31]

While sharing the same social commitments as Warrior's *Tribal Secrets*, Jace Weaver's *That the People Might Live: Native American Literatures and Native American Community* uses values articulated first within Native oral traditions as the basis for what he calls "communitist" literature: "It is formed by a combination of the words 'community' and 'activism.' Literature is communitist to the extent that it has a proactive commitment to Native community, including what I term the 'wider community' of Creation itself."[32] Weaver's communitism avoids judgments based upon the explicit political ideology of a text, instead expanding his interpretive apparatuses to include a definition of Native literature that is inclusive of multiple diverging viewpoints and voices, both from the past and the present.

Craig Womack's *Red on Red: Native American Literary Separatism* extends Warrior's and Weaver's work on Native intellectual and theoretical traditions by focusing on a particular indigenous nation, Womack's Creek Nation. Through studying the relationship between Muscogee Creek oral traditions, Muscogee writers, and their ties to Creek notions of nationhood, Womack argues for the existence and importance of tribally specific Native national literatures. Womack shows how oral traditional stories and Creek written narratives provide the concepts upon which Creek nationalism is built, arguing explicitly for the interpretive use of oral traditional models of nationalism when analyzing written literature: "Critics create literary theory in relation to literature, and one would expect nothing less from national literatures—that the oral tradition would generate vital approaches for examining Native literatures. Oral tradition, then, becomes central to Native political analysis and the development of Native literary theory rather than fodder for backing up critics' pet theses on performance and translation, a discussion that has become largely redundant."[33] Like Warrior's and Weaver's, Womack's work argues that the relationship between Native literature and Native communities is arguably the greatest concern of current criticism.

In her essay in this volume, "Land Claims, Identity Claims: Mapping Indigenous Feminism in Literary Criticism and in Winona LaDuke's *Last Standing Woman*," Cheryl Suzack illustrates the directions mode-three criticism may take when it maintains its dual focus on intellectual sophistication and commitment to Native communities. Suzack identifies an oppositional space in which gender identity becomes "an analytical category" through which "discussions of tribal politics and community values" may be engaged. What is both powerful and insightful about Suzack's methodology is that she is able to borrow both from mainstream notions of criticism, including feminist theory, and from theories of Native community and gender relations that are expressed in the form of the novel. Suzack does not simply apply a theory to LaDuke's novel or retrofit mainstream feminism to serve as a critical lens; instead she approaches *Last Standing Woman* as a source of theory, perhaps one of the better explorations of the ways Native American women activists come to "recognize their common identity and are moved to political action." But, beyond theorizing, Suzack challenges mainstream notions of the common boundaries between criticism and the world beyond academia by anchoring her discussion of gender in terms of the real ways the White Earth band of Chippewa Indians was categorized within the White Earth Land Settlement Act (WELSA). Criticism, theory, and practice come together in such a way that they mutually support each other.

Essays such as Suzack's share with some of the most influential works of Native American literary studies in the past ten years an expressed goal of clarifying not just the connections, but the responsibilities that Native writers, Native writings, Native communities, and critics of Native literature all share. Terms such as Warrior's "intellectual sovereignty" and, just recently, "intellectual trade routes"; Weaver's "communitism"; Cook-Lynn's "anti-Indianism"; Womack's "Red Stick" approach—all these terms, which are the markers of literary theoretical concepts, are unintelligible outside the context of Native community history, politics, and needs. They are critical terms used in theorizing the relationships between indigenous peoples and colonial powers, and as such they may be applicable to the struggles of indigenous communities around the world.

The directions in which mode-three criticism is headed require considering a general definition of Native American literary theory. In some ways, a definition of "theory" may be a little late in coming for Native American literary studies, since scholars of Native literature have surely been theorizing, creating concepts, and defining terms for years. But as the contours of the field become clearer in focus, it is certain that there is no general understanding of what constitutes theory as it is applied. And, in light of the topic of this volume, it is important to at least suggest one working definition of theory as it applies to American Indian literatures. As an example of a mainstream definition of theory, I quote Jonathan Culler:

1. Theory is interdisciplinary—discourse with effects outside an original discipline.
2. Theory is analytical and speculative—an attempt to work out what is involved in what we call sex or language or writing or meaning or the subject.
3. Theory is a critique of common sense, of concepts taken as natural.
4. Theory is reflexive, thinking about thinking, enquiry into the categories we use in making sense of things, in literature and in other discursive practices.[34]

Glaringly absent from this definition, and what makes it, as it stands, an inappropriate definition of theory as applied to Native literary studies is a reference to the social existence and obligations of theory. A fifth characteristic would perhaps read: "Theory arises out of the dialectical relationship among artists, arts, critics, and Native communities." In Culler's definition, the subject and object of theory is itself. In Native theory the subject is Native experience, the object, Native community.

What is crucial at this moment in the field of Native American literary studies is to continue to develop terms and concepts that can further the study of American Indian experience in all its richness. And just as many contemporary writers, including Lisa Brooks in this volume, are more than ever revisiting early Native writers with an eye toward constructing a genealogy of Native critical thought, it is also important to return to more recent canonical texts and replace them within the paradigms of contemporary Native American literary criticism. What increasingly seems to be the case is that writers, both creative and nonfiction, are always at least a couple critical steps ahead of the work of scholars in our field. A reading of the concept of "vision" in N. Scott Momaday's well-known *The Way to Rainy Mountain* illustrates more clearly the potential for developing alternative interpretive strategies and critical terms drawn from reading Native literature through the lens of oral traditional paradigms. In *The Way to Rainy Mountain* Momaday shows performatively how a concept may be constructed within a sociocritical context.

Reading a Concept of "Vision" in *The Way to Rainy Mountain*

In *The Way to Rainy Mountain*, the concept of "vision" entails movement from alienation to knowledge, from lack of connection to a relationship with place, from a lack of cultural identity to a deeply felt cultural identity. More than an extension of physical sight, vision is a process of mediation that includes both physical sight and intellectual and emotional insight. As a story about the migration of the Kiowas from the mountains to the plains, *Rainy Mountain* is not just about the narrator's identity, but also about the Kiowas' quest to reconceive themselves, to increase their "stature" as a people and to imagine who they could be. Throughout the text, metaphors of sight conceptualize the way the Kiowas and, eventually, the narrator understand themselves. When the Kiowas come down from the mountains and onto the plains, the newfound ability to see into the "distance" answers a fundamental need. Expressing their living relationship with the places that would become their homelands, the ability to "see far" is the physical expression of a worldview. The intellectual counterpart of this worldview theorizes insight as an ever-deepening exploration and understanding of life through the mind's eye. When the capacity for sight and insight is honed and kept vibrant, the members of a culture may attain a sense of vision that encourages actions that contribute to health and survival. In *The Way to Rainy Mountain*, this type of vision lies near the core of the culturally specific Kiowa idea of imagination that is first expressed in language and is intertwined with the relationship between a people and a land.

The introduction to *Rainy Mountain* explores how vision is nurtured by charting the narrator's process of developing a Kiowa way of seeing. As the text makes clear, vision is not pregiven. As we see and think, we are interpreting the world. This process of reflection and self-reflection is characterized by its mutability; it represents an ever-expanding dialectic between sight and insight, place and human beings. The more we see, the more we think; the more carefully we think, the more deeply we see. Although an individual may initially base his acquisition of vision on the sight and insight gained from the physical experience of a place, this process cannot be abstracted from culturally specific uses of language, memory, thought, and emotion. As the narrator finds out, vision is necessarily a communal concept, one that depends upon the concept of relationship and finds its most complete expression in the shared vision of a people.

In *Rainy Mountain*, the narrator's quest focuses largely on learning to "see" the lands that have shaped Kiowa identity from within a Kiowa perspective. In the opening paragraph of the introduction, the narrator describes the land surrounding Rainy Mountain, geographically placing it and then naming it. The narrator states: "The hardest weather in the world is there. Winter brings blizzards, hot tornadic winds arise in the spring, and in summer, the prairie is an anvil's edge." Despite his attention to changes in the land, the narrator's vision of Rainy Mountain at first lacks a sense of interrelationship that the storytelling tradition so deeply values. The narrator claims that "Loneliness is an aspect of the land" and "All things in the plain are isolate; there is no confusion of objects in the eye, but *one* hill or *one* tree or *one* man." Analyzed from the perspective of physical sight, the narrator's perceptions are clear;

objects do stand out more clearly on the plains. But, from the Kiowa cultural perspective, the narrator's understanding of Rainy Mountain is misinformed. His reading of the land as lonely, isolating, and divided into singular objects shows his limited understanding of both relationship and place. While he uses the dialectic of sight and insight to create a partial vision of Rainy Mountain, he does not yet have the cultural tools—such as stories, histories, and even his own reevaluated experiences—to understand his ancestors' relationships to that very land.[35]

The narrator's misapprehension of place grows. In the next line he says, "To look upon that landscape in the early morning, with the sun at your back, is to lose the sense of proportion. Your imagination comes to life, and this, you think, is where Creation was begun." Once again, the narrator's physical sight is clear; his interpretation is not so clear. While a loss of proportion could be read as a way of seeing all things in creation equally, in relation to a tribal worldview predicated on balance it marks a sickening loss of dimension, a disruption of proper relationships. Gradually, the narrator's perceptions move from sight to insight. By actively reading the land, he engages in a process of creating a vision of Rainy Mountain; thus, his imagination does "come to life." But vision gained through individual experience alone is not powerful enough to create the culturally informed understanding of place the narrator seeks. While the narrator might "think" creation began at Rainy Mountain, we later learn that the Kiowa creation story is older than their relationship with that place. Because the narrator does not yet fully understand the cultural processes from a Kiowa perspective, his interpretation of Rainy Mountain is his alone. Thus, it is fitting that, at this stage in his development, the narrator stands with his "back" to the sun, looking away from the source of light that is the Kiowa god.[36]

While developing vision is important to the narrator's cultural growth, the ability to imagine what one cannot physically see is equally crucial. Momaday argues that the imagination can stand in as a surrogate for sensation as a whole, including physical sight, and he gives several examples of this process. Of the narrator's grandmother, Aho, Momaday writes, "the immense landscape of the continental interior lay like memory in her blood. She could tell of the Crows, whom she had never seen, and of the Black Hills, where she had never been." Aho's way of seeing is deeply informed by her immersion in Kiowa oral tradition, which sees no contradiction between valuing both experiences of the body and experiences of the mind. For Aho, stories are as vivid as physical reality; her imaginative construction of reality is not bound by space, time, or sensation. The "memory" that lives in Aho's "blood" suggests that Aho understands herself as continuous with the past by means of body, mind, "blood," and "memory." The blood and the memories have been passed down to her in a chain of stories that have transformed her body and mind. Lacking this understanding of the oral tradition, the narrator has a limited concept of reality. His imagination is not yet expansive enough to immediately accept the reality of his mind as seamless with the reality of the physical world. Still, he builds on the thoughts he has gained through physical sight and states, "I wanted to see in reality what she had seen more perfectly in the mind's eye, and traveled fifteen hundred miles to begin my pilgrimage." The difference between his sight and Aho's imaginative vision signals cultural, epistemological, and perceptual differences between him and his grandmother. Recognizing these differences, the narrator sets out on a literal and figural "pilgrimage" to try to understand Aho's culturally constructed Kiowa vision.[37]

In the Yellowstone country of the Kiowas' origin, the narrator attempts to engage the epistemological processes his ancestors used to construct and understand their world. He begins by exploring his emotional responses to the land: "Yellowstone, it seemed to me, was the top of the world, a region of deep lakes and dark timber, canyons and waterfalls. But, beautiful as it is, one might have felt the sense of confinement there." The narrator's ability to imagine what his ancestors "might have felt" on their journey from the Rockies to the plains shows his evolving trust in the epistemic status of his emotional responses. As his vision grows, he becomes more confident in his speculations, claiming, "There is a perfect freedom in the mountains, but it belongs to the eagle and the elk, the badger and the bear." The narrator creates a nascent theory of "freedom" as a creature's suitability to its environment, which has a direct impact on the creature's ability to become what it desires to become. Empowered with this knowledge, which began as intuition, a feeling, a hunch, the narrator is able to make a full-fledged epistemological claim about his people: "The Kiowas reckoned their stature by the distance they could see, and they were bent and blind in the wilderness." The narrator's cultural understanding has been transformed through his experience of the Rockies and through theorizing the meaning of those experiences. The dialectic between sight and insight transforms his epistemology. He can now offer a more culturally integrated Kiowa theory of place. The experience of a place and the epistemology of a people are coextensive; physical "distance" and metaphysical "freedom" are dependent on each other for definition. By theorizing his emotions in relation to the land, he imaginatively constructs a theory of how the Kiowas "reckoned" themselves as a people.[38]

As he continues to trace the journey of his ancestors, the narrator intuits the motivational force behind the Kiowa migration: the feelings of wonder and delight. Descending from the mountains, he writes, "the earth unfolds and the limit of the land recedes. Clusters of trees, and animals grazing far in the distance, cause the vision to reach away and wonder to build upon the mind." As with Aristotle's concept of beauty and Kant's concept of moral duty, the Kiowan concept of the "good life" begins with wonder. The physical ability to see far into a limitless landscape is linked metaphorically to intellectual openness and curiosity, imagination motivated by wonder. As the narrator's vision grows, so too does his capacity to imagine not only what his people might have felt looking upon the plains, but *how* they felt it.[39]

As with vision, wonder is a culturally dependent concept that grows with and builds one's knowledge of how to see and interpret the world. Recounting the Kiowas' journey from the mountains to the foothills, the narrator states, "There the Kiowas paused on their way; they had come to a place where they must change their lives." As with his own previously inadequate theory of place, the narrator claims that the Kiowas were at first metaphysically unequipped to understand the land they saw: "[T]hey must wean their blood from the northern winter and hold the mountains a while longer in their view." Their conception of themselves was rooted in an epistemology born of their relationship with the mountains. But by acquiring the sun-worshiping Tai-me religion from the Crows, they also acquired the intellectual and emotional means to understand the plains, for "Precisely there does it [the sun] have the certain character of a god.". The process of building relationships in a foreign land and transforming it into a homeland requires arduous intellectual and physical work.[40]

Experiencing an unfamiliar place can be dangerous and frightening. As the narrator's initial experiences at Rainy Mountain show, in the absence of a culturally grounded understanding of a place, the natural features of a landscape may seem lonely, isolating, and proportionless. With a more developed sense of vision, the narrator comes to understand the Kiowa cultural imperative of confronting the unfamiliar with story, thereby integrating it into an existing web of relations. Seeing Devil's Tower, the narrator writes, "Two centuries ago, because they could not do otherwise, the Kiowas made a legend at the base of the rock." This story tells of seven sisters who are chased by their brother, who has turned into a bear. They climb a tree to escape their brother, and the great tree carries them into the sky where they become the Big Dipper. The seven sisters, the bear, the rock tree, and the stars all play a necessary role in explaining a cosmology that reaches from earth to sky and is defined by interconnectedness. Experiencing a new land compelled the Kiowas to reconsider their world, but that reconsideration retains a sense of fundamental relationships: "From that moment, and so long as the legend lives, the Kiowas have kinsmen in the night sky. Whatever they were in the mountains, they could be no more." Telling a story in response to a new place creates an interrelationship between the land and the Kiowas; their cultural identity is changed through relating to the land upon which they live. In a reciprocal relationship, their perception of the land is also forever changed.[41]

Once he develops his understanding of how Kiowa vision is composed of many elements—thought and emotion, imaginative reality, story, and the concept of wonder—the narrator can interpret the most imaginative of Kiowa conceptualizations, their origin story. As Momaday writes, "According to their origin myth, they entered the world through a hollow log. From one point of view, their migration was the fruit of an old prophecy, for indeed they emerged from a sunless world." Moving from darkness into the light, from the mountains to the plains, the Kiowas engage in the process of growth embedded within this story. By coming to understand the story, the narrator brings his concept of vision into accord with a Kiowa explanation of their origin. Like his ancestors' journey before him, the narrator's journey to Rainy Mountain contains elements of both the contingent and the determined. Called out onto the plains by their origin story that is at once a mandate and an invitation to wonder, the Kiowas define their epistemology as a process of growth.[42]

Employing a socially constructed and culturally informed process of seeing and thinking, the narrator revises his understanding of the landscape. As the introduction draws to a close, the narrator's vision of Rainy Mountain has changed. Whereas before the narrator saw a proportionless, isolating, and lonely land, he now says of the houses on the plain: "They belong in the distance; it is their domain." The narrator's maturing vision allows him to see objects on the plains as ordered and having their place, rather than as contingent and disconnected. His vision signals a development of a Kiowa sense of imagination: "There, where it ought to be, at the end of a long and legendary way, was my grandmother's grave. Here and there on the dark stones were ancestral names." His grandmother's grave, like everything else at Rainy Mountain, has its rightful place on the land, and the narrator's new knowledge of where things "ought to be" shows his developed understanding that the land and the people are one. As imagination develops, story shapes insight into a way of seeing into the distance, as the Kiowas intuited when they looked out onto the plains. That sense of imagination is carried within a person, for as the narrator states at the end of the introduction, "Looking back once, I saw the mountain and came away."[43]

As American Indian criticism continues to develop, it becomes increasingly important for scholars of Native literature to create linkages between diverse forms of linguistic expression and critical thought. This process should begin with acknowledging the ways in which critical thought comes out of social relationships articulated both orally and in print, in the past and in the present. Exploring what those terms and concepts are gives us the tools to do our work well and to give back to those communities to which we are indebted. Native literary concepts such as Momaday's "vision" need to be drawn out and contextualized from within the oral traditional paradigms that Native texts both engage and articulate, and mode-three criticism should explore and use such terms. Native American literatures, both oral and written, have been theorizing, but too many of us have had our heads in the clouds for too long. Like Dayunisi, its time we critics dive into the deep waters.

Notes

1. Ong, *Orality and Literacy*, 74; Havelock, *Muse Learns to Write*, 120; Brill de Ramirez, *Contemporary American Indian Literatures*, 6.

2. Ong, *Orality and Literacy*, 9.

3. Ibid., 113–14.

4. Krupat, *Turn to the Native*, 17.
5. Robert Warrior, *People and the Word*, 6.
6. Krupat, *Turn to the Native*, 21–22.
7. Hudson, *Southeastern Indians*, 120.
8. Nabokov, *Forest of Time*, 47.
9. Ibid., 92.
10. Smith, "Protecting and Respecting," 210.
11. Robert Warrior, *People and the Word*, xiii, xx, xiv.
12. Alfred, *Peace, Power, Righteousness*, xvii, xviii.
13. Robert Warrior, *People and the Word*, xv.
14. Alfred, *Peace, Power, Righteousness*, xvi.
15. Tedlock, *Popol Vuh*, 22, 56, 21, 63, 17.
16. Robert Warrior, *Tribal Secrets*, xvii.
17. Wiget, *Native American Literature*, 13.
18. Krupat, *Turn to the Native*, 48.
19. Krupat, *Red Matters*, x.
20. Konkle, *Writing Indian Nations*, 50, 51.
21. Pulitano, *Toward a Native American Critical Theory*, 22.
22. Owens, *Other Destinies*, 19.
23. Ashcroft et al., *Empire Writes Back*, 15.
24. Pulitano, *Toward a Native American Critical Theory*, 22.
25. Ashcroft et al., *Empire Writes Back*, 30.
26. Robert Warrior, *Tribal Secrets*, xxiii.
27. Robert Warrior, *People and the Word*, 184; Pulitano, *Toward a Native American Critical Theory*, 188–91.
28. Robert Warrior, *People and the Word*, 181, 185, 187.
29. Robert Warrior, *Tribal Secrets*, 91, 97–98.
30. Ong, *Orality and Literacy*, 74.
31. Robert Warrior, *People and the Word*, 97–98, xii.
32. Weaver, *That the People Might Live*, xiii.
33. Womack, *Red on Red*, 67.
34. Culler, *Literary Theory*, 14.
35. Momaday, *Way to Rainy Mountain*, 5.
36. Ibid.
37. Ibid., 7
38. Ibid., 7.
39. Ibid.
40. Ibid., 7, 8.
41. Ibid., 8.
42. Ibid., 7
43. Ibid., 11, 12.

Honoring Ni'Wahkomakanak

JANICE ACOOSE

Preface

Way back in June 2002 Craig Womack invited me to participate in the creation of a volume of Native-authored literary criticism. The idea for the writing project, he explained, grew out of a conversation among Sean Teuton, Daniel Justice, Malea Powell, Jim Ottery, Janice Gould, Jace Weaver, Robert Warrior, and himself. According to Womack, the group concluded that "theory, in and of itself, is not the problem: it is the kind of theorizing that has taken place that has been sometimes disappointing." The proposed book, he said, would "specifically address Native literary theory . . . create Native knowledge." The group envisioned that someday the existence of such a volume would serve as a declaration that it is "possible to teach a class on Native literary criticism using all Native authors."

I received Womack's letter in the midst of a confusing and frustrating period in both my professional and personal life. Professionally, I felt alone and isolated because for too many years I was the only indigenous graduate student of indigenous literatures in the English Department at the University of Saskatchewan. Personally, I was anticipating the birth of my first *No'sim* while coping with the emotional pain associated with both the preparation of my "statement of claim" against the Indian residential school I had attended and the end of my marriage. Thus, I responded enthusiastically to Womack's invitation to participate in this scholarly writing project. So enthusiastic was I to finally work with other indigenous scholars that my first draft dealt more with the frustrations I felt in my professional life and less with "literary theory" or "making knowledge."

I rewrote the majority of my essay after I read Craig Womack's, Chris

---

Janice Acoose's roots stem from the Sakimay Saulteaux First Nation and the Marival Métis Colony in Saskatchewan, Canada. She currently works as an associate professor at the First Nations University of Canada in Saskatoon. A literary critic, Acoose has written Iskwèwak Kah Ki Yaw Ni'Wahkomakanak: Neither Indian Princesses nor Easy Squaws *and contributed to* Looking at the Words of Our People: First Nations Analysis of Literature *and* (Ad)dressing Our Words*:* Aboriginal Perspective on Aboriginal Literatures, *Canada's only two books of Native-authored and Native-published literary criticism.*

Tueton's, and Daniel Justice's comments on my work. Craig Womack wrote, "I hope that you, Tol Foster, and Kim Roppolo will get a conversation going since Tol is arguing for regionalism and Kim for an intertribal rhetoric, making a case for the power of the literature to reach beyond its tribally specific boundaries." Chris Tueton suggested connections to Tol Foster's and Cheryl Suzack's work, which he maintained both "point toward pan-tribal and pan-cultural influences and allegiances." Daniel Justice wrote, "The best moments throughout are those when your ideas are in dialogue with some of the larger issues and concerns in the discipline, and when you reach back to your roots to engage with broader socio-political realities of native peoples in a colonialist regime." As I revised, I attempted to balance my voice, tone, subject, and focus with the other contributors' essays while maintaining the integrity and strength of my original ideas. Kimberly Roppolo reacted to my changes by making a connection to "her own growth as a writer during the course of developing this volume."

As I read over the essays of others, Kimberly Blaeser's piece—which is not included in this final collection—sated my hunger for appetizing theoretical approaches. Nourished by Blaeser's tone and posturing, I was encouraged to continue the practice of bringing my own lived experiences to my theoretical analysis of literary texts. Like Blaeser, I have had experiences with readers/critics who too often dismiss as "uncritical" or "romantic/nostalgic" my lived experiences, which are rooted in Nêhiyawak-Métis-Nahkawè cultures. Now, despite academic snobbery or cultural insensitivities, I will continue to perform theory by bringing my ancestors, cultures, and languages to my critical work. (Oh no, here she comes dragging her whole tribe along with her. Sound familiar?)

I read the final draft of Kimberly Roppolo's "Samson Occom as Writing Instructor" (this volume) with a more attentive focus than I'd brought to her first draft. I was particularly encouraged by her references to Lisa Brooks's quotation of Robert Warrior, who called for a respectful critical conversation, and by the way she connected to her Native relatives for guidance during this important writing project. However, as I've written in the pages ahead, as critics, we have to be prepared to rock the boat, challenge, question, and metamorphose existing criticism. Roppolo also correctly makes the point that my theoretical approach to indigenous literatures—a culturally specific approach—is to be viewed as a "baseline." Indeed, I am not advocating that the culturally specific approach should cancel out all other theoretical approaches: in the pages ahead, I model a culture-specific theoretical approach to reveal *possibilities* for the interpretation of indigenous literatures.

I read with interest too Roppolo's discussion of "Indian country today," which she refers to as the "zone" in which this book is happening. This empowering region, she maintains, encompasses the entire hemisphere and is a region of our own creation. A region created of resistance, Indian country creates imaginatively intellectual sovereignty, according to Roppolo. While I find this idea (at least the essence of this idea) fascinating, something about "imagined" sovereignty just isn't enough for me. I'm even more convinced of the shortcomings of "imagined" sovereignty when I think about the Natives, Indians, full-bloods, half-bloods, and aboriginals whom I discover when I turn my attention to indigenous literatures "who have ceded not only vast territories of land, but also the territories of imagination and voice as well."

In Roppolo's essay too she maintains that as indigenous peoples we must decolonize our minds, theories, methodologies, and relationships with each other. And, again, while I don't disagree with the essence of this idea, I wonder why we have to bring the "colonial" into our relationships with each other? I believe that we have the resources and capacities within our cultures and territories to work out relationships with each other. In ceremonial spaces here in this land Nêhiyawak, Nahkawè, Dakota, Nakota, and Dene peoples gather together frequently. Perhaps as critics we might learn something from these shared ceremonial spaces.

I was interested, too, in Tol Foster's final draft, entitled "Of One Blood." My own skepticism of contemporary theoretical claims from the academy has indeed been influenced by theory-driven approaches that have for too long set up binary oppositions between "them" and "us." I have, like Foster, argued here and in other scholarly publications that "generalized theories have done real damage to Native communities" and that some contemporary theoretical approaches are too limited for indigenous literatures. Like Foster, I believe that we must value and critique the "historical and cultural archive as a theoretically sophisticated site of its own. [Indeed, that one's] history and experience can provide a testable and portable framework for understanding relations between individuals, institutions, and historical forces." Thus, in the pages ahead I model a culturally specific way of valuing and critiquing some aspects of the Nehiowè and Nehiowè-Métis historical cultural archive.

Foster's references, however, to the "new regionalism" leave me feeling just a tad bit uncomfortable and somewhat confused. His eagerness to embrace regionalism confuses me because of his statements regarding the limitations of contemporary theories. On one hand, he refers to the historical and cultural archives as "sophisticated" sites, while on the other hand, he relies on critical terminology like "tribal cosmopolitanism" to enhance an already sophisticated, all-my-relations' philosophy.

I want to address here, too, Foster's comment about postmodernism, which he suggests has made the emergence of Native knowledge and truth claims possible in the academy. When I read this statement I called up in my memory the numerous challenges I faced as I attempted to bring "Native ways of knowing" into the academy. It certainly wasn't postmodernism that fueled those challenges. My years within the academy were fueled by my rootedness to this land, my cultures, and "all my relations."

Foster also suggested in an earlier draft of his essay that "attention toward developing our own canon has been extremely fruitful for us, but we are now at a point where we can confidently engage with other canons that intersect with our own." I agree that most of us, as critics, are now in positions that inspire confidence and allow us to enjoy certain privileges. I also agree that we can engage with other intersecting canons. However, I want to suggest that we research our own cultures of origin and, from our respective cultures, initiate cultural restoration projects by building culture-specific literary canons. As critics, we can support these projects by working within our own cultures first, and then engaging with other indigenous canons cross-culturally. I imagine those critical bodies interacting and engaging in a critical landscape that honors cultural differences and celebrates cultural similarities: Honoring cultural differences, we can respectfully work toward understanding; celebrating cultural similarities, we can enter into dialogue with each other. But I'm passionately committed—perhaps even blinded—by a political conviction that insists on "honoring my relations" whose spiritual presence continues to influence my life and work. We cannot, after all, arrive at the destination "indigenous" without having journeyed through life in particular communities/culture-specific places. Or can we?

There has been some discussion, too, about our use of English to communicate cross-culturally. In "Theorizing American Indian Experience" (this volume), Craig Womack writes, "Some Indian thinkers have taken to pitting themselves against an 'enemy's language,' claiming a radical incommensurability in relation to English. . . . In viewing English as a forced imposition on Native people, it seems to me that only the victimization end of the spectrum is being considered. What about when Indians have enthusiastically taken up English and reading? Before there were ever Canadian residential and U.S. boarding schools, for example, forcing Indians students to learn English, there were several thousand New England Indians reading and writing. . . . So, why were they interested, those who were? Were they simply trying to 'reinvent' something profoundly deficient or did a few Native thinkers see some kind of intrinsic tribal merit in the English language?" To respond to this, I offer for consideration here excerpts from Nêhiyaw-Métis scholar/writer Emma LaRocque's "Tides, Towns, and Trains." LaRoque explains that she was born into a complex community that was open to natural change but that simultaneously experienced forced change. She explains that

> change was not and is not new to Indian and Métis culture. The issue is to differentiate between change that is imposed and change that comes from free choice. And change that is forced is oppression. Oppression over time, such as that of the colonizing of Native peoples in Canada, has had various and varying effects on different generations. I believe changes came slower for my parents than for me, but my parents experienced changes that were more directly forced upon them by Canadian society, especially in regard to their children and schooling. It may be harder to unravel the effects of changes that were at once forced and

sought after. School was forced on me, too, yet I actually fought my parents in order to go to school. At the time, I did not know that school was an institution of colonization invading and disturbing the way of life of my family, my community, and my ancestors.[1]

Honoring *Ni' Wahkomakanak*

I am a *Koochum* now, and *No'simak* Alijah-Blue and Angelina-Nicole are "beautiful-brown-bouncing-bubby-babies," as I often sing to them when I cradle their precious little bodies in my arms.[2] In those tender moments when our eyes meet and our spirits join, the significance of words and energy becomes clear to me. The transformative power of words becomes even clearer when I watch them with their maternal Chilean relatives, who construct the world around them with English-Spanish. I imagine them as young children running into my arms and calling, "*Hola, Co-Co.*" I imagine the myriad of Nahkawè-Nêhiyaw-Métis-Chilean ancestors whose energies flow through their blood brought alive in the voicing and joining of the Spanish greeting, "*Hola,*" with the Nêhiyaw-Métis-Nahkawè term of address, "*Koochum/Co-Co.*" I imagine instructing them to always call me "*Co-Co*" rather than the culturally slippery and seductive term "grandmother"—just as my Nêhiyaw-Métis *Koochum* taught me. I imagine passing on ancestral stories of Quewich, Ekos, and Acoose just as *Nimosom* passed these heirlooms on to me.[3] In those imaginings of *No'simak* futures, I realize the wisdom of *Nokom's* and *Nimosom*'s teachings: the language and stories they passed on to me carry "culture from past generations to present, and so on into the future."[4] And so I honor my relations *Nokom*, *Nimosom*, and *No'simak* for encouraging me to remember the power of storied words.

Writing Cultural Bodies into Being

In "Coming Home through Stories" Neal McLeod writes, "Every time a story is told, every time one word of an Indigenous language is spoken, we are resisting the destruction of our collective memory."[5] Thus, I introduce this paper by honoring *Ni'Wahkomakanak* from both a writing and speaking *Koochum* place that, like Nêhiyaw-Métis-Nahkawè ceremonial traditions, invokes the spirit-presence of ancestors as well as the living presence of "all my relations." When I make connections to cultural memory and living traditions, my text fuses writing and speaking by merging written English criticism with Nêhiyaw-Métis-Nahkawè systems of knowledge. When I place in the written text *Nokom*, *Nicapan*, *Nimosom*, they become speaking voices of Nêhiyaw-Métis-Nahkawè culture-specific stories that interrupt conventional forms of textual criticism and create spaces for cultural differences in the discourse of indigenous literatures. When I name and place *No'simak* Alijah-Blue and Angelina-Nicole in this text, they become rooted in collective memories and linked to the past; their textual presence ensures that future generations will always re-member Nêhiyaw-Métis-Nahkawè storytelling traditions. When I name and place in this written text my Nêhiyaw-Métis-Nahkawè cultures, ceremonial traditions, ancestors, and present system of relations, I perform an "honoring" cultural ritual that both invites culturally like-minded readers and welcomes cultural outsiders. I signal in the text a welcome to culturally like-minded readers by naming my writerly-speaking self Nêhiyaw-Métis-Nahkawè. I invite into my text cultural outsiders:[6] I signal their cultural-outsider position by acknowledging their originating culture or referring to them as "indigenous," a term I prefer because it connotes the political realities of cultures "growing naturally" from the land. And I acknowledge the many cultural-outsider places from which creative imaginings grow by utilizing the plural form of literature: thus, the term "indigenous literatures" appears throughout the text.

My writing-self has been educated culturally by Nêhiowe-Métis-Nahkawè stories that transfuse culture, but I have also been swayed by the contemporary rhetoric of indigenous political leaders, brilliant scholars, and astute lawyers who speak of sovereign nations and self-determining peoples. Thus, I turn to contemporary indigenous-Canadian literatures written in English with great expectations. With great expectations, I fervently search the pages for reflections of an author's nation of origin, ancestors, language, and expressions of national sovereignty. Often I am saddened to "discover" Natives, Indians, full-bloods, half-bloods, and aboriginals (to use just a few choice nomenclatures) who have ceded not only vast territories of land, but also the territories of imagination and of voice. Amid these seemingly perplexing identity crises, there are some contemporary indigenous-Canadian writers talking back to the great white way as they transform fluidlike ancient stories into "lily white words" with "picket fence sentences / and manicured paragraphs / one wrong sound and you're shelved in the Native Literature section."[7] Like my own efforts to ensure cultural survival by translating to the written page culture-specific stories and criticism, the works of Marilyn Dumont, Emma LaRocque, Jeannette Armstrong, Armand Ruffo, Neal McLeod, Maria Campbell, and Paul Seesequasis talk back to overshadowing colonial authorities as they bundle their own cultures into the fabric of written English.[8] Their culturally infused texts reject internal colonial conditioning that acquiesces to "*Keyam, Keyam*," which according to Emma LaRocque's brilliant prose in "Tides, Towns, and Trains" loosely translates from Cree to mean "among other things, let it be—don't rock the boat. Don't question. Don't challenge."[9] Their voices rock the textual layers of written English, question their own culture's practices, and challenge morbid myths of the vanishing Indian. Like these writers, I attempt to metamorphose previously sedentary (and sedimentary) critical practices by substituting English with Nêhiyaw and Nahkawè in strategic textual places. Rather than interrogate pan-indigenous critical practices, I model a culture-specific theoretical performance. By doing so, I call into question the continued reliance on seemingly convenient practices that become uncritical with overuse and too often privilege a singular and fictitious pan-indigenous culture over the numerous and distinct living cultures. My own critical performance reveals *possible* theoretical approaches: I enter texts from both insider and outsider positions. From a cultural-insider position, I engage personally with the text as I draw upon my own cultural knowledge and lived experience within that culture. From a cultural-outsider position, I approach others' texts cognizant of similarities but eager to learn from cultural differences.

When I leave my own cultural landscape to enter the contemporary indigenous-Canadian critical terrain, I note that Jeannette Armstrong attempts to "bring to life" culture-specific bodies of literature. Two important critical anthologies live in Canada as a result of Armstrong's literary midwifery efforts: *Looking at the Words of Our People: First Nations Analysis of Literature* and *(Ad)dressing Our Words: Aboriginal Perspectives on Aboriginal Literatures.* A self-described Okanagan, she saturates her creative fiction, poetry, and criticism with cultural values, teachings, philosophies, and in specific cases, her language. Armstrong reaffirms cultural integrity by vitalizing written English with Okanagan. Carrying Okanagan with her to written English, she explains: "the Okanagan person will take the spiritual, the understanding, and the connection with the spiritual, and the attempt is to materialize that, to bring that forward into the physical plane, because it's not knowable, it doesn't have voice in the physical plane. And so when we materialize that, we bring it into a physical plane, either through words or through movement or through carving or through paint or through social construct." Through her work with the En'owkin Centre in British Columbia, Armstrong supports the revitalization of "outsider" cultures too.[10]

Because Armstrong is cognizant of the "many different cultures producing different kinds of literature," she resists attempts to stifle them as one category. A staunch proponent of indigenous literary sovereignty, she grew into a noteworthy critic through her involvement with such writing projects as *Looking at the Words of Our People: First Nations Analysis of Literature.* Between the covers of this volume, indigenous critics speak about our own literatures, articulate possible literary theories, and perform viable critical practices. Armstrong asserts a sovereign position when, in the "Editor's Note," she declares unequivocally: "First Nations Literature *will be* [my emphasis] defined by First Nations writers, readers, academics, and critics and perhaps only by writers and critics from within those varieties of First Nations contemporary practice and past practice of culture and the knowledge of it."[11]

One of the essays included in this first critical text is Armand Ruffo's "Inside Looking Out." Although he employs the term "Native" in his subtitle and in places in his text, his essay offers some useful considerations. Assuming a cross-cultural critical position, this self-described Anishnaabe scholar/writer quotes Laguna Pueblo poet/critic Paula Gunn Allen to make the point that those professing to teach American Indian materials "must study carefully the traditions, history, and present day settings of the tribe from which the document comes or to which it refers . . . context and continuity are two of the most important areas to be taken into account." Thus, Ruffo suggests that readers must culturally initiate themselves to avoid superficial readings: he calls upon critics to clarify symbols, allusions, and perceptional-interpretive systems within their originating cultural epistemologies. From a cultural-insider position, he maintains that there is "an elaborate system of coding which subsumes a complex body of information . . . information which is not readily available to the culturally uninitiated."[12]

In the follow-up to the first critical edition, *(Ad)dressing Our Words: Aboriginal Perspectives on Aboriginal Literatures*, Ruffo calls attention to a gap in Canadian critical theory when he writes, "since the publication of that first critical text there has been no other collection of literary criticism solely by Aboriginal people." Like Armstrong, Ruffo advocates sovereignty when he makes the declaration that the contributors "come to their subject 'culturally initiated,' and thus well aware of the 'territory' of which they write." Although Ruffo does not reject outright Western literary theories, he advises critics to apply and contextualize such theories within "Indigenous ways of knowing."[13] In "Coming Home through Story," Neal McLeod employs a postcolonial interpretive methodology. His critical position proves useful for his cultural restoration project, although I remain cautiously guarded about nonindigenous theories that could enclose and stifle the culture specificity of critical/creative work.

In "Coming Home through Stories," McLeod performs an honoring Nehiyâwiwin ritual when he places in written-English signifying language, his storytelling ancestors, and Nehiyâwiwin oral and written stories. His efforts produce a practice that "resists the destruction of collective memory." His text thus functions as an important vehicle for cultural transmission. Respectful of his cultural inheritance, McLeod maintains that as long as Nêhiyawak "choose to take the time to learn the stories and language," Nehiyâwiwin will survive. He therefore bundles medicined Nehiyâwiwin words into the fabric of written English. As the medicine-powered words transfuse the text, organisms within the cultural body become revitalized. McLeod's ritualizing critical performance adheres to important cultural protocol that honors Nehiyâwiwin being, both spiritual and physical. And he speaks from a sovereign position when he pronounces himself *Nêhiyawak* and the territory, *Nêhiyâwaskiy*. He makes clear, too, how Nehiyâwiwin was seriously compromised by the spatial and the ideological diaspora, which culminated in "*ê-mâyihkamikahk* ('where it went wrong'—The North West Resistance of 1885)." Plagued by *ê-mâyihkamikahk*, a psychic disease that spread throughout their territory after thousands of buffalo drowned themselves, Nehiyâwiwin endured *pâstahowin*, or the transgression from Nehiyâwiwin to colonial order. Following the examples of his storytelling relatives, McLeod, too, mediates contemporary *pâstohowin* that exiles Nehiyâwiwin to "liminal space," a discursive space that influences his postcolonial posturing.[14]

From his postcolonial position, McLeod critically surveys Nehiyâwiwin discourse, a discursive space disrupted by colonial presence and Nehiyâwiwin storytelling relatives. Resisters and challengers of colonial hegemony are honored and celebrated in the text. Resister Nehiyâwiwn names such as Mistahi Maskava, Minahikosis, and Payipwât are distinguished Nehiyâwiwin markers here, while their English names appear enclosed in parentheses: (Big Bear), (Little Pine), and (Piapot). McLeod's text likewise welcomes oral storytelling relatives such as *Capan, Kokom, Mosom*, and Uncle Big John, while including the published storytellers Wilfred Tootosis, Andrew Ahenakew, and Edward Ahenakew, and the translated voices of Nehiyâwiwin such as Peter Vandale, Kataayuk (Frizzly Bear), Jerry McLeod, John McLeod, and John Tootosis. He adheres carefully to Nehiyâwiwin storytelling protocol that requires naming each successive story voice, as well as his relationship to that teller: "It was told to my Great-Great-Grandmother *Kekehkiskwew* (Hawk Woman), then to *Nimosom* (my grandfather), and then to my father." The practice of placing his ancestors, their stories, and Nehiyâwiwin storytelling protocol into written English transforms the text into a viable transmitter of culture.

As a vehicle for cultural transmission, McLeod's text mirrors significant historical events and echoes voices of oral stories of survival. A mirror of history, the text reflects Nehiyâwiwin struggles with colonial power that were manifested in the North West Resistance of 1885, the English fur trade, the Treaty #6 process, and the Indian residential schools. Echoed voices of Nehiyâwiwin ancestors reverberate through written English as their stories prophesy demarcation of traditional lands, resist colonial order, tricksterize treaty discourse, testify to the horrors of residential schools, sing protective medicine songs, and recall "great historical and social change."[15]

McLeod's text also becomes a transmitter of culture by interrogating exterior and interior discourse: as an interrogator of outside discourse, the text "talks back" to colonial authorities; as an interrogator of inside discourse, the text challenges internal colonial conditioning. Talking back to overshadowing colonial authorities, the text implicates

> [t]he English [who] through a systematic process attempted to alienate *Nêhiyawak* from our land and in turn alienate us from our collective traditions. . . . [T]he process of alienation occurred in two interrelated ways (and these were concurrent). First, the English gradually alienated *Nêhiyawak* from our land, a process which was accelerated with the Fur Trade winding down and also through the Treaty process (which was accompanied by increased settlement). Second, the English alienated *Nêhiyawak* from our stories and languages, and set up coercive legislation in regards to our religious ceremonies. These ceremonies were outlawed in the Indian Act (Section 114) and mandatory attendance to residential schools was imposed.[16]

McLeod's text also functions as an internal interrogating voice of culture. The text indicts Nêhiyawak as a colonizing power: "The Cree (*Nêhiyawak*) . . .

displaced other groups such as the Blackfoot and Dene in their territorial expansion of the late seventeenth to the first half of the nineteenth century." It also reveals Nêhiyawak complicity in colonial relations of power by the absence of *Wîtihkokan's* Dene cultural narratives, although McLeod explains that *Kokocis* "negotiated between the world of Christianity and the world of traditional Dene/Cree hunting beliefs." The text interrogates intertribal relations between Chief Atâhkakohp and an unnamed Swampy Cree medicine man. Rather than pitting colonizer against colonized, the evidence of internal struggles suggests that during the 1870s and 1880s there "was widespread use of bad medicine." As an internal interrogating voice, the text reveals Nehiyâwiwin adapting, growing, and changing, as the Nêhiyawak presence erases "vanishing Indians."[17]

Once referred to rhetorically as "the mother of us all,"[18] Maria Campbell continues to occupy a prestigious place among indigenous-Canadian writers in English. Campbell's *Halfbreed* (1973) initiated the practice of carrying to written English important elements of culture, dynamic storytelling ancestors, and a distinctive language. *Stories of the Road Allowance People* continues Campbell's Nehiowìwin-Métis cultural revitalization project. Like McLeod's narrative, Campbell's text adheres to a culture-specific storytelling protocol. She places in written English "Old Uncle" and pipe-carrying Old Ladies who come to the storytelling circle on a cold winter night. In the voice of Old Uncle, Campbell privileges Nehiyâwiwin as she welcomes readers: "*Hahaa Kiyas mana Kisayanoo Kah Kee achimoot*. . . . Long time ago the old man told us this story." The Old Ladies validate Old Uncle's truth telling by bringing their pipes to the story circle; they nod their approval of his storytelling authority when they reply: "*Tapwe Anima* . . . Yes, yes it is true." Campbell also places in written English her culture-specific copyright when she explains that she has been given permission to tell old men stories that she paid for with "gifts of blankets, tobacco, and even a prize Arab stallion." Re-creating in textual form a Nehiyâwiwin "giveaway" ceremony, Campbell offers readers the stories "in the dialect and rhythm of my village and my father's generation."[19]

One of the included stories, "Jacob," functions as a transmitter of collective memory that links Nehiyâwiwin tribal memory with an emerging Nehiyâwiwin-Métis cultural body, thereby ensuring Nehiyâwiwin-Métis live on into the future. Like McLeod, Campbell invokes the spirits of storytelling ancestors whom she honors by creating discursive space within written English. Granmudder Mistapuch—a figurative presence of Nihiyâwiwin collective memory —"knowed lots of stories . . . even knowed the songs." Granfawder Kannap—a figurative creation of Nehiyâwiwin ancestry—appears in the text as a dis/membered body. Jacob—the discursive body of Nehiyâwiwin in transition—has been ripped away from the relatives, community, and way of life. The storyteller gives voice to an emerging Nehiyâwiwin-Métis body that ruptures the textual surface of English as it demands discursive presence.[20]

Campbell writes that Granmudder Mistapuch "he come from Muskeg . . . before he was a reserve."[20] The reference to "Muskeg" is important here.

Cultural insiders and culturally initiated readers will immediately recognize this place as one of Wisahkecahk's creations: as his body tumbles toward earth from the moon, he calls for the creation of a soft spot to cushion his fall: "And so it was that he fell into a soft place. The earth being obedient to his call, formed itself into a soft spot. Wisahkecahk fell in—head first! He wiggled and wiggled. He squirmed for a long time trying to free himself. Finally, he was free. He was all covered in mud and was looking so pitiful. He was blinking his eyes, but with all the mud. He was really having a hard time. He was standing there trying to look so dignified. He did look funny!" Wisahkecahk cursed in anger at the soft spot of earth: " 'When man inhabits the earth,' he said, 'such spots as this will be waste land and will be of no use whatsoever to anyone. They will be called 'muskegs.' " Wisahkecahk's presence becomes erased by written legislation as the place becomes "reserved" for Indians.[22]

On the other hand, the figure of Granfawder Kannap appears in the text as dis/membered, a body disconnected from cultural memory and relations. A figurative creation of Nehiyâwiwin ancestry, he appears as Granfawder:

> his name he was Kannap
> but the whitemans dey call him Jim Boy
> so hees Indian name he gets los.
> Dats why we don know who his peoples dey are.
> We los lots of our relations like dat.
> Dey get dah whitemans name
> Den no body
> He knows who his peoples dey are anymore.

A dis/membered body, Granfawder Kannap goes to Mistupuch for doctoring. She re/members him through story, which the storyteller voices in text: "All I can tell you now / is about Jim Boy / an hees story hees not very ole."[23]

In transition, Nehiyâwiwin negotiates discursive space as Jacob, a figurative body in written English. As the figurative body of Nehiyâwiwin, Jacob becomes disconnected from cultural referents such as stories and place; thus, he returns to an unnamed community orphaned and voiceless. However, Nehiyâwiwin collective memory—Granmudder Mistupuch—reclaims Nehiyâwiwin—Jacob—through a translated voice of Nehiyâwiwin-Métis—the storyteller.

The teller of "Jacob" emerges in written story as an unnamed cultural body. Connected to Nehiyâwiwin telling, the voice of the emergent cultural body negotiates a discursive space between the oral and written traditions. Thus, the text appears disrupted by a peculiar dialect and rhythm: cultural insiders and culturally initiated readers will recognize this written English as the culturally specific voice of Nehiyâwiwin-Métis.

Like that of McLeod's text, the voice of Campbell's text performs an interrogative function of Nehiyâwiwin-Métis and thus ensures that the cultural body survives. Her text interrogates exterior discursive presence by naming and indicting colonial manifestations of power. Signaling exterior discursive challenges as "dis trouble," the storyteller names "whiteman's" patronymic system, which displaced "Indian names," as the disturber of the peace. Catholic priests armed with written legislation and policemen with guns are indicted as agents of colonial authority: in the presence of these colonial agents, "none of the mans / they can do anything" as wagons full of kids are carted off to indoctrinating residential schools. The residential schools are named and indicted as colonial institutions which dis/membered Nehiyâwiwin from collective memory:

> Dem peoples dat go away to dem schools
> an come back you know dey really suffer.
> No mater how many stories we tell
> we'll never be able to tell
> what dem schools dey done to dah peoples
> an all dere relations.[24]

Here Nehiyâwiwin suffers, its storytelling capabilities and cultural relations disabled. But the Nehiyâwiwin-Métis storyteller enables voice and literally connects relations within written English. Speaking in a translated voice, the storyteller connects Nêhiyawak to Nehiyâawiwin cultural memory and a cultural body: Jacob is linked through oral story to Granmudder Mistupuch and Granfawder Kannap through written "hees story."

Campbell's text ensures cultural survival by functioning as internal interrogator of Nehiyâwiwin-Métis. The text challenges cultural discourse that accommodates uncritically patriarchal hegemony of white rules by "talking back" to gendered relations:

> Dats dah way he use to be a long time ago.
> If dah woman he work
> den the man he help him an if dah man he work
> dah woman he help.
> You never heerd peoples fighting over whose job he was
> dey all know what dey got to do to stay alive.[25]

As an internal interrogating voice, the text also implicates certain Nehiyâwiwin practices that privilege patriarchy. Within the text, Nehiyâwiwin is figuratively re-created as a cultural body dis/membered from the voice of collective memory. The story also challenges patriarchal complicity within colonial relations of power: men appear powerless and disabled while old women sing their healing songs, death songs, re/member the stories, give birth, and doctor dis/membered bodies.

By placing "Indians" as literal referents, as opposed to cultural referents, the text finally calls into question the practice of outside naming. As "Indians" figure into text, Nehiyâwiwin cultural memory fades: once the place named by the Cree-ator, Wisahkecahk, Muskeg becomes land reserved for Indians; Mistupuch, once a healer within a Nehiyâwiwin context, becomes an Indian doctor; Granfawder Kannap's Nehiyâwiwin name becomes a lost Indian name; once noteworthy horsemen, Nehiyâwiwin become Indians with few horses; and once self-sufficient, Nehiyâwiwin must learn Indian living. Perhaps the place within the text that speaks most clearly of dis/membered Nehiyâwiwin is in the priest's translation of Jacob's father's name, incorrectly translating "Star" from "Awchak": a slip of the tongue confuses the word for star, *acahkos*, with the word for spirit, *ahcahkw*.

When this priest translates Nehiyâwiwin, he sets in motion a series of tragic events: hearing the name of Jacob's father, his unnamed wife believes him to be her father and, in shame, kills herself; Jacob becomes "dead" inside and deaf to the Old Women's healing songs. The birth of a girl child to Jacob's adopted daughter then encourages him to re/member healing songs. Subsequently, through the translated voice of the storyteller, Jacob emerges as an enabled and a re-constituted Nehiyâwiwin cultural body:

> An all hees life
> he write in a big book
> dah Indian names of all dah Mommies and Daddies.
> An beside dem
> he write dah old names and
> dah new names of all dere kids.[26]

The storyteller intervenes in Nehiyâwiwin discourse, an emergent cultural Nehiyâwiwin-Métis body. Fusing written and oral forms of knowledge, Nehiyâwiwin-Métis figures into the liminal space created by Jacob's resistance to colonial presence. Ultimately, Jacob not only reclaims the power of naming, but also appropriates the priest's/whiteman's property of the written record.

In "The Republic of Tricksterism," Paul Seesequasis playfully wrestles with both oral and written authorities. As a self-described Cree[27] "mixed-blood urban orphan," he has been culturally mis/placed by the de/cree/ing Indian Act legislation and culturally dis/placed by authoritative Indian Act-ing Indians. To help him sort out this cultural conundrum, Seesequasis invokes a trickster spirit who materializes in the text as a mixed-blood shape-shifting *rigoureau*. Culturally initiated readers/critics may assume that the invocation to the trickster will summon up all forms of Nêhiyawak spirits, particularly the Nêhiyawak trickster Wisahkecahk. The culturally uninitiated reader/critic may decide that a trickster is a trickster, but to Nehiyâwiwin-Métis people educated in oral stories, the *rigoureau* is not the Nêhiyawak trickster, Wisahkecahk.

I approached Seesequasis's "Republic" armed with my academic weaponry and shawled in Nehiyâwiwin-Métis storytelling memories. My academic approach was bamboozled quickly when I came face-to-face in the text with the mythical *rigoureau* of Métis oral story. Without a Nehiyâwiwin-Métis storytelling education, I would have scurried back to the ivory-towered academy when I encountered *Pakakos*, Hairy Hearts, *Wetigoes*, and the Little People, who—along with the *rigoureau*—seemed to be creating pandemonium by destabilizing the foundational structure of written English narrative. Amid such chaos, trying to perform theory was practically impossible. Following the *rigoureau,* spirit rodents and scavengers scampered into the story, pulling out of the so-called sacred realm of Nêhiyawak oral myth a variety of mean-spirited Hairy Hearts, bushed Little People, and insatiable *Wetigoes.* When Nêhiyawak mythological figures spirit onto the page, narrative/storytelling voices shift shape, story seams bust wide open as truth turns into fiction, and myths spill into each other. Lingering over the textual carnage, the mixed-blood *rigoureau* shifts shape into a fictional character named Uncle Morris, who changes into the legendary Métis activist, Malcolm Norris. As a mixed-blood *rigoureau,* he tricksterizes readerly assumptions and teases cultural conditioning.

Having grown up with *rigoureau* presence, I wasn't scared off by all the mythical scurrying about or the hemorrhaging textual carnage: so I pondered the motley crew of characters that Seesequasis assembled onto former cultureless white pages. Besides all the spirits materializing profusely and Uncle Morris shifting shapes, Cree urban mixed-bloods become orphans on the page. The "full blood Cree" mother-Mary is de/creed by written authority, while Tobe becomes an imaginary full-blood Indian Act-ing Indian.

The urban mixed-blood orphans occupy the liminal space between written English and Nehiyâwiwin oral story. Having fallen between the seams of oral and written cultures, they appear in the text de/creed, left without status by the legislative Indian Act and banished from the Re-served-Place-of-Indian culture/storytelling. However, they shift the Re-served place of culture by transplanting it into an un-Edenic plot: shopping malls and beer parlors are their sacred grounds and Clashing Sex Pistols their tribal drums. Without status in the status-symbol world of written authority, the urban mixed-bloods learn to live without defining-Indian-Act-ing-de/cree-ing-papers and to play without culturally confining Cree-centric leashes.

The figurative mother-Mary of Nehiyâwiwin oral storytelling (not unlike her biblical counterpart) lies silently and submissively in written narrative form: "Mary Seesequasis, aka Ogresko, was born on Beardy's reserve on January 20, 1934. The first child of Sam Seesequasis, of Beardy's reserve, and Mary Rose Nahtowenhow, of the Sturgeon Lake band. . . ." But the trickster-spirit of Nehiyâwiwin humor transforms the silenced facts of Mary's life into storytelling images as "*nimosom* dance[s] through life with gentleness and humour" and *nokom* becomes a bear, hunts rabbits, decapitates chickens, and farts "in the direction of bureaucrats and posers." Daughter of *mosom* and *kokom*, Mary comes into the text woven into Nehiyâwiwin cultural traditions of orality that resist de/cree-ing authority. Her familial-oral connections rupture the textual surface of written English and align her with inverted gender roles: with gentleness and humor, her father, *nimosom*, dances through life while mother, *nokom*, farts, hunts, and decapitates chickens. Already connected through *mosom* and *kokom* to shape-shifting gender roles, Mary continues to challenge de/cree-ing authority and unwritten codes of segregation when she falls in love with a white man.[28]

In stark contrast to Mary, the grand-chief-to-be appears in the text as a symbolic figure of the written authority's de/cree-ing legislation. He materializes without form, a smelly presence emanating between *nokom's* farts: *nokom* farted . . . [t]he grand-chief-to-be lived downwind from my grandmother's farts." But he is provided form through written English: "Tobe was born mixed-blood, his father Cree, his mother white. . . . He would grow up as mixed-raced pure blood, purer than thou and given to exaggerating the quantity of his half cup of tribal blood." Privileged within both oral Nêhiyaw and written English patriarchy, Tobe's so-called pure "Indian" blood is not affected by the de/cree-ing legislation. Thus, he becomes enabled as a fictional Indian-Act-ing-Indian and is subsequently empowered as Chief Tobe in a rotting and fermenting Indian organization. After the pronouncement of Bill C-31, a government de/cree that restores "Indian" status, he becomes the disfigured, part legend, part lie, Honorable Heap Big Chief.[29]

Uncle Morris, a mixed-blood *rigoureau*, shifts the shape of both oral and written forms, upsets cultural expectations, and plays with dogmatic truth when he whorls onto the page. A figure of Métis mythology, the *rigoureau* straddles both oral and written traditions, but he teases readers with parodying performances of sacred myths and tickles them with mimicking gestures toward authoritative forms. Teasing and tickling, he disrespects, even dares to disregard, conventional story forms. As a mythical *rigoureau*, he mimics written forms when he shifts shape from a fictional Uncle Morris into a legendary Métis activist, Malcolm Norris. Seemingly by accident, or perhaps by a slip of the tongue, a Métis legend slides onto the written page as "Malcolm," a Métis activist who attempts to unite all "urban skins." His fictional counterpart, Uncle Morris, envisions urban reserves liberated from Nêhiyawak mythological cannibal spirits and hairy hearts. The *rigoureau* frustrates cultural purists with parodying performances of so-called sacred stories: he tricks their Nehiyâwiwin cultural expectations as he transforms into the *rigoureau* rather than the Nêhiyawak trickster, Wisahkecahk, and he taunts Christian dogma by mocking the Christ's crucifixion and resurrection. As a Christlike figure, he is persecuted and condemned to death for blasphemous challenges to "noble and sacred institutions." Notions of the sacred are drenched in irreverent humor when the sacred myth of the crucified Christ spills into pan-indigenous symbols of oral myth. Persecuted and condemned by authorities of both written and oral traditions, Uncle Morris is "nailed to a metal medicine wheel, his arms and legs spread in four directions." He chews sacrilegiously at both biblical and oral authorities when he transforms, rather than resurrects, into a pesky termite rather than a holy spirit.[30]

Seesequasis draws on a rich cultural inheritance from both oral and written traditions when he creates a mythic republic for urban mixed-blood orphans. Orphaned on the pages of written authority, the mixed-bloods become *rigoureau's* children in an unlikely Platoean republic. But unlike in Plato's republic, meaning falls apart as the pesky termite chews away at notions of truth, and the *rigoureau* shadows sacred stories of both oral and written authority. In the mixed-bloods' republic, notions of cultural purity disappear too as the urban orphans transplant culture to the city, mocking traditions and pissing on rituals. Even the powerful patriarchal protectors of pure blood contort into imaginary full-blood Indian-Act-ing Indians.

Seesequasis's "Republic of Tricksterism" dismantles theoretical efforts to domesticate complex bodies of culture-specific myths and figures. Attempts to fix the tricksterlike *rigoureau* into a Nehiyâwiwin oral form prove unmanageable as the mythological figure slips in and out of cultural contexts.As a *rigoureau,* he evades rigorous attempts to place him in deadening cultural bodies that no longer offer spirit sustenance. Emerging from the rigor mortis of both oral and written bodies, the *rigoureau* defies deadening enclosures.

Reading Seesequasis's work from a Nehiyâwiwin-Métis cultural-insider position requires demystifying layers of so-called sacred Nehiyâwiwin and putting aside authoritative written conventions. Peeling away layers and putting aside written conventions, Seesequasis's story becomes an important model for the re-creative, reaffirming, and revitalizing possibilities of culture-specific stories in written English: he revitalizes written English by re-Cree-ating a powerful story-myth that fills the mixed-bloods' psychological abyss.

Seesequasis, Campbell, and McLeod are rooted in cultural communities very similar to my own. My maternal relatives are Nehiyâwiwin-Métis and our community is named Marival. Although most of the Old People who inhabited the Marival Halfbreed Colony have returned to the Earth, they live in remembered stories passed on by writerly-speaking voices of my generation. A Nêhiyaw-Métis-Nahkawè voice of my generation, like McLeod I return "home" through story. Although the "colony" has long been dismantled, the land transfuses my memories of stories so that my writerly-speaking voice remembers Nêhiyaw-Métis ancestors—*Down Koochum*, *Mosom* Jimmy, *Mosom* Dad, *Koochum* Philomene. Re-membering them, I connect them here to cultural bodies; like McLeod's ancestors, my Nêhiyaw-Métis relatives were exiled from "home"—the place that rooted them in nation, territory, family, and community. Consequently, like Campbell's Jacob, my parents "[dey] was jus plain pitiful / . . . [dey] can talk [dere] own language . . . don know how to live in dah bush."[31] Because their voices have fallen—like Seesequasis's urban orphans—through the seams of written and oral cultures, Nêhiyaw-Métis and Nahkawè collective memories were interrupted.

So, following the path marked by McLeod, Campbell, and Seesequasis, I carry my ancestors, language, and stories here into written English. Following Seesequasis's example, I carry my mother—Harriet Beaudin-Acoose—into my text. I borrow from Seesequasis's text, "hisqueau,"[32] a textual figure that traces her colonial condition. "His," a prefixed pattern of her place within the patriarchal colonial system. "Queau," a patterned sound that re-members her to Nehiyâwiwin: the place of memory, land, language, ancestors, and story. Following McLeod's prints in text, I borrow the term "liminal space" to create discursive presence for my Métisness. Following Campbell's textual figure, Jacob, I use my text to marry Nehiyâwiwin to Métis. Em-bodying Nehiyèwiwin to Métis, I use my text to create a textual figure that transfuses Nehiyâwiwin-Métis in written English.

My parents, not unlike Seesequasis's parents, wrought untold *ethos-tropy* when they married: a "half-breed" and an "Indian." I create the textual figure —*ethos-tropy*—to name the merging of cultural bodies, as well as the turning of cultural spirit. Nehiyâwiwin-Métis-Nahkawè: merged cultural bodies turned cultural spirits.

Following McLeod, Campbell, and Seesequasis, I bundle memories, create medicine words, and tie my medicine bundle in the fabric of written English. With medicine-powered words, I create a textual presence and discursive space for Nêhiyaw-Métis-Nahkawè. Like Campbell's Jacob, I write in books so that my sons Blair and Blue, my daughter-in-law Nicole, and *No'simak* Alijah-Blue and Angelina-Nicole will always re-member "dah old names and / dah new names of all dere kids."[33] As a *Koochum*, I occupy written English and mark it as my "home," my place of memory.

Notes

1. LaRoque, "Tides, Towns, and Trains," 82.

2. About these terms: *Ni'Wahkomakanak* loosely translates in English as "all my relations." In regard to spelling Nehiyâwiwin and Nêhiyaw-Métis words, I've tried to write the words as they are phonetically pronounced. However, I acknowledge other ways of spelling, which I include in quotations and specific content. *Koochum,* translated to English, suggests a kind of grandmotherly relation, although within both my maternal Nêhiyaw-Métis and paternal Nahkawè cultures, *Koochum* asserts considerable influence and assumes greater responsibility over *No'simak*. A shortened form of it appears in the text as *Co-Co*. *No'simak* is a term of address reserved for grandchildren. *No'sim* Angelina's birth encouraged me to make life-changing decisions. She came into the world three months before her expected date at a little over two pounds. For the first three months of her life, I was only able to touch her "spiritually," since she was kept in isolation in the neonatal unit for premature babies. During those spiritual encounters I called upon the spirit energies of "all my relations" to help me anchor her in the world. To those spirit helpers, I pledged to have a feast and a giveaway once she was safely rooted in this world. As I write this essay, I am trying to figure out a way to balance my need to host these ceremonies with my professional commitments.

I want to register here my preference for the capitalization of such terms as "Indigenous" and "Aboriginal"; however, I have necessarily deferred in this instance to the editorial policy of the Press.

3. Quewich, Ekos, and Acoose are the paternal names of *Nicapanak* (my great-

grandfathers) and *Nimosom* (my grandfather), whose legendary feats are kept alive in oral stories of the Nahkawè as well as written stories/articles/essays by this writer. The term *Mosom* refers to "grandfather (*nimosom*, "my grandfather"), although as with the term *Koochum, Nimosom* asserts greater influence and accepts a great deal of responsibility in the rearing of grandchildren.

4. Niatum, "History," 64–82.

5. McLeod, "Coming Home," 3.

6. Because my text relies primarily on the English language and the critical essay form, nonindigenous readers already assume a place of readerly privilege.

7. Dumont, "Devils Language," 391.

8. See also Gregory Scofield, Louise Halfe, Basil Johnston, Richard Wagamese, Tomson Highway, and Alexander Wolfe, whose English texts are infused with their culture-specific languages.

9. LaRocque, "Tides, Towns, and Trains," 82.

10. Armstrong, *Looking at the Words*, 151–52.

11. Ibid., 135, 7.

12. Ruffo, "Inside Looking Out," 163.

13. Ruffo, *(Ad)dressing Our Words*, 6, 7, 8.

14. McLeod, "Coming Home," 31, 18.

15. Ibid., 32, 23.

16. Ibid., 18–19.

17. Ibid., 18, 25, 24. Cultural relations, blood relations, and story relatives are aligned/allied in Neal McLeod's and Maria Campbell's work. And some of the same figures inhabit Paul Seesequasis's work.

18. See interviews with Beth Cuthand, Jordan Wheeler, and Daniel David Moses in Lutz, *Contemporary Challenges*.

19. Campbell, *Stories*, 2.

20. Ibid., 89.

21. Ibid., 86.

22. Ahenakew et al., Wisahkewcahk, 24–26, 28. This story is one of *No'sim* Alijah-Blue's favorites. He insists I read it to him over and over, and his eyes twinkle with mischief as he laughs at Wisahkecahk's misfortune.

23. Campbell, *Stories*, 87, 89.

24. Ibid., 98, 92.

25. Ibid., 87.

26. Ibid., 102.

27. I use the culture-specific term "Nêhiyawak" to name the people Seesequasis refers to as Cree.

28. Seesequasis, *Republic*, 411.

29. Ibid.

30. Ibid., 412, 415.

31. Campbell, *Stories*, 92.

32. Seesequasis, *Republic*, 412.

33. Campbell, *Stories*, 102.

Digging at the Roots

Locating an Ethical, Native Criticism

LISA BROOKS

Craig Womack tells us, in his groundbreaking work on Native literary criticism, *Red on Red*, that we have been "whipped into believing that we have no intellectual history of our own making that might provide frameworks for analysis."[1] Although a growing body of scholarship supports Robert Warrior's vital affirmation, in *Tribal Secrets*, of a long-standing Native intellectual tradition, "Native literature" and "Native American studies" continue to be regarded, within the academy and the popular imagination, as "new" or "emerging" fields. At this moment, we face a critical juncture in our discipline. Many English departments are pushing for the incorporation (or assimilation) of Native American literature as a branch of American literature, to be studied alongside other "ethnic" literatures, such as African American, Chicano/a, and Asian American, which together form a body of interdisciplinary and perhaps, interchangeable, subjects. Scholars are encouraged to acquire some textual knowledge in each of these fields, and to compare them, using, as the foundation of their analysis, the tools of critical theory as they exist within mainstream cultural studies. Native American literature is perceived as a relatively undeveloped area of inquiry, which can benefit from the application of the longer tradition of European-based literary theory to its growing field of texts. This approach is all well and good, except when it is privileged over the current efforts of many Native studies scholars to emphasize the depth and breadth of indigenous intellectual traditions—for, concurrently, there is a push among Native literary critics to move toward a deeper

---

Lisa Brooks (Abenaki) is assistant professor of history and literature and of folklore and mythology at Harvard University. She received her PhD in English, with a minor in American Indian studies, from Cornell University. Her book, The Common Pot: Indigenous Writing and the Reconstruction of Native Space in the Northeast *(forthcoming), focuses on the role of writing as a tool of social reconstruction and land reclamation in the Native Northeast. In addition to her academic work, she also serves on the advisory board of Gedakina, a nonprofit organization focused on indigenous cultural revitalization, educational outreach, and community wellness in northern New England.*

analysis of and sovereignty over Native literature, with a focus that is more tribally specific and much more entrenched in the study of our own systems of knowledge.

I believe that for us, at this moment, there can be no move more important than establishing that our work, our writing is part of an extensive indigenous intellectual tradition. What we have at stake is not only the recognition of the validity of our knowledge, but the sustenance of indigenous epistemologies. As Womack writes, "tribal literatures are not some branch waiting to be grafted onto the main trunk. Tribal literatures are the *tree*, the oldest literatures in the Americas, the most American of American literatures. We *are* the canon."[2] Native texts cannot merely be added into American literature as one constituent of a multicultural melting pot of emerging voices. The field of American literature itself has been deeply lacking in the context of Native America. We still need to do the work to bring informed Native standpoints to the fore. Our indigenous education—grounding in our own intellectual and cultural traditions—puts us in a unique position in our approach to texts. Our claims to an indigenous perspective don't rest on identity politics, or some inherent connection to ancestral voices; it's about understanding literature from a perspective embedded in long-standing sources of knowledge. We are part of a philosophical conversation, which did not emerge only in the last twenty years but has been ongoing on this continent for millennia. To deny the existence of our epistemological roots is to buy into the myth that we have no tradition of thought, a myth, ironically, that is contradicted by our own "mythology." We may have much to lose if we do not make education in these traditions our priority. This book raises some important questions for our ongoing conversation: What is an indigenous literary tradition? What is an ethical indigenous criticism? If "tribal literatures are the tree," as Womack suggests, what are its roots?

Origin Stories

In the first published version of the Wabanaki creation story, Penobscot Joseph Nicolar highlighted the central ethics of community life. "Three things of Klose-kur-beh's teaching are held more sacred than all others," he wrote. "The first was the power of the Great Spirit," which inhabits "the sun—moon—stars—clouds of heaven—mountains—and even the trees of the earth." "Second," he continued, "the land the Great Spirit gave them they must never leave, and the third, they must never forget their first mother."[3] Simple enough, really, and certainly the most central of the values my own father taught me: honor the spirit that runs through all beings, don't abandon home, remember your mother. So, for me, as an Abenaki student and scholar, certain questions emerge from these foundational principles. How can we keep our writing home? In other words, how can we write from home, and in ways that can speak to and contribute to our own communities, including all of the beings, human and nonhuman, that constitute them? How can we simultaneously honor the geographic, political, and experiential space we share, the streams that connect us? Finally, who is our mother? Or more directly, what are the sources of our intellectual tradition and what can we learn from them about practicing an ethical criticism?

In my own work, I have turned to three sites for answers to these questions: language, traditional stories, and the texts of the northeastern Native writing tradition. Two of the literary critics who have strongly influenced my thinking, Kathryn Shanley and Robert Warrior, offer important reasons for seeking out these philosophical wellsprings. Shanley points to language and oral literature as being the most "evident" resources for "Native American peoples' critical language."[4] This "metalanguage," Shanley writes, "can be key to the literature." For me, Shanley's use of the term "key" has a double meaning. The "metalanguages" present in language and oral literatures are "key," that is, important, to analysis because of their embeddedness in written literatures, but they also offer crucial interpretive "keys" that unlock meaning in Native-authored texts. Without knowledge and comprehension of oral literary traditions, the criticism and interpretation of Native literature, at best, will tend away from depth and complexity, and at worst, will be shallow and misleading. Of course, the frameworks we use for this interpretation must be grounded in particular places. As Janice Acoose observed (in an earlier version of her essay for this vook), "Taken out of context, or retold without some relevant understanding of our history, beliefs, language, traditions, spiritual practices, and values, the stories simply become legendary references to so-called vanished Indians." Furthermore, as Chris Teuton noted, in an earlier version of his essay in this volume, while "academic criticism often recognizes the importance of American Indian epistemologies, spiritual beliefs, and moral theories," particularly those grounded in the "oral tradition," as subjects of study, "these bodies of thought have not been placed at the center of scholarly interpretive or theoretical frameworks." This is a state of the field that I hope is open to change.

These oral traditions, for me, are inextricably intertwined with the written traditions that have taken root and grown up alongside them over the past few hundred years. Rather than privileging oral sources over written texts, Robert Warrior urges us to consider the extensive source of "intellectual history" available in the writings of the "Native writers and scholars" who preceded us. "When we take that tradition seriously," he asserts,

> we empower our work. First, we see that, far from engaging in some new and novel practice that belongs necessarily to the process of assimilating and enculturating non-Native values, we are doing something that Natives have done for hundreds of years—something that can be and has been an important part of resistance to assimilation and survival. Such a generational view . . . provides a new historical and critical site that invites us to see contemporary work as belonging to a process centuries long, rather than decades long, of engaging the future contours of Indian America. Second, we stand on firmer ground in our

interlocutorial role with Eurocentric scholarly theories and categories. . . . Third, critically reading our own tradition allows us to see some of the mistakes of the past as we analyze the problems of the present.[5]

Language: Writing/Criticism as Transformative Activity

I'll begin, then, with a reading of a simple word, drawn from one of the first Abenaki-authored texts to root our oral language in print. To call myself "Native" in Abenaki, I would use the term *alnôba,* or its longer version, *alnôbawôgan.* The latter is neither truly an adjective nor a noun, as the labels "Native," "American Indian," or "Native American" are in English. Rather, as the writings of nineteenth-century preacher Pier Pôl Wzokhilain tell us, *alnôbawôgan* means both "human nature" and "birth." Literally, it can be translated as the activity of "being (or becoming) human." Thus, in Abenaki philosophy, the very nature of being human is rooted, not in the consciousness of our mortality, but our natality, and the active state of transformation that birth implies. This concept provides a striking contrast to the stereotypical European constructions of Native "tradition" as static and potentially destructible (mortal), while confirming the idea of tradition, so present in much of contemporary Native literature, as an ongoing process, both cyclical and transformative.[6]

In line with this process, the word *alnôbawôgan* has been transformed within the Abenaki language to denote "being Native." This contemporary usage evokes those central Wabanaki principles that Nicolar recorded, rooting Abenaki indigeneity in our birth from a particular (mother)land. The word, in its active form, also signifies the activities with which we are engaged, the transformations that constitute the ongoing process of "being human" within a multifaceted world. The questions this concept raises for all of us Native lit crits might be: How do we *do* criticism as human beings? How can writing be an activity of sustenance, transformation, and conversation within our communities, both those of our home country and those of the Native, and broader, academic networks to which we belong? As Womack observes, language can have an invocatory, transformative power. It has the potential to "actually cause a change in the universe."[7] What sorts of transformation do we want to make?

Traditional Literature: Writing/Criticism as Participatory Thinking

In concert with these concepts present in language, traditional northeastern creation stories often link the emergence of human beings in the land to the transformative process of birth. To elucidate the complex conceptions present in traditional literature, I'd like to turn to a story of birth that is probably familiar to us all. Through its travel within Native networks and its wide-reaching publication, the Haudenosaunee (Iroquois) story of Sky Woman has become one of the most widely known indigenous narratives of creation.

Several Native writers have published versions drawn from communal oral narratives, including John Norton (Cherokee/Mohawk), David Cusick (Tuscarora), Arthur Parker (Seneca), and more recently, Joseph Bruchac (Abenaki) and the combined effort by Joanne Shenandoah (Oneida) and Doug George (Mohawk). Cusick's version has even made it into the *Norton Anthology of American Literature*. Sky Woman may be one of the most canonical Native texts in our literary tradition.[8]

In the traditional story, only a mass of water exists beneath the sky, and the water animals are its only inhabitants. When they see a woman falling from a hole in the Sky World, the animals "council together . . . to devise a way to provide for her."[9] Each animal dives to the bottom of the sea, striving to take up some dirt. Each returns, gasping for air, but empty-handed. Finally, muskrat, it is said, dives deep down into the water until he can go no further, grasps a handful of earth in his paw, and rises to the surface. He gives up his life, but in his last breath, he releases the dirt onto turtle's back. The geese fly up to catch Sky Woman in their wings, and, as they lay her on the bower of turtle's back, the woman releases a seed she carried from the Sky World, and the earth is born.

Rather than emerging from a void of existence filled by a divine male creator, the earth materializes through the interrelated activity of its inhabitants. Moreover, the creation of the earth requires thought. The story emphasizes the resourceful intelligence of all the water animals, and of Sky Woman herself. The thinking that results in creation is cooperative, drawing on the insights and abilities of all the members of the community to solve the problem at hand. As the newest arrival in the group, Sky Woman becomes a participant rather than being portrayed as an outsider. Before falling though a hole in the Sky World, she reaches out to grab a seed from a tree, with the thought of earth in mind. When she arrives, she plants the seed, making her own contribution, as the grandmother of all humans, to creation. Sky Woman tells an important story about the potential in imaginative inspiration and the power of group deliberation. Only through the interaction of both of these processes can the earth be born.

This story also has a great deal to say about how we might participate as humans in the processes that transform and sustain the land we inhabit. Sky Woman not only carried the seed of the earth in her hand, but the seed of its human inhabitants in her womb. In John Norton's words, "When she had fallen on the back of the Turtle, with the mud she found there, she began to form the earth, and by the time of her delivery had increased it to the extent of a little island. Her child was a daughter, and as she grew up the earth extended under their hands." Sky Woman's daughter soon became pregnant with twins, and these sons battled over their emergence into the world. Norton's version continues: "At the time of her delivery, the twins disputed which way they should go out of the womb; the wicked one said, let us go out of the side; but the other said, not so, lest we kill our mother; then the wicked one pretending to acquiesce, desired his brother to go out first: but as soon as he was delivered, the wicked one, in attempting to go out at her side, caused the death of his mother." The twins, known as "Skyholder" and "Flint," are often referred to as the Good Mind and the Bad Mind in English translation, but these labels can be deceptive. As Onondaga linguist Kevin Connelly explains, the real difference between the two is rooted in the relationship between thought and action:

> In the Iroquoian telling of creation, twins are born in this world. They are beings but not human beings. Collectively, they can be referred to as Two Minds and they go about transforming this world, creating. Eventually humans are created. Two Minds becomes two human cognitions; what I refer to as being versus analysis, and participant versus doer. Culturally, presently, the two minds are given the moral labels of Good Mind and Bad Mind in English. Culture privileges and nurtures "the given," that is, two created cognitions, uniquely. In Onondaga being and participant are treasured, analysis and doer are reined in tightly.[10]

A direct translation of the Sky Woman story confirms Connelly's interpretation of the "Two Minds." In the Oneida version published by Floyd G. Lounsbury and Bryan Gick, the Oneida tellers Demus Elm and Harvey Antone relate, *na?tehoti-?nikul-ó:t*, meaning, "they had different kinds of minds/thoughts."[11] This translation also emphasizes the distinction between participant and doer. Skyholder walks through the land "considering" what might contribute to it, acting constructively from *within* the environment, while Flint "arranges" without deliberation, acting *upon* the environment in careless and destructive ways. In David Cusick's version of the story, Flint does not act out of inherent malice, but is "moved by an evil design."

The distinction is critical. Flint's destructive action occurs because he is not thinking clearly, in concert with his relations, and thus, he responds rashly to impulse. Skyholder, on the other hand, demonstrates concern for the effect his brother's act will have on their mother and "endeavors to prevent his [brother's] design."

The literal translation of Skyholder's emergence, in the Oneida version, is "he was born, for one to be born human," echoing the Abenaki association of human "being" with birth. Furthermore, both Connelly's Onondaga translation and this Oneida version suggest that to "be human" in a good way is to participate in the ongoing activity of the birth/transformation/creation of the land that we inhabit. As in the Wabanaki writings of Nicolar and Wzokhilain, Haudenosaunee philosophy connects indigeneity to birth from a common mother/land and sustained participation in the processes that continually create that land. Yet it is important to emphasize that humans are not the only, or even the primary, participants in this process. If we look back to Norton's version, we can see the fullness of Haudenosaunee participatory cosmology. Rather than writing, "they extended the earth," he writes, "the earth extended under their hands," confirming the idea that creation occurs through the cooperation of multiple beings—between the water animals and Sky Woman, and here, between "the earth" and the two women. Other versions also demonstrate the conceptualization of an active, participatory "earth." One translation maintains that Skyholder could only perform his generative role in shaping the land because "this earth is alive." Oneida historian Anthony Wonderley relates that this version suggests that "the miraculous growth of our world results from the generative power of 'our Mother,' the earth."[12]

Connelly's analysis of Onondaga linguistics sheds important light on this conceptualization of an active earth. By focusing on the grammatical category of aspect in Onondaga oral texts, he reveals the centrality of space and participation in Haudenosaunee language and cosmology. Summarizing one of his central arguments, Connelly writes, "Since Onondaga is an aspect language and is not a time-line-tense language, a completely different-kind-of-existence is portrayed. The English speaking reader has to draw heavily on imagination to create a world that is completely free of time-line-tense; a world where time is inevitable but neither necessary nor 'good' (according to cultural bias). Instead, there is a favored world of pristine spatial existence, and the space is in motion, it is dynamic, and we are participants."[13]

As I understand it, in Onondaga cosmology, the earth and its beings are neither subjects nor objects, in the English sense of nouns, but rather "participants" or even, states of being, in a constantly transforming space of activity. Creation occurs through interaction, not through one being acting upon another. Human *participation* is highly valued because it attempts to work in concert with the activity of creation, as opposed to acts motivated only by individualistic desire and will. This is not to say that will does not play a strong role in creation. Think about how hard each of the water animals tries to get soil from the bottom of the sea. It takes a great deal of desire and willpower, sometimes, to act in concert with creation. However, the important distinction between participation and "doing" is that the water animals and Skyholder draw their ideas from group deliberation and consideration for how their activities will affect their fellow inhabitants. They act in awareness of the need for careful thought and action in response to the change in their environment represented by the arrival of Sky Woman. Flint, on the other hand, acts impulsively, without consideration for the consequences his actions will have on the whole.

Our literary traditions emphasize the power of thought in transformation. They tell us that the thinking that creates the world is an ongoing activity with which we, as human beings, are engaged. Any work we do as Native scholars operates as part of a long indigenous intellectual tradition, beginning with Sky Woman and her many and varied sisters. How might we follow the example of the water animals, of Sky Woman, of Skyholder in our own writing? The academy asks us to think about our careers, our professional progress as individuals, and our production of knowledge, with little regard for our position as members of Native communities. Does this necessitate following Flint's rocky path? How can we ensure that our scholarship does not destroy our mother? What would it mean to participate in criticism, to make our writing participate in and create community? This volume may be an important start. It seems that what Robert Warrior called for some years ago in *Tribal Secrets* was for Native scholars to participate in a critical conversation, rather than merely to "do" criticism. This volume, I believe, is born of that call.

Relational Frameworks: "Thinking in Skin"

So let me begin this next section with an attempt to think in concert with what my fellow contributors have said so far, to make the theory I've developed in these last few pages participate in our developing conversation. As I've read through these essays, it has occurred to me that both the Abenaki concept of *alnôbawôgan* and the Haudenosaunee story of Sky Woman have something to say to key issues raised in this volume. For instance, *alnôbawôgan* offers an alternative way of conceptualizing the English word "Native." The Abenaki word *alnôba* first describes the state of being human within a particular environment, not as opposed to other humans nor as a marker of national or racial identity, but as opposed to, and in relation to, all the other beings—animal, plant, rock, spirit—who also inhabit this land. Secondly, it evokes a particular way of being human that seems to work well in this particular land. Thirdly, as the term has evolved over the last few hundred years, it recognizes the affiliation of that particular understanding of "human" with the English terms "Native," "Indian," or "indigenous," although even then, the word *alnôba* is generally reserved for Indians who share a commonality within this particular region, those with whom we have some familial and cultural relationship.[14] Therefore, "Native" in the Abenaki language is not a term that is used to separate and distinguish us from other "races" but is rooted in the recognition of relationship to other humans with whom we share common experience and common bonds. Identity is thus always relational, and grounded in a particular place and its history.

The Sky Woman story also emphasizes relationality, and I want to spend a bit more time reflecting on the two brothers and how they speak to the critical approaches we have taken in this volume. In the story, even opposition is relational, the two minds are brothers, the closest of kin, enmeshed in a "creative contest." The real conundrum of the story emerges when we realize that "the world as we know it" is the direct result of this "contrapuntal" dynamic.[15] So the question I would pose to my fellow contributors is, what might we learn from more fully examining the relationships between those concepts that we have put in opposition? This question arises, not only from my own theoretical strategies, but from contemplating the intersections between the many voices gathered here and from Craig Womack's particular interrogations herein of the "false dichotomy" between thought and experience, oral and written, nationalism and pan-tribalism.[16]

In an earlier version of his valuable overview essay, "Theorizing American Indian Literature," Chris Teuton provided a thoughtful synopsis of Paula Gunn Allen's interpretive framework from *The Sacred Hoop*, which values "concrete experience as opposed to abstract comprehension."[17] Allen roots this opposition in a difference between Native interactive understandings of the "mythic" and European objectification of Indian "myths." Allen's analysis seems to mirror the story of the two brothers, in which a "participatory" approach to story and scholarship is valued over a "detached, analytical, distanced observation of myth." However, I wonder if the real issue at hand is not one of experience versus abstract thought—a dichotomy that, as Womack points out, is much more rooted in Cartesian dualism with its separation of body and mind than any Native tradition with which I am familiar—but rather a position of "detachment" and "distance" versus participatory mental engagement. Teuton, in conversation with Allen, observes that "the Western scholarly tradition has, historically" privileged "objective, distanced" analysis of oral literature, while Allen advocates a "mode of interpretation" that "includes the interpreter as part of the story: the listener/reader participates in the creation of meaning by embedding the story in his/her life, which takes place as part of a real community."

I have come to most value scholarship that recognizes intellectual work as an activity that has effects on and participates in the "real" world that we inhabit. Perhaps the concern to which we should turn is the need for thought that acknowledges its embeddedness in experience, which cultivates and expresses an intimate relationship with the world in which it thinks. In his essay here, Robert Warrior highlights a phrase from Joy Harjo that may be very useful to us: I crave both literature and scholarship that shows us "thinking in skin."[18]

Similar questions about the relationship between oppositions may be asked of the presumed dichotomy between the oral and written traditions. As Craig Womack notes, all of the "oral" accounts that I have referenced thus far are drawn from written texts. Even those stories that I have heard firsthand have textual traditions and are inevitably in dialogue with those texts. As he rightly observes, we now have a written oral literary tradition—often the stories that have been recorded, or versions of the stories that are recorded, are those most likely to be recovered and retold. Likewise, a simple textual fragment of a story that was thought to be lost, in the hands of a Native storyteller who is entrenched in her national literature, can be reborn in oral form. I've seen it happen many times. My own reading of these texts is inextricably entwined with the way they have been told and interpreted in my lifetime. I do not crave a "pure" form, only one that is alive and is participating in my community, in my own comprehension of the world.

One of the most prominent oppositions within this book is the debate between tribally specific and pan-tribal approaches to literature and criticism. Janice Acoose has raised critical questions about the potential for pan-tribal or generic "Native" approaches to participate in the erasure of cultural specificity and diversity, as well as the dissolution of national sovereignty. Such approaches, she suggests, may even pose a threat to cultural and political survival. Furthermore, she contends that Native readers often turn to literature to feed a hunger to know themselves, to see the particularities of their own history, culture, and experience reflected back to them. Kim Roppolo, conversely, argues for the possibility of pan-tribal approaches that may nourish the relationships between us. She writes of the need for "an intertribal rhetoric" to facilitate conversation and communication across constructed national, social, and racial boundaries and urges us to enter the "rhetorical borderland," a space in which we will certainly be challenged, but from which we might also grow. This is a debate that emerges across the volume, and I hope that these two authors will forgive my admittedly simplified rendering of their complex positions. What I want most to explore, in the pages that follow, is the historical relationship between nationalism and intertribalism, as well as its connection to the intertwined roots of Native political experience and participatory writing here in the Native Northeast. For this, my friends, is a very old and ongoing debate.

Nations within Networks: The Tradition of Writing in the Native Northeast

To my knowledge, the earliest recorded Native articulation of the concept of "Indian" in North America emerged from here on the Algonquian coast. Recognizing the need for an intertribal alliance some time before the emergence of King Philip and long before Tecumseh, the Narragansett leader Miantonomi traveled throughout the Northeast, appealing to his relations:

> For so are we all Indians as the English are, and say brother to one another; so must we be one as they are, otherwise we shall be all be gone shortly, for you know our fathers had plenty of deer and skins, our plains were full of deer, as also our woods, and of turkies, and our coves full of fish and fowl. But these English having gotten our land, they with scythes cut down the grass, and with axes fell the trees; their cows and horses eat the grass, and their hogs spoil our clam banks, and we shall all be starved. Therefore it is best for you to do as we, for we are all the Sachems from east to west, both Moquakues and Mohauks joining with us, and we are all resolved to fall upon them all, at one appointed day."[19]

Significantly, the first use of the word "Indian" to denote the relationships between those peoples within a particular region who share a common experience was in response to the direct and dire threat of colonization. As in my own exploration of the word *alnôbawôgan*, Miantonomi's concept of "Indian" is spatially and historically specific, emerging not just from the English conceptualization of a particular racial identity, but from the need for recognizing a common identity in order to form the alliances that might ensure the sustenance of the land, and the nations it contains, in response to a force that threatens to destroy it. In our own debates around this issue, we might consider the trade networks, shared histories, and specific relationships between nations that have been so much a part of our common experience within this land. Might not these old networks, which existed long before colonization, provide an alternative model for conceptualizing contemporary intertribalism, not just because they are "traditional," but because the system seems to have worked?

In *Tribal Secrets,* Robert Warrior asked us not only to engage in critical conversation with each other, but with our literary ancestors, encouraging us to pay attention to "American Indian writers of earlier periods," in part, because they "confronted similar situations."[20] Taking up his call, I would like to turn to the writings that emerged from the intertribal networks of the Native Northeast in the eighteenth and nineteenth centuries. These texts, composed by the descendants of Miantonomi and his relations, provide an especially fertile ground for exploring the questions we've raised thus far. In particular, I want to ask: What models for writing as a participatory and transformative activity exist within this literary tradition? What can we learn from our intellectual ancestors about the relationship between analytical thought and political action, between the oral tradition and writing, between nationalism and intertribal relations?

Scholars who have employed oppositional frameworks that focus on the tension between the "Indian" and "white" worlds have often failed to see a full picture of the northeastern landscape. Most critics have portrayed early Native writers either as individuals "caught between two worlds" or as "subjects," who, even as they may have resisted or challenged the colonial world, struggled to exist within it. The question of the degree to which they were corrupted by writing, by Christian religion, and by their presence in European circles is almost inevitably raised. However, if we shift our gaze and instead look closely at the relationships and communications *between* these writers, a network of indigenous intellectual exchange comes to the fore, in which leaders *used* writing to reconfigure, reimagine, and reclaim "Native rights" and "Native land." Far from being "corrupted" by writing, Algonquian and Haudenosaunee people frequently resisted the role designed for them by their missionary teachers and used the skills they acquired to compose petitions, political tracts, and speeches; to record community councils and histories; and, most importantly, to imagine collectively the means through which their communities could survive.

These points are especially true for Samson Occom and William Apess, the most well known of early Native writers. Critics and instructors have focused largely on their autobiographies, perhaps because those texts best mirror the European definition of literature as individual self-expression and fit easily into the American literary tradition. However, of all their writings, the autobiographies are most out of place in Native literary traditions, and both were produced in order to establish status within colonial circles. Occom wrote his autobiography under pressure from outsiders who questioned his identity and his loyalty, due in large part to controversy over the active role he played in the Mohegan land case. He authored the brief narrative just before embarking on a tour of England to raise funds for Indian education, when establishing his credibility was crucial to his success. As his first publication, Apess's autobiography is the most conservative and cautious of his collected works and truly the beginning point of his own intellectual and political journey in print.[21]

In focusing on those texts that conform to European literary genres, scholars have minimized the significance and power of the writings that most affected Native communities in the Northeast. During the infamous Mohegan land case, for instance, Samson Occom assumed a leadership role in the struggle to reclaim his Native home. He wrote the first Indian-authored petition to the king of England and corresponded with Sir William Johnson, the powerful agent of Indian affairs in Iroquoia and husband to the influential Molly Brant. Occom circumvented the power the Connecticut colony had imposed over his nation and utilized his considerable writing skills and his connections within indigenous networks to participate actively in community preservation.

Occom became notorious in New England during the 1760s for challenging the overseers appointed by the colony of Connecticut, opposing the schoolteacher at Mohegan (whom he believed was failing to educate the community's children), and rallying his relations to stand up for their land rights. Robert Clelland, the schoolteacher whom Occom opposed, complained to the governor of Connecticut Colony that Occom "wrote a Letter agst this Colony with his own hand to the King of G Britain, and amongst many other things, he says they have not a foot of land. . . . He has behaved very ungratefully to the worthy & kind overseers who has spent no small time to protect them & manage their affairs, repeated complaints he has Sent up to Sir William Johnston & it is said he is gone up to him this Season. It is trew I suppose that he said he would ly down & die if he got not his Will. . . . If Samson could be gain'd the rest would come easily over, at present his is all in all with them."[22]

Even when the missionary board that funded his teaching called Occom to task for his "ill conduct," forcing him to make a "confession" in which he promised not to "act in that affair" of the land claim "unless called thereto and obliged by lawful authority," he later told a Mohegan woman that he had "outwitted" the commissioners.[23] He proceeded to push the case through William Johnson, seeking "authority" from the internal "obligation" to his community and appealing to the "lawful authority" of higher colonial powers. Writing to Johnson on behalf of the Mohegans, Occom explained their situation: "We are imposed upon by our overseers, and what our overseers have done, we take to be done by the [Connecticut] Assembly. By what they have already done, we think they want to render us as cyphers in our own land. They want to root us out of our land, root & branch. They have already proceeded with arbitrary power over us, and we want to know from whence they got that power or whether they can maintain such power justly over us."[24]

In this letter, Occom invokes a metaphor for indigeneity that "roots" the Mohegans in their land, making it clear that it is the destructive behavior of the Connecticut settlers that threatens the continuance of their tree and the growth of their "branch." Occom questions the legitimacy of the power these interlopers have asserted "in our own land," an authority the governors of the colony (and some Mohegans) took for granted. Occom was invested not only in reclaiming a sense of Mohegan sovereignty, but also in reasserting the Mohegans' nation-to-nation relationship with the British. In concluding his letter, Occom appealed to British law, asking Johnson "whether the kings Instructions Concerning the Indian Lands, aren't as much for us as any Tribe." He referred to the 1763 royal proclamation, and a critical passage in which the king "strictly enjoin[ed] and require[d] all persons whatever, who have either willfully or inadvertently seated themselves upon any Lands . . . which, not having been ceded to, or purchased by Us, are still reserved to the said Indians as aforesaid, forthwith to remove themselves from such Settlements." In Occom's analysis, the proclamation could be applied to any Indian nation that had not ceded its territory, and in his reading of the documents of the land case, Mohegan certainly qualified.[25] Occom utilized his reading skills to review and interpret the laws that might provide for the preservation of his nation's rights and then sought to communicate directly with the source of those laws. At about the time Occom wrote the letter to Johnson, a report came to the governor of Connecticut from Mohegan that "Samson wrote a letter to the King of England wherein he said these Indians joined the English when few in Number, but when they increased they took their Lands from them after they set up stakes for their bounds, and now their widows suffered as they had no land to plant, or kept creatures on & that in truth they had not land of their own."[26]

Samson Occom brought the power of literacy home and made it participate in the community of Mohegan. It is important to recognize that Occom was not an anomaly or a "special case." He was only one of many educated Indians who returned home from missionary schools and used the knowledge they had gained to advocate for land cases and community rights, and to record and interpret documents crucial to community preservation.[27] Occom and other educated Mohegans like Samuel Ashpo and Joseph Johnson also used writing within their community to communicate with each other and to record community councils. For example, Occom recorded the following council for his nation: "April 28, 1778: In the evening, the Tribe met together, to Consult about the Disposal of the Rent money, and as it has been agreed unanimously heretofore once and again, that we shall look upon one another as one Family, and will call or look upon no one as a Stranger, but will take one another as pure and true Mohegans; and so at this time, we unanimously agreed that the money does belong to the whole Tribe, and it shall be disposed of accordingly for the Benefit of the Whole."[28]

This passage from Occom's papers reveals the continuance of an indigenous ethical system at Mohegan, despite the divide-and-conquer tactics practiced by the Connecticut colony. The Mohegan land case had split the nation, and Occom, in particular, advocated for unity. He wrote to William Johnson, "Understand Sir, this Tribe has been in 2 parties, the Government Pretended to befriend the Indians, and Mr. Mason pretended the Same, and each had a Number of Indians, and there is a few of us that Seems to Stand between the two." Even the deposed sachem Ben Uncas, whom Occom and the majority of the Mohegans regarded as a puppet of the colony, expressed his concern over the division of the community. Writing to the Connecticut governor about "our melancholy situation at Mohegan," Uncas related, "I am really afraid murder will be committed here soon" and admitted that "Samson is as uneasy as ourselves."[29] When the Mohegans confirmed themselves as "one Family," those who participated in the council were actively reconstructing their community. Recognizing the role colonialism played in their division, they reclaimed an Algonquian ethic of familial inclusiveness.

The record of this council demonstrates the kind of participatory thinking that is evident in the story of Sky Woman, with the Mohegans deliberating together to make communal decisions for the "benefit of the whole" nation. Writing solidified their decision, invoking action and making their words manifest, while also providing a record of the event for future generations. Throughout northeastern Native networks, writing took on a role that was complementary to wampum, ensuring that spoken words would be honored and that agreements would be remembered. It generated and recorded transformations in Native Space. Samson Occom and his relations used writing as a transformative activity to reclaim land, to maintain relationships, to send news between communities, and to preserve and enact the decisions of "the whole." It is this kind of "literature" that makes Mohegan writing an important part of an indigenous intellectual tradition.

While utilizing writing in service to his nation, Occom also relied on wider, regional alliances to carry the power of his writing through. During his time in Iroquoia, Occom mastered the diplomatic rhetoric and fostered the relationships that would later enable him to call on the services of Mohawk ally and relation William Johnson, who could then work within his political networks to advocate the Mohegan case before the English king. This relationship was bolstered by the alliance that the Mohegans had made with both the Mohicans and the Mohawks during the so-called French and Indian wars. (Note as well, that these same alliances, particularly the three nations' close ties to the British, also made them adversaries to Wabanakis who continued to resist British expansion in the north.) Occom and the Mohegans operated as one nation within an intricate intertribal network, recognizing that the relationships between nations were essential to the survival of "the Whole."

Sometimes we look down so pitifully on Occom, censuring his acceptance of Christian dogma and lamenting the colonial yoke under which he lived, but we forget the degree to which he was a fully participating member of a Native nation, a leadership figure, and a representative, as well as the ways in which he used his skills as a writer and preacher for the empowerment of the Mohegan people. We also forget the degree to which Christianity became a part of the fabric of the region of New England, including its Native networks, and the ways in which those nations participated in political relations with their colonizing neighbors with as much variation as we do today.[30]

We could apply the same faulty logic today in our own choice of teaching within the institution of academia versus working in our tribal office or living a subsistence existence up in the northern woods (choices I am personally conscious of having made). I think it's defeatist to ask if that makes us "less Indian"—only future generations will be able to evaluate our choices and their impacts on the long-term sustenance of our environments and communities, and I can only hope that they will evaluate our roles as participants and contributors, rather than on a contrived scale of corruption and purity. I hope that they will want to look carefully at the work we were doing, in part because this is one of the activities in which Indians were engaged at the turn of the twenty-first century. Most importantly, I want to emphasize the need to look at the relationships between Native people and forces like Christianity within particular places and contexts. Evaluating and analyzing the work of people like Occom, who emerge (as we all do) from unique regional, cultural, and historical landscapes, in a framework that relies on a generic understanding of Indian identity can be a precarious move, especially when it fails to take historical relationships into account. As Tol Foster has suggested (in a previous draft for this volume) in his own analysis of John Joseph Mathews and Will Rogers, when such texts are utilized as "signifiers" of the "radical otherness" of Indians, they are often denied a "full literary and cultural range" and lose the "particular cultural and aesthetic resonances" for which we might most value them as literature.

To further explore the potential in a critical framework suggested by Foster's "Native regionalism," I'd like to turn to Pequot author William Apess, who was writing his relations into a narrative of continuance at a time when the rest of New England was heavily invested in the tragic story of extinguishment. Of all of Apess's published writings, *Indian Nullification of the Unconstitutional Laws of Massachusetts Relative to the Mashpee Tribe; or The Pretended Riot Explained* is the least utilized in both critical inquiry and teaching, and yet this multivoiced narrative probably had more significance for Native New England communities than all of his other publications combined. *Indian Nullification* tells the story of the "Mashpee Revolt," a moment in the early nineteenth century when the Mashpee Wampanoags declared their reserve to be Native Space and thereby "nullified" laws enacted by the Commonwealth of Massachusetts to manage and control them as dependents of the state. The Mashpees faced continual battle with land encroachment, an oppressive guardianship system, wood poaching of their carefully sustained forest, and a missionary who used their meetinghouse and their resources to serve the non-Native neighboring community.[31] During the "revolt," Apess and the Mashpees not only asserted their claim to self-governance, but enacted it, organizing their own councils and implementing their own regulations regarding "outsiders" from the commonwealth.

In his travels as an itinerant preacher, William Apess had heard conflicting reports about his relations at Mashpee; some people suggested that the people were "well provided," while "others asserted they were much abused." Apess had been told that the Mashpees had a missionary "who took care of their lands," but when he arrived there in 1833, and spoke with his "brethren," he found that in reality, their lands had been taken over. As Apess related in *Nullification,* he gave sermons at Mashpee in which he read from his "pamphlet" on the "history of the Indians of New England," illuminating connections between their shared past and the current state of affairs. Drawing on his readings of published histories and the oral traditions he heard while traveling among Native communities, Apess composed his own history, not only to inform and challenge broad New England audiences, but to empower his relations with a sense of themselves as actors in an indigenous counternarrative to the mythology of disappearance in which New England Indians were intelligent survivors, rather than tragic victims destined to fade away. One of Apess's standard arguments was to demonstrate to whites and Indians alike that "Indian degradation" was neither the result of racial nature, nor an inevitable tendency to vanish in the wake of civilization, but of quite specific laws and actions designed to dispossess Indians of their land. He connected the Mashpees' struggle with those of Indians all over the Americas, from the arrival of Columbus to the Cherokee removal that was so hotly debated at the time. Apess thus brought writing into service for the larger Algonquian network, helping Native communities to reconstruct communal narratives that would ultimately empower them to reclaim the space of home.[32]

In writing *Indian Nullification*, Apess allowed for multiple voices to participate relationally in the text. The narrative included the Mashpees' own "Declaration of Independence" from the commonwealth, their petition as "the red children of the soil of America" to "the White People of Massachusetts . . . the descendants of the pale men who came across the big waters to seek among [us] a refuge from tyranny and persecution," and the general notice published by the "National Assembly of the Marshpee Tribe" proclaiming their right to govern themselves and control their resources, as "the free-born sons of the forest." Apess also integrated the responses of the opposition into the text of *Nullification*, as well as excerpts from the heated debate that raged in the Massachusetts press for nearly a year.[33]

According to Apess, the "Mashpee Revolt" became such a popular issue in Massachusetts that when the controversy hit the statehouse, the Mashpees addressed an overflowing audience that broke out into spontaneous applause at the conclusion of their speech. Under this public pressure, as the *Boston Daily Advocate* reported, "The Mashpee Act, restoring the rights of self-government in part, to the Mashpee Indians, of which our legislation has deprived them for 140 years, passed the Senate of Massachusetts yesterday, to the honour of that body, without a single dissenting vote." Under the act, Mashpee was incorporated as an "Indian District," its inhabitants were "granted the right to elect selectmen," and all persons outside of the community were forbidden to "ever cut wood, or transport the same therefrom."[34] The writings that the Mashpees published in print and press were instrumental to the success of their case. In calling the larger community of Massachusetts to task for their destructive impulses, the Mashpees raised awareness that the problems in their village were those of the whole commonwealth. Acting and speaking inclusively, the Mashpees then asked their neighbors to participate in deliberation, to find a solution that would ultimately, in its justice, serve them all.

After the passage of the act, Apess composed the narrative of *Indian Nullification* for publication, with a mixture of voices woven together by a story of indigenous resistance, transformation, and survival. Apess's central message was encapsulated in the pamphlet's title, which contained elusive multiple meanings. While alluding to the nullification debate regarding states' rights that would gradually build into a civil war, it also evoked issues more central to the Mashpee case. Apess's narrative testified to a moment when Indians "nullified" the unjust laws of a colonial state and challenged the very idea of Indian "nullification." While American authors were writing the story of the vanishing Indian, Apess imagined regeneration and used writing to bring the reconstruction of Algonquian New England into being.

Apess's writing within the networks of Native New England may provide a strong model for a regional approach to understanding the relationship of nation to network. In "Of One Blood," Tol Foster provides a strong argument for the validity of regionalism as a theoretical framework for Native studies. As he wrote in an earlier version of this essay, one of the dilemmas posed by the inclusion of Native literatures in courses and anthologies of American literature is the question, "How do we cogently present anthologies, courses, and monographs on Native texts that do not leave out some of the crucial connections that bind and separate the peoples of those five hundred plus nations?" For Foster, the answer lies in honoring the particularities and relationships within specific regions, as well as the applications of the problems and concerns of a "given region" to issues "that are unresolved in the larger world and therefore of national or cosmopolitan interest."

In publications like *Indian Nullification* and the *Eulogy on King Philip*, William Apess addressed the struggles and histories that were particular to his region, but also connected them directly to the pressing political issues of his day, including slavery, removal, states' rights, and postrevolution republicanism. Apess insisted on including the Bostonians he addressed in his regional, familial landscape, on the basis of a shared—albeit bloody—history. To confront that history of violence, and to regenerate and heal the social and physical landscape, Apess proclaimed that if his white "brethren" wanted to preach their prayers for justice across the nation, their "work" had best begin at home, with respect for Native rights, "in New England." Apess built his arguments with references to a regional history that everyone in his audience would recognize, but grounded his telling with an Algonquian interpretation, insisting that both speaker and listeners were participants in a continuing Native landscape, and therefore agents responsible for its future.[35]

While Apess's work was instrumental in reclaiming Native Space in the region of New England, other northeastern writers envisioned the continuation of wider indigenous networks, even as the United States claimed the continent, physically and imaginatively, as its own. Mohawk leader Joseph Brant and Mohican leader Hendrick Aupaumut have received much less critical attention than figures like Occom and Apess, although each produced enough writing to fill volumes, and both men's influence on early American Indian policy was considerable. They wrote petitions on behalf of their communities' land rights, engaged in a vast correspondence with Native and colonial leaders, and participated in the creation of communal histories for their nations. As active community leaders, they used their writing skills to record local councils and multinational treaties and to relay communications between their many relations, while using their diplomatic skills to negotiate with British, American, and multiple Native nations under pressure from a rapidly transforming political landscape.

Brant and Aupaumut both served as mediators in the Ohio Valley after the Revolutionary War, when the United States was attempting to expand its territories into the West. Their encounter in the valley is especially significant because of the conflict that erupted between them and the volume of writing they produced. Contained within Brant's and Aupaumut's journals, speeches, and correspondence are intricate articulations of their particular visions for peace. Both men were empowered by their nations, and by their respective colonial allies (Britain and the United States), to mediate a peace between the Native nations in the Ohio Valley and the newly formed United States. Their distinctive visions arose from competing conceptualizations of Native Space, rooted in each man's particular cultural tradition.

Hendrick Aupaumut believed Native continuance was rooted in the preservation of the village space. Algonquians needed to ensure they had a specific place to "hang a kettle, whereof they and their children after them might dip out their daily refreshment." He promoted a view among his western relations that Native nations needed to secure particular territories, bound by writing, as he had done for his own community, because in his experience, land encroachment was unstoppable. To Aupaumut, each nation was both a "kettle" unto itself and a part of the larger Algonquian network of relations that connected all villages together in mutual support and sustenance. During his journeys west, he reconstructed the "path of my ancestors," reconnecting his nation to the larger Algonquian community and encouraging his relations to strengthen their own "kettles" in order to preserve the network as a whole.[36]

Joseph Brant drew on Haudenosaunee and Algonquian political ideology to envision the "Dish with One Spoon," a multinational Indian alliance to preserve common lands. Brant sought to unite Native people from Haudenosaunee country to the Ohio Valley, recognizing from long experience that division was the greatest threat to Indian survival. In the councils that followed the Revolutionary War, he worked to build a confederation called the United Indian Nations as "one body" and "one mind" dedicated to maintaining the Ohio Valley as shared Native Space. Brant sought a return to the foundational principles of the Great Law but had to assure his western Algonquian allies that participating in the United Indian Nations would not signify their submission to a Haudenosaunee Confederacy that they had come to regard as a hierarchical and often oppressive body.[37] Building a common language between Haudenosaunee and Algonquians, Brant invoked the Algonquian metaphor of the "Dish with One Spoon" to articulate his vision. As Brant explained the concept in a letter to Alexander McKee, a British agent and trader with strong relational and political ties to the Shawnee:

> We have been told that such a part of the country belongs to the Six Nations. But I am of the opinion that the country belongs to the confederated Indians in common. If we say that such a part of the country belongs to one nation and such a part to another the Union cannot subsist, and we cannot more effectively serve our enemies whose whole aim has been to divide us. . . . Upwards of one hundred years ago a moon of wampum was placed in this country with four roads leading to the center for the convenience of the Indians from different quarters to come and settle or hunt here. A dish with one spoon was likewise put here with the moon of wampum. This shows that my sentiments respecting the lands are not new.[38]

The land of the valley was held in common, consisting of a network of shifting riverside villages within a larger shared hunting territory of grasslands and forests, all fed and connected by the Ohio River and its tributaries, enabling an efficient and diplomatic utilization of resources. The political vision of the confederation rested on recognizing equality and building consensus among all the nations who ate from the "dish," a coming together of minds that would enable the political system to mirror the geographic one. In speeches and in writing, Brant urged Algonquians and Haudenosaunee alike to engage in "deliberation" together so that they might achieve "unanimity" in their dealings with the young American nation and thus preserve a large territory in the West that would remain exclusively under Native control.

The writings of Brant and Aupaumut demonstrate the application and sustenance of indigenous epistemologies, embedded in tribally specific traditions that enabled distinctive strategies for dealing with colonization. Any reading of their journals demonstrates the need for those of us who analyze their writings to be highly educated in and aware of the nuances of those traditions. Without education in the culture, diplomacy, and history of our specific nations, we as critics cannot fully comprehend these texts, or analyze their philosophies. At the same time, we can see in Aupaumut's "kettle" and Brant's "dish" the long-standing oppositional debate between nationalism and intertribalism as strategies for combating colonization, as well as two different conceptualizations of the relationship between the nation and the larger network to which it belongs. It is crucial to recognize that both of these conceptualizations operated within the same landscape, overlapping and intersecting within political and geographic space.

The United Indian Nations operated in a broad international space that included multiple Iroquoian and Algonquian nations, as well as the newly formed United States, the Canadian British, and the "backcountry settlers" who were inundating their lands.[39] At the councils in the Ohio Valley, there was a mixing of languages and diplomatic traditions that constituted a kind of "rhetorical borderland," to use Colleen Burke's term (cited by Kim Roppolo herein). One of the most difficult tasks facing the people who gathered there was to create a statement that would relay their final word in regard to the "dish" they all shared. This statement had to honor all the traditions from which it sprang *and* clearly communicate the needs of the whole to the leaders of the United States. Thus, the United Indian Nations was constantly engaged in the pursuit of an "intertribal rhetoric" that would facilitate communication within the confederation's councils and that would also translate to the non-Indians who shared their political and physical space. The difficulty of such a task is quite evident in the journals of Brant and Aupaumut, especially as they each describe the eventual breakdown in communication that ushered in the Battle of Fallen Timbers.[40]

I want to consider, first of all, that a historically and spatially specific intertribalism—which is based on the actual relationships between individuals, families, nations, and places, as well as a continuous attempt to build and maintain communication and relations—might be distinguished from a pan-tribalism that assumes a unified concept of Indian identity. The ideal of cross-cultural communication needs to take into account the differences, commonalities, and relationships *between* Native nations, not just between "Indian" and "non-Indian." (Even the frequently used metaphor of the "cultural broker" often fails to consider the long tradition of treaty making and exchange *within* Native Space, where intermediaries were required to master many different languages and political practices.) Those of us who value tribal specificity and national sovereignty would do well to take into account the long-standing tradition of intertribal exchange, especially as we consider how to interact within the many networks to which we belong today. We can think of intertribalism in a tribally and culturally specific framework, that is, in terms of the historical and ongoing relationships between us, incorporating the kind of deeply rooted scholarship called for by Janice Acoose, Phillip Morgan, and Tol Foster while honoring the need for work that seeks ways of reading in-between cultures, as Kim Roppolo suggests, reaching across national boundaries to find sites of commonality, conflict, and exchange. It may even be possible to develop a language of commonality, at least in this volume, that builds a strong and valuable conversation within *and* seeks to clearly and diplomatically represent the voice of the whole to the outside.

Within this whole, surely there will be opposition, but hopefully, we will be able to see and reflect on the relationships between our divergent viewpoints and understand their rootedness in our particular political, cultural, and social positions.[41] One of the hardest aspects of Robert Warrior's call for a critical conversation is imagining ways to challenge each other that will not put briars in each others' paths. The journals of Joseph Brant and Hendrick Aupaumut are particularly valuable in this regard, because they reveal the ways in which Native leaders critiqued and challenged each other. We may have as much to learn from the relations between early Native writers as we do from the writings themselves. Occom, Aupaumut, and Brant knew each other well and shared many experiences and acquaintances in common. Brant and Aupaumut, at times, nearly regarded each other as enemies, and at other times, as friends. Occom and Brant were both Wheelock students, and Occom even attended Brant's wedding during one of his diplomatic visits to William Johnson. Occom and Aupaumut became close friends in the final years of Occom's life, when both men were living in reconstructed Algonquian villages at Oneida. All three men belonged to a large interrelated network of writing Indians, with whom they interacted and corresponded. Any analysis of the connections between them only scratches the surface of the political and social communities in which they participated.

Within these networks of writing Indians, a profound exchange of knowledge was taking place. While Occom became fluent in Haudenosaunee language and diplomacy, enabling the reconstruction of his nation, Brant cultivated a common political language between Algonquian and Haudenosaunee people to articulate his intertribal vision of unity in the Ohio Valley. Conversation and debate about the state of political affairs, which took place in both writing and speech, was prolific in this environment. The texts of the northeastern Native tradition emerged from within this indigenous space of exchange, not, as is often portrayed, from displaced Indian individuals reflecting on the state of their lives in relation to the colonial world. Occom, Brant, Aupaumut, and Apess weren't individuals "caught between two worlds;" they were Native thinkers who inhabited many spaces of interaction, just as we do today.

Writing as Tool and Resource

In content and form, early Native writings reflect their authors' embeddedness in indigenous cosmologies. Brant and Aupaumut's journals are multivoiced narratives, similar in form to Apess's *Indian Nullification,* relating the perspectives of various communities and individuals as well as their own critical analysis. Similarly, the communal histories that Brant and Aupaumut helped to compose were participatory projects, drawn from councils and created in conjunction with other leaders, for the purpose of sustaining indigenous knowledge and educating a wider non-Native audience.

In the recording of councils and the production of communal histories, writing took on a role similar to wampum, serving as a vehicle for remembrance and solidifying group identity. However, it is important to observe that writing did not *replace* wampum in indigenous networks. These tools seemed to act interchangeably. As Aupaumut observed, speech unaccompanied by either "writing or wampum" was regarded as "an empty message." The narratives of Apess, Aupaumut, and Brant attest to this interrelationship between oral and written literature within northeastern Native communities, where writing is informed and infused by oral tradition, and the continuance of oral tradition is aided by the tool of literacy. Indeed, this particular way of adapting writing to the indigenous landscape seems to extend well beyond the Northeast, as Phillip Morgan relates herein. His essay on the writings of Choctaw intellectual James L. McDonald demonstrates how the "new literacy" in the English language was assimilated *by* the Choctaw community "into older, more established language art forms" and "incorporate[d] . . . as a fully viable tool of discourse." This important parallel between regions underscores the idea that "writing Indians" like Occom, Apess, and McDonald were hardly anomalies or exceptions, but were rather part of a larger landscape of adaptation in which Native people learned quite quickly how to make use of new tools and adapt them to old ways, without either replacing the other. Although it has long been a widely held belief that the adoption of literacy cancels out orality, this assumption just does not bear out in the face of the ever-growing body of indigenous writing. What Morgan writes about McDonald (this volume) can also be extended to the network of Indians writing in the Northeast (and beyond): "There is no evidence in his scrutiny that suggests that he expects literacy to replace orality, or orality to subdue literacy. It is more accurately inferred that he expects each to perform a transforming and edifying work on the other. We may choose to regard this as what Womack refers to as a foundational principle of indigenous criticism." Thus, it is the intertwining of the oral and the written, and the utilitarian value placed on writing as both tool and resource for community continuance, that forms the root of an indigenous American literary tradition.

As Morgan suggests, these "foundational principles" bear direct relevance to our critical conversations today and may indeed serve as a model for understanding how we utilize both literature and criticism. Writing can operate like wampum, forging connections between nations and generating conversation across the extensive networks of this continent. Writing can also operate like a birch-bark scroll, a textual map of a nation's communal history. The creation of and exchange of books, like wampum, can be central to our gatherings, whether they be a writers' conference in Tahlequah, a cultural festival in Montreal, an assembly of indigenous leaders at the UN, a potluck anywhere in Indian country, or a book like this one. I do believe that there is a link between the early writers and our burgeoning literary movement, our networks of Native writers, our work as scholars—much of this has to do with how we value writing as a resource for the sustenance of our selves and our communities. Perhaps a key question, to respond to Womack's reflections on the early writers, is whether the possibility now exists to use writing as a tool in the way Occom, Apess, Aupaumut, Brant, and McDonald did, in a way that will not just represent the landscape, but will participate in it, and whether, as politically conscious writers, we have some kind of a responsibility to try to imagine ways that we can do just that, not because of a prerogative that could potentially hierarchize politics over creativity, or experience over abstraction, but because our writing and imagining might actually be useful. Yet perhaps the production of literature in which a "proactive commitment to Native community" is central, as Jace Weaver argues in his book, *That the People Might Live*, is a process that is already ongoing. Perhaps the early writers merely exemplify how long writing has been playing a key role in these conversations between us.[42]

If we think of writing as a tool of the political imagination, it may mean that we need to expand the boundaries of what we define as literature. While honoring the more recent roles that poetry and fiction have begun playing in the imagination and sustenance of our nations, we might also look to what Scott Lyons calls battles "waged on the textual frontier." What he observes about the struggles over Chippewa treaty rights and the naming of the Washington Redskins might also be said for the early writers: "These victories were won by Native people who learned how to fight battles in both court and the culture-at-large, who knew how to read and write the legal system, interrogate and challenge cultural semiotics, generate public opinion, form publics, and create solidarity with others. . . . Both initiatives arose from the grassroots, each in their own way fought over questions of land and identity, and the ultimate outcome of both was an honoring of 'a whole way of life,' another productive step in the perpetuation of the people."[43] In expanding our view of literary production—geographically, temporally, and stylistically—we reimagine the bounds of the relationships that Native people have to writing. We are challenged to consider how multiple kinds of texts might serve the multiple needs of Native communities; we are moved to contemplate how writing can operate as a living force of change and sustenance in the landscape.

In this volume, Cheryl Suzack explores this potential in "literature as an imaginative site of social reconstruction" through her reading of Winona LaDuke's *Last Standing Woman*. In a way that harkens back to the earlier writers, *Last Standing Woman* is informed by LaDuke's own experiences as an active member of White Earth. The novel arises from her direct involvement in the Anishinaabe struggle to regain their lands and revitalize their nation, and reflects a consciousness of the Anishinaabe historical landscape as well as the author's own place within that storied environment. She is engaged in the process of narrating the nation in a way similar to Apess and Occom, in that her vision is not of individual empowerment and healing but of communal regeneration and sustenance, with all the complexity of contemporary relations that reflects the engagement of the author with the on-the-ground struggles of Native communities.

At the same time, LaDuke is intensely concerned with the relationships between nations, demonstrated with particular force in the novel by the personal alliance formed between two women characters, Ishkwegaabawiikwe and Situpiwin, who originate from nations which had long been in opposition. Suzack roots LaDuke's concern with intertribal relations not only in the historical relations between nations on the plains, but in the global indigenous women's network to which she also belongs. "The novel," Suzack writes, "privileges women's acts of resistance as engendering an alternative vision of community identity that focuses on intertribal communal relations rather than autonomous ones." The "kinship union between Ishkwegaabawiikwe and Situpiwin," according to Suzack, represents "a symbolic act of resistance." As Womack suggests herein, for the early writers, and certainly for Winona LaDuke, writing is both a social experience and a political act. The imagination, and the imagination of nations (to which several of the writers in this book refer) is an embodied experience, a part of the "process" through which sovereignty is enacted, a necessary part of the communal "journey."

Yet I want to be cautious about advocating for writing that is so fully aware of its political stance or suggesting that writing should serve primarily as a tool of advocacy. Perhaps the oppositional framework of which we should be most wary is a critical stance that divides "pure" art and thought from embodied action, poetry from the political. As Robert Warrior demonstrates in his exploration of Joy Harjo's "thoroughly embodied" erotics (this volume), the beauty of poetic writing is as essential to our political health as anyone's direct action. As the writing of Audre Lorde, on which Warrior draws, suggests, sometimes just to be fully in our bodies, to engage with other beings, whether through erotic expression, through fishing a stream walked by our fathers for generations, participating in tribal deliberation and dance, or picking ripened high bush blueberries in the marsh—these acts, their interpretation and representation, their transformation through thought, and then the written word can be an incredibly powerful political act, especially when the author's particular way of experiencing the world has been suppressed, denied, and romanticized to a fault. Simply to speak the truth to the world as we know it, as a good friend recently reminded me, is essential to our survival, essential to the sustenance of the whole.

We need to seek out the political vision in Louise Erdrich as much as we need to trace the literary history of Winona LaDuke; as Womack suggests, we need to hear *and read* treaty oratory in dialogue with creation stories; we need journeys of the imagination that envision the complexity of our past and the possibilities of our future in dynamic relationship with each other. Our need for sustenance demands both. Indeed, literature may be one of the crucial resources we rely on for our continuance. Janice Acoose reminds us that many readers turn to tribally specific texts to feed their hunger to know themselves. Literature can be a map, in Tol Foster's words, to aid us in finding our ways "home." Suzack reminds us, in her reading of LaDuke, that literature can feed the imagination of nations. Robert Warrior tells us that we also need the food that is exchanged between nations, recalling (in an earlier version of his essay that appears here) how "the poetry of Joy Harjo acted as a kind of connecting tissue for my emerging sense of what my work as an Osage intellectual would be. . . . I would read Harjo's poetry literally every day." Perhaps literature is the food that makes us think in our skins.

I think again of the story of Sky Woman, how all those water animals came to council together, to imagine an earth on which the falling woman from the sky could be sustained. I recall how Sky Woman combined the thought in her mind with the body of the seed in her hand to contribute to the land's imagination. I think of the brave thought and action of the earth diver (whether it be muskrat, beaver, or in the Cherokee versions told by Chris Teuton and Daniel Justice herein, water beetle or water spider) in bringing a small piece of dirt from the world below. I think of the embodied land itself—in the form of mud, in the form of water creatures, and in the form of Sky Woman herself—that creates the world. I look out my window now on this land, as it begins to turn, from the deep wet green of summer to the sweetening dry decay of fall, and I imagine the burst of color that will come just before the snow sets in. I look at the squash growing on the vine, I hear the crickets singing from the pine-strewn forest floor, I see the beech leaves stretching out toward the sun, I watch the wind as it moves through the branches, then stills; and I have to believe that these words that I write are somehow part of that conversation. The activity of creation is ongoing. It has to be. The existence of the world depends on it, literally.

As Native scholars, we have ways of seeing the world that we've acquired from our parents and other relations, from community leaders and teachers, and through our own efforts to engage with our traditions. We are participants in the ongoing process of that "tradition." We are part of a vast exchange that informs the literature and informs our ability to interpret the literature. One way to ensure that we do not fall into the trap of generalization or ossification (as Robert Warrior sees happening, for instance, in some of the critical analysis of the 1980s), and therefore subject ourselves to accusations of essentialism, is to root our work in analysis that is spatially and historically specific, that is grounded deeply in knowledge of our particular cultural, political, and intellectual traditions and the places that we call home. I would argue that this knowledge cannot be gained through traditional methods of scholarship, but is only *fully* accessible through interaction within the multifaceted indigenous networks to which we belong.

I am not denying the importance of acquiring literacy in the cultural theory that is currently being practiced in the university. We need that knowledge in order to achieve, and such knowledge might even prove beneficial to our communities. It is certainly crucial to communication within larger networks. However, it is equally important that we acquire literacy in our own theoretical traditions, because as Native scholars we can contribute a great deal to both our home communities and academic communities by applying our minds to understanding the depth and complexity of our literary traditions. Native languages, traditional stories, and written texts contain incredible insights into what it means to be a human being, what it means to write, and what it means to participate in a thinking world. On all of the ideas cultural theory seeks to understand, to deconstruct, or to reconstruct, our traditions have much to say. The more we can bring that idea to the fore, and show our thinking in operation, the more we have to contribute to the academy, not just as scholars but as participants in multiple intellectual communities.

Notes

1. Womack, *Red on Red*, 12.

2. Ibid., 7.

3. Nicolar, *Life and Traditions*, 14. The term "Wabanaki" refers to all of the related "Dawnland" peoples, including my own Abenaki Nation, which inhabits the western region of the Dawnland (present-day Vermont, New Hampshire, and Southern Quebec) and the Penobscot, Passamaquoddy, Mik'maq, and Maliseet who inhabit the eastern region (present-day Maine and the Maritimes). Wabanaki people are part of the extensive Algonquian language/culture group that extends throughout the northeast woodlands to the south and west.

4. Shanley,"Writing Indian,"141.

5. Warrior, *Tribal Secrets*, 2.

6. This idea appears centrally in many contemporary works of Native literature. In particular, I am thinking of Leslie Marmon Silko's novels and Joy Harjo's poetry.

7. Womack. *Red on Red*, 17.

8. See Cusick, *Sketches of Ancient History*, and Cusick's version of the Iroquois creation story in the *Norton Anthology of American Literature.* See also Norton, *Journal of Major John Norton*; Parker, *Seneca Myths;* Bruchac, *Iroquois Stories;*. and Shenandoah and George, *Skywoman*. Note that although Norton had intended to publish his journal during his lifetime, the text never actually made it into print until historians Carl Klinck and James Talman rediscovered it, in the castle of Norton's Scottish patron, in the 1960s. Norton was born in Scotland to a captive Cherokee and a Scotswoman. He served in North America with the British army as a young man, became enmeshed in the Native networks of the Ohio Valley, and befriended Joseph Brant. The Mohawk leader adopted Norton as his nephew, and

the two worked together in a leadership capacity at Grand River, where Norton married a Mohawk woman, raised Mohawk children, and resided for much of his adult life. According to his journal, he eventually traveled to Cherokee country and reunited with his father's relations. Norton's Native identity, to some historians, remains questionable, but his contributions as a member of the Mohawk community were considerable. See Klinck and Talman's introduction to Norton's journal, as well as Benn, *Iroquois in the War of 1812*; Fogelson, "Major John Norton,"250–55; and Kelsay, *Joseph Brant*.

9. Parker, *Seneca Myths*, 62.

10. Connelly, "Textual Function," 75.

11. Elm and Antone, *Oneida Creation*, 77–79; Cusick, *Sketches*, 9.

12. Elm and Antone, *Oneida Creation*, 8, 76; Norton, *Journal*, 88.

13. Connelly, "Textual Function," 75.

14. Day, *Western Abenaki Dictionary*, 31.

15. Wonderley, "Elm-Antone Story," 19.

16. As Womack argues in his essay in this volume, it is surely problematic to hierarchize or even assume a divide between a "pure" embodied experience and "corrupt" abstract thinking, especially considering that all this thinking that we do occurs within these bodies that we inhabit. Abstract thinking has a relationship to embodied experience, although they may sometimes challenge each other as the mind interprets and relates the body's perceptions of reality.

17. Allen, *Sacred Hoop*.

18. Harjo, *Map to the Next World*, 101.

19. "Lieft Lion Gardener," 3:154. Miantonomi gave this particular speech to the Montauks (on Long Island) in 1642; however, colonial reports suggest that Miantonomi's alliance involved Indians from the Wabanaki coast to the Mohawk River. Oberg, *Uncas*, 96–97. For analysis of Miantonomi's speech, see Salisbury, *Manitou and Providence*, 13–24, 231–32.

20. Warrior, *Tribal Secrets*, xiii, 2.

21. For an important exploration of Apess's intellectual journey, and "his contribution to Native intellectual history," see Robert Warrior, *People and the Word*. One of the central purposes of my own research has been to explore how the writing that came from Europe was incorporated into Native systems for communicating and recording knowledge. Rather than focusing on Native texts that fit into English literary genres, I've tried to open up the category of "literature" to include any writings created by Native people. In doing so, I have found that the most common forms that Native writing took in the eighteenth and nineteenth centuries reflect the formats and purposes of earlier Native traditions, such as birch-bark maps and messages and wampum belts. Birch-bark messages became letters and petitions, wampum council records became treaties, song pictographs became hymns, journey pictographs became written "journals" that contained similar geographic and relational markers, and finally, histories recorded on birch bark and wampum became written communal narratives. All of these genres were prolific in the Northeast long before Indian people began writing poetry and

fiction. A central contention of my dissertation is that these texts that emerged from within the Native Space of the Northeast represent a uniquely indigenous literary tradition. I apologize for summarizing simplistically a complicated process of cultural transformation. For a more rigorous and detailed analysis, see Brooks, *Common Pot* (forthcoming from the University of Minnesota Press).

22. "Robert Clelland to Governor Thomas Fitch," 314–15. For background on the Mohegan land case, see Conroy, "Defense of Indian Land Rights," 395–424; De Forest, *History;* Joseph Johnson, *To Do Good;* William Love, *Samson Occom;* Peyer, *Tutor'd Mind;* and Joseph Smith, *Appeals.*

23. "Minutes of the Connecticut Correspondents," quoted in William Love, *Samson Occom,* 127; Ben Uncas, Letter to Governor Thomas Fitch, May 24, 1765, *Indian Papers*, series 2, vol. 258, Connecticut Archives, Connecticut State Library, Hartford. For context and analysis, see also Peyer, *Tutor'd Mind,* 72–74.

24. Samson Occom Papers, folder 2, Connecticut Historical Society Museum, Hartford.

25. The relevant part of the proclamation stated, in full:

> And whereas it is just and reasonable, and essential to Our Interest and the Security of our Colonies, that the several Nations or Tribes of Indians, with whom We are connected, and who live under Our Protection, should not be molested or disturbed in the Possession of such Parts of Our Dominions and Territories as, not having been ceded to, or purchased by Us, are reserved to them, or any of them, as their Hunting Grounds . . . no Governor or Commander in Chief in any of Our other Colonies or Plantations in America, do presume, for the present, and until Our further Pleasure be known, to grant Warrants of survey, or pass Patents for any Lands beyond the Heads or Sources of any of the Rivers which fall into the Atlantick Ocean from the West and North West, or upon any Lands whatever which, not having been ceded to, or purchased by Us as aforesaid, are reserved to said Indians, or any of them. . . . And we do further strictly enjoin and require all persons whatever, who have either willfully or inadvertently seated themselves upon any Lands within the Countries above described, or upon any other Lands, which, not having been ceded to, or purchased by Us, are still reserved to the said Indians as aforesaid, forthwith to remove themselves from such Settlements.

In line with Occom's analysis, historian Louis DeVorsey observes, "The Proclamation Line is often shown in elementary texts and historical atlases as representing the western limits of the British colonies during the period preceding the American Revolution. This is an incorrect assumption which overlooks a very important phrase in the proclamation." After quoting the key phrase that demonstrated the proclamation's application to "any lands whatever which" had not "been ceded or purchased," DeVorsey adds: "It is to be emphasized, in the light of this stipulation, that the Proclamation of 1763 did not extend British dominion over the whole of the area located to the east of 'the heads or sources of any of the rivers which fall into the Atlantic Ocean from the west and northwest.' This is a point which has often been overlooked in non-specialist presentations." DeVorsey, *Indian Boundary,* 38. Special thanks to the John Carter Brown Library for access to the original broadside, "By the King, a Proclamation."

26. Bill, "Statement of Charles Bill," William Samuel Johnson Papers, Museum of Connecticut History, Hartford.

27. These included many of the students who attended Eleazar Wheelock's Indian Charity School, and its successor, Dartmouth College, such as the famous Mohawk leader Joseph Brant; the Delaware interpreter John Pumshire, who played an important role in Delaware Treaty councils and land dealings with the state of New Jersey; and the Narragansett leaders John and Tobias Shattuck, who served as scribes and advocates in their nation's land struggles. See Boyd, *Indian Treaties;* Love, *Samson Occom;* Kelsay, *Joseph Brant;* Konkle, *Writing Indian Nations;* McCallum, *Letters of Eleazar Wheelock's Indians;* Peyer, *Tutor'd Mind;* Wheelock, *Plain and Faithful Narrative;* and Wyss, *Writing Indians.*

28. Samson Occom Papers, folder 16, Records of the Mohegan Tribe, Museum of Connecticut History, Hartford.

29. "Ben Uncas to Governor Fitch," May 24, 1765, *Indian Papers,* series 2, vol. 258, Museum of Connecticut History, Hartford; Occom Papers, folder 2, Museum of Connecticut History, Hartford.

30. As in many indigenous communities, the practice of Christianity in Native New England was syncretic, combining indigenous and European spiritual practices, taking on its own character in relation to particular brands and movements of Christianity, and becoming a staple of life for many families, thus part of the fabric of communal identity and history. Now, we might not *like* that so many of our ancestors sought refuge in Christianity, and we may be able to see clearly in retrospect the damaging impact of such choices, but we should not deny our own histories and what we might learn from them or fall into the illusion that those choices made them somehow less Indian. Rather, as Womack rightly argues in this book, "If we include Occom's Christianity as part of [his] Mohegan experience, then we change the rules in significant ways . . . we include possibilities that can open up, instead of close down, our understandings of what constitutes Native experience."

31. Mashpee became a center of sustenance for Massachusetts Indians when increasingly forceful settlement left many New England Natives "wandering" through their own homeland. This Wampanoag Indian town was able to support its sizeable population, according to historian Daniel Mandell, "in large part because of [its] large, resource-rich" land base, which was maintained through indigenous management practices. *Behind the Frontier,* 178. Although surrounded by deforested Massachusetts towns, Mashpee remained a comparatively healthy woodland environment and was thus a prime target for poaching of resources, especially timber. For more on Mashpee history and the "Revolt," see Nielsen, "Mashpee Indian Revolt," 400–420; Campisi, *Mashpee Indians;* and Mandell, *Behind the Frontier.* For background on Apess, see O'Connell's introduction in Apess's *On Our Own Ground.*

32. Apess, *On Our Own Ground*, 172–73, 212–14.

33. Ibid., 179–80.

34. Ibid., 241; Campisi, *Mashpee Indians*, 108.

35. Apess, *On Our Own*, 310.

36. Aupaumut, "Extract," 9:101; Aupaumut, " Narrative of an Embassy," 9:76. For background on Aupaumut, see Taylor, "Captain Hendrick Aupaumut," and Ronda, "As They Were Faithful." I am drawing much of my analysis from Aupaumut's journals of his journeys to the Ohio Valley in 1791–1793 in the Timothy Pickering Papers, v. 59–62, at the Massachusetts Historical Society. For background on the Ohio Valley, see White, *Middle Ground*.

37. The phrases "United Nations," "United Indian Nations," etc., were commonly used by the Iroquois Confederacy to refer to themselves and the nations "united" under them during the French and Indian wars, but as it was used in the Ohio Valley during the period following the revolution, the phrase invoked a uniting of equal nations, all invested in maintaining a clearly bounded Native geographic and political space, especially in opposition to claims the United States made that all territory between the Atlantic Ocean and the Mississippi River was American space.

38. Joseph Brant Manuscript (microfilm copy at Dartmouth College), 11F204-5. The American leadership had a particular vision for the Ohio Valley. If Indians were to remain there at all, they would be contained on small, limited plots, while the bulk of the valley would be divided up into lots and sold to settlers to fill the nearly empty national treasury. Thus, Aupaumut's vision could be interpreted either as pragmatic forethought, based on knowledge of the force of colonial settlement, or as acquiescence with a nascent colonial policy that claimed "Indian tribes" as part of American space. Brant and the United Indian Nations, in invoking the "Dish with One Spoon," sought to bolster a much older vision of the Ohio Valley. Richard White has observed that the "greatest political accomplishment" of the confederation was the "acceptance" among all "that the land belonged equally to all Indians of the *pays d'en haute*, could not be ceded without the consent of the entire confederation, and would be defended by all." *Middle Ground*, 435. On the formation of the confederation, see White, *Middle Ground*, 413–68; Kelsay, *Joseph Brant*, 344–47, 399–405; and Stone, *Life of Joseph Brant*, 248–54, 264–72. Isabel Kelsay was the first historian to call attention to Brant's use of the metaphor of the "Dish with One Spoon." See Kelsay, *Joseph Brant*, 410, also chapter 20. Richard White mentions it briefly, noting, "To eat from a common dish was a standard Algonquian metaphor of peace, alliance, and friendship" (441).

39. The nations gathered included, in Brant's words, "the Five Nations, the Hurons, Delawares, Shawanese, Ottawas, Chippewas, Powtewattimies, Twichtwees, Cherokees, and the Wabash confederates," as well as a few delegates from the Creeks and Mohicans.

40. The Battle of Fallen Timbers was the culmination of General Anthony Wayne's campaign in the Ohio Valley, which took place on the heels of the breakdown in negotiations between the United Indian Nations and the United States and represented an attempt of the United States to impose their conceptual map

of American national space through physical force. For more background, see sources cited above.

41. I am especially struck by the clear, insightful analysis offered herein by Daniel Justice and Cheryl Suzack in their relational readings of the critical opposition between Elizabeth Cook-Lynn and Louis Owens. I am pleased to see Native writers offering culturally and historically specific readings of criticism as well as literature.

42. Weaver, *That the People Might Live.*

43. Lyons, "Rhetorical Sovereignty," 466.

Of One Blood

An Argument for Relations and Regionality in Native American Literary Studies

TOL FOSTER

> [Y]ou will unite yourselves with us, join in our great councils, and form one people with us, and we shall all be Americans. You will mix with us by marriage. Your blood will run in our veins, and will spread with us over this great island.
>
> —Thomas Jefferson, to representatives of the Delaware and Miami, Washington, D.C., 1808

> We have given to the European people on this continent our thought forces—the best blood of our ancestors having intermingled with [that of] their best statesmen and leading citizens. We have made ourselves an indestructible element in their national history.
>
> —Chief Pleasant Porter, Creek Nation, to U.S. Senate Committee, 1906

The story of Native peoples has long been told in terms of binary oppositions based in weighted political frames crafted by and favorable to the colonizers: prehistorical peoples against historical peoples; savages against citizens; superstitious children of nature against realist technological innovators

---

Tol Foster (Anglo-Creek) was raised in the Afro-Anglo-Creek-Lebanese village of Bristow, Oklahoma, on the western edge of the old Creek Nation. A PhD graduate of the University of Wisconsin–Madison, he is an assistant professor in the American studies department at the University of North Carolina at Chapel Hill, where he teaches American Indian literatures and cultural studies. He is preparing his dissertation on the multiethnic communities of Oklahoma for publication.

and pragmatic Christians; lazy Indians, either the casino-endowed kind or the affirmative-action enabled, depending on the context, against hardworking and hard-bitten immigrant Americans who are the true inheritors of the land; Esau against Jacob.

Natives, in this narrative, have always been American history's Other.[1] This approach, for better or worse, is a theory-driven one. It is not of the sort of theories that are in favor in the academy today, but nonetheless it is a highly portable theoretical approach that facilitates powerful narratives and constructions. Such generalized theories have done real damage to Native communities, so it is of little wonder that Native theorists are skeptical of even contemporary claims emanating from the academy. This concern with the danger of theory, of course, is somewhat ironic, given that a central contribution of contemporary theory has been support for this very skepticism. For example, Foucault built upon Nietzche's *Geneology of Morals* to disrupt theories that masked themselves as natural facts by both historicizing dominant claims and documenting silenced alternatives. Recognizing the danger of such naturalized claims to truth, Foucault was resistant to falling into such a trap himself and instead pursued a more careful approach of historicist and localized, contingent claims. Hubert L. Dreyfus and Paul Rabinow summarize this approach:

> Foucault combines the best of philosophical reflection with scrupulous attention to empirical detail. Nonetheless, he remains consciously, frustratingly elusive when it comes to capturing our current condition in general formulae. . . . But Foucault is being consistent to the consequences of his analysis, viz. that such generalities are either empty or that they can serve as the justification for promoting just what Foucault wants to resist. Once one sees the pervasiveness, dispersion, intricacy, contingency, and layering of our social practices, one sees that any attempt to sum up what is going on is bound to be a potentially dangerous distortion.[2]

Foucault's methodology of hesitation and recovery forms a sound approach for theorists studying the Native archive because it resists generalized claims that are potentially dangerous. Theory arises out of historical events and in response to particular contexts, and if transported too carelessly it has tremendous capacity for damage.[3] Anyone attempting general claims that fit all Native societies is bound to be wrong, which is why Native people have been the shoals upon which social scientists have crashed ever since the beginning of the twentieth century. Foucault is far more nimble than the anthropologists, but because of his skepticism for all truth claims, his work does not offer a grounding for Native theoretical claims. It is in following Foucault to this point that contemporary theory seemingly tailored for Native people, such as postcolonial theory, becomes too limited for recovering indigenous voices and subjectivities, let alone articulating Native truth claims and calls for justice.[4] Attention to specificity, locality, and contingency is the key contribution that thinkers such as Foucault provide us, not some theory that will liberate and explain indigenous people.[5]

Instead of looking for some theory to import into indigenous communities, we yield a far more rigorous understanding by both valuing *and critiquing* the historical and cultural archive as a theoretically sophisticated site of its own. One's history and experience can provide a testable and portable framework for understanding relations between individuals, institutions, and historical forces. Given these claims, I argue here that tribal figures like the Cherokee writer Will Rogers are historically situated actors who utilize the counternarratives of their communities as a theoretical base from which to conduct anticolonialist and cosmopolitan critique.

An emphasis on the historical and cultural archives as well as theoretical approaches yields the most sophisticated readings of Native people and their texts and returns us to a long-standing trajectory of interest in indigenous work disrupted by the academic U.S. nation-building project of the twentieth century. In American literary and cultural studies, the primary American literature was Native, long before Europeans arrived, and centuries old, engaging in a historical rather than prehistorical context across and between continents.[6] After contact, to colonizers like Thomas Jefferson, Natives were *the* indigenous Americans, the personification of a continent whose nature was equal to the best of European culture, at least within the rhetoric of revolution *from* Europe. As Robert Dale Parker in his book *The Invention of Native American Literature* notes, even the study of Native American literature under the Boasian "salvage anthropology" school preceded literary studies focused on American literature, the study of the literary output of the settlers.[7] Despite these beginnings, American studies focused during its institutional formation on the city and the immigrant, and American history focused on the tangential relation of New England religious communities to the U.S. Constitution to the exclusion of other founding constituencies such as Dutch New York and the Iroquois Confederacy.[8] American literature focused on writers who could rival the best of Europe and canonized the writers who represented American individuality and ideals in the face of Soviet Communism.

Mainstream focus on the great Others of the United States in its founding century, African Americans and Native Americans, came only in the twentieth century, through the civil rights battles of the sixties and the Indian Claims Commission (1946–1978).[9] Progress in both areas was partially the result of the Cold War, inasmuch as the inequality of blacks and the injustice to Natives served as the basis of developing world Communist arguments against U.S. hegemony. After the Cold War, literary studies became one of the first disciplines to incorporate Native and black scholarship into its structure, but this scholarship continues to be compartmentalized in an adjunct relation to the primary American canon. This is somewhat acceptable for African American studies, as it traces (forced) immigrant groups whose goal is to be full constitutive members of the American project. It does not work for Native studies, for Natives have their own nations and traditions and have consistently articulated their own literature and identities outside the American nation-state.

Thus it is in American history scholarship, not literary studies, that the Native perspective has become fundamental to the re-visioning of our understanding of this continent, and it is history, with its renewed attention to the multiple constituencies that crafted our current nation, that serves as the model for an accurate and engaged discipline, not because it includes Native Americans, but because there are no Native American Others left in its narratives. There are only Creeks allied to British suppliers allied against the westward-expanding United States; the Spanish empire with its redoubts of mission Natives in California at war with Apache and Comanche raiders; elite Cherokee slave-holding Southerners against poor Georgian gold-seeking squatters. American history has broken the binaries, and American cultural studies has followed in its wake. American literature studies has not yet caught up.[10]

The answer for Native Americanists to this failure of American literary studies in the academy is not, however, *separation*. Native and settler histories and culture are not capable of being separated. As the epigraphs above suggest, both Chief Pleasant Porter of the Creeks and President Thomas Jefferson yoked Native and settler into a common family. For Jefferson, the gesture of intermixture would make American settlers the just inheritors of the land; for Porter, intermixture would ensure the survival of tribal people within the national body; it would indeed *make* the United States into a tribal nation. Though working from different power relations and positions, both Jefferson and Porter were suggesting amalgamation and adoption as the solution to struggles between Natives and settlers, and that is what has happened on the cultural and historical level.[11]

The historically and theoretically astute regionalism I propose as a frame allows us to mediate and engage the claims of these very different speakers and their positions against and in dialogue with one another. Thus engaged, we can understand the relation between *Native* and *America* in a way that privileges the local and the tribal. In cultural studies, our existing interpretative models might be able to account for Jefferson's perspective, built partially on a valorization of Native people and partially on a concern that possession of Indian lands occur with a modicum of honor, but these models fit poorly with the long-standing tradition of Creeks to incorporate others into their confederacy and with the relatively new strategies of southern acculturation and intertribal coordination that Porter's comments represent.[12]

Relational Regionalism

It is only through the regional focus that we can understand fully Porter's claim, which is both tribally specific and informed by a committed strategy among the elite of the Indian Territory to marry United States whites in order to participate as full and protected citizens. A neglect of any of the national, regional, or tribal frames would create an insufficient narrative arc. In this collection a number of writers have emphasized the centrality of the tribally specific framework for reading Native texts, and it could be very easy to read my own regional frame as a challenge to such readings, but I actually see a regional framework as one that is not actually coherent without more specific tribal studies that serve to buttress and challenge it. Perhaps one of the strongest voices for the prioritization of tribal voices in this conversational collection is that of Janice Acoose, who notes that particular communities precede other frames in priority. Writing in dialogue with this piece, she notes that though

> we can engage with other intersecting canons . . . I want to suggest that we research our own cultures of origin and, from our respective cultures, initiate cultural restoration projects by building culture-specific literary canons. As critics, we can support these projects by working within our own cultures first, and then engaging with other indigenous canons cross-culturally. I imagine those critical bodies interacting and engaging in a critical landscape that honors cultural differences and celebrates cultural similarities: Honoring cultural differences, we can respectfully work toward understanding; celebrating cultural similarities, we can enter into dialogue with each other. But I'm passionately committed—perhaps even blinded—by a political conviction that insists on "honoring my relations" whose spiritual presence continues to influence my work. We cannot, after all, arrive at the destination "indigenous" without having journeyed through life in particular communities/culture-specific places. Or can we?

I certainly have no disagreement with the claim that we speak first from our own subject position and our tribal perspective, or that we must primarily engage in our own tribal studies to be able to speak intelligibly across tribal and regional boundaries. Indeed, particularity—whether that be tribal or regional—if considered in a nuanced enough way, can be a perfectly dynamic and coherent way to address new regions and peoples. If we understand our own tribal histories and cultures thoroughly enough, we might discover within them all the tools we need to interpret the larger world, without having to delve into the work of such foreigners as Foucault, for example.

Indeed, the tribally specific framework is a necessary basis for much of the most important work of recovery and reading happening in Native studies today, and it begins, often as not, with a recovery of one's own relations, which is a central honoring act, as Acoose suggests. Witness Phillip Morgan's tribally specific recovery work in which he traces Choctaw voices such as J. L. McDonald and Peter Pitchlynn to argue for a primacy of those Choctaw voices in determining Choctaw values and texts. Indeed, without McDonald, Pitchlynn, and—I would argue—Morgan, we are in danger of having an impoverished conversation about Native literary practice even on the intertribal level. We need one another so much, if only as scholars, because Native cultural practice is so rich and so vast no single one of us could pretend to research it all. More importantly, it is often only those of us with particular tribal connections who even know what to look for in the first place, and this search is often as not spurred on by a curiosity about our own identities and roots, as Morgan notes in his call for Native scholars to engage

> with primary research in the library, museum, tribal government, and private archives that have in the past been the academic terrain of historians and folklorists but largely ignored by literary critics. The search and discovery experiences for me rank among the most personally and professionally enriching of my life, because to actually *read* (rather than to imagine the dispositions of) McDonald, Pitchlynn, Brant, or Aupaumut connects and validates me as a writing Indian across a gulf of time with relatives grappling with virtually identical issues 175 or more years ago.

The tribal archive overall is vast, and there are many voices in it that we need to hear again. Yet McDonald and Pitchlynn, who are so central to the project of Indian Territory, do not even appear in my work on that area, because the way I conceived the project as a regional framework necessarily left them and many other important voices out. Thankfully, Morgan recovers them. And this is indeed a central task for us as tribally affiliated scholars, because we are called to know our own tribes, if for no other reason than to serve as a resource for others in our tribes as they seek to pass these bodies of knowledge on to their children.

But my interest in the regional frame—that is, looking outside the tribal archive—is also in a strange way tribally specific. We find relations in the strangest of places. For example, in pursuing my approach of looking regionally I discovered for myself that the African American poet Melvin Tolson is also Afro-Creek, and this led me to a very different reading of some of his material than now exists in the scholarship. Had I been looking merely for Creeks, I never would have found this one—perhaps "our" greatest poet before Louis "Littlecoon" Oliver and Joy Harjo. Thus, as I continue to speak of the regional frame through this article, I wish to stress that I see the connection of the tribal and the regional to be acts pursuing the same project of knowing ourselves and the world. Indeed, if we take up the example of Tolson, we might find the tribally specific in the world "out there" and find that the exclusion of Tolson is part of that world's influence on our tribe "in here." To be tribally specific and be Creek, perhaps, means that I must seek out the Afro-Creek Melvin Tolson.

The danger, then, of the tribally specific frame is that it too often leads us to close off voices that do not obviously seem to be part of the tribal community and to privilege the more conservative voices in that community. Worst of all might be the privileging of tribally specific values and attitudes merely because they are traditional, without asking whether or not they are useful or helpful. I believe that through the work of Craig Womack, Joy Harjo, and others, for example, the case can easily be made for an outward-looking, dynamic cosmopolitanism based in notions of relation as the central "tradition" of Creek cultural life. Thus, the sort of relational regionalism that I wish to propose could be read as the central tenet of Creek "traditional" life and practice.

To illustrate this point, then, I wish to use the story of Choffee, the rabbit trickster of the Creeks, in which it is related that, through trickery, he stole fire from elsewhere and gave it to the Creek people. This fire became so central to the Creeks' sense of self that they carried the fire from each of their towns all the way along the various trails of tears to their new homes in Indian Territory. Those fires—for these Creeks—represented home. When the fires were transposed upon the new territory, even if fed along the way by different fuels, the Indian Territory *became* home. I could use as my source the traditional ethnographic materials collected by John Swanton,[13] but instead I choose to read from the version done by middle-school Creek children as a school project with the assistance of the Cherokee animator Joseph Erb.[14] Their version is entirely spoken in Creek, with English subtitles, and is a mixed-media DVD video made of claymation figures, digital animation, and conventional diorama sets. In their version of the tale, Choffee, to help the freezing Creeks, travels through space *to Paris*, and there—gathered around a fire populated by Frenchmen in berets and with long mustaches—teaches them a Creek stomp dance. While circling their fire, Rabbit grabs a coal from their fire, puts it on his forehead, and then absconds with it, again flying through space to bring fire to the Creeks. While Swanton might have thought this a tale about how southeastern rabbits get that distinctive smudge above the bridge of their noses, I think the central lesson of the tale is the one that the students demonstrated by putting Paris—that locus of conventional cosmopolitanism —at the center of their tribal tale. By imagining the Creek fire as dependent on Frenchmen, and the French themselves as tribal people, all in a medium introduced to them by American culture and by a Cherokee teacher, these students were engaging in an act of tribal sovereignty that refused to recognize borders as limitations. They refused to see Parisians as nontribal peoples with something to offer—fire—which would become the heart of the Creek Nation, and something to gain—the stomp dance—which would become a primary signature of tribal culture worldwide.

This call for a regional approach attempts to open debates rather than freezing them, and thus I find Kim Roppolo's suggestion (this volume) of using such a framework to describe an unbound "Indian Territory" to be an exciting idea, especially if it is expanded to indigenous networks in North, South, and Central America that are so often left out of the U.S.- and Canada-based notion of "Indian country." Or, most provincially, the notion of Indian country bounded by the borders of the United States (the national-colonial frame) that Janice Acoose's explorations of Native Canadian writers should explode. And this notion of an extended Indian country does point to a concomitant set of relations, for as Daniel Justice demonstrates in his rebuttal to Delphine Red Shirt, to understand contemporary Lakotas, one might also need to understand the historical Pequots, who "acted as a buffer that protected many western communities [such as Red Shirt's] from the full brunt of White expansion." If, as Justice notes in his essay,"[e]mpires can't survive by acknowledging complexity," neither can tribal or regional communities, even —especially—in resisting those empires. Anywhere the story is simple, we can be assured that it is incomplete and that some crucial member of the community has been silenced. This is the central disciplining function behind my notion of the regional frame—and it carries with it the radical notion that tribally specific work is necessarily incomplete if it does not have multiple perspectives and voices within it and is even incomplete *if it does not acknowledge voices without as well.*

Thus the regional frame is not necessarily ancillary to tribal specificity, but is actually at times the very center of a given tribal practice. This particular Creek story, for example, suggests that the very center of our culture was exchanged with (or taken from) some other people and place. Thus the center might be out there, among presumptive strangers. Further, I would argue that it is within the regional frame that we most effectively witness the *interzones* where different constituencies collide and, as a result, renegotiate their communal cultural frames.[15] The regional frame focuses on the tension between communities, the borderlands, the contact zones, or whatever we might wish to call them. I would argue that this is the most challenging space to focus on critically, for it lacks the clarity of the other frames. The regional frame is by definition the least theoretically or culturally pristine space, for it is effectively only the edge of other constructions, and it is always by definition incomplete.[16]

I must, by the way, distinguish this regional frame from the regionalism that was dominant from the 1890s to the 1930s in America among settler communities. That earlier regionalist impulse was largely driven by a fear of modernity and an uncritical and provincial boosterism. Yi-Fu Tuan notes that the "frontier settlements of North America lacked a venerable past; to attract business and gain pride their civic leaders were obliged to speak with a loud voice."[17] Patricia Nelson Limerick, one of the most important scholars of New Western History, lists the modifiers tagged to such studies: "Provincial, antiquarian backwaters. Unanalytical. Unreflective. Nostalgic," and "uncool."[18] These complaints are valid inasmuch as regional studies take on a part of the whole and attempt to make of it the whole. Another problem with regional studies is that they are often undertaken for no greater reason than to glorify the region under study. The danger of the regional study of central Iowa is that the foregone conclusion will be that the center of the American literary world is central Iowa. Writing from Madison, Wisconsin, I am thinking of the rows upon rows of such studies that lie dusty on the shelves of the Wisconsin

Historical Society, most of which were written out of the intersection of provincialism and boosterism of the late nineteenth century and the early twentieth. These studies were failures because they did not effectively weave themselves into the larger struggles of their time.

Relational regionalism accepts the constructedness and contingency of the notion of a region in both time and space. A region can be configured differently, depending on which element and historical moment is being traced. However, in order to be effective, the new historicist and regionalist impulse must include and articulate the frames of the region's constitutive members without privileging or silencing unsavory components of those frames. In the tribal context this means that we need to start acknowledging dissent within the community in a muscular fashion, as well as pointing out unsavory elements of our home community's practice openly. The regional identity arises out of the interaction of these frames and can be identified, but does not do so uniformly, because of differences of power.

In contrast to earlier uncritical regional articulations, we should emphasize that regional space and the regional frame are not utopias. They are anything but, for they always provoke the tension between similarity and difference among, and often within, their constituents. This revelation of difference is also present in tribally specific studies. The regional frame, however, because it foregrounds interactions and conflicts between communities, often is more fully documented and traceable. Yi-Fu Tuan notes, for example, that though even casual observers can notice differences between neighboring villages, they "may conclude that . . . [each particular] village is one place, a unified community conscious of its identity vis-à-vis neighboring communities. This is true, yet the village itself is divided."[19] Further, the regional frame traces contributions and collisions between communities as those events and practices become constitutive of the communities themselves. By considering communities and individuals through the regional frame, we would seek the exact opposite phenomenon of a Boasian anthropologist out to record a "pure" cultural articulation before it becomes intermixed with that of other communities, and thus "lost." This regional impulse celebrates adaptation by communities, and assumes that there is very little that is culturally pure in this way. Canoes are a central technology for settler nature lovers, and few Oklahoma Natives could imagine a world without their pickup trucks. There is nothing tragic in such adaptations. For Native studies, the regional impulse foregrounds not only the Cherokee adaptation of the governmental model of the United States to their own tribal government, but also the key role of Cherokees in helping their neighboring Creeks engage the United States as well.[20]

Relational Regionalism in the Postmodern Frame: Fires That Travel

Postmodernism in the academy invokes images of fluidity without restraint or ethical boundary. But there is another sense of postmodernity as a historical moment.[21] If modernity begins with the Renaissance and the Enlightenment (which themselves were dramatically provoked by the presence of the people of the New World who confounded the literalist biblical narratives upon which medieval Europe legitimized itself), postmodernity begins with the acceptance not only of scientific relativity, but of cultural relativity, a concept that challenges totalizing (and totalitarian) knowledge systems that seek to control others through (de)legitimization. For Western philosophy, this means simply that no one culture has the absolute patent on truth, and it suggests that truth is perspectival, that different cultures see things differently.

For Jace Weaver, this is not a problematic situation for tribal communities; they are, in the words of the philosophers McPherson and Rabb, "polycentric."[22] Their worldviews are not closed to revision and are not totalitarian. They are, like the best scientific practices, tested, sufficient, and contingent on new experiences. That is to say, they are revisable in the right circumstances. This is how we are here today; our tribal forebears were able to radically revise their lifeways, to be postmodernists in the best sense, and to play sometimes contradictory games in order to survive.[23] But, as Weaver notes, this polycentric position is not merely relativist, for "though no culture's worldview can be privileged in any universal sense, it can and must be privileged *for that particular culture.*"[24]

Weaver illustrates this claim through a story gleaned from George Tinker's "An American Indian Theological Response to Ecojustice":

> Imagine two Indian communities who live in close proximity to each other, separated by a mountain. A non-Native visitor arrives as the first community [and] . . . is informed that the tribe's council fire is the center of the universe [and] . . . [t]he following day, the outlander and representatives of the first tribe travel to the other community. The elders of the new tribe declare that their council fire is the center of the universe, and the members of the first tribe nod their assent. Confused, the visitor asks her host, "I thought you said that your fire was the center." The Indian replies, "When we're there, that is the center of the universe. When we are here, this is the center."[25]

Cultural centers are revisable and flexible, and they travel.[26] They are contingent rather than absolute. In the Western tradition this is a new realization and has been extremely productive in both the sciences and humanities, but as the story above suggests, it is not a new concept to Native communities. What is new, however, is that postmodernism has made the emergence of Native knowledge and truth claims possible in the academy and has led to the emergence of alternative and sometimes oppositional fields of study there, including but not limited to women's studies, cultural studies, and, of course, Native studies courses.[27]

Given this new historical possibility for the consideration of differing accounts of the world, let us imagine then not merely that individuals constitute multiple identities among the various collectives of which they are a part, but that the collectives themselves are in constant motion, both within the collective and outside of it, in relation to other communities. This state of cultural *transmotion*[28] is the innermost process of collective cultural formation and renewal, and it is a process I believe is most clearly articulated in organized tribal societies. However, transmotion can also occur as well for identities constructed by the axes of ethnicity, sexuality, and regionality, to name a few. Because the tribal collective is more clearly a model for this understanding than others, it is privileged in my argument about the influence of a regional identity. Tribal people have both a clear practice-based identity and a cultural-political identity. It is through particular practices and legal representations that tribal people are tribal people, and these elements of our identities represent dynamic possibilities for both tribal and nontribal peoples *and texts*. Thus I see readings that foreground tribal perspectives as useful for deployment, even outside tribal texts. I hear a call for this in Kim Roppolo's point (in an earlier version of the essay that appears in this volume) that "[i]f we are simply doing mainstream academic argumentative analyses using pieces of tribally specific literature as a lens for reading, are we really doing anything very different?" Roppolo goes on to suggest that Native scholars "need more focus on *employing* our cultural epistemologies and hermeneutics, to decode texts, written and otherwise." Tribally specific epistemologies are based in particular practices and histories and are a dynamic collection of traditions that have *long* been conversant with elements of uncertainty and ethics that the contemporary academy is only now discovering. Thus, why could we not deploy those bodies of knowledge as a theoretical frame even over the output of our regional neighbors by imagining them as our relations? I suggest that to do that we follow models such as that demonstrated in Roppolo's essay, and I hope that by both celebrating and critiquing Will Rogers within a Native context of relations, I am doing just that.

It is in the interaction of Tinker's two tribes, above, that we see a shift from a tribal to a regional identity. Neither militates necessarily against the other because they are relational to each other and spatial within themselves. This is to say that within the first community, the fire is indeed the center of their universe of relations, and when an individual from that community interacts around another group's fire, their cultural practices become the central mediating influence for that individual *within that space*.

The relation of these two groups together is more determinate than the particular space that they occupy. The physical space, the land, has obvious and material implications for them and does impact the forms in which their culture can be expressed, but I have very little interest in claiming some form of geographic determinism. Rather, in articulating this point about regionalism as a constituent factor in identity formation, I focus on the way in which relational space (region) allows constituent identities to formulate themselves both internally (us) and externally (not them).[29] This process of interrelated positionality traces the way that these communities coevolve. Over time, those internal characteristics of a given culture draw from strategies and ideas posited by neighboring cultures. The borrowing culture rejects some ideas and incorporates others into the idiom of the borrowing culture. We adapt some of what makes them toward what makes us, and we understand them by positing that we share common understandings. The more flexible and expansive our relational frame, the more easily we can accept, like the Creeks, the idea that someone else's fire might become the center of our own. The ability to participate in both of those communal fires is to be cosmopolitan, to belong to multiple spaces and embrace them on their own terms.[30] I believe that this claim is compatible with Daniel Heath Justice's call for what he calls kinship criticism (this volume), in which we nurture "relationships and the attentive care we give to the ongoing processes of balanced rights and responsibilities that keep kinship going in a good way. Kinship, like Fire, is about life and living; it's not about something that *is* in itself so much as something we *do*—actively, thoughtfully, respectfully." Tribes, I argue, are largely sustained by just such a cosmopolitan tradition, what might in other terms be considered postmodernist.

None of this, however, compromises the basic unit of the community, the tribe.[31] Let's return to the notion of the tribal fires. As the wood exhausts itself in the center of the sacred fire, the outer parts are pushed into the center to continue it. The vital center is replaced by what was at the margins, which becomes the new center. Further, let us imagine that the tribe, which has traditionally fed the sacred fire with red oak, is somehow disrupted and removed from areas that provide red oak, so that the sacred fire is now nourished instead with mesquite. There has been a disruption, certainly, but the essential character of the tribe has remained the same. Whether fed on mesquite or red oak, the fire remains sacred and the tribal structures coherent.

If we accept that this sort of process is central to that of tribal communities, then we can understand how, in an epistemological way, tribal peoples are not disrupted by either the notions of modernity or postmodernity. In a recent lecture on modernity, in which she argued for multiple modernities at different historical junctures, Susan Stanford Friedman described her curiosity about the very term "modernity" in tribal languages. I do not believe there is any such word in Muscogee, but I suspect that if there is, it is probably "pickup truck."[32] By this I mean to suggest that if my metaphor of tribal epistemology is correct, there is no notion of modernity within it because there is no such disruption to its understanding of itself. There most certainly is a disruption in relation to other communities, but not in terms that cannot be articulated within its own hefty discourse of power and greed.[33] Others who act on tribal people will certainly be considered Other, but they will not be considered "modern" against some sort of tribal premoderns. This is a construct, we should notice, of the antitribal nation-state, which wishes to posit historical breaks as a way of building up an incommensability between then and now, just as tribal stories often construct a vague rupture between now and the time when crucial myths were in play. That was then, but this is now, we hear the government judge proclaim, but for tribal people, such explanations are inadequate, and indeed dangerous. Following from Native epistemology we must add to such narratives of difference the notion of the relational. History and events are part of the story, but they are not the determinate parts. Relations are the primary axis through which we can understand ourselves and each other.

Human communities are all related, and relatable. It is this similarity that serves as the basis of critique both within and outside our particular communities. S. P. Mohanty presents a thorough development of this notion in his book, *Literary Theory and the Claims of History: Postmodernism, Objectivity, Multicultural Politics* (1997). In it, he writes, "To believe that you have your space and I mine . . . [and] there can be no responsible way in which I can [develop] . . . a set of general criteria that can have interpretive validity in both contexts . . . is to assert that all spaces are equivalent [and] . . . I . . . need not . . . think about how your space impinges on mine or how my history is defined together with yours."[34] Therefore, to say that we are all related is emphatically not to suggest that all narratives are equal or that all spaces are the same. Rather, it is the grounding for thorough critique, even across historical moments.[35]

We have all heard the Native expression that we are all related. In his 1978 article, "Civilization and Isolation," Vine Deloria, Jr., contrasts Western frames toward knowledge with Native intellectual training by noting that though the phenomena do not change, the Western intellectual worldview, in dividing elements and building up hierarchies of knowledge, often ends up discounting and degrading "phenomena [which] do not fulfill our expectations" and thus "the opportunity to come to grips with another facet of reality escapes us." In contrast Natives, Deloria writes, focus on synthesizing seemingly disparate forces in their intellectual work, and "relatedness characterized their experiences of the universe." This model of "[r]elatedness is a much better description of the Indian way of looking at the world," and it functions not merely as a generic philosophical principle, but as a materialist and scientific one.[36]

Deloria goes on to describe the Osage tribal practice of planting their corn in Missouri and then heading to Colorado and Wyoming for their summer hunting season. When a particular mountain flower began to turn to seed, they knew that it was time to return to Missouri, where the corn would be ready for harvesting at their arrival. Deloria writes, "Such behavior may seem the utmost of simplicity except that to accomplish such a task required that they know the relationships of plants, animals, and lands over a distance of some 2,000 miles and know these complex relationships so well they could transfer an abstract sense of time, time in the sense of organic growth, from plant to plant over the distance and use the growth of a mountain plant as a gauge or calendar for their corn."[37] In this illustration we see that within the

Osage intellectual framework, the land and the other plants served as accurate and relatable predictors of each other. The maturation of the mountain flower marked the coming maturation of the corn, and the Osage were able, through observation, to conceive of the land itself as a form of technology and instrumentation. This is to say that when the Osage perhaps thought to themselves that "we are all related," they meant this not merely in holistic or spiritual terms, but also in materialist and scientific terms.

Deloria's notion of relatedness is precisely the term I am gesturing toward in limning a relational regional framework. Relatedness in this sense is emphatically *not* the leveling of distinction or hierarchy, the contention that we are all the same, but that even within the constraints of hierarchy and different levels of maturity and expertise we are nonetheless intricately bound to each other. For example, the Colorado mountain flower does not go to seed at the same time or in the same way as the Missouri corn; they are strikingly different, with different cycles, and it is this very difference—that the flower goes to seed so much earlier than the corn—on which traditional Osage scientists relied.

This example also makes easily understood the idea of presence or personhood for nonhuman elements, for though the mountain flower was, indeed, technology for the Osage, it was also a living thing, and its way of being was of value to the Osage. That is to say, it provided the Osage with a tool, a gift, out of its own being that made their lives more sustainable and full, and it had a knowledge that the Osages, without it, would not be able to have on their own. I see this idea as an expression of a tribal cosmopolitan tradition, for it suggests that there are bonds and commonalities across community boundaries—between humans and animals, or animals and spirits, for example.[38] I suggest that we consider the regional frame as the way to explore that tribal cosmopolitan tradition and that we see the regional frame as relational rather than fixed to any particular space or history. A cosmopolitan tribal identity is one shaped not only by a nuanced and realist understanding of one's own group, but of the many relations it has with groups outside of it.[39] Thus, if we are all related, as the Native American truism suggests, the central story should be to elucidate exactly how that is so without allowing particularly powerful institutional histories and canonical events to shape exclusively how we understand our relations to one another. The more perspectives that can be incorporated into the narrative, the more accurate it will be.[40]

I have limned here, in broad terms, the reason that I believe the regional frame should be utilized particularly for contextualizing and understanding Native texts and communities, and I wish now to place the Cherokee humorist and film star Will Rogers within the nexus of a particularly complicated example of the points about relationality and regionalism that I have been advancing. I wish to start by articulating how focusing on the regional frame reveals crucial relations that other frames lack, which in this case is a very tribally specific racial antipathy toward African Americans on the part of many of the Five Tribes, and particularly the Cherokee. I use this issue as a way of recovering a crucial story that is constitutive of the relation between southern Native tribes and their neighbors, and as a way of demonstrating how this new regionalist approach *must* be willing to tell problematic and uncomfortable stories because the primary reason for this approach is *not* to engage in simplistic or positive stories of encounter, but rather to focus on deeply divisive relations between communities.[41] I then focus on Rogers, who was not immune from this racial antipathy, to argue that his tribal regionalist perspective nonetheless allowed him to articulate a powerful anticolonial critique by positing relations between people, rather than difference based on particular histories and cultures. It is this cosmopolitan approach that dampens the influence of Cherokee racial antipathy on Rogers, and it is this notion of relation as grounds for critique that makes him such a central figure in the Native intellectual tradition. So these moves, considered together, will both demonstrate the explanatory capacity of the regionalist frame and also demonstrate how the cosmopolitan impulse in tribal traditions serves as a basis for critique.

The Stars and Bars at the Powwow: Misreading Cherokee Identity

A recent *New York Times Magazine* article titled "The Newest Indians" featured a group of southern Cherokees who are fighting for recognition. The *Times* journalist cast them as southern whites with a liminal relation to their Cherokee heritage, and, as the final coup de grace in his characterization of this group, he described a young man at their powwow:

> I was distracted by another handsome teenage boy with light brown hair, the head grass dancer, who didn't seem to have made the full transition to Indian yet. His outfit was a painstaking interplay of beads and feathers and a series of striking variations of white and red shapes sewn onto his vest, which for some reason caught my eye and seduced me into leaving the bleacher seats in order to wander closer to the rail; elbowing my way out in front of even small children to peer more carefully and to make absolutely sure that the tiny red rectangles were—yes, indeed, no doubt about it—little Confederate battle flags.[42]

This passage ends the first section of the article, standing without gloss. The reporter describes an absurd image of himself charging in front of young children to reveal the secret at the heart of these new Indians—they are really just white poseurs, people who look, he writes, just like "regular Alabama white folks"! The proof, for the reporter, is the interwoven battle flags of the Confederacy. These battle flags signify to the reporter that the boy "didn't seem to have made the full transition to Indian." However, to those familiar with the full Cherokee history, the battle flags could be read, actually, as signification of an *authentic* Cherokee experience. Within the national imagination, the Confederacy is synonymous with white racism. Lost in that concept, of course, is the history of southern Native people who also owned slaves and who also aligned themselves with the Confederacy.

Like the country as a whole, these tribes split over this conflict, but only the tribes of Indian Territory lost territory because of their participation in the war.[43] Few of the readers of the *New York Times*, and few New York–based journalists can be expected to know the very complicated history and relation Cherokees have not only with the South, but with African Americans. Although the Cherokee Trail of Tears is well known, people often are not told about the strategy among many Cherokees to adopt the culture and conventions of their white southern neighbors. There were numerous Cherokees, by the time of removal, who had black slaves and large plantations and were the envy of their white neighbors. Certain members of the Cherokee tribe, and of the other removed tribes as well, believed that the adoption of a tribal constitution that resonated with the influence of the U.S. Constitution and the adoption of white southern-style slavery would serve them in getting along with their American neighbors. After removal, a powerful faction of the Cherokee tribe of Indian Territory (Oklahoma) sided with and fought for the Confederacy, and after the war this same constituency worked to have tribal people considered white under the definitions of the new state of Oklahoma, which they were. The Cherokees demonstrate, as Grace Hale notes in her book, *Making Whiteness*, that the construction of whiteness itself is "always contingent, always fragile, always uncertain" because becoming white was for them a maneuver to avoid being controlled and constrained by the white state, as blacks were. For the Cherokees, creating a difference of space between themselves and blacks protected their own space. Hale elucidates this point in relation to the dynamics of the American South: "It is important to place southern segregation, then, within this contradictory historical context of representational fluidity and spatial grounding. Geographically separating peoples as a way of making and fixing absolute racial difference occurred across the nation. By the early twentieth century, segregation laws and more localized conventions affected Native Americans, Asian Americans, and African Americans, and the separation has remained visible in our very language."[44]

Protecting their own space in order to create distinction with blacks did not exempt Cherokees from Reconstruction, in which the federal government forced them and the other removed tribes of Indian Territory to adopt their former slaves as full citizens after the Civil War. This adoption of the Cherokee freedmen was a divisive issue, not the least because it created a potential division of loyalties within the already fractured Cherokee Nation. The fear was that these freedmen would favor tribal dissolution and the division of assets and would be a constituency more loyal to the United States than to the tribe. Thus, throughout the nineteenth century as they fought federal efforts to break apart the tribe, Cherokees in Oklahoma, like many of the other removed tribes from the South, continued to have antipathy toward blacks, not merely out of a bid to be considered structurally white, but also as a move to protect sovereignty and cohesion within their polity. A primary tension of this imposition of tribal members against the will of the tribal majority was its attack on sovereignty, on the ability of the tribe to dictate its own membership. Such is the tricky and difficult nature of this example, that the protection of a tribe's right to control its membership, which all Native Americanists agree is a crucial component of sovereignty, should mean the maintenance of an oppressive and unjust racial caste system and that U.S. federal imperialism over the tribes should effect a change that is socially just, but imposed as a way of dissolving the tribal structure itself.

The imposition of people upon the tribes in Indian Territory did not end with the incorporation of the freedmen, who turned out to be loyal Natives after all.[45] Indian Territory was a space reserved for tribal members, federal agents, and specially licensed Americans only.[46] However, with the construction of the railroad lines through the territory, the population boomed with illegal immigrants from the South, both white and black, who overwhelmed the Native population and began to use their critical mass to push for legal rights. Technically the Cherokees could expel illegal white and black intruders, but the federal government protected white (propertied) citizens.[47] Black citizens, however, were opportune targets for anti-American ire. Many American blacks, therefore, found a symbiotic relationship with the tribal freedmen, particularly in the Creek towns neighboring the Cherokee nation. As they moved into these towns, Creek freedmen were able to count them as residents and to thereby expand their representation in the tribal government.[48]

The Regional Context: African Americans and the Seminoles, Creeks, and Cherokees

A crucial approach of the regional frame is to demonstrate the subtle differences between neighboring communities; the way in which neighboring tribes in Indian Territory dealt with Afro-Native and African American people is elucidative in this regard. Slave ownership was common throughout the tribes of the Southeast, including the Creeks and Seminoles, who would become neighbors to the Cherokees in the new Indian Territory out west. The Cherokees, Creeks, and Seminoles all had many decades of experience with African American slaves before being removed to Indian Territory, and each group had distinctive modes of slavery that changed over time due not only to internal tribal conditions but also to influence from other neighboring tribes and from directives from both the United States and the Confederate states.[49] Although there is some debate over whether or not slavery as it was practiced by these three tribes was more lenient than that of the American South,[50] there is little debate that Natives—particularly Native elites—realized that claims to whiteness and racial superiority depended on antipathy and discrimination toward African Americans. After the Civil War the United States forced all three tribes to free their slaves and to include these African American freedmen in their tribal structures. The Seminoles incorporated their freedmen and intermixed people the most of the three tribes, and as Daniel Littlefield as shown, this was related to the deep tribal history of the Seminoles and their interdependence with African Americans as co-insurgents against the colonizing U.S. forces before removal— and against U.S. and Confederate forces during the Civil War. After the Civil War, Brevet Major General John B. Sanborn was assigned in October of 1865 to the task of "regulating the relations between the Freedmen in the Indian Territory and their former masters." Sanborn found that the traditionalist proletarian Seminoles considered the freedmen their equals and "were in favor of incorporating them into their tribe with all of the rights and privileges" of other Seminoles, though the pro-Confederate Seminoles likely felt quite otherwise. The postwar treaty with the United States, agreed upon on August 16, 1866, stipulated that the freedmen be incorporated into the tribe. At the time, the commissioner of Indian affairs noted that incorporation would be easy in this particular tribe because "there had already been a considerable intermingling of the races before the tribe removed from Florida."[51]

The Seminoles at the time saw these Afro-Seminole peoples as a buttress against attempts by their Creek neighbors to incorporate them all back into the Creek Confederacy.[52] The Creeks also had a tradition of slavery, but they were less reliant on African Americans for the survival of their tribe itself. Daniel Littlefield writes: "Except on the plantations of a few mixed bloods, slavery at first appeared to be a 'convenience' to the Creeks. Slaves were allowed to accumulate property, by means of which they purchased their freedom, and there was little prejudice against intermarriage between Indians and blacks. However, by 1824, the Creeks had written a code which began to restrict the activities of their blacks."[53] After removal, the Creeks, like the Cherokees, hardened their slavery and antiblack laws in a format that closely proximated that of the American South.[54] Littlefield suggests that a dominant reason for this harmonization with the slavery laws of the old South had much to do with the massive influx of whites who intermarried into all of the tribes, except the Seminoles, in great numbers.[55] Slavery created deep divisions within the Cherokee Nation and played a part in leading a group of traditionalists, the Keetoowah band, to split off from the tribe, in resistance to the main Cherokee body, which was dominated throughout the nineteenth century by a slave-holding elite.[56]

Considered regionally, the issue of black settlement and autonomy among the tribes is largely related to interaction among the tribes themselves. After the Civil War the Seminoles were most hospitable to African Americans, and as immigrants—both white and black—from the United States came into Indian Territory, they settled predominantly in the superior farmland areas of the Creeks, who had adopted their freedmen with little problem, mostly because they had intermarried so much with Afro-Creeks.[57] In contrast, the Cherokee elite, of which Will Rogers's father, Clem, was clearly a member, fought the inclusion of the African American former slaves of the Cherokee into the tribal citizenship rolls, largely because of the fear that these African American "citizens" would betray the tribe in favor of federal prerogatives, a claim that cannot be easily dismissed given the antagonism toward them by the Cherokee elite.[58]

The United States demanded that the Cherokees make citizens of their former slaves, so resisting the former slaves was also, in some ways, fighting for tribal sovereignty against the United States. The Cherokees were forced to adopt their former slaves, but the tribespeople created such a hostile space for the Cherokee freedmen that they did not develop tribal townships or political representation within the tribal structure to the degree that Creek freedmen did. Cherokees and Creeks both worried about the influx of American citizens of all races from the American South, but they were concerned that federal officials would force the tribes to add American southern blacks as freedmen as a way of internally dividing the tribes. The Cherokees were more organized in resisting American black settlement than the Creeks, whose freedmen towns began actively incorporating these Americans into their communities in order to gain polity within the Creek national system, which was based on the long-standing Creek tradition of incorporation of other cultural groups into their confederate polity of townships.[59] The danger for all tribal people, freedmen or otherwise, was the post–Civil War immigration of individuals who refused to recognize the sovereignty of tribal laws over their persons as citizens of the United States rather than guests of the tribes. As this intruder population overwhelmed tribal members numerically, the tribes found it too difficult to dislodge the "foreigners" whose status between the United States and the tribes created difficulties of enforcement and restraint.[60]

Muskogee, a railroad town in the Creek Nation, founded by intruders on the border with the Cherokee Nation, illustrates some of the differences between the two tribes and connects directly to Will Rogers, as I will discuss later. Whereas the Cherokees had "platted their railroad towns and sold the lots to citizens only" in order to keep noncitizens out of the tribal nation, the Creeks "were suspicious of any action that might be construed as a surrender of their jurisdiction, and no provision for the growth of Muskogee was ever made" because the Creek government refused to acknowledge it at all.[61] Muskogee grew to become a point of entry for intruders into both nations, intruders who, with the completion of the railroads into Indian Territory, advocated for and received the opening up of the lands to American settlement.

This historical context shapes our understanding of Will Rogers, whose father was a prominent Cherokee politician and cattleman, a member of the Cherokee elite and a veteran of the Confederate army. Clem Rogers had much to lose if the Cherokee Nation was dissolved and Indian Territory was incorporated into the United States, for he would lose Native title to all of his rangeland.[62] This, combined with attitudes inherited from the American South, led men of Clem Rogers's position to resent intruders of all creeds, but particularly blacks and the Creeks who incorporated them, for endangering Indian Territory as a whole.

This blame was partial, and misplaced, as the following anecdote demonstrates. Cherokee cattlemen often did not recognize the authority of predominantly Afro-Creek police officers (lighthorsemen) on their borders. When they and their partner cattlemen from Texas allowed their animals to graze on Creek pastures without paying fees to the Creek Nation, their cattle, unsurprisingly, were sometimes "speedily converted to beef" by the resident Creeks. Thus, considerable tensions arose between Afro-Creeks and Cherokees in ways that are far more involved and complex than simple mainstream racism. Both Afro-Creeks and elite mixed-blood white Cherokees saw the other as endangering the integrity of Indian Territory. Thus, when lighthorsemen from the Afro-Creek town of Marshalltown disarmed a couple of young prominent Cherokee ranchers on Christmas Day in 1878, a Texas friend "undertook to reduce the negro officers to their proper place in the universe," an approach that led to a gunfight. The position of the elite Cherokee ranchers is that the Creeks were endangering tribal sovereignty by incorporating "negros," but in this episode, it was the Cherokees and their Texas confederate who did so. Cherokee white mixed-bloods could imagine themselves as being loyal Cherokees rather than American sympathizers, but they could not extend the same precedence of tribe over race to their Afro-Creek neighbors.[63]

Placing Will Rogers

Incidents like these considerably enrich our understanding of Will Rogers, who was born in Indian Territory in 1879, just after the incident described above. Rogers grew up wealthy, the possessor of thousands of acres of rangeland in Indian Territory. With the dissolution of Indian Territory in 1906 and creation of Oklahoma in 1907, Rogers's family had to buy back their land, having lost Native title to it. Rogers himself, in fact, left for South America in part to regain somewhere abroad the large landholdings that his family had lost. Though he found South America inhospitable to such dreams, it was through this adventure that he entered show business as a traveling trick roper named "The Cherokee Kid" and eventually reached the stage of Ziegfield's Follies in New York City. There, he supplemented his roping tricks with humorous quips about current events, and it was his humor rather than his roping that gained him a career as a nationally syndicated humor columnist and film star. From there Rogers became one of the most enduring and successful American actors and comedians in history, making more money in 1934 than any other individual in the United States, save one Henry Ford.[64]

Rogers's texts are more important than his films for Native Americanist scholars, and the collection is vast. Donald Day notes that "Will's writings . . . constitute the best blow-by-blow history of a period ever written . . . from December 31, 1922 to August 15, 1935," but even more important than his account of the events of his time were Rogers's contributions to programming for the new mass-communication media of the twentieth century, particularly film and radio, as well as to the increasingly consolidated national newspaper industry.[65] These new media outlets, with their constant demand for material, provoked Rogers toward topical jokes, humor that both depended on the national reach of the media and compelled it. The result of this, naturally, was a content that no one would consider narrowly regional or tribal in any fashion. And indeed if we consider the canon that has embraced Rogers's work, it is not Native studies, but rather the popular culture canon.[66]

Rogers produced perhaps more writing than any other Native author, before or since, yet he is largely absent from Native studies—and is considered in that field a minor figure. I wonder if it is this particular dynamic of finding the *Native* in Native American that has left discussions of Will Rogers largely out of our canon—that his extensive oeuvre in print, on film, and on the radio on nearly every subject of his historical moment too deeply blurs his particularly Cherokee contributions to the national and global discourse. Unlike a figure like Charles Eastman, Rogers does not have a clearly "Native American" text that fits nicely into syllabi. However, Rogers, whose quotes are probably as durable today as they were when he wrote them, and still surprisingly ubiquitous, really does not need much recovering from the margins of American culture as do so many of his Native peers. Rogers is not a marginal figure who can be brought to our critical attention through the regional frame; on the contrary, he is a national figure whose regional roots have been poorly traced. Rogers is enigmatic because he does not fit easily into a tribal, regional, national, or internationalist frame, but inhabits all of these. He authored a series of humorous travel sketches while globe-trotting as "America's Ambassador to the World." He articulated through his columns topical events in national and regional politics and their relation to international forces, and he commented often on his own face-to-face encounters with locals as he traveled around the country. He was even mayor of Hollywood!

Given all of this prominence, the most likely reason that Rogers has been neglected in Native studies is the latent racism that appears in his texts, a trait particularly evident in his work with Stepin Fetchit and in his discussions of the predominantly black population of Muskogee, Oklahoma. Whereas Rogers was opposed to much of the mythology of white superiority and ethnocentric claims of superiority, some of his most famous films feature his participation in America's racialist nostalgia for the "the good ol' days" of slavery and the country's relentless will to control African Americans through ideological stereotypes of the compliant or ridiculous Sambo. We should find it deeply troubling that in such movies as *David Harum* (1934) and *Judge Priest* (1934) Rogers, who was on other fronts adamant to recuse himself from scripts that would alienate his "family values" audience, willingly participated in—indeed, seemed to have no interest in challenging—scripts that derived much of their humor from the debasement of the Stepin Fetchit character, a classic "Sambo" or "Coon" character. We might be able to excuse Rogers's problem here in noting that Stepin Fetchit's career was clearly independent of that of Rogers, and that racist attitudes toward African Americans (and tribal peoples) went hand in hand with the national ideology of white superiority. Still, we cannot but find it bitterly ironic that these two actors, who are the first in their minority groups to achieve national success in films, participated so heartily in these colonial fantasies.

Rogers, in these moments, severely undermines his credibility in counteracting American colonial narratives by participating in systems that attempt to build white privilege at the expense of African Americans, especially given that a close reading of his personal letters reveals the discrimination and suspicion with which he himself was handled by the family of the white woman he was to marry. Rogers had firsthand knowledge of white racism and stereotypes from the wrong end, and still he participated in them.[67] As George Lipsitz notes in his book *The Possessive Investment in Whiteness*, "The power of whiteness depended not only on white hegemony over separate racialized groups, but also on manipulating racial outsiders to fight against one another, to compete with each other for white approval, and to seek the rewards and privileges of whiteness for themselves at the expense of other racialized populations."[68]

Lipsitz's point leads us to the further realization that Rogers's participation in this particular American colonialist fantasy was not exclusively related, perhaps, to the influence on him of the "cosmopolitan" elites in New York and Hollywood, or to an unanalytic relationship to his culture.[69] Nobody who reads Rogers's articles closely believes the carefully constructed mask of ignorance that Rogers constructed for himself. The thesis that Rogers learned his racism through cosmopolitan contact is incorrect; it was homegrown, literally. Here is his description of the route to his hometown, Claremore: "Now, before reaching Claremore, you will pass, even though it's in the middle of the day, a place where you think it's night and you won't know what is the matter. Well, that's Muskogee, Oklahoma, and this darkness is caused by the color scheme of the population, so put on your headlights and go on in."[70] More than any other element, Rogers's racism is particularly rooted in the way in which he, as a Cherokee, identified with his tribal history. His position as a dispossessed scion of the Cherokee elite led him to displace upon freedmen and American blacks the loss of his nation's sovereignty and his family's loss, even as this very same tribal identification served him as an anticolonial lens through which he was able to provide a powerful and useful critique of twentieth-century corruption and state power. Finally, his travels helped him broaden and reinforce his critique of this process. In some ways his tribal perspective was narrow and problematic, and in others cosmopolitan and anticolonial, not to mention widely influential.

If Rogers's racism was historically mediated and tribally specific, rather than just an echo of the larger racism prevalent in the America of his day, then it is a component of Native American practice that needs to be acknowledged and critiqued. Such a critique can be fashioned in the tribal idiom, even after the postmodern turn. Returning briefly to the image of the two fires, we can imagine this anecdote as a merely relativist statement: When I am over that mountain, *that* is the center of the world, but when I am here, *this* is the center. But these are not absolute claims on the empirical world, they are theory- and culture-mediated and productive practices. The important insight of the anecdote is *not* the two fires or the communities themselves, but the revelation that the person who moves between them can mediate—relate—the two. It is the Native idea of relations that allows us to accept both ideas and practices not our own as potentially useful or harmful to us. In relation to Rogers, it is the concept of relations that allows us to critique the tribal element that blamed, and continues to show antipathy toward, Afro-Native people as constitutive threats to the tribal community.[71] Focusing on the Creeks, the historian David Chang has demonstrated that in Indian Territory, at least, such people were, in fact, united with their tribal brethren against the supersession of the territory by the state of Oklahoma.[72] Even if they had been party to some sort of betrayal of tribal sovereignty, as many tribal factions have been in the past and the present, tribal members like Will Rogers should have critiqued them not through an appeal to race—that is, some sort of notion of incommensurable difference—but rather in terms of relation—shared practice and expectation. This is exactly how Afro-Creek people mediated the influx of American blacks into their communities, an event that they could not resist. They extended a notion of relation as a way of bringing such people into the community and harmonizing goals and expectations.

Craig Womack's study of Creek literature, *Red on Red*, is for me the premier example of a good tribally specific approach to this sort of relation. In the book's innovative mise-en-scène chapters, Womack stages discussions between different tribal perspectives that argue with and against Womack and each other, together.[73] These voices do not silence each other, but rather work to harmonize their differences. Womack's discussions are modeled on Alexander Posey's Fus Fixico columns, in which Fus Fixico and his friends, who represent different factions of the tribe, sit together drinking a fermented corn drink called *sofky* and relating the events of the day to the tribal community with humor rather than acrimony. I would argue that the Creek community and tribal identity is in the center of that sort of discussion—amendable but present.

Will Rogers and Native Cosmopolitanism

Will Rogers is an important and valued Native presence because of just this capacity for relation. Rather than articulate relations within his own tribal community, or relate merely from his subject position as a colonized Cherokee, Rogers extended his notion of community outwards to the United States itself. Rogers engaged in a rhetoric, and I would argue, a pedagogy, of relation by imagining himself in relation to his colonizers, and imagining a relation between his colonizers and the colonized of the world. He pursued his critique not through an argument of particularized experience (though that is where he learned it) but through the notion of a common relation.

Even his difference—as a Native American writing to settler Americans—is articulated through common math anxiety as a way of establishing identity in Cherokee, rather than American governmental terms: "My father was one-eighth Cherokee Indian and my mother was a quarter-blood Cherokee. I never got far enough in arithmetic to figure out how much 'Injun' that makes me, but there's nothing of which I am more proud than my Cherokee blood. My father was a senator in the tribe . . . and was a member of the convention that drafted the constitution of . . . Oklahoma."[74] His account of his lineage pokes fun at the post-Dawes Commission anxiety that is placed (still) on the blood quantum of Indians. Even while citing the numbers, Rogers obscures them. They are his "Injun" certificate of authenticity officially, but he is telling us here that they are unimportant, useful only in the BIA office in Washington. More useful is his emphasis on his father's position as a member of the Cherokee government, elected and esteemed by Cherokee citizens, and by his father's service to that community and to Oklahoma. Rogers is introducing a more tribally specific and administratively flexible notion of Native identity as community-mediated and practice-based. In tribal communities, one is not just born a tribal person, but instead becomes one through practices and behavior that serve the community, which then recognizes the individual as a member.

Rogers performs all of this work while still representing himself as an Everyman whose simple words are nonetheless loaded with irony. Writing in a different context, Paul de Man notes: "It helps a little to think of it in terms of the ironic man, in terms of the traditional opposition between *eiron* and *alazon*, as they appear in Greek or Hellenic comedy, the smart guy and the dumb guy. . . . You must keep in mind that the smart guy . . . always turns out to be the dumb guy, and that he's always being set up by the person he thinks of as being the dumb guy, the *alazon*."[75] Rogers, in prose directly similar to that of Alexander Posey's *Fus Fixico Letters*, with their misspelled and run-on *este charte*, uses his poor grammar and spelling but erudite observations to critique the smart guys, be they captains of state or commerce, with quips that reveal the serious mode as an absurdity. In this moment, Rogers invokes his father's history within the tribe and as a founder of the state to explain that no matter how marginal his and his father's blood quantum may be, his father (and he, by association) was a true Indian and a true Oklahoman, a representative of both tribe and place.

Just as Rogers is careful to recoup his father from fascist blood-quantum games, we must recognize in his extensive writings not just the application of "cracker-barrel humor" but also the distinctive marks of Ind'n humor, perhaps directly due to the influence of Cherokees and other tribal peoples in his region such as Alexander Posey (Creek), whose work has been revived in

Native studies, largely due to the excellent scholarship of Daniel F. Littlefield, Jr. Just as many of the *Fus Fixico Letters* begin with "Well, so," as in "Well, so Hotgun he say they was something doing all the time and the newspapers was had lots a things to talk about," Rogers's syndicated columns began with "Well all I know is just what I read in the papers."[76] The very concept of progress is up for ridicule in these invocations. Rogers positions himself as a critic not just in the quotidian world of the papers but, repeatedly, outside them. What Rogers "knows" is that the news is rarely new but instead repeats very old human stories of colonization and aggression.

Rogers, who gained such fame as the voice of common America, instead becomes the voice of the trickster,[77] deflating the rhetoric of ever-progressing societies with insights literally based in the experience of Indian country, even as he profits from it as a columnist for his mainstream New York–based employer. In taking Ind'n humor and critique into the very center of the mainstream discourse, Rogers stands as the Fus Fixico that went to New York and made it his own. In "Red Men Got Big Laugh," one of Rogers's weekly articles, he uses Calvin Coolidge's appearance at the dedication of a new dam in Arizona to critique the old story of land theft that gets obscured in mantras of progress and change. The project is supposed to serve as a reservoir to irrigate crops, but Rogers muses whether the Apaches, whose land was confiscated for the project, will gain anything. He notes:

> Here was the old warlike Apaches that fought to hold all they had, and most of them wound up in jail, but there was a Washington that fought for his tribe against invaders and wound up with a flock of Statues and a title of Father of his Country. And yet I expect . . . the old Apache Chiefs went through more and fought harder for their Country than George did. But George won, that's the whole answer to history, it's not what did you do, but what did you get away with at the finish. . . . [So] we were out there on Indian land dedicating a Dam to get water for white people to come out and use and gradually take more Indian land away. There is going to be nothing different. . . . The more so-called civilized we get the more we kill and take. But I bet many an old Indian got many a quiet laugh out of the speeches of "good fellowship" there that day, *that were meant to be serious.*[78]

Struggles over the land provide a moment to delve into "history," which writes the scripts for how to submerge the traces of Indian holdings under floodwaters of progress even as the rest of the land is demarcated with statues to the "great white father."

Rogers's critique, we notice, is an analogy based in the tribal notion of relation—the United States is imagined as a *tribe*, like the Apaches. The critique gains momentum through this intertribal extension of relation. Washington's Euroamerican tribe will not recognize the Apaches' right to a national sovereignty like their own, because they want to imagine, for their own purposes, a radical incommensurability between tribal nations and their own. For Coolidge, there can be no Apache George Washington. The position of radical incommensurability shields the Americans from an ethical responsibility to the Apaches. Coolidge and the others are giving speeches to people whose view they themselves refuse to hear. Unlike Coolidge, Rogers imagines the United States in the terms of his own tribal community and holds it accountable to those terms. Indeed, Rogers imagines America as a tribal community, made up of a heterodox but related polity in which no members are silenced.

However, the Apaches have their own monuments to their land, their own connections and memorials within this space which is to be flooded. They did not need dams to live in that area, for they have found ways to live within it. Rogers suggests that what the Indian might do to get water or what the Indian might say about the annexation of the land is the true understanding of this event, an understanding that the politicians "seriously" will not understand. The Apaches understand that concepts such as "civilized" and "savage" are predicated largely on issues of power, and Rogers flips this assumption of the whites—that they are acting in a "civilized" manner—by pointing out that it is "the so-called civilized" who "kill and take."

The Indians, who the whites treat as their *alazon*, their dumb guy, get the last laugh, even as they lose the lands. In a sense, they have become *eiron*, the smart guys, because they know, unlike the speechmakers, who "meant to be serious," that this idea of "progress," if not corrected, will mean perpetual warfare and struggle. After this excerpt, Rogers goes on to make just this point in relation to Japanese aggression in China, and thus extends his argument as one not against whites, that is, not one based on racial difference, but against societies that act unjustly toward their neighbors. This injustice begins with the articulation of difference through linguistic masking. Just as Americans justify their treatment of Natives under the banner of "civilization," the Japanese invade their neighbors in the name of "modernization." When Japanese modernity attacked American civilization at Pearl Harbor, such masks became absurd. However, in the immediate term, the Apaches are clearly the losers. They lack the power to continue resisting militarily. Instead they resist in careful ways, ways that the politicians choose to recognize only as silence. It is this silence that Rogers attempts to articulate. It is Rogers who hears the "quiet laugh" of the "old Indian," and it is Rogers who most fully makes legible the Native critique that those in the mainstream are only too happy to hear as silence.

In another passage, Rogers uses the battlefield of the Little Bighorn to note that, in flying over the entire United States "and seeing the millions of acres that we don't use anyway, . . . it does look like America was big enough that they could have staked off say at least a fourth or a fifth of it and give it to [the Natives] for all time to come. Then I wouldent [*sic*] have seen Custer's battleground and hundreds of other graves in all those lonely old western forts."[79]

Rogers's observation at first seems like a tacit acceptance of land appropriation by the United States which has the right to "give" a portion of the land to its original owners, but instead it exemplifies his rhetorical tribal *We*. In this move, Rogers is taking the medium of Benedict Anderson's imagined community, the newspaper, and using it to construct an imagined relation from the tribal perspective in which *we* still have the capacity to return the land to its tribal owners which *they*, those nineteenth-century politicians, took. After this rhetorical presentation, Rogers's reader might not be surprised at feeling more connected to Rogers than to the American politicians. Yet Rogers's argument ironically mirrors that of Andrew Jackson, who removed the Cherokees to Indian Territory, and other nineteenth-century American political leaders who argued that land under Native control was not being used and therefore could (indeed should be) put to work. Here, the land could find its true purpose as a relational gesture in the field of social justice, a manifestation of the land as a shared place where Custer would not have had to die and the land would not be populated with forts and the massacred ghosts they created.

Rogers's overall oeuvre of books, films, newspaper articles, radio broadcasts, and many speeches and public appearances clearly demonstrate how he used his domination of the mass media to bring to the national "imagined community" a sensitivity not only to the Apache situation, but also to the struggles for freedom internationally and here at home. His work also focused attention on debates about wealth distribution and fairness that had a lasting and powerful influence on the discourse and temperament of Americans toward each other. I would argue further[80] that Rogers is perhaps the central figure—on a myriad of fronts—in instilling into the American "imagined community" a coherent ethos of commonalities that superseded ethnic, regional, economic, and racial distinctions but that nonetheless valued those distinctions as contributions—not failings—in the American multicultural project.

Rogers's very public comedy provided him with an opportunity to critique the power structures of his day, but he did not alienate himself from any of his many constituencies—powerful or not—and in this regard he was able to serve as an acceptable social locus for a whole range of consumers. Regardless of their political affiliation or ethnic background, most—if not all—Americans could find in the work of Rogers something that they could agree with, because he adopted them into his intertribal American nation. And Rogers was a ubiquitous presence in the 1920s and 1930s, both domestically and abroad, not just as a comedic reporter of the news, but as a crucial narrative voice that helped others construct a coherent picture of a society that was acknowledged to be one of dramatic sociological and technological change. In an era when Americans began to yield more and more autonomy to professional "experts" in the government, sciences, and industry, Rogers became a comforting and normalizing voice of a simpler, less mediated time, even as

Rogers himself served as a cultural mediator between the people and the events of the world and the nation. Internationally, Rogers's narratives of people in Russia—and in other countries he visited as America's "self-made diplomat"—served many Americans as their sole "personal" account of the world outside their borders during a time when the influence of mercantile America was being acutely felt internationally and just before the events that would thrust America into superpower status with the events of World War II.

Rogers's coherent narrative of the world and of the nation is clearly grounded in his identification with the Cherokees and their mistreatment by the United States, and his vision of the world is a relational one, a thread in the fabric of tribal cosmopolitanism. Because this perspective is so readily in the archive, commenting on a myriad of subjects, we should utilize it as *a* central Native critical voice of its time against other Native and non-Native voices, not merely as someone commenting on or protesting events, but as someone carrying on a national debate between positions in his work, and in certain instances as a determinant voice in shaping that debate.[81]

Rogers is also the figure of this new regionalism limned here, a frame for exploring the notion of relations between communities. His critique engages the local, regional, national, and the global and is based in a particular tribal history that is both productive and problematic. Through the rhetoric of relation, which is the tradition of tribal cosmopolitanism and outward-looking transmotion, he managed to relate and inhabit the contradictions in the global community like few individuals before or since. His work is rightly valued outside the field of Native American studies, and it is time that we bring him back into the tribal canon from which he arose.

Notes

1. I use the term "Natives" to speak generally about North American Natives within the United States. There are significant complications and qualifications attached to this generalization, both within and outside that frame, as should be apparent through the course of this essay.

2. Dreyfus and Rabinow, *Michel Foucault,* xxvi.

3. Recent attention has been given to the historicity of critical theory. For example, in *Historicizing Theory,* Peter Herman writes, "Even though the last thirty years or so have witnessed a resurgence of historical studies, a resurgence largely predicated upon rejecting the New Critical paradigms of the verbal icon and discoverable, transhistorical meaning, the discussions surrounding theory and its career in the academy are more often than not surprisingly ahistorical" (1).

4. Postcolonial theory is useful enough that it should be actively attended to by scholars interested in Native work, to be sure, but Natives have always existed in a colonial milieu of resistance, not a postcolonial one, and until postcolonial studies evolves to a degree that it can articulate adequately the status and voice of oppressed indigenous people and minorities around the globe, rather than claiming they cannot be expressed except as absences and subalterns, it will be inadequate

to the needs of either Native American or global indigenous studies. For a general critique of postcolonial claims, see S. P. Mohanty, *Literary Theory*; for a polemical but thorough critique of postmodernism generally, see Terry Eagleton, *Illusions of Postmodernism*; for a critique of postcolonialism, see Louis Owens, *Mixedblood Messages*, 50–53. Owens deepens this critique in "As If an Indian Were Really an Indian" in his posthumously published collection of essays, *I Hear the Train*.

5. S. P. Mohanty and a range of critics are engaged in critiquing and revising postmodernist claims under the banner of what Mohanty calls postpositivist realism. Linda Martin Alcoff provides an excellent discussion of this approach and of the limitations and contributions of Foucault in her article, "Objectivity and Its Politics."

6. Jack Weatherford's book *Indian Givers* relates quite well the relations between Native and non-Native peoples as modern co-equals. Some scholars have eschewed the idea that Europeans were the only people to make contact with Natives of the Western hemisphere. From the Pacific, Nancy Yaw Davis's *Zuni Enigma* suggests that Japanese people interacted with the Zuni as early as 1350. In his masterful introduction to *When Brer Rabbit Meets Coyote*, which he also edited, Jonathan Brennan provides an overview of scholarship positing connections between Africa and the Americas (2–3). Enrique Dussel contextualizes European modernity itself within the context of other and earlier empires and "centers" in his essay, "Beyond Eurocentrism.".

7. Parker, *Invention of Native American Literature*.

8. In relation to Dutch New York and its influence on the United States, see Russell Shorto's provocative popular article, "All Political Ideas Are Local," particularly pages 58 and 60. Considering the Iroquois Confederacy and Dutch New York as central sites for America's ideological founding is a crucial move in what I consider the new regional impulse in American studies.

9. For a brief overview of the Indian Claims Commission (ICC), see Francis Paul Prucha's *Great Father*, 341–43. Prucha does not take up the Cold War relations of the ICC.

10. American studies, by the way, though the obvious inheritor of American history's bounty and potential midwife to American literature's maturation, has been mostly AWOL in relation to Native studies. Philip Deloria, in his article "American Indians, American Studies, and the ASA" has argued quite carefully that the ASA, for example, has not yet conceded the necessary colonialist space to make true dialogue with Native studies possible, and Daniel Heath Justice's provocative essay "We're Not There Yet, Kemo Sabe" argues that the ALA has been openly hostile to Native critiques and claims. During its founding period—from the thirties to the fifties—when, as Leo Marx has written in "On Recovering the 'Ur' Theory (121)," Americanists identified themselves and aligned with America as an immigrant nationalist project, tempered by the best of the Enlightenment and progress, this might have been excusable. Now, however, it is not.

11. This is emphatically *not* to say that the tribes, by being incorporated into the United States culturally and geographically, have conceded their status as legally

sovereign tribal nations or have been assimilated. Rather, Natives and settlers are related to each other by a great degree of shared culture, history, outlook, and—of course—actual familial relations.

12. For an articulation of Creek efforts to incorporate into the United States in the twentieth century, see David Chang's unpublished dissertation, "From Indian Territory to White Man's Country."

13. Swanton, *Myths and Tales*.

14. "Rabbit Brings Fire" (DVD); *http://www.blackgummountain.com/store/index.html*.

15. I use the term "interzone" from Kevin Mumford's study of twentieth-century black neighborhoods that were carved out by progressive whites to serve as "sin districts" rather than the more well-worn metaphors of space and identity like Gloria Anzaldua's borderlands, Mary Louise Pratt's contact zones, or Richard White's middle ground because I want to emphasize an imbalance of power and to foreground the ability of the dominant community to set the terms of these encounters in the space of the subordinate groups. See Mumford, *Interzones*, especially pages 20–21 for Mumford's own articulation of the term. My area of special interest, Indian Territory, was created in 1803 by Jefferson, who saw the Louisiana Purchase as a convenient outlet not only for migrating whites but for southern Natives. This is exactly what Indian Territory became—a subaltern space fashioned by those in power over them, an interzone.

16. The regional framework posits that there are always more voices being silenced, but their presence is pointed to in the texts available. I work this out in my dissertation chapter on John Joseph Mathews, particularly in relation to the Osage members of the Native American Church and the nonhuman persons of Mathews' Osage Blackjacks.

17. Tuan, *Space and Place*, 174.

18. Quoted in Peter Applebome's article "Out from under the Nation's Shadow," B7.

19. Tuan, *Space and Place*, 167.

20. Angie Debo, in *The Road to Disappearance*, writes that in May of 1824 John Ridge and David Vann, young educated Cherokees, helped the Creeks draft a statement of policy in the face of settler aggression. To wit: "[W]e have . . . [decided] to follow the pattern of the Cherokees, and on no account whatever will we consent to sell one foot of our land, neither by exchange or otherwise" (88).

21. Terry Eagleton's *Illusions of Postmodernism* proposes a thorough and convincing critique of a somewhat broad postmodernism that is a useful and necessary corrective to the concept. A crucial part of his critique is his attention to the historical genesis of postmodern ideas as a type of capitulation to global capitalism (38–39).

22. Weaver, *That the People Might Live*, 32.

23. That is to say that at times of great peril central "rules" of a culture may be broken in order to save the culture itself. I am thinking here, actually, of the Judaic tradition that one may break the laws between God and man in order to save lives.

This suggestion allows one to break injunctions against working on the Sabbath, for instance, in case of emergencies.

24. Weaver, *That the People Might Live*, 33. Emphasis in original.

25. Ibid., 33.

26. In a personal conversation with Louis Owens (October 16, 1999) we agreed that the metaphor of a tornado was fitting to this concept. The tornado is defined by the force at the edge of the vortex, which is always bringing into itself new material and which, consequently, is made visible by this material. Like a tornado, a culture is often defined against what surrounds it, and yet a fundamental element of its form is determined by its appropriation of material outside itself. There is the land; there is the vortex. The land is not the vortex, the vortex not the land, but they are nonetheless intricately tied to the other. Furthermore, like a culture, the tornado is defined at is margins, so it is often most legible there. The center of the tornado, its heart, is calm and stable. Likewise, the cultural center is often unarticulated; it resides in the silences. It is stable, and within the context of the culture, it does not change. However, the entire culture, even while maintaining this coherent structure, is moving. Owens added to this notion the further idea that, of course, like tornados, some cultures fade away, some are peripheral, and some are like looming forces of nature, seemingly rending the very landscape to which they relate.

27. Native knowledge has perhaps most impacted the sciences in the form of knowledge of medicinal plants and has been the primary resource for ethnopharmacology and the attendant corporate bio-pirates of whom Vandala Shiva writes. Therefore, though Native knowledge has been taken up by the sciences (often as "local knowledge"), the pattern of its acceptance has followed the old colonial paradigm of exploitation and erasure.

28. In *Fugitive Poses*, Gerald Vizenor defines transmotion as "that sense of native motion and an active presence, [which] is sui generis sovereignty. Native transmotion is survivance, a reciprocal use of nature, not a monotheistic, territorial sovereignty. Native stories of survivance are the creases of transmotion and sovereignty" (15). I take this interplay between motion and presence as the interplay between individual members and the group identity and between individual communities in relation to each other. Vizenor's term is explicitly *not* linked to national borders or official documents, but instead to a cultural outlook and the stories that create it.

29. Even within Native communities, we see this impulse, and there are strategies—gentle yet honest—that can serve as a corrective to them, as with Kimberly Roppolo's anecdote, presented in an earlier version of her essay for this collection, about teasing her Cheyenne relations into remembering that their identity is now inclusive of other tribal people, most notably herself.

30. This articulation of cosmopolitanism is largely epistemic and political rather than aesthetic, as it is generally referenced in Western contexts. It is also emphatically not the cosmopolitanism articulated by Arnold Krupat in *Red Matters*, where he argues that "Native American literature today proceeds from either a

nationalist, indigenist, or cosmopolitan perspective" (ix). While Krupat argues that these distinctions reflect "hard" camps, we should instead recognize these perspectives as contingent rhetorical positions that work in concert toward developing consensus and strategies of survivance. In my study, the cosmopolitan is not counterpoised to the grounded, regional mode (Krupat's nationalist/indigenist), which I define as the "relational regional" frame, because I see all of these frames as elements of the same intensely tribally specific cosmopolitan impulse. Indeed, my focus on historical contextualization is meant to suggest that some "provincials" are born "cosmopolitan" through the complexity of their identity constructions and that tribal traditionalists are often the most cosmopolitan of voices in their communities. Further, tribal dialogues demonstrate a tremendous flexibility not explored adequately by Krupat's "hard" camps. No tribe, or tribal position, is easily disentangled from another. This awareness of multiplicity within an ostensibly unified self provides a realm of both nuance and hybridity. The Native community is not sterile or monolithic, nor capable of being boiled down to three (really two) distinct positions; Native American cultural practice argues that even the "empty" woods constitute a busy and conflicted place, full of human and nonhuman communities in relation to one another, whether others choose to see that or not. Thus Native cosmopolitanism (which when paired with outside communities can be called relational regionalism) is the practice of noticing and interacting with the multiple communities of any given place. Even among Krupat's "three" camps, there is a failure to recognize that though the rhetoric and emphasis among various tribes and their members may be different, the goals—sovereignty, cultural survivance, and respect for the interdependence of all life—are values and assertions held in common. Different rhetorical poses, rather than suggesting differences of opinion on these topics, signify instead the clear tribal understanding that diverse specialization is good for the group and that different approaches might sustain those goals more effectively.

31. For an amplification of this, see Justice (this volume) on defining Cherokee community. The notion of differences within a tribe or allegiances outside of it *can* dissolve the community. Tribes and communities can fall apart, but the absence of single particularities (absence of a land base, absence of a tribal language, etc.) do not in themselves demonstrate that a particular group is not a "real" tribe, as Delphine Red Shirt attempts to claim in relation to eastern tribal peoples. Had Red Shirt taken an attentive look at the history and context of tribal and nontribal peoples in the area she lives in—as Justice does—she would have seen the inadequacy of her claim that "Pequot, Mohegan, Paugussett, Paucatuck or Schaghticoke" are "not Indians."

32. See, for example, Martin and Mauldin, *Dictionary of Creek/Muskogee*. In Creek there are no references to "disruption," "modern," "modernity," "progress," "civilized," "civilization," "event," or "rupture." The word for pickup truck, by the way, is *esconeckuce*.

33. Of course, I am not arguing that Native people are ahistorical and that Native communities are not disruptable or extinguishable. Indeed, there are a number of

historical moments and processes that could be argued as the introduction of modernity to Native peoples, not the least of which was the pandemic of European-introduced diseases that killed off up to 90 percent of Native people. The point made here is that indigenous societies do not have the historical notion of themselves as disconnected from the historical and cultural past. For example, in literature, Native artists do not attempt to make space for themselves by attacking those who came before them, as is common in mainstream literary America, where for the most part the cultural field follows the mercantile field in its desire to, as Ezra Pound said, "make it new." Of course, and perhaps ironically, Ezra Pound himself was polemically against this very fetish for the new in commerce.

34. Mohanty, *Literary Theory*, 131.

35. It is often said that people in earlier historical periods are like radically different cultures, and this is true. However, as human beings in communities, they each created expectations and structures that responded to their times and that are plausibly related to actions we would have taken. Their difference is only of interest to us because of their relation and similarity to us. Thus we are interested in the history of the ancient Greeks, but not of ancient lions. Of course, *radical* claims to relatedness, particularly in the Native context, do attempt to concern themselves with the perspective of nonhuman communities—as I articulate in my chapter on John Joseph Mathews in my forthcoming book. Within the Native intellectual context, Robert Warrior in *The People and the Word* makes an intriguing claim for what he calls "synchronicity," the way in which the themes and claims of Native writers overlap across tribes and historical moments (xx).

36. Deloria, "Civilization and Isolation," 140, 141.

37. Ibid., 141.

38. See Anna Lee Walters, *Talking Indian,* as Roppolo cites her in this volume: "[E]verything we two-leggeds know about being human, we learned from the four-leggeds, the animals and the birds, and everything else in the universe. None of this knowledge is solely our own. . . . Everything we are was taught us, you see?"

39. I would argue that the fictional text that best exemplifies a reading with this Native relational framework is Leslie Marmon Silko's work, particularly *Almanac of the Dead*, which unsettles conventional notions to force the reader into powerful and suppressed narratives with real histories. Silko's text so adroitly opens conversations that it apparently provoked Subcommandante Marcos to contact Silko herself. Even if this is apocryphal, the text brings crucial discussions and relations to the fore like none other in Native American literary studies.

40. Following from Mohanty, I should point out that different perspectives offer sometimes unique narratives that are necessary for understanding the actual relations between communities. The more perspectives included in creating this understanding the better, but there is a way to test and evaluate these perspectives in relation to one another that allows us to value them differently, as long as we understand that conditions change and that our notion of such relations is fallible, contingent, and always in need of revision.

41. My emphasis on disagreements and conflicts as the primary reason for this

approach does not imply that it is the only way to apply it. The reason for emphasizing difference, in fact, is to engage in a materialist and historically astute dialogue toward mutual understanding. Though the regional frame I propose highlights differences, it depends intimately on a notion of shared relation. A good example, within the tribal (rather than regional) context, of this approach is the position that Warrior takes within his chapter on the Osage constitution in his book *The People and the Word.* Thus the principle of intertribal relation is an extension of that concept within tribal space, and I see no reason why the model I am suggesting could not be applied even outside tribal texts and critics.

42. Hitt, "Newest Indians," 36–41.

43. Prucha, *Great* Father, 142–43. Unlike others of the Southern tribes, notably the Seminole, who fought largely, if not entirely, for the North, the Cherokees were paid for their western lands by the federal government.

44. Hale, *Making Whiteness,* 8.

45. See, for example, Chang, "From Indian Territory," 94–95, in relation to the Creeks. As will be seen later in this essay, the Cherokees and Creeks had different relationships with Afro-American and Afro-Native people, so it is unclear to what extent Afro-Cherokees were loyal to the Cherokee Nation and its leaders.

46. Debo, *And Still the Waters Run,* 140.

47. Ibid., 242–44.

48. Chang, "From Indian Territory," 105–106.

49. Scholarly opinion on the relations between African-Americans and Natives is particularly complex. Some of the more important texts that have considered these issues among the three tribes are Angie Debo, *And Still the Waters Run*; Bill Sampson, "Justice for the Cherokees"; Daniel Littlefield, Jr., *Africans and Seminoles*; Theda Perdue, *Slavery and the Evolution of Cherokee Society*; Jack Forbes, *Africans and Native Americans*; Rennard Strickland and William M. Strickland, "Beyond the Trail of Tears"; Katja May, *African Americans and Native Americans*; David Chang's "From Indian Territory"; and Circe Sturm, *Blood Politics.*

50. See Sturm, *Blood Politics*, 68–69, for a good discussion of these debates.

51. Littlefield, *Africans and Seminoles*, 188, 191, 193.

52. The Seminoles were made up of peoples who split off from the Creek Confederacy over the eighteenth and early nineteenth centuries. See Littlefield, *Africans and Seminoles*, 3–4.

53. Ibid., 200.

54. The Choctaws and Chickasaws, the other two members of what were once called the "Five Civilized Tribes," are also important in these regards but are not considered here only because of space limitations. For a full exploration of this issue, see Daniel Littlefield's excellent study, *Chickasaw Freedmen.* Because of the way that the April 28, 1866, Reconstruction treaty was written, sovereignty of these two tribes was interlocked in the way they were to deal with their former slaves. Because the Chickasaws and Choctaws had to have the same legislation, the issue went unresolved for many years (see Littlefield, *Chickasaw Freedmen,* 39–40). Thus the Choctaw, though willing to adopt their former slaves, were restrained from doing so because the Chickasaws refused such an action (66).

55. Littlefield, *Chickasaw Freedmen*, 202.

56. McLoughlin, *Cherokees and Christianity*, 119.

57. A precise study by Katja May notes that after the Civil War "[a]mong the Creeks, African Americans held elective political offices as council members, judges, and policemen. This was not the case among the Cherokees. Nevertheless, African Americans among the Cherokees had access to Indian status signifiers, e.g. education and allotments, enough to differentiate them from 'state Negroes,' who were African Americans immigrating from the surrounding states" (May, *African Americans*, 3–4). May goes on to suggest that of the five tribes of the region, the Seminole were the most tolerant and the Choctaws and Chickasaws were the least tolerant, with the Creeks and Cherokees in the middle. I should note that this schema, roughly accurate, also corresponds closely to the settlement of non-Native groups. The lands of the Choctaws and Chickasaws, for example, are now considered "Little Dixie," because they were settled by ex-Confederates and their dependants. These immigrants, I suggest, might have influenced the lack of tolerance among their Native neighbors, particularly the Scotch and Anglo-Chickasaw elites who shaped much of the political life of the tribe and who themselves had utilized African slaves the most fully since their introduction to the tribe in the early nineteenth century (see Littlefield, *Chickasaw Freedmen*, 5). This is yet another example of the careful and complex interplay of tribal and nontribal people that a Native regionalism would focus on. Of course, the Chickasaw, for example, were concerned with questions of political polity as much, if not more so, than questions of racial or tribal superiority, and this could explain, more than either internal or external racism, the legal prejudice against Afro-Chickasaws. After the Civil War, the Chickasaws numbered about five thousand people, with about two thousand Afro-Chickasaws (Littlefield, *Chickasaw Freedmen*, 31). Had the Afro-Chickasaws been incorporated as voting members of the tribe, the fear was that they would give away tribal prerogatives and land and work to become U.S. citizens. Littlefield quotes Chickasaw governor B. F. Overton as noting in 1875 that if the Chickasaw legislature were to adopt the former slaves, "you sign the death-warrant of your nationality with your own hands; for the negroes will be the wedge with which our country will be rent asunder and opened up to the whites; and then the grand scheme so artfully devised by the treaty of 1866, will have been effected, and the ends of the [federal] conspirators attained" (66).

58. Debo, *And Still the Waters Run*, 221.

59. The Cherokee elites who fought for the South and shared southern value systems and the Afro-Cherokees who were liberated from these elites by the U.S. federal government became natural enemies. The 1866 treaty between the Cherokees and the federal government stipulated that the freedmen be included among the Cherokee, but by 1883 the Cherokee tribal council excluded them from per capita payments of money from the sale of lands to the United States (Sturm, *Blood Politics*, 76). This action set off a passel of federal interventions and lawsuits between the Afro-Cherokees and the Cherokee Nation that continue to this day.

60. Debo, *And Still the Waters Run*, 229, 253.

61. Ibid. 231–32. May suggests instructively that looking at settlement patterns in

the land reveals the degree of Creek tolerance and Cherokee antipathy toward African Americans, both Native and non-Native: "The greater African American immigration to the Creek Nation led to the foundation of some twenty-three all-black towns (only three or four were African Creek towns). In the Cherokee Nation there were only two or three dispersed black settlements which were barely tolerated by neighboring Cherokees and white settlers" (*African Americans,* 255). Sturm's text dramatizes this distinction: "How many times had she heard local [Cherokee and white] people say, 'Yeah, we got rid of all our blacks, pushed them down south to Muskogee'" (*Blood Politics,* 192).

62. Because land in the Cherokee Nation was claimed through usage, Cherokee ranchers like Clem Rogers could "own" land simply by fencing it off and employing it for labor. Before the Civil War, in which he fought for the Confederate army in Stand Watie's Cherokee Mounted Rifle Regiment, Clem Rogers's lands included "approximately 60,000 acres of excellent bluestem grassland" for his many head of cattle (Halliburton, *Red over Black,* 74). After the war, allotment forced Clem and other wealthy landowners to give up title to almost all of their land, which they then had to buy back from American and Cherokee allottees.

63. Debo, *And Still the Waters Run,* 253.

64. Yagoda, *Will Rogers,* 47, 59, 306.

65. Rogers, *Autobiography,* xv.

66. Rogers noted, in a piece describing his approach to humor, that, in order to generate enough material for all the many outlets with which he was contracted, he had to parody the latest news. The content demands of his job required him to develop a routine built around a daily response to the news of the day. This technique defines the humor of David Letterman and Jay Leno. Indeed, Rogers may be the father of the late-night "in today's news" routine, a very American format.

67. The eminent critic of popular culture, Lary May, has published a chapter on Rogers that is essential reading in its study of Rogers's films in this context. My dissertation chapter on Rogers comes to a conclusion different from that of May in relation to this question. See May, *Big Tomorrow.*

68. Lipsitz, *Possessive Investment in Whiteness,* 3.

69. Racism and race consciousness in its most virulent and legalistic sense emanated in this country from scientific and mercantile elites. One potential explanation of Rogers's nascent racism is his association with these elites—which is documentable. But Rogers was a big star, known for exercising autonomy over his work and was not unanalytic about any of it. Any study of the man demonstrates that his 'cracker-barrel' persona belied his extensive knowledge and awareness of others and of his own language. Lary May excuses Rogers for his racism. My own take diverges from May—most respectfully—in refusing to excuse Rogers for endorsing the nascent racism of his time.

70. Rogers, *Weekly Articles,*, vol. 1, 100.

71. Historically, the Cherokee elite like Clem Rogers saw the freedmen as non-Cherokees whose participation in the Cherokee government and in elections

would undermine the tribe in favor of pro-United States policies and perhaps even lead to the dissolution of the tribe itself in exchange of a percentage of the tribe's assets. Up to contemporary times, descendants of the freedmen have been denied the vote in the Cherokee Nation because they cannot prove a degree of Indian blood. However, times are changing. Early in 2006 the Cherokee Nation Judicial Appeals Tribunal in a 2 to 1 decision recognized Cherokee freedmen as members of the tribe. (See Teddy Snell, "Freedmen."). The reaction of tribal officials and citizens to this decision has been mixed but has largely moved along two poles: anxiety about a greater strain on tribal resources from a new client base for health care and other services as well as anxiety about the movement away from citizenship by blood relation to a Cherokee Native against the argument that this is the historical and culturally correct thing to do—to bring back together the freedmen and the Natives in one community. For one Cherokee citizen's opinion expressing this latter view, see Jennifer Sparks, "Freedmen Are Citizens of Cherokee Nation." Recently Chief Chad Smith has called for an election among citizens to decide if the Cherokee constitution will be amended to restrict citizenship to members by blood. The central claim of those who wish to exclude descendants of freedmen is based on the issue of sovereignty, and the central claim of those who wish to include the descendants is based on issues of relationship and antidiscrimination. In a special tribal election in March 2007 an overwhelming majority of Cherokees (6,693 to 2,040) voted to exclude freedmen from citizenship. For background on this debate, see *http:///indianz.com/News/archives/000930.asp*. See also S. E. Ruckman, "Tribe Membership Challenged."

72. In 1894, Creek freedmen were united with other Creeks against allotment (Chang, "From Indian Territory," 94–95). By 1895, the Creek elite, sensing the futility of resistance, wanted to accept allotment on favorable terms (96). Congress decreed that if the Five Tribes did not conclude an agreement with the government by October 1, 1898, the federal government would abolish the tribal judicial system and take over unilaterally. On April 1, 1899, after the matter had been decided, all citizens, regardless of their particularities, rushed to get the best allotments. Chang's account suggests that the Creek freedmen were no more pro-allotment than others in their social class in the Creek Nation and that in fact it was the elites who, out of resignation, became the first pro-allotment faction.

73. Womack, *Red on Red*.

74. Rogers, *Autobiography*, 5.

75. de Man, *Aesthetic Ideology*, 165.

76. Posey, *Fus Fixico Letters*, 124.

77. Rogers is using trickster discourse as a way to liberate. It is interesting that Native peoples have often created trickster stories that respond to dangerous hegemons and to Euroamericans in particular. The trickster sense that I am invoking comes from Gerald Vizenor, but not only from Vizenor. The trickster of the southeastern tradition—Rabbit—is present in Rogers's reference to himself as "Rabbit." For example, Rogers writes, "I looked like a promising End. I could run pretty fast. In fact my nickname was and is to this day among some of the old

timers 'Rabbit.' I never could figure out if that referred to my speed or my heart" (*Weekly Articles*, vol. 4, 68) and "I was pretty fast as a runner. Down in the old Indian Territory they used to call me 'Rabbit'" (*Weekly Articles*, vol. 6, 183). However, like so many things that are deeply tribally specific and yet shared, the trickster traveled in stories between tribes. The trickster travels and is one of our clearest manifestations of the Native cosmopolitan tradition.

78. Rogers, *Weekly Articles*, vol. 4, 125–26. Emphasis mine.

79. Ibid., vol. 3, 19.

80. Rogers is a central figure in my ongoing dissertation that deals with the rise of multiculturalism in America and its relation to regional triethnic communities, using Oklahoma as a case study.

81. Rogers's influence and persuasiveness in American culture cannot be definitively measured, but it can be traced, as I do in greater detail in my dissertation project.

Samson Occom as Writing Instructor

The Search for an Intertribal Rhetoric

KIMBERLY ROPPOLO

In the final chapter of this volume, Craig Womack asks, "Might English *be* one of our Indian languages?" I think the Creek dialect sections of his *Red on Red*, in particular, show that we have, as he suggests in this current text, colonized English as much as it has colonized us. The importance of *how* language is used to convey meaning is just as important in analyzing how our English texts work as our belief in the efficacy of our tribal languages to change reality is in understanding *how* language works in ceremonial ways. Anna Lee Walters, in *Talking Indian: Reflections on Survival and Writing*, says:

> "It's for the old stories and songs that you grieve," he said. "That's what you want and need. . . . You came all the way back here for a story. You came all the way back here to hear someone, anyone, talking Indian, didn't you? . . . For what you are searching is right here. . . . This will give you life. . . . You were right to come back. . . . It is important and curious to remember that everything we two-leggeds know about being human, we learned from the four-leggeds, the animals and the birds, and everything else in the universe. None of this knowledge is solely our own. . . . Everything we are was taught us, you see? This is what the stories are, the teachings of who we are. . . . That's why we need the stories. Without them we grieve. For ourselves, for direction, for meaning. . . . Now I sit here, sixty years later, telling you the exact same thing my old folks told me as a teenager. The only thing that's different is I'm talking a foreign language, one forced on us, but nevertheless, I'm still talking Indian. It's ironical."[1]

Kimberly Roppolo is of Cherokee, Choctaw, and Creek descent and teaches in the Native American studies department at the University of Lethbridge. Beside publishing in academic journals, she has received the 2004 First Book Award for prose from the Native Writers' Circle of the Americas for her book-length manuscript entitled "Back to the Blanket: Reading, Writing, and Resistance for American Indian Literary Critics." She is the associate national director of the Wordcraft Circle of Native Writers and Storytellers.

In our home communities, even in English, some of us still "talk Indian." In my classrooms, my use of English varies, depending on the demographic composition of the class. In fact, my English varies throughout my daily life, depending on whom I am with in the community. If I went to Watonga, Oklahoma, or out to either reserve outside of Lethbridge speaking like I am writing here, people *would* understand what I was saying, but they *wouldn't* understand *me*. In other words, non-Native use of English—and I mean that in a totally different way than English as a second language—would mark me as someone who doesn't know how to communicate in the community properly and doesn't want to learn—in other words, someone no one would listen to. Certainly, using standard English in a Native church setting, where I might have the right to speak, implies a false sense of the speaker's own superiority. The privileging of standard English in the academy also causes other complications for those of us who go off to "get an education" when we try to come back and work with our peoples. Some once very traditional young people come home and are impatient with tribal modes of discourse, with the time traditional speaking takes, and with the communality of decision making when dialogic discourse is used, as it takes more time than even the sometimes seemingly endless competing monologues do. If we are sending our young people away so that they might come back and help their own peoples, we need to academically validate our own English discourse that grows out of our home communities.

But we have to start by studying it before we can apply it. Despite the fact that a significant amount of material exists on rhetoric and communication among many other subgroups of the American population, very little has been published about American Indian rhetoric and communication, and even less has been published *about* the subject *by* American Indians, that is, by people who have firsthand experience with Native American modes of discourse. The general gap left in the area of rhetorical studies by the disdaining of Native rhetorics as inferior or the entire ignoring of these rhetorics was pointed out as early as 1972 by Choctaw scholar Jerry D. Blanche in his article "Ignoring It Won't Make It Go Away." And the gap has closed very little since then. There is one anthology of articles on the subject being compiled currently by Ernest Stromberg, which will include work by Native scholars. Additionally, Scott Lyons (Annishinaabe), author of "Rhetorical Sovereignty: What Do American Indians Want from Writing?" and "The Incorporation of the Indian Body: Peyotism and the Pan-Indian Public, 1911–1923," also investigates rhetorical sovereignty in his book. Malea Powell (Miami) has published a book on the rhetoric of "survivance" in Sarah Winnemucca Hopkins's and Charles Alexander Eastman's work, and her article, "Blood and Scholarship: One Mixed-Blood's Dilemma," was included in Keith Gilyard's *Race, Rhetoric, and Composition*. And there is a Caucus for American Indian Scholars and Scholarship at the annual College Composition and Communication Conference, with members making presentations in several sections. Non-Native authors have also made a few contributions in this area. Notably, Patricia Bizzell has an article entitled "The 4th of July and the 22nd of December: The Function of Cultural Archives in Persuasion, as Shown by Frederick Douglass and William Apess." Danna Gibson has written an article entitled, "The Community of the Eastern Cherokee: Enacting Community via Discourse." George Kennedy makes brief mention of Native rhetorics in his *Comparative Rhetoric: An Historical and Cross-Cultural Introduction*, and Bruce Ballenger has an article entitled, "Methods of Memory: On Native American Storytelling." There are also writings from the field of linguistic anthropology that have application to the topic at hand, particularly Anthony K. Webster's article, "Sam Kenio's Coyote Stories: Poetics and Rhetoric in Some Chiricahua Apache Narratives," and Joel Sherzer and Anthony C. Woodbury's *Native American Discourse: Poetics and Rhetoric.*

Though all of these sources deal with American Indian rhetorics to some extent and from a variety of viewpoints—and, in fact, I will refer to some of them later in this chapter—the most useful material published thus far on the structure of Native American discourse and several other rhetorical elements comes under the guise of literary criticism: Craig S. Womack's (Creek/Cherokee) *Red on Red: Native American Literary Separatism.* Womack argues in this text that to suggest Native viewpoints exist despite colonialism is not essentialist; rather, these "radical Native viewpoints . . . are called for to disrupt the powers of the literary status quo as well as the powers of the state—[because] there is a link between thought and activism." And Métis scholar and activist Howard Adams points out that "the state, rather than the Indians, controls 'the mental means of production.'"[2] With this view in mind, Womack proceeds with a Creek literary analysis of Creek and Cherokee writing with a tribal, in contrast to an intertribal, perspective. Womack structures his text by weaving narratives written in Creek dialect in between his chapters of literary analysis written in mainstream discourse mode—narratives that communicate, or that are intended to communicate, the same point to a Creek audience that the chapters do to an academic audience. While this discourse is "Creek" English, I would imagine it is understandable by and profitable for a non-Creek audience to varying degrees. I have to say "imagine" here because I cannot know how much my familiarity with Creek discourse informs my own reading. While I have no problem at all following Womack's dialect sections and find them much richer than mainstream academic writing—in fact, I think the Creek parts are the best literary criticism I have ever read—I am not sure how an audience unfamiliar with this dialect responds.

But I do feel that most potential readers can get at least the gist of the dialect sections, and this supports my notion that we might develop an even more intertribal mode of discourse that might be used for academic writing and speaking to communicate to a dual audience of scholars, Native and non-Native alike, as well as to the general Native American community. Both Lee Hester's "Pishukchi: One Choctaw's Examination of the Differences in English and Choctaw Language Use" and Patricia Penn Hilden's "Ritchie Valens Is Dead: *E Plurbius Unum*" are evidence of this fact. And Dean Rader's presentation, structured as intertribal discourse and given at the American Literature Symposium on Native Literary Strategies for the Next Millennium (held in Puerta Vallarta, Mexico, November 29–December 23, 2000), was extraordinarily successful with a mixed audience of many of the top scholars in the field of Native literature. Rader, moreover, is non-Native, proving that this discourse cannot only be understood by, but can also be *constructed* by, those non-Natives who choose to become culturally literate in their field of specialty rather than isolating themselves in the halls of academe and calling themselves experts on something with which they have only a superficial familiarity.

Further analyzing the term "rhetoric," an organized system of language whose primary function is to convey an idea, an argument, would be useful, particularly considering that an intertribal scholarly rhetoric that utilizes the English language and crosses cultural borders—tribal boundaries, those that divide Native cultures from the mainstream, and those that divide the academy from the larger U.S. society—falls into what Colleen Burke calls a rhetorical borderland. Burke utilizes in her definition Richard Ohmann's five patterns of classical rhetorics: (1) "a way to persuade an audience to believe or to act in a certain way"; (2) "the truth at which an author or spokesperson believes he or she has arrived and wants to convey to an audience"; (3) "a vehicle that absorbs truth and abandons subterfuge"; (4) "an avenue that embodies an author or spokesperson's character, voice, and style"; and (5) "discourse that reflects a worldview."[3] By contrast, I see a rhetorical borderland as a liminal zone where things are much murkier because of the lack of homogeneity; because of a lack of shared beliefs, values, and assumptions; because of the lack of communal interests or goals; because of a lack of trust. Burke claims that in these borderlands, "depending on what the author or spokesperson wants to achieve, rhetoric can create a sense of well-being, incite an audience to action, propagate fear, engender trust, or . . . present a semblance of the truth."[4] Working in this liminal area, we need to be careful not to create the kind of fear that causes the reactionary stances taken in recent years by some non-Native critics against Native critics, those that gave rise to charges of "essentialism." But we also need to keep in mind that this liminal area can be a zone of change, a space in which fuller readings of Native literature can develop, created by both Native and non-Native critics, and a space within which the kind of positive and productive interaction between Native and non-Native scholars that we need in our field can exist.

Though there are similarities, there is also a great deal of difference between Native American and mainstream arguments. There is a difference in the appeals to ethos. In Native culture, experience in general—whether the experiences of the culture encoded in story, the experiences of an authoritative elder, or the experiences of an individual who shares the same cultural values

—is held as evidence. In fact, this is precisely what invests a person with "authority" in Native cultures: experience that leads to maturity. Vine Deloria asserts that

> maturity, in the American Indian context, is the ultimate goal of all human existence . . . the ability to reflect on the ordinary things of life and discover both their real meaning and the proper way to understand them when they appear in our lives. . . . Maturity is a reflective situation that suggests a lifetime of experiences that, through an increasing ability to reflect on experience, has produced a personal hierarchy of relationships. This hierarchy has three major components that, because of the intense personal nature of experience, are appropriately related to the experiences of the individual and, on the tribal level, the group. Some components are weighted heavily because of the intensity of their content, others because of their inherent rationality and capability to explain everyday occurrences and others are simply a matter of personal preference, originating in a number of ways, although greatly influenced by the particular environment, social and natural, of the person who has reached maturity.[5]

There are also differences in purpose. I would suggest that Native American oratory, when addressed to a culturally and racially mixed audience, carries messages intended for Indians and other messages intended for both those outside the culture and within it. The messages intended for Indians carry the same purpose as narrative in Native cultures, to bring the people back into the circle, back into balance. The oratory, in other words, carries the intention of "homing" that William Bevis has noted in Native American novels. The messages intended for both those inside and outside of the culture are intended to *do* something for the people, whether this is to obtain a boon, negotiate terms of an agreement between cultures, or simply to express how some cross-cultural interaction has affected the people. In all instances, these messages are examples of Margaret Szasz's "culture brokering," texts coming from someone serving in the capacity of a cultural go-between. While I do not want to relegate those of us who are American Indian literary critics to the role of the mixed-blood in *A Man Called Horse*—"I've got a lot to learn, and you, Metis, you are going to teach me"—it is one of the roles we do fall into by nature of our association with the academy. Perhaps more important, it is one of the roles we fill as "a network . . . of writing Indians," if we see ourselves working in much the same way that Lisa Brooks sees the writing Indian community of Occom, Brant, Aupaumut, and others. I hope for us that there is just as "profound" an "exchange of knowledge."

There are also many other differences, not the least of which is the valuing of, as opposed to the need to resolve definitively, paradox in the argument. Confusion *can be* a positive value, it is the nexus of growth, as it makes people think for themselves. Betty Booth Donahue shares that

> In an interview, the Reverend Mr. Randy Jacob, a Choctaw scholar from Broken Bow, Oklahoma, explains that the well composed American Indian text is designed to confuse the hearer or reader. In the oral tradition, good story tellers do not tell all of the story. The hearer/reader must supply the missing parts of a narrative and comprehend the point of the work by means of his or her own intellectual efforts. For this reason, many oral works do not move along a chronological plot line in which first one event happens and then another. Works in the oral tradition seldom demonstrate cause and effect. Events transpire, and the hearer/reader must infer possible cause and effect, significance, and chronology if such categories are necessary for comprehending the meaning of a narrative. Since a narrative assumes different meanings as the interpretive abilities of the hearer/reader change with age and experience, narrative, like the hearer/reader, stays in a constant state of interpretive motion. All of this is not to say that there is no truth to a story; it is to say, however, that truth or meaning must be perceived by a Choctaw in his own time and in his own way.[6]

Duane Big Eagle puts it this way: "Many American Indian people have a greater acceptance of paradox than is common in many European and Western cultures. Pointing out to a Native American that they have just said something contradictory might only bring the response: 'So?' . . . Paradox may be seen as the essential nature of existence."[7] Vine Deloria says, "American Indians . . . [recognize] that premature analysis will produce anomalies and give incomplete understanding. When we reach a very old age, or have the capability to reflect and meditate on our experiences, or even more often have the goal revealed to us in visions, we begin to understand how the intensity of experience, particularity of individuality, and the rationality of the cycles of nature relate to each other."[8]

Before proceeding with an analysis of two articles I see as rhetorical models, I would like to summarize the elements I envision as possibly being included in a rhetoric for Native American literary discourse. Then I would like to show how some of these elements work to create meaning in Samson Occom's "A Short Narrative of My Life."

A rhetoric for Native American literary discourse would be tribally centered, with intertribal connections. In fact, it would recognize the connectedness of "All My Relatives." Janice Acoose does just that in this volume when she says, "I introduce this paper by "honoring *Ni' Wahkomakanak* from both a writing and speaking *Koochum* place that, like Nêhiyaw-Métis-Nahkawè ceremonial traditions invokes the spirit-presence of ancestors as well as the living presence of 'all my relations.'" Tol Foster, moreover, reminds us in his analysis of Will Rogers that our predecessors writing in English did this as well. He says, "Rogers engaged in a rhetoric, and I would argue, a pedagogy, of relation by imagining himself in relation to his colonizers, and imagining a relation between his colonizers and the colonized of the world."

This rhetoric would use an indirect form of discourse, based on synthesis rather than analysis, and be nonlinear/holistic, with meaning-filled gaps (that which in the oral appear as pauses and appear in my writing here as dividing lines between sections of text). Our penumbras, in other words, are the universe, are all of creation, as a Native worldview would posit the criticism as part of the ongoing Story of All Our Relations.

Criticism written in this vein would show an awareness of the power of words. Again I refer to Acoose's work in this volume for an example:

> When I place in the written text *Nokom*, *Nicapan*, *Nimosom*, they become speaking voices of Nêhiyaw-Métis-Nahkawè culture-specific stories that interrupt conventional forms of textual criticism and create spaces for cultural differences in the discourse of indigenous siteratures. When I name and place *No'simak* Alijah-Blue and Angelina-Nicole in this text, they becomes rooted in collective memories and linked to the past; their textual presence ensures that future generations will always re-member Nêhiyaw-Métis-Nahkawè storytelling traditions. When I name and place in this written text my Nêhiyaw-Métis-Nahkawè cultures, ceremonial traditions, ancestors, and present system of relations, I perform an "honoring" cultural ritual that both invites culturally like-minded readers and welcomes cultural outsiders.

Additionally, Acoose finds this in McLeod's work: "He therefore bundles medicined Nehiyâwiwin words into the fabric of written English. As the medicine-powered words transfuse the text, organisms within the cultural body become revitalized. McCleod's ritualizing critical performance adheres to important cultural protocol that honors Nehiyâwiwin being, both spiritual and physical."

This proposed Native critical discourse would include repetition and recursivity, which Ron McFarland points out is "perhaps the fundamental tool of rhetoric . . . [and] is one of the basic features of traditional Native American poetry and is typical of oral poetry in general."[9] This carries over to the contemporary, as McFarland points out in regard to Sherman Alexie's work. Joy Harjo's poems and the entire body of Leslie Silko's work provide other excellent examples.

Like Native literature, the critical work would defy genre boundaries. Greg Sarris's *Keeping Slug Woman Alive: A Holistic Approach to American Indian Texts* provides an example of this and is seminal to all progression toward changing the terms of discourse in the field, though I do feel it is closer to reader-response than it is to what I am envisioning. Also notable in this regard, though in a different discipline, was J. L. Vest's presentation "Comparative African and American Indian Philosophy" at the American Philosophical Association Pacific Division Conference held in Albuquerque, April 5–8, 2000.

Our criticism would allow for paradox, recognizing it as a nexus of growth. As a Native reader, Acoose does not feel she *has* to resolve Seesequasis's Uncle

Morris/Malcolm Norris. She allows the character to retain his shape-shifting identity as well as his religious and sacrilegious nature. An even better example in this volume is the analogy of the two fires borrowed by Foster:

> Imagine two Indian communities who live in close proximity to each other, separated by a mountain. A non-Native visitor arrives as the first community [and] . . . is informed that the tribe's council fire is the center of the universe [and] . . . [t]he following day, the outlander and representatives of the first tribe travel to the other community. The elders of the new tribe declare that their council fire is the center of the universe, and the members of the first tribe nod their assent. Confused, the visitor asks her host, "I thought you said that your fire was the center." The Indian replies, "When we're there, that is the center of the universe. When we are here, this is the center.[10]

The Native critical discourse I desire would value communally made meaning, as Native cultures have since time-immemorial, and, in connection with this, it would utilize an experiential-based auctoritas. Just as in Native discourse, authority is centered in my experiences primarily, but I can refer to what I know of my peoples' experiences—both my tribal peoples and my peoples in my field. This appears in Native discourse as "what I've been told," often preceded by a "they say" or similar construction based on tribal language devices for referring to an authority beyond the realm of personal knowledge.

This discourse would have an accruing context of meaning, one that mimics the continual acculturation that occurs with maturation and results in the elders being those who are the most accultured, the most mature, who have the greatest body of contextual knowledge. This is what is so impressive to me about Acoose's work here, despite our differences. Her positioning of herself as *Koochum* reflects not only her individual and familial identity, not only her cultural grounding and use of communally made meaning, but also her own growth as a writer during the course of developing this volume. Her chapter itself *layers* meaning, mirroring the development of the very knowledge it conveys. I honor her here as my critical Elder, deserving of our respect in the academic Native community as our elders are in our traditional communities.

Like American Indian oratory and everyday discourse, this critical framework would not only take into account, but be grounded in, the identity of the speaker. Who I am has a direct bearing on what I know, as I can only know what I have experienced personally. I can *believe* what I have heard from (read of) others, but I can only report it as such. Traditional introductions give this information as well as a context for listeners that goes beyond it. Eugene Blackbear, Jr., says,

> I just follow that standard format. I talk about good deeds. I talk about the credentials of that person. I talk about the reputation of that person. I talk about genealogies. In regard to good deeds, what I usually like to do is give some information about hospitality and etiquette. As far as

reputation, I give some information about accomplishments, ceremonial standing, belonging to a member of a traditional group, warrior society, or traditional chieftainships. Genealogies depend on tribe. For instance, for the Cheyenne, this would be paternal relationships, going back for four or five generations so that people in the crowd will know how they are related to that person.[11]

Traditional introductions let the hearer/reader know who the person is and what they have accomplished in relation to his or her people. This is why Mary Crow Dog (née Brave Bird) starts her book by saying, "I am Mary Brave Bird. After I had my baby during the siege of Wounded Knee they gave me a special name—Ohitika Win, Brave Woman, and fastened an eagle plume in my hair, singing brave-heart songs for me. I am a woman of the Red Nation, a Sioux woman. That is not easy."[12] Mary Crow Dog lets us know who she is—in intertribal terms, because of her involvement with the Indian movement, and in tribally specific terms—and gives us a recount of her coup, a coup that marked her as a warrior among her comrades. She spends the rest of the first chapter building on this, giving histories and genealogies of both her and her (now ex-) husband's families, as well as personal history in regard to what she is about to relate. She gives us the context from which she is speaking, what gives her the right to say what she is about to say.[13]

This does not mean that only Indian scholars should write about American Indian literature or teach it. As Patrice Hollrah says, white scholars are, admittedly, "limited by their position, but at the same time, not all of them attempt to speak with the authority of cultural insiders. There are white scholars who consciously listen to what the Native scholars and critics prescribe in terms of approaches to the literature, whether those are tribal-specific cultural and historical contexts, issues of sovereignty and connections to the land, and/or literary criticisms developed from the literature of the tribe in question." Hollrah quotes Wahpetonwan Dakota history scholar Angela Cavendar Wilson, who "suggests that white scholars consult American Indian sources for the cultural insiders' perspectives, and if they do not, they should acknowledge the limitations of their white perspectives in their work."[14]

As I mentioned earlier, Womack's *Red on Red* includes within the analysis of Native literature some very insightful rhetorical analysis as well; I would like to return to it as a source for two additional elements, both of which I feel are very important. In *Red on Red*, Womack claims that "Native literary aesthetics must be politicized and that autonomy, self-determination, and sovereignty serve as useful literary concepts." He further explains, "I will seek a literary criticism that emphasizes Native resistance movements against colonialism, confronts racism, discusses sovereignty and Native nationalism, seeks connections between literature and liberation struggles, . . . roots literature in land and culture, . . . and attempts to find Native literature's place in Indian country, rather than Native literature's place in the canon."[15]

Or, as the character of Stijatti says in one of the interchapter sections:

> How can Native Lit Critters carry on a discussion of Creek culture as a conversation *with* Creek people rather than speaking *for* Creek people? How can white Lit Critters become helpers, rather than Indian experts? How can they promote the work of Native people over their own, and still was keep up their own good efforts at contributing to Native literary development? How can Indian Lit Critters do the same thing—encourage the budding talent in their own tribes, the young ones who have new things to say, the kids singing themselves back together?

Womack's work suggests, and I agree, that a Native literary discourse must be political, must be mimetic, as the literature is, and must be a radical act of love for the Peoples.

On the basis of his analysis of Louis Oliver's work, Womack proposes that the inclusion of humor, an essential element of Indian discourse, even when the subject matter is serious or sacred, can aid in "analyzing Native literature in a manner that Indian people can immediately recognize and relate to." Womack's analysis, moreover, of Alexander Posey's writing, gives a breakdown of some of the rhetorical devices used in Indian humor—the humorous situations that often arise because of cultural differences when Indians have to function in a "changing world"; the humor that can be found even in the dark circumstances of Indians cooperating in colonial/assimilationist actions against their own tribes; the humor derived from naming (i.e., a character's name can have humorous implications regarding personality); Indian slang; unusual expressions; reworked clichés; botched English; onomatopoeic puns; sexual humor (it is important to note here that Native cultures traditionally took a very relaxed and natural approach to sexuality, both hetero and homosexuality, and that sexual situations and humor are a vital part of the oral tradition); and, finally, understatement.[16]

Let me add one last note on a rhetorical element of Indian humor that Womack mentions later in his book, an element that is not only illustrated in the Creek dialect passages between the chapters, but that is a function of Indian joking on a daily basis—Indian "talk" is filled with "Indianized" allusions. In short, contemporary Native American discourse continually takes in and absorbs dominant culture by making elements of it Indian.[17]

As I have mentioned previously, I believe our strongest rhetorical models in print have come from other areas within Native studies. Lee Hester, Choctaw philosopher and coeditor of *Ayaangwaamizin: The International Journal of Indigenous Philosophy*, has written an academic paper using a traditional Native rhetoric. This article, entitled "Pishukchi: One Choctaw's Examination of the Differences in English and Choctaw Language Use," illustrates the same principles and rhetorical structures seen throughout Native American written and spoken discourse.

Hester begins his article by briefly contextualizing who he is: "I must admit that I am Choctaw, a citizen of the Choctaw Nation of Oklahoma." He admits his limitations. "I'm a . . . learner. Though I learned some Choctaw at my grandmother's knee, she had already lost much of her language and I was forced to learn it more as a second language." Throughout, he employs indirect discourse[18] combined with humor, all the while being "polemic" in a positive sense of the word. For instance, he explains that the word "Choctaw" was once used colloquially in English to refer to unintelligible speech, but says that "it turns out that even when Choctaws speak English, it is still 'strange or incomprehensible.' If you look at historical documents and are at all familiar with how Choctaws talk, you see instance after instance where the Choctaws failed to make themselves understood. Officials of the United States government, try as they might, have been unable to crack the Choctaw code and are as much in the dark now as they were 200 years ago." Moreover, the whole purpose behind his paper is double-edged; while the paper is ostensibly about language differences, the choice of the outside material he uses to develop his argument—the words of government officials during the removal process and Choctaw oratorical reactions to them—at the same time builds a case that his people were wronged in this process. As most academics are unfamiliar with this style of discourse and, as the paper *is* about language use differences, Hester points out his use of indirect discourse directly; he "culture-brokes." After Hester employs a personal narrative regarding something he learned from Choctaw elder Aleckton Davis in support of his argument—another aspect of a tribal-centered discourse—he says,

> This story in itself probably explains all the differences between Choctaw language use and English language use. Indeed, if this were a completely Choctaw paper, I would only smile and thank you for your attention at this point and consider the presentation clear. I have said all I can say. From a Choctaw perspective, from here on it is up to you. If you think hard and long, if you build up enough stories like this, you'll eventually come to understand the differences in Choctaw and English language use. It would be almost insulting you if I were to presume to continue and explain the differences. Politeness—respect—would prevent me from ever being so presumptuous . . . the key here is thought and context. To understand many instances of Choctaw language use, you have to think about what is said and bring as much context and outside knowledge into your thoughts as possible. What is more, you have to be willing to suspend judgement about what was ostensibly said. It may not be and often isn't the most important message. This is hard for an academic. . . . The rest of this paper, and all that came before, is not all that I am saying. In some cases it may not even be what I'm saying. Since I am not as subtle as my ancestors, portions of this exercise will be obvious—I hope this is not insulting. It is my failing, not yours, if the answers come too easily. With luck some of the answers may not appear for years.[19]

In conclusion, Hester uses, at least in a modified form, a tribally centered style of discourse to convey an academic message, one that though the presenter is

Choctaw and his language use is based on Choctaw English models, is, I would suggest, familiar to most other American Indian speakers of English. Unlike dialect writing,[20] Hester's writing is understandable to an intertribal audience (even if they've never met a Choctaw or heard a Choctaw talk) as well as to academics.

The anthology *As We Are Now: Mixblood Essays on Race and Identity*, edited by William S. Penn (Nez Perce/Osage), offers yet another model that I see as appropriate. Penn says that the selections in this book

> Cross boundaries in the fields of storytelling, ethnography, history, psychology, dance, music, and art—and are often narrative and non-linear: rooted as they must be in the overwhelming respect for the power of words and the oral tradition of "telling" or "saying," . . . the new generation of Native American writers is appropriating the genres and modes of the Western tradition to its own purposes. . . . This narrative mixture of mode is often produced by the act of reclamation, an imaginative act of identity and selfhood that must be reenacted every time a mixblood writer sets out to write, an act that always involves recognizing the gap, entering the dialogue between disagreements (European or Native American, linear or circular, direct or indirect, historical image or historical actuality), and then finding a way to bridge that gap—or to express it.[21]

Particularly of note in this collection is Patricia Penn Hilden's "Ritchie Valens Is Dead: *E Pluribus Unum*," a synthesis that epitomizes William Penn's description above and, at the same time, is recognizable within a traditional tribal framework. This essay, for me, is the best written example of a mode of discourse I label as "ndn," postmodern, but not postcolonial, as we are indeed still colonized, a polycultural outgrowth of tribal discourse, layered with code-switching allusions in the spirit of WaWa Calachaw Bonita Nunez: "I am a seeker of Truth. / And [I] search out all things regardless where."[22]

Penn Hilden, like Hester, introduces herself as a mixed-blood at the beginning of the essay and does acknowledge in a sense her limitations—she is three-quarters Anglo.[23] Also like Hester, she employs indirect discourse throughout the essay, but she does so in more structural terms, using multiple headings and subheadings, leaving the reader to fill in the gaps himself or herself between sections of her essay such as pieces of law, quotes from elders, a negative review of Disney's *Pocahontas*, bits of poems by Sherman Alexie and Wendy Rose, and her own expository prose and personal narratives. Additionally, she appropriates allusions from mainstream culture and makes them her own, the title being a perfect example of this, her indirect commentary on the subject of her essay, California ideals of "real" American identity and whiteness and the reality of its mixed-blood past and present. As Penn says in the introduction to the volume:

> The classical Maya wrote their histories by recording and *giving context to* the events considered to be most important to the people. Narrative essays, I suggest, do the same. Thus, in contextualizing ideas, they may well seem loose, nonlinear, fractured, or digressive. But in reality, they are carefully structured, and each structure may be both described and defended. They are not loose, but oral and even conversational—as though talking to a really imagined audience; they are nonlinear only in the sense that for most of us all things are connected, and thus to give a proper context dialogue rarely follows from A to B to Z; they are not digressive but, as I have begun to insist, "augmentative"—and augmentation . . . adds connection and context, gives life to dull "facts," and celebrates the power of imagination, metaphor, and the cross-connections between the speaker and the listener, which is another way to claim that narrative essays work toward community, toward inclusion and not to the exclusivity of colonization. The narrative essay is, in my opinion, where scholarly or academic writing is heading, or where it will head if it wants to revive its relation to an audience greater than seven.[24]

I believe readings based on models such as these offer possibilities for a more tribal-centered discourse, one that is both open-ended and respects the texts and authors as subjects negotiating meaning rather than dissecting them as objects.

> Oratory receives . . . little . . . understanding on the part of the white public, owing to the fact that oratorical complications include those of Indian orators.
>
> Luther Standing Bear
> "What the Indian Means to America"

Much of the critical writing on Samson Occom, Mohegan Indian, Christian minister, and author of the work A. LaVonne Brown Ruoff calls "the first Indian best-seller,"[25] centers naturally on his role as a mediator between Indians and whites in the colonial era and on the role Christianity played in colonization and assimilation. The works of Dana D. Nelson, Eileen Razzari Elrod, David Murray, Michael Elliot, Margaret Connell Szasz, and Bernd Peyer have all focused on some aspect of how Occom manages to address both colonizing and colonized audiences at once, offering a plurality of meaning in one piece of discourse. Of course, all of this scholarship grows out of an increasing interest in applying a Bakhtinian dialogic to the study of written Native literature, a literature that for a variety of reasons is inevitably cross-cultural. But as Kimberly Blaeser has pointed out in "Native Literature: Seeking a Critical Center," even in studies that attempt to create a "dual vision to adequately appreciate the richness of Indian Literature, the native half to that vision has still been conspicuously absent."[26]

To a reader familiar with Native rhetorics, what is "conspicuously absent" in the studies of Occom's heteroglossia is any mention of indirect discourse. Though several scholars arrive at interpretations at times that are similar to those that can be derived with an awareness of this phenomena in Native speech, often their cultural distance has caused them to arrive at conclusions divorced from a Native reality. Even when their interpretations are more harmonious with those based on Native rhetorics and epistemologies, studying how Occom uses, or more accurately, adheres to, this "rule" of politeness enriches and expands their readings. When someone has done something either wrong or foolish, when an error needs to be addressed, care is often taken, at least traditionally, that that person does not feel "put on the spot," that he or she can remedy his or her mistake without losing honor. Implication, rather than explication, is the usual means of conveying this message. Barbara Duncan recalls the time she told her Cherokee friend, Hawk Littlejohn, about some relationship difficulties she was experiencing. Rather than telling her she was co-dependent, Littlejohn told her this story:

> "You know, once there was an old man crossing over Soco Gap . . . going East from Cherokee towards Maggie Valley. And it was the fall of the year, and it was cold. And just as he got over the top of the gap, and was starting down, he looked down and saw a rattlesnake laying there beside the trail. And it was frozen, about frozen to death. And because he was ani-yunwiya, one of the real people, he had had compassion on his relative. And he reached down and picked up that rattlesnake and put it inside his shirt to warm it up. Well, he was coming down the mountain, and he felt the snake move a little bit. And he came down a little further, and the snake moved a little bit more. Come on down the mountain, and the air was getting warmer, and the snake was moving around. Come on down a little more, and the snake was moving around, and it bit him. And he reached inside his shirt and pulled the snake out and said, 'Why'd you bite me? I picked you up and saved your life, and now you've bitten me and I might die!' And the snake said, 'You knew I was a rattlesnake when you picked me up.' "
>
> I sat there for a minute taking this in. "You knew I was a rattlesnake when you picked me up," Hawk repeated.
>
> "Uh huh," I said, "and this means?"
>
> "If you know somebody's a rattlesnake," he said, "you don't have to pick them up."[27]

Straightforwardly saying that the person in question was bad for Duncan would have been rude, not only because talking badly of people is typically considered rude, but also because Duncan's foolishness would have been pointed out. Additionally, despite the emphasis on the group among tribal peoples, Native Americans have a great deal of regard for an individual's autonomy in making personal decisions. Littlejohn, while he obviously cares enough for his friend that he would like to see her out of a destructive relationship, avoids directly telling her what to do. Had Duncan been accustomed to indirect discourse, the story alone would have sufficed. Even when she indicates with her question that she does not see how the story relates to the earlier portion of their conversation, Littlejohn finds other ways to imply this rather than fully explicating his "reading" of her situation.

Violating this rule of polite speech brings censure. Choctaw attorney Scott Kayla Morrison tells of the time her aunts were giving her advice after she had graduated from college. One aunt, Aunt Opal, an alcoholic who rarely contributed to these sessions, joined in with a comment.

> Aunt Little Al's raised eyebrow at Aunt Opal's remark was the only indication of surprise. Aunt Opal was still able to be coherent, as this rare moment of sharpness indicated. The aunts exchanged bare glances, not at Aunt Opal, but at Little Al for showing surprise. She was still not ready to be called plain "Alice," and a helluva long way from being called "Big Al." Children seeking counsel from elders called for a certain decorum, decorum which comes from internal control over individual emotions. This solemn discussion concerned the collective interest of the community. It did not relate to the individual concern of Aunt Opal being sober. "Big Al" would have known that. Even plain "Alice" may have suspected that. But Little Al did not, and thus had acted on her impulse. She had a long way to go, but the aunts were in no hurry.[28]

Alice's foolish or childish behavior in showing surprise, albeit without actual speech, is enough to be impolite.[29]

Knowing that Occom uses indirect discourse as a way to avoid offending anyone's honor, even when this meant he had to show respect to those who had shown him none, can make a great deal of difference in how we understand his intentions. Near the end of "A Short Narrative of My Life," Occom parenthetically interjects, "I speak like a fool, but I am Constrained,"[30] a phrase that has been commented on by various scholars. Elrod suggests that Occom makes an association here between himself and the apostle Paul by quoting 2 Corinthians 11, making a related association between the white missionaries and "the ungrateful and recalcitrant Corinthians."[31] Nelson reads the interjection as evidence of "Occom's own sense of self-division . . . a pained awareness of the contradictions that finally may have no resolution within the (mono)logic of colonialism. " She argues that "the cultural hegemony of colonialism . . . undercuts Occom's attempt to argue his own worth . . . exactly at that moment that he compares himself to a white missionary." As Occom makes this self-commentary right before he mentions his having acted as his own "interpreter," one example of how he should deserve at least as much, if not more pay, than white missionaries, Nelson feels it ironic that "as he asserts a fuller worth *because* of his ability to speak his native tongue, he finds himself compelled to apologize for his lack of eloquence in English."[32] While both Elrod and Nelson may have valid points, I feel that Occom makes this interjection because he feels forced to speak rudely, that is, directly, pointing out the un-Christian behavior of his superiors on the missionary boards. Despite his repeated appeals to Wheelock for help, despite the hardships he had endured in "Instructing [his] poor Kindred" because of his "uncommon Pity and Compassion to [his] Poor Brethren According to the Flesh,"[33] Occom has been treated abominably. The round of accusations leveled at him after his breaking with Wheelock—that he was not really Mohegan, that he was only recently converted for the purposes of the fund-raising tour—along with accusations of drunkenness and family troubles, leave Occom feeling as if he must defend himself forthrightly. But like "Little Al" in the excerpt from Morrison above, Occom would look *foolish* within his own cultural context for speaking so frankly, and he indeed seems to feel so.

The next section of his narrative, the anecdote of the "Poor Indian Boy" beaten by a young man in his white master's family, is evidence of Occom's use of indirect discourse as a rhetorical technique. Even though in this context he somewhat explicates himself—having already "made a fool of himself" anyway—Occom avoids pointing out that the ministers who have beaten him metaphorically, complaining of his service, are not his masters. Rather, they, like the young man in the story, are subject to answering to the master themselves. David Murray's interpretation of this passage, that it is "almost . . . an expression of solidarity" for Indians mistreated by whites, is too cursory.[34] Realizing that this passage of an Indian rhetorical device used in a Christian religious context, albeit a syncretic one, makes clear that Occom is suggesting that whites will have to answer to God for their treatment of him based on nothing more than his race, and he refuses to sacrifice his dignity any further by spelling out for them the moral that derives from their own scripture.

Occom clearly used indirect discourse in communicating with other Indians in ways that they recognized. In a letter to Wheelock regarding his work among the Oneidas, Occom relates this speech, in which the Oneida leaders give their consent to having him stationed as a missionary among them:

> Father, We are very glad you have come among us with the good Word of God, or God's News: And we think we are thankful to God, and give you Thanks, and the good Men who assisted you up here.
>
> We will, by the Help of God, endeavor to keep the Fire which you brought and kindled among us; and we take our *old Customs, Ways, and Sins,* and put them behind our Backs, and never look on them again; but will look straight forward, and run after the Christian Religion.
>
> Whenever we shall attempt to erect Schools among us, we beg the Assistance of good People your Way.
>
> *We intreat the great Men to protect us on our Lands, that we might not be encroached on by any People.*

> We request that the great Men would forbid Traders bringing any more Rum amongst us; for we find it not good; it destroys our Bodies and Souls.
>
> This Belt shall bind us together firm in Friendship for ever.[35]

The belt, a gift of wampum, places the exchange in an Indian context, the gift sealing what we now must view as an oral and written ("in shell" rather than "in stone") contract. And clearly Occom has implied to these chiefs, leaders who at this time were finding it impossible to fulfill their traditional obligations to their people, that the agreement to become Christian would do more than provide for their peoples' spiritual salvation, as the colonizers purported it would. Both sides for which Occom was a go-between had expectations not detailed in this oral contract. Occom recorded in his diary just prior to this event that the English had been demanding to extradite an Oneida accused of killing a Dutchman. While we cannot know what Occom's intentions were, we do know that a similar case, that of Moses Paul, involved alcohol, and we do know how devastating alcohol was, and is, to traditional Native cultures and in the lives of individual Native peoples. Additionally, Sir William Johnson, who negotiated with the Oneida regarding this incident, reports in his diary that the Oneidas were "in a very wretched situation . . . for the want of provisions . . . they were starving." And Wheelock's own correspondence suggests that his real reason for sending Occom and his brother-in-law, David Fowler, was not to establish a mission, but rather to recruit more students: " 'a fine Opportunity this to obtain Boys Judiciously chosen for our Design from remote Nations.' " The collusion of Christianity in the form of missionizing and capitalism in the form of alcohol trade once again *really* add up to nothing more than methods of colonization.[36]

While Peyer indicates that the Oneidas might expect the "requests" they make in this "meeting," as he terms it, will be fulfilled by Occom's residing among them as a missionary, an understanding of indirect discourse in combination with the knowledge that this is an oral and written contract reveals even more. Obviously, Occom has implied to the Oneida leaders, whom he would not wish to offend by pointing out directly their failure to fulfill traditional obligations to their people, that whites will tolerate their continued existence if they will assimilate, that this will be the only way in which they will now be able to care for their people. *Sin*, for these Indian Christians, is the maintenance of traditional *Customs* and *Ways*. Occom's strictness with the Oneidas in this regard, noted by Gideon Hawley, a white missionary, as stricter than necessary, is his attempt to save them physically by making them appear less Indian. And Occom's concern over the alcoholism induced in the people by the machinations of empire, which Wheelock refers to in a letter to Rev. George Whitefield, admittedly one likely cause of their impoverished circumstances, also is a concern that they are being stereotypically Native in the eyes of the colonizers, making them even more susceptible to attacks on their sovereignty.[37]

An experience Occom had on the way to the Oneidas offers convincing evidence that Occom himself could not have believed that "acting white" necessarily made one a Christian. Having traveled on the outskirts of New York City, Occom records his shock in his diary, a forum in which he is obviously much more straightforward about his opinions:

> But I never Saw a Sabbath Spent so by any Christian People in my Life as some Spent it here . . . Drunkards were Realing and Staggering in the Streets, others tumbling off their Horses, there were others at work in their farms, and if ever any People under the Heavens Spoke Hells Language, these People did, for their Mouths were full of Cursings, Prophaning Gods Holy Name—I greatly Mistake if these are not the sons and Daughters of Belial . . .
>
> I have thought there was no Heathen but the wild Indians but I think now there is some English Heathen, where they Enjoy the Gospel of Jesus Christ too. Yea, I believe they are worse than ye Savage Heathens of the wilderness.[38]

Occom, in this state of mind, cannot truly believe the Oneidas should give up their mode of dress and change their hairstyles in order to be more Christlike. Rather, as the agreement between them implies, Occom believes these changes necessary to prevent their being uprooted by whites.

These few examples of how the Indian rhetorical tradition of indirect discourse informs Occom's writings suggest to me that further examination of his works from a Native viewpoint to see what we can learn for our own writing is warranted. His "A Sermon Preached at the Execution of Moses Paul, an Indian," delivered to a mixed audience, does offer itself up to a dialogic examination like his other works do, as the scholars mentioned in my introduction indicate by their methods. But including the Indian half of this equation is the only way we can access a fuller interpretation. Michael Elliot asks of the sermon, "Did Native Americans understand that Occom was delivering a different message to them than to his Anglo audience? Could Anglo-Americans see that he questioned their treatment of American Indians? To what degree did any of his listeners or readers question the sincerity of Occom's Christian faith?"[39] While Elliot acknowledges that Occom uses a "pluralistic rhetoric," a familiarity with Indian rhetorics is plainly needed to answer his questions fully. It will only be then that Occom's role as "cultural broker," to borrow Szasz's term, can be more comprehensively understood. I would also suggest that further studies of Native rhetorics in other texts, written and otherwise, might be fruitful in developing our own methodologies and praxis. Moreover, this kind of study would give us as Native scholars the support we need to validate Native ways of constructing arguments in the academy. As Acoose bemoans, "With great expectations, I fervently search the pages for reflections of an author's nation of origin, ancestors, language, and expressions of national sovereignty. Often I'm saddened to 'discover' Natives,

Indians, full-bloods, half-bloods, and aboriginals (to use just a few choice nomenclatures) who have ceded not only vast territories of land, but also the territories of imagination and of voice." If we want our texts, our critical works, to "reach home" in our communities and not just in the academy, we need to speak to our communities in ways that are culturally *acceptable* and *recognizable.* By doing so, we will also reinforce to our Native students, no matter what tribe, that *their* ways of arguing, their elders' ways of speaking, are productive, are useful, and offer up different results from mainstream arguments. We can send them, as well as their texts and ours, back home with intellectual, hermeneutic, and rhetorical sovereignty intact.

Notes

1. Walters, *Talking Indian*, 30–41.
2. Womack, *Red on Red*, 5.
3. Burke, "Teaching American Indian Literature."
4. Ibid.
5. Vine Deloria, *Spirit and Reason*, 13–14.
6. Donahue, "Observations," 68.
7. Big Eagle, "Notes for Teachers," personal communication.
8. Vine Deloria, *Spirit and Reason*, 14–15.
9. McFarland, "Sherman Alexie's Polemical Stories," 28.
10. The stomp-dance grounds at Stoke's in the deep woods of eastern Oklahoma, it might be mentioned, are, as many other grounds are, "polycentric" in this way. Of course, the fire that is at the center of the dance circle and is crucial in ceremonial terms does not change, but what it represents changes with the songs, alternating Cherokee discourse with Creek. That is, both Creek and Cherokee people use the grounds simultaneously, and the only way I personally know to distinguish whether the upcoming song will be Creek or Cherokee is to listen for the "Lu-ga!" or "Dak-si!" at the beginning of it. Maintaining tribal sovereignty while working together to preserve common ceremonial ways has been worked quite well for a long period of time. For instance, some people differ on the appropriate time of year for stomp dancing, so those people do not come out to dance when they feel it is inappropriate. There are other differences as well, in the stories of how fire was brought to Oklahoma, for example, but few if anyone, even those who believe the Creeks were the only ones who brought fire, would consider all the Cherokees, many of whom have Creek ancestry, to be Creek, though Cherokees by definition are "people of one fire," a very important point both culturally and spiritually.

Foster's analysis of this, by the way, provides proof for "constant flux," a key component of Leroy Little Bear's Native paradigm, so feared as too general by those who only endorse tribally specific approaches. Because of this embracing of paradox, I would argue against Foster's focus on "deeply divisive relations between communities" as an exclusive—double-entendre intended—approach. We must be inclusive as well as exclusive; we must look at similarities as well as differences.

Finding these similarities as I have done in "Back to the Blanket" and as Leroy Little Bear has done throughout his nurturing of a contemporary academic oral tradition here at the University of Lethbridge and at Harvard is anything but "simplistic." Rather it requires, I would suggest, long-term analysis of holistic synthesis, something I gather Little Bear has done through sheer experience and I know that I have only acquired through a combination of academic study and traditional study under the instruction of Eugene Blackbear, Sr. Traditional epistemology—with physical, spiritual, mental, and emotional sacrifice—is grueling, but a thirty-thousand-year-old pedagogy offers up much to the learner.

11. Blackbear, personal interview, September 7, 2001.

12. Crow Dog, *Lakota Woman*, 3.

13. Unlike Sherman Alexie's character Marie Polatkin, whom Patrice Hollrah reminds us has an issue, like some Indian and non-Indian scholars, with "as told to" texts, I do not believe Mary Brave Bird Crow Dog's voice is erased or subsumed by Richard Erdoes in their jointly authored book. Neither do I believe that Wilma Mankiller's voice is erased by Michael Wallis in her book. Both of these women are strong, powerful, and unlike the early "as told to" authors, very much alive. I do believe either would speak out if she felt erased in her "own" text.

14. Hollrah, "Sherman Alexie's Challenge," 32, 33.

15. Womack, *Red on Red*, 11. Womack's point is developed throughout the book; see, in particular, his introduction, 75, 150–51, and 205–206.

16. Ibid., 210, 136, 156–58.

17. Ibid., 178. This can easily be observed by attending a powwow and hearing a good emcee turn mainstream jokes into Indian jokes or by viewing American Indian humor sites on the web. For instance, from *http://twist.lib.uiowa.edu/amerind/ndnhumor.html* comes the following story:

Back in the 1950s, this old comedian/ventriloquist from back east was touring the rez. While he was on his little show circuit, he would stay and visit with some of his Navajo friends. They would share jokes, mostly pertaining to Hopis. As they sat and visited, they would think up ways he could use his little dummy to tell the jokes and they'd laugh for hours into the night.

A couple of nights later, he had a big gig in Gallup. He performed to a full house of mostly Navajos. He got the biggest response when he told the Hopi jokes.

So he went on and on with them, bringing the room to laughter as loud as thunder. Then all of a sudden what seemed to be out of nowhere, this man stood up from the middle of the crowd and yelled out loudly, "How dare you! I can't take this anymore!" and the room fell dead silent!

The ventriloquist turned pale white as sweat glistened on his brow under the spotlight.

"Who the hell do you think you are, insulting my people like that? You think us Hopis, we're all stupid, don't you?' yelled the Hopi man. "How dare you insult my people! Especially being a white guy and coming around here insulting me and my people. You know we're not as stupid as you and all these Navajos think we are. I come from a proud group of people and I am proud of who I am! We're not stupid! What do you have to say to that?"

The ventriloquist was mortified and replied, "I am *so* sorry, sir. I did *not* mean any disrespect. I'm only doing a show and I knew that this region here being mostly Navajo it would go over really well. Again I truly do apologize, sir, and . . ."

When abruptly the Hopi man interrupted and shouted back, "Shut the hell up and don't even speak to me! I don't even want to hear you! Besides, I'm not even talking to *you* anyway. I'm talking to that little guy on your damn lap!"

18. Here, as in my work elsewhere, I use the term "indirect discourse" to denote a common Native American speech phenomenon in which the speaker avoids directly stating something to the listener or listeners, instead implying meaning and expecting those hearing to make meaning for themselves.

19. Hester, "Pishukchi," 81–82, 82–84.

20. The Fus Fixico letters of Alexander Posey provide an excellent example of dialect humor.

21. Penn, *As We Are Now*, 3.

22. Quoted in Allen, *Spider Woman's Granddaughters*, v.

23. But Penn Hilden does not, as I admittedly wish she would have, let the reader know that her tribal heritage is Nez Perce. This is likely because she is sufficiently well known enough at this point to assume her readership knows this.

24. Penn, *As We Are Now*, 5.

25. Ruoff, *American Indian Literatures*, 62.

26. Blaeser, "Native Literature," 57.

27. Duncan, *Living Stories*, 16.

28. Quoted in Duncan, *Living Stories*, 94–95.

29. The tendency to use indirect discourse or other hints rather than offending someone's honor is so strong that Native Americans will sometimes violate other taboos just to avoid speaking directly. At a recent powwow I attended, a dancer had dropped an eagle feather without noticing it. Dropping an eagle feather is taken to be a very bad sign, and certain procedures have to be followed by the dancer in order to avoid repercussions and in order to show proper respect for the sacred nature of the feather. In cases like this one, where the dancer did not notice, it is the responsibility of the arena director to let the dancer know so he "can honor the feather out" properly. However, the arena director himself had failed to notice, giving those of us who had seen the feather fall a big dilemma. This arena director had been violating decorum all evening, upsetting many people greatly and, in general, making the evening tense for many of us. Despite this, and perhaps even because of it, no one wanted to offend his honor by pointing out the feather to him, showing him, in effect, that he had not been doing his job, that he had not been behaving properly all evening, and that now, his ill behavior was coming back on us all, manifesting itself there on the floor where we avoided stepping on it as if it were a sleeping baby or a sleeping copperhead. No matter how much we all stared at the feather each time we passed—and my husband says we all looked like a bunch of GIs who had just dropped the American flag at a state funeral—the arena director did not seem to catch on. Finally, in the confusion of people moving on and off the floor between dances, someone broke the taboo against touching the feather and retrieved it, leaving it on the emcee's table for the

arena director to find later and take care of. In this way, he would be able to come to terms with his misbehavior on his own, without being made aware of it publicly, even by those whom he himself had wronged earlier.

30. Occom, "Short Narrative," 618.
31. Elrod, "I Did Not Make Myself So," 142.
32. Nelson, "I Speak Like a Fool," 58.
33. Occom, "Short Narrative," 615.
34. Murray, *Forked Tongues*, 54.
35. Quoted in Blodgett, *Samson Occom*, 63–64. Emphasis added.
36. Ibid., 60, 61, 55.
37. Ibid., 64–65, 67.
38. Ibid., 56–57.
39. Elliot, "This Indian Bait," 235.

Blind Bread and the Business of Theory Making, by Embarrassed Grief

AS TOLD BY LEANNE HOWE

Introduction

She said, *"Let me tell."*

People assume that a writer begins a story with a blank piece of paper. But it's quite the opposite. First there is a question, a longing to know one thing, then another that causes a story to stalk the writer like a hunter after prey. When I began to write about how Natives reason together to translate the stories of our world, Embarrassed Grief appeared. My need to know, and perhaps my dreams, brought her across time and space to help me tell the story. She is the narrator, I am the translator. To be any good at translation, one must do a kind of disappearing act, which, in a way, signifies the trope of Native existence in America. We remain invisible. Yet we continue.

For the purposes of this volume, I will be substituting the word "theory" with "story" and engaging the essays of Christopher Teuton and Cheryl Suzack, but it will be through my characters that you will hear the story.

Overture

In the weeks before the passage of NAGPRA, the Native American Graves Protection and Repatriation Act, Embarrassed Grief stands weeping at the

---

LeAnne Howe (Choctaw) is currently the John and Renee Grisham Writer in Residence at the University of Mississippi, Oxford. She is also associate professor at the University of Illinois, Champaign-Urbana, in the American Indian studies program and in the MFA program in creative writing in English. Her first novel, Shell Shaker, *received an American Book Award in 2002 from the Before Columbus Foundation, and the French translation,* Equinoxes Rouge, *was a 2004 finalist for Prix Medici Estranger, one of France's top literary awards. Her collection of poetry,* Evidence of Red, *received an Oklahoma Book Award in 2006. She has also served as the narrator and screenwriter for* Indian Country Diaries: Spiral of Fire, *a ninety-minute PBS documentary. Her second novel,* Miko Kings, an Indian Baseball Story, *is forthcoming.*

corner of Dubuque and Clinton in Iowa City, Iowa—as is her custom. It is a ritual she's adopted from a photograph she saw in *National Geographic* illustrating how Quiché women protest against the Ladino-controlled government by weeping daily in the streets of Guatemala. However, Embarrassed Grief is not weeping for the remains of our ancestors stored in the bowels of the Smithsonian. At least that's not what her sign says. It reads: "Peace will come only when America recognizes its Native people."

I cringe. Embarrassed Grief doesn't look anything like the Quiché women in the photograph. Nor does she look particularly Native. She has green eyes, the pale skin of a dried cornhusk, and long colorless hair. No one on any reservation would ever mistake Embarrassed Grief for a rez girl because she's wearing rings on every finger, sandals, and a long swishy robe like Jesus. But she fits in here. This is Iowa City, Iowa, the "Athens of the Midwest," and Embarrassed Grief is vice president of the American Indian Student Association (AISA). She is also a graduate teaching assistant in the Department of English at the university. When she sees me, and a group of Indians, across the street, she dabs a white paper napkin at the corners of her puffy eyes, then heads straight for us.

I make an immediate about-face, hoping to avoid her, but she runs like a hulking bear and grabs me around the neck. It is amazing how fast she is for a woman her size.

"I hate the IHS in Tahlequah," she says, sobbing on my T-shirt. "Indian Health Services—they're killing my parents."

Under normal circumstances I would return her bear hug. (Oklahoma Choctaws are big huggers.) I would tell her that her parents are going to be all right. (Oklahoma Choctaws are also known for giving erroneous advice.) I would then offer to buy her a cup of coffee. But these are deviant times. I work at the University of Iowa and I'm totally out of my element, a duck out of water, a Choctaw out of Oklahoma. I'm surrounded by cranky academics. They question everything. They've got me doing it too. But to tell you the truth, I've always been a little cantankerous. I make no secret that I'm antagonistic toward Embarrassed Grief.

"You're right," I say. "The IHS is full of conniving murderers who would dissect the cadavers of their own mothers. If I were you, I'd tell my parents to give up their Cherokee identity and pretend to be starving, homeless white people. They'll get better health care on welfare."

Embarrassed Grief seems startled at the verve of my honesty and her eyes tear up again. "But we could change the IHS," she says sniffling. "I have an idea that . . ."

"Forget it. Go home and take your parents to real doctors. That's how you can truly be of service to them." I walk away, hoping she will stop pestering me. And stop making a spectacle of herself on behalf of Indians.

Later, at the Chicano and American Indian Cultural Center, when the subject of Embarrassed Grief comes up, I hiss in a menacing voice. "Something must be done about that woman. She's not Embarrassed, she's embarrassing. I've never seen an Indian woman cry like that in public."

"She's upset about her parents," says Debbie Begay. "Don't pick on her; she's had a difficult life. I heard what you told her."

Debbie is a young Navajo student and the mother of three children. She came to the University of Iowa to study economics.

"And what's up with her name?" I ask.

"Indians often change their names."

"The ones avoiding the law."

"Lots of tribes have naming ceremonies."

"The Cherokees around Tahlequah don't."

"How do you know?"

"I know."

Debbie sits cross-legged on the sofa and cradles her sleeping baby in one arm. "Besides," she says, opening a textbook with her free hand, "her name was changed for her."

"By whom?"

"Someone in the Philippines."

"Oh, sure."

"It's true. When she studied abroad to learn Spanish, she was drawn to a convent in Manila, and that's the name the sisters gave her. But she decided against becoming a nun."

"Why?"

"Because they told her she would have to give up playing softball."

I lean toward Debbie and whisper conspiratorially. "Do you hear yourself? These kinds of things just don't happen to real people."

"Maybe not to everyone," says Debbie, "but some people live extraordinary lives."

"You'll believe anything," I say, taking a couple of apples from my sack.

"Diné people will give the benefit of the doubt. You Oklahoma Indians are so mean. Leslie Silko is right about that."

I offer a slice of apple to Debbie. "Silko said what?"

She waves it away. "It's in all her stories. Oklahoma Indians think they're superior to Pueblo and Diné people."

"Define superior."

"What's the capital of Mamlaktu-al Bahrayn?" asks Debbie.

"Manama," I say, slicing another piece of apple. "The kingdom is east of Saudi Arabia in an archipelago of the Persian Gulf. But why are you using the country's formal Arabic name?"

Debbie looks sorrowful. "I didn't think you'd know it."

"Every Oklahoma Indian knows it," I quip. "We're from oil country, too, you know!"

We stare at each other for a moment. Other students are coming into the center with their children in tow. For now we realize our geography wars are over.

"Look," I say, "Embarrassed Grief is all drama and no substance. I don't care if she is a great softball player and a failed nun. White people are going to think we're all as wacky as she is."

"C'mon," says Debbie, "she's not hurting anyone."

Debbie smiles at her baby. "Have a little compassion. We're all Indians."

A month goes by and I try to forget about Embarrassed Grief and her weekly protests in downtown Iowa City. While I still believe she is an oversized chameleon, always taking up ludicrous causes—her most recent is a letter-writing campaign to U.S. congressmen, urging them to pass a law to regulate the earnings of taxicab drivers—Debbie Begay has made me feel self-conscious about my hostility. Why does Embarrassed Grief bother me so much? Am I wary of Embarrassed Grief because she has strange ideas and is willing to act on them? I haven't counted on my own intellectual deficiency as the cause of my dislike. That's hard to take. So later in the semester when Embarrassed calls a meeting of AISA, I decide to support her, no matter what kind of screwy idea she's come up with.

At the meeting, she does seem different. Gone are the sandals and robe. Instead, she wears a T-shirt and jeans. Before she gets up to speak, I sit with my dog-eared copy of *The Dialogic Imagination*, worrying that she has arranged to have us all arrested.

"I've been thinking about our old stories," she says. "While the bones of our storytellers still reside in the Smithsonian, they won't be there much longer. So in order to celebrate the passage of Public Law 101-601, and their imminent freedom, we should feed the homeless population in Iowa City on Thanksgiving Day. What a statement that will make, especially since Indians have been feeding the tired, the poor, the huddled, homeless masses yearning to breathe free since 1492. We should continue that tradition."

Her politics have agency in our group. Everyone (including me) becomes animated over the idea of taking control of our history. We vote to host a frybread giveaway and marshal our resources. We come up with about five hundred dollars to buy all the ingredients necessary to make enough frybread and bean soup to feed the local homeless. I volunteer to make the dough, and Debbie Begay offers to fry it. Embarrassed is in charge of publicizing the event and gathering the homeless.

On Thanksgiving Day we prepare the soup and frybread. When the first homeless people arrive at the door of the Chicano and American Indian Cultural Center, Embarrassed greets them with open arms. Throughout the day, over one hundred people arrive to be fed by the American Indian students.

In the beginning, Embarrassed is a very animated hostess. Often she converses in Spanish. Sometimes Chinese. She theorizes on the temperature at the center of the earth with one scruffy-looking gentleman as she offers him a second piece of frybread.

I am only able to catch fragments of her conversations.

"*Bakhtin, Foucault, Derrida*," she chants in a high-pitched voice. "Yes, I've known them all. Derrida once kissed me flush on the mouth. Drink plenty of liquids if you go out with him."

She doesn't wait for a response but moves on to the next person in line for frybread.

"Pluto isn't the farthest planet in our solar system," she says.

"I didn't know that," says an old gentleman. It's obvious he's too busy eyeing his plate of food to formulate a further response, so he just shrugs.

"Oh, don't doubt me, Sir," says Embarrassed. "I've been in outer space and there are seven more planets yet to be discovered."

"It could happen," I say in a low voice to Debbie.

Debbie and I are responsible for making the bread. As I roll out another dough ball and pass it to her, I add, "I've read about such things happening in the *National Enquirer*."

"Shush!" says Debbie. "Not another word."

Toward the end of our feast, Embarrassed Grief is showing signs of growing anxiety. She's talking faster, and more incoherently, about her theories on life, liberty, and the pursuit of happiness. She begins to wring her hands. When the last homeless couple has left the building, she sobs.

"Is Rome burning, or is it the frybread? You know St. Embarrassed was a Christian martyr during the Roman Empire. She was killed because she rescued the bodies of her slain brothers. I saw her in a dream once. I'm still trying to make sense of it so I can write a paper on her true identity."

"She's very keyed up," whispers Debbie.

"Overstimulation of the motor nerves," I say. "A serious case."

Debbie flashes me a cruel look and says that *our* friend is in bad shape and that we must take her to the hospital. "Are you going to help her, or just make jokes?" she asks testily.

"Okay, okay, I'll help."

I ask Embarrassed to step outside with me so we can talk over the politics of reciprocity among Indian tribes. As we breathe in the crisp November air of Iowa, I tell her that her idea of using our past to feed the future was a good idea.

"What's going to happen?" she asks, wiping her tears.

"Maybe you need to go home for a good rest," I answer.

We lock eyes. In that moment I realize that she has heard "Tahlequah" in the word "home." Place, land, home hold a more tribal meaning for her than I imagined. Embarrassed stands up, dries her eyes, and we fall silent and watch our breath make vapor rising in the night air.

Eventually, Debbie Begay drives her car into the parking lot of the Chicano and Native American Cultural Center. Other American Indian students have come to help Embarrassed Grief into the 1983 Oldsmobile along with Debbie's three children, a stray dog, and a sack of frybread. Before they drive away, Embarrassed rolls down her window and waves a piece of bread in the air.

"Home is like blind bread," she says to all of us in the parking lot.

"How's that?" I ask.

"Both nourish anyone who partakes of it, regardless of where they come from or who they are. I have a theory about that."

I wave until the car is out of sight. Since it is my turn to clean up the kitchen at the center, I use the time to think. Ever since I first met Embarrassed Grief, I thought something "big" was going to happen to her, but my scenarios have usually involved the police. I'd never imagined that I would learn from her.

Slowly life returned to normal at the Chicano and American Indian Cultural Center. For many months I continued to think about Embarrassed Grief and what might have happened to her after she left the university. In some ways she was like the woman in the Choctaw story *Ohoyo Chishba Osh*,[1] who came from far away only to leave left behind a strange gift that would benefit the people. The story goes something like this: Two Choctaw hunters are out traveling when they encounter a woman they've never seen before. The strange woman tells them she is from a place very far away. She then trades with the hunters, giving them seeds for their roasted hawk meat.

From these few seeds, the Choctaw were able to grow corn. In other words, through the exchange of stories, and a gift, corn changed the people in ways they could have never imagined. Today, corn remains one of America's leading exports, and according to the Kentucky Corn Growers Association, some thirty-five hundred foods and consumer and industrial products contain some form of corn.

Stories Are Theories

Native stories by Native authors, no matter what form they take—novel, poem, drama, memoir, film, or history—seem to pull together all the elements of the storyteller's tribe, meaning the people, the land, multiple characters, and all their manifestations and revelations, and connect these in past, present, and future milieu. (Present and future milieu means a world that includes non-Indians.) The Native propensity for bringing things together, for making consensus, and for symbiotically connecting one thing to another becomes a theory about the way American Indians tell stories. Oral or written, I have called this genre "tribalography."[2]

Embarrassed Grief is not unlike Redford McAlester, Tema Billy, and Adair Billy, all characters in my novel, *Shell Shaker*. All have traveled widely, traded information, adopted new tools, and then returned home with new ideas that are both dynamic and destructive. They are international and intertribal, reflecting a larger worldview that would have been as important in the past as it is in the present. That's the nature of tribal interactions—and for me that's when a story really begins to cook. I, as the translator of these events, want to know what comes next.

In "Blind Bread and the Business of Theory Making," Embarrassed is a

Cherokee from Tahlequah who travels to Manila to study abroad. She is adding experience and knowledge to her belief system. For reasons that aren't fully realized in the excerpt, Embarrassed leaves Manila and makes her way to Iowa before going back home to Tahlequah. One thing, though, is clear: being so far from "home" takes its toll on her emotional health.

In *Shell Shaker*, Redford McAlester also leaves home and tries organized religion. He preaches the Gospel and even travels to the Baptist seminary in Fort Worth, Texas, before going to schools back east. Eventually he returns home to run for chief of the Choctaw Nation of Oklahoma, and his emotional health affects the entire tribe.

Both sisters Tema Billy and Adair Billy also leave home. Tema Billy moves to New York and becomes a stage actress. When she returns home to help her family, she is able to save her sister Auda Billy by reciting lines from "The Conference of Birds," a twelfth-century mystical poem by Sufi author, Farid Ud-Din Attar. When Tema encounters an intruder in her mother's home she remembers an oral story about Choctaw warriors. Combining the oral Choctaw story with her experience in acting, Tema is then able to kill the invader. Anthropologist Jason Jackson has said that "linking the narratives in the present to speech and action in the past is an expression of what Richard Bauman, Dell Hymes, and others have called traditionalization."[3] In other words, my characters are doing some of the same things that Choctaws have done in the past. They link the stories they've heard about their ancestors with the stories they are living. This linking of the narratives breathes meaning into their world (as well as breathing life onto the pages of written stories).

In Christopher Teuton's essay in this volume, "Theorizing American Indian Literature" he makes it clear that he sees oral stories as a template for the ethical codes and social context of contemporary Cherokees. I could not agree more. While Teuton uses Cherokee creation stories as one example, the concept he elucidates plays out in the actions of my Choctaw characters. Two sisters, Delores and Dovie Love, in *Shell Shaker* enact the oldest Choctaw traditions concerning bone picking and burial. Their Choctaw elders taught them the stories.

Redford and Tema and Adair Billy all share similar characteristics with Embarrassed Grief in that they idealize their tribe's past. Embarrassed is also angry with her tribe for allowing the federal government to make a mess of her parents' health care. As her new name suggests, she's developed into a kind of perpetual sacrificial victim. The irony is that by allowing her name to be changed to that of a martyred saint, she loses the thing she wants to hold onto.

Cheryl Suzack argues in "Land Claims, Identity Claims" (in this collection) that indigenous feminism is crucial to changing tribal politics: "I examine how American Indian feminist critics have theorized a relationship between community identity, tribal history, and women's collective agency in connection with gender identity in order to create an oppositional space from which to restore gender identity as an analytical category in discussions of tribal politics and community values." In other words, American Indian women must assert themselves in tribal governance if tribes are to survive.

As vice president of the American Indian Student Association, Embarrassed Grief has a political role, as do many of the female characters in my stories. She argues for combining two federal events, the Thanksgiving holiday and the passage of Public Law 101-601, NAGPRA. In a metaphorical way, she's trying to link to Foucault's "archaeology of knowledge" in a literal way. NAGPRA, as most people are aware, provides a process whereby museums and federal agencies can "return" to their original homelands certain Native American cultural items—human remains, funerary objects, sacred objects, and objects of cultural patrimony—to lineal descendants, culturally affiliated Indian tribes, and Native Hawaiian organizations. Most American Indians (and ethnographers) consider their elders to be living libraries. Elders are great sources of history and story. Embarrassed and the other students link NAGPRA to Thanksgiving in America's history and story and acknowledge that the bodies of those held captive in the Smithsonian are sacred. Such sacred texts must therefore be returned to their tribal libraries, their homelands. In "Blind Bread and the Business of Theory Making," it is evident that insane or sane, healthy or sick, useful or useless, dead or alive Indians must return home. Indians[4]—the ones I know, the ones I admire, the ones I admonish, the ones I'm interested in writing about—go home. Embarrassed will do the same. Who knows what will happen to the Cherokees after she runs for tribal council? This is the beginning of the story equation that Native writers make for their readers. We link one thing to another thing.

Another point I want to stress is that Embarrassed Grief uses Bakhtin's ideas on how language registers conflicts between groups. Her protest sign reads, "Peace will come only when America recognizes its Native people." She's tried Foucault's ideas on objectivation and subjectivation and has determined she is both—objectified and subjectified.

Embarrassed also claims she's gone out with Derrida. She has swallowed deconstructionism and even talks about kissing him/it flush on the mouth. She argues that AISA should make a point of feeding the homeless on Thanksgiving in order to subvert the meaning of the holiday. What is implied is that Embarrassed, the other students, and even the narrator have read the many histories of contact between Indians and non-Indians. They've been reading the words that the ethnographers wrote down that their ancestors said—and they are now subverting the assumptions and challenging those same "nation-state" stories. Embarrassed says, "I've been thinking about our old stories," which signifies that she is doing what Jason Jackson says the Yuchi do when they read the stories of their ancestors in the texts and interpret them. "They possess a strong willingness to make new inquiries among themselves to reflect upon and refine their own interpretations of myth and ritual, and to extrapolate deeper interpretations based on further consideration and new evidence. . . . For the Yuchi today, the ethnographic record, rather than codifying belief and stifling this process, provides another resource enabling contemporary ritualists to maintain a dialogue with the old people who served both as consultants to earlier researchers and as the previous generation of Yuchi community leaders."[5]

In *Shell Shaker,* Auda Billy, Redford McAlester, and the Jesuit priest Renoir are engaged in this same process. Auda Billy, a historian, knows the oral stories of her family, and she has the material culture to prove it: burden baskets that belonged to her ancestors Haya and Anoleta. What does Auda do? She *writes* a story, a history of the Choctaws that is both from her oral history and from documents. In one scene Auda tries to tell what happened at an eighteenth-century Choctaw battleground, only to be challenged by her audience at an Oklahoma Historical Society event.[6] In other words, the audience does not agree with Auda Billy's theory of events that shaped her tribe's past.

At this point, it is important to stress again that "theory" and theories are themselves stories that literary critics tell. When Craig Womack asked us to write a collective document on theory that would guide future generations of American Indian and non-Indian scholars who teach American Indian, Alaska, and Native Hawaiian literatures, I was both pleased and skeptical. He asked *us* to create Native knowledge. I did not think I could do this alone, and I said so. However, as this book evolved, the process was revealed, and I realized I wasn't writing (or creating) alone. My characters, as well as the other authors in the volume, would create theory with me.

This is not unlike the way I work in fiction. When I'm in the writing zone, there are dozens of people standing around my computer screen watching what I type. First, there are my grandmothers, my mothers, uncles, aunts, ancestors, my children, and my characters. Next, other Indian writers enter my office and stand around the computer—N. Scott Momaday, Leslie Silko, Maurice Kenny, Simon Ortiz, Susan Power, Craig Womack, Joy Harjo, Phil Deloria, Brenda Child, Jean O'Brien, and Vine Deloria, Jr.—all Native writers who are somehow engaged in their tribal communities and homelands.

Why *Shell Shaker* Is about Choctaws

In the beginning there are Choctaw stories. There are Cherokee stories. There are Diné stories. There are Lakota stories. I am trying to say that we, the people, are derived from creation stories. We are people of specific landscapes, and our specific stories are told about our emergence from a specific place.

I came up with the term "tribalography" because I didn't agree that American Indians tell strictly autobiographical stories, nor memoir, nor history, nor fiction, but rather they tell a kind of story that includes a collaboration with the past and present and future. Hence the term "tribalography." In the case of the Haudenosaunee, their story has remained consistent over the many decades. They have said their confederacy was founded on the core values the Peacemaker proposed: freedom, respect, tolerance, consensus, and brotherhood. Under the terms and spirit of the *NeGayaneshogowa*, or the Great Law of Peace, all parties pledged themselves to the confederacy's body of laws. United we thrive, divided we fall.

Historian Robert Venables says that the Haudenosaunee influenced the founding fathers to unite the people of the Old World. This is literary praxis at its best. A native story taught the immigrants the value of unification. In that sense a native story created America.

This is not unlike how tribes were created. In the case of the Choctaw, the Nanih Waiya (Bending Hill) is the story of where we came from, both literally and metaphorically. To some, the mound is Ishki Chitto, or Great Mother; to others our birthplace is where our ancestors crawled up out of the cave, *near* Nanih Waiya, and combed their long hairs to become people. I am not attempting to say whose story is the oldest, nor am I going to delineate them all, but in using the following accounts I am highlighting the fact that today, as in the past, the mound located in Winston County near Philadelphia, Mississippi, is recognized by Choctaw people as a symbol of our ancient existence in the Lower Mississippi Valley.

One story told by Hopakitobi (Prophet That Kills) says that he considers himself a part of the people who came from inside the Earth: "The Great Spirit created the first Choctaws, and through a hole or cave, they crawled forth in the light of day. Some say that only one pair was created, but others say that many pairs were created."[7]

Choctaws defined where we came from. The language is full of descriptive old town names that tell a story, or the history of a specific space: Kashtasha, Fleas Are There; Halunlawansha, Bullfrog Place (Philadelphia, Mississippi); Kati Oka hikia, Thorn-bush Standing in Water; and Kafi talaia, Sassafras Thicket; to give a few examples.

Nakshobi is another Choctaw place-name that is very specific. The Choctaw word, "Nakshobi," means, "to stink" and is indicative of "bad-smelling waters." Eventually Nakshobi was transliterated to "Noxubee." Over time Noxubee in Mississippi has become a powerful metaphor for spiritual life and death—and political corruption. Hernando de Soto's destructive sixteenth-century expedition brought European diseases into this site; Europeans introduced Christianity and alcohol in Noxubee; a Choctaw civil war took place there in 1748–1749; in the 1812 Creek-Choctaw war an estimated five hundred people were killed in Noxubee County. The controversial Dancing Rabbit Creek Treaty was signed there on September 27, 1830, which forced the relocation of eight thousand Choctaws to present-day Oklahoma. The site in Noxubee County was near a poisoned spring, so named by the Choctaws because rabbits staggered with convulsions after drinking the bad waters.

Noxubee County is also the birthplace of Peter Pitchlynn, a Choctaw leader in the early 1800s who told this story of Choctaw emergence. In his story, Pitchlynn states that the people he is associated with came from the Gulf of Mexico and immigrated north onto the prairie lands:

> According to the traditions of the Choctaws, the first of their race came from the bosom of the magnificent sea. Even when they first made their appearance upon the earth they were so numerous as to cover the sloping and sandy shore of the ocean, far as the eye could reach, and for a long time did they follow the margin of the sea before they could find a place suited to their wants. The name of their principal chief has long since been forgotten, but it is well remembered that he was a prophet of great age and wisdom. For many moons did they travel without fatigue, and all the time were their bodies strengthened by pleasant breezes, and their hearts, on the other hand gladdened by the luxuriance of a perpetual summer.[8]

A Choctaw woman named Pisatuntema tells another story. Her account appears originally in *Myths of the Louisiana Choctaw*, by David Bushnell, Jr.

> Soon after the earth (*yahné*) was made, men and grasshoppers came to the surface through a long passage that led from a large caravan in the interior of the earth, to the summit of a high hill, Nane chaha. There deep down in the earth, in the great cavern, man and the grasshoppers had been created by Aba, the Great Spirit, having been formed of the yellow clay. For a time the men and the grasshoppers continued to reach the surface together, and as they emerged from the long passageway they would scatter in all directions, some going north, other south, east or west.[9]

I use these few accounts to show how Choctaw stories collected by ethnographers inform our contemporary written stories. In fact, the oral stories are the legal primacy we used to make our original treaties with foreign nations. In the nineteenth century Andrew Jackson's men believed that Choctaws stories were true. Otherwise how can we explain the treaties they made with us? Why would a foreign government make a contract to trade for land if they didn't believe we [the Choctaws] weren't the original holders of the land?

Tribalography in Indian Literature

When my birth mother told me stories about our origins, she talked about the land in Mississippi, the Nanih Waiya, and she said described us as "Eastern people." I was never really sure what she meant until I researched the Choctaw Confederacy and learned that our tribe was divided between eastern factions and western factions, as well as other designations. Mother also told me stories of the Little People who once harassed my uncle when he came home late at night. She talked of the strange water spirits that live around Choctaw lakes and rivers in Mississippi and Oklahoma. She told me stories of the blue lights. And she told stories about my grandfather, aunts, uncles, and our relatives who are not related by blood. One example of our fictive kin is my

Choctaw grandfather's "adopted" white brother. Even after the "brother" had grown to manhood, he was regarded as a member of our family, though he was not Choctaw.

All this is my way of explaining how *Shell Shaker* is also a tribalography. I used some oral stories from my birth mother. I found documents in the historic record; I used stories of Choctaws who were gourd dancers, and stories of women who shook shells, and stories of dancers who covered themselves in white powder before they danced. I also used stories about the women who made sashes from porcupine skins. Many of these traditions and events were forgotten in the twentieth century. So why did I choose "Shell Shaker" as a title for my novel, knowing that most Choctaws do not shake shells? The main reason is that I wanted to remind my community that a long time ago Choctawans had many different dances and ceremonies and customs, and yes, there is evidence that some communities shook shells. If I wrote about some of them, I hoped the others would begin to rise up out of the land where they've been kept—waiting on us to remember to call them out.

Only this past summer, in order to enlarge Green Corn celebrations, a Choctaw-Chickasaw man talked of reclaiming another old chief's grounds in southeastern Oklahoma. While he was talking, I was reminded again that dreams and stories and songs don't just visit one or two of us. Eventually they come to many of us. The revival of Green Corn grounds in Oklahoma over the past twenty years has done a lot to reinvigorate our communities. Perhaps this is the reason I didn't invent a tribe in *Shell Shaker*. By writing, by interacting with my tribe, I am a part of the future stories that will rise up. My mother helped me write the Choctaw language in *Shell Shaker*. Choctaw was her first language. While the novel is "fiction," much of the history is as accurate as I could interpret it, especially the skirmishes in 1738 and 1739 between the Chickasaws, who supported the English, and the Choctaws, who supported the French.

Choctaws suffered our first civil war in 1747 with the assassination of war chief Red Shoes on June 22. I wanted to write about self-destruction and the horrors of war through the vehicle of Red Shoes's soliloquy. This following section is told from Red Shoes's point of view. He is narrating the future, but in present tense, as if it were happening to him at that very moment. I also wanted to follow the example of my family who tell all their stories of the past in present tense.

> "But my story is not finished," I argue. "I will caress the inevitable coming to life in front of me. My head on a pole branches like the red leaves of autumn pruned too late to heal. On the longest day of the year when the eye of the Sun finally closes, an assassin will set fire to my body, then remove my head. Then nothing, not even breath can come between Anoleta and me in a place where the net of air and earth have been rearranged for this purpose. It is she and Haya who will track me

> down on the road to Couechitto. After the slaughter at the Alibamu Conchatys, after the hundreds dead, I decide I *do* want to sacrifice myself. I will help in my own death, but when heat rising from the fire makes me vomit the last bite of moisture out of me, I don't want to end. Red smoke sizzles on my tongue. A hot tingling runs over the top of my head, I am being roasted alive. Flesh oozes down my cheek, tears of light run down my face. I am no longer one who is here, yet I am here. A chorus of frogs, deep voices, announces my departure, and I understand, there will be no birds coming for me. Everything around me is moving away, unsteady. I am raining down on the ground dissolving in a blood clot of sadness. In my last solemn moments I pray for a reflection, a shape that will defy the astounded dead. I will not be a stone without eyes. I will not live where no one sees me or knows my name. I will return, I sing. I will return, I sing. I will return."
>
> *You are raving.* The wind says.
>
> "Huh! A road does come for me. There is a whistling sound, searing. A meat-whistling that shrivels everything."[10]

With the above passage, I am writing the red history of our tribe and illuminating the dynamic nature of Choctaw time. In it, the "we" is ever-present, which is how I believe Choctaws express spirituality. The spirit is ever-present. The present is ever-spirit. Red Shoes was killed as he made camp, the evening of June 22, 1747. His assassin tracked him down and chopped off his head. It was then posted on a post, and burned, as was the rest of his body.

In the next passage, Isaac Billy is visiting his grandmother, Nowatima, who explains the interaction between the Natchez, the Choctaw, and the French—from a Choctaw point of view.

> Isaac digs in his pocket and takes out a tiny gray stone no bigger than his thumb. It resembles a skull and once belonged to his great-grandmother Nowatima. After he returned home from boarding school, he'd sit with her for hours in front of their fireplace. Night after night she would draw stories in his mind. He saw a hurricane so powerful that it made the Mississippi run backwards. At the river *Ahepatanichi*, he saw kettling birds of an unknown species dropping excrement on the heads of Spanish invaders. "What the Hispano didn't realize," smiled Nowatima, "was that magical excrement containing the seeds of potatoes had been dropped on them. So the invaders would unknowingly spread potatoes to starving people everywhere. A gift from our Seven Grandmothers." Isaac witnessed a war between the Natchez and the French that began over the slaughter of trumpeter swans. Nowatima said the French didn't know that they built their fort over a bird refuge, a place protected by the Natchez. When the Natchez leader, Stung Serpent, and his son brought a pair of mated swans to Chépart, the fort's commander, he threw them out of his house and shot the birds just to show

how little he regarded their gift. This so enraged the Natchez that they killed Chépart and two hundred and fifty other Frenchmen. Then they planted the French heads on pine posts in the center of the fort. Food for birds. Eventually the Choctaw helped the Natchez move in with the Ouachitas who were living along the Red River. "You see," said Nowatima, "that is how the Choctaws saved the French, our allies. Otherwise the Natchez would surely have wiped them out. Now you know how a people in the swamp can slip into another name as easily as food slips inside your mouth. But the real truth of my stories is that nothing ever dies." Isaac removes his bulky glasses and brushes a small tear away. Sunlight glints on his face like a mirror, the morning sky is bright blue.

Many years after Nowatima's death, he asked Auda to find out what the historians wrote about the Natchez war. She told him it happened in 1730, but that the French had called the swans worthless waterfowl.

Hekano, he does not question Nowatima's stories. Her words were confident, rich with details. A long time ago—she would say. Isaac drifts into the world she made for him and the stone warms his hand.[11]

In my view, the above paragraphs illustrate my theory, or story, about Choctaw events. The French military officers in their letters first told the story of the Natchez war. Later in the 1750s, the French travel writers retold this same story from another point of view. Then in the twentieth century, American historians and ethnographers wrote about the Natchez war and the Choctaw's involvement. Two centuries later, while writing *Shell Shaker*, I would finally recapture this story and tell another version of it. By using French documents, and by using stories my uncles told about World War II, and by using my dreams, I was able to reimagine our history from many point of views: mine, my relatives, and our ancestors. I hope I am talking through our ancestors, the ones whose words were written down in the documents, and untangling the stories within stories within stories—and smoothing them out for the future, so that some other Choctaws will write their version of our stories.

In this essay, I've translated for Embarrassed Grief, other characters, and my relatives. I've even talked about my writing methods to explain what a tribalography is and how it is an ethical Native literary praxis. In this story within a story it is the characters who have shown how a Native writer remains in conversation with the past and the present to create the future. We are makers of theory bread, and we hope that our reasoning together will not only inform but nourish you.

Notes

1. For a full account of the story, see H. B. Cushman's *The History of the Choctaws, Chickasaws, and Natchez Indians.* While Cushman has been widely criticized for his fanciful use of language, I believe there are some useful cultural markers

found within this story. Specifically useful is Cushman's attention to the "call and response" song that the unknown woman brings to the two Choctaw men. It should be noted today that Choctaw songs are famous for their call-and-response motifs.

2. Howe, "Story of America."

3. Jackson, *Yuchi Ceremonial Life*, 114.

4. The most academically acceptable term I know is "Native," but I will most likely use "Indian" and "American Indian" throughout this essay.

5. Jackson, *Yuchi Ceremonial Life*, 240.

6. Howe, *Shell Shaker*, 44.

7. Swanton, *Source Material*, 35.

8. Ibid., 31.

9. Bushnell, "Myths," 527.

10. Howe, *Shell Shaker*, 173–74.

11. Ibid., 78–79.

Your Skin Is the Map

The Theoretical Challenge of Joy Harjo's Erotic Poetics

ROBERT WARRIOR

The poetry of Joy Harjo has long been for me a primary standard against which I measure the work I do as a critic and theorist. Her poetry has been an ethical model for me of the sorts of challenges both creative and theoretical work need to be responsive to. This is primarily because Harjo never takes the easy way out. Instead, she addresses topics and explores aspects of Native experience that far too often drop out of academic discourse in Native American studies.

Here I am interested in working out how Harjo treats one of those topics—the erotic—and how her poetic explorations of the erotic challenge the development of Native theory. Specifically, Harjo's erotic poems provide the fullest expression of her commitment to embodiment. That commitment speaks to the work of Natives doing theory, serving as a reminder that theory, however abstract, is something that is done in our bodies. For those of us committed to theoretical approaches that seek to address and make changes to the material realities that people in Native communities face, then, Harjo's erotic poetry is a challenge to understand that our bodies, including our intellects, are connected to those material realities.

In an earlier version of her essay that appears in this volume, Kimberly Roppolo argued, "As we 'decolonize' our minds, our theories, our methodologies, we must also decolonize our relationships with each other." Harjo's commitment to embodiment, expressed most fully in her erotics and the relationality that is part of it, is a reminder that our relationships to our bodies, as much as to our minds, are also in need of our attention. Similarly,

---

Robert Warrior (Osage) is the author or coauthor of four books: American Indian Literary Nationalism *(with Jace Weaver and Craig Womack);* The People and the Word: Reading Native Nonfiction; Like a Hurricane: The Indian Movement from Alcatraz to Wounded Knee *(with Paul Chaat Smith); and* Tribal Secrets: Recovering American Indian Intellectual Traditions. *He is Edith Kinney Gaylord Presidential Professor at the University of Oklahoma.*

Daniel Justice argues that an "ethical Native literary criticism . . . is about relationships, about attending to the cultural, historical, political, and intellectual contexts from which Indigenous texts emerge." The presence of the erotic in Harjo's texts is a challenge, a confrontation, that at its best shocks us into a recognition that our bodies and the erotic selves who live in them are also necessary contexts of our work.

Harjo's poetry, of course, has been important to the landscape of Native literature since she started publishing in the mid-1970s. Phrases from the work she did even before her landmark book, *She Had Some Horses,* are firmly embedded in critical discourse on Native literature and culture, including "angry woman are building" and "That's what she said."[1] Various poems of hers, including "She Had Some Horses," "The Woman Hanging from the Thirteenth Floor Window," "I Give You Back," "For Anna Mae Pictou Aquash, Whose Spirit is Present Here and in the Dappled Stars (for we remember the story and must tell it again so we may all live)," and "Perhaps the World Ends Here" are among the most beautiful and striking poems to come from the Native world.[2] If we have classics, Harjo is responsible for a remarkable number of them.

Looking at the sweep of her work, I would argue that one reason she has been such a compelling figure is that she, more perhaps than any other Native poet, includes the fullness of Native experiences, including eroticism, in her work. That eroticism can be quite explicit, as when she writes of what she calls her "heart's dogs" going out in search of her lover. "They smelled your come on my fingers, my face," she writes. "They felt the / quivering nerve of emotion that forced me to live."[3] More typical is the poem "Motion," in which Harjo writes,

> We get frantic
> in our loving . . .
> I tremble and grasp
> at the edges of
> myself; I let go
> into you. . . .
> . . . we exist
> not in words, but in the motion
> set off by them, by
> the simple flight of crow
> and by us
> in our loving.[4]

Such eroticism has always been for me as a reader attractive—okay, sexy—in and of itself, but it is more than that. Harjo has recognized Audre Lorde's foundational insight, from her essay "Uses of the Erotic: The Erotic as Power," that the erotic can be a crucial source of power in the struggle for justice. Suppression of the erotic, according to Lorde, has happened for specific reasons. "Every oppression," writes Lorde, "must corrupt or distort those various sources of power within the culture of the oppressed that can provide energy for change."[5] The line from Lorde to Harjo is, importantly, a direct one, as Harjo acknowledges at the beginning of *In Mad Love and War* and in a later interview.[6]

In her groundbreaking essay, "Erotica, Indigenous Style," Kateri Akiwenzie-Damm argues that the process of suppression Lorde describes in her essay has happened throughout the indigenous world. "When the colonizers arrived," she writes, "who we are as Indigenous peoples was disrupted and controlled," including attitudes toward sex and sexuality. Akiwenzie-Damm posits robust traditions of eroticism in indigenous ceremonial and story traditions, traditions that the process of colonialism has eroded and erased. The result, she argues, has been "in terms of sexuality, many of our communities were at least as repressive (and hypocritical?) as the colonizing cultures that surround us."[7]

Deborah Miranda agrees with Akiwenzie-Damm's assertion that the erotic has become an invisible part of Native life. She describes her frustration at the way Native women poets have regularly been ignored in larger discussions of the erotic in American poetry in spite of numerous examples of Native women writing in the erotic mode. She argues, "The amount of energy that a serious scholar of American poetry would have to invest in missing these Native authors and books must be tremendous." This invisibility frustrates Miranda because, as she says, "American Indian women's erotics make a more 'real,' less stereotypical, artificially constructed American Indian woman visible, and this writing allows us to fully experience our creative strengths—something no one now alive on this continent has yet truly seen."[8] The erotic, on Miranda's reading, is an exemplar of what Cheryl Suzack suggests in this volume when she argues that we need to "create an oppositional space from which to restore gender identity as an analytical category in discussions of tribal politics and community values."

This is in line with what Lorde argues. The erotic, for Lorde, "rises from our deepest and nonrational knowledge" and stands opposed to a "system which defines the good in terms of profit rather than in terms of human need, or which defines human need to the exclusion of the psychic and emotional components of that need."[9] To engage the erotic is to challenge the power of the psychic structures that keep us in our place. In this way, I would argue, engaging the erotic also helps us as we theorize.

Importantly, the erotic for Lorde is never merely sex and is never dangerous, brutal, or coercive. Human sexuality, of course, always runs the risk of involving any of those things, but Lorde presents the erotic as being self-consciously committed to being a force for human liberation. While abandoning oneself to bodily pleasure is not for Lorde a calculated process wrapped up in rationality (thank goodness), it is nonetheless purposive.

Indeed, one could argue that what Lorde strives for is an erotics that overcomes more nihilistic forms of pleasure-seeking, whether through substances or the body. As Lorde says,

> For once we begin to feel deeply all the aspects of our lives, we begin to demand from ourselves and from our life-pursuits that they feel in accordance with that joy which we know ourselves to be capable of. Our erotic knowledge empowers us, becomes a lens through which we scrutinize all aspects of our existence, forcing us to evaluate those aspects honestly in terms of their relative meaning within our lives. And this is a grave responsibility, projected from within each of us, not to settle for the convenient, the shoddy, the conventionally expected, nor the merely safe.[10]

The erotic, thus, is a key to affirming the worth and the wholeness of the self. Its expression is an act of resistance and colors all other such acts. In this way, the erotic becomes a way of measuring a life, with that measure being more about the quality of life in our bodies than achieving a set of specific goals.

Approaching the erotic causes a rethinking of the work of Native poetry and, by extension, Native theory. As Vine Deloria says in an oft-quoted introduction to an anthology of Native poetry, "Only the poet in his [or her] frightful solitude and in his [or her] ability to transcend chronological existence can build that spiritual bridge which enables individuals to travel the roads of [human] experiences." What poets give us, according to Deloria, is "a raging beyond nobility that calls for recognition of the humanity and nationality of Indian existence."[11] The theoretical extension here is the necessary obviating of those things that poetry makes cryptic and the erotic maintains, as is appropriate, at a nonrational level.

Lorde's argument about the erotic, especially as it is represented in poetry, provides the sort of bridging process that Deloria describes. The erotic, she says, "forms the bridge . . . between the spiritual and the political."[12] That bridging, thus, is much more than bringing together past and present or the need to bring together the personal and the political or the spiritual and the social. It is the creation of a connection between an embodied self and the world in which that self exists.

Harjo, by engaging the erotic, does more than provide poetic work that confirms the need for justice, the prevalence of violence in the lives of Native people, or the importance of language in the articulation of our future. Hers is a world of history, tradition, the struggle for justice, the naming of enemies, the love of language, and a call for articulating experiences. But it is also a world of the body, one in which new realities come from the related themes of the erotic and the reproductive. Her inclusion of the erotic confirms Akiwenzie-Damm's contention that "To deny the erotic, to create an absence of erotica, is another weapon in the oppressor's genocidal arsenal. When this part of us is dead, out future survival is in jeopardy."[13] Indeed, even—or especially—for those of my fellow contributors to this volume who focus on oral traditional material, including Chris Teuton and Janice Acoose, Akiwenzie-Damm's work is a reminder of how subtle and sophisticated those materials can be.

The connection between the erotic, bodies, and Native survival is vital. It would be easy to say that the erotic is something individual, something luxurious, and something that needs to take a second seat to more pressing issues like land claims, sovereignty, and funding next year's budget. But what if Akiwenzie-Damm is right that our oppression as Native people has resulted in a denial of who we are erotically? Isn't reclamation of our erotic selves its own sort of victory? I will have more to say about this in concluding, but it's worth thinking about such connections and the way the deprivations of history have not been merely a matter of one or two things (bad policies, stolen land, evil intentions, cultural loss, or misguided decisions), but of a systematic assault on the wholeness of who we are.

Harjo provides a way of thinking about how Indian people can reclaim themselves by embracing the erotic. Importantly, her embrace of the erotic is at times complemented by images of giving birth and connections to a transformed world. As she says of the main character in "For Alva Benson, And for Those Who Have Learned to Speak," "She learned to speak for the ground / the voice coming through her like roots that / have long hungered for water." In giving birth to her own daughter, the poem's main character continues a history of linking humans with the landscape: "Mt. St. Helens / erupts as the harmonic motion of a child turning / inside her mother's belly waiting to be born / to begin another time."[14]

This concern for reproduction appears in the numerous poems Harjo has written for her children, Phil and Rainy Dawn, and her several grandchildren.[15] Among these is the title poem for her 2000 collection, *A Map to the Next World*. Dedicating the poem to one of her granddaughters, Desiree Kierra Chee, Harjo writes, "In the last days of the fourth world I wished to make a map for those who would climb through the hole in the sky." Though the overt reference is to Hopi beliefs in this being a fourth incarnation of the world that will sometime soon emerge into a fifth incarnation, Harjo's poem also contains references to her own Muscogee world. She speaks of the need, for instance, to "carry fire to the next tribal town, for renewal of spirit."[16]

Recognizing "that Harjo's work is deeply Muskogean," according to Craig Womack, is important, "not to detract from her other influences but to name what I feel is the very foundation of her work." Womack's argument is a powerful one, as it challenges readers of Harjo's poetry to consider the depth of her tribal knowledge and experiences, even as they encounter the global reach of her perspectives and creativity. Being open to the world, in fact, is for Womack a deeply Creek trait, making Harjo's poetry part of what he calls "a very old song."[17] Later in "Map," Harjo indicates that this old song is one that must continue to be nurtured in each generation. Upon ascending a ladder to the next world, she offers a warning to "Remember the hole of our shame marking the act of abandoning our tribal grounds."[18]

Harjo fills this poem of renewal and transformation with advice, admonitions, and warnings for her newborn granddaughter. She writes of the society in which her granddaughter will grow up as needing transforming: "Take note of the proliferation of supermarkets and malls, the altars of money. They best describe the detour from grace. / Keep track of the errors of our forgetfulness; the fog steals our children while we sleep." Penultimately, Harjo indicates the constancy with which the next world must be sought, writing, "Crucial to finding the way is this: there is no beginning or end." This comes before she concludes the poem by saying, "You must make your own map."[19]

Appropriately, the erotic is not a theme in this poem, though Harjo does reference the procreative act that led to birth when she says, "The place of entry is the sea of your mother's blood, your father's small death as he longs to know himself in another."[20] Late in the book, in "traveling through the dark," when she describes physical travel and traveling in dreams, she returns to the idea of a map. As she writes,

> Another mode of travel is lovemaking which is similar to the travel of the spirit in dreaming; you bring your skin with you. Your skin is the map, the means through which you experience the transformation, the deep. You can skim the surface quickly, or you can dive through many layers into the deepest unknown territory of intimacy. It is there you will find the quivering raw essence of humanness, there at the center of power. This journey is fueled by the most powerful energy in this universe, and energy more potent than jet fuel or uranium or solar blast. It is called desire.[21]

A few pages earlier, Harjo speaks of "thinking in skin and our pleasure" as she declares, "there is something quite compelling / about this skin we're in."[22] For Harjo, then, our bodies—or our skins, which are the parts of us that most immediately touch and relate to the rest of the world around us—are not only the most immediate site of the battle for our selves, but also the primary guide to where we ought to be headed. Our skin, as Harjo puts it, is the map.

Throughout *A Map to the Next World*, Harjo is concerned with traveling to and from a "ceremony / to rid us of the enemy mind," so lovemaking as a mode of travel is important to the overall themes of the book. She worries, in fact, about how, because of forgetfulness, "any of us are going to make it / through the bloodstream to the ceremony / for returning from the enemy." The fourteen-part poem, "Returning from the Enemy," and the poems that lead up to it refer once again to this ceremony, and Harjo indicates that the poems in the book exist on both sides of the ceremony.[23]

This can be seen even earlier than *A Map to the Next World*. The idea of erotic love as a means of traveling to a new or alternative reality also shows up in "City of Fire," a poem from *In Mad Love and War*. "Come, sweet," she writes, "I am a house with many rooms. / There is no end. / Each room is a street to the next world. / . . . And you have made / a fire in every room. / Come. / Lie with me before the flame." Here, the transformation is fundamental, as "I take you apart raw. / . . . We will make a river, / flood this city built of passion / with fire, / with a revolutionary fire."[24]

Harjo's affirmation of the erotic as the way toward "the center of power" provides a way of reading the erotic imagery of all of her earlier work. This idea of the skin being a map that leads us to our "quivering raw essence of humanness" provides a way of seeing what has been the trajectory of Harjo's erotic poetics from the beginning of her published work. As she has said in reflecting on her early work, "I have changed as much as these poems have through the years.... When I look back over the many lives between then and now I remember a very young woman at her typewriter, entering the field of imagination with a great trust, even wildness. And there were the horses, shimmering in the sun and rain on the battleground of wins and losses, always revealing the possibility of love."[25]

Love, of course, has many aspects and types. But erotic love for Harjo very often creates the space in which all other love lives and thrives. In an interview, she has said, "To be 'in the erotic,' so to speak, is to be alive. . . . Eroticism presents political problems, cultural difficulties, religious problems because the dominant culture can't function with a society of alive people."[26] This, then, is an active strategy of resistance against what Akiwenzie-Damm points to when she says, "It seems to me that the repression of erotic art is symptomatic of our oppression and signifies a deep psychological and spiritual break between a healthy and holistic tradition and an oppressed, repressed, shamed, and imposed sense of reality."[27]

Rather than being a luxury that must wait for some other struggle to be won, then, the erotic becomes central to all struggle. As Harjo writes in "Heartshed," "I walk into another room inside / your skin house. / I open your legs with my tongue. / The war is not over but inside you / the night is hot / and my fingers walk their way up your spine."[28] And it is within this space, liberated by sensuality, that the work of transformation takes place.

That transformation happens against a background of personal and tribal histories of violence and abuse—the generational effects of being surrounded by an enemy. Speaking of a friend's lifetime of demons, she writes, "I've seen the shadow of the monster, seen it try to pin him down, sensed the wrench of grief. I know it in myself."[29] Harjo posits two ways of dealing with such monsters. One is simply to forget. As she says, "Forgetting is so easy in this illusion and I understand the need to sleepwalk." Sleepwalking numbs the pain of contemporary life, but only by remembering that pain, she indicates, do we create a chance for healing. She says, "The field of hurt is immense and to venture outside the lines can be tricky and difficult. It's too much to bear sometimes. But the complexity of the mind behind the larger system of knowledge is stunning and will break through any way it can."[30]

Venturing outside the lines, then, is fundamental to Harjo's work and nowhere is this more clear than in her uses of the erotic. "How can we be healthy in a holistic way," Akiwenzie-Damm asks, "if we are deprived of this view of ourselves or if we only see ourselves portrayed as damaged and unhealthy?"[31] An ideal illustration of how Harjo works through that question in her poetry is the character Noni Daylight, who shows up in several of Harjo's early poems.

When Noni Daylight first appears in *What Moon Drove Me to This?* she is, to put it mildly, messed up. Plotting to keep her lover from leaving her, she attempts suicide by taking a bunch of pills. "It worked," Harjo writes, "daylight survived and her lover / was oh so guilty and promised / never / to love anyone else again." Daylight maintains something of that dysfunction throughout the poems she appears in, but Harjo also introduces the idea early on that she is seeking a better life. Using the theme of travel that figures so prominently in *A Map to the Next World*, Harjo takes Noni Daylight to the edge of the Grand Canyon, pondering the Hopi idea that the canyon is the birthplace of their people and thinking that, in fact, "most of the world / must have originated / from that point. / . . . she thinks / she must still be traveling from there. / But not very far at all." Harjo presents Noni Daylight as a far from perfect person traveling toward something—or back to it—or both.[32]

She is a flawed character, but one who is open to love, especially sensual love. In "Someone Talking," she yearns for a former lover, numbing herself with bourbon as she "tastes the Old Crow. / Yellow fire all the way into/ her belly." The presence of her lover becomes palpable as she longs for his presence. Harjo writes, "The man of words outlines wet islands / with his lips / on Noni Daylight's neck."[33]

Noni Daylight makes her last appearance in Harjo's poetry in "She Remembers the Future," a poem that stands in stark contrast to that first image of Noni Daylight nearly dead by her own hand. Here, she expresses a sense of vibrant hope. "[H]er skin / responds" to the beauty of the natural world "like a woman / to her lover." She is intent, though, to bring what Harjo calls her "otherself" along with her into her healthy imagined future. She asks, "should you ride colored horses / into the cutting edge of the sky / to know / that we're alive / we are alive."[34]

The sort of healthy transformation that we see in Noni Daylight is a theme that reappears throughout Harjo's work. One example is the poem "Deer Dancer," where an intriguing woman comes into an Indian bar one night, drawing the attention of those attracted to her and the ire of those they came in with. After putting money into the jukebox, she climbs on top of a table, "And then she took off her clothes. She shook loose memory, waltzed with the empty lover we'd all become."[35]

This beautiful, naked woman is the opposite figure of most deer woman stories, in which a temptress leads a married man astray only to reveal herself as a grotesque monster. Harjo's deer dancer leads the people in the bar to their better selves. "She was the myth slipped down through dreamtime," Harjo writes, "The promise of feast we all knew was coming. The deer who crossed through knots of a curse to find us. She was no slouch, and neither were we, watching."[36] She awakens those in the bar to an alternative reality, bolstering their sense of their own worth.

Such images are the antidote Akiwenzie-Damm is looking for when she says, "We need to see images of ourselves as healthy, whole people. People who love each other and who love ourselves. People who fall in love and out of love, who have lovers, who make love, who have sex. We need to create a healthy legacy for our peoples."[37] Harjo's erotics point in the direction of wholeness and healing. As is the case with Lorde, Harjo and Akiwenzie-Damm point toward an erotics that defines itself as healthy and evaluates sexuality on the basis of the extent to which it makes our lives a more complete expression of the best we can imagine for ourselves.

Harjo has seemingly been moving all along toward what she calls in *A Map to the Next World* a ceremony for returning from the enemy. And getting there has everything to do with engaging the sensual. Harjo's formulation of the erotic shares an important aspect of Tol Foster's essay on regionalism in this volume—the development of the erotic in Native discourse need not focus on utopias.

The erotic, then, leads to a transformed, nonutopic self. This is perhaps no more evident than in Harjo's poem "The Myth of Blackbirds." The poem takes place in Washington, D.C., a dystopic city that recalls for Harjo visits from tribal leaders, including her own direct ancestors, to treat with the U.S. government. "The first time I visited there," she writes later in *The Woman Who Fell From the Sky*, "I suffered from vertigo and panic attacks. I saw rivers of blood flowing under the beautiful white marble monuments that announced power in the landscape."[38]

Yet, in this city that houses the apparatuses of power over the lives of Native American people, Harjo manages to find love and intimacy in the embrace of another person. The world of "whirring calculators" and "computers stealing names," Harjo writes, "is the world in which we undressed together." "[Y]ou touched me and the springs of clear water beneath my skin were new knowledge," she says. "And I loved you in this city of death."[39] Erotic contact in this case becomes an act of defiance in the face of power, again an act of resistance through reclaiming her own body and that of her lover.

The poem is about being able to see things in and of themselves. Thus, the act of undressing and being intimate with a lover become the keys to being able to deal with what Harjo calls "the loop of mystery between blackbirds and the memory of blackbirds." That loop of mystery is a "spiral of power" that links the past to the present. So, as she honors her ancestors, she also says, "And I particularly admire the tender construction of your spine which in the gentle dawning is a ladder between the deep in which stars are perfectly stars, and the heavens where we converse with eagles."[40]

The erotic, then, is a bridge that gives Harjo access to her own history and also a way of countering the history of damage that history represents. Yet that act of defiance doesn't end with her standing face to face with the enemy, but side by side, sweetly, with her beloved. The poem ends with Harjo saying, "And I am thankful to the brutal city for the space which outlines your limber beauty. . . . To the ancestors who do not forget us in the concrete and paper illusion. To the blackbirds who are exactly blackbirds. And to you sweetheart as we make our incredible journey."[41] This passage shows Harjo bridging memory and history, collective politics and individual struggle. The bridging not only involves, but requires, awareness of the body. Perhaps most important of all, the journey across the bridge happens in relation to someone else, someone beloved who heightens the sense of embodiment.

The history that "The Myth of Blackbirds" invokes is specifically Muscogean in the way that Womack argues is true for so much of Harjo's work. Yet, in line with Womack's argument, the specific Muscogean aspects give rise to intertribal sharing. This comes through in Harjo's usage of the word "sweetheart" in the last line of the poem, which I read as an allusion to the "49" song that Harjo quotes twice before in her poetry. As those familiar with the social traditions of the Indian world know, a 49 is a late-night intertribal gathering of young Indian people, usually following a powwow or dance. A 49 typically takes place on back roads or someplace else where law enforcement won't intrude. These are boisterous events filled with laughter and bravado, a sort of temporary liberation of space and time. 49 songs are typically about love and romance, 49s being prime hunting grounds for "snags," or romantic entanglements.

In both *She Had Some Horses* and *A Map to the Next World*, Harjo uses lines from one of the most famous of 49 songs: "when the dance is over, sweetheart / I will take you home in my one-eyed Ford." In *Map*, Harjo goes on to say of the song, "That song was destined to become a classic." Harjo also titles one of her poems in *What Moon Drove Me to This?* "There Was a Dance, Sweetheart," which carries the same feeling of sociality as these more direct references to the 49 tradition.[42]

The one-eyed Ford song, then, is about finding a snag, which is, needless to say, a richly layered term. The layers and ambiguity are why I see Harjo referring to this social tradition in "The Myth of Blackbirds." Harjo presents the world as a complicated place where Indian people are faced with enormous problems and challenges. To bring this echo from the liberated space of the 49 to the erotically liberated space of a Washington hotel room is a way of connecting these disparate aspects of the Native world. The lover is a sweetheart, a snag whose complication may add to life's difficulties, but who can provide a place through which to experience a defiant transformation.

Making this kind of physical connection is a way to recognize the deepest levels of human want and desire. The "sensual ache /. . . of wanting you against me," she writes, ". . . is the connecting secret."[43] Again, similar to Foster's concept, it is not utopian, perfect love that Harjo's poem invokes, but something that echoes from "A Map to the Next World" when she says to her granddaughter, "An imperfect map will have to do, little one."[44] Harjo's world is one in which people make mistakes, get wrapped up in relationships that don't work or which aren't right. She makes reference throughout *A Map to the Next World* to a long relationship she ended in 1996. In reference to that relationship, she makes this bittersweet declaration:

> I will never forget you. Your nakedness
> haunts me in the dawn when I cannot distinguish your
> flushed brown skin from the burning horizon, or my hands.

> The smell of chaos lingers in the clothes
> you left behind. I hold you
> there.[45]

The physicality of love, its smell and touch, are a risk, as Harjo seems to acknowledge, and seeking out the erotic is to risk the destructive aspects of human relationships. But the risk of heartbreak and dysfunction is as important as the realization of love. Even in the pain of the end of a relationship we can read a sense of the liberated body finding, ironically, in absence a stronger sense of itself.

Harjo's erotics are a universal invitation to live in our own skin and to learn to be in the world in a different way. She invites us to understand our desires as being part of who we are and to understand ourselves as capable of feeling our way to a new reality. But her erotic challenge is also one that speaks specifically and especially to those from her world, the Indian world, who confront the same history of suppression that she does. As Audre Lorde says,

> But when we begin to live from within outward, in touch with the power of the erotic within ourselves, and allowing that power to inform and illuminate our actions upon the world around us, then we begin to be responsible to ourselves in the deepest sense. For as we begin to recognize our deepest feelings, we begin to give up, of necessity, being satisfied with suffering and self-negation, and with the numbness which so often seems like their only alternative in our society. Our acts against oppression become integral with self, motivated and empowered from within.[46]

This is the direction Harjo has pointed toward through all of her erotic poetry, from Noni Daylight to her latest work.

What this means for Native theory comes back to the deep embodiment of Harjo's idea of our skin being a map. The map is not a policy, a political strategy, or an ideology. It is, for Harjo, the body. Flawed, scarred, and embattled, it is also beautiful, capable, and trustworthy. It is the most basic location of our memories and our stories.

Harjo's insistence on embodiment is a reminder that our bodies are a legitimate site for theorizing and that one of the important links between theory and experience is the fact that theorizing is something we do in our bodies. We can be abstract while remaining deeply aware that no thought occurs outside of life in the body. An embodied criticism is one that helps all of us see the importance of saying no, of refusing the sort of bigotry that Daniel Justice writes about, and embracing the idea that our intellectual dissent can be a healthy step toward one sort of healing that all of us need.

Concomitantly, literature is something that also comes from the body. Language that articulates the depths of that embodiment can defy continuing assaults on who we are as Native people. "Five hundred years of colonization and its many painful wounds," Miranda argues, "have resulted in many Native women living basic survival-level emotional lives. We accept being made invisible as a kind of Novocain rather than endure the constant grinding of historical traumas that directly targeted Native women's bodies and our ability to express ourselves in language and literacy."[47] To succeed at such expression, far from a luxury, is a crucial part of a broader struggle. And it won't just happen. While it is difficult to disagree with Kim Roppolo that "we need to speak to our communities in ways that are culturally *acceptable* and *recognizable*," I hope my analysis of the erotic also shows the need for Native critics to challenge what is acceptable and to question what has come to be recognizable in Native communities.

Akiwenzie-Damm argues that "To reclaim and express our sexuality is part of the larger path to de-colonization and freedom."[48] Harjo, throughout her work, affirms this need for Indian people to come to grips with their own desires as part and parcel of reaching for justice, which to me is the key to ethical theorizing. "What motivates us is mystery," she writes toward the end of *A Map to the Next World*, "how the aloof stone desires more than anything / to be opened, shivering and wet with love."[49]

Notes

1. Harjo, "Conversations between Here and Home," in *Last Song*, 13, and "Old Lines," in *What Moon Drove Me to This?*, 39, 69.

2. Harjo, "She Had Some Horses," in *She Had Some Horses*, 63–64; "Woman Hanging," in *Horses*, 22–23; "I Give You Back," in *Horses*, 73–74; "For Anna Mae," in *In Mad Love and War*, 7–8; "Perhaps the World," in *Woman Who Fell from the Sky*, 68.

3. Harjo, "Nine Below," in *Mad Love*, 60.

4. Harjo, "Motion," in *Horses*, 54.

5. Lorde, "Uses of Erotic," 53.

6. On a page of acknowledgments in the front of *In Mad Love and War*, Harjo says, "I wish also to thank Audre for her warrior self, her fierce and tender poetry. You helped me affirm that the erotic belongs in poetry, as in the self." See also Harjo, *Spiral of Memory*, 108.

7. Akiwenzie-Damm, "Erotica," 144, 146.

8. Miranda, "Dildos," 136, 145.

9. Lorde, "Uses of the Erotic," 53, 55.

10. Idid., 57.

11. Deloria, foreword, x, ix.

12. Lorde, "Uses of the Erotic," 56.

13. Akiwenzie-Damm, "Erotica," 145.

14. Harjo, "For Alva Benson," in *Horses*, 18.

15. See, for instance, "Rainy Dawn," in *Mad Love*, 32; "The Naming," in *Woman Who Fell*, 11–13; "Sonata for the Invisible," in *Woman Who Fell*, 49–50; and "Promise," in *Woman Who Fell*, 62–63.

16. Harjo, "Map," in *Map to the Next World*, 19.
17. Womack, *Red on Red*, 260, 261.
18. Harjo, "Map," in *Map*, 21.
19. Ibid., 19, 21.
20. Ibid., 20.
21. Harjo, "traveling through the dark," in *Map*, 102–103.
22. Ibid., 101.
23. Harjo, "Instinct," 16; "Forgetting," 41; and "Returning from the Enemy," 69–96, all in *Map*.
24. Harjo, "City of Fire," in *Mad Love*, 41.
25. Harjo, *Horses*, 6.
26. Harjo, *Spiral of Memory*, 108.
27. Akiwenzie-Damm, "Erotica," 147.
28. Harjo, "Heartshed," in *Mad Love*, 62.
29. Harjo, "Twins Meet Up with Monsters," in *Map*, 51.
30. Harjo, *Map*, 44.
31. Akiwenzie-Damm, "Erotica," 147–48.
32. Harjo, "The First Noni Daylight," 27, and "Origin," 33, in *What Moon*.
33. Harjo, "Someone Talking," in *What Moon*, 47.
34. Harjo, "She Remembers," in *Horses*, 46.
35. Harjo, "Deer Dancer," in *Mad Love*, 6.
36. Ibid.
37. Akiwenzie-Damm, "Erotica," 148.
38. Harjo, "Wolf Warrior," in *Woman Who Fell*, 46.
39. Ibid., 28, 29.
40. Ibid., 28, 29.
41. Ibid., 29.
42. Harjo, "Backwards, in *Horses*, 20; "The Psychology of Earth and Sky," in *Map*, 14; "There Was a Dance," in *What Moon*, 21–22.
43. Harjo, "There Are Oceans," in *What Moon*, 49.
44. Harjo, "Map to the Next World," in *Map*, 20.
45. Harjo, "Songs from the House of Death," in *Map*, 37.
46. Lorde, "Uses of the Erotic," 58.
47. Miranda, "Dildos," 138.
48. Akiwenzie-Damm, "Erotica," 151.
49. Harjo, "Four Songs," in *Map*, 104.

Theorizing American Indian Experience

CRAIG S. WOMACK

Part One

The problem I wish to examine in the first section of this essay is whether or not a historical and materialist theoretical commitment can adequately explain experience. Some of the motivation for this comes from reading the work of the promising new theorists who call themselves "postpositive realists" and whose ideas are best summarized in their anthology, *Reclaiming Identity: Realist Theory and the Predicament of Postmodernism.* I want to offer alternatives to their insistence on the rejection of foundationalism. Then, in the second part of the essay, I will focus on our own text, authored by Native critics, where many of our claims for theoretical legitimacy depend on how we view experience. Of particular concern to me in the concluding section will be the problem of privileging certain kinds of supposedly more authentic experiences over others by relegating intellectual endeavors to a second-rate role. And I will point out the contributions of those who have managed a more integrated philosophy of experience.

Realist theory, as espoused in *Reclaiming Identity*, is a reaction to the extremes of postmodernism—its seeming inability to make normative truth claims and its descent into a relativistic abyss where all things are equally fictitious, an egalitarianism that some critics have found less than liberatory, especially minority scholars. Somewhat unhappily, the rise of minority-area studies within the university has occurred simultaneously with the burgeoning radical skepticism that questions the very legitimacy of the kind of racial identity categories that minority studies has often embraced, many theorists problematizing long-held notions of any kind of collective identity, emphasizing their constructedness and the fluidity between inside and outside boundaries and deemphasizing any kind of essential, inherent, or universal basis for such identities.

Just when minorities are insisting on telling their own histories, it would seem, they find out that history is fiction—and, perhaps, not fiction having the virtues that novelists and storytellers celebrate. This is bad timing, to say the least, for those who want to enter the canonical fray of history. Minority scholars discover that the very notion that they constitute a "they," a distinct group with the ability to distinguish itself from other groups and claim a right to speak on its own behalf, is a constructed notion that "only" exists inside their heads (albeit I have to admit here that most postmodernists would argue that ideas are their own kind of powerful reality, an important notion that holds a great deal of validity).

In the turn toward linguistic as much as material realities, some of the wary might see in all this an insidious political move on behalf of European critics, a concerted effort of those already privileged to protect their positions of power. There may be some truth to this—no doubt individuals have abused positions of power—but such conjecture enters into issues of intentionality, which are difficult to gauge, and the theoretical problem of creating a monolithic group of so-called white critics. I have chosen to deal with the philosophical underpinnings of particular scholars rather than attempt to scrutinize the motivations of a huge body of people.

In terms of legitimating identity in today's theoretical environment, whatever genetic evidence might be offered for insider status, or any other kind of evidence, according to prevailing arguments, it will never be completely independent of the world of interpretation, which is mediated by the slippery effects of language. Racial identity involves an act of interpretation as much as fiction does—powerful fiction maybe but a fiction always rooted in all the same biases of perception as everything else in the fiction and nonfiction world. The degree to which identities might relate to anything real is simply indeterminable in any absolute sense. Race is an idea as much as a DNA code. Whatever the phenotypical and genetic differences might be will always be determined by the stories people tell about them. Racial difference is culturally determined, often, if not always, in relation to systems of power.

This school of thought insists on the inventedness of all things, construction by culture, and relationships to power that reward certain ideas and punish others. In the latter regard, postmodern theorists readily admit the existence of power and its abuses. The "predicament" that postpositive realist theorists point out in relation to postmodernism is that, given a world where oppression is a reality, evaluative judgments are necessary to identify things that are potentially harmful; yet, because of the death of any kind of universalized, essentialized truth, postmodernism puts us in the position of needing to make such judgments without a normative basis from which to make them. Moral claims are always relative, not absolute; they are constructed by culture, subjective perceptions affected by those doing the perceiving rather than objective realities that are determinable outside the biases of the perceiver. Anyone can make a claim but how does one determine its validity under these circumstances? A person wanting to effect change is left with the strategy of constructing her own fiction to compete with, to challenge all the other fictions. Who should win these narrative shooting matches when the rules, like the stories themselves, are inventions, fictions, culturally arbitrated?

In response to this conundrum, postpositve realists have sought ways to make normative truth claims once again possible. In some ways, the realists might be described as "having their cake and eating it too." They want to retain the theoretical sophistication of postmodernism in terms of looking at how history and culture give rise to ideas that are always mediated by human knowledge (rather than consisting of some kind of preexistent foundation) while also insisting that truth claims can be judged *relatively* true or false, thus, making it possible for minorities to assert their histories, claim identities, deem insider viewpoints relevant and meaningful, and so on. The key word, here, however, is "relatively"; this is the rub, whether or not postpositivists can effectively resist relativism.

The postpositive theorists, like their postmodern counterparts, cannot escape the theoretical bias against foundationalism. Part of this, I suspect, is a natural defensiveness because of the way minority scholars have been dismissed as naive essentialists rooted in some kind of primal approach to culture, one in which DNA, or ancestral spirits, or other supposedly ahistorical factors create a people, if in fact such things are ahistorical. Of course, one could never be happy with a theoretical approach that simply attempts to prove to "white folks" that one is not stupid, and the postpositive theorists have a lot more going for them than that. However thorny the path they travel, they are looking for ways to turn their attention to the social realities that surround us.

The realists are trying to react against theoretical movements that could potentially dismiss history—in the case of minorities their own history, which has not had the advantage of several centuries of domination before it was proclaimed a fiction. The kinds of questions the realists are tackling are essential ones in determining whether or not minority insider viewpoints are possible and distinguishable from outsiders' viewpoints. There is much good, obviously, in what they have set out to do.

The dilemma, as I see it, the way in which the postpositivists have failed to escape their own "predicament of postmodernism," is their insistence on a strong antifoundationalism as the basis for their theorizing. While they admit the existence of reality, this reality is only understandable through human knowledge. If one wants to rescue intellectualism from a relativistic morass—yet one still clings to the notion that the world consists only in terms of human intervention, at least whatever we can know of the world as humans—then how does one ever escape the rules of postmodernism? The only alternative is a version of postmodernism that describes much the same theoretical commitment as the old version, without any real theoretical difference but with a new theoretical jargon constituting its main distinctive feature. It is an irony—perhaps a necessary one but an irony nonetheless—to call oneself a realist and then make the real world only approachable through interpretation.

My position is no less problematic, yet I believe it has some validity, and I have the right to express it.

Why is my position problematic? Because once one subtracts interpretation from how we perceive the world, what is left? We know something is left, but we cannot describe it without interpretation, since the very act of describing it *is* an interpretation. Examining the effects of eliminating interpretation and searching for what is left will always be a purely theoretical exercise since none of us can actually do this.

What is left, apart from human mediation though, to take a stab at my own question, is the possibility that some essences actually exist: that is, some forms of knowledge, experiences, realities, and so on, outside the ones humans ponder in their heads, create through discourse, reward or punish through cultural institutions. I do not know for sure, but perhaps postpositive realists do not consider the viability of essentialism for fear of being seen as naive, as religious lunatics, as theoretical Luddites—or because of the admittedly difficult, some would say impossible, chore of saying just what exists outside the human imagination when one is himself or herself a human. I believe this leaves them with social construction, with mediation, with interpretation, with the discursive turn that insists that everything is contained within language that determines its subject (as well as its object), perceiver, as well as perceived. In other words, they are left with postmodernism, the very body of knowledge they hope to challenge. I say this in a spirit of dialogue, hoping that some of them might respond, and we can talk to each other.

One might wonder then whether or not postpositive theory is a paradigm shift as much as a slightly altered focus, well within the rules of postmodernism, that allows realists to judge historical, and other, claims as "relatively" more true or false in relation to other historical claims without committing to whether or not any of these things can be definitively linked to actual reality. (Although it is certainly important to note, and this is a theoretical core of postpositivism, that epistemic status, particularly race, gender, and class, is an extremely important factor when considering if something is "relatively" true or false. A foremost endeavor is matching claims with reality, even if it can never be asserted with full confidence in any absolute sense if the "match" is accurate.) A certain claim then might seem to describe a particular set of circumstances better than others—even if one can never absolutely determine what the true relationship between the claim and reality actually is. Realists make normative value judgments while still admitting that those judgments are mediated rather than inherently true in any sense. The word "relatively" shows up over and over again throughout *Reclaiming Identity*, possibly hundreds of times. (Obviously I have not done a word count.)

And the word, to give the realists their due, is an important one because one of the most important insights of postmodernism is that master narratives that claim a single truth that cancels out all others often end up being oppressive.

Postpositivists, by still embracing a postmodern skepticism in regard to master narratives while retaining the possibility of normative truth claims, have simply pulled postmodernism back toward a more centrist position, away from the radical skepticism that potentially could dismiss history as a discipline, not to mention minority studies as a legitimate site of knowledge. What the realists have not established is what the real basis for their history might be, and they will not be able to address that issue without tackling essentialism in some kind of serious way. Theirs is a useful position, in terms of reining in postmodern extremes, but I am the sort who wonders how we can be certain that there are no essences, that throughout history there have been no forms of knowledge that are intrinsic, even apart from human knowledge of them.

I see some trickiness in postpositivist definitions, some circular reasoning. If one starts talking about an essence for experience, the realists might object that the theorist is then proposing some kind of pure, unmediated experience, which is never possible. That critique works for them, however, because their definition of experience is mediation. Experience, for them, is the interpretation of an experience. They will, in fact, admit that interpretations are often rooted in events that have actually occurred.

Their point, of course, is that the experience can never be separated from the interpretation. In terms of my own "constituency," however, and here I am borrowing Sean Teuton's useful word, I doubt that everybody in the Native world defines experience as interpretation of some reality that can never actually be apprehended. This bothers me—this possible gap, this difference between my community's ideas and prevalent theory, as difficult as it is to measure on either side of the theory line or the social line or to know what one can do to remedy the situation and bring the two groups together. The challenge of such dilemmas has underscored much of my own work.

There is a strong chance that I may not understand postpositive commitments and have thus distorted their position; therefore, I highly recommend that people read *Reclaiming Identity* for themselves and carefully consider these arguments, since the ideas of this group seem like an important beginning step in the right direction. It is very important to note that the mainstay of their theory is an insistence that race, class, and gender are both real and substantial markers, in some kind of significant sense, that affect experience and that these markers of epistemic status can be applied in evaluating truth claims. These, of course, are important claims.

In advocating for a compassionate criticism, I do not want to reject their work because it fails to toe a particular theoretical line (though I certainly want to try to scrutinize their position). One might hope that we could garner the same respect for Indian critics from them as they learn about what we do. I would like to see a creative and life-affirming scholarship ever opening itself up to new ideas instead of closing them out. Disagreeing with critical positions can be inspired, I believe, by love of one's own community rather than by hatred of those one disagrees with. A harmony ethic is not a weakness but a fully realized engagement with the world and the consequences of one's actions. We are already poisoned enough by hatred in the academic world and the world at large.[1]

My first aim in this essay, then, will be to come out of the essentialist closet, so to speak, and to argue for a reexamination of the validity of certain kinds of essentialisms in relationship to experience. My second goal (not in terms of priority but in terms of the order in which I will address these issues), once I have argued the theoretical validity of experience, including considering foundationalism as a possibility, will be to say something about a recurring problem I see in Native studies, where certain experiences—namely, those associated with atttending ceremonies, telling or hearing oral stories, and being present in cultural milieus—are privileged over other kinds of experiences such as reading, interpreting, or authoring books; articulating theoretical notions; teaching university courses; engaging in various intellectual practices; and so on. Such a stance is based on a false dichotomy that opposes a mental world against a physical, culturally rich one.

These false binaries are corrosive and, at their most reactionary, treat difficult intellectual work as a tool of the enemy. They presume that participation can only be defined in physical terms, claiming physical experience as the only viable form of Native experience, thus valorizing forms of myopia that undermine sociopolitical sovereignty. The binaries assume culture without intellect or, at least, make intellect a second-class citizen, in effect sterilizing *both* thought and participation.[2] Lisa Brooks talks about the delicate balance between both and the way in which each has to be mediated by community deliberation rather than by individual decisions.

As I approach this task, I am aware of certain ironies, namely, my own insistence, in relation to the postmodern debate, on a physical reality having its own kind of presence that may constitute a form of knowledge that is as important as human knowledge. It may sound like my own theoretical stance also depends on a split between the mental and physical realms. A main purpose in this essay, then, will be to discuss how the *interdependence* of reality and interpretation does not cancel out the *independence* of either world. Reality and interpretation, to borrow a metaphor, are each sovereignties, and, like all sovereignties, they interact across their borders. Yet each can be imagined, in powerful ways, as an independent nation, which is not the same as an isolated nation.

I want to address some questions: Is human knowledge the only kind of knowledge there is? Is there ever an essence, a spiritual reality that coheres? If so, what are some of the limitations of our theoretical commitments that prioritize material and historical viewpoints? What are the possibilities we have yet to consider? How can we understand our own experience in a meaningful way? How can we understand the experiences of others?

I believe that what is needed is a reexamination, rather than a simple rejection, of essentialism. All too frequently charges of essentialism involve name-calling rather than a philosophical commitment. We have to get over this—the fear of exploring new ideas because someone might call them "essentialist"—as well as the tendency to label someone else as "essentialist" simply because we do not agree with them.

I would argue that "not all essentialisms are created equal." Some of them are useful. We need to understand the moments in critical history—our fears, reservations, critical advances, critical failings—that led to our abandonment of essentialism in the first place. I believe we can reject many of the problems that arise with universalizing, but I do not think it is wise to reject essentialism entirely.

I will turn briefly to some examples of essentialisms in the discipline I teach in, Native American studies. A teaching methodology, still popular, emphasizes an idea called the "Native perspective" or the "Native paradigm." I would have no problem with either of these approaches if we could simply add an "s," that is, pluralize perspective and paradigm so they become perspectives and paradigms. But it is the very singularity of the terms that is most insisted upon. This is a model that argues for a universal system of Native thought. If there are differences among tribes and across histories, its proponents would evidently argue, the amazing similarities far outweigh them.

In one of its worst manifestations, the teacher of the Native perspective persuasion draws a line down the middle of the blackboard. On one side there is a column labeled "Traditional Values" or some such. In this column goes all the good stuff, all the Indian stuff. The "Native mind" is nonlinear. Everyone and everything is related in the Indian world. There are no hierarchies. Humans do not place themselves above the rest of creation. Time is a river. The earth is sacred and always a mother. Sexuality is part of the natural world.

White people get to go on the other side, whoever these white people may be. Don't drink out of the Indian fountain, can't you see the sign? This category is variously labeled; it is often called, "Contemporary Values." This is where all the bad stuff goes; the workers of iniquity are cast into the lake of contemporary values where all those belong who do not love the earth. We learn from this column on the blackboard that "they" think oppositionally; they hierarchize things; they have a material, rather than a sacred, view of the planet; time is a straight line instead of a river; sexuality is sinful; and so on.

Freshman students tend to take this model apart rather handily, usually in about fifteen seconds, a fact that does not discourage the supporters of the Native perspective or the Native paradigm or the "Indian mind." These students raise their hands and say things like, "Up there on that side of the board where you've got all that stuff about white people? I'm not like that." This is when the mystical Indian look is most appropriate (it helps to have a window in the classroom, so you can stare off into the distance), as in "we have entered waters you can never understand, my white brother, but thanks for taking the class anyway." Docile students might mutter, "Yes, Kemo Sabe," or some such; more belligerent ones will keep arguing or drop the course.

I guess I do not need to belabor the point about the problems inherent in such a teaching methodology. A most obvious one is that it takes hundreds of different tribes and millions of individuals and dehistoricizes their experiences. It lifts its arguments outside time and space, history and geography: it is a philosophy removed from the land, from a specific sense of place or culture. According to its own arguments, it is a most un-Indian way of looking at the world. It is universalism taken to its most logical extreme in regard to both "whites" and Native people.

It is internally contradictory. It claims that Indians do not hierarchize the world, yet presents two columns that do just that by always prioritizing the "traditional" over the "contemporary." It often opposes a "Western perspective" against a "Native perspective," another popular way of titling the columns, in which the Western perspective is critiqued by virtue of its Judeo-Christian roots when, in fact, the Native perspective itself uses Christian arguments by arranging its presentation into what is largely an opposition of good versus evil.

When we start talking about "the white man," some might wonder which one we mean. Similarly, when we come up with the "Indian mind," just whose brain are we dealing with? The strengths of looking for those things that unite us across tribes can be undermined by an unrelenting insistence on a unitary Indian worldview. Indian viability depends on a radical incommensurability with "white" culture rather than its own integrity. Ironically enough, one's definition of things Indian will always depend on a "white" center, in this case, one that forms the basis of the opposition.

At its *very* worst, the Native perspective approach to teaching does not even require a chart. The strategy is to simply repeat the words "Native perspective" as many times as one can in a fifty-minute class hour, or an hour and fifteen minutes for classes that meet twice a week. By virtue of hearing "Native perspective" over and over again, the student can only assume that the term must mean something really important. Especially if the teacher is able to effectively convey the aforementioned guilt trip that "if you don't get it, don't worry, only Indians can understand." And if Indians give you any trouble, then only *real* Indians can understand.

Even a concept as obviously defective as *the* Native Perspective, however, can be made more credible by simply adding an "s" to the end of the word (and maybe getting rid of the singular "the" and a capital letter) so that it becomes "Native perspectives." Native perspectives then involve any Indian articulating an opinion. The discipline of Native studies becomes the scholarly endeavor to examine those opinions and assess their value and meaning, or, in some cases, to critique their lack of value and meaning in relation to the historical, cultural, legal, geographical, governmental, and other surrounding contexts that inform them.

Native scholarship, at its best, like Native culture, is a dynamic, living expression of intellectual, cultural, artistic, spiritual, and relational experiences and understandings. We do not presume an unchanging taxidermic worldview.[3]

Even some of those teaching the singular, capitalized "Native Perspective" may do it better than others. Some teachers, because of their own rich tribally specific backgrounds and sense of history, can support their universalist claims with examples from their own tribes, for instance. They can move back and forth between the universal and the local. Ultimately, all of us who teach have to make generalizations about the world, and we all seek some kind of balance between statements of abstraction and of exemplification. We cannot simply descend into an impotent relativism where all cohesive claims are impossible.

I want to bring home my point here that any given essentialism may be more nuanced than we are often willing to admit: In order to appreciate the position of those teaching from this Native perspective viewpoint, we have to understand that it represents a certain moment in Native studies history that has to do with where Native studies is as an academic discipline, the kind of environments that the people grew up in who advocate such a position, and so on. That discussion is beyond the scope of this particular essay, but a lot could be said about the protectionist and defensive mode that an academic discipline goes through in the early phases of its history, as well as about an older generation of Native scholars who grew up with a keen sense of guarding a much-abused system of knowledge that was in real danger of being co-opted and compromised. Theirs was a compelling understanding of a need for establishing and guarding some universal principles, some guidelines, some rules. In other words, before evaluating the Native perspective approach, we would need to consider the history of this particular essentialism.

As weak as the essentialism "*the* Native Perspective" is (depending on how it is taught), still other essentialims seem, well, essential. In Native studies we believe that the sovereign status of Native nations is central to the physical and cultural survival of tribes. Tribal sovereignty is not *necessarily* an essentialism, given that it is shaped by historical and material realities, but in today's theoretical world, if one considers the very extremes of poststructuralism, there are some who call into question *any* raced-based notions and/or collective identities. Tribal sovereignty depends not only on notions of race but on the idea of nation, and these are times when any kind of group identity can potentially be dismissed—not to mention the problem of equating nationalism with forms of oppression.

We now also face an internal critique in relation to sovereignty. Recent Native scholarship has questioned the validity of sovereignty because of its supposed European origins. The problem with this kind of analysis is that we end up with the etymological approach to Native studies, that is, a kind of point-of-origin argument. Whatever we are talking about, if it origniated in Europe, it is therefore irrelevant. This makes no sense because it is impossible to legitimate a culture, or a government, only to the degree to which it goes undetected, hidden from outside influences, isolated from Europe or anywhere else. Further, I think it is arguable that tribes had forms of sovereignty before European contact. The English origin of the word does not necessarily cancel out the relevance of the concept to Indians before or after contact. We know that means of identifying community members, understanding geographical relationships with neighbors, and working out jurisdiction have always existed among tribes, even if such understandings have changed over time or differ in significant ways from European jurisprudence.

When I talk about sovereignty, I hope it is understood that I believe that it has multiple dimensions. There is, for example, the kind of sovereignty often spoken of in Canada in the language of court cases and the Royal Commission reports that say that indigenous sovereignty is an "inherent, not a derivative right." Unfortunately, U.S. courts, and Congress, have failed to pick up on this important language, which insists that tribal sovereignty is not granted by courts; in fact, it preexists them. In Canada, First Nations sovereignty, in a sense, arises out of the very soil of the country and predates the British Crown, the Articles of Confederation that created the nation of Canada in 1867, the Repatriation Act of 1981 that gave Canada control of its own constitution, and so on. The concept of inherent rather than derivative rights applies in the United States, even if courts have been slow to recognize them: Native peoples, like all peoples, have rights to self-determination that do not originate in legislation, even though legislation becomes of utmost importance in regard to the outcomes of those rights.

So, this is one kind of sovereignty in its broadest, most expansive sense, sovereignty that is inherent rather than derivative. Another kind of sovereignty has to do with the political realities Native people have had to face, such as the plenary powers of Congress, which have been used, often successfully, to define, by limiting, sovereignty. A third form of sovereignty is imagined sovereignty. A tribe can win all the court cases in the world, but if its members are not sovereign inside their heads, the court victories will not do them much good. One of the primary vehicles for imagined sovereignty is oral and written literature and its attendant criticism. Stories provide key opportunities for community members to present images of themselves on their own terms, another powerful form of sovereignty.

In short, sovereignty is multifaceted, and I concur with Robert Warrior's arguments in *Tribal Secrets* that there is great potential in viewing sovereignty as an open-ended process rather than a terminal definition. When Native critics protest the European origins of sovereignty, I think they are using the wrong argument, one based on point-of-origin analysis, but the good thing is that they are trying to open up sovereignty to alternative definitions and are seeking ways in which Native realities might broaden our concepts of sovereignty. If the argument, however, is to simply change the name to "peoplehood" or self-determination or any other number of terms, we are still dealing with words in English, a point Jace Weaver makes in the book *American Indian Literary Nationalism*, and I wonder how they escape the supposed dangers of the Euro-origins of their own alternative terms. The point should be the transformative potential of sovereignty rather than only the etymological history of the term used to describe it.

Given this multifaceted view of sovereignty, we can hold out hope for self-determination, for example, for terminated or nonrecognized tribes, since one aspect of sovereignty is the way it is an inherent right practiced by self-determining communities rather than a derivative one granted by colonial governments. These nations are self-determining by virtue of their understanding of themselves as such as much as by their recognition by the United States. They are faced with political struggles with governments that circumscribe their rights or their understanding of themselves—or, in some cases, even with other Native people who might claim they are less than "real" for a host of different reasons (lack of ratified treaties and any other number of possibilities). Sovereignty does not solely rest on U.S. recognition. A history of internal recognition, practice, and exercise of sovereignty also comes into play. (And, to be sure, the degree of recognition *outside* the self-determining community by other tribes is a determining factor also. Simply proclaiming sovereignty is not the same thing as deserving it. Sovereignty is exercised across borders in relation to sovereign neighbors as well as within borders.)

Historicizing sovereignty, then, is one way of teaching Native studies. This approach is different from one that is based on generalizing terms such as "the Native perspective." Sovereignty positions, when rooted in historical inquiry such as specific court cases, legislation, and events inside and outside Indian country, can be analyzed with all of the favorite tools of today's scholars. This is to say, they can be studied and assessed in relation to history, cultural contexts, theories, interpretations, and—to use a favorite phrase—their "linguistic turn" or degree of constructedness. And they can thus be found useful or found wanting. They are not somehow inherently naive.

I have given an example of an essentialism that does not hold up under close scrutiny, the singular Native perspective. I have suggested that it becomes a viable concept when pluralized and taught in relation to historical particulars. I have presented another possible essentialism (if one sees collective identities as potential essentialisms) that is meaningful in Native studies, the concept of sovereignty. Since I am a literary specialist, I want to consider more closely issues of language and give an example of one more "good essentialism." What, for example, does Kiowa author N. Scott Momaday mean when he says, "A word has power in and of itself. It comes from nothing into sound and meaning; it gives origin to all things. By means of words can a man deal with the world on equal terms. And the word is sacred. A man's name is his own; he can keep it or give it away as he likes. Until recent times, the Kiowas would not speak the name of a dead man. To do so would have been disrespectful and dishonest. The dead take their names with them out of the world."[4]

I will try to explain what I believe Momaday means by giving two examples, one from my personal experience and another from a powerful body of southeastern literature, the Cherokee incantations. Racially, culturally, and spiritually (and in other important ways), I am connected to the Muscogee Creek Nation and, to a lesser extent, to the Cherokee Nation. I want to discuss an example taken from my own religious community at Tallahassee Wakokiye

Creek ceremonial grounds. There are other people, certainly, far more qualified to talk about Creek religion than I am—to be specific, elders, fluent Creek language speakers, medicine people, leaders at Creek traditional grounds, pastors of Creek Baptist and Methodist churches, to name only a few. So, I hope to make personal observations rather than speak from some kind of ethnographic, or other, position of authority. At the same time, I don't want to dismiss my own private experience of these matters. Most importantly, I will use these ideas to analyze the role of language within literature, a situation I am more comfortable with than saying anything definitive about Creek religion.

The highlight of the religious year for Creek ceremonialists (a common distinction is made in the tribe between the ceremonialists and Creek Christians) is the Green Corn ceremony, a yearly ritual of renewal and celebration that involves rebuilding the arbors, remaking the sacred fire, and relighting fires in the camps of the participants. There are men's dances, women's dances, and the night dances where both men and women have central roles. There is medicine-taking for religious reasons that have to do with health and spiritual well-being. And in this regard I want to make an observation. We male members of the grounds sit out under the arbors for many hours while the *hillis heyya*, the medicine maker, makes the medicine. I do not intend to go into detail here about the specifics of what happens with the medicine because first of all I do not know; this requires a particular kind of training and experience that involves a lifetime of knowledge undertaken by certain qualified people. Secondly, even if I were one of the people who knew the details of these rituals, there would probably be matters with certain limitations as to public exposure. In short, I do not know what the medicine person is saying while he chants over the medicine, nor would I divulge this if I did.

I simply want to make a point about language. The medicine man speaks over the medicine for a very long time, and it is my understanding that it is this process of prayerful speaking that turns a tub full of what seems to be everyday water and a particular root that grows in our country into medicine that not only has pharmaceutical qualities but spiritual properties that help us dance, stay awake, and endure and that, in the coming year, will provide spiritual protection. Some people might say all of this is "just in our heads," the power of it socially conferred rather than inherent. It is my belief, however, that not all of this can be explained as social practice, and it is an insistence on human chauvinism and the inability to deal with spiritual reality that limits theoretical opportunities today. We have movements in theory that emphasize a sounder engagement with the material world but only inasmuch as that practice can be attributed to culture, that is, the social practice of humans. The fact that water, however, is always composed of both hydrogen and oxygen molecules together does not mean there is no such thing as hydrogen or oxygen apart. Spiritual reality is mediated through human social practice, but that does not mean spirits do not exist apart from humans or that ceremony only exists in the meanings humans give it.

The medicine I describe has the power to reconstitute physical reality, to turn a rather ordinary-looking washtub full of stuff, actually very particular stuff, into medicine infused with spirits. The singing, the dancing, the proper care of the fire, the medicine itself, and other factors that happen over the course of many days are part of a reconstitution where ordinary reality is transformed, and spirits become participants alongside humans. "Touching medicine," as we say over home, cannot be fully explained by social construction and/or human mediation to my way of thinking, a view admittedly influenced by the religious nationalism of Green Corn practice that has such a long history within the territory, and before the territory in the home country in Georgia and Alabama.

I want to extend this argument to the literary realm. A particularly rich body of literature among southeastern Indian peoples is contained in the incantations that are used to go to water (a monthly purification ritual), to ward off evil, to lure a love interest, to attract deer in successful and respectful hunting relationships, to cure specific physical ailments, and so on. Modern readers often describe this substantial body of written and oral discourse as poetry, given that the language is intensely imagistic, artistic, and aesthetically different from everyday speech. To be sure, it is poetry in a very special sense. The distinction has to do with the specific performative and ritualistic aspects of the poems as well as the expected outcomes from having said them. These poems are astounding in the quality of their images, even in their English translations. To my way of thinking, they are world-class literature. Much could be said about the use of these songs, chants, and poems.

For my purposes here, I will note the special performative nature of these incantations, which are spoken next to running water, facing east, at sunrise or sunset, depending on what the desired effect is. There are complicated narrative connections here, rooted in stories, but the idea is that this is the most magical time of day, when the night world and day world have merged in a perfect unity and that these moments contain the greatest potential for enacting the supernatural. Tobacco is often involved, and the belief is that by the time the incantation is spoken, usually in patterns of four and seven, the tobacco will no longer be ordinary tobacco. It will be supernatural tobacco, the smoking of which will cause certain things to happen such as a cure, the attraction of a love interest, the appearance of deer for the hunter, or the warding off of evil.

At a certain point the chant reaches a crescendo, where the things being spoken of begin to occur. Jack and Anna Kilpatrick, both Cherokees and Cherokee speakers, captured something of this idea in the title of their master work of translation, *Walk in Your Soul: Love Incantations of the Oklahoma Cherokee.* The title refers to a particular line in one of the incantations, "I am now walking in the very middle of your soul." By the time the speaker reaches that line, the resistant lover has already had his or her will redirected, so much so that if the recalcitrant lover wants to continue to be resistant, that person might have to counteract with his or her own medicine. Before the incantation ends, the chant has had a real effect on the Cherokee cosmos, sometimes one that can be gauged by visual observation of one's immediate environment: a change of heart in the reticent or resistant object of one's affections; a physical cure in the case of an illness addressed in a healing poem; the appearance of deer after singing a hunting song.

In this essay, I am more interested in the philosophy of the language itself in the incantations. These chants are something like participating in a very complicated chess game where spiritual forces are played off each other. The words become active and actually move spiritual entities about in beneficial alliances. This has to do with an extremely complex system of "symbolism"—I admit this is not a very good word for the language of this particular poetry—where spiritual forces from the Cherokee pantheon that inhabit the Upper, Lower, and Middle Worlds have to be arranged into a complex balance through the words of the poem. It is the language itself (the language is a heightened religious language much different from everyday spoken Cherokee), and saying it under these special ritual circumstances next to water at dawn or dusk, that will actually cause these spirits to realign themselves in ways beneficial to the speaker or his or her patient.

The idea, however, goes far beyond the notion that the words can make things happen. What is fascinating is that the words themselves can become entities; they step into being. There are special verb forms that involve actualization,[5] and language is no longer referential; the words have become what is being spoken about. This is especially true in regard to the invocation of the color red in the incantations, where red is no longer an adjective; red becomes a "thing," a spiritual force to be reckoned with, an increase in the speaker's spiritual potency. The "red lines" from one of the incantations read thusly,

> Now under the morning Red, now under the treetops I
> just submerged myself . . .
> My Red Attire, desired by Red Eyes, I have just come to
> spread out. . . .[6]

Jack and Anna Kilpatrick explicate these lines:

> There is no equivalent in English for the Cherokee term that means the glow of the morning sky, the *Morgenrote,* just before the sun rises; for built into the word is the connotation that this auroral phenomenon is impregnated with miraculous creative power. Like a disembodied spirit, says the incantator, he has bathed in this sea of magical red up there at the level of the treetops; he is now clothed in radiant enchantment, and can say to a rival: "I speak with supernatural authority!" and can say to himself: "I lay down my own Pathway (i.e., future)!" He knows that he is the object of envious admiration, which he extracts merely to add to his already overpowering glory.[7]

I have tried, then, to cautiously critique a particular essentialism, in this case the Native perspective, while advocating the power of a different essentialism that has to do with the sacred dimension of language as experienced in Muscogee ceremony and Cherokee literature. I cannot somehow "prove" the power of this kind of medicine to the skeptic, though my claims seem to me as reasonable as most claims made by theorists of various persuasions. I am not a secular critic. I do not believe that secular criticism is inherently more analytical or that religious criticism is, by default, only committed to faith instead of reason. It is the quality of the criticism that counts, and secular criticism is no more guarantee of objectivity than religious criticism is assurance of bias. My rhetorical strategy in relation to essentialism, moreover, has been the easily recognizable "don't throw out the baby with the bathwater" school of logic. Do not take a bad essentialism, in other words, to mean that all essentialisms are bad.

In terms of spiritual essences, then, I am not willing to attribute the whole of Native religions to the way they are created through language, discourse, mediation, and human knowledge. I want to leave space open for other spiritual presences besides my own and that of my own species—such as water, wind, landforms, spirits, ancestors who have passed on, stomp dance singers long since dead who join their voices with ours at the grounds as we sing during the night dances, any number of other lives we share the planet with who help shape our, and their own, realities. Maybe they have a whole discourse of their own, that is to say, their version of what constitutes discourse. Why wouldn't they? The fact that I do not know much about the stories they tell, or whatever realities they experience for themselves, does not excuse me from an ethical imperative to try to imagine them if I want to be responsible for living on a planet I share with many others. Though no one can know all the stories, neither can one get by very effectively by listening only to (or telling only) his or her own. It is a mistake, a rather glaring one, to look at the difficulty of the chore of listening to nonhuman others and to thus conclude, okay, then I will concentrate only on human discourse and forget about the rest or, even more problematically, assume that everything is contained within human imagination.

Terry Eagleton, in a recent assessment of postmodernism, has made these points well in relation to the problem of assuming that all of reality can be located inside cultural theory:

> To convert the whole world into culture is one way of disavowing its independence of us, and thus of disowning the possibility of our death. If the world depends for its reality on our discourse about it, then this seems to lend the human animal, however "decentered," an imposing centrality. It makes our existence appear less contingent, more ontologically solid, and so less of a prey to mortality. We are the precious custodians of meaning, since we are all that stands between reality and utter chaos. It is we who give tongue to the dumb things around us. Culturalism is right that a natural event like death can be signified in a

> myriad cultural styles. But we die anyway. Death represents Nature's final victory over culture. The fact that it is culturally signified does not stop it from being a non-contingent part of our creaturely nature. It is our perishing, not our bestowals of meaning, which is necessary. The dumb things around us fared perfectly well before we happened upon the scene. Indeed, they were not at that time dumb at all, since it is only we who define them as mute. Death, however, which sketches an intolerable limit to the omnipotent will, is too indecent an event to be much spoken of in the society (the United States) from which a good deal of culturalist thought springs, which may be one reason why such thought can prosper there.[8]

I would simply add to Eagleton's Marxist-influenced insights that religious questions might also be at the very heart of these matters. The idea of presence and nonpresence, which is part of the language debate in relation to signification, is a spiritual matter, especially if one argues, as I do, for the possibility of presence, of inherency. To argue for presence, however, or a metaphysical dimension of language, does not cancel out the way language is also socially constructed. These two phenomena are not mutually exclusive. In addition to the magical properties of the aforementioned chants, there are all the ways humans ponder, interpret, and act on them. Their realities, obviously, are also socially conferred; however, I would argue not exclusively so. As I have said, water does not cancel out the existence of hydrogen and oxygen any more than human mediation cancels out the nonhuman world that exists apart from humans.

This brings me, then, to the next important part of my argument. While acknowledging a spiritual world and presenting Native religion as a rich source of critically engaged theory, I do not want to deny a material or historical one. In regards to Indian country I want to be able to talk about treaties, and their roots in the U.S. Constitution, as comfortably as I talk about Native spirituality. People who have worked or lived in treaty-based tribal communities know that treaties, in fact, are part of a sacred discourse in which spiritually based beliefs cannot be separated from a complicated legal history. There is a whole body of oral storytelling that never gets recorded in the hundreds of so-called Indian oral tradition collections that continue to be published, which has to do with Indians talking about the history of treaty signings, what people understood, the intentions of the signers, the treaty's relationship to earlier agreements, the implementation of the treaty, and so on.

Evidently, the Indian experts who publish anthologies do not perceive stories about treaties to be Indian enough. Only talking-animal stories seem to qualify, alongside monster slayers, trickster tales, and creation accounts. Tribes are still almost always viewed exclusively as cultures rather than also as legally defined political entities, a misperception that radically affects the representation of all things Indian, including what is believed to be Indian literature. Treaty stories often have a sense of the sacred about them as strong as that surrounding any creation account. (Lest I be mistaken, let me say it is not my intention to dismiss the power of creation accounts or their accuracy in explaining how Native people came to be on this continent and any other number of realities.) Every year we have more (sometimes shallow) writings about oral traditions, literary "tricksters," and the like, with little scholarship focused on treaties, and the stories that contextualize them, as literature. To talk about treaties is to discuss living nations; it is more palatable to an Indian-hating public to present Indians as historical artifacts.[9]

Let me move on to another of the questions I raised at the beginning of this essay, which has to do with not only understanding our own experience but that of others. This becomes a crucial issue for the social or literary critic. Like it or not, even if we are not consciously aware of such a role, we are often in the rather precarious position of summarizing human experience, that is, abstracting experience into critical theories.

What is the relationship between our theories and the people we are theorizing about? Do the subjects of our theorizing see themselves in the same way as we describe them in books, journal articles, classroom lectures, and so on? How do we bring their self-representations into our theorizing? I see this as one of the most salient, as well as the most difficult, ethcial questions in my life as a scholar. When I am writing about Muscogee Creek people, or other Native people, obviously I cannot send out a survey and compile the results to see if my literary depictions and interpretations are on the mark. I cannot simply turn my work over to the tribe and get it returned with a stamp of approval or rejected with an accompanying restraining order. Who would the tribe pick to be responsible for the "official tribal opinion"? I have to depend on a lived relationship that is a lifelong process and never an easy one (although certainly joyous at times).

In my own work, I have made a symbolic attempt at stressing this point. I have taken great pains to imagine a Muscogee Creek response to my own theorizing and even written literary criticism that includes comic dialect letters where Creek people talk back to my text (that is to say, Creek people who I have invented in my imagination, not actual letters from Creek readers, though I get those too). This is an imperfect measure of the community, to be sure; nonetheless, this is my attempt to try to think about how those I am writing about might respond to what I am saying about them, or at least to consider that. I use the one tool most immediately available to me to unite my experience with theirs—my imagination.

Imaginative vision provides one of the best means for accessing and understanding this vast field we call experience. This is both a rational and a spiritual exercise. The presence of spirits has never precluded human interactions and interventions or the use of our minds (although religion in its worst sense sometimes discourages the use of the mind). A classic example of cooperation between humans and spirits is found in Leslie Marmon Silko's massive

1991 opus, *Almanac of the Dead*, which says that the spirits are whispering to people all over the world that Indians are going to get North America back. The novel makes clear, however, that humans working out this spiritual mandate, especially in relationship to the ruling power structures, find it to be a very complicated matter indeed. When Momaday says, then, that a word "has power in and of itself. It comes from nothing into sound and meaning; it gives origin to all things," I believe he implies an interaction between the spiritual and material worlds. Giving language inherency, or essence, however, does not cancel out the effect that human beings have on these spiritual entities we often call words. Once they come into sound and meaning they are circulated among humans who also begin exerting their influences on *them*. It goes both ways. My concern in this essay is the theoretical tendency to privilege subject positions, that is, human perceptions. (One might even wonder why it is a given that humans always occupy the subject positions.)

The theorists keep reminding me that experience can never be separated from mediation. If that is true, then we also have to acknowledge the converse: that mediation can never be separated from the experiences where interpretations originate. In today's theoretical climate, we put more emphasis on the interpretations. We might claim to do so because of the impossibility of accessing the experience itself in its pure unmediated form, but we cannot proceed as if that means that the experience itself was never there, that it never had a site of origin. And there may be some value in trying to at least imagine how any given experience came into being before it was filtered through various levels of discourse, even if this imagining of a pure, emergent experience is an act of fiction-making. I am a novelist. I am a strong proponent of good fiction.

Discourse itself, of course, has a point of origin, or maybe many points of origin, as difficult as it is to say where they all might be. It is built out of words, after all. A word is never completely separated from its origins, from the story of its emergence or the emergence itself. The evolution of a word is, at least partially, in a physical act, that of speaking, which involves air and sound and movement and vibration and expulsion and breathing in and breathing out and a whole host of other physical experiences. Even when we read a word, rather than hear one spoken, we imagine its sounds, imagine it being said out loud, hear a voice. Imagining itself is a real event. There are even neurons and electrical impulses set off in the physical world during acts of the imagination. Words, in fact, *do* bear a relationship to their referents, to the act of speech from which they have evolved, even when they are in print. Printed words continue to also be spoken. And imagined. Speech emanates from the human body, specifically from the heart, the source of blood and breath. Another referent for language, then, is our bodies. And, of course, there are many other referents. And these bodily referents exist independently of our interpretation of them, though these many worlds also join forces. Whoever is reading this essay right now has a body, whether or not I imagine the reader's body inside my head. And I have a body, whether or not she or he imagines me. We are not created 100 percent by human discourse.

The human body, as I will discuss in the second half of this essay, is a key turning point for any materialist philosophy. Terry Eagleton also claims the body as a foundation for ethics:

> To say that morality is basically a biological affair is to say that, like everything else about us, it is rooted ultimately in the body. As Alasdair MacIntyre observes, "Human identity is primarily, even if not only, bodily and therefore animal identity. It is the mortal, fragile, suffering, ecstatic, needy, dependent, desirous, compassionate body which furnishes the basis of all moral thought. Moral thought puts the body back into our discourse. Friedrich Nietzsche maintained that the roots of justice, prudence, bravery and moderation, indeed the whole phenomenon of morality, were essentially animal. In this sense, ethics resembles aesthetics, which started life in the mid-eighteenth century not as a language about art, but as a way of investigating bodily experience. . . .
>
> It is because of the body, not in the first place because of Enlightenment abstraction, that we can speak of morality as universal. The material body is what we share most significantly with the whole of the rest of our species, extended both in time and space. Of course it is true that our needs, desires and sufferings are always culturally specific. But our material bodies are such that they are, indeed must be, in principle capable of feeling compassion for any others of their kind. It is on this capacity for fellow-feeling that moral values are founded; and this is based in turn on our material dependency on each other.[10]

The challenge, of course, is just *how* do we get beyond a manic anthrocentric chauvinism and assumptions of human experience as the only possible measure of lived experience, interpretation, and knowledge? If we advocate a relational approach to the world and to our scholarly endeavors, how do we engage with other realities and nonhumans?[11] Being a human myself, my answer to this question must be a tenuous one. Yet I am willing to venture that the defining markers of this engagement are qualities of imagination, contemplation, and compassion. I must confess I do not know all the answers. In the opening passages of *Talking Indian,* Anna Lee Walters acknowledges that we must approach language respectfully by admitting there are some things we do not understand about it, even suggesting the power of that which remains in mystery. I am going to make a leap of faith in my discussion by relying on an age-old tribal religious practice, that of vision.

Carefully considered imaginative vision is one of the ways we understand these relationships between humans and nonhumans. Vision has to do with going beyond the "facts," which one might note is also a key critical move in theorizing. An interpretation has to do with coming up with some kind of meaning out of the "raw data," if you will, and making speculative leaps toward understanding its implications.

Vision provides one of our best hopes for accessing and understanding experience. In my own work, especially in *Drowning in Fire,* I have applied this to linking historical accounts that one reads or hears with personally lived experience. I have argued that history means very little until we develop a relationship with it that in this cyberage we might call "interactive." We can grow up with history books or even as the recipients of a powerful oral tradition. Until we imagine these stories for ourselves, however, they mean little more than facts and dates, undifferentiated names and places, the kind of "capital H" History that most people have resigned themselves to, even historians. Especially historians. I am talking about more than developing a capacity to empathize with people from our pasts. This has to do with placing ourselves inside their stories, becoming participants in history, more specifically, turning our selves into characters in a story. History must be dreamed. It has to be authored. It must be turned into a fiction before it can ever be true. This is not only the job of history professors; in fact, some of them may be the least qualified for the position. This is the responsibility of any human being who desires an ethical relationship to her past. History is a vision quest, the quintessential religious experience. How else, if not through vision, can we access these experiences from the past so we may also experience them?

One of the best descriptions of historical vision that I know of occurs in N. Scott Momaday's essay "The Man Made of Words." Momaday's unique encounter with Kiowa history occurred after he had penned the last words to his multigenre masterpiece, *The Way To Rainy Mountain.* He had written about a historical figure, a Kiowa woman by the name of Ko-sahn, who remembered and told of the last Kiowa sun dance. Momaday had known her in his childhood when she was already very old, but she had long since passed away by the time he had written his book. To the author's great surprise, she insisted on giving him a history lesson before she would let him declare his work completed. This is a rather long quotation but important enough to include in its entirety:

> For some time I sat looking down at these words on the page, trying to deal with the emptiness that had come about inside of me. The words did not seem real. I could scarcely believe that they made sense, that they had anything whatsoever to do with meaning. In desperation almost, I went back over the final paragraphs, backwards and forwards, hurriedly. My eyes fell upon the name Ko-sahn. And all at once everything seemed suddenly to refer to that name. The name seemed to humanize the whole complexity of language. All at once, absolutely, I had the sense of the magic of words and of names. Ko-sahn, I said, and I said again KO-SAHN.

Then it was that that ancient one-eyed woman Ko-sahn stepped out of the language and stood before me on the page. I was amazed. Yet it seemed entirely appropriate that this should happen.

"I was just now writing about you," I replied, stammering. "I thought —forgive me—I thought that perhaps you were . . . that you had . . . "

"No," she said. And she cackled, I thought. And then she went on. "You have imagined me well, and so I am. You have imagined that I dream, and so I do. I have seen the falling stars."

"But all of this imagining," I protested, "this has taken place—is taking place in my mind. You are not actually here, not here in this room." It occurred to me that I was being extremely rude, but I could not help myself. She seemed to understand.

"Be careful of your pronouncements, grandson," she answered. "You imagine that I am here in this room, do you not? That is worth something. You see I have existence, whole being, in your imagination. It is but one kind of being, to be sure, but it is perhaps the best of all kinds. If I am not here in this room, grandson, then surely neither are you."

"I think I see what you mean," I said meekly. I felt justly rebuked. "Tell me, grandmother, how old are you?"

"I do not know," she replied. "There are times when I think that I am the oldest woman on earth. You know the Kiowas came into the world through a hollow log. In my mind's eye I have seen them emerge, one by one, from the mouth of the log. I have seen them so clearly, how they were dressed, how delighted they were to see the world around them. I must have been there. And I must have taken part in that old migration of the Kiowas from the Yellowstone to the Southern Plains, near the Big Horn River, and I have seen the red cliffs of Palo Duro Canyon. I was with those who were camped in the Wichita Mountains when the stars fell."

"You are indeed very old," I said, "and you have seen many things."

"Yes, I imagine that I have," she replied. Then she turned slowly around, nodding once, and receded into the language I had made. And then I imagined I was alone in the room.[12]

Momaday's poetic riff on the word "imagine" functions to develop various imaginings within imaginings, that is, the author's imagining of Ko-sahn and Ko-sahn's imaginings of the Kiowa emergence from the hollow long, the much later movement from Yellowstone to the southern plains in the 1700s, and the falling-star event that occurred in 1833.

This is how we approach the paradox we are up against. How can we ever know what experience is in its original forms, apart from mediation, interpretation, our perceptions? We cannot. Reality may exist with or without us, but whatever we can know is affected by our thoughts, no matter how spiritual the message. But we can imagine the places where experiences originate.

We can see the emergence story of an experience, like Ko-sahn sees the orignal Kiowa emergence from below the earth and up into the larger landscape through the hollow log, in hers—and in our—mind's eye. And this imagining is essential. Ko-sahn claims that it takes on a life of its own. I am arguing that we need to imagine the origins of experience instead of merely focusing on all the levels of discourse it gets refracted through. Even if we are "making up" these emergence stories of experience.

This story serves to illustrate Momaday's famous statement in the same essay that "the greatest tragedy that can befall us is to go unimagined."[13]

Dreaming the origin stories of experience puts us in an active, rather than a passive, or unexamined, relationship to experience. In the aforementioned fiction writing of mine I have argued that inheriting a culture is not enough. It is not sufficient, that is to say, to simply be a recipient. We also have to create our own personal cultures that dream, imagine, scrutinize, talk back, challenge, revise, corroborate the culture that we have inherited. We can have history imposed on us or we can create our own. It might not be particularly easy to affect the power structures that control official history, the official story, so to speak, but we all have a wonderful source of personal authority in our imaginations. The way we understand our own experience in relation to collective experience is through a process of vision. This puts us in a different relationship to others—and I do not mean here only human others—when we dream their stories, one that demands, ultimately, that we examine our lives in light of theirs and their lives in light of ours. We cannot bear witness to a culture alone; we need to imagine others who can help us. We can only have so much physical contact with other members of our communities, past and present. Much has to be dreamed.

I hope for a dynamic and engaged relational understanding of culture and scholarship, one in which we are active participants in the continual creation of the people as well as the intellectual and artistic products of the people. I want to challenge the static taxidermies of so much of contemporary criticism as it is applied to Indians.[14] It is my hope that this criticism can be oriented toward community activism and an analysis of material circumstances. Liberated imaginations may look beyond social realities in order to dream of better ones that do not exist yet, but this need not be the same as abandoning the material world.

In psychoanalytical terms, one's dreams are the playground for the subconscious. Those (feelings) who cannot come out to play during the day come out at night. This kind of dreaming is somewhat beyond our control, though evidently some people can manipulate some of the images in their dreams. A dreamer can be a victim of frightening dreams. Or surprised and delighted by them. It's a crapshoot.

But there are ways we can dream in our waking hours where we control free play yet still let it take us on wild rides to those places we normally cannot go—such as the origin points of experience. We can always choose to investigate the mirror, the images of experiences, the many layers they get refracted through, the simulations, the discourse, and so on. But some dreamers might wonder about what caused the image to appear in the mirror in the first place, the source of the image. We access this through our imaginations. The theoretical stance that all experience is mediated may be true enough in a factual sense but not in a visionary sense, where there are probably more possibilities, where experiences can be approached at their places of origin, where we can stand off in the tree line, as Ko-sahn did (and Momaday did) and we readers do, and watch the Kiowas emerge out of the hollow log.

Of course, there is also a cautionary note in all of this, and this is where our theory becomes very useful to us. One can imagine oneself (or others) inaccurately. The postpositive notion of epistemic status is apropos here, the idea that race, class, and gender are both real and substantial markers that affect experience. Numerous people in other eras, as well as today's New Agers, have gone loco on universalism while forgetting about the ways in which their own histories establish certain parameters that limit the degree to which they can "become" something they are not. For an in-depth discussion of these matters, I direct readers to Geary Hobson's, Leslie Silko's, and Wendy Rose's now-famous essays on the issue of white shamanism.

In short, a key issue here is universalism, the assumption that there is a stream of spirituality that everyone can tap into. Carl Jung discussed archetypes that serve as a kind of entry point into a universalized spiritual accessibility, the idea that certain motifs from dreams, visions, and literatures occur across cultures and time periods and mark a shared human religious reality. Joseph Campbell's important work, *The Hero with a Thousand Faces*, also advances the idea of certain universal literary archetypes. Another incredibly important influence on these ideas is orthodox Christianity in which the gospels are believed to be universally applicable; indeed, they must be preached to all peoples, rather than maintained only in a particular community marked by geogrpahy, culture, national boundaries, ethnicity, and so on. In Christ, according to the apostle Paul, there is neither Jew nor Greek; the gospel message must be proclaimed to the ends of the earth.

Some readers might note that my call to imaginative vision is suspiciously like this notion of tapping into a universal spiritual stream, a dangerous romanticism, and, indeed, there is potential for abuse. It is important to note, however, that, like the realist theorists, I am convinced that epistemic markers such as race, gender, and class (and I would add to the list some other factors such as geographies, landmarks, jurisdictions, citizenships, affiliations, sovereignties) are incredibly important factors in evaluating claims about spiritual access. Tribal claims can be evaluated in relationship to these real-world benchmarks. If someone says he is an Indian or says he has had a spiritual experience or says he is an Indian because he has had a spiritual experience, there are material criteria I can use to evaluate that claim.

At no point in history has it been more imperative to allow compassionate spirits into our theorizing and to check those spirits against the social realities that surround us. While human technology increased faster in the twentieth century than in all the centuries before, spirituality has declined at some kind of exponential rate. We live with more violence and brutality against fellow humans, and nonhumans, than any epoch before ours, including the medieval ages. In the First World we have the privilege of hiding our faces from the suffering of others, forever blinding ourselves with our absolute faith in progress. The United States's recent, and ongoing at the time of this writing, bombing of Iraq is an example of a nation that is technologically advanced while spiritually bankrupt (nonetheless producing as much religious noise as any place on the planet about its own righteousness, politicians and others somehow claiming a gospel basis for their immorality). A religious position, in and of itself, is no guarantee of human decency; thus my claim for vision must also vigorously insist on a rigorous critique of "vision." We cannot simply turn traditionalism, in this case in the form of vision, into another sacred cow.

The power to dream, imagine, and, especially, to empathize seems lost on the United States. In our most recent history, the Iraq war was possible only because of our ability to distance ourselves from it rather than imagine the tremendous suffering it has inflicted. At least once in his life, N. Scott Momaday tells us, a person needs to concentrate on the remembered earth. Iraq is part of the earth we all share, and it is critical we imagine it, remember it, become involved in re-membering rather than dis-membering it. We need as well to imagine the effect of this war on our home landscape, our economy, our educational system, and, most important, our families who continue to lose sons and daughters, husbands and wives, brothers and sisters.

Morality is the most important question theorists face today, and it is mostly ignored, relegated to the organizationally "religious," who have a long history of spiritual incompetence. Theory cannot simply opt out of the issues of our time, religious or otherwise. Wading through the minefield of philosophical traps inherent in theory is challenging, but I would like to suggest that Native critics should turn toward their religious traditions, not away from them, in confronting these issues. Moreover, they must confront these traditions as critics not merely as cheerleaders. If *ofunka*, the Creator, has given me a job, say, the job of being a critic, then I should do my job: I should criticize in the best, creative, compassionate sense of the term. To the degree I am capable, I would like to suggest strategies rather than offer the usual clichés around the aphorisms of "just listen to the elders" and "respect traditions," since both those processes are complicated, mediated endeavors that are never easy or straightforward and are weighed down in complex issues of interpretation themselves.

In concluding this first section I would like to say that interpretations and experiences outside those of the human are interdependent, but they also manifest powerful independences. If for one reason or another, human life ends on earth—a possibility that becomes more likely every year because of the apparent inability of the political leadership of the United States and its citizens to imagine themselves in relation to the remembered earth—much will still remain whether or not we're here to interpret it. The land and other forms of life will still be here. They would continue to exist without being contained in human thought and discourse. I would like to think the land would miss us, but I may be overestimating our importance or attributing my own understanding of "feelings" to the land. Subject positions, then, are powerful, but they are not all-powerful. My perceptions influence what I see, but what I see has its own vitality, its own spirit, and it does not simply depend on me. I suspect that the land constitutes its own knowledge, though I am not able to explain exactly how, since the instant I discuss this I am coming to the subject through my human viewpoint. The objects of my perceptions, nonetheless, have their own stories, not just the ones I impose on them. This does not release me from the responsibility, however, of imagining their stories.

I would like to spend at least part of my time, then, dreaming what those stories might be or even straining to hear what these potent others have to say for themselves.

Part Two

Why take up the subject of Indian experience? Might we say that experience is its own teacher? One of our Americanisms certainly tells us it is the *best* teacher. Who needs to theorize it?

The heart of the critique against tribal literary nationalism hinges on denying the validity of Indian experience. Let me begin by making my thesis clear: I will argue that insider viewpoints are relevant and necessary in the examination of tribal literature. An unspoken code—or, at the very least, a state of affairs everyone has gotten far too used to—has emerged in our discipline: Indians write the stories, poems, and plays, and non-Indians tell us what they mean. Claiming that Indians can do both, I hope to make the case that tribal experience can provide a useful foundation for effectively studying tribal literature. This is not the same as saying that all Indians are naturally predisposed to insightful revelations about their experience or its application to literature. While it is ludicrous to claim that every Indian is a born literary critic, it is equally absurd to imply that it is impossible for an Indian to apply her insights about being Indian to the study of Native literature. It is also ludicrous to argue that all non-Native critics are incapable of understanding Native literature and culture.

I want to use Elvira Pulitano's book, *Toward a Native American Critical Theory*, as an example of why we must address the crucial question of experience. (I address it here much more briefly than I have elsewhere and with quite a different focus.) Pulitano writes, in relation to my own work, "Womack's Creekcentrism runs the risk at best of repeating the errors pointed out by Fanon and other Third World intellectuals and at worst of turning into a reductionist Nativism." She also goes a step further by claiming that tribal literary nationalists actually continue the work of colonialism. She says, "by celebrating an authentic Native difference, they ultimately end up perpetuating further versions of colonialism, colonialisms in which the Native is once again significantly Othered."[15] Discussing Native difference, of course, has a lot to do with whether or not Indian experience is distinguishable from other kinds of experience.

A main point of Pulitano's is the impossibility of any claim to a Native perspective, given the inherent hybridity of Native cultures after five hundred years of contact with Europeans. Recovering some kind of precontact Native essence, she argues sensibly, is impossible. It is too late to escape each other, and our destinies are profoundly mutually dependent. Less sensibly, she says that claims to insider status are immediately suspect because insider/outsider implies mutual dependencies rather than natural oppositions. Whatever constitutes Native experience cannot be differentiated from non-Native experience. There is no autonomous tribal culture that anyone can draw on, so the argument goes, as a philosophical basis for theory or praxis. There are only hybridized cultures deeply affected by a diversity of influences on one another. Attempts to describe forms of Native knowledge become, Pulitano writes, "a hope to recover a precolonial cultural purity, thereby creating some kind of national consciousness entirely independent of the European colonial enterprise."[16] By examining his own tradition, the nationalist at the same time fixes that tradition in the past, turning it into a cultural artifact rather than an ever-changing, living body of knowledge.

Pulitano extends these ideas to Native texts and the body of criticism that surrounds them. In her introduction, she writes that "any attempt to recover a 'pure' or 'authentic' form of Native discourse, one rigidly based on a Native perspective, is simply not possible since Native American narratives are by their very nature heavily heteroglot and hybridized."[17] In applying her ideas to readings of Native literature, Pulitano, then, takes issue with the old saying "you cannot use the master's tools to dismantle the master's house." According to Pulitano, for better or worse, the master's tools are the only tools left—or, more accurately, it is no longer possible to differentiate where the master's tools leave off and the Indian tools begin. There is no independent theoretical framework that can be built upon an autonomous tribal culture because neither exists, that is, neither an autonomous theory nor an autonomous culture. It is also pointless to determine whether or not there is any essential difference between the master's tools and the Native's after five hundred years of European contact. The concept of "decolonizing the mind," a term that gained some currency in the 1990s, is now defunct, since we know there is no "them," no "us," and it is futile to eliminate forms of colonial discourse from anyone's consciousness because our very consciousness is created by European contact and colonial discourse.

Tribal literary nationalists, those scholars who believe Native communities might contribute something to an evaluation of their own literatures, are guilty of a host of errors. Ignorant of her own profound hybridity, the tribal nationalist engages in meaninglessness in any assertion of Native literary aethetics, since such aesthetics originate in hybridized cultures. The Native novel, poem, short story, and play are not indigenous to North America but rather to Europe. As far as I can tell from reading Pulitano, all other phenomena are indigenous to Europe as well, including Indians, since they originate in the European mind. Point of origin seems to be a pivotal claim, a kind of etymological approach to Indian studies.

Fiction itself is claimed as an inherently hybridized form of discourse. In terms of literary analysis the tribal nationalist who claims the importance of including Native scholars in his bibliography is merely fooling himself since the Native writers he draws upon are cosmopolitan by virtue of education, experience, and their cultures of origin. The Native literary critic's job is to create a multicultural collage in which non-Native critical voices and Native critical voices are in constant dialogue. There are no discernible differences between the two modes of discourse, yet each must continuously interrogate the other. Literary nationalists have deluded themselves by claiming to write works of difference; an examination of their narratives reveals the same arguments as found in Western texts. The use of English by Native writers makes it impossible to claim any Native distinction.

When quoting Native sources, the critic must prove her honesty by always telling her readers about the inevitable nature of the Indian writer's non-Indianness. Whatever Indian experiences these sources might represent can never be unraveled from their European intertwinings. If Indian experience even exists, it is so muddled after five hundred years it is impossible to say just what it is.

A central failure of the tribal literary nationalist has been what the twelve-step groups call denial. We are in denial about our hybridity. Pulitano calls on us to finally 'fess up. We need to constantly examine, and state within our criticism, our complicity with Western discourse and culture. Referring to Paula Gunn Allen and Gayatri Spivak, the latter a superior critic according to Pulitano, Pulitano writes, "Unlike Allen, Spivak acknowledges her complicity."[18] I can hear it now: "Hello, I'm Gayatri, and I'm a complicitous hybrid." Pulitano argues that confession is our first act before we proceed with anything else, confession before communion. She writes, "Any from of discourse involving notions of tradition, sovereignty, and commitment to communities should at first acknowledge the level of complicity between Native intellectuals (regardless of the kind of community in which they operate) and the dominant academic discourse."[19] In my own case I need special treatment, interrogation, because I should be the subject of an investigation. Pulitano writes, "Interrogating only his investigating tools when he should also be interrogating his position as a critic and subject of investigation, Womack voices simulations of tribal identity."[20] The critic should always be examining himself, sharing generously with his readers all the problems inherent in his methodology, as well as his indebtedness to Europe. We might very well term such a critical commitment "Europhilia."

In spite of this love for all things European, the main goal of Native literary critics, Pulitano insists, must be subverting Eurocentric discourse. She writes, "my critique of Allen's ethnographic stance aims at showing the limitations of such a methodology in the context of a Native American theoretical discourse whose main goal is to challenge the analytic tools of Eurocentric theory while dismantling romantic definitions of Indians."[21]

The authority of Western theoretical paradigms must be challenged by tribal scholars and their energies directed toward reinventing and reimagining the language of this authoritative discourse. The tribal literary nationalist who might be interested in studying his tribal literature for its relevance to his own community has missed the boat since he should not be promoting nationalism but transnational solidarity, and he has no autonomous literature or history anyway, only a hybridized one as deeply European as it is Indian. In fact, any study of tribal history is an attempt to fix that history and to make claims about authenticity based on an idealized past, that is, on an autonomous, pure culture. European discourse is insufficiently subverted by the tribal literary nationalist because such critics simply act as if European theory does not exist or they deem it irrelevant.

It is important to note that Pulitano does not reject the work of all Native literary critics. In fact, she creates a hierarchy of Native-authored criticism on the basis of which critics, in her view, most successfully challenge Eurocentric hegemony. She deems Gerald Vizenor the most convincingly subversive, Greg Sarris and Louis Owens running a close second, and myself, Robert Warrior, and Paula Gunn Allen running almost neck-and-neck—Allen a nose behind—for dead-ass last, having supposedly rejected any possibilities for dialogue outside the Indian world at all. As Pulitano concludes,

> More forcefully and more provocatively than the other theorists I have discussed, Vizenor combines revolutionary content and revolutionary style, presenting a significant alternative to Western hermeneutics. Rejecting any form of separatism and essentialism as far as Indian identity is concerned, he celebrates a discourse that is communal and comic. Like Sarris and Owens, Vizenor embraces a crosscultural approach, one merging Native epistemology with Western literary forms. His approach, however, is more revolutionary than theirs, attempting as it does to fuse at every level of discourse, the tribal with the nontribal, the old with the new, the oral with the written.[22]

In proposing the second- and third-string critics, Pulitano says, "Unlike Allen, Womack, and Warrior, who take separatist approaches to a Native discourse, Sarris and Owens insist on the necessity of displacing the margin-center opposition, not by remaining outside in the margin and pointing an accusing finger at the center, but by implicating themselves in that center and sensing the politics that makes it marginal."[23]

In addition to the finger-pointing, the tribal literary nationalist does more harm than good by simply reversing hegemonic categories, making Native people the center, and shifting someone else into an oppressive margin, retaining asymmetrical power relations, becoming another colonial invention, and not challenging anything. Now that the playing field has finally been leveled, since no one has experiential knowledge from home communities, a literary critic living and teaching in Geneva, Switzerland, who may have never met a Creek person, knows as much about Creek people as any given Creek citizen. Creek experience does not shed light on Creek literature, Creek history, or Creek anything and to claim that it does amounts to ironically reversing the terms of ethnography and claiming privileged insider status. Pulitano writes, "I discuss Womack's separatist approach, showing how his call for a Native American literary separatism and for a Native perspective ultimately reinscribes colonial definitions of Indianness and simply reverses the Western binary structure of an us/them universe through which Native American studies continues to be the Other of Euramerican discourse."[24] The tribal nationalist who argues any point about the literature of her home community becomes an abusive ethnographer who has claimed a position as a privileged insider. Having a literary thesis, if you are a tribal critic, equates to setting yourself up as an informant claiming insider authority.

A commitment to sovereignty is a separatist position that perpetuates Western binary thinking. "What, if not a 'parochial question of identity and authenticity,'" Pulitano muses, "is Warrior's reliance on such problematic categories as *self-determination, tribal,* and, most important, perhaps, *sovereignty*?"[25] Sovereignty, Pulitano insists, is a European, not an Indian idea but, as stated earlier, all things in her paradigm seem to be European, since Europe is everyone's and everything's creation story. She says that "to appeal to terms such as *self-government, nation, sovereignty, or self-determination* as parameters of authenticity is self-defeating, an exercise doomed to failure, because these concepts are of European origin and do not express indigenous realities."[26]

As if all this is not enough, the Native critic is also a privileged elite whose contact with her home community is a delusion. The nationalist critic who has no contact with her own people, nonetheless seeks theories rooted in her homeland. Even a rez resident viewing herself as a community member only elicits further problems, since Native communities involve multiple locations that go far beyond the reservation. The nationalist, according to Pulitano, lives a great geographical distance from her home, and the metaphorical distance is even greater. This Native critic's education, university position, and efforts to publish works of literary criticism move her continually away from her community. Tribal nationalists publish books with university presses, and this eliminates any possibility for a tribal perspective. The very language the tribal nationalist employs in his work distances him from his community no matter what that language is. The distance is an inherent condition that cannot be mediated by anything the nationalist does to make the language relevant. His audience is academics, not Native communities. To quote Pulitano, "*Red on Red* remains, therefore, a sophisticated work of literary criticism and, as such, inaccessible to those members of a Native audience who cannot approach it from a similarly privileged position."[27]

Even the tribal nationalist who lives on a reservation or in an Indian community is still not home since his privilege cancels out any contact he might think he is having with his people. Pulitano writes, in relation to my own scholarship, that "Womack's position resembles that of the privileged diasporic Third World so often critiqued by fervent opponents of postcolonialism, people such as Aijaz Ahmad, who argues that postcolonial theorizing is a matter of class and institutional privilege and a flight from collective socialities into the abstraction of metropolitan theory."[28] The Native nationalist then must come out of her own community, end her isolation, and engage in dialogue with the outside world while at the same time face charges that she is distant from her community. Come out of your community, you are isolating yourself, is one of Pulitano's messages. You are too far from your home community and no matter what you do you will never be any closer, is the other.

One wonders about the implications of all this for research. If Indian experience is an ironic illusion fostered by Indians on themselves, why would any researcher, Native or non, need to check his or her claims against oral, written, and other community sources? Why would the researcher need to be in a lived relationship with those he or she writes about? The researcher is "freed" from contact with humans, and her involvement need only be textual. The last couple decades, marked by an insistence that those writing Native history consider a broader range of sources than the usual suspects, have been a waste of time. Pulitano's own claim that Vizenor, Sarris, and Owens revolutionize their work by drawing on an oral tradition is meaningless if Indian experience is an impossibility. Pulitano, as well as some Native critics, need to carefully think through their commitments to poststructuralism.

This summary of Pulitano's work, even though I have addressed other aspects of it elsewhere, is essential to the subject of this essay because the issue of Indian experience is where we are taking direct hits from the critics who make it theoretically impossible for us to even speak if we wish to maintain that there is something Indian about our voices. The validity of experience, both personal and tribal, becomes one of the key issues in Native studies, if not *the* key issue, because a prevalent reality of postcontact life is that Indians have not had the primary role in representing their own cultures to the outside world; that is, others have reported on their experiences.

Of the thirty thousand or so books written about Native people only 10 percent are authored by Indians. In Native American studies we want to pay special attention to the 10 percent because we are interested in what Native people have to say for themselves. If we prioritize the non-Native-authored works about Indians, one wonders how any given Native studies course is significantly different from its counterpart outside of Native studies, that is, how a history course in the Native studies department can distinguish itself from a course about Indians in the history department. In Native studies we endeavor to present Native perspectives, and we assume that one cannot present Native perspectives without Natives, in this case without Native-authored texts, since university courses depend significantly on textual representations as a core feature of their instruction. One cannot make the argument for the importance of Native-authored texts if Indian experience does not mean anything.

If Indian experiences are not distinguishable, then why *shouldn't* the historians and anthropologists be doing Native studies instead of us? What would we need Native studies programs for? A key question is whether the Indian difference I advocate is a radical incommensurability involving cultural traits that are like no one else's, or are there other ways of claiming the simple right of Native people, like all other people, to tell their stories, present their viewpoints? Does claiming the integrity of Native experiences depend on some kind of cultural purity, on its lack of "contamination" from the outside world, or are there more important factors to consider?

Just such questions permeate Native literary studies at this point in our history when some of the non-Native participants who have dominated our field, as well as some of our Native colleagues, embrace notions of hybridity, mediation, cosmopolitanism, and other theoretical notions that question the validity of any kind of "pure" Native experience, literary or otherwise. Instead they emphasize the many outside influences on Native cultures that are the inevitable result of five hundred years of contact. How can we deny their compelling case that Indians have been influenced by non-Indians?

We cannot. But one might wonder what the point is. Saying that cultures are influenced by other cultures is like saying humans breathe. Does anyone know of a culture that *isn't* influenced by those with whom it has come in contact? Why do the hybridity theorists claim this as a central feature of their theorizing? Are there more mature ways of understanding our intellectual legacy that might move us beyond this static moment when we are giving a huge amount of our energy to a project that restates, over and over again, the obvious—like none of us have ever been told at least a thousand times and in a thousand different ways that "these days Indians drive pickups"? Might we seek a criticism with the capacity to surprise and delight us instead, something both rigorous as scholarship and artistically evocative? A generative scholarship may be of more lasting and meaningful impact than the endless deficit-theory criticism that too often, even if unintentionally, sees us as the tragic victims of history.[29]

While it is true that my Indian experience does not guarantee that I will be insightful when I write or speak about things Indian, neither does it guarantee that I will be *uninsightful.* Sure, any given Native critic could simply be lazy and write or say something without doing his homework. He could also lack substantive connections with his tribal community or be just plain stupid for that matter. Tribal affiliation does not guarantee tribal insight, tribal connection, or even intelligence. It is ludicrous, however, for a critic to claim that, by definition, a Creek person cannot say anything intelligent about being Creek, or a Native person about being Native, because the terms "Creek perspectives" and "Native perspectives" are oxymoronic. As long as there are Creeks they will have various perspectives, and Natives will continue to have perspectives. Indian experience, carefully considered and intelligently articulated by Indians, means something. Indian experience is distinguishable because Indian people, like all peoples, have the right to describe their experiences and claim them as their own. Given a five-hundred-year history of people speaking on behalf of Natives, it becomes even more critical that Native people have opportunities to tell their own stories, describe and claim their own experiences. This, obviously, is not the same as claiming that those descriptions will be automatically insightful because they are articulated by privileged insiders. Even more foolish is to claim that we do not need the insiders' opinions about their own cultures or that we only need them if they prioritize investigating their European underpinnings.

I want to look at the work of four of the essayists in this volume in an attempt to uncover a more balanced view of experience. Cheryl Suzack's essay is entitled, "Land Claims, Identity Claims: Mapping Indigenous Feminism in Literary Criticism and in Winona LaDuke's *Last Standing Woman.*" One of the many striking features of Suzack's work is an insistence on feminism as a valid theoretical commitment in spite of the way some Native women intellectuals have characterized feminism as incompatible with their own cultures. Suzack problematizes culturally based rejections of feminism that ignore the diversity in Native communities and dismiss potential alliances with the outside world that might benefit Native women.

Suzack cites Navajo poet and critic Laura Tohe's article, "There Is No Word for Feminism in My Language." In reaction to the title of the Tohe piece and the general direction of the article, which expresses a discomfort with feminism, Suzack questions the rejection of feminism because "it isn't Navajo enough," or "it isn't Navajo at all." Here I might add that Suzack is not trying to debate what constitutes Navajo realities but rather the notion of accepting or dismissing ideas in relation to how well they describe narrowly defined, tribally specific practices that fail to acknowledge the tribe's own diversity or its relationships to the outside world. While Tohe concluded that "there was no need for feminism because of our matrilineal culture,"[30] Suzack found this claim to be "a somewhat hollow rhetorical argument for the exceptionality of Diné women's matrilineal culture since it disavows a larger commitment to building a future for American Indian women's feminist community, a commitment that can work against asymmetrical power relations in several cultural and/or tribal locations."

Suzack's critique of Tohe's seeming disavowal of feminism gets to the heart of a controversy that affects most of the essays in this book, the notion "my culture didn't (or doesn't) have feminism (or some other philosophy) as part of our tradition; therefore, feminism (or another commitment) must be bad." I cannot help but tell a story, and I will try to be brief.

When I was at Lethbridge one of my colleagues was teaching a Native women's issues class. One of the things I heard students saying—I was asked to visit the class on a couple of occasions—was in relation to the level of violence against women on the Blood Reserve. One student said, "Well, you know, traditionally, Blackfoot men never used to hit women." The philosophical problem is pretty apparent, but it is surprising that not very many people talk about it. For the sake of argument, let us say that a group of elders could assert confidently that traditionally Blackfoot men *did* used to hit women, would that then mean that Blackfoot men should continue to hit women today? My colleague who taught the course oftentimes ended up in this cultural trap where practices were deemed justifiable on the basis of whether or not they could be "proven" traditional. And this, of course, was always a losing battle, and not only in terms of deciding who got to be the final arbiter of tradition, an obvious problem in and of itself, given the rez reality of power struggles among traditionals about which groups are the most authentic.

In terms of the women's issues course, where would students go to read up on these practices from back in the good ol' Indian days to prove whether or not a practice was traditional? Of course, they would end up checking out works of anthropology in the library. And then they had to try and figure out if the anthropological depictions were accurate, and most often the questions about their accuracy simply could not be answered, even in a community such as southern Alberta where a number of nontextual sources, that is, community traditional leaders, were readily available. The authenticity of books could certainly be discussed, but the "traditional" backdrop against which this matter could be measured was diverse, dynamic, difficult to pin to any single fixed opinion.

Apart from the problematic reliance on questionable books, this positing of a transhistorical tradition unaffected by politics, material realities, and so on still seems to me a rather anthropological way of looking at the world, ironically enough given the prevalent Indian distrust of anthropology, and an approach that constitutes old-fashioned out-of-mode anthropology at that. The questions that surround all of this continue to haunt me: Is tradition a transparent ahistorical foundation, as inerrant and unquestionable as Holy Writ for fundamentalist Christians, a version of the pope speaking ex cathedra from a Vatican balcony, or is tradition something else? How do we evaluate its legitimacy? Most often we answer the question with what the computer guys used to call an endless loop. We say, "Just listen to the elders." This is pretty much something like saying, "If you want to know whether or not what the elders say is true just listen to the elders." This has application in the literary world as well: Is the oral tradition, for example, the default study for all of Native literature? Surely, we can do better than this. Doesn't it matter *what* the elders are saying and *how* we respond to it? In terms of Indian experience, valuing the elders' statements and living examples also relies on evaluating that experience. It does not come in a syringe we can simply inject ourselves with; we have to scrutinize what they tell us.

What happens when the elders, in the name of tribal tradition, for example, advocate kicking out all their tribal citizens from the nation who have black skin, a particularly virulent injustice in southeastern tribes? What happens when one studies those particular tribal histories honestly and discovers that southeastern political traditions in the late nineteenth century included "full-blood" traditional politicians who advocated a vote for all black tribal citizens and opposed the mixed-blood faction of the tribe that dominated the government and ran on platforms of disenfranchizing those same black citizens? During this late-nineteenth-century time period, one can look at old photos, and it is often the black southeastern Indians who look more "traditional" than the mixed-blood Indians running the tribal government. Today we have a complete turnaround in which some claim the "traditional" thing to do is to deny black Indians their citizenship. Obviously, "traditionalism," in this instance, is historically variable and contingent on a number of factors.

Returning to Native feminism, what does Suzack call for then in terms of a legitimate critical practice that takes into account the realities of Native women? She emphasizes multiple registers of community affiliations in which feminism functions as an important consideration among other tribal concerns. She says that the kind of criticism she "would call for . . . would get beyond the self-evident form of discursive practice that relies solely on 'telling our story' criticism. . . . Such a practice would articulate the relationship between congressional legislation as it has been inherited and imposed within tribal communities and a standpoint feminist perspective that privileges subordinate group claims."

While one might question why "telling our stories" would necessarily involve rejecting a materialist critical practice, a fairly clear picture emerges of a philosophy that seeks to identify relevant community affiliations that are multiple and interdependent rather than monolithic and privileged, even when they are perceived as "authentic." Further, this philosophy would be measured in relation to how well it describes material conditions in the community of which it speaks.

Suzack says, "The central conflict in the novel [*Last Standing Woman*] illustrates LaDuke's concern to articulate a form of collective community identity that enables the social reconstruction of members' historically fractured lives without reassembling them at the expense of individual interest groups and without reconfiguring social justice issues as race relations." Citing Nakota critic Kathryn Shanley as a scholar whose practices are compatible, Suzack says, "The genealogy that Shanley constructs of a gendered identity dispersed across multiple inheritances of history and family provides a model of American Indian identity that is circular and provisional, yet conceives of the space of feminist critical work as a site for reconstructing and reimagining connections among women through the cross-cultural work of the critic." Suzack also comments on the ways feminist critics Joan Scott and Gayatri Spivak have contributed to this conversation:

> Yet [Joan Scott's] explanation for this neglect—that feminist critics have had "[difficulty] incorporating the term 'gender' into existing bodies of theory and convincing adherents of one or another theoretical school that gender belongs in their vocabulary"—continues to resonate as an important materialist insight for feminist criticism, especially in light of ongoing reformulations of history that are being written with what Gayatri Chakravorty Spivak calls the "tools for developing alternative histories," that is, with analytic frameworks that read history through the multiple determinations of "gender, race, ethnicity, [and] class."

In applying these ideas to LaDuke's work, Suzack says,

> The novel thus privileges women's acts of resistance as engendering an alternative vision of community identity that focuses on intertribal communal relations rather than autonomous ones and foregrounds the necessity for a dual approach to reconfiguring the history of the Anishinaabeg community, one that not only illustrates the multiple identifications through which community affiliations occur, but also represents as constitutive the relationship between the cultural and sexual exploitation of tribal women and the political and territorial dispossession of the Anishinaabeg people.

Two important components of Suzack's critical practice, then, are both an emphasis on subordinate groups and a consideration of the larger histories that surround them. Identity does not have to be based on opposition, on pitting an "us" against a "them" or arguing for a radical incommensurability between communities of people: "Such a recognition on LaDuke's part reconfigures the boundaries of identity politics away from an oppositional stance that privileges race identity and asymmetrically organized race relations toward a communal position that envisions a common humanity." One of the strengths of Suzack's philosophy is that it manages to avoid recent accusations that tribal theorists suffer from a fundamental naivete that denies the interrelatedness of cultures or sees culture as a bucket with a hole in it—"Soon it will be all be gone but please don't fill it with anything from the outside because we have to protect what's leaking from contamination."

An identity based solely on opposition necessarily depends upon the opposing force for its very existence. It is, in the end, a debilitating perspective. Identity, in my view, must be seen as a transformative process rather than measured in terms of its purity. What is relevant is not the degree to which the identity is contaminated from European views or free from such contamination; the point is the way in which Native people make identities meaningful for themselves and their communities. Native identities, perspectives, and experiences, in spite of what Pulitano argues, can, in fact, be claimed, relative to the degree that Native people find them meaningful.

Suzack insists that personal tribal experience reverberates with political experience and corroborates the notion that Audre Lorde and others have drawn upon that the personal *is* political: "The resonances between [Janine] Littlewolf's physical act of repudiation in signing away her children [in La-Duke's novel *Last Standing Woman*] reverberates symbolically with the political act of dispossession resulting from the treaty and allotment arrangements through which the Anishinaabeg people were perceived to have sealed away their allotment land with 'the stroke of a pen on a sheet of paper.'"

While Suzack insists on a philosophy that can account for Native women's material realities, she does not do so at the expense of spirituality. One of my concerns about the postpositivists' interest in the epistemic status of race, gender, and class in the anthology *Reclaiming Identity* is the way in which that work fails to consider the interaction of spirit with an assessment of material realities, that is, what would seem like a rationalist bias in the project. I see this as a leftover legacy from poststructuralism in its problematization of various forms of presence. This might work for the postpositivists, and if it serves their needs there is something to be said for their theory, but I have my doubts whether many Native critics will be able to accept a materialist commitment unless it is modified by some interest in spiritual concerns (at least in a more serious manner than what is currently being addressed in theory. I add this disclaimer because some might argue, fairly convincingly, that material concerns *are,* in fact spiritual concerns). This, I think, represents a fruitful area where we might have some dialogue with those who share compatible interests. Suzack comments on the interplay between law and spirits in *Last Standing Woman*:

> La Duke's vision of the formation of White Earth as a place constructed through divine intervention that transports the Anishinaabeg people from a liminal state of existence, where they "undulated between material and spiritual shadows," to a new beginning in the observance of the "Creator's law" and in recognition of a "season[al] round," not only connects the Anishinaabeg to the land through a spiritual purpose that disavows its formation as a remnant of the treaty process in which the Anishinaabeg people become the victims of colonial management, but also articulates their relationship to the land as a material fact in recognition of their historical agency. Thus, in LaDuke's view, the Anishinaabeg people's right to the land cannot be superseded by secular issues that privilege the relations of law and government over the relations of the metaphysical. For LaDuke, the Anishinaabeg people's material and spiritual connections to the land are fused such that they cannot be distinguished through quantifiable blood connections or illegally imposed colonial patterns of ownership.

Suzack's argumentative stragegy manages to keep land redress as a central issue. Her essay concentrates on the WELSA legislation at the White Earth Reservation and how it has affected those seeking land reform, thus taking up a central concern of tribal critics like Elizabeth Cook-Lynn who see return of homelands as one of the central ethical imperatives of literary criticism. (Suzack, however, critiques the mixed-blood debates of Cook-Lynn and Louis Owens, arguing that both the castigation and the celebration of mixed-blood identity foregrounds a problematic category that combines a diverse group of thinkers, obscures their tribal and political affiliations, and remains tied to federally imposed definitions.) By emphasizing both the material and spiritual nature of land claims, Suzack allows us to consider whether race, class, and gender are the only epistemic measures of experience. What about race, class, gender, land, and spirits, for example? At the same time that Suzack concerns herself with land issues, she does not seek a criticism that cancels out the groundwork of feminist thinkers whose histories she examines in light of her own. Suzack avoids a theoretical stance that is isolationist and exclusionary, one that would demand a vigilant watch over some kind of tribal purity best gauged by its avoidance of outside cultural "contamination."

Like another contributor to this volume, Robert Warrior, who deals with erotic power in the poetry of Joy Harjo, Suzack sees personal and communal emotions as a valid aspect of experience, an understanding that can lead to historical, and other kinds of, knowledge: "LaDuke links the concept of intergenerational disinheritance and social isolation represented by Situpiwin's deprivation of her family and the loss of Anishinaabeg members through death, disease, and residential schools to the contemporary predicament of Anishinaabeg women who endure systemic poverty and emotional despair as a result of their 'accumulation of intergenerational grief.'" Given Suzack's claim here that grief has an effect on women's material circumstances, what role, then, do emotions play in theorizing?

To further address this question, I want to turn now to the essay just alluded to, Robert Warrior's "Your Skin Is the Map: The Theoretical Challenge of Joy Harjo's Erotic Poetics." To address a subject like eroticism, one so strongly rooted in individual subjectivity, is not easy in the present theoretical climate, where subjectivity is posed as an inescapable barrier that will always obscure any kind of absolute truth and throw all perceptions into the realm of the indeterminable. Depending on how one looks at it, subjectivity can be distrusted as an obfuscating force that distorts reality or a cause of celebration for the way it permeates every perception and challenges the hegemony of disciplines that claim unassailable objective or scientific viewpoints. In short, it is not always easy to know how to handle a discussion of subjectivity. How do we evaluate those ideas that arise from feelings like eroticism, from emotions long held by artists, and many others, to be sources of inspiration, of creative power? Warrior explores these notions as they were articulated by feminists of color, specifically Audre Lorde, in the 1980s. He also summarizes the way one Native critical thinker, Kateri Akiwenzie-Damm, has more recently described the erotic as a potential source of resistance against colonialism.

Lorde's "foundational insight," to use Warrior's term, is the recognition "that the erotic can be a crucial source of power in the struggle for justice." Warrior describes a direct line between Lorde and Harjo, a connection that Harjo herself acknowledges. Harjo understands that the erotic challenges submission to power structures. Warrior quotes her in his essay: "To be 'in the erotic,' so to speak, is to be alive. . . . Eroticism presents political problems, cultural difficulties, religious problems because the dominant culture can't function with a society of alive people." He also quotes Lorde as she indicates an understanding of how the erotic challenges authority: "[A]s we begin to recognize our deepest feelings, we begin to give up, of necessity, being satisfied with suffering and self-negation, and with the numbness which so often seems like their only alternative in our society."

One of the key features of Lorde's theorizing on the erotic is that she opens it up to many possibilities of life-affirming excellence beyond physical sexual acts, that is, to a "grave responsibility, projected from within each of us, not to settle for the convenient, the shoddy, the conventionally expected, nor the merely safe." I strongly suspect that Lorde, for example, might describe authoring her essay as an aspect of the erotic; such a perspective would at least be philosophically consistent with her ideas. Warrior puts it well when he says the erotic can function as "a call for articulating experiences." Wed with contemplation, physical experiences can inspire us to consider what we think about the world around us.

This begins a stream of thought I wish to explore: that the body itself is a site of theoretical knowledge and not only as a subject but also as a site of theoretical departure. There are experiential modes of theorizing that consider the necessary interconnections between body, mind, emotions, and spirit. By opening up the erotic to a much wider range of experience than having sex, by including any striving for excellence, and centralizing carefully considered ideas, retrospection, intropsection, and so on as part of the erotic, Lorde breaks down the opposition between mind and body, between spirit and flesh that the West has labored under for so long. In Lorde's philosophy, eroticism, or sexuality, is not a roadblock, something to overcome, on the journey toward spirituality. Eroticism and sexuality are *the very means* of achieving spirituality. In breaking down the spirit/flesh, head/heart oppositions, physical experience becomes integral to theory making, as well as lovemaking. Lorde helps us claim that personal, bodily experience means something and can be claimed as insight. The validity of the insiders' viewpoints can be based on the idea that a person can at least claim the knowledge his body teaches him—to whatever degree he can articulate that insight convincingly.

Ideas become so central to the erotic that they are pivotal in Lorde's famous—and controversial—distinction between eroticism and porn; the latter avoids facing the truth, denies feelings, replaces ideas with sensation. The idea of a "heady eroticism," and its challenge to the problematic split between mind and body, becomes a central theoretical notion in relation to this volume and what I see as a false opposition in which bodily participation in ceremonies, in listening to stories, and through any kind of physical presence in what are seen as culturally rich milieus is privileged over theorizing, authoring books, reviewing manuscripts, teaching courses, and so on—where these latter activities are frequently seen in terms of a cultural deficiency associated with bodily absence from primary cultural sources. I will say more about this later in relation to particular essays. (Of course, all of this could be carried to logical extremes—one thinks of the "indigenous" scholar who has never had any "bodily" contact with his or her home community and all the problems that poses for community-based theory.)

In Harjo's own poetry, as reflected in the title of Warrior's essay, the skin can be a map. In the Harjo poem "The Myth of Blackbirds," the poetic speaker says, "You touched me and the springs of clear water beneath my skin were new knowledge." One of the most profound manifestations of this knowledge is the way in which the erotic "moment" becomes much larger than itself. As Warrior acknowledges, "Venturing outside the lines . . . is fundamental to Harjo's work and nowhere is this more clear than in her uses of the erotic." Warrior goes on to describe Harjo's erotics "as a means of traveling to a new or alternative reality."

Harjo's poetry, of course, is famous for moments of grace when a person sees connections between herself and multiple worlds that cross both spatial and temporal distinctions, as well as many other boundaries. A woman may see the ways in which she is composed of other genders; a Creek historical moment may intersect with the experiences of many other tribes; indigenous perspectives may reach outside the Americas; language might be opened up to aspects of communication that are nonverbal; a personal experience might be revealed in terms of the larger world of myth, and on and on it goes. This cosmopolitanism, we might note, is still claimed as part of the Indian world rather than as primarily hybrid. The erotic, in Harjo's work, often functions as the entry point, the way in, the hole through which emergence occurs, and, of course, the sexual and birthing nature of this latter image is relevant here. What makes the erotic become sensually evocative is that these meanings are not lost upon the participants. As an important part of the physical act itself, they interpret it. They become theorists. I believe that theory is as simple as that, the way in which we contemplate our experiences. Like many simple things it has profound implications.

By contemplation of the erotic we become more aware of the inner and outer dimensions of our world. These acts have transformative possibilities in which joy may become a gateway to enlightenment. This kind of celebration is at least as important as the deficit theory that points out all the ways Indians are no longer Indian as well as other forms of aestheticism and self-denial so rife in the academy. Relational connections have the potential to make us more aware of our responsibilities and the needs and desires of others within this contemplative experience, not just of our own desires. This knowledge, of course, is not guaranteed in erotic encounters; it is qualitative and dependent on the willingness of the participants to engage it.

Part of the process of turning the erotic into knowledge, then, involves the participants claiming the experience rather than blindly going on their way without considering the meaning of what has happened. This is why it is so important that we insist on a theoretical space where Indians can claim the validity of Indian experience and contemplate its significance. We have rights over our bodies and the way our bodies provide experiences that turn into knowledge. Claiming experience is essential to Native perspectives. Much has been taken away from us in the Indian world, and we must not allow anyone to tell us that we cannot legitimately claim the experiences that emanate from our own bodies and the bodies of our ancestors. When someone tells us that Native perspectives, or Creek perspectives, are impossible, they are cutting us off from our very bodies. This we cannot allow, and we must protest—another erotic act because of the way in which the protestor insists on her own rules rather than those imposed on her.

Akiwenzie-Damm historicizes erotic power specifically in relation to its threat to colonial authority, which is why various forms of Native eroticism have been repressed and controlled. (One might note the way in which ethnographic collections have often erased sexual references in Native oral traditions and important contributions of women. Less obvious might be the various ways Native cultures have been "straightened" by both Indians and non-Indians representing them, who ignore the substantial contributions of gays and lesbians.) Suppression of the erotic involves a *homogenization* of *heterogenous* cultures. I might argue that it makes Indians less interesting, or, as proponents of the erotic would say, "less alive." It makes it even easier to turn Native people into ethnographic objects readily available for reductive categorizations and generalizations, which, of course, is a means of controlling a people and controlling outsiders' beliefs about a community.

In terms of resistance, Warrior says the erotic "challenge[s] the power of the psychic structures that keep us in our place." Lorde believes the erotic is resistant because it is a form of nonrational knowledge that threatens a culture where everything is based on profit rather than human needs. While agreeing with Lorde's insight about "psychic structures," I might add as a gay man that I hail from the state of Oklahoma where until a very recent supreme court decision I could be thrown in jail for my loving, a somewhat more tangible threat than psychic structures, even though the state may face enormous difficulty in effectively enforcing their sodomy codes. We all know, nonetheless, that in Oklahoma and elsewhere, gay men have landed in jail for having sex. I make the simple point here that in some cases erotic suppression can be pretty tangible. On May 3, 2004, our Democratic governor, Brad Henry, signed a piece of legislation that said that the gay and lesbian parents of adopted children were no longer their legal guardians. This act of aggession against the state's own citizenry passed by an overwhelming 97-11 margin in the state legislature.

I want to return to the theoretical questions with which I opened up this discussion. How do we give credence to the erotic, given its close relationship to subjectivities? How might the erotic be relevant in evaluating truth claims? In today's theoretical climate it is not so much that subjectivities are more distrusted than they were in the past. Instead, the interpretational biases often formerly associated primarily with subjectivities are applied to all realms of thought so that the boundaries between subjectivities and objectivities are blurred. Simply put, areas of discourse that could formerly be viewed as factual and distinguishable from opinions, feelings, and emotions are now viewed differently. Subject positions, and the mediating role of interpretation, affect all realities. There is an objective world, but human perceptions will always affect reality because *what* we see is influenced by *how* we see. Searching for the corrrect *how*, the scientific or religious or personal or communal view of the world that is the one true way of seeing it, will not solve the problem since there is no way of locating that vision in the realm of some kind of universalized, essentialized, stable, final, uncontestable truth claim. There will always be competing claims or the possibility of competing claims, and perceptions of truth are not stable across time periods and cultures.

Subjectivities, then, are not especially distrusted; *everything*, including areas of knowledge formerly thought of as objectivities, is distrusted as far as absolute claims about any given phenomena go. Reality is affected by human viewpoints, according to this human-biased view. That is why this particular philosophical standpoint is sometimes called "radical skepticism." The predicament of subjectivities, at one time more closely associated with the personal, is now a unilateral challenge. Relativism becomes a critical issue because identity claims are so deeply rooted in various forms of experience, of individual and communal subjectivities. These problems have far-reaching implications. For example, how do minorities claim the validity of their experience in such a way that area studies, like Native American studies, are justifiable? While the Bureau of Indian Affairs, or tribes, may have—justifiably or unjustifiably, depending on how one looks at it—what is claimed as quantifiable criteria for tribal membership, there is no such test for including Native American studies in the academy. The discipline is validated by claims about history, identity, and experience, the three areas hardest hit by the theorizing of the last three decades. For those of us who teach Native American studies in university settings, theoretical relativism might be a threat to our jobs, to put it in terms that are more concrete than all this abstraction. On another plane, something as fundamental as claiming a Creek, or a Native, perspective and presenting it in a book becomes contestable, as recent reactions to Native scholarship have shown.

An important question is how do we claim subjectivities in such a way that they make normative truth claims possible? Perhaps one aspect of a compassionate criticism is the gift of humility we can bring to bear upon our work. We can acknowledge that we are not the ultimate arbiters of experience and knowledge; we are part of a larger conversation of relational, varied voices.[31]

An essayist I have found helpful in these regards is Minh T. Nguyen, author of " 'It Matters to Get the Facts Straight': Joy Kogawa, Realism, and the Objectivity of Values." Nguyen argues that intuition, emotions, and love have epistemic worth. She examines Joy Kogawa's novels and argues against the stereotypically ephemeral view of subjectivities, where memory, for example, grows dimmer and less accurate over time. Instead of emphasizing disintegration, the kind of realist theory expressed by Nguyen might view changes in memory as *growth* over time in which a person has been affected by learning, new theoretical frameworks, moral and political maturation, and other new ways of understanding. In other words, the instability of memory could just as easily be an upward spiral as a downward descent, so to speak; Nguyen assumes that subjectivities have just as much capacity to lead *toward* the truth as *away* from it.

Nguyen sees emotions as theory-laden, part of the materials from which theories are built: "emotions are intimately connected to our beliefs and judgements."[32] In fact, theories must be linked to emotions before they can become persuasive. Nguyen quotes the subject of her study, Joy Kogawa, on these matters: " 'Documents and facts are intended to direct our prejudiced hearts but rarely provide direction by themselves. I have boxes and boxes of documents but what I need is vision and vision comes from relationship. Facts bereft of love direct us nowhere.' "[33]

Nguyen summarizes this viewpoint by saying, "Kogawa's moving assertion strengthens the realist claim that objectivity is inextricably tied to love and personal and social relationships; we attain objectivity not by disregarding it or disavowing our emotions and values but by interrogating their epistemic character to assess the relevant insights they might provide. It is *interested* inquiry, then, that allows us to perceive and interpret our reality more accurately."[34] Emotions can be analyzed. Along somewhat similar lines, religious experiences can, and must, be subjected to critical scrutiny—they should not be granted a special dispensation making them immune from criticism. A serious intellectual does not have to be a secular critic. If he is a religious critic, however, he does have to remember that criticism constitutes half of his job title. Religious critics may very well find themselves at odds with religious practitioners, though not because faith and reason can never be compatible.

A theory that makes all the right moves on the philosophical chess board but fails to convince anyone of its validity will not accomplish much. Theory has to *move* people in order to attract them to its ideas. Many of Nguyen's insights remind me of the way in which more than one of our contributors, including myself, has leaned on Momaday in arguing that history must be imagined and felt in order to be interpreted, and, I believe, this holds true for theory as well. Our iconographic arrow maker in *The Way to Rainy Mountain* puts himself at risk when he takes time to imagine and speak to his enemy, who could avail himself of this critical moment and strike first. Yet this vulnerability leads the arrow maker *closer* to, not *further* from, a clearer understanding of his world; by trusting his emotions he does not descend into relativistic uncertainty but saves himself and his family from imminent danger.

I think that one of the important values of some of the good old-fashioned New Critics of the 1930s, though I do not agree with the tenets of their "text-only" formalism, was that they often tried to write critical pieces that were as artistic and evocative as the novels, poems, and plays they were analyzing. They hoped to emulate the spirit of the art they were centrally involved in. Some of them *were* novelists, and one cannot help but wonder if having a stab at writing a novel might teach a person something about the act of interpreting one. There seems to me a certain kind of ethics in saying, "Yes, I criticize art, but I have also had a go at creating it, so I know something firsthand about what that feels like." (Another, argument, obviously, that personal experience means something. A corrollary might be arguing that a Native viewpoint might be meaningful in analyzing Native literature or significant for a job teaching Native literature.) I think some of the New Critics provide examples of ways in which theorists sought emotional immediacy in their criticism. Such immediacy, at its best, can seek engagement on a visceral level that leads us back to our bodies, and our feelings, as pathways to knowledge. The fact that a creative writer or a Native person might have his or her own insights obviously does not preclude the participation of "nonnovelists" or non-Natives in criticism.

Nguyen emphasizes that the possibility for error (rather than absolute truth) becomes a means of sharing and learning with others. A person can act in concert with her communities and seek ways of joining the fragments; a postmodern vulnerability need not result in stasis. One is again reminded of the Harjo line, "[Y]ou touched me and the springs of clear water beneath my skin were new knowledge," as well as the call by Lisa Brooks, one of our contributors, for participatory thinking. As Nguyen says, "Kogawa urges us to embrace 'the paradoxical power in mutual vulnerability.' She does not view vulnerability as a weakness; for her, it is a source of strength because it lays the groundwork for establishing trust and empathy with others."[35]

Subjectivity, then, may not be an obstacle on the path to theorizing, or even simply an inevitability that permeates all our theoretical choices; it may be the very path along which one travels toward a more mature philosophy, especially if one holds out hope for a passionate, as well as a compassionate, criticism. I hope for an engaged passion in our intellectual endeavors, one that requires deep contemplation about the ethics and responsibilities within which such a passion is rooted. I worry about criticism that is not funny. I worry about criticism that is not moving. I have, therefore, a good deal to worry about. Comedy and emotion in criticism, it seems to me, are essential critical aesthetics.

Critics can be passionate without being *com*passionate. One's criticism, in other words, needs be checked against the reality of one's own body, one's experiences, the knowledge that comes of these intersections. It also, however, must be checked against other bodies, experiences, knowledges. I am not talking about a group grope. First, I am saying that, given our human limitations, the fact that we are incapable of millions of conversations with human and nonhuman others, empathetic imagination becomes vital. Second, I claim that personal vision must be checked against social reality.

Of course, I cannot deny that there are theoretical challenges that remain, ones that may arise out of the inevitabilities of our human condition; I confess that I do not have the answers for these challenges. What happens when we have *competing* truth claims, whatever their basis in emotions, in subjectivities, in objectivities? Let us say, for argument's sake, that we have competing claims among tribal members. In other words, how do we come up with a philosophy, as Cheryl Suzack reminds us, that "articulate[s] a form of collective community identity that enables the social reconstruction of members' historically fractured lives without reassembling them at the expense of individual interest groups"?

When the inevitability arises that one group is going to have to be privileged over another, how does anyone make those decisions? Honestly, I do not know the answer to that question, but I would hope that a primary goal would be something as old-fashioned and humanistic as insisting that compassion—a subjectivity—be foregrounded as a criterion. Further, this is where the practice of theory becomes incredibly important to us. In a world of competing claims, in order to make decisions, we have to evaluate how competently those making the claims justify them. This is an inescapable theoretical act that goes as far back as schools of classical rhetoric, where evidence has to be provided and justifications given that explain how the evidence backs up the claim. It is foolish to simply shrug this off as a "European" tradition, therefore irrelevant to Native people: in Indian cultures we have a long tradition of evaluating claims in reference to how well they describe the real world. (One is reminded, to cite one of scores of examples, of the core argument in *God Is Red* that Christianity becomes interested in abstract dogma to the exclusion of material reality, whereas many Native traditions correlate philosophies with the geographies where they originate.)

Each of the contributors I cite here is interested in material conditions, legislation, court cases, histories—in short, in judging the accuracy of representations according to their "degree of fit" in reference to lived tribal realities. This makes our work quite different from the formalist extremes of Elvira Pulitano's *Toward a Native American Critical Theory* with its utter lack of historical references or analysis of social policy.

In terms of remembering compassion in an environment of potential conflicting interests, even among tribal members, I have been especially impressed by the growing optimism in the poetry of Joy Harjo. For instance in *The Woman Who Fell from the Sky* she argues that love is the very force at the heart of physics, and Harjo has great hope that love can transform human beings across many kinds of boundaries. This argument may seem incredibly unlikely in the present political climate at home and abroad, but what else is there? Does anyone have any better ideas? I am not being hopelessly naive; I am calling for a love that is critically engaged, one rooted in historical, cultural, and legal particulars. When these highly contested debates shake the communities to their foundations, such as the tragic disenfranchisement of the freedmen from Oklahoma tribes, a tradition that should have been applied is the concept of *anogetchka,* in Creek, simply "love." When we lose that concept no one will be enfranchised any longer, whatever their skin hue.

It might seem like a contradiction is emerging. Earlier, I said I wanted to challenge those who privilege physical participation over other kinds of experience stereotypically seen as more cerebral and less authentic. Now I seem to be claiming the validity of emotional states that are so intimately tied to physicality—they emanate, in a very real sense, from our bodies, given that our minds constitute an important part of our physical being. I think this theoretical commitment is consistent, however, if one recognizes that emotions involve a broad range of both physical and introspective experiences. We interpret our emotions. In addition to being emotionally moved during a ceremony, or in some other primary cultural milieu, I can be quite moved, and experience love and any other number of emotions, in reading a book or participating in a conference. Lorde insists on contemplation as a central value of the erotic.

I want to turn now to some historically specific views of experience, in this case Lisa Brooks's depiction of a nineteenth-century New England network of Native intellectuals in her essay for this volume, "Digging at the Roots: Locating an Ethical, Native Criticism." Brooks carefully builds an argument for what she calls "participatory thinking," an approach that grounds itself in New England oral traditions and written traditions without privileging one over the other. In fact, the phrase itself is a useful one in resisting oppositional splits between physical and mental experience, since it merges participation with thinking. Neither does Brooks shy away from delineating the pitfalls possible in regard to either physical or mental activities undertaken without attention to proper balance.

In her analysis of the familiar Iroquoian Sky Woman story, she warns of the dangers inherent in "Flint's rocky path," to borrow her phrase about an oral-tradition character who illustrates that critical thinking can be undertaken (1) without sufficiently engaging others who might contribute to and revise one's theories and (2) without group deliberation that considers the effects of ideas on the larger, extended community.

Brooks, however, does not turn her analysis into the clichéd morality tale the tradition usually suffers in which oral stories stand for the dangers inherent in individualism. She reads her tradition as a call, instead, for intellectual activity that becomes a network of participatory thinkers who are responsible for group deliberation and who do not shy away from difficult intellectual tasks. Brooks provides further evidence that these participatory thinking networks also existed outside creation stories, that networks of New England Native writers demonstrated these traditional values through their interactions with one another. Brooks says,

> The journals of [Mohawk leader] Joseph Brant and [Algonquian leader] Hendrick Aupaumut are particularly valuable in this regard, because they reveal the ways in which Native leaders critiqued and challenged each other. We may have as much to learn from the relations between early Native writers as we do from the writings themselves. Occom, Aupaumut and Brant knew each other well and shared many experiences and acquaintances in common. Brant and Aupaumut, at times, nearly regarded each other as enemies, and at other times, as friends. Occom and Brant were both Wheelock students, and Occom even attended Brant's wedding during one of his diplomatic visits to William Johnson. Occom and Aupaumut became close friends in the final years of Occom's life, when both men were living in reconstructed Algonquian villages at Oneida. All three men belonged to a large interrelated network of writing Indians, with whom they interacted and corresponded. Any analysis of the connections between them only scratches the surface of the political and social communities in which they participated. . . .
>
> The texts of the northeastern Native tradition emerged from within this indigenous space of exchange, not, as is often portrayed, from displaced Indian individuals reflecting on the state of their lives in relation to the colonial world.

For Brooks, this volume, *Reasoning Together*, represents one possibility for living out such networks in our own day and applying her two northeastern oral-tradition aesthetics of (1) engaging other Native thinkers and (2) deliberating as a group the possible effects of our theorizing. Brooks sees this as a fulfillment of a specific critical juncture, which she traces back to an influential work: "It seems that what Robert Warrior called for some years ago in *Tribal Secrets* was for Native scholars to participate in a critical conversation, rather than merely to 'do' criticism. This volume, I believe is born of that call. . . . [Warrior] asked us not only to engage in critical conversation with each other, but with our literary ancestors."

I am reminded here of another critical undercurrent that led up to this volume, Pomo-Miwok author Greg Sarris's groundbreaking work, *Keeping Slug Woman Alive*, which argued for the validity of self-conscious attention to our personal stories as part of our critical interpretations. Here we are adding another dimension to that earlier call: We are asking for attention not only to our own but to *each other's* stories, that is, the stories of those of us who write Native literary criticism as we reason together.

In order to avoid accusations of engaging in unwarranted essentialism, Brooks recognizes the importance of "root[ing] our work in analysis that is spatially and historically specific," as well as in a profound understanding of our own intellectual traditions. By drawing on the examples of the Sky Woman story and the New England writers, however, she includes a further criterion: "I would argue that this knowledge cannot be gained through traditional methods of scholarship, but it is only *fully* accessible through interaction within the indigenous networks to which we belong."

Brooks broaches the subject of competing Native critical viewpoints, suggesting they be handled with the careful consideration delineated in her oral-tradition account, that is, with attention to not only how our theories will affect the outside world and our communities but how our challenges will affect *one another* as Native intellectuals: "One of the hardest aspects of Robert Warrior's call for a critical conversation is imagining ways to challenge each other that will not put briars in each others' paths." We are in the process of constructing a space for an ethical Native criticism. As we read each others' writing, and respond with our own thoughts, an important question to contemplate is: how do we create this book as a participatory, thinking community?

This goes beyond simply avoiding offending each other—it has to do with articulating theory that includes a discussion of the way the theory corroborates or challenges the Native critical environment that surrounds it. This has to do with a time period where we might act less like free agents (a term Warrior uses in *Tribal Secrets* to describe the isolation of Native intellectuals in the 1920s and 1930s) and more in concert together, since we have the privilege of a readily identifiable community of Native writers who have both the incredible gift—and the responsibility—of coexisting with each other, at the very least trying to understand the work others have done.

This need not imply an imposed uniformity of opinion but a consideration of the shape and contour of the critical moment we exist in so that we do not simply reinvent the wheel by rehashing the same efforts already well established, nor act as irresponsible lone gunmen whose ideas, creative as they might be, result in setbacks to our discipline. At minimum, a baseline requirement should be that we read and cite each others' books, that is, the books of other Indian writers. Further, if we are going to criticize European literary theory, we should have at least read some of it or else keep quiet about things we know nothing about. I regret that this needs to be said at all, but Indian scholars, like anybody else, have to do their homework. If we want to be professionals in literature departments we need to do as much as any of our colleagues to understand our own field and even engage some things that go beyond our specialized areas of interest. Such efforts, after all, only help us delineate what it is we do both in relation to, and in distinction from, others.

Brooks's rich beginning has the power to suggest other studies to come. A central question in relation to the nineteenth-century writers is how did we get from point A to point B? That is, how did we get from these men and women authoring political tracts, petitions, letters, and many other forms of political organizing, to the world of fiction and its attendant literary criticism that we have today (as well as to the world of Native nonfiction)? In describing William Apess among the Mashpees, Brooks says, "During the 'revolt,' Apess and the Mashpees not only asserted their claim to self-governance, but enacted it, organizing their own councils and implementing their own regulations regarding 'outsiders' from the Commonwealth." Can we imagine some of today's fiction writers in such a role? What has happened?

Can the difference simply be relegated to some kind of incommensurability between creative and nonfiction work? Most of the nineteenth-century authors did not write novels or literary criticism, but took up "real-life" concerns. Why is it that the broader fabric of these earlier writers' lives has had so little impact—until recently—on both the authorship and criticism of Native fiction, poetry, and drama? Could a fiction writer today have a role as a community activist the way these earlier writers did? I do not know of any who, like William Apess, have spent thirty days in jail for participation in protests. I do not think this necessarily delegitimates their work, but I am simply wondering about the differences in historical circumstances.

In the contemporary period that some have characterized as the "Native American literary renaissance," the nature of the politics of many fiction writers seems to be quite different from that of other writers who preceded them and even from their nonfiction contemporaries like Vine Deloria, Jr. In the fiction writers, to varying degrees, there is a striking *disengagement* with politics, at least the overt politics of these other writers. In the "homecoming novels," to borrow another phrase that comes out of this time period, there seems to be a turn, instead, to culture, to oral tradition, to ceremony. I realize I am creating a false opposition between culture and politics in order to make a point, and my statement about the apolitical holds up only to varying degrees, depending upon which work is under consideration. But, in a certain sense, we saw a radical period in the sixties and seventies and yet had a conservative fiction.

One might compare Alexander Posey's turn-of-the-century Fus Fixico letters to *House Made of Dawn,* or Pequot author William Apess's 1830s essay "An Indian's Looking Glass for the White Man," or Sarah Winnemucca's 1880s autobiography, *Life among the Paiutes,* or Vine Deloria's 1973 benchmark comparative religion text, *God Is Red,* and I think the differences in the polemical nature of the mostly nonfiction discourse, compared with the fiction that gets the most attention today, will be striking—whatever some might claim about the political subtleties of Momaday's creative writing.

While I think many people will defend the so-called renaissance writers and argue against their apoliticism, I think it is hard to miss the point that the politics in the contemporary fiction often feels quite different from these other writings. We might wonder about the nature of this political shift and how it came about. Striking is the fact that the United States did not produce a

"Red Power novel" about the sixties and seventies while Canada did—Jeannette Armstrong's *Slash.* We have quite a burgeoning literature on the nineteenth century, but the question "What does it mean for us in relation to today's writing?" has gone largely unanswered. Brooks's essay stands as a challenge for us to understand these historical relationships and offers a way to describe what a workable Native critical network might look like today.

In her concluding discussion of the Sky Woman story, instead of simply assuming the oral tradition as an intellectual foundation, Brooks admits that the tradition leaves it up to us to continue the work of analysis and interpretation. Rather than advocating the much-heard call to return to tradition, as if the oral tradition is a transparent set of interpretational principles and a standard for living, Brooks realizes the way in which the tradition itself demands critical work from us. The oral tradition, like the elders' advice previously alluded to, is not an injection available from a syringe. It requires an analytical engagement, the work of criticism, interpretation, and especially, historicization that occurs in response to storytelling.

It is also interesting to note that Brooks's discussion of the oral tradition relies exclusively (and legitimately) on written texts by tribal authors. Our oral traditions now have an underlying written foundation that is unmistakable. The oral tradition can no longer be completely separated from authorship. There is much potential in future scholarship that might examine the *textual* underpinnings of the contemporary oral tradition. Many works are available that emphasize ways in which Native novels are influenced by the oral tradition but none yet on how the oral tradition is influenced by books, on how it has even *become* a process of authoring written texts. This probably constitutes a missing piece of our literary puzzle.

Brooks, then, contributes in important ways to a growing understanding of experience by further breaking down the opposition between physical and mental experience, oral and written, through her demonstration of the link between activism and authorship prevalent in the nineteenth century and by examining Native critical experience through the ways it is refracted through other Native thinkers.

Tol Foster attempts an expansion of definitions of Native experience in his essay, "Of One Blood: An Argument for Relations and Regionality in Native American Literary Studies." Foster argues convincingly that Native literature is marked by an ability to reach outside its own tribal boundaries to multiple audiences and purposes. Foster calls for looking at Native literature in regional contexts rather than only in tribally specific ones. In an earlier version of the essay that appears in this volume, he cited John Joseph Mathews's Latin motto in *Talking to the Moon* as evidence that an Osage text, like other tribally centered texts, cannot simply be analyzed in terms of its Osage background knowledge: "I have the motto of my life in the blackjacks painted in Chinese red on the face of my mantel in Roman lettering: VENARI LAVARI LUDERE RIDERE OCCAST VIVERE. It was once the motto of some unit of the Third

Augustan Legion and was placed over the entrance of the officers' club at a fort . . . along the Roman frontier of the first century [and . . .] I think it a good motto in the original . . . when translated: to hunt, to bathe, to play, to laugh—that is to live."[36]

According to Foster, "Mathews forces us to see that the Osage Mathews and the Oxford Mathews are very compatible creatures and this rhetorical flanking maneuver demands that we consider their similarities as well as their differences. Mathews is placing Osage lifeways on an even terrain with Roman ones, whilst our tendency to read Mathews within the context of Native America attempts to corral the text into a sometimes false and limited comparison to the Euroamerican canon." Foster goes on to carefully build a case throughout the essay for a Native regionalism that allows literature some breathing room outside the tribal world.

Foster's example of John Joseph Mathews's Latin motto is certainly a vivid way of driving home his point that reading *Talking to the Moon* consists of more than simply unfolding its Osage cultural references. There is a question, however, I want to consider. Are Native contexts doomed to "corral" the text? Is the nature of the critical challenge too much interest in locating the tribally specific references in these works, or, more generally, their "Indianness"? Or is the real problem the inability to see the Roman motto *as part of Mathews's Osage experience?* The Roman motto is not an Osage idea necessarily because it has in common some essential attitude that Osages also share with Romans about hunting, bathing, playing, and laughing (although they might, who knows?). It is an Osage idea because John Joseph Mathews, an Osage, values it and relates it to his Osage experience in the Blackjacks.

If we shift the discussion this way, by opening up Mathews's Osage experience to many possibilities that involve Osages making their own cultural choices, exercising their personal sovereignties, it changes the playing field. In addition to noting the regional qualities of Native literature when it makes references outside Native culture, we can also mark the many possibilities for tribal experience, finally allowing our discussion of it to actually reflect tribal realities (like Presbyterian preachers, Oxford-trained biologists, and so on). We can develop a more mature sense of tribal realism, given that tribal reality has never consisted exclusively of traditionalists and their practices; nor have the traditionalists been completely isolated from other worlds that surround them; neither have traditionals been easily described by any single set of characteristics.

I would argue that it is quite possible to be intensely interested in the "Osageness" of Mathews's text by including the Roman motto and other things like it (such as Mathews's extended metaphor of the four natural stages he observes among the Blackjacks that symbolize the United States' naivete in thinking it can forever dominate global affairs) *as part of the Osage cultural references.* Osage sovereignty, it seems to me, can, and must, concern itself with events outside of Osage country. One might cite, for example, the history of Osages attending prominent universities as evidence that Mathews's educational interests in classical cultures, as well as his orientation as a natural scientist, match Osage realities. (I thank Tol for allowing me to playfully interrogate his earlier ideas, which he later revised.)

In terms of my own defense of tribally specific approaches (in this case the claim that they can coexist with regional approaches without being replaced by them because of any inherent superiority of the latter), my analysis of Alice Callahan's novel *Wynema* comes to mind. My criticism of that work has never been that the novel is not traditional enough in terms of a lack of depiction of the ceremonialists and their practices (though I certainly deal with the quality of those particular representations). My protest is that Callahan's work somehow manages to avoid almost any Creek reality whatsoever, whether it is the history of the Creek Baptist and Methodist churches; the slave-holding Creek Confederate faction her own father was a member of (I do not know if Samuel himself had slaves, but it is interesting that the novel has a strong suffragist voice and absolutely no abolitionist commitment); the strong presence of Creek African Americans within the tribe; the Creek businessmen within the nation; Creek jurisdiction over a geographically defined territory; or virtually anything that would identify Creek material, social, religious, political, or historical realities. In other words, I have critiqued the dearth of Creek experience in the novel, without, I hope, limiting Creek experience to a forced definition of traditionalism or any single prioritized lifestyle or faction, hoping instead to emphasize the very complicated fabric of Creek life, given the tremendous diversity within the nation at the time of Callahan's writing.

Creek experience of the late nineteenth century could be anything from working in a mercantile in North Fork Town like G. W. Grayson did before he enlisted in the Confederacy to being a Creek Methodist pastor leading services in the Muscogee language to serving as a medicine maker at the ceremonial grounds to being an African American Creek with close ties to the churches or grounds or being an African American Creek who identified more strongly with non-Indian blacks in the territory to being a Creek author raised outside Creek jurisdiction in Texas, like Callahan herself, but returning as an adult for stints as a Creek teacher. And so many possible points in between that, of course, to name them all would be impossible. The problem with *Wynema* is not so much that it does not identify some "officially sanctioned" form of Creek experience but that it largely fails to identify any recognizable form of Creek experience at all. If the novel did not claim to be about the Creek world, perhaps this would not be a problem—but it does. I hold out the real world as a standard of measure, in this case the Creek real world, but I hope the critique accomplishes exactly what Cheryl Suzack suggests—that it allows for the presence of multiple community affiliations within that society and even outside it.

To return for a moment to the Mathews example, at the heart of the oppositional schism that shrinks from identifying Mathews's Oxford experience as Osage experience is an attitude that goes to the core of language. Some Indian thinkers have taken to pitting themselves against an "enemy's language," claiming a radical incommensurability in relation to English. (Though surely not all associated with the phrase see English in such absolute terms, nonetheless I want to play with the notion for a little bit.) If we are facing off with an "enemy's language," then we ourselves are the enemy since most of us are English-speakers. Many making claims about the "colonizer's English" have never spoken anything but English, and the English language is the source of all their writings. In viewing English as a forced imposition on Native people, it seems to me that only the victimization end of the spectrum is being considered.

What about when Indians have enthusiastically taken up English and reading? Before there were ever federal Canadian residential and U.S. boarding schools, for example, forcing Indian students to learn English, there were several thousand New England Indians reading and writing by the time Sam Occom penned his autobiography in 1770. I am willing to venture that not all of them were forced to speak English, that they were not all the victims of literacy. So why were they interested, those who were? Were they simply trying to "reinvent" something profoundly deficient or did a few Native thinkers see some kind of intrinsic tribal merit in the English language?

I do not think it a certainty that the English language is the colonizer's language. Once it landed in the New World, English picked up a lot of tribal influences from Indians, from Africans in the Caribbean, and so on. Literally, there are thousands of Indian words in English. Maybe Indians colonized English instead of the other way around. At any rate, it is unlikely that English could ever be some purely authoritative European discourse without picking up tribal, and other, influences that kept it in flux, moderated its Eurocenteredness and its authority. Is it not possible that Indians experience English as more than oppression?

Might English *be* one of our Indian languages? It is hard to argue against the fact that today English is the most commonly spoken language among Indians—at least in much of the United States and Canada. Does that not make English an Indian language? Obviously, Indians seem to find some value in speaking it unless we are total victims with no agency whatsoever. If I could still go around speaking Creek everyday like my granddad's siblings and relatives were able to do growing up around places like Weleetka and Eufaula in the early part of this century, that would be a dream come true. I would still, however, be quite interested in English, as were many Creeks during my grandfather's time and even earlier. (George Stiggins, G. W. Grayson, Alice Callahan, and Alexander Posey might be some prominent examples.) English is a great language, after all, the one that brings me William Shakespeare, Mark Twain, James Baldwin, Dorothy Allison, and Audre Lorde, not to mention the great bulk of the written literature from my own tribe and others. No one can doubt the mind-boggling abuses/losses that occurred from residential and boarding schools, and forced imposition of English, but it is also possible that these systems of abuse do not describe the only relationship that Indian people have had with English.

This carries over into issues of translation in interesting ways. In terms of translation of Native languages, everyone always seems to see the hole instead of the donut. The emphasis is usually on loss. When one reads a translated Gabriel Garcia Marquez novel, one might hear a comment about the excellence of the English translation. One does not hear this, however, about translated Native materials. Rather than emphasizing its diminishment and the second-class nature of Native literature, however, what if we want to claim that Native literature is so excellent that some of that excellence survives in English? That is to say, what if we want to argue that Native literature is world-class literature, as Foster would remind us, so powerful that it can cross different kinds of boundaries? We may need a different argument than the prevalent emphasis on incompatibility, which leaves us with something that is second-rate because of translation. I am more interested in arguing that Native literature is first-rate, able to compete with the best literary artistry anywhere in the world.

There is no doubt that translated material is different from the original. Is difference, however, always bad? What if there are certain ways that the translated story *improves*, at least for its English-speaking audience? We are always told that jokes and humor fall flat when translated from tribal languages to English. Perhaps this is true (one wonders how much of this might be related to differences between live performance and appearance in print rather than issues of linguistic incompatibility), but what if there are other aspects of the story that are rendered "better" in English?

Further, many people make dubious claims about the gender biases of English. Of course, we know that languages do have grammatical structures that vary from culture to culture. If one investigates some of these "genderless" tribal languages, however, I suspect that one will find that they too have ways to indicate gender, simply different ways from how it is indicated in English. It is interesting to note that the tribes with the supposed "genderless" languages are far from feminist utopias. The point is, I think these differences may be important, but I would like to see people offer some linguistic evidence as to what the differences actually mean rather than offering reductive generalities that, in the end, may not help us argue the excellence of tribal literatures.

In the political sphere, arguments for saving Native languages, which are a central tribal issue of grave importance, can be made in reference to the integrity, excellence, and value of indigenous languages rather than claiming their radical incommensurability in relation to English or denigrating English itself, a language hugely important to us. Native languages should be saved because they are beautiful and of great intrinsic worth, not because of the way they compare to an English that is supposedly inferior for conveying Indian ideas. The argument based on the cultural superiority of Indian languages over an inferior English simply reverses oppressive categories based on forms of dominance and does not even serve our own interests. Indian languages, Indian experiences, Indian perspectives can, in fact, be claimed by Indians without relying on arguments of isolation, purity, incommensurability. They are Indian because Native peoples, like all peoples, have the right to speak, to teach languages, to claim experiences, to articulate perspectives. Given five hundred years of history where others have spoken so frequently on their behalf, a claim for the validity of Native perspectives is far from an essentialist one. There is nothing essentialist about saying it is just and fitting to allow Native people to speak for themselves in regard to their experiences, especially in light of a history that has not allowed them to do that.

One might wonder if these various open-ended approaches to tribal experience threaten the kind of tribally specific practices I have outlined in my own work. I do not think they do, simply because I have tried to demonstrate the many ways in which tribally specific experiences are constantly expanding, even beyond their own borders and out into non-Indian realms. I have also tried to critique those elusive searches for cultural purity that seek a shrinking world rather than one inclusive of the realities and opportunities that surround it. I have consistently emphasized the futility of categorizing things according to their level of purity or taintedness, a theme I explored in *Red on Red*. The example I have had the most fun with over the years is a dialect letter in that book that insists that intense interest in Alfred Hitchcock movies could be an important part of a Creek perspective. The difference between my own approach and those that have dominated hybridity theories is an insistence that Creeks talking about Alfred Hitchcock films do not constitute some kind of hybridized cultural moment but that dissecting an Alfred Hitchcock film can be counted as a profoundly Creek experience.

This is not necessarily because there is anything inherently tribal about Hitchcock (though there may be, who knows?) but because Creeks may choose such works for their own reasons. The freedom to make these choices, I believe, is part of what constitutes intellectual sovereignty, a concept Robert Warrior introduces us to in his milestone work, *Tribal Secrets.*

Readers may recall my claims at the beginning of this section about the importance of being able to distinguish Native experience from non-Native experience in order to claim Native studies as a discipline autonomous from anthropology, history, and other academic units. Distinguishing Indian experience, then, has to do with recognizing the rights of Native people to speak of their own experiences and with evaluating their claims in relation to Native realities, not the purity of Indian experience—that is, keeping it uncontaminated by avoiding outside cultural influences. By this point, I think it should be obvious that my argument that a Native person might have special insight into Native studies—or into Native experience—is not the same as claiming that all Indians will always have special insights into Native studies—or Native experience. Not all humans, after all, are insightful.

It *is*, though, an argument for privileging Native viewpoints as a response to their erasure, which has characterized several centuries of history, as well as a claim that Native experience has the *potential* for special insight into Native culture, one that should be encouraged in as many ways as possible, including advocating for autonomous Indian studies departments. Such departments, at their best, provide alternative viewpoints, though it is certainly not a given that they will necessarily produce them, just as it is not a given that any academic department will achieve excellence.

While a discussion of the current state of Native studies departments would require another paper, practical methodologies are readily available for such departments to distinguish themselves from other disciplines. One obvious one is the insistence on teaching courses using Native-authored texts. Does this guarantee the books will be better than non-Indian-authored works? Obviously not. A cornerstone of Native studies is Native people telling their stories. This makes Indian-authored books indispensable in Native studies departments. If one uses all Native texts to teach a course on nineteenth-century Indian history, relying on works such as autobiographies, tribal histories, conversion accounts, and so on, the course is going to be different from a nineteenth-century Indian history class in the history department. But shouldn't it be? Isn't that the point? Surely, this is a happy separatism.

Have I built a contradiction into the essay, having just advocated distinguishing our discipline from others, on the one hand, while arguing that Indian experience is infinitely varied, interrelated, on the other? If Indian experience can be anything, how do we define it? I seem to have circled back to the dilemmas in the first section of this essay in asking, What is a Native perspective? Rather than a universalized form of truth, I have suggested that a Native perspective is any perspective articulated by a Native person and that, given the many Natives articulating perspectives, we have many Native perspectives rather than *the* Native perspective in the singular. An "anything goes" attitude, however, is not the end of the story.

The critical chore we face becomes the challenge of assessing those perspectives in terms of how well they describe the material, social, political, spiritual, and other Indian realities in the Native worlds to which the perspectives refer. In suggesting that Indian experience is anything Indians experience, I find it important to acknowledge that this, as well, does not constitute the end of the story. As scholars we are still left with the responsibility of analyzing the strengths and weaknesses of these experiences in relation to particular community criteria that we must struggle to define and legitimate. Not all Indian experiences will be of equal value.

In Osage author Charles Red Corn's compelling novel about Osage religious change during the 1920s entitled *A Pipe for February*, the young character Molly makes the following speech to her elders, recalling one older mentor she disagreed with in her childhood:

> *I remember once when we were children. My cousin Wa-tsa-ka-wa and my cousin Wah-ni-un-tah and I, we huddled next to one of those bark lodges and we listened while the grown people talked about burying a Pipe.*

> *The Non-hon-zhin-ga said we children would be taught by white people and we would speak like white people. He said we would not know Osage ways. I remember that. It is clear in my mind.*
>
> *The man who spoke was a good man and I respect him. Still one thing he said was not right. It will take more than white teachers to make us think like white people.*
>
> *There is much we do not know about the teachings of the clans. Still when the people buried the Pipe, they did not bury our thoughts. We still have those thoughts and we remember those things our parents taught us.*
>
> *It is true we are different from the generation of Osages before us, just as the generation after us will be different from us. Generation after generation we have changed some things to make a way for ourselves on earth. Still, the things that are important have remained the same.*
>
> *It is true we sound like white people when we speak their language, and yet before we learned the language of the white people, we spoke Osage and our thoughts are Osage thoughts.*
>
> *Things in the mind and things in the heart make people what they are, and I know we were born with hearts that are Osage. That does not change."*[37]

Our challenge as Indian intellectuals goes beyond simply advocating an open-ended definition of Indian experience. We cannot descend into a relativistic abyss. We have to imagine, I believe, a core of Indian values, an essence, the "important things that remain the same." The way I envision this Native core right now is as a mass of fiery energy. While it is protean in nature, ever changing in shape, new things coming into it, old things leaving, that doesn't mean the ball of fire I see in my mind's eye, these essences of tribalism, do not exist. We have to create a theoretical space that allows for this tribal core, for people like Molly who want to imagine ways to be Osage based on a continuity with the past. (And it is important to note that Molly insists that this includes a responsibility to think critically about the past, about tradition and traditionalists. Simply put, she disagrees with an elder speaking on Osage tradition.)

The open-ended process this essay suggests cannot, and should not, avoid the intellectual challenge of making normative tribal judgments; we cannot dismiss essentialism in its entirety. Various tribal communities can, and will, have to determine criteria as to what constitutes their core values and how to apply them. In this essay I have tried to demonstrate that one criteria, isolationism, has not served us very well. "Contact" has been a problematic word for us, not to mention a traumatic experience, but perhaps we are at a historical juncture where tribal experience can be strengthened and challenged by contact rather than simply diminished by it. Perhaps even, instead of being on the receiving end of contact, we can become the contactors instead of the contactees in ways that emphasize sharing rather than displacing.

The real challenge to sovereignty studies, if they are to mean anything at all, is not in establishing their validity relative to hybridity theories. Rather, the task at hand is establishing their validity in the tribal world in terms of moving them beyond a series of affirmations for all things Indian and into the arena of contested power struggles to see if they have enough integrity to resist oppressive realities such as the disenfranchisement of the freedmen in the southeastern tribes and the hate legislation such as anti-gay-marriage amendments being passed by some tribal governments. If not, sovereignty studies will remain theoretical in the worst sense of the word—that is, the opposite of the applied theory argued for at every turn throughout this volume. Given the fiery core of a historic tradition that needs both its protectors and challengers, our job is daunting. My hope is that we lean in favor of those literally and symbolically disenfranchised within, and by, the tribal world. To my way of thinking, this is the heart and soul of activist scholarship, a commitment to the powerless as much as the powerful.

Notes

1. This paragraph was inspired by Daniel Heath Justice's written comments on an early draft of my essay.
2. These comments on false binaries also come from Daniel Heath Justice's remarks on my essay.
3. Again, a nod to Daniel Heath Justice, who inspired this brief paragraph.
4. Momaday, *Way to Rainy Mountain*, 33.
5. See chapter 2, "Transformational Language," in Alan Kilpatrick, *Night Has a Naked Soul.*
6. Jack and Anna Kilpatrick, *Walk in Your Soul*, 25–26.
7. Ibid., 26–27.
8. Eagleton, *After Theory*, 162–63.
9. This sentence is yet another one inspired by Daniel Heath Justice's comments on my essay.
10. Eagleton, *After Theory*, 155–46.
11. The opening two sentences of this paragraph also come from Daniel Heath Justice's remarks.
12. Momaday, "Man Made of Words," 164.
13. Ibid., 13.
14. This paragraph is indebted to comments on my essay by Daniel Heath Justice.
15. Pulitano, *Toward a Native American Critical Theory*, 99.
16. Ibid., 94.
17. Ibid., 13.
18. Ibid., 40.
19. Ibid., 74.
20. Ibid., 85.
21. Ibid., 27.
22. Ibid., 185–86.

23. Ibid., 14.

24. Ibid., 80.

25. Ibid., 67. Emphasis in original.

26. Ibid., 71.

27. Pulitano, *Toward a Native American Critical Theory*, 92.

28. Ibid., 92.

29. I am indebted to Daniel Heath Justice's comments for the sentence that concludes this paragraph.

30. Tohe, "There Is No Word," 110.

31. I am indebted to Daniel Heath Justice comments on my essay for this particular sentence.

32. Nguyen, "It Matters," 186.

33. Ibid., 200.

34. Ibid. Emphasis in original.

35. Ibid., 194.

36. Mathews, *Talking to the Moon*, 194.

37. Red Corn, *Pipe for February*, 229–30.

Bibliography

Ahenakew, Freda. *Wisahkewcahk Flies to the Moon*, Winnipeg, Man.: Pemmican Press, 1999.

Akiwenzie-Damm, Kateri. "Erotica, Indigenous Style." In *(Ad)dressing Our Words: Aboriginal Perspectives on Aboriginal Literatures,* edited by Armand Ruffo. Penticton, B.C.: Theytus, 2001.

——, ed. *Without Reservation: Indigenous Erotica.* Wiarton, Ont.: Kegedonce Press, 2003.

Alcoff, Linda Martin. "Objectivity and Its Politics." *New Literary History* 32 (2001): 835–48.

Alfred, Taiaiake [Gerald R]. *Heeding the Voices of Our Ancestors: Kahnawake Mohawk Politics and the Rise of Native Nationalism*. New York: Oxford University Press, 1995.

——. *Peace, Power, Righteousness: An Indigenous Manifesto*. Don Mills, Ont.: Oxford University Press, 1999.

Allen, Paula Gunn. *The Sacred Hoop: Recovering the Feminine in American Indian Traditions.* Boston: Beacon Press, 1992.

——. *Spider Woman's Granddaughters: Traditional Tales and Contemporary Writing by Native American Women.* New York: Ballantine Books, 1990.

——. *The Woman Who Owned the Shadows.* San Francisco: Spinsters, Ink, 1983.

Anzaldua, Gloria. *Borderlands/LaFrontera: The New Mestiza.* San Francisco: Aunt Lute Press, 1987.

Apess, William. *Indian Nullification of the Unconstitutional Laws of Massachusetts Relative to the Mashpee Tribe, or, The Pretended Riot Explained*. Boston: Jonathan Howe, 1835.

——. "An Indian's Looking-Glass for the White Man." In *On Our Own Ground: The Complete Writings of William Apess, a Pequot*. Edited by Barry O'Connell. Amherst: University of Massachusetts, 1992.

——. *On Our Own Ground: The Complete Writings of William Apess, a Pequot.* Edited by Barry O'Connell. Amherst: University of Massachusetts Press, 1992.

Applebome, Peter. "Out from under the Nation's Shadow." *New York Times*, February 20, 1999: B7.

Armstrong, Jeannette, ed. *Looking at the Words of Our People: First Nations Analysis of Literature.* Penticton, B.C.: Theytus, 1993.

——. *Slash.* Penticton, B.C.: Theytus, 1985.

Ashcroft, Bill, Gareth Griffiths, and Helen Tiffin. *The Empire Writes Back: Theory and Practice in Post-colonial Literatures*. New York: Routledge, 1998.

Aupaumut, Hendrick. "Extract from an Indian History." *Collections of the Massachusetts Historical Society*, 1st series (1826) 9:101.

——. "Narrative of an Embassy to the Western Indians." *Collections of the Massachusetts Historical Society*, 1st series (1826) 9:76.

Baird, David. *Peter Pitchlynn: Chief of the Choctaws*. Norman: University of Oklahoma Press, 1972.

Ballenger, Bruce. "Methods of Memory: On Native American Storytelling." *College English* 59 (1997): 789–800.

Barnard, Ian. "Gloria Anzaldua." *The Gay and Lesbian Literary Heritage: A Reader's Companion to the Writers and Their Works from Antiquity to the Present*, edited by Claude Summers. New York: Henry Holt, 1995.

Barreiro, José, ed. *Indian Roots of American Democracy*. Ithaca, N.Y: Akwe:kon, 1992.

Baumgardner, Jennifer. "Kitchen Table Candidate." *Ms. Magazine*, April/May 2001: 47–53.

Bell, Betty Louise. "Almost the Whole Truth: Gerald Vizenor's Shadow-Working and Native American Autobiography." *A/B* 7, no. 2 (1992): 180–95.

Benn, Carl. *The Iroquois in the War of 1812*. Toronto: University of Toronto Press, 1998.

Berkhofer, Robert F. Jr., *The White Man's Indian: Images of the American Indian from Columbus to the Present*. New York: Vintage Books, 1978.

Bevis, William. "Native American Novels: Homing In." In *Critical Perspectives on Native American Fiction*, edited by Richard Fleck, 15–45. Washington, D.C.: Three Continents Press, 1993.

Bhabha, Homi. "By Bread Alone: Signs of Violence in the Mid-nineteenth Century." In *The Location of Culture*. New York: Routledge, 1994.

Big Eagle, Duane. "Notes for Teachers on Native American Cultures." Personal communication to Kim Roppolo, August 26, 1999.

Bill, Charles. Statement. William Samuel Johnson Papers. Connecticut Historical Society Museum, Hartford.

Birchfield, D. L. *The Oklahoma Basic Intelligence Test*. Greenfield Center, N.Y.: Greenfield Review Press, 1998.

Bird, Gloria. "Breaking the Silence: Writing as Witness. In *Speaking for the Generations: Native Writers on Writing*, edited by Simon Ortiz. Tucson: University of Arizona Press, 1998.

Bizzzell, Patricia. "The 4th of July and the 22nd of December: The Function of Cultural Archives in Persuasion, as Shown by Frederick Douglass and William Apess." *College Composition and Communication* 48, no. 1 (1997): 44–60.

Blackbear, Eugene, Jr. Personal interview with Kim Roppolo, September 7, 2001.

Blaeser, Kimberly M. *Gerald Vizenor: Writing in the Oral Tradition*. Norman: University of Oklahoma Press, 1996.

——. "Native Literature: Seeking a Critical Center." In *Looking at the Worlds of Our*

People: First Nations Analysis of Literature, edited by Jeannette Armstrong, 51–62. Penticton, B.C.: Theytus, 1993.

Blanche, Jerry D. "Ignoring It Won't Make It Go Away." *Journal of American Indian Education* 12, no. 1 (1972). http:///jaie.asu.edu/v12/v12S1ign.html.

Blodgett, Harold. *Samson Occom*. Hanover, N.H.: Dartmouth College Press, 1935.

Bonnin, Gertrude [Zitkala Sa]. *American Indian Stories*. Lincoln: University of Nebraska Press, 1985.

Boudinot, Elias. "An Address to the Whites." In *Cherokee Editor: The Writings of Elias Boudinot,* edited by Theda Perdue, 65–83. Athens: University of Georgia Press, 1983.

Boyd, Julian P., ed. *Indian Treaties Printed by Benjamin Franklin, 1736–1762*. Philadelphia: Historical Society of Pennsylvania, 1938.

Brant, Beth, ed. *A Gathering of the Spirit: A Collection by North American Indian Women*. Toronto: Women's Press, 1992.

Brantlinger, Patrick. *Crusoe's Footprints: Cultural Studies in Britain and America.* New York: Routledge, 1990.

Brennan, Jonathan, ed. *When Brer Rabbit Meets Coyote: African-Native American Literature*. Champaign-Urbana: University of Illinois Press, 2003.

Brill de Ramirez, Susan Berry. *Contemporary American Indian Literatures and the Oral Tradition.* Tucson: University of Arizona Press, 1999.

Brooks, Lisa. *The Common Pot: Indigenous Writing and the Reconstruction of Native Space in the Northeast.* Minneapolis: University of Minnesota Press, 2008.

Bruchac, Joseph. *Iroquois Stories: Heroes and Heroines, Monsters and Magic.* Trumansburg, N.Y.: Crossing Press, 1985.

Bruhm, Steven. "Queer Today, Gone Tomorrow." *English Studies in Canada* 23, nos. 1 and 2 (March/June 2003): 25–32.

Burke, Colleen. "Teaching American Indian Literature with Black Elk Speaks." Master's thesis, St. Cloud State University, 2001.

Burkhart, Brian Yazzie. "What Coyote and Tales Can Teach Us: An Outline of American Indian Epistemology." In *American Indian Thought,* edited by Anne Waters, 15–26. Oxford, U.K.: Blackwell, 2004.

Bushnell, David, Jr. "Myths of the Louisisan Choctaw." *American Anthropologist* N.S. 12 (1910): 526–35.

Butler, Judith. *Gender Trouble: Feminism and the Subversion of Identity.* New York: Routledge, 1990.

Callahan, S. Alice. *Wynema: A Child of the Forest.* Lincoln: University of Nebraska Press, 1997.

Campbell, Joseph. *The Hero with a Thousand Faces.* Princeton, N.J.: Princeton University Press, 1949.

Campbell, Maria. *Halfbreed.* Toronto: McClelland and Stewart, 1973.

——. *Stories of the Road Allowance People.* Penticton, B.C.: Theytus, 1995.

Campisi, Jack. *The Mashpee Indians: Tribe on Trial.* Syracuse, N.Y.: Syracuse University Press, 1991.

Castillo, Susan Perez. "Postmodernism, Native American Literature and the Real: The Silko-Erdrich Controversy." *Massachusetts Review* 32 (1991): 285–94.

Chang, David A. Y. O. "From Indian Territory to White Man's Country: Race, Nation, and the Politics of Land Ownership in Eastern Oklahoma, 1889–1940." Dissertation, University of Wisconsin-Madison, 2002.

Chomsky, Noam. *For Reasons of State*. New York: Pantheon, 1973.

——. *On Power and Ideology: The Managua Lectures*. Boston: South End, 1987.

Churchill, Ward. *Fantasies of the Master Race: Literature, Cinema and the Colonization of American Indians.* Edited by Annette Jaimes. Monroe, Maine: Common Courage Press, 1992.

Clelland, Robert. Letter to Governor Thomas Fitch, New London, December 26, 1764. *Collections of the Connecticut Historical Society* 18, Hartford, 1860–1967, 314–15.

Clifford, James, and George Marcus, eds. *Writing Culture: The Poetics and Politics of Ethnography.* Berkeley: University of California Press, 1986.

Cobb, Amanda. Unpublished manuscript in possession of the collective.

Colson, Elizabeth, ed. *Autobiographies of Three Pomo Women.* Archeological Research Facility, Department of Anthropology, University of California, 1974.

Conley, Robert J. *Cherokee Medicine Man: The Life and Work of a Modern-Day Healer.* Norman: University of Oklahoma Press, 2005.

——. *The Witch of Goingsnake and Other Stories.* Norman: University of Oklahoma Press, 1991.

Connelly, Kevin A. "The Textual Function of Onondaga Aspect, Mood, and Tense: A Journey into Onondaga Conceptual Space." Dissertation, Cornell University, 1999.

Conrad, Joseph. *Heart of Darkness.* Garden City, N.Y.: International Collectors, 1902.

Conroy, David W. "The Defense of Indian Land Rights: William Bollan and the Mohegan Case in 1743." *Proceedings of the American Antiquarian Society* 103 (1933):395–424.

Cook-Lynn. "American Indian Intellectualism and the New Indian Story." *American Indian Quarterly* 20 (1996): 57–76.

——. *Anti-Indianism in Modern America: A Voice from Tatekeya's Earth*. Urbana: University of Illinois Press, 2001.

——. *Aurelia: A Crow Creek Trilogy*. Boulder: University Press of Colorado, 2002.

——. "Literary and Political Questions of Transformation: American Indian Fiction Writers." *Wicazo Sa Review* 13, no. 1 (1995): 46–51.

——. "Who Gets to Tell the Stories?" *Wicazo Sa Review* 9, no. 1 (1993): 60–64.

——. *Why I Can't Read Wallace Stegner and Other Essays: A Tribal Voice*. Madison: University of Wisconsin Press, 1996.

Cronin, Mary Elizabeth. "Activist/Author Looks to the Future." *Seattle Times*, April 23, 1998, and July 16, 2002. http:///seattletimes.nwsource.com/news/lifestyles/html98/altduke_042398.html

Crow Dog, Mary, with Richard Erdoes. *Lakota Woman*. New York: Harper, 1990.

Culler, Jonathan. *Literary Theory: A Very Short Introduction.* Oxford, U.K.: Oxford University Press, 2000.

Cusick, David. "The Iroquois Creation Story." In *Norton Anthology of American Literature*, 4th ed., vol. 1, edited by Nina Baym et al. New York, Norton, 1994.

——. *Sketches of Ancient History of the Six Nations: Comprising a Tale of the Foundation of the Great Island (Now North America), the Two Infants Born, and the Creation of the Universe.* Lockport, N.Y.: Niagara County Historical Society, 1961.

Davis, Lennard. "Thirty-two Letters on the Relation between Cultural Studies and the Literary." *PMLA* 112, no. 2 (1997): 257–86.

Davis, Nancy Yaw. *The Zuni Enigma: A Native American People's Possible Japanese Connection.* New York: Norton, 2001.

Day, Gordon. *Western Abenaki Dictionary*, vol. 1. Hull, Quebec: Canadian Museum of Civilization, 1994.

Debo, Angie. *And Still the Waters Run: The Betrayal of the Five Civilized Tribes.* Princeton, N.J.: Princeton University Press, 1973.

——. *The Rise and Fall of the Choctaw Republic.* Norman: University of Oklahoma Press, 1961.

——. *The Road to Disappearance.* Norman: University of Oklahoma Press, 1941.

De Forest, John W. *History of the Indians of Connecticut from the Earliest Known Period to 1850.* Hartford, Conn.: Hamersley, 1851.

Deloria, Ella. *Speaking of Indians.* Lincoln: University of Nebraska Press, 1988.

Deloria, Philip. "American Indians, American Studies, and the ASA." *American Quarterly* 55, no. 4 (December 2003): 669–80.

Deloria, Vine, Jr. "Civilization and Isolation." In *For This Land: Writings on Religion in America*, edited by James Treat. New York: Routledge, 1999.

——. *Custer Died for Your Sins: An Indian Manifesto.* Norman: University of Oklahoma Press, 1988.

——. Foreword. In *New and Old Voices of Wah'Kon-Tah*, edited by Robert Dodge and Joseph McCullough. New York: International, 1985.

——. *God Is Red: A Native View of Religion.* Golden, Colo.: North American Press, 1994.

——. "Self-Determination and the Concept of Sovereignty." In *Economic Development in American Indian Reservations,* edited by Roxanne Dunbar Ortiz, 22–28. Albuquerque: University of New Mexico Press, 1979.

——. *Spirit and Reason.* Golden, Colo.: Fulcrum, 1999.

de Man, Paul. *Aesthetic Ideology.* Edited by Andrzej Warminski. Mineapolis: University of Minnesota Press, 1996.

DeVorsey, Louis. *Indian Boundary in the Southern Colonies, 1763–1775.* Chapel Hill: University of North Carolina Press, 1961.

Donahue, Betty Booth. "Observations of Another Trotline Runner: A Critical Discussion of D. L. Birchfield's *Oklahoma Basic Intelligence Test.*" *SAIL* 11, no. 3 (1999): 66–79.

Donaldson, Laura E. "Noah Meets Old Coyote, or Singing in the Rain: Intertextuality in Thomas King's *Green Grass, Running Water*." *Studies in American Indian Literatures* 7, no. 2 (1995): 27–43.

Dreyfus, Hubert L., and Paul Rabinow. *Michel Foucault: Beyond Structuralism and Hermeneutics*, 2d ed. Chicago: University of Chicago Press, 1982.

Dumont, Marilyn. "The Devil's Language." In *An Anthology of Canadian Native Literature in English*, edited by Daniel Moses and Terrie Goldie. Toronto: Oxford University Press, 1998.

Duncan, Barbara, ed. *Living Stories of the Cherokee*. Chapel Hill: University of North Carolina, 1998.

Dussel, Enrique. "Beyond Eurocentrism: The World System and the Limits of Modernity." In *The Cultures of Globalization*, edited by Fredric Jameson and Masao Miyoshi, 3–31. Durham, N.C.: Duke University Press, 1998.

Eagleton, Terry. *After Theory*. New York: Perseus Books, 2003.

——. *The Illusions of Postmodernism*. London: Blackwell, 1996.

Easthope, Anthony. *Literary into Cultural Studies*. New York: Routledge, 1996.

Eastman, Charles Alexander [Ohiyesa]. *From the Deep Woods to Civilization*. Lincoln: University of Nebraska Press, 1977.

Elliot, Michael. " 'This Indian Bait': Samson Occom and the Voice of Liminality." *Early American Literature* 29, no. 3 (1994): 233–53.

Elm, Demus, and Harvey Antone. *The Oneida Creation Story*. Edited by Floyd G. Lounsbury and Bryan Gick. Lincoln: University of Nebraska Press, 2000.

Elrod, Eileen Razzari. " 'I Did Not Make Myself So . . .': Samson Occom and American Religious Autobiography." In *Christian Encounters with the Other*, edited by John C. Hawley, 135–49. New York: New York University Press, 1998.

Erdrich, Louise. *The Beet Queen*. New York: Bantam, 1987.

——. *Love Medicine*. New York: HarperCollins, 1984.

Fey, Harold E., and D'Arcy McNickle. *Indians and Other Americans: Two Ways of Life Meet*. New York: Perennial–Harper and Row, 1970.

Fixico, Donald L. "Call for Native Genius and Indigenous Intellectualism." *Indigenous Nations Studies Journal* 1, no. 1 (2000): 43–59.

Fogelson, Raymond D. "Major John Norton as Ethno-ethnologist." *Journal of Cherokee Studies* (Fall 1978): 250–55.

Forbes, Jack. *Africans and Native Americans: The Language of Race and the Evolution of Red-Black Peoples*. Champaign-Urbana: University of Illinois Press, 1993.

Freeman, Michael. "Puritans and Pequots: The Question of Genocide." *New England Quarterly* 68, no. 2 (June 1995): 278–93.

Freire, Paulo. *Pedagogy of the Oppressed*. Translated by Myra Bergman Ramos. New York: Continuum, 1989.

Garroutte, Eva Marie. "The Racial Formation of American Indians." *American Indian Quarterly* 25, no. 2 (2001): 224–39.

Geertz, Clifford. *The Interpretation of Cultures: Selected Essays*. New York: Basic Books, 1973.

Gibson, Danna. "The Communiity of the Eastern Cherokee: Enacting Community via Discourse." http:///acjournal.org/holdings/vol2/iss1/essays/gibson.htm.

Gilley, Amy. "Cherrie Moraga." In *Gay and Lesbian Literary Heritage: A Reader's Companion to the Writers and Their Works from Antiquity to the Present*, edited by Claude Summers. New York: Henry Holt, 1995.

Glover, David. "Thirty-two Letters on the Relation between Cultural Studies and the Literary." *PMLA* 112, no. 2 (1997): 257–86.

Goebel, Rolf, "Thirty-two Letters on the Relation between Cultural Studies and the Literary." *PMLA* 112, no. 2 (1997): 257–86.

Gramsci, Antonio. *Selections from the Prison Notebooks of Antonio Gramsci.* Edited and translated by Quintin Hoare and Geoffrey Nowell Smith. New York: International, 1971.

Greenberg, David F., ed. *Crime and Capitalism: Readings in Marxist Criminology.* Philadelphia: Temple University Press, 1993.

Gubar, Susan. "What Ails Feminist Criticism?" *Critical Inquiry* 24 (Summer 1998): 878–902.

Guerrero, Marie Anna Jaimes. "Civil Rights versus Sovereignty: Native American Women in Life and Land Struggles." In *Feminist Genealogies, Colonial Legacies, Democratic Futures,* edited by M. Jacqui Alexander and Chandra Mohanty, 101–121. New York: Routledge, 1997.

Guillen, Claudio. "On the Edge of Literariness: The Writing of Letters." *Comparative Literary Studies* 31, no. 1 (1994): 1–24.

Habermas, Jürgen. *The Structural Transformation of the Public Sphere.* Translated by Thomas Burger, assisted by Frederick Lawrence. Cambridge: MIT Press, 1989.

Hale, Grace Elizabeth Hale. *Making Whiteness: The Culture of Segregation in the South, 1890–1940.* New York: Vintage Books, 1998.

Halliburton, Rudyard. *Red over Black: Black Slavery among the Cherokee Indians.* Westport, Conn.: Greenwood Press, 1977.

Hames-García, Michael. *Fugitive Thought: Prison Movements, Race, and the Meaning of Justice.* Minneapolis: University of Minnesota Press, 2004.

Harjo, Joy. *In Mad Love and War.* Middletown, Conn.: Wesleyan University Press, 1990.

——. *The Last Song.* Albuquerque, N.M.: Puerto del Sol, 1975.

——. *A Map to the Next World: Poems and Tales.* New York: Norton, 2000.

——. *She Had Some Horses.* New York: Thunders Mouth Press, 1983.

——. *The Spiral of Memory: Interviews,* edited by Laura Coltelli. Ann Arbor: University of Michigan Press, 1996.

——. *What Moon Drove Me to This?* New York: Reed Books, 1979.

——. *The Woman Who Fell from the Sky.* New York, Norton, 1994.

Harris, Cheryl. "Whiteness as Property." *Harvard Law Review* 106 (June 1993): 1707–91.

Hartsock, Nancy. "The Feminist Standpoint: Developing the Ground for a Specifically Feminist Historical Materialism." In *The Feminist Standpoint Revisited & Other Essays,* 105–132. Boulder, Colo.: Westview Press, 1998.

Hau, Caroline S. "On Representing Others: Intellectuals, Pedagogy, and the Uses of Error." In *Reclaiming Identity: Realist Theory and the Predicament of Postmodernism*,.edited by Paula M. L. Moya and Michael R. Hames-García, 133–70. Berkeley: University of California Press, 2000.

Havelock, Eric. *The Muse Learns to Write: Reflections on Orality and Literacy from Antiquity to the Present.* New Haven, Conn.: Yale University Press, 1986.

Herman, Peter C. "The Resistance to Historicizing Theory." In *Historicizing Theory*, edited by Peter C. Herman, 1–16. Albany: State University of New York Press, 2004.

Hester, Thurman Lee, Jr. "Pishukchi: One Choctaw's Examination of the Differences in English and Choctaw Language Use." *Ayaangwaamizin: The International Journal of Indigenous Philosophy* 1, no. 1 (1997): 81–90.

Hitt, Jack. "The Newest Indians." *New York Times Magazine*, August 21, 2005: 36–41.

Hobson, Geary. *The Remembered Earth: An Anthology of Contemporary Native American Literature.* Albuquerque: University of New Mexico Press, 1979.

——. "The Rise of the White Shaman as a New Version of Cultural Imperialism." In *The Remembered Earth*. Edited by Geary Hobson. Albuquerque: University of New Mexico Press, 1979.

Hoggart, Richard. *The Uses of Literacy: Changes Patterns in English Mass Culture.* Fair Lawn, N.J.: Essential Books, 1957.

Hollrah, Patrice. "Sherman Alexie's Challenge to the Academy's Teaching of Native American Literature, Non-Native Writers, and Critics." *SAIL* 13, no. 2–3 (2001): 23–35.

hooks, bell. *Teaching to Transgress: Education as the Practice of Freedom*. New York: Routledge, 1994.

Howe, Adrian. *Punish and Critique: Towards a Feminist Analysis of Penality*. New York: Routledge, 1994.

Howe, LeAnne. *Shell Shaker*. San Francisco: Aunt Lute Books, 2001.

——. "The Story of America: A Tribalography." In *Clearing a Path: Theorizing the Past in Native American Studies,* edited Nancy Shoemaker, 29–48. New York: Routledge, 2002.

Hudson, Charles. *The Southeastern Indians.* Knoxville: University of Tennessee Press, 1976.

Hymes, Dell. *In Vain I Tried to Tell You: Essays in Native American Poetics.* Philadelphia: University of Pennsylvania Press, 1981.

Inglis, Fred. *Cultural Studies.* Cambridge, Mass.: Blackwell, 1993.

Irving, Washington. *The Sketch Book of Sir Geoffrey Crayon, Gent.* London: John Murray, 1820.

Isernhagen, Hartwig. *Momaday, Vizenor, Armstrong: Conversations on American Indian Writing.* Norman: University of Oklahoma Press, 1999.

Jackson, Jason Baird. *Yuchi Ceremonial Life: Performance, Meaning, and Tradition in a Contemporary American Indian Community*. Lincoln: University of Nebraska Press, 2003.

Jameson, Fredric. *Marxism and Form: Twentieth-Century Dialectical Theories of Literature*. Princeton: Princeton University Press, 1971.

Johnson, E. Pauline. "A Strong Race Opinion." In *Tekahionwake: Collected Poems and Selected Prose*. Toronto: University of Toronto Press, 2002.

Johnson, Joseph. *To Do Good to My Indian Brethren: The Writings of Joseph Johnson, 1751–1776*. Edited by Laura Murray. Amherst: University of Massachusetts Press, 1998.

Justice, Daniel Heath. "We're Not There Yet, Kemo Sabe." *American Indian Quarterly* 25, no. 2 (Spring 2001): 256–69.

Keating, Ana Louise. "Feminist Literary Theory." In *Gay and Lesbian Literary Heritage: A Reader's Companion to the Writers and Their Works from Antiquity to the Present*, edited by Claude Summers. New York: Henry Holt, 1995.

Kelsay, Isabel Thompson. *Joseph Brant, 1743–1807, Man of Two Worlds*. Syracuse, N.Y.: Syracuse University Press, 1984.

Kennedy, George A. *Comparative Rhetoric: An Historical and Cross-Cultural Introduction*. Oxford, U.K.: Oxford University Press, 1998.

Kidwell, Clara Sue. *Choctaws and Missionaries in Mississippi, 1818–1918*. Norman: University of Oklahoma Press, 1995.

Kilpatrick, Alan. *The Night Has a Naked Soul: Witchcraft and Sorcery among the Western Cherokee*. Syracuse, N.Y.: Syracuse University Press, 1997.

Kilpatrick, Jack, and Anna Kilpatrick. *Walk in Your Soul: Love Incantations of the Oklahoma Cherokee*. Dallas, Tex.: Southern Methodist University Press, 1965.

King, Thomas. *The Truth about Stories: A Native Narrative*. Toronto: House of Anansi, 2003.

Kipnis, Laura. "Feminism: The Political Conscience of Postmodernism?" *Social Text* 21 (1989):149–66.

Konkle, Maureen. *Writing Indian Nations: Native Intellectuals and the Politics of Historiography, 1827–1863*. Chapel Hill: University of North Carolina Press, 2004.

Krupat, Arnold. *Red Matters: Native American Studies*. Philadelphia: University of Pennsylvania Press, 2002.

——. *The Turn to the Native: Studies in Criticism and Culture*. Lincoln: University of Nebraska Press, 1996.

——. *The Voice in the Margin: Native American Literature and the Canon*. Berkeley: University of California Press, 1989.

Laclau, Ernesto, and Chantal Mouffe. *Hegemony and Socialist Strategy: Toward a Radical Democratic Politics*. New York: Verso, 1985.

LaDuke, Winona. *All Our Relations: Native Struggles for Land and Life*. Cambridge, Mass.: South End Press, 1999.

——. "The Indigenous Women's Network: Our Future, Our Responsibility." United Nations Fourth World Conference on Women. Beijing, China. August 31, 1995. http:///www.igc.org/beijing/plenary/laduke.html.

——. *Last Standing Woman*. Vancouver, B.C.:Rainforest Books, 1997.

LaRocque, Emma. "Tides, Towns, Trains." In *Living the Changes*, edited by Joan Turner, 76–90. Winnipeg, Man.: University of Manitoba Press, 1990.

Lawrence, Bonita. *"Real" Indians and Others: Mixed-Blood Urban Native Peoples and Indigenous Nationhood.* Vancouver: University of British Columbia Press, 2005.

Leitch, Vincent, ed. *Norton Anthology of Theory and Criticism.* New York: Norton, 2001.

Lenin, V. I. *Imperialism: The Highest Stage of Capitalism*. New York: International Publishers, 1939.

Leon-Portilla, Miguel, ed. "Introduction." In *The Broken Spears: The Aztec Account of the Conquest of Mexico.* Boston: Beacon Press, 1992.

Lewis, David, Jr., and Ann T. Jordan. *Creek Indian Medicine Ways: The Enduring Power of Mvskoke Religion.* Albuquerque: University of New Mexico Press, 2002.

"Lieft Lion Gardener, His Relation of the Pequot War." *Collections of the Massachusetts Historical Society,* 3d series, 3:154.

Lincoln, Kenneth. *Native American Renaissance.* Berkeley: University of California Press, 1983.

Lipsitz, George. *The Possessive Investment in Whiteness: How White People Profit from Identity Politics.* Philadelphia: Temple University Press, 1998.

Littlefield, Daniel F., Jr. *Africans and Seminoles: From Removal to Emancipation.* Westport, Conn.: Greenwood Press, 1997.

——. *The Chickasaw Freedmen: A People without a Country.* Westport, Conn.: Greenwood Press, 1980.

——, and James W. Parins, eds. *Native American Writing in the Southeast: An Anthology, 1875–1935*. Jackson: University of Mississippi Press, 1995.

Lorde, Audre. "The Uses of the Erotic: The Erotic as Power." In *Sister Outsider: Essays and Speeches.* Freedom, Calif.: Crossing Press, 1984.

Love, William DeLoss. *Samson Occom and the Christian Indians of New England.* Syracuse, N.Y.: Syracuse University Press, 2000.

Lyons, Scott. "The Incorporation of the Indian Body: Peyotism and the Pan-Indian Public, 1911–1923." In *Rhetoric, the Polis, and the Global Village*, edited by C. Jan Swearingen and Dave Pruett, 147–53. Mahwah, N.J.: Lawrence Erlbaum, 1999.

——. "Rhetorical Sovereignty: American Writing as Self-Determination." Dissertation, Miami University, 2000.

——. "Rhetorical Sovereignty: What Do American Indians Want from Writing?" *College Composition and Communication* 51, no. 3 (2000): 447–67.

MacCallum, James Dow. *The Letters of Eleazar Wheelock's Indians.* Hanover, N.H.: Dartmouth College, 1932.

McDonald, James L. Letters to Peter Pitchlynn. Peter Perkins Pitchlynn Collection, Western History Collections, University of Oklahoma, Library, Norman.

——. "The Spectre and the Hunter, a Legend of the Choctaws." Manuscript in the

Peter Perkins Pitchlynn Collection, Western History Collections, University of Oklahoma.

McFarland, Ron. "Sherman Alexie's Polemical Stories." *SAIL* 9, no 4 (1997). http://www.richmond.edu/faculty/ASAIL/SAIL2/94.html

McLeod, Neal. "Coming Home through Story." In *(Ad)dressing Our Words: Aboriginal Perspectives on Aboriginal Literatures,* edited by Armand Ruffo, 17–36. Penticton, B.C.: Theytus, 2001.

McLoughlin, William G. *The Cherokees and Christianity, 1794–1870: Essays on Acculturation and Cultural Persistence.* Athens: University of Georgia Press, 1994.

McNickle, D'Arcy. *Native American Tribalism: Indian Survivals and Renewals.* New York: Oxford University Press, 1973.

——. *The Surrounded.* Albuquerque: University of New Mexico Press, 1978.

——. *Wind from an Enemy Sky.* Albuquerque: University of New Mexico Press, 1988.

McPherson, Dennis H., and J. Douglas Rabb. *Indian from the Inside: A Study in Ethno-Methaphysics.* Thunder Bay, Ont.: Lakehead University Press, 1993.

Maddox, Lucy. *Citizen Indians: Native American Intellectuals, Race, and Reform.* Ithaca, N.Y.: Cornell University Press, 2005.

Mandell, Daniel. *Behind the Frontier: Indians in Eighteenth-Century Eastern Massachusetts.* Lincoln: University of Nebraska Press, 1996.

Manypenny v. United States. 125 F.R.D. 497 U.S. Dist. Ct. D. Minn. 1989.

Manypenny v. United States. 948 F. 2d 1057 U.S. Ct. App. 1991.

Mao Tse-Tung. *On Contradiction.* Peking: Foreign Languages, 1960.

Martin, Jack B., and Margaret McKane Mauldin. *A Dictionary of Creek/Muskogee.* Lincoln: University of Nebraska Press, 2000.

Marx, Karl. "Theses on Feuerbach." In *The Marx-Engels Reader,* rev. ed., edited by Robert C. Tucker, 143–45. New York: Norton, 1978.

Marx, Leo. "On Recovering the 'Ur' Theory of American Studies." *American Literary History* 17, no. 1 (Spring 2005): 118–34.

Mathews, John Joseph. *Sundown.* Norman: University of Oklahoma Press, 1988.

——. *Talking to the Moon: Wildlife Adventures on the Prairies of Osage Country.* Norman: University of Oklahoma Press, 1981.

——. *Wah'Kon-Tah: The Osage and the White Man's Road.* Norman: University of Oklahoma Press, 1981.

May, Katja. *African Americans and Native Americans in the Creek and Cherokee Nations, 1830s to 1920s: Collision and Collusion.* London: Routledge, 1996.

May, Lary. *The Big Tomorrow: Hollywood and the Politics of the American Way.* Chicago: University of Chicago Press, 2000.

Meyer, Melissa. *The White Earth Tragedy: Ethnicity and Dispossession at a Minnesota Anishinaabe Reservation, 1889–1920.* Lincoln: University of Nebraska Press, 1994.

Miranda, Deborah. "Dildos, Hummingbirds, and Driving Her Crazy: Searching for American Indian Women's Love Poetry and Erotics." *Frontiers* 23, no. 2 (2002): 135–49.

Mittleman, Leslie. "Is Letter-Writing a Dying Art?" *World Literature Today* (Spring 1990): 221–26.

Mohanty, Satya P. *Literary Theory and the Claims of History: Postmodernism, Objectivity, Multicultural Politics*. Ithaca, N.Y.: Cornell University Press, 1997.

Mohawk, John C. "Indians and Democracy: No One Ever Told Us." In *Exiled in the Land of the Free: Democracy, Indian Nations, and the USA Constitution*, edited by Oren Lyons and John C. Mohawk, 43–71. Santa Fe, N.M.: Clear Light, 1992.

Momaday, N. Scott. *House Made of Dawn*. New York: Perennial-Harper, 1968.

——. "The Man Made of Words." In *The Remembered Earth*, edited by Geary Hobson. Albuquerque: University of New Mexico Press, 1979.

——. *The Names: A Memoir.* Tucson: University of Arizona Press, 1976.

——. *The Way to Rainy Mountain*. Albuquerque: University of New Mexico Press, 1969.

Momaday, Natachee. *American Indian Authors.* Boston: Houghton Mifflin, 1972.

——. *The Owl in the Cedar Tree.* Flagstaff, Ariz.: Northland Press, 1975.

Mooney, James. *Myths of the Cherokees*. New York: Dover, 1995.

Moraga, Cherrie, and Gloria Anzaldua. *This Bridge Called My Back: Writings by Radical Women of Color.* Waterbury, Mass.: Persephone Press, 1981.

Morgan, Lewis Henry. *Ancient Society*. Calcutta: Bhareti Library, 1877.

Moses, Daniel, and Terrie Goldie. *An Anthology of Canadian Native Literature in English.* Toronto: Oxford University Press, 1998.

Mourning Dove (Christine Quintasket). *Cogewea; the Half-Blood*. Lincoln: University of Nebraska Press, 1981.

Moya, Paula, and Michael Haimes-Garcia. *Reclaiming Identity: Realist Theory and the Predicament of Postmodernism.* Berkeley: University of California Press, 2000.

Mumford, Kevin. *Interzones: Black/White Sex Districts in Chicago and New York in the Early Twentieth Century.* New York: Columbia University Press, 1997.

Murray, David. *Forked Tongues: Speech, Writing, and Representation in North American Indian Texts*. Bloomington: Indiana University Press, 1991.

Mygatt, Matt. "Two Worlds Collide." *Albuquerque Journal*, February 5 and 6, 2000.

Nabokov, Peter. *A Forest of Time: American Indian Ways of History*. Cambridge, U.K.: Cambridge University Press, 2002.

Nelson, Dana. "I Speak Like a Fool but I Am Constrained": Samson Occom's Short Narrative and Economies of the Racial Self." In *Early Native American Writing: New Critical Essays*, edited by Helen Jaskoski, 42–65. Cambridge, U.K.: Cambridge University Press, 1996.

——. "Reading the Written Selves of Colonial America: Franklin, Occom, Equiano, and Palou/Serra." *Resources for American Literary Study* 19, no. 2 (1993): 246–59.

News from Indian Country. Multiple issues cited.

Nguyen, Minh T. " 'It Matters to Get the Facts Straight': Joy Kogawa, Realism, and the Objectivity of Values." In *Reclaiming Identity: Realist Theory and the*

Predicament of Postmodernism, edited by Paula Moya and Michael Haimes-Garcia. Berkeley: University of California Press, 2000.

Niatum, Duane. "History, Nature, Family, Dream. In *Looking at the Words of Our People: First Nations Analysis of Literature,* edited by Jeannette Armstrong, 64–82. Penticton, B.C.: Theytus, 1993.

Nicolar, Joseph. *The Life and Traditions of the Red Man*. Bangor, Me.: C. H. Glass, 1893.

Nielsen, Donald M. "The Mashpee Indian Revolt of 1833." *New England Quarterly* 58 (1985): 400–20.

Norton, John. *The Journal of Major John Norton, 1816*. Edited by Carl Klinck and James Talman. Toronto: Champlain Society, 1970.

Oberg, Michael Leroy. *Uncas: First of the Mohegans.* Ithaca, N.Y.: Cornell University Press, 2003.

O'Brien, Sharon. *American Indian Tribal Government.* Norman: University of Oklahoma Press, 1989.

——. "The Struggle to Protect the Exercise of Native Prisoners' Religious Rights." *Indigenous Nations Studies Journal* 1, no. 2 (2000): 29–49.

Occom, Samson. Papers. Folders 2: Correspondence 1761–65. Manuscript stacks, Connecticut Historical Society Museum, Hartford.

——. Papers. Folder 16: Records of the Mohegan Tribe. Manuscript stacks, Connecticut Historical Society Museum, Hartford.

——. "A Sermon, Preached at the Execution of Moses Paul, an Indian." In *The Harper American Literature*, vol. I,, edited by Donald McQuade et al., 472–80. New York: Harper and Row, 1987.

——. "A Short Narrative of My Life." In *Norton Anthology of American Literature*, vol 1, edited by Nina Baym et al., 612–19. New York: Norton, 1998.

Ong, Walter. *Orality and Literacy: The Technologizing of the Word.* New York: Routledge, 1982.

Ortiz, Alfonso. *The Tewa World: Space, Time, Being, and Becoming in a Pueblo Society*. Chicago: University of Chicago Press, 1969.

Ortiz, Simon J. *Earth Power Coming: Short Fiction in Native American Literature.* Tsaile, Ariz.: Navajo Community College Press (Diné College), 1983.

——. "Towards a National Indian Literature: Cultural Authenticity in Nationalism." *MELUS* 8, no. 2, *Ethnic Literature and Cultural Nationalism* (Summer 1981): 7–12.

——. *Woven Stone*. Tucson: University of Arizona Press, 1992.

Oskison, John Milton. *Brothers Three.* New York: Macmillan Company, 1935.

Owens, Louis. "As If an Indian Were Really an Indian: Native American Voices and Postcolonial Theory." In *I Hear the Train: Reflections, Inventions, Refractions,* 207–226. Norman: University of Oklahoma Press, 2001.

——. *Mixedblood Messages: Literature, Film, Family, Place*. Norman: University of Oklahoma Press, 1998.

——. *Other Destinies: Understanding the American Indian Novel.* Norman: University of Oklahoma Press, 1992.

Parker, Arthur Caswell. *Seneca Myths and Folk Tales.* Edited by William Fenton. Lincoln: University of Nebraska Press, 1989.

Parker, Robert Dale. *The Invention of Native American Literature*. Ithaca, N.Y.: Cornell University Press, 2003.

Penn, William S. *As We Are Now: Mixblood Essays on Race and Identity*. Berkeley: University of California Press. 1997.

Penn Hilden, Patricia. "Ritchie Valens Is Dead: *E Pluribus Unum.*" In *As We Are Now: Mixblood Essays on Race and Identity,* edited by William S. Penn, 219–52. Berkeley: University of California Press, 1997.

Perdue, Theda. *Slavery and the Evolution of Cherokee Society, 1540–1866.* Knoxville: University of Tennessee Press, 1979.

——, ed. *Cherokee Editor: The Writings of Elias Boudinot*. Athens: University of Georgia Press, 1983.

Peterson, Jr., Michael Edward. "That So-Called Warranty Deed: Clouded Land Titles on the White Earth Indian Reservation in Minnesota." *North Dakota Law Review* 59 (1983):159–81.

Petrone, Penny. *Native Literature in Canada: From the Oral Tradition to the Present.* Toronto: Oxford University Press, 1990.

Pevar, Stephen. *The Rights of Indians and Tribes: The Authoritative ACLU Guide to Indian and Tribal Rights*. New York: New York University Press, 2004.

Peyer, Bernd C. *The Tutor'd Mind: Indian Missionary-Writers in Antebellum America*. Amherst: University of Massachusetts Press, 1997.

Phillips, Lily. "Thirty-two Letters on the Relation between Cultural Studies and the Literary." *PMLA* 112, no. 2 (1997): 257–86.

Posey, Alexander. *The Fus Fixico Letters.* Edited by Daniel F. Littlefield, Jr., and Carol A. Petty Hunter. Lincoln: University of Nebraska Press, 1993.

Powell, Malea. "Blood and Scholarship: One Mixed-Blood's Dilemma." In *Race, Rhetoric, and Composition*, edited by Keith Gilyard, 1–16. Portsmouth, N.H.: Heinemann-Boynton/Cook, 1999.

——. "'I Write These Words with Blood and Bone': Two Nineteenth Century American Indian Intellectuals and a Rhetoric of Survivance." Dissertation, Miami University, 1998.

Pratt, Mary Louise. "Arts of the Contact Zone." In *Ways of Reading: An Anthology for Writers*, edited by Davis Bartholomae and Anthony Petrosky. Boston: Bedford Books, 1996.

Prucha, Francis Paul. *The Great Father: The United States Government and the American Indians,* abridged. Lincoln: University of Nebraska Press, 1986.

——, ed. *Documents of United States Indian Policy*. Lincoln: University of Nebraska Press, 1990.

Pulitano, Elvira. *Toward a Native American Critical Theory.* Lincoln: University of Nebraska Press, 2003.

Rader, Dean. "Native Screenings." ALA Symposium/Native American Literary Strategies for the Next Millennium. Puerta Vallarta, Mexico, December 2, 2000.

Rampell, Ed. "Feminist Dream or Nightmare: The Green Party." *Women's Interna-*

tional Net Magazine 38 (June 11, 2001). http:///winmagazine.org/issues/is sue38/win38e.htm

——. "Towards an Inaugural Pow-Wow." *Women's International Net Magazine* 44 (June 8, 2001). *http:///www.winmagazine.org*

Red Shirt, Delphine. "These Are Not Indians." *American Indian Quarterly* 26, no. 4 (Fall 2002): 643–44.

Red Corn, Charles. *A Pipe for February*. Norman: University of Oklahoma Press, 2002.

Restall, Matthew, Lisa Sousa, and Kevin Terraciano, eds. *Mesoamerican Voices: Native-Language Writings from Colonial Mexico, Oaxaca, Yucatan, and Guatemala.* New York: Cambridge University Press, 2005.

Rich, Adrienne. "Compulsory Heterosexuality and Lesbian Existence." *Signs* 5 (1980): 631–60.

Ridge, John Rollin. *The Life and Adventures of Joaquin Murieta, the Celebrated California Bandit.* Norman: University of Oklahoma Press, 1955.

Riggs. Lynn. *The Cherokee Night* (play, 1936).

——. *The Cream in the Well* (play, 1940).

——. *Green Grow the Lilacs* (play, 1933).

——. *The Year of Pilar* (play, 1940).

Rogers, Will. *The Autobiography of Will Rogers.* Edited by Donald Day. Boston: Houghton Mifflin, 1949.

——. *Will Rogers's Weekly Articles*, vols. 1-4. Edited by James M. Smallwood. Stillwater: Oklahoma State University Press, 1980.

Ronda, James P. "'As They Were Faithful': Chief Hendrick Aupaumut and the Struggle for Stockbridge Survival, 1756–1830." *American Indian Culture and Research Journal* 3, no. 3 (1979): 43–55.

Rosaldo, Renato. *Culture and Truth: The Remaking of Social Analysis*. Boston: Beacon, 1989.

Roscoe, Will, ed. *Living the Spirit: A Gay American Indian Anthology.* New York: St. Martin's Press, 1988.

——. *The Zuni Man-Woman.* Albuquerque: University of New Mexico Press, 1991.

Rose, Wendy. "The Great Pretenders: Further Reflections on White Shamanism." In *The State of Native America*, edited by M. Annette Jaimes. Boston: South End Press, 1992.

Ross, Luana. *Inventing the Savage: The Social Construction of Native American Criminality*. Austin: University of Texas Press, 1998.

Rothenberg, Jerome. *Shaking the Pumpkin: Traditional Poetry of the Indian North Americas.* Garden City, N.Y.: Doubleday, 1972.

Ruckman, S. E. "Tribe Membership Challenged." *Tulsa World*, July 30, 2006: A22.

Ruffo, Armand. "Inside Looking Out: Reading Tracks from a Native Perspective." In *Looking at the Words of Our People: First Nations Analysis of Literature*, edited by Jeannette Armstrong, 161–75. Penticton, B.C.: Theytus, 1993.

——, ed. *(Ad)dressing Our Words: Aboriginal Perspectives on Aboriginal Literatures.* Penticton, B.C.: Theytus, 2001.

Ruoff, A. LaVonne Brown. *American Indian Literatures: An Introduction, Bibliographic Review, and Selected Bibliography*. New York: Modern Language Association, 1990.

Ruppert, James. *Mediation in Contemporary Native American Fiction.* Norman: University of Oklahoma Press, 1995.

Said, Edward W. *Culture and Imperialism.* New York: Knopf, 1993.

——. *Orientalism*. New York: Vintage, 1994.

Salisbury, Neal. *Manitou and Providence: Indians, Europeans, and the Making of New England, 1500–1643*. New York: Oxford University Press, 1982.

Sampson, Bill. "Justice for the Cherokees: The Outlet Awards of 1961 and 1972." Master's thesis, University of Tulsa, 1972.

Sarris, Greg. *Keeping Slug Woman Alive: A Holistic Approach to American Indian Texts.* Berkeley: University of California Press, 1993.

Scarry, Elaine. *The Body in Pain: The Making and Unmaking of the World*. New York: Oxford University Press, 1985.

Scott, Joan. "Gender: A Useful Category of Historical Analysis." In *Gender and the Politics of History*, 29–50. New York: Columbia University Press, 1988.

Seesequasis, Paul. "The Republic of Tricksterism." In *An Anthology of Canadian Native Literature in English*, edited by Daniel Moses and Terrie Goldie, 411–16. Toronto: Oxford University Press, 1998.

Selinger, Bernard. "*House Made of Dawn*: A Positively Ambivalent Bildungsroman." *Modern Fiction Studies* 45 (1999): 38–68.

Sequoya-Magdaleno, Jana."Telling the *différance*: Representations of Identity in the Discourse of Indianness." In *The Ethnic Canon: Histories, Institutions, and Interventions*, edited by David Palumbo-Liu, 88–116. Minneapolis: University of Minnesota Press, 1995.

Shanley, Kathryn W. "Blood Ties and Blasphemy: American Indian Women and the Problem of History." In *Is Academic Feminism Dead?* edited by The Social Justice Group at the Center for Advanced Feminist Studies, University of Minnesota, 204–232. New York: New York University Press, 2000.

——. " 'Talking to the Animals and Taking Out the Trash': The Function of American Indian Literature." *Wicazo Sa Review* 14, no. 2 (1999): 32–45.

——. " 'Writing Indian': American Indian Literature and the Future of Native American Studies." In *Studying Native America: Problems and Prospects*, edited by Russell Thornton, 130–51. Madison: University of Wisconsin Press, 1998.

Shenandoah, Joanne, and Douglas M. George. *Skywoman: Legends of the Iroquois.* Santa Fe, N.Mex.: Clear Light Publishing, 1998.

Sherzer, Joel, and Anthony C. Woodbury. *Native American Discourse: Poetics and Rhetoric.* New York: Cambridge, 1987.

Shorto, Russell. "All Political Ideas Are Local." *New York Times Magazine*, October 2, 2005: 54–61.

Silko, Leslie Marmon. *Almanac of the Dead.* New York: Penguin, 1991.

——. *Ceremony*. New York: Penguin, 1977.

——. "Here's an Odd Artifact for the Fairy-Tale Shelf: Review of *The Beet Queen*." *Studies in American Indian Literatures* 10 (1986): 177–84.

——. "An Old-Time Indian Attack Conducted in Two Parts: Part One: Imitation 'Indian' Poems. Part Two: Gary Snyder's *Turtle Island*." In *The Remembered* Earth, edited by Geary Hobson. Albuquerque: University of New Mexico Press, 1979.

Smith, Graham Hingangaroa. "Protecting and Respecting Indigenous Knowledge." In *Reclaiming Indigenous Voice and Vision*, edited by Marie Battiste, 209–224. Vancouver: University of British Columbia Press, 2000.

Smith, Joseph Henry. *Appeals to the Privy Court.* New York: Columbia University Press, 1950.

Smith, Paul Chaat, and Robert Allen Warrior. *Like a Hurricane: The Indian Movement from Alcatraz to Wounded Knee*. New York: New Press, 1996.

Snell, Teddy. "Freedmen Added as Citizens of Tribe." *Tahlequah Daily Press*, March 8, 2006: 1, 3.

Sparks, Jennifer. "Freedmen Are Citizens of Cherokee Nation." *Tulsa World*, June 11, 2006: G4.

Spivak, Gayatri Chakravorty. "Can the Subaltern Speak?" In *Marxism and the Interpretation of Culture*, edited by Cary Nelson and Lawrence Grossberg, 271–313. Urbana: University of Illinois Press. 1988.

——. "Three Women's Texts and a Critique of Imperialism." *Critical Inquiry* 12, no. 1 (Autumn 1985) 243–61. Reprinted in *Feminisms: An Anthology of Literary Criticism*, edited by Robyn Warhol and Diane Price Herndl, 798–814. New Brunswick, N.J.: Rutgers University Press, 1991.

——. "Who Claims Alterity?" In *Remaking History*, edited by Barbara Kruger and Phil Mariani, 269–92. Dia Art Foundation Discussions in Contemporary Culture No. 4. Seattle, Wash.: Bay Press, 1989.

Standing Bear, Luther. *Land of the Spotted Eagle*. Lincoln: University of Nebraska Press, 1978.

Strickland, Rennard. *Fire and the Spirits: Cherokee Law from Clan to Court*. Norman: University of Oklahoma Press, 1975.

——, and William M. Strickland. "Beyond the Trail of Tears: One Hundred Fifty Years of Cherokee Survival." In *Cherokee Removal: Before and After*, edited by W. L Anderson, 112–38. Athens: University of Georgia Press, 1991.

Stripes, James. "Beyond the Cameo School: Decolonizing the Academy in a World of Postmodern Multiculturalism." *Wicazo Sa Review* 11, no. 1 (1993): 24–32.

Sturm, Circe. *Blood Politics: Race, Culture, and Identity in the Cherokee Nation of Oklahoma*. Berkeley: University of California Press, 2002.

Swanton, John R. *Myths and Tales of the Southeastern Indians*. Norman: University of Oklahoma Press, 1995.

——. *Source Material for the Social and Ceremonial Life of the Choctaw Indians*. Bureau of American Ethnology Bulletin No. 103. Washington, D.C.: Government Printing Office, 1931.

Szasz, Margaret Connell. "Samson Occom: Mohegan as Spiritual Intermediary."

In *Between Indian and White Worlds: The Cultural Broker,* edited by Margaret Connell Szasz, 61–78. Norman: University of Oklahoma Press, 1994.

Taylor, Alan. "Captain Hendrick Aupaumut: The Dilemmas of an Intercultural Broker. *Ethnohistory* 43, no. 3 (1996): 431–57.

Tedlock, Dennis. *The Spoken Word and the Work of Interpretation.* Philadelphia: University of Pennsylvania Press, 1983.

——, trans. *Popol Vuh: The Definitive Edition of the Mayan Book of the Dawn of Life and the Glories of Gods and Kings.* New York: Touchstone, 1996.

Teuton, Sean. "Internationalism and the American Indian Scholar: Native Studies and the Challenge of Pan-Indigenism." In *Identity Politics Reconsidered,* edited by Linda Martin Alcoff et al., 264–84. New York: Palgrave, 2006.

——. "Placing the Ancestors: Postmodernism, 'Realism,' and American Indian Identity in James Welch's *Winter in the Blood. American Indian Quarterly* 25 (2001): 626–50.

——. "A Question of Relationship: Internationalism and Assimilation in Recent American Indian Studies." *American Literary History* 18, no. 1 (2006): 152–74.

——. *Red Land, Red Power: Grounding Knowledge in the American Indian Novel.* Durham: Duke University Press, 2008.

——, and Vera Palmer. *Art across Walls.* Ithaca, N.Y.: Cornell University and Willard Straight Hall Art Gallery, 1999.

Thompson, Stith, ed. *Tales of the North American Indians.* Mineola, N.Y.: Dover, 2000.

Tohe, Laura. "There Is No Word for Feminism in My Language." *Wicazo Sa Review* 15, no. 2 (2000): 103–110.

Tsosie, Rebecca. "Privileging Claims to the Past: Ancient Human Remains and Contemporary Cultural Values." *Arizona State Law Journal* 31, no. 2 (Summer 1999): 583–677.

Tuah, Yi-Fu. *Space and Place: The Perspective of Experience.* Minneapolis: University of Minnesota Press, 1977.

Uncas, Ben. Letter to Governor Thomas Fitch, May 24, 1765. *Indian Papers,* series 2, volume 258, Connecticut Archives, Connecticut State Library, Hartford.

——, Zachary Johnson, and Simon Choychoy. Letter to Governor Thomas Fitch, May 18, 1765. William Samuel Johnson Papers, Connecticut Historical Society Museum, Hartford.

United States Senate. Select Committee on Indian Affairs. "White Earth Indian Land Claims Settlement." *Hearing before the Select Committee on Indian Affairs.* 99 Congress, 1st session, S. 1396. Washington, D.C.: Government Printing Office, 1985.

Velie, Alan R. *Four American Indian Literary Masters: N. Scott Momaday, James Welch, Leslie Marmon Silko, and Gerald Vizener.* Norman: University of Oklahoma Press, 1982.

Vest, J. L. "Comparative African and American Indian Philosophy." American Philosophical Association Pacific Division Conference, Albuquerque, N.M. April 5–8, 2000

Vizenor, Gerald. *Bearheart: The Heirship Chronicles*. Minneapolis: University of Minnesota Press, 1990.

——. *Darkness in Saint Louis Bearheart*. St. Paul, Minn: Truck Press, 1978.

——. *Fugitive Poses: Native American Indian Scenes of Absence and Presence*. Lincoln: University of Nebraska Press, 1998.

——. *Landfill Meditations: Crossblood Stories*. Middletown, Conn.: Wesleyan University Press, 1991.

——. *Manifest Manners: Postindian Warriors of Survivance*. Hanover, N.H.: University Press of New England, 1994.

——. *Narrative Chance: Postmodern Discourse on Native American Indian Literatures*. Norman: University of Oklahoma Press, 1993.

Walters, Anna Lee. *Talking Indian: Reflections on Survival and Writing*. Ithaca, N.Y.: Firebrand, 1992.

Warrior, Clyde. "The War on Poverty." In *Great Documents in American Indian History*, edited by Wayne Moquin, 355–59. New York: Da Capo Press, 1995.

Warrior, Robert Allen. "The Native American Scholar: Toward a New Intellectual Agenda." *Wicazo Sa Review* 14, no., 2 (1999): 46–54.

——. *The People and the Word: Reading Native Nonfiction*. Minneapolis: University of Minnesota Press, 2005.

——. *Tribal Secrets: Recovering American Indian Intellectual Traditions*. Minneapolis: University of Minnesota Press, 1995.

Waters, Anne, ed. *American Indian Thought*. Oxford, U.K.: Blackwell, 2004.

Weatherford, Jack. *Indian Givers: How the Indians of the Americas Transformed the World*. New York: Crown, 1988.

Weaver, Jace. "From I-Hereneutics to We-Hermeneutics: Native Americans and the Post-Colonial." In *Native American Religious Identity: Unforgotten Gods*, edited by Jace Weaver. New York: Orbis Books, 1998.

——. *That the People Might Live: Native American Literatures and Native American Community*. New York: Oxford University Press, 1997.

——, Craig Womack, and Robert Warrior. *American Indian Literary Nationalism*. Albuquerque: University of New Mexico Press, 2006.

Webster, Anthony K. "Sam Kenio's Coyote Stories: Poetics and Rhetoric in Some Chiricahua Apache Narratives." *American Indian Culture and Research Journal* 23, no. 1 (1999): 137–63.

Welch, James. *Fools Crow*. New York: Penguin, 1986.

——. *Winter in the Blood*. New York: Harper & Row, 1974.

Wheelock, Eleazar. *A Plain and Faithful Narrative of the Original Design, Rise, Progress and Present State of the Indian Charity School at Lebanon, Connecticut*. Boston: Richard & Samuel Draper, 1763.

White, Richard. *The Middle Ground: Indians, Empires, and Republics in the Great Lakes Region, 1650–1815*. New York: Cambridge University Press, 1991.

White Earth Land Settlement Act. 100 Stat. 61 (1986).

Wickman, Patricia Riles. *The Tree That Bends: Discourse, Power, and the Survival of the Maskókî People*. Tuscalossa: University of Alabama Press, 1999.

Wiget, Andrew. *Native American Literature.* Boston: G. K. Hall, 1985.

Wilkinson, Charles. *American Indians, Time, and the Law: Native Societies in a Modern Constitutional Democracy.* New Haven, Conn.: Yale University Press, 1987.

Williams, Raymond. *Culture and Society, 1780–1950.* New York: Columbia University Press, 1958.

——. *Marxism and Literature.* New York: Oxford University Press, 1977.

Williams, Walter. *The Spirit and the Flesh: Sexual Diversity in American Indian Culture.* Boston: Beacon Press, 1986.

Wilson, Michael. "Speaking of Home: The Idea of the Center in Some Contemporary American Indian Writing." *Wicazo Sa Review* 12, no. 1 (1997): 129–147.

Womack, Craig S. *Red on Red: Native American Literary Separatism.* Minneapolis: University of Minnesota Press, 1999.

Wonderly, Anthony. "The Elm-Antone Story in Comparative and Historical Context." In *The Oneida Creation Story*, Demus Elm and Harvey Antone, edited by Floyd G. Lounsbury and Bryan Gick. Lincoln: University of Nebraska Press, 2000.

Woolf, Virginia. *The Death of the Moth and Other Essays.* New York: Harcourt, Brace, 1942.

Wyss, Hilary E. *Writing Indians: Literacy, Christianity, and Native Community in Early America.* Amherst: University of Massachusetts Press, 2000.

Yagoda, Ben. *Will Rogers: A Biography.* Norman: University of Oklahoma Press, 2000.

Young Bear, Ray. *Black Eagle Child: The Face Paint Narratives.* Iowa City: University of Iowa Press, 1992.

Youngbear-Tibbets, Holly. "Without Due Process: The Alienation of Individual Trust Allotments of the White Earth Anishinaabeg." *American Indian Culture and Research Journal*, 15, no. 2 (1991): 93–138.

Zavarazadeh, Ma'sud, Teresa L. Ebert, and Donald Morton, eds. *Post-Ality: Marxism and Postmodernism.* Washington, D.C.: Maisonneuve Press, 1995.

Index